Targeting JNCIA

Study Guide for Exam JN0-201

By

Jeffrey Ringwelski, John Jacobs,
Tyler Wessels

This book is a work of non-fiction. Names and places have been changed to protect the privacy of all individuals. The events and situations are true.

ISBN: 1-4107-6496-6 (e-book)
ISBN: 1-4107-6495-8 (Paperback)

Library of Congress Control Number: 2003094108

This book is printed on acid free paper.

Printed in the United States of America
Bloomington, IN

1stBooks - rev. 07/28/03

Acknowledgements

The authors would like to thank, in no particular order of appreciation:

Evan Mennillo for his great work and continued attention to detail. Max Gabriel and Brandon Gaither for feedback and assistance.

All those who contributed, in their own way, to a project that ended up a bit more complex than originally thought.

Contents

Figures

Chapter One
Preface

Targeting JNCIA

Overview

The explosive growth in packet switched computer networks in general, and the public Internet specifically, continues to fuel a need for skilled technicians and engineers at every enterprise and service provider level. Likewise, the need for certification testing to maintain a benchmark for measuring those skills continues to be a necessity. Juniper Networks® builds and services a line of routers designed around Internet Protocol (IP) that are upon the leading edge of packet switching network technology.

Since the inception of the Juniper M40 backbone router, it has become increasingly apparent to industry specialists that there is a new contender in a market that was previously dominated of Cisco Systems. As Juniper expands its visibility both at the core and edge of modern networks, it is becoming increasingly important for employers and employees alike to recognize the special skills and tasks required to work with these devices.

Introduction

The Juniper Networks Technical Certification Program (JNTCP) is a multi-tiered program that demonstrates a competence with Juniper Networks M and T-Series routers, JUNOS software, and general inter-networking ability. Complete information on the certification program as well as the most up to date information regarding the exams can be found at www.juniper.net.

The current four tiers that constitute the JNTCP are:

Juniper Networks Certified Internet Associate (JNCIA) – A written exam administered by Prometric (www.prometric.com) consisting of 60 multiple choice questions that ensure an essential foundation of basic knowledge necessary for troubleshooting and debugging a variety of routing issues involving Juniper Networks devices. A minimum of 70% is required to pass. This is the base level for Juniper certifications. The JNCIA is valid for 2 years and may be renewed by taking the current version of the test.

Juniper Networks Certified Internet Specialist (JNCIS) - Testing for this level of certification is made up of a 75 question, multiple choice written exam available from Prometric testing centers. A minimum of 70% correct is needed for a passing grade. Pass/Fail results and scoring are available immediate after the test. Certification is valid for 2 years. A valid JNCIS is required for taking the JNCIP practical exam. There is no prerequisite for attaining the JNCIS certification.

Juniper Networks Certified Internet Professional (JNCIP) – The JNCIP is the first of the two full-day practical examinations (the JNCIE is the second). Test candidates have 8 hours to configure and troubleshoot a variety of routing problems using current Juniper Networks technology. Pass/Fail results and scoring are available within ten business days after the test. Certification is valid for 2 years. A valid JNCIS is required for taking the JNCIP practical exam.

Juniper Networks Certified Internet Expert (JNCIE) – A valid JNCIP certification is a prerequisite to begin the JNCIE exam. The JNCIE is the second full day hands-on practical exam. It requires expertise in configuring and debugging a variety of complex routing situations utilizing Juniper Networks technology. Pass/Fail status is available within 10 business days of taking the exam. The JNCIE is valid for 2 years and may be re-certified by taking the current JNCIS written exam.

Objective

The focus behind *Targeting JNCIA* is to enable the reader to have a working understanding of TCP/IP routing and the Juniper platform sufficient to allow him or her to pass the Juniper Networks Certified Internet Associate (JNCIA) certification written test. Before beginning this book, the reader should have a basic knowledge of TCP/IP and routing concepts. This includes: the OSI model, routing versus routed protocols, IP addressing and subnetting.

For a complete understanding of command and configuration syntax, access to a working M-series router with JUNOS is recommended. However, it is understood that access to such devices is a luxury that is not commonly available. As such, relevant examples of the output that can be expected from specific commands as well as configuration sections to help clarify potentially confusing material have been included.

This book is not designed to be network design handbook. Rather it is a study guide and may be used as a quick reference. As your knowledge of networking increases, it will become evident to you that many of the concepts and protocols presented here are much more complex and contain many additional features and caveats. Some of the more academic information has intentionally been omitted to ensure proper focus on the facts pertinent to passing the JNCIA examination. Study material for those interested in detailed discourse on protocols is noted at the end of every chapter by listing the Request for Comments (RFC) whitepapers that are stored at the IETF (www.ietf.org). Additionally, there are a number of detailed network design guides available for those planning on furthering their knowledge.

Using this Book

The primary objective of this book is to adequately prepare you for the JNCIA exam and get you on your way to achieving technical certification. *Targeting JNCIA* is broken into a number of sections to allow for ease of locating information.

The beginning section includes this preface, along with a refresher on IP sub-netting, OSI model layers, and overview of the Internet. The next section deals with the Hardware of Juniper Networks various devices, highlighting the similarities and differences between different platforms. The routing sub-section includes information on the major routing protocols and routing concepts which will be tested on the JNCIA exam: RIP, OSPF, IS-IS, BGP, MPLS, and Multicast. Included at the end of every chapter you will find a listing of additional reference material that, while it may not be covered on the test, may increase your understanding of the fundamental concepts previously covered.

To reiterate, *Targeting JNCIA* should not be thought of as a comprehensive guide to all things IP, rather it is a resource to prepare you for taking and passing the Juniper certification exam.

We have used different fonts in an attempt to prevent confusion about which sections of text represent router output, input, configuration sections, terms, and the like. Sample output and configuration sections will appear similar to:

```
jncia@my.router>
```

All configuration statements and router commands are listed so that optional parameters are enclosed in <angle brackets>.

```
jncia@my.router> show interface <interface-name>
```

Tokens that should be replaced with actual interface or address information are *italicized.* In the above example, "interface-name" is optional for this command to function. If it is desired to view a specific interface, the actual name of that interface must be typed in to replace the string *interface-name.* Configuration commands that require an entry, but have multiple choices, are enclosed in [square brackets]. Be aware that JUNOS configuration levels are also noted with [square brackets]. In the example below, the level must be entered. Either a value of '1' or '2' can be configured. The interface name is also required, and data must be entered by the user to specify.

```
[edit protocols isis]
jncia@my.router#  set  interface  interface-name  level
[1|2] [enable|disable]
```

Again, *italicized words or strings* must be replaced with user data for the command to function. Optional commands are enclosed in <angled brackets>. Lastly, when data must be entered, but there are multiple values from which to choose, all appropriate values are enclosed in [square brackets] and separated with the pipe "|" character.

It is also important to note that most commands within JUNOS can have tags added to the end of them ('brief', 'detail', 'extensive'). Not all possible command outputs are addressed when listed in this book. Most commands are truncated to maintain focus on the key points necessary for the exam.

Additionally, most configuration snippets will appear in their JUNOS tree format. Key terms and concepts will be *italicized* the first time they appear. As with most telecommunications guides, there is a considerable number of acronyms used throughout. Acronyms will be expanded the first time they are encountered and will be followed by their common abbreviation. We have included a glossary of terms to alleviate problems.

Finally, a number of diagrams are including using graphic icons to represent nodes and devices. The icons are standard router and switch representations and should be easy to recognize and understand.

In general, physical device connections are represented with a solid line between devices and logical connections (routing protocol adjacencies, for example) are illustrated via a dashed line between network elements.

We apologize that the font size is often altered with respect to configuration and output display. This was necessary to ensure all pertinent information stayed on the same line as frequently as possible and was therefore more legible.

The following sections are designed to give some background and a light refresher for material that forms the foundation for moving on to more advanced routing concepts and practices. These sections are not intended to teach someone who is totally unfamiliar with TCP/IP routing subject matter, but may clear up some trouble points for those who are just beginning or perhaps haven't been in practice for awhile. In particular, be certain you are comfortable with the idea of *classless inter-domain routing* (CIDR) and subnetting, especially being able to derive subnets and masks as it *will* play an important part in the JNCIA.

The Internet

The Internet is a worldwide collection of private and public computer networks which are interconnected to each other via a system of telecommunication service providers who transport data between end points. As with most consumer services, the nuts and bolts of the Internet are largely transparent to the average user. However, to those who must maintain and service sections of this huge "network's network", an understanding of these inner workings are critical. In order to set some type of standard on networks and interconnection that would ensure interoperability without compromising innovation, the *International Organization for Standardization* (ISO) developed a model for computer networking called the *Open Systems Interconnect* (OSI) reference model. The OSI model is broken down into 7 levels:

Layer 7 : Application
Layer 6 : Presentation
Layer 5 : Session
Layer 4 : Transport
Layer 3 : Network
Layer 2 : Data Link
Layer 1 : Physical

Table 1.1 OSI Model

The OSI model describes the flow of data in a network, from the lowest layer consisting of pulses on cables up to the highest layer containing the end user's software application. Data going to and from the network is passed layer to layer. Each layer is able to communicate with the layer immediately above and below it. Every one is written as an efficient, streamlined software component. When two computers communicate on a network, the software at each layer on one host is communicating with the same layer on the other. For example, the Application layer of one computer communicates with the Application layer of another. The Application layer on either host has no regard for how data actually passes through the lower layers of the other, nor does it have any control in how those lower layers behave. In a sense, the lower layers are transparent when communicating to another host.

While knowledge of the OSI model and the functions of its groups will help you to better understand TCP/IP and networking in general, the JNCIA examination utilizes very practical test questions. The main job of a router is to deliver data to physically diverse, logically grouped devices. This is the domain of the Network layer, the third level of the model. As such, the exam and this book concentrate upon the bottom three layers with a primary focus on layer-3.

IP Addressing

Internet Protocol (IP) is the de facto system for exchanging packets of data between nodes on the public Internet. This protocol defines the rules that must be followed for end hosts to communicate successfully using the network. Everything from email and streaming audio to web pages and voice traffic is "packetized" and moved from a source to a destination using IP. Digital bits are the basis for digital network communication. A bit can be either on or off, meaning this particular bit has a value of 1 or 0. Expanding this will illustrate the logical progression:

# bits	Possible Combinations
1	0 or 1
2	00 or 01 or 10 or 11
3	000 or 001 or 010 or 011 or 100 or 101 or 110 or 111

Table 1.2 Binary Bit Combinations

You can see that the combinations begin to add up rather quickly. This exponential rise is the basis for a common rule in addressing called 2^n. A group of eight bits is known as a *byte.* This gives a byte 256 possible combinations. The confusing part of this is that the first number is actually 0 (all bits 'off'). This means that these 256 combinations represent numerical values from 0 to 255.

When bits are organized in a byte, the bits on the left are high order bits while those on the right are low order. If we say that the positions begin on the right hand side, the value of each bits value is '2' to the power of its position if it is 'on' or zero if it is 'off'. Remember that binary numbering begins from 0. With that, the lowest order bit has a value of 2^0, or 1. The next higher bit has a value of 2^1, which is either 2 or 0. Next, 2^2, 4 or 0. Next 2^3, 8 or 0. Next $2^4 = 16$, $2^5 = 32$, $2^6 = 64$ 2^7 (the eighth bit, because numbering begins at 0!) is 128. So, if we layout the eight bits of a byte and assign them their values:

Bit Position	8	7	6	5	4	3	2	1
Value	128	64	32	16	8	4	2	1

Table 1.3 Binary Values

If we fully expand a byte in binary notation with bits being either 1 or 0 we can see how these values are derived. Because of this we can see that some of the possible combinations are:

00000001 = 1	00000010 = 2	00000011 = 3
00000100 = 4	00001000 = 8	00001101 = 13
00010000 = 16	00100000 = 32	00010111 = 23
01000000 = 64	10000000 = 128	11111111 = 255

IP addresses are in the format of 32 bits, or 4 bytes, usually given in familiar dotted decimal notation *x.x.x.x.* This gives a theoretical range of 0.0.0.0 to 255.255.255.255. Other times addresses will be given in expanded binary form. In such an expanded form, we would see 128.31.127.255 as:

10000000.00011111.01111111.11111111

IP Subnetting

Each unique node on an interconnected network requires a unique IP address to identify it. Each address has two parts: one which identifies a unique network and a second which identifies a unique host on that network. The concept of dividing hosts up into unique network identifiers is known as *subnetting*. Traditional 'classful' addressing defined groups of varying network size depending upon the value of the leading byte.

Address Class	# Network Bits	# Hosts Bits	Decimal Address Range
Class A	8 bits	24 bits	1-127
Class B	16 bits	16 bits	128-191
Class C	24 bits	8 bits	192-223

Table 1.4 Address Classes

Even to this day, IPv4 addresses are sometimes called by their historical class. This means that the class of an address can be identified simply by looking at the first octet. 12.123.240.101 belongs to the traditional space of a Class A address because the first octet (12) falls within the 1-127 range.

Certain addresses are reserved for specific uses. Two such types are broadcast and network addresses; when the host segment is all 'on' or all 'off', the binary equivalent of having all 1's or all 0's. The lowest address is considered the network and highest is the broadcast. This is what is frequently referred to as '2^n-2', the common formula for determining the useful number of addresses for a given power.

Keeping in mind that the number of hosts is determined by subtracting two addresses (2^n-2), one for the network and the other for broadcast, using the old Class A, B, and C addressing scheme the Internet could support the following:

- 127 Class A networks that could include up to 16,777,214 hosts each
- Plus 65,000 Class B networks that could include up to 65,534 hosts each
- Plus over 2 million Class C networks that could include up to 254 hosts each

Because Internet addresses were generally only assigned in these three sizes, there were a lot of 'wasted' addresses. For example, if you needed 10 addresses for your network you would be assigned the smallest address available (Class C). However, that still meant 244 unused addresses. As the number of nodes on the Internet continued to grow, it became apparent that the classful addressing scheme was not going to scale. While the Internet faced an "address crunch", less than 10% of assigned addresses were actively used. To help combat the encroaching exhaustion of address space and simultaneously eliminate some of the waste, a system known as classless inter-domain routing (CIDR) was devised. CIDR was developed to be an efficient replacement for the old process of assigning Class A, B and C addresses with a generalized network "prefix". Instead of being limited to network identifiers (or "prefixes") of 8, 16 or 24 bits that corresponded to bytes, CIDR uses a *variable length subnet mask* (VLSM) to adjust the size of the sub-network. Thus, blocks of addresses can be assigned to a single host or networks as small as 2 hosts to those with over 1 million. This allows for address assignments that much more closely fit an organization's specific needs.

A subnet mask can be thought of as just that, a mask which is laid over the IP address to determine the network and host information. For this reason, IPv4 masks are also 32 bits, normally given in 4-byte x.x.x.x notation. Subnet masks are started from the left hand side and continue right. Any bit that is part of the mask is used to determine the network portion of the address, and is turned 'on' (1). Because the network ID must be continuous, the subnet mask ends when a bit on the right is turned 'off' (0). All subsequent bits are then 'off' as well. For example, a default Class C subnet mask includes the first twenty-four bits of the network section. This translates to the first three octets being 'on'.

11111111.11111111.11111111.00000000 binary
or 255.255.255.0 in decimal notation.

When a subnet mask is used with an IP address, bits that fall to the right of the network section are the bits usable for host IDs. It is often easier to understand the bit pattern interaction of addresses and masks when they are expanded into binary notation. The binary equivalent of the IP address 192.168.12.100 is:

11000000.10101000.00001100.01100100

If we use a /24 subnet mask on this address:

11000000.10101000.00001100.01100100 address
11111111.11111111.11111111.00000000 mask
Network. Network . Network . Host

We can see from the above that the host portion is made up of the last octet. So, the .100 portion of the IP address identifies the unique host.

A CIDR address includes the standard 32-bit IP address and also information in the form of a subnet mask to determine how many bits are used for the network prefix. For example, in the CIDR address 10.10.134.192/30, the "/30" indicates the first 30 bits are used to identify the unique network and the remaining 2 bits describe the unique host. This is also sometimes noted, especially in writing router configurations, as a decimal subnet mask of 255.255.255.252. Looking at the last octet we can see that the rightmost two bits have not been included.

11111111.11111111.11111111.11111100

CIDR continues to follow the 2^n-2 rule in that there are 2 addresses subtracted for network and broadcast identifiers. There is one exception, any address with a /32 address denotes a single specific host. There is no network or broadcast address associated with a /32. Below is a partial listing of available VLSM CIDR addresses. In each case, the number of hosts available corresponds to 2^x - 2, where x is the length of the address in bits (32) minus the number of bits in the subnet mask (the number behind the /). So, 10.10.134.192/28 has 32-28= 4 bits. X=4 gives us 2^4-2=14 unique hosts available.

CIDR Block Prefix	**# Equivalent Class C**	**# of Host Addresses (2^n-2)**
/30	1/128th of a Class C	2 hosts
/27	1/8th of a Class C	30 hosts
/26	1/4th of a Class C	62 hosts
/25	1/2 of a Class C	126 hosts
/24	1 Class C	254 hosts
/23	2 Class C	510 hosts
/22	4 Class C	1,022 hosts
/21	8 Class C	2,046 hosts
/20	16 Class C	4,094 hosts
/19	32 Class C	8,190 hosts
/18	64 Class C	16,382 hosts
/17	128 Class C	32,766 hosts
/16	256 Class C = 1Class B	65,534 hosts
/15	512 Class C	131,070 hosts
/14	1,024 Class C	262,142 hosts
/13	2,048 Class C	524,286 hosts

Table 1.5 CIDR Blocks

Despite the advent of CIDR, concerns about the exhaustion of IP address space have become more prevalent recently simply given the number of nodes residing on the Internet. The present scheme of addressing with 4 bytes is known as IPv4 (version 4). IPv4 is over 20 years old, and has presided over a period of unprecedented, explosive growth. A new system, called IPv6 or Ipng (Next Generation) attempts to alleviate concerns of IPv4, most notably IP address exhaustion. Where an IPv4 address is 32 bits, an IPv6 address is 128 bits in length. This allows for a gargantuan number of addresses, over 340 unidecillion, or 3.4×10^{38} – over 1 billion addresses per person on the planet.

IPv6 is *not* a requirement for the JNCIA.

Key Points

- The OSI networking model contains 7 Layers:
    - Layer 7: Application
    - Layer 6: Presentation
    - Layer 5: Session
    - Layer 4: Transport
    - Layer 3: Network
    - Layer 2: Data Link
    - Layer 1: Physical
- IP addresses consist of 32 bits separated into network portion and a host portion.
- A subnet mask is used to determine the break between network and host subsections of an IP address.
- VLSM allows for conservation of address space by allowing the subnet mask to allocate bits across the entire range of the IP address.
- An address where all the host bits are set to 1 is the broadcast.
- An address where all the host bits are set to 0 is the network.
- There are 2^n-2 addresses in a CIDR block, where N is the number of host bits.

RFC

For more detailed technical information search for the following:

- RFC 1517: Applicability Statement for the Implementation of CIDR
- RFC 1518: An Architecture for IP Address Allocation with CIDR
- RFC 1519: CIDR: An Address Assignment and Aggregation Strategy
- RFC 1520: Exchanging Routing Information Across Provider Boundaries in the CIDR Environment
- RFC 1631: IP Network Address Translator (NAT)
- RFC 1812: Ipv4 Router Requirements
- RFC 1878: Ipv4Variable Length Subnet Table
- RFC 1918: Address Allocation for Private Internets
- www.ipv6.org
- www.ietf.org

Chapter Two
Hardware

Chapter 2: Hardware

Overview

M-series routers have two major architectural components: the *Routing Engine* (RE) and the *Packet-Forwarding Engine* (PFE). The RE and PFE separate the control plane and the forwarding plane within the router. The RE contains routing protocol overhead and route table information. The PFE's primary function is the forwarding of production traffic given the information supplied by the RE. While operating independently, the RE and PFE communicate to each other over a 100 Mbs internal link (known as fxp1). This separation of the control and forwarding planes allows the RE to process control packets, such as routing updates, without negatively impacting the performance of the PFE or throughput of the router.

Introduction

This chapter will cover the hardware of Juniper Networks M-series routers. While there are a number of subtle differences between the platforms, Juniper has endeavored to make their routers have a common feel to them, regardless of model. This will no doubt become apparent when you review the software section, but also rings true for hardware. The most notable common thread for the M-series routing architecture is the separation of the control plane from the forwarding plane. This design allows the router to process routing updates without reducing its ability to maintain line-rate forwarding. By the end of this chapter you should be able to:

- ✓ Identify the different M-series routers.
- ✓ Recognize different hardware components and how they relate to the boot process.
- ✓ Identify the primary hardware components of each M-series router.
- ✓ Understand the Application Specific Integrated Circuit (ASIC) layout.
- ✓ Explain packet flow through the ASICs.

The JNCIA focuses upon the widely available M-series Juniper routers. Recently, Juniper has unveiled its next generation of core routers, the T-Series. However, as the current exam does not focus upon these particular routers, neither will this chapter.

M-series Routing Engine (RE)

The primary function of the RE is to maintain the routing tables and control the routing protocols. The RE is also responsible for all software processes that control interfaces, chassis components, system management, and user access to the router.

All routing protocol packets are sent directly to the routing engine for processing. The software processes are run separately so that the failure of one process doesn't affect the other processes. The advertisement, filtering, and modification of routes are handled by the RE according to the configured routing policy. The RE is responsible for building and maintaining multiple routing tables. It derives the active routes from each routing table and creates the *forwarding table*. The master forwarding table is located locally on the RE and a copy is sent to the PFE (via fxp1). The copy of the forwarding table on the PFE is the instance used to actually switch packets through the router. The RE has the ability to update the forwarding table that resides in the PFE without disrupting packet flow.

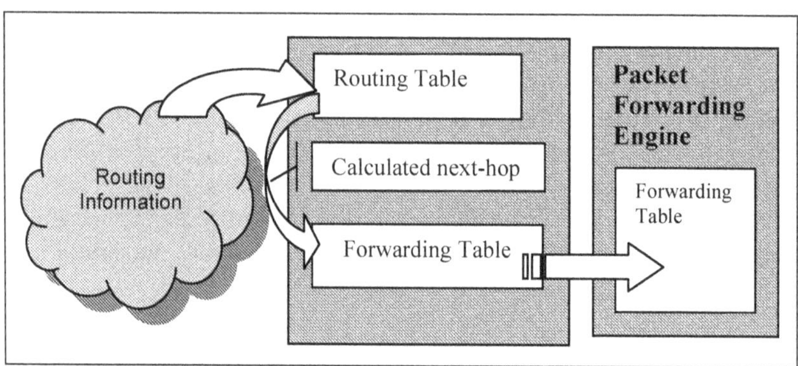

Figure 2.1: Flow and maintenance of the Routing and Forwarding Tables

The routing engine is the also the primary storage device for the router. Configuration files, JUNOS software, and microcode are stored and maintained in RE storage systems permitting local and remote upgrades.

The RE consists of a CPU, SDRAM, compact flash, rotating hard drive and a removable PCMCIA device. The CPU is a Pentium-class processor running JUNOS software. The SDRAM holds the routing table and forwarding table as well as other RE processes. Compact flash provides primary storage for JUNOS software images, microcode and two configuration files. The hard disk provides secondary storage for log files and memory dumps and an additional eight previous configuration files.

The boot source for an M-series router is as follows:

1) PCMCIA or ATA flash card (not often used)
2) Compact flash (also referred to as the non-rotating media)
3) Hard disk (also referred to as the rotating media)
4) Management Ethernet (network)

The RE controls all interfaces for out-of-band management access such as console ports, auxiliary (AUX) ports and the management Ethernet port. For more information on the software processes run on the RE, see Chapter 3, *JUNOS*.

M-series Packet-Forwarding Engine (PFE)

The primary responsibility of the PFE is to provide layer-2 and layer-3 packet switching. The PFE performs these functions through the use of *Application Specific Integrated Circuits* (ASICs). Each M-series router's PFE shares many of the same ASICs. The physical location of ASICs in the system varies between platforms, but the responsibilities and functions of the ASICs remain the same. Unlike the RE, which is a single component, the PFE is a distributed group of a number of hardware elements centered on optimizing packet forwarding. Unfortunately for those taking this exam, the group of components that make up the M-series PFE are not consistent across platforms. The larger, more robust, routers tend to have more individual, discrete components. The smaller boxes lean toward hardware consolidation to lower costs.

M-series PICs & FPCs

All media types (fiber, coax, UTP, etc.) require a physical connection to the router. The *Physical Interface Card* (PIC) is the first place a packet is received by the router and the last point it exits before going onto the transmission media. There are numerous types of PICs, varying by port speed, media type, port density, and so on. All M-series routers utilize them, but not every type of PIC can be used in every model of router.

For high-throughput routers like the M160, M40, and M20, PICs are arranged on removable *Flexible PIC Concentrators* (FPCs). On the smaller M5 and M10 routers, the FPCs are built into the *Forwarding Engine Board* (FEB). The major function of an FPC is to house PICs, shared memory for those PICs, *I/O Manager ASICs*, and *Packet Director ASICs*. These last two hardware components are discussed below.

M-series PFE ASICs

Application Specific Integrated Circuits (ASICs) are special chips designed to perform specific tasks. They are ideally suited for network devices as once a routine can be performed by a hardware chip, it is inherently faster than the same routine run on software. The hardware components that make up the PFE house the ASICs. The types of hardware components and location of the ASICs vary between M-series routers.

Each type of PIC is equipped with an ASIC that is designed to perform the media specific control functions for that type of interface. Encapsulation, de-capsulation, framing and checksums are some of the control functions provided by the media specific PIC ASICs.

The Packet Director ASIC is only utilized by M160 and M40e routers. The Packet Director ASIC's primary function is to distribute incoming packets to the I/O Manager ASICs and to distribute outgoing packets to the correct PIC.

The I/O Manager ASIC has 2 primary functions. The first is to divide incoming packets into 64-byte data cells (also called J-cells) and transfer the cells to the *Distributed Buffer Manager* (DBM) ASIC. The second function is to retrieve the 64-byte data cells from shared memory and reassemble the packet.

Each M-series router has 2 Distributed Buffer Manager ASICs. One Distributed Buffer Manager ASIC is responsible for managing and distributing the 64-byte data cells to shared memory banks that reside on the FPCs. The other is responsible for transferring outgoing packets to the correct FPC.

Route lookups are performed by the Internet Processor II ASIC using the forwarding table stored in RAM. This ASIC is located on different hardware components based upon the model of M-series router. The Internet Processor II ASIC is also responsible for transferring exception and control packets to the RE. Any packet that is required to be processed by the routing engine is considered to be an exception packet.

The below picture illustrates the sequential flow of a packet through the M40 and M160s ASICs. These ASICs make up the Packet Forwarding Engine. The Packet Director ASIC is only utilized by M40s and M160s.

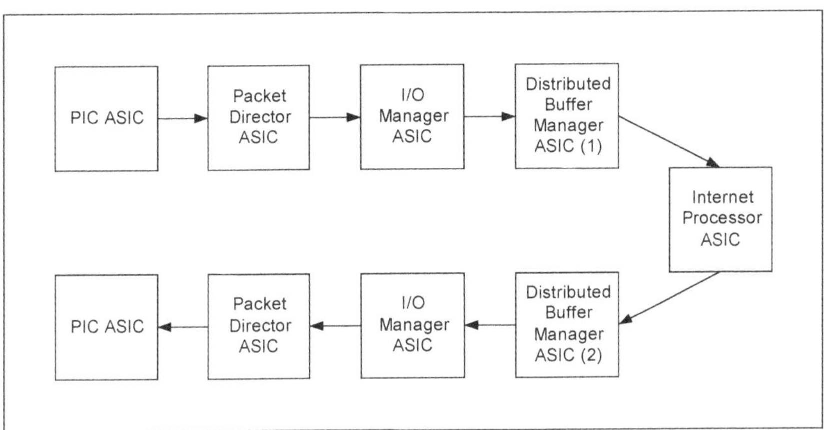

Figure 2.2 M160 & M40e packet flow (logical ASIC view)

The below picture illustrates the sequential flow of a packet through the M5/10 and M20 ASICs. These ASICs make up the Packet Forwarding Engine. Notice the lack of a Packet Director ASIC.

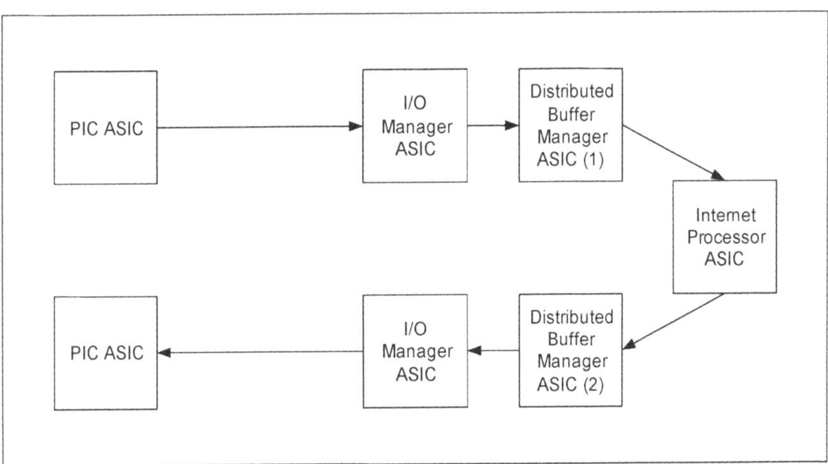

Figure 2.3 M5, M10, M20, and M40 packet flow (logical ASIC view)

M160 Overview

The M160 is an internet backbone class router offering high-speed SONET/SDH, ATM, and Gigabit Ethernet media types. This router is designed for large networks such as those used by *Internet Service Providers* (ISPs). The M160 has an aggregate throughput of 160 Gbps and can forward up to 3 Gbps at line-rate on each original FPC1 and up to 10 Gbps at line-rate on each next-generation FPC2.

M160 Chassis

The chassis is the structure that houses all the individual hardware components. The primary component is the *midplane*, which is located vertically towards the back of the chassis. Each component that is installed in the chassis connects to the midplane. The midplane is responsible for transferring packets from one component to another, distribution of power to each component, and signal connectivity that is used for monitoring and control of the entire system.

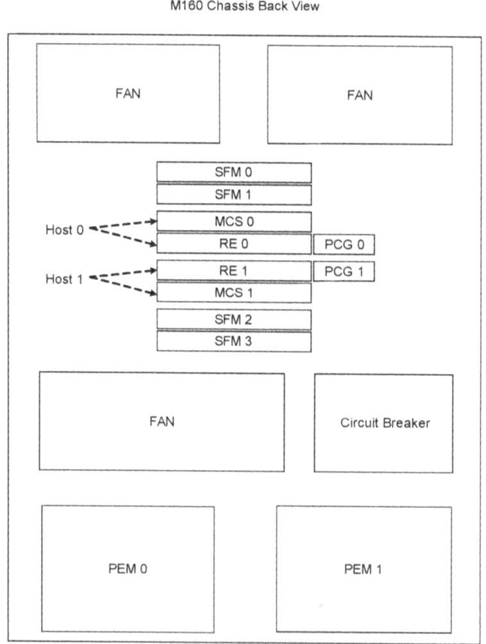

M160 Chassis Front View

Craft Interface								
CIP	FPC 0	FPC 1	FPC 2	FPC 3	FPC 4	FPC 5	FPC 6	FPC 7
mgmt aux	PIC 0	PIC 0	PIC 0	PIC 0	PIC 0	PIC 0	PIC 0	PIC 0
con	PIC 1	PIC 1	PIC 1	PIC 1	PIC 1	PIC 1	PIC 1	PIC 1
mgmt aux	PIC 2	PIC 2	PIC 2	PIC 2	PIC 2	PIC 2	PIC 2	PIC 2
con	PIC 3	PIC 3	PIC 3	PIC 3	PIC 3	PIC 3	PIC 3	PIC 3

Figure 2.4 M160 Chassis View (Front and Rear)

M160 Flexible PIC Concentrator (FPC)

FPCs are inserted at the front of the chassis connecting to the chassis midplane and house various PICs. There are eight vertical FPC slots located at the front of the M160. The slots are numbered from left-to-right where the leftmost slot is 0; the rightmost slot is 7. Each allows up to four PICs to be installed. If a slot is not occupied by an FPC, or if an FPC is not fully populated with PICs, a blank cover must be used to allow proper airflow and cooling within the chassis.

There are three basic types of FPCs: *type 1, type 2, and OC-192.* Type 1 FPCs (FPC-1s) support such interfaces as single-port OC-12 and Gigabit Ethernet (GigE) PICs. Type 2 FPCs (FPC-2s) support higher speed PICs such as OC-48 and 2-port GigE. The last type is an OC-192. This model does not have four individual connectors for PICs, but rather the entire FPC is dedicated to a single OC-192 interface. Type 1 and OC-192 FPCs are produced in two forms: standard and enhanced. Enhanced cards have advanced QOS capability and an additional 2MB of RAM.

All FPCs are hot swappable. The chassis does not have to be powered down to remove or install an FPC. An FPC whose PICs are not carrying live traffic that is removed will cause slight forwarding latency while the shared memory is flushed. One configured with PICs carrying live traffic cannot be removed without causing a network outage and packet loss.

FPCs connect the PICs to the rest of the router, allowing packets entering a PIC to be forwarded across the midplane to the SFMs and ultimately to the destination port. Each FPC contains a shared memory pool and two types of ASICs: one Packet Director ASIC and up to four I/O Manager ASICs. The primary role of the Packet Director ASIC is to accept packets from the PICs installed on the FPC and prepare them to be passed on to the I/O Manager ASIC. The I/O Manager ASIC divides each packet into 64-byte memory blocks that will be stored across all FPC shared memory by the Distributed Buffer Manager ASICs (located on the SFMs).

M160 Switching & Forwarding Modules (SFMs)

The SFMs are located in the rear of the chassis and constitute the majority of the PFE. Up to four of these hot-swappable components can be installed to provide full packet forwarding capability. Removing an SFM does disrupt forwarding performance as the PFE reconfigures the distribution of packets to the remaining SFMs. At least one SFM must be online for the router to continue forwarding packets.

The primary functions of the SFM are route lookup, buffer management and switching packets to a destination FPC. Each SFM has an Internet Processor II ASIC that performs route lookups using the forwarding table that is stored locally in SRAM. The Distributed Buffer Manager ASIC also resides locally on the SFM and is responsible for allocating incoming (from an FPC) packets to the shared memory pool located on all FPCs. There is a second Distributed Buffer manager ASIC that is responsible for forwarding outgoing (outgoing from the SFM) packets to the FPCs. Another function of the Internet Processor II ASIC is to transfer control and exception packets to the microprocessor on the RE. Any errors detected by the SFM's microprocessor are sent to the routing engine in the form of a syslog message that describes the error.

M160 Packet Flow

The following steps walk through packet on a M160 router:

- Packets first enter the router via a PIC interface.
- They are then sent to the Packet Director ASIC on the FPC.
- The Packet Director ASIC distributes the packets in a round-robin fashion to the FPC's I/O Manager ASICs.
- The I/O Manager ASICs process the packet header and divide the packets into 64 byte cells, forwarding the cells through the midplane to the inbound Distributed Buffer Manager ASIC on the SFMs. Note that *Quality of Service* (QoS) queuing takes place within this ASIC.
- The Distributed Buffer Manager ASIC distributes the 64-byte cells throughout the shared memory banks of each FPC.
- The Internet Processor II ASIC on the SFM performs the lookup and makes a forwarding decision.
- The Internet Processor II ASIC notifies the outbound Distributed Buffer Manager (DBM) ASIC on the SFM of the forwarding decision.
- The outbound DBM ASIC forwards the notification to the I/O Manager ASIC of the FPC that houses the outgoing PIC.
- The I/O Manager ASIC retrieves the 64-byte cells from the shared memory banks and reassembles the packet with the results of the route lookup done by the Internet Processor II ASIC.
- The I/O Manager ASIC then forwards the reassembled packets to the FPCs Packet Director ASIC who forwards the packets to the correct outgoing PIC.
- The PIC finally transmits the packets out the appropriate interface.

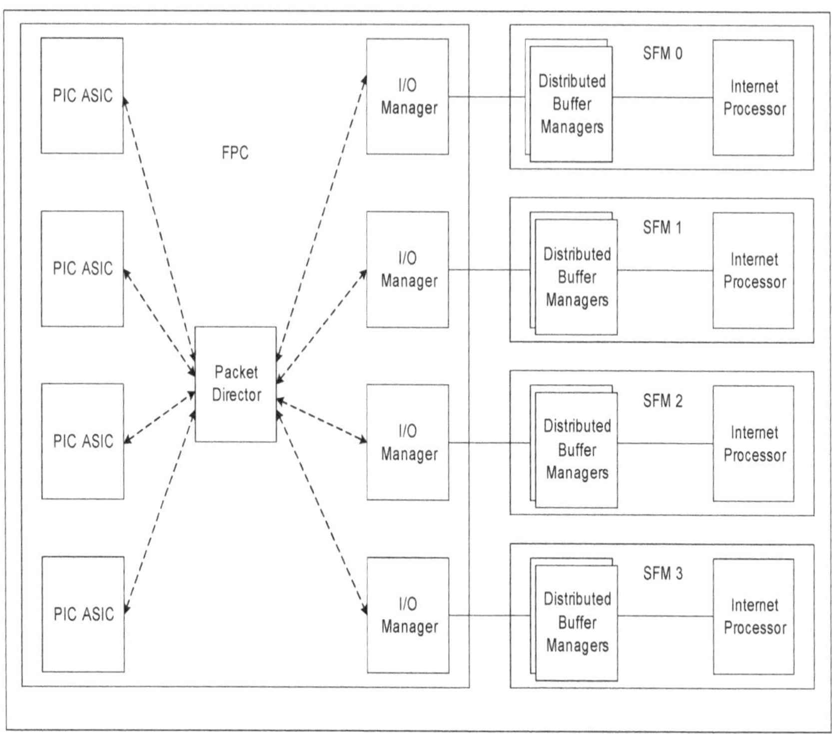

Figure 2.5 M160 Packet Flow (ASIC placement view)

Physical Interface Cards (PICs)

PICs are the connections to various network media types such as SONET/SDH, ATM, and Gigabit Ethernet. They transmit and receive network packets. PICs are responsible for the encapsulation, framing, and line speed signaling for its specific media type. PICs are hot swappable. If the PIC is carrying live traffic and is removed, packets will be dropped and a network outage will occur.

M160 PFE Clock Generators (PCGs)

The M160 router is configured with two PCGs located at the rear of the chassis. The RE dictates one as the primary and the other as the secondary. Each contains a 125 MHz system clock generator. The clock generator is used to provide timing and synchronization to the components of the PFE.

M160 Host Module

The host module actually refers to two separate hardware components that rely heavily upon the function of each other. An RE and *Miscellaneous Control Subsystem* (MCS) are physically separate, but function logically as a single unit. The router supports up to two host modules (two REs and two MCSs). An RE cannot operate without an adjacent MCS. If two host modules are installed, one is designated as active and the other as backup. Upon failure of the active host module, the backup module assumes the primary role.

M160 Miscellaneous Control Subsystem (MCS)

The MCS is installed at the rear of the chassis connecting to the midplane. As mentioned in the RE section, up to two MCSs can be installed. Each MCS installed requires an adjacent RE. The primary function of the MCS is to work with the RE in providing control and monitoring of the various router components. The MCS also provides the SONET clocking for the router while the PCGs provide system clocking.

The MCS monitors each component of the router for failures and alarms. Statistics from each component are collected by the MCS and then relayed to the RE, which will then generate the appropriate log message or alarm condition. For all components that have a master/backup relationship, the MCS dictates which of the two devices will be master.

M40e Overview

The M40e router is identical to the M160 except that it only supports up to two SFMs, unlike the M160 which supports up to four. If two SFMs are installed, one is active and the other is backup. This router's throughput capacity is subsequently reduced to 40 Gbps.

M40 Overview

The M40 has an aggregate throughput of 40 Gbps and can forward up to 3 Gbps at line-rate on each FPC. The M40 chassis has eight vertical slots for FPCs to be installed. The major architectural difference between the M40 and M40e/M160 is the PFE. The M40 PFE consists of a backplane, *System Control Board* (SCB), FPCs and PICs.

The same ASICs that are used on the M40e/M160 are also used on the M40. The only difference being the location of some of the ASICs. On the M40e/M160, the Internet Processor II ASICs are located on the SFMs. On the M40, the older Internet Processor I ASIC is located on the SCB (the Internet Processor I performs the same functions, but is not capable of some enhanced firewall features, as noted in the Policy chapter). On the M40e/M160, the Distributed Buffer Manager ASICs are also located on the SFMs. On the M40, they reside on the backplane.

M40 Front

Cable Management Tray

FPC 0	FPC 1	FPC 2	FPC 3	SCB	FPC 4	FPC 5	FPC 6	FPC 7
PIC 0	PIC 0	PIC 0	PIC 0		PIC 0	PIC 0	PIC 0	PIC 0
PIC 1	PIC 1	PIC 1	PIC 1		PIC 1	PIC 1	PIC 1	PIC 1
PIC 2	PIC 2	PIC 2	PIC 2		PIC 2	PIC 2	PIC 2	PIC 2
PIC 3	PIC 3	PIC 3	PIC 3		PIC 3	PIC 3	PIC 3	PIC 3

Craft Interface

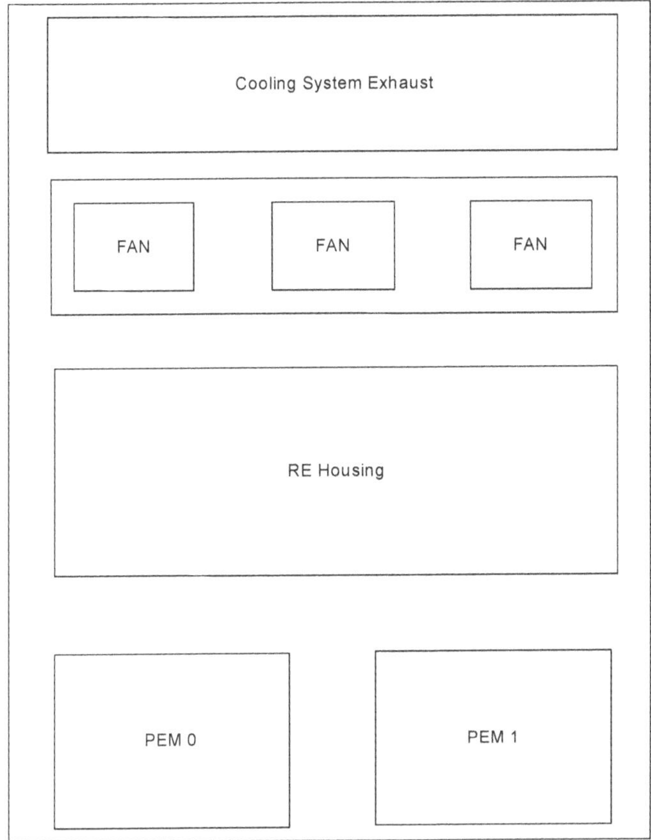

Figure 2.6 M40 Chassis View (Front and Rear)

M40 Backplane

The M40 backplane performs many of the same functions as the M40e/M160 midplane. The backplane is part of the PFE and performs 3 major tasks: power distribution, signal connectivity to the various router components, and housing of the Distributed Buffer Manager ASICs, which manage the shared memory on the FPCs.

M40 System Control Board (SCB)

The SCB connects to the backplane from the center vertical slot at the front of the chassis. It is part of the PFE and performs 4 major functions:

route lookups, system component monitoring, exception and control packet forwarding, and FPC control.

The Internet Processor I ASIC resides on the SCB and is responsible for performing route lookups. They are performed using the forwarding table that is stored on the SCB's *synchronous SRAM* (SSRAM). Similar to the MCS on the M40e/M160 platform, the SCB is responsible for monitoring the various router components for alarms and failure conditions. It also collects component statistics and relays this information to the RE, where the appropriate log message is generated or alarm condition is triggered. In addition to the standard component monitoring, the SCB has the ability to initiate an automatic reset of an FPC should such a problem or error arise.

M40 Packet Flow

The packet flow through the M40 is identical in theory to the packet flow through the M40e/M160 with regard to the ASICs. The various ASICs that make up the PFE are located on different components of the router, as noted, but the type and order of packet flow through the ASICs remains unchanged.

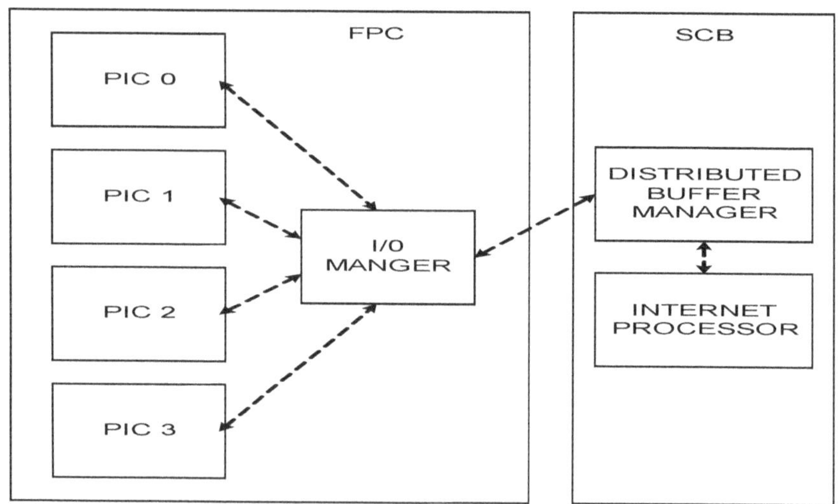

Figure 2.7 M40 packet flow (ASIC placement view)

M20 Overview

The M20s aggregate throughput is 20 Gbps and forward at line rate up to 3 Gbps on a single FPC. The chassis supports up to 4 horizontal FPCs that are installed at the front of the chassis connecting to the backplane.

Front

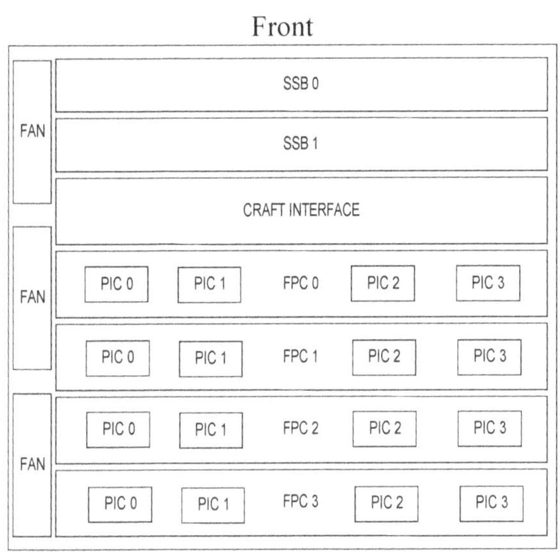

Rear

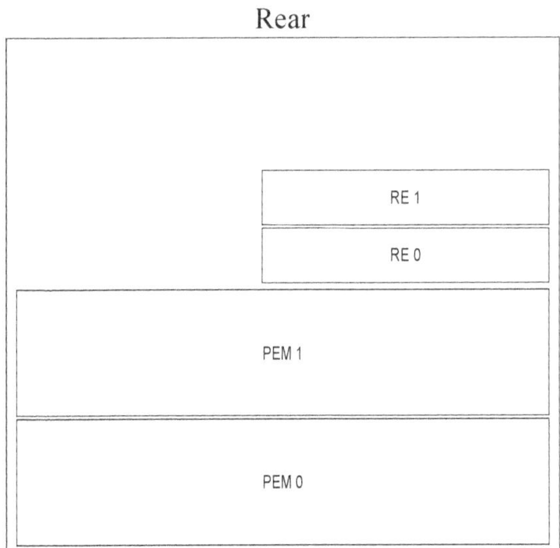

Figure 2.8 M20 Chassis View (Front and Rear)

M20 Packet Forwarding Engine

The M20 PFE consists of 4 components: the midplane, *system and switch board* (SSB), FPCs and PICs. The midplane forms the rear of the card cage where the FPCs and SSBs are connected and is responsible for power distribution and signal connectivity.

The SSB installs horizontally at the front of the chassis connecting to the midplane and houses the Internet Processor II ASIC and Distributed Buffer Manager ASICs. The SSB is responsible for much of the packet forwarding and overall system control. Some system control functions such as component monitoring and statistics collecting take place on the SSB. It monitors and collects statistics about alarm and error conditions of each of the router components. The system data that the SSB collects is passed on to the RE where the appropriate log message or alarm state will be set. The SSB also has the ability to reset FPCs if an alarm or error state is detecting that warrants a reset.

FPCs

The major difference in M20 FPCs is in the number of I/O Manager ASICs and the lack of a Packet Director ASIC. Because M20 FPCs only have a single I/O Manager ASIC, there is no need for a Packet Director ASIC whose purpose is to distribute packets to multiple I/O Managers. The FPCs perform the same functions as the FPCs from other M-series routers.

M-5/M-10 Overview

The major difference between the M5 and M10 routers is the number of PICs each supports. The M5 router supports up to four PICs while the M10 supports up to eight. The aggregate throughput of both is 6.4 Gbps. The M5 can forward up to 3 Gbps at line-rate for any combination of PICs, the M10 can forward up to 6 Gbps at line-rate for any combination of PICs.

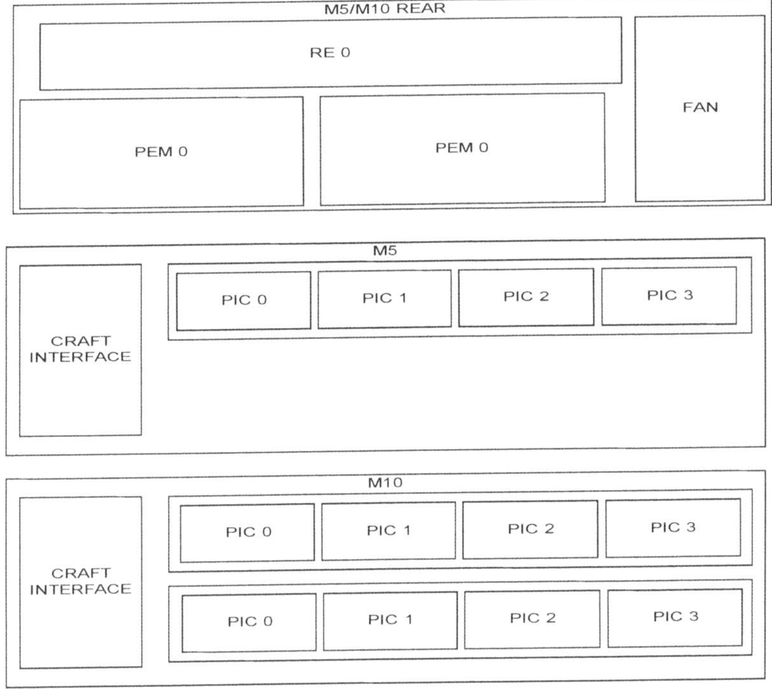

Figure 2.9 M5/M10 Chassis View (Front and Rear)

M5/M10 PFE

The PFE consists of 3 major components: the midplane, Forwarding Engine Board (FEB), and PICs. The midplane occupies the center of the router chassis where the FEB, PICs and other components connect. The midplane provides power distribution and signal connectivity.

The FEB is located at the rear of the chassis above the power supplies. It houses the Internet Processor II ASIC and two Distributed Buffer Manager ASICs. The Internet Processor II ASIC performs route lookups using the forwarding table that is stored in SSRAM on the FEB. It is also responsible for transferring exception and control packets to the RE for appropriate log message and alarm condition creation.

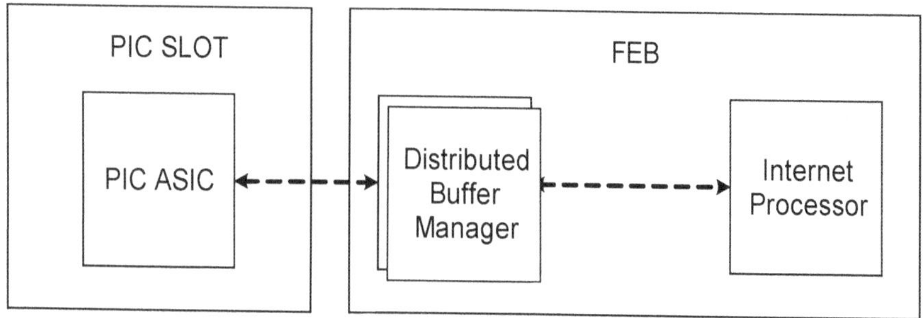

Figure 2.10 M5/M10 packet flow (ASIC placement view)

Key Points

- The two major components of every M-Series router are:
  - Routing Engine
  - Packet Forwarding Engine
- JUNOS software is kept on compact flash, a back-up is stored on the hard disk.
- The boot series for M-series routers is:
  1) PCMCIA or ATA flash card (not often used)
  2) Compact flash (also referred to as the non-rotating media)
  3) Hard disk (also referred to as the rotating media)
  4) Management Ethernet (network)
- The RE uses information from all protocols to build the Routing Table, which contains all destinations the router is aware of.
- The best next-hop addresses are used to build the Forwarding Table.
- The RE keeps a master copy of the Forwarding Table and sends a copy to the PFE over fxp.1.
- QoS queuing takes place on the I/O Manager ASIC.
- The PFE is made up of distributed components, and utilize ASICs to provide hardware forwarding functions. The key chips for each platform are noted below:

  M160/M40e ASICs:
  - PIC ASICs
  - 1 Packet Director per FPC
  - 4 I/O Managers per FPC
  - 2 Distributed Buffer Managers per SFM
  - 1 Internet Processor II ASIC per SFM

  M40:
  - PIC ASICs
  - 1 I/O Manager per FPC
  - 2 Distributed Buffer Managers on the backplane
  - 1 Internet Processor I ASIC on the SCB

  M20:
  - PIC ASICs
  - 1 I/O Manager per FPC
  - 2 Distributed Buffer Managers on the SSB
  - 1 Internet Processor II ASIC on the SSB

M5/M10:

- PIC ASICs
- 2 Distributed Buffer Manager ASICs on the FEB
- 1 Internet Processor II ASIC on the FEB

➢ Packet Flow for the M160/M40e:

1) Packets first enter the router via a PIC interface.
2) They are then sent to the Packet Director ASIC on the FPC.
3) The Packet Director ASIC distributes the packets in a round-robin fashion to the FPC's I/O Manager ASICs.
4) The I/O Manager ASICs process the packet header and divide the packets into 64 byte cells, forwarding the cells through the midplane to the inbound Distributed Buffer Manager ASIC on the SFMs. Note that *Quality of Service* (QoS) queuing takes place within this ASIC.
5) The Distributed Buffer Manager ASIC distributes the 64-byte cells throughout the shared memory banks of each FPC.
6) The Internet Processor II ASIC on the SFM performs the lookup and makes a forwarding decision.
7) The Internet Processor II ASIC notifies the outbound Distributed Buffer Manager (DBM) ASIC on the SFM of the forwarding decision.
8) The outbound DBM ASIC forwards the notification to the I/O Manager ASIC of the FPC that houses the outgoing PIC.
9) The I/O Manager ASIC retrieves the 64-byte cells from the shared memory banks and reassembles the packet with the results of the route lookup done by the Internet Processor II ASIC.
10) The I/O Manager ASIC then forwards the reassembled packets to the FPCs Packet Director ASIC who forwards the packets to the correct outgoing PIC.
11) The PIC transmits the packets out the appropriate interface.

➢ Packet Flow for the M40/M20:
(Note that the M20 has an Internet Processor II and an SSB rather than the Internet Processor I and SCB of the M40.)

1) Packets first enter the router via a PIC interface.
2) They are then sent to the FPC I/O Manager ASIC.

3) The I/O Manager ASIC process the packet header and divide the packets into 64 byte cells, forwarding the cells to the Distributed Buffer Manager ASIC on the SCB. Note that *Quality of Service* (QoS) queuing takes place within this ASIC.
4) The Distributed Buffer Manager ASIC distributes the 64-byte cells throughout shared memory.
5) The Internet Processor I ASIC on the SCB performs the lookup and makes a forwarding decision.
6) The Internet Processor I ASIC notifies the Distributed Buffer Manager ASIC on the SCB of the forwarding decision.
7) The outbound DBM ASIC forwards the notification to the I/O Manager ASIC of the FPC that houses the outgoing PIC.
8) The I/O Manager ASIC retrieves the 64-byte cells from the shared memory banks and reassembles the packet with the results of the route lookup done by the Internet Processor I ASIC.
9) The I/O Manager ASIC then forwards the reassembled packets to the correct outgoing PIC.
10) The PIC transmits the packets out the appropriate interface.

- Packet Flow for the M5/M10:
  1) Packets first enter the router via a PIC interface.
  2) They are then sent to the Distributed Buffer Manager (DBM) ASIC on the FEB
  3) The Internet Processor II ASIC on the FEB performs the lookup and makes a forwarding decision.
  4) The Internet Processor II notifies the DBM on the FEB of the forwarding decision.
  5) The DBM ASIC then forwards the packets to the correct outgoing PIC.
  6) The PIC transmits the packets out the appropriate interface.

Chapter Three
JUNOS

Chapter 3: JUNOS

Overview

JUNOS is the common operating system that is run on all Juniper M-series routers. All processes that control the router run on a UNIX kernel. The *command-line interface* (CLI) is a shell process that parses and inputs all user commands to JUNOS. This command set controls all aspects of the hardware and routing instructions. By the end of this chapter you should understand and be able to define:

- ✓ The router boot sequence.
- ✓ Features of the CLI.
- ✓ Processes of JUNOS.
- ✓ The JUNOS configuration tree.
- ✓ How to edit the configuration file.
- ✓ How to view traceoption logfiles.
- ✓ How to view and identify configuration groupings.

Introduction

JUNOS is the brain of a Juniper router, without it not much can get done. It is precisely because of this necessity that it is often overlooked in favor of studying the hardware it interfaces with and the data it processes. There are a number of things that need to be noted about this otherwise transparent layer of code to best prepare for the exam.

All M-series routers run the same JUNOS code. There is no special revision for M160's that will not work on an M5. This is contrary to some vendors who make specific code for specific platforms. Indeed, Cisco IOS® has many different trains of code within a specific platform's IOS depending on the feature set desired. This means that while there are hardware specific commands that may differ due to the chassis, such as the absence of SFMs on the M5, the overall command set is the same. This translates into increased productivity for a technician who no longer needs to recall different command conventions.

The JUNOS software resides on the compact flash (often called the non-rotating media or RAM disk) on the routing engine. The backup/alternate copy is stored on the hard drive (or 'rotating media'). The current/active configuration and the three previous configurations are stored on the internal flash drive for quick access. Meanwhile, the six previous configurations are stored on the hard drive (numbered 4 through 9).

Boot Process

The boot process is fairly lengthy and displays a large amount of information on the console. One of the key factors to acknowledge is from where the software has booted. If not from flash (either removable PCMCIA or compact), the router will post a message upon login stating that it has booted from alternate media.

Upon start up, the router will attempt to find a useable copy of JUNOS. The boot sources for an M-series router are as follows:

1) PCMCIA or ATA flash card (not often used)
2) Compact flash (non-rotating media)
3) Hard disk
4) Network (Ethernet)

If any of the above hardware components are missing or the code stored therein is corrupt, the router will move down the list to the next candidate media. It is recommended by most support personnel that the flash card be removed from the router as it is not often accessed and for this reason may hold an outdated version of software and configuration. This will force the router to boot from the compact flash and subsequently the hard drive if problems are encountered.

Processes (Daemons)

For the most part, the individual processes (called *daemons* in the UNIX world) that make up the full feature set of JUNOS software run independently. Each of these processes runs in an individual memory space and can most often be halted or restarted without impacting others. Diagnostic or cosmetic output processes, such as the *SNMP daemon* (snmpd), could be stopped or restarted with little impact to the overall packet forwarding of the router. However, it is fairly obvious that when a daemon such as the *routing process daemon* (rpd) is interrupted, service will be impacted.

Command Line Interface (CLI)

After working with an M-series Juniper, the thing you will become most accustomed to by far is the CLI. It is the means with which the user most often interfaces with and queries the router. A great deal of planning and engineering has gone into the CLI to make it intuitive and user friendly. This allows the end user to focus on gathering information and performing job duties rather than muddling with syntax and fighting every command phrase.

As was mentioned before, JUNOS runs a number of independent processes. Of primary concern to the CLI is the *management daemon* (mgd). You can think of the mgd as the process through which the command line hands its queries and requests to other processes. It is more complex than that, but for the purpose of the JNCIA those differences are academic. When a user accesses the router, a CLI process is started for that user and the mgd spawns a child management daemon process to support that user. Therefore, each individual logged into the router has a separate CLI and mgd-child process supporting them.

The CLI can run in two modes: *operational* and *configuration*. After first logging into an M-series, you will be placed in the operational mode. From this main prompt, troubleshooting, diagnostics, and information gathering take place. The configuration mode is a special, restricted set of commands that can be used to modify the router configuration file. Both modes run in the same manner; they use the same control keys, a similar structure, and identical interface. The only difference is the sub-set of commands available in each mode. Let us consider the things common to both modes.

The command hierarchy is broken into a logical tree, beginning at a general level and narrowing to a specific focus. When entering commands into the CLI, EMACS key associations can be used to manipulate the cursor (for some of the more common key-bindings, see Figure 3.1).

Moving the Cursor	
Control-b	Back-up one character
Alt-b	Back-up one word
Control-f	Move forward one character
Alt-f	Move forward one word
Control-a	Move to the beginning of the line
Control-e	Move to the end of the line
Deleting Characters	
Control-h	Delete the character before the cursor
Control-d	Delete the next character
Control-k	Delete all characters from the cursor to the end of the line
Control-x	Delete all characters on the command line
Scrolling through the command history	
Control-p	Cycle backward through the recent command history
Control-n	Cycle forward through the recent command history
Control-r	Search through the command history for a matching string

Figure 3.1 EMACS Editor Keys

JUNOS stores a history of the last commands entered. One can cycle through the history using the control-p and control-n combinations. This is helpful if a number of commands are being cycled through, or if a similar command is issued a number of times requiring only a small change.

In addition to the mundane use of separating commands, each time the space bar is pressed the CLI attempts to parse what is on the command line. Thus, partially typing a command followed by a space will attempt to complete the name of the command automatically. If there is more than one possible completion, pressing the space bar multiple times will echo back all possible endings. For example, typing in "sho" and a space, will allow the CLI to auto-complete "show". This ensures that a router administrator doesn't get to the end of a long and complex command string before the CLI errors out. As soon as a non-acceptable command is entered, JUNOS "complains" that it is not a valid input. Erroneous input is underscored with a carat (^) at the first point JUNOS is unable to complete the command. This is, of course, completely a matter of syntax. JUNOS will not complain about poor configuration design if the command structure is correct. So, typing 'sho osp int' will echo back 'show ospf interface' and then display the command output. But mistyping 'show opsf' will return a syntax error because 'opsf' is not a recognized command.

```
jncia@my.router> show opsf
                      ^

syntax error, expecting <command>.
```

At any point within monitoring or configuring a router, the "?" key can be used to display all commands available at that level. The "?" can either be used in at the end of a word to see valid completions, or in the place of a word to see all possible selections.

```
jncia@my.router> show os?
Possible completions:
  ospf              Show information about OSPF

jncia@my.router> show ospf?
Possible completions:
  database          Show OSPF link-state database
  interface         Show OSPF interface status
  io-statistics     Show OSPF I/O statistics
  log               Show OSPF SPF log
  neighbor          Show OSPF neighbor status
  route             Show the OSPF routing table
  statistics        Show OSPF statistics
```

Additionally, help files are stored on the router's hard drive and can be accessed at any time using the commands:

`Help topic` *`topic`* (general information about this subject)

`Help reference` *`topic`* (more detailed information and configuration guidelines).

Operational Mode

As was noted previously, operational mode is where the user is first placed after logging in. This familiar prompt contains the username logged in at the device name followed by a chevron, sometimes referred to as a 'greater than' (>):

```
jncia@my.router>
```

Commands available from the main level of operational mode are:

```
jncia@my.router>?
Possible completions:
  clear        Clear information in the system
  configure    Software configuration information
  file         Perform file operations
  help         Provide help information
  monitor      Real-time debugging
  mtrace       Multicast trace source to receiver
  ping         Ping a remote target
  quit         Exit the management session
  request      Make system-level requests
  restart      Restart a software process
  set          Set CLI properties, date, time,
               display
  show         Show information about the system
  ssh          Open a secure shell to another host
  start        Start a software process
  telnet       Telnet to another host
  test         Diagnostic debugging commands
  traceroute   Trace the route to a remote host
```

The range of 'show' commands are by far the most useful when troubleshooting a network event. They are non-intrusive, informative commands about the protocols, hardware, and processes running on the router.

What follows is a partial list of the more useful commands within JUNOS. For the protocol dependent ones, more detailed descriptions will be given in their respective chapters.

show system uptime	Displays the amount of time the system has been running since the last reload.
show chassis hardware	Reports a list of the installed hardware components and serial numbers.
show chassis fpc	Reports the status of the Flexible PIC Concentrators
show chassis sfm	Reports the status of the Switch Fabric Modules
show log *logfile*	Displays the contents of a configured traceoptions logfile.
show version	Shows the current code revision running on the router.
show configuration	Displays the currently running configuration.
show interface terse	Gives a complete listing of all operating interfaces.
show interface description	Reports the configured name for all interfaces.
show bgp summary	Lists all BGP neighbors and session information.
show bgp neighbor *<neighbor>*	Displays detailed information about a specific BGP peer.
show ospf neighbors	Shows all ospf neighbors that are currently configured.
show ospf interface	Lists all currently active OSPF interfaces.
show isis interface	Lists all currently active IS-IS interfaces.
show route x.x.x.x	Displays current routing information for a specific prefix.
show policy *<policy-statement>*	Lists the policy configured with the given name.
monitor interface traffic	Displays real-time throughput statistics for active interfaces
monitor interface *interface*	Reports real-time traffic, error, and physical layer statistics
monitor interface traffic	Real-time traffic monitoring of all logical interfaces
monitor start *<logfile>*	Logs information to CLI as it occurs. Useful for debugging.
monitor stop *<logfile>*	Ceases the display of *logfile* information to the screen.
monitor stop all	Ceases the display of all logfile information to the screen.

(Note that the 'clear' commands will reset all possible targets if one is not specified)

clear interface statistics <*interface-name*>	Resets the traffic and error counters
clear bgp neighbor <*neighbor*>	Resets BGP adjacency
clear ospf neighbor <*neighbor*>	Resets OSPF adjacency
clear rsvp session <*name*>	Resets RSVP adjacency
clear ldp neighbor <*neighbor*>	Resets LDP adjacency
clear mpls lsp <*lsp-name*>	Resets MPLS label switch path.

request support information	Displays verbose technical information used by Juniper to assist with troubleshooting router issues.
request system snapshot	Creates back-up files used to restore a router in event of failure. Useful before conducting maintenance.
request system halt	Gracefully exits active system processes.
request system reboot	Reloads the router.

Configuration Mode

The active configuration (plus several backup configurations, as discussed below) is stored on the routing engine's compact flash drive. To configure routing and hardware parameters within JUNOS, you enter "edit" or "configuration" mode. The configuration level, like the operational prompt, is hierarchically arranged from less specific to more specific entries. Options available from the main level of edit mode are:

```
[edit]
jncia@my.router#?
Possible completions:
  <[Enter]>     Execute this command
  activate      Remove the inactive tag in a statement
  annotate      Annotate the statement with a comment
  commit        Commit current set of changes
  copy          Copy a statement
  deactivate    Add the inactive tag to a statement
  delete        Delete a data element
  edit          Edit a sub-element
  exit          Exit from this level
  help          Provide help information
  insert        Insert a new ordered data element
  load          Load configuration from an ASCII file
```

```
  quit          Quit from this level
  rename        Rename a statement
  rollback      Roll back database to previous version
  run           Run an operational-mode command
  save          Save configuration to an ASCII file
  set           Set a parameter
  show          Show a parameter
  status        Display users currently editing
  top           Exit to top level of configuration
  up            Exit one level of configuration
  update        Update private database
```

As can be seen, the main level does not directly lead to sub-portions of the configuration. This level contains the operators that will add, change, or delete portions of the configuration. Actual protocol, interface, and policy options need to be accessed with their specific statements. Those specific layers of the file can be reached with 'edit', 'insert', 'de/activate' and 'delete'. The levels of configuration reachable with operators include:

```
jncia@my.router# edit?
Possible completions:
  access               Network access configuration
  accounting-options   Accounting data configuration
  chassis              Chassis configuration
  class-of-service     Class-of-service configuration
  firewall             Define a firewall configuration
  forwarding-options   Control packet sampling
  groups               Configuration groups
  interfaces           Interface configuration
  policy-options       Routing policy option configure
  protocols            Routing protocol configuration
  routing-instances    Routing instance configuration
  routing-options      Protocol-independent options
  security             Security configuration
  snmp                 Simple Network Management
                       Protocol
  system               System parameters
```

The branches of the hierarchy to pay most attention to for the JNCIA are the firewall, interface, policy-options, protocols, and routing-options levels. This is by no means a complete list of what is possible with the robust and powerful configuration options. Rather, it is a partial set of what the JNCIA will focus upon. For a complete and detailed discussion of configuration options it is best to consult the Juniper Networks user guides or www.juniper.net.

The configuration highlights that should be studied for firewall and policy-options will be covered in the Policy chapter. Likewise, the study points for protocol configuration will be dealt with in their specific chapters. The remaining topics of interface and routing-options, will be dealt with later in this chapter.

[edit firewall] – This statement allows for the creation of packet filters and options for the firewall policy. This is covered in the *Policy* chapter.
[edit interface] – This statement allows access to configure physical and logical aspects of the interfaces, including addressing, sub-interface units, and encapsulation.
[edit policy-options] – Protocol routing policies, as-path expressions, and prefix-lists are accessed with this statement. See the *Policy* chapter.
[edit protocols] – The various routing protocols are configured at this level. Thisincludes: RIP, BGP, OSPF, IS-IS, LDP, RSVP, MPLS, DVMRP, IGMP, MSDP, and PIM. See the protocol specific chapters as well as the *Multicast* and *MPLS* sections.
[edit routing-options] – The options for configuring static routes, the Router ID (RID), and the BGP autonomous system number (ASN or AS) are accessed with this statement.

Table 3.2 Basic Configuration Statements

For example, routing protocols are configured separately, but they are all covered under the logical group 'protocols'. To configure BGP, one must enter edit mode and then go to the protocols hierarchy level. From `[edit protocols]`, OSPF, BGP, RIP, and IS-IS may all be accessed, but they are all logically different groups under 'protocols'.

From the operational CLI, the "show configuration" command will display the configuration in its hierarchical logical tree. Simply typing "show" in configuration mode will give the same output. Once under any sub-level of "edit" configuration hierarchy, such as `[edit protocols bgp]`, typing "show" will not list the entire configuration but rather will list the configuration for that level of the configuration only. For example:

```
[edit protocols bgp]
jncia@my.router# show
    group internal {
        type internal;
        local-address 192.168.1.1;
        neighbor 192.168.1.100;
    }
}
```

Curly braces separate information with the configuration, much akin to C programming. An open brace, also called a left brace ({), indicates the beginning of a logical grouping of configuration commands. In order to be syntactically correct, the closing brace (}) must follow and end the last part of the group. More simply, every { must be followed by a } at some point.

Below is a look at this with an expanded view of how 'show configuration protocols' might appear for a very simple configuration. Don't concentrate on the portions of the configuration that might be unfamiliar, but rather try to locate braces and the logical grouping of components.

jncia@my.router>: show configuration protocols	
protocols{	This brace begins 'protocols'
bgp {	This brace begins 'bgp'
group internal {	Begins/Opens group 'internal'
type internal;	
local-address 192.168.1.1;	
neighbor 192.168.1.100;	
}	Closes/Ends group 'internal'
}	Closes 'bgp'
ospf {	Begins 'ospf'
area 0.0.0.0 {	Opens 'area 0.0.0.0'
authentication-type md5;	
interface so-3/0/0.0 {	Opens 'interface so-3/0/0.0'
metric 20;	
authentication-key	
}	Closes 'interface'
}	Closes 'area 0.0.0.0'
area 0.0.0.3 {	Opens 'area 3'
authentication-type md5;	
interface so-4/0/0.0 {	Opens 'interface so-4/0/0'
metric 20;	
authentication-key	
}	Closes 'interface'
}	Closes 'area 3'
}	Closes 'ospf'
}	Closes 'protocols'

Figure 3.3 'Show Configuration Protocols' Sample

To modify or add portions to the configuration from the command line the 'set' syntax is used. If we were to configure the router-id and AS number by means of the CLI, we can utilize 'set' commands. Both of these options are defined under routing-options. To correctly configure them, one would:

Enter edit mode.

```
jncia@my.router> configure
Entering configuration mode

[edit]
jncia@my.router#
```

Notice the prompt is now below a header that indicates our relative position in [edit] and has changed to a hash (#). The CLI has now entered configuration mode. Because the options that will be changed are at the routing options level, we will make the changes there:

```
[edit]
jncia@my.router# edit routing-options

[edit routing-options]
jncia@my.router#
```

Notice how we are now at the `[routing-options]` level of configuration and how that is now indicated in the prompt. From this level we can more easily access all of the options below this tier, but none of the ones above it. Adding the Router ID is now a matter of using *set*.

```
[edit routing-options]
jncia@my.router# set router-id 10.10.100.101
```

'Set' can be used at any level along the tree as long as a valid path to that option exists from the present location. Remember since we are at `[routing-options]` we can access and modify the information at this level and below, but cannot access anything that is above it. For instance, if we need to change the router hostname, we will not be able to access it from this level.

```
[edit routing-options]
jncia@my.router# set hostname
                     ^
syntax error.
```

The hostname option is under the `[system]` portion of the configuration tree, and thus is not configurable from here. Indeed, JUNOS will not allow you to proceed typing a hostname at this point. Attempting to enter the space after hostname will likewise echo back a syntax error as the software cannot find a valid completion for that command at this level.

It is important to note that configuration commands within JUNOS are somewhat different than Cisco IOS in that the exact command you type does not appear in the configuration file.

Examine this example of a basic BGP configuration:

```
[edit protocols bgp]
jncia@my.router# show

     group ebgp-peer {
          peer-as 123
          type external
          neighbor 10.0.0.1
     }
```

You see the familiar hierarchical tree format. However, to set these parameters you could simply type one line:

```
[edit]
jncia@my.router# set protocols bgp group ebgp-peer
peer-as 123 type external neighbor 10.0.0.1
```

Or, you could enter these commands one at a time:

```
[edit]
jncia@my.router# edit protocols bgp group ebgp-peer

[edit protocols bgp group ebgp-peer]
jncia@my.router# set peer-as 123

[edit protocols bgp group ebgp-peer]
jncia@my.router# set type external

[edit protocols bgp group ebgp-peer]
jncia@my.router# set neighbor 10.0.0.1
```

Notice how neither of these resemble what is displayed when typing '`show`'. The command statements have been parsed and placed in the correct logical grouping with the correct braces. JUNOS takes care of all that. Note as well that the entire subsection could be entered with four command statements, or with one slightly longer, more complex `set`. Finally, take note of the fact that in the second example we move down the command tree several levels at once, four levels to be exact: [protocols], [bgp], [group] and the group-name [ebgp-peer]. This could have been accomplished in four separate steps as well. Just as the first example configured multiple options at once, the second moves down several levels at once.

We have seen how entering `[edit <sub-section>]` allows us to progress down the tree. There are three ways to travel back up the command hierarchy as well: `exit,` `up,` and `top`.

Exit – This returns the user to the last level that was active. If the user had gone to a [edit protocols bgp group ebgp-peer] with one command, exit will return the CLI to the top level. If the user had gone to [group ebgp-peer] from [protocols bgp], exit will return to [protocols bgp]. Exiting from the main configuration CLI will return the user to operational mode.

```
[edit]
jncia@my.router# edit protocols bgp group
ebgp-peer

[edit protocols bgp group ebgp-peer]
jncia@my.router# exit

[edit]
jncia@my.router# edit protocols bgp

[edit protocols bgp]
jncia@my.router# edit group ebgp-peer

[edit protocols bgp group ebgp-peer]
jncia@my.router# exit

[edit protocols bgp]
jncia@my.router# exit

[edit]
jncia@my.router# exit
Exiting configuration mode

jncia@my.router>
```

Up – This command moves to the level immediately above the present tier by a specified number of steps. If the user had gone to specific level four lower than the general top level of edit, up will move the CLI to a level three lower than general edit. Entering 'up 4' will have the same effect as exit. The default is one level.

```
[edit]
jncia@my.router# edit protocols bgp group ebgp-peer
```

```
[edit protocols bgp group ebgp-peer]
jncia@my.router# up
```

(Note that this moves up both `[group]` and `[group name]`, as they are logically one level)

```
[edit protocols bgp]
jncia@my.router# up

[edit protocols]
jncia@my.router#
```

Top – This command moves to the root, or main, edit prompt regardless of current level or how many steps were taken to get there.

```
[edit protocols bgp]
jncia@my.router# top

[edit]
jncia@my.router#
```

Candidate Configuration and Commit

Two extremely useful points regarding system configuration are the idea of the candidate configurations and the `'commit'` statement.

Once in the configuration mode `[edit]`, the active configuration can be modified in any way. As soon as you enter configuration mode, the aspects you are altering become known as the *candidate configuration*. The candidate configuration does not replace the running configuration until the 'commit' command is entered. If there is a syntax error upon committing the candidate, the process will report an error and continue running from the pre-commit configuration. Note as well that if the configuration is modified and the user exits from edit mode without committing the changes, the router will still be running the original configuration but will have a modified candidate buffered in edit. If someone later re-enters edit mode to make different changes, they may well end up unknowingly committing changes someone else had made previously.

Loading files

There are also a number of ways to import sections of a configuration from ASCII files with the `load` command. This takes the requested file and places it in the candidate configuration. It is important to note that the ASCII file must have the configuration in the correct hierarchical format. This means that JUNOS is expecting commands that are in the correct tree syntax, complete with accurate brace placements around the correct groupings ({,}). A file filled with '`set`' command statements will not work with '`load`'. There are three options when loading a file:

```
[edit]
load [merge|override|replace] [terminal|filename]
```

Load merge – This command statement adds the contents of the file to the current configuration and places the combined file into the candidate. If there are any conflicts between the loaded file and the current one, the loaded parameters over-write them.

Load override – This command disregards the existing configuration. The requested file, and the requested file alone, becomes the candidate. For this reason it is imperative that the loaded file contain a **complete** configuration.

Load replace – This final possibility copies the current configuration into the candidate and attempts to match and substitute the contents of the loaded file. The loaded file must contain the `replace:` tag prior to the configuration options changed to work correctly.

One further option that may be requested is to manually enter the data rather than load a pre-typed file. By specifying '`terminal`' as the source rather than a file name, the configuration CLI allows a user to input data in a field and terminate input with control-d when finished. This data field becomes the source file for the candidate load. Again, this data must be in the correct hierarchical format, complete with braces. For this reason, this option is not really meant for a user to manually type in the data; instead it is a great way to quickly cut-and-paste in a desired pre-assembled snippet. Manually configuring the router is always best done with `set` commands.

Rollback

There have been a number of notes mentioned about how JUNOS keeps backup copies of previous configurations on hand for quick access. As was mentioned previously, any configuration changes made to the router do no take effect until a commit is performed. But what happens if there is an unforeseen problem after the commit is made? With certain types of network gear, there might be no choice but to manually undue each of the configured changes by explicitly deleting each change that was made. In extreme cases, an entire backup configuration might have to be loaded. JUNOS eases this not altogether uncommon problem of configuration mistakes and allows for easy reversal. By keeping the latest configuration handy in flash memory, if a problem is encountered the technician can immediately take advantage of the *rollback* command to reload the pre-changed file. In a sense, it is a shortcut `load override` with a locally stored file.

```
[edit]
jncia@my.router# rollback ?
Possible completions:
  <[Enter]>        Execute this command
  <number>         Numeric argument
  0                2003-03-11 09:33:44 UTC by john via cli
  1                2003-02-13 09:32:52 UTC by jeff via cli
  2                2003-02-09 18:29:02 UTC by tyler via cli
  3                2003-01-20 21:18:23 UTC by root via cli
  |                Pipe through a command
```

The rollback will replace the modified config file with the back-up. This is the equivalent of loading any locally stored file and must still be committed for the router to take it. Because the router keeps the 9 most recent modifications, a complex, multi-step maintenance gone wrong can still be somewhat painlessly backed out. This should not, however, be considered an excuse for not having adequate remote back-ups of configuration files. Accidents and system crashes do occur, as do maintenances with a dozen modifications.

We can see from the previous example that the configuration was modified four times. The actively running configuration file is numbered 0. We can also see a timestamp for when changes were made. Upon entering:

```
[edit]
jncia@my.router# rollback 1
```

File number 1 is loaded as the candidate configuration. It will not take effect until a '`commit`' is issued. Note that rollback commands must be given from the top level of `[edit]`.

If we were instead to edit and commit an additional change, each number would increment by 1. There would be a new active file 0 written with the current timestamp, and there would then be 5 files total.

Traceoptions

One of the unique and extremely helpful features of the JUNOS software is the ability to setup and monitor detailed logging information. This logging information is known in JUNOS as *traceoptions*. They are extremely versatile and may be applied at practically any and all levels of the configuration. The log information is stored, by default, on the router hard drive. The default logfile is named *messages* and it contains information about interface and protocol flaps as well as general error output. Additional logs and more specific traceoptions, called flags, can be configured. Logs can be viewed by issuing the "show log *logfile-name*" command at the operational CLI. Additionally, "show log?" will display the available files that have been configured for traceoptions. Another useful command is "monitor start *logfile-name*", which continually prints new output to the file as it is posted to the log. This is extremely useful for real-time debugging of routing problems. The display of this information can be stopped by "monitor stop *logfile-name*" or "monitor stop all".

Introduction to Routing

Routing is the process by which data is delivered to and through the correct nodes in a network. The rules followed by particular nodes that make routing possible are called *protocols*. A *routing* protocol is one which determines paths and delivery, or routes, of data packets. Examples of routing protocols include OSPF, BGP, IS-IS, RIP, and the Cisco proprietary E/IGRP. A *routed* protocol is one which carries the data, such as IP, IPX, Appletalk or the like. Juniper routers are optimized for routed IP, as indeed is most of the Internet, and as such the Juniper certifications are based upon IP only. Similarly, Juniper routers utilize open standards routing protocols.. Consequently the JNCIA will exclusively focus upon RIP, OSPF, IS-IS, BGP and multicast protocols.

The JUNOS software architecture maintains routing information in two related databases: the *Routing Table* and the *Forwarding Table*. The Routing Table contains all routing information learned by all routing protocols running on the Juniper. The Forwarding Table contains only the routes that are actually used to forward packets to their destinations. In a sense, the Routing Table holds all possible routing information for all destinations known to the router. Meanwhile, the Forwarding Table holds only the best path per destination, called the *active route*. By only holding the active route, the Forwarding table is minimized in terms of size, while still being able to reach every known location.

By default, JUNOS software maintains multiple routing tables. The following are the important tables to remember for the exam:

- inet.0 - Default unicast table
- inet.1 - Default multicast table
- inet.2 - Multicast RPF checks
- inet.3 - MPLS path information
- mpls.0 – MPLS label-swapping table

(*inet* is an abbreviation for Internet)

The mpls.0 table lists the next hop router for each label switch path, allowing transit routers to forward packets along the LSP. See the *MPLS* section for more details.

More detailed information regarding the process prefixes travel through before becoming installed into the forwarding table will be covered more in-depth in the *Hardware* section.

There are a number of different routing protocols with which a router might learn how to get to a particular address. Because of this, the device needs a system to determine which route it will prefer. Each prefix put into the routing table of a Juniper router is listed along with the protocol from which it is learned. While the JUNOS software might have many routes to a particular host, only the active route is installed into the forwarding table and used to route packets. Each protocol is assigned a *preference*, a number from 0-255, with lower numbers being more preferable. Generally, a better preference indicates a more reliable protocol and hence a more desirable path. The table below illustrates how the protocol preferences are broken down.

How route is learned	Default Preference
Directly Connected	0
Static	5
MPLS	7
OSPF Internal	10
IS-IS Level 1	15
IS-IS Level 2	18
Redirects	30
RIP	100
Point to Point	110
Aggregate	130
OSPF External	150
BGP	170

Table 3.4 Route Preference

So if a router knows of two paths to a particular destination, one through RIP and another via OSPF, it will choose OSPF with a preference of 10. It may seem a bit counter-intuitive to think lower preference is better, but this is one of the few cases where this is true. Keep in mind that these preferences can be modified from their default value through configuring *policy* (to be covered later in this book).

If a router has more than one equal-cost path to the exact same destination, it will randomly install one of those routes into the forwarding table. In order to install multiple routes, policy must be applied to load balance traffic between the paths.

Static vs Dynamic Routes

Routing protocols such as OSPF are examples of how a router learns *dynamic routes.* Dynamic routing utilizes information exchanged by protocols between neighboring routers to monitor and modify route information as the network topology changes. Routes may be manually configured by an administrator. Such routes do not change unless the configuration is updated and do not reflect the overhead 'work' of a dynamic routing protocol. Such routes are called *static routes*. The configuration for static routes is relatively straight-forward and simple, but it does not provide a robust system of routing or the advantages of automated redundancy common to dynamic protocols.

Once configured, static routes remain active and do not respond to topology changes. The exception to this is if the change is local to the router, such as if the static route is associated to an interface or next-hop that goes away. Static routes are installed in inet.0.

Configuring Static Routes

Static routes do not have a protocol per se, and are therefore configured under the [routing-options static] level of edit mode. There must be a valid next-hop address for the static address to work. A null value is considered valid for this. The syntax is:

```
[edit routing-options static]
jncia@my.router# set route destination-address/subnet-
mask [discard|reject|next-hop <next-hop-
address>|<interface-name>]

[edit]
jncia@my.router# show routing-options

routing-options{
      static {
            route 192.168.100.0/24 next-hop 10.1.134.2;
            route 192.168.200.0/24 next-hop so-1/0/0.0;
            route 192.168.220.0/24 discard;
            }
}
```

If an IP address or interface is not given for a next-hop, one of the null values must be used. When a null route is configured, packets matching that route are dropped. The difference between the `reject` and `discard` null value is in how they respond to dropping the packet. A `reject` null route will return an ICMP "prohibited" message. A static route with a `discard` null value will silently drop the packet, returning no message.

There is a fourth option, `receive`, for static routes. This indicates that packets matching the static are to go to the RE. Static routes with the `receive` option are not covered on the JNCIA.

Each of the dynamic protocols on the JNCIA exam will be covered in a dedicated chapter later in this book. The advantages and challenges of each will be detailed at that time. At this point, suffice it to say, the additional configuration complexity and overhead are generally accepted because of the benefits of less administration and dynamic fault tolerance. The router uses static routes when it does not have a route with a lower (better) preference (see the above), when it cannot determine the route to a specific destination, or when forwarding un-routable packets.

It should also be noted that the individual routing protocols can be manually configured to have a different preference, thus allowing a different route to be selected. An example of this would be someone configuring a static route of last resort and stipulating a preference of 200. This way, any other identical route coming from a dynamic protocol will be selected first.

Interface and Routing-Options Configuration

As was mentioned before, protocol and policy relevant configuration will be covered in their specific chapters. The configuration areas that remain and should be given consideration for the examination will be covered here.

Interface Configuration

One of the two main levels of configuration that need attention is:

[edit interfaces] – Access to configure physical and logical aspects of the interfaces

Configuration options at the interface level of edit mode allow the user to define interfaces addresses, sub-interfaces, encapsulations, and the routing family with which it will forward packets. Juniper routers have two types of interfaces, *permanent* and *transient*. Any interface installed as a PIC is a transient interface. This includes all the mixes of SONET, ATM, Ethernet, and serial ports. Permanent interfaces are automatically detected by JUNOS and begin with the identifier *fxp*. The management Ethernet interface for out of band connectivity is `fxp0`. The internal Ethernet interface that allows communication between the RE and the PFE is `fxp1`.

When installing transient interfaces, JUNOS automatically recognizes the hardware and provides a physical tag for it. The physical interface tag is given in the format of <type>-<fpc>/<pic>/<port> where:

- Type = The media type (a complete list is in the *Appendix*)
    a) so = SONET
    b) at = ATM
    c) fe = Fast Ethernet
    d) ge = Gigabit Ethernet
    e) lo = Loopback
    f) t1 = T1 interface
    g) t3 = T3 interface
- FPC = The FPC slot in which the PIC resides
- PIC = The PIC location on the FPC
- Port = The PIC port number

When reading the physical interface tags, it is important to remember that numbering begins with zero. For example, `so-0/1/2` describes the physical SONET interface that is located on the first FPC slot (numbered 0), PIC slot 1, and port 2 on that PIC. This physical tag is used for identifying the particular interface a user wishes to view or configure and is not the same as the interface description, which may be set with the `description` option under `[edit interfaces]`. It is user defined and may be any string. However, JUNOS requires any string that includes spaces to be enclosed in double quotes ("description").

```
[edit interfaces]
jncia@my.router# set so-4/0/0 description "OC3 to
Chicago"

[edit interfaces]
jncia@my.router# show

so-4/0/0 {
        description "OC3 to Chicago";
}
```

The physical interface requires an encapsulation type to successfully establish a layer-2 link with the remote interface. Encapsulation types vary by physical interface, but they are all configured under the interfaces level of edit mode. Enabling Point-to-Point protocol on our sonet link looks like:

```
[edit interfaces]
jncia@my.router# set so-4/0/0 encapsulation ppp

[edit interfaces]
jncia@my.router# show
    so-4/0/0 {
        description "OC3 to Chicago";
        encapsulation ppp;
}
```

Each physical interface may have one or more logical, or virtual, interfaces mapped to it. Multiple logical sub-interfaces can be useful in ATM, Frame Relay, and Ethernet networks when creating virtual circuits or VLANS on a single physical port.

These sub-interfaces are configured under `[edit interfaces]` level with the `unit` command statement.

```
[edit interfaces]
jncia@my.router# set so-4/0/0 unit 0

    so-4/0/0 {
        description "OC3 to Chicago";
        encapsulation ppp;
        unit 0
}
```

Each logical interface descriptor can have one or more *family* descriptors to define the protocol family that is associated with and allowed to run over the logical interface. Families referred to for the JNCIA are listed below. A complete list is included in the *Appendix*.

- Internet Protocol, version 4 (IPv4)
- International Organization for Standardization (ISO)
- Multiprotocol Label Switching (MPLS)

The Internet family, commonly referred to as 'family inet', is used when considering IP protocols such as OSPF, BGP, and RIP. 'Family iso' is used in conjunction with IS-IS, while 'family mpls' is, of course, used by MPLS forwarding. Multiple families may be configured on a single interface. Simply put, this means that the interface must be configured for the types of protocol families that will be used upon it. An interface must have a family type enabled before it will allow network traffic to utilize the link.

```
[edit interfaces so-4/0/0 unit 0]
jncia@my.router# set family inet

[edit interfaces so-4/0/0 unit 0]
jncia@my.router# set family mpls

    so-4/0/0 {
        description "OC3 to Chicago";
        encapsulation ppp;
        unit 0 {
            family inet;
            family mpls;
        }
    }
```

Additionally, the address for a particular family is designated beneath the family level of configuration.

```
[edit interfaces so-4/0/0 unit 0]
jncia@my.router# set family inet address
192.168.10.1/30

    so-4/0/0 {
        description "OC3 to Chicago";
        encapsulation ppp;
        unit 0 {
            family inet {
                address 192.168.10.1/30;
            }
            family mpls;
        }
    }
```

Configuring Routing-Options

The second area of configuration that does not fit under a specific protocol or other area is that of routing-options. There are three areas important to the JNCIA at this configuration level of which you should be aware.

```
[edit routing-options]
jncia@my.router# set?
Possible completions:
      autonomous-system   Autonomous system number
      router-id           Router identifier
      static              Static routes
```

(These are not all the possible completions, only the ones that may concern the examination.)

We have already seen the concept of static routes and the methods for configuring them previously in this chapter.

```
[edit]
jncia@my.router# show routing-options

routing-options{
      static {
            route 192.168.100.0/24 next-hop 10.1.134.2;
            route 192.168.200.0/24 next-hop so-1/0/0.0;
            route 192.168.220.0/24 discard;
            }
}
```

The Autonomous System Number (ASN) is necessary for BGP to function properly. However, since it actually defines the administrative group to which the router belongs, it is configured below routing options:

```
[edit routing-options]
jncia@my.router# set autonomous-system as_number
```

Where `as_number` is the desired ASN 1 through 65535 inclusive.

Likewise, the Router ID (RID) is a crucial component used by a number of processes. It is defined with the command statement below:

```
[edit routing-options]
jncia@my.router# set router-id address
```

Key Points

- JUNOS runs on a UNIX kernel.
- Software processes run in separate memory space for increased stability.
- The main JUNOS image resides on compact flash.
- A back-up image is kept on the hard-drive.
- The standard boot sequence for JUNOS:
    - PCMCIA flash
    - Compact flash
    - Hard-drive
    - Network
- The CLI has an operational and configuration mode.
- Static routes are manually configured and go into inet.0.
- Static routes must have a valid next-hop or null value configured.
- Dynamic routes are learned via routing protocols.
- JUNOS uses administrative preference to choose between multiple routes. Lower preference is better.

Directly Connected	0
Static	5
MPLS	7
OSPF Internal	10
IS-IS Level 1	15
IS-IS Level 2	18
Redirects	30
RIP	100
Point to Point	110
Aggregate	130
OSPF External	150
BGP	170

- Interface configuration controls:
    - Sub-interfaces
    - Protocol families
    - Addressing
    - Encapsulation
- Routing-option configuration controls:
    - Static routes
    - Autonomous System Number (ASN)
    - Router ID (RID)

Chapter Four
RIP

Chapter 4: RIP

Overview

In this chapter, we will discuss Routing Information Protocol (RIP). We will cover the differences between RIP version 1 and version 2, functionality, limitations, and configuration on a Juniper router.

RIP is arguably the easiest dynamic routing protocol to configure and run. Many of the concepts that follow will also be present in the more robust, complex protocols that appear later on in the book. By the end of this chapter, you should be able to understand and apply the following concepts:

- ✓ Understand why administrators implement dynamic routing
- ✓ RIP best path selection.
- ✓ Establishing and maintaining RIP neighbors.
- ✓ Route updates in RIP.
- ✓ Routing loop prevention within RIP.
- ✓ Configuration of RIP in JUNOS.

Introduction

You have already learned how the Juniper router organizes destination prefixes in the routing table and uses that to establish the forwarding table. Additionally, you have seen how to manually configure a next hop, called *static routing*. We now move on to cover the idea of *dynamic routing protocols*. Routing protocols are just that, rules by which two systems can exchange information on how to route packets. Unlike static routes, which must be manually updated, dynamic protocols can learn about topology changes, add new routes, and optimize routing without outside intervention. This translates into a more scalable network with less administrative overhead. There are a number of different routing protocols, each one offering its own advantages and challenges.

Dynamic routing protocols are generally grouped into two types: *distance vector* and *link-state*. We will discuss the concepts behind link-state protocols in the IS-IS and OSPF sections. RIP is a distance vector protocol. Distance vector protocols use *hop count* to determine the distance to get to a network, where each router that the traffic passes through is considered a hop. In this way, routers can determine which path will cross the least number of nodes. This is assumed to be the quickest/best path. RIP routers advertise their directly attached networks and the distance (hop count) to the networks they can reach via their RIP neighbors. Each neighboring router that hears advertised routes will then add one to the hop count and advertise them to its neighbors. This is how RIP routers form their view of network topology.

Protocol Fundamentals

Routing Information Protocol (RIP) is a simple distance-vector routing protocol used in fairly small and/or stable network environments. Timers are implemented at set intervals to communicate with its determined neighbors to exchange routing information and updates. RIP uses UDP port 520 for communication between network hosts and the Bellman-Ford algorithm to determine best path selection. Unlike other *Interior Gateway Protocols* (IGPs), RIP uses only a fixed metric (*hop count*) to select a route. The longest network path cannot exceed 15 hops with this routing protocol. A route metric of 16 or more is unreachable. This is what makes RIP best suited for use in smaller, stable networks

Version 1 vs. Version 2

Everything you hear and read about RIP will most likely be referring to version 2. Version 1 is old technology and is not widely used. However, it is important to know the differences between these versions for the JNCIA exam.

Version 1 does not support classless routing. This is to state that the route received by a RIPv1 neighbor is assumed to be class-full. If a version 1 router receives an update for the route 120.1.2.3, it will be automatically assumed to be 120.0.0.0/8 (the Class A equivalent route). This precludes the use of VLSM in RIP version 1.

In version 1, the neighbor's address is always assumed to be the next-hop address for the destination (not efficient in an Ethernet or other multi-access environment). Version 2 adds a field in route updates for the next-hop address.

Version 1 broadcasts messages. Version 2 uses multicast to the specific address of 224.0.0.9. All RIPv2 routers listen for this address, but do not forward the messages.
Version 2 supports route-tags (information carried from protocols redistributed into RIP), and is backward compatible with Version 1.

Authentication was not introduced until RIP version 2. The RFC for version 2 specifies plain-text passwords, but JUNOS allows plain-text and MD5 encrypted keys.

Communication between RIP hosts

As noted earlier, RIP uses UDP for all communication. This means that the communication of messages is "connectionless and unreliable". That is to state, there is no confirmation when routing updates are sent out to a neighboring host. Because of this fact, timers are padded to allow for the occasional loss of messages. Once an interface is configured for RIP, it will immediately begin transmitting its known and configured networks to all established neighbors. The transmit interval is user configurable, with the default set to occur every 30 seconds.

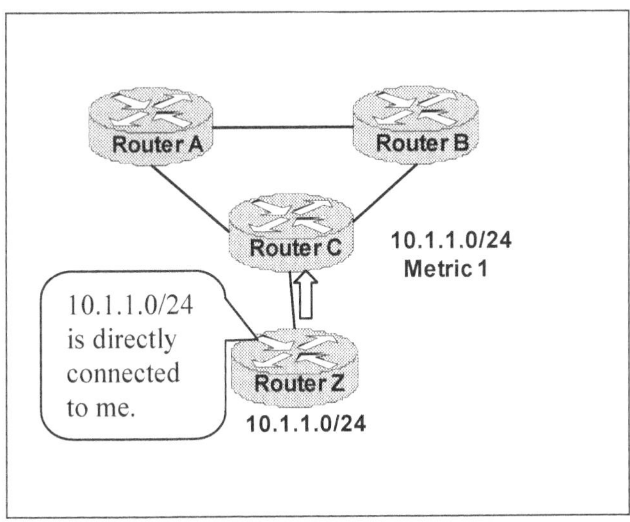

Figure 4.1 RIP Route Update

In Figure 4.1, Router Z is directly connected to network 10.1.1.0/24 and begins to advertise this in its updates with a hop-count of zero. Router C receives this update and increments the metric by one, indicating the destination is one hop away. Checking its routing table and seeing it has no better path, it installs the route and passes the information along in its own route updates that it sends to its neighbors.

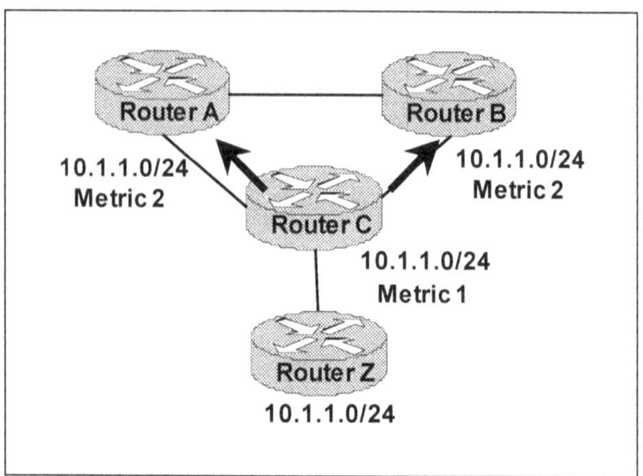

Figure 4.2 RIP Route Propagation

In Figure 4.2, C updates neighbors A and B with the route. They in turn increment the hop count and install the route as well. In the simple topology of 4.2, A and B will update each other with the route to 10.1.1.0/24. However, since the hop count will again be incremented, the metric for that path will then be three. Neither A nor B will choose to install that update as it already has a valid route with a lower metric of 2 by way of going through C.

Neighbors continue to pass RIP route updates hop by hop throughout the network. No neighbor will have a complete view of the topology until it has received all the updates. For this reason, RIP is sometimes called 'routing by rumor', as a router is only aware of what its neighbors are telling it. It is easy to see that this behavior, coupled with the 30-second update timer, could result in very large convergence times. A change propagating over 10 routers would require up to 300 seconds to be fully communicated throughout the network. However the period of the update timer must be balanced with the conservation of network overhead. Because RIP updates include the entire contents of the routing table they can be quite large. Forcing the timers to speed up can easily congest low bandwidth links and spike CPU usage on routers.

Another problem to contend with in RIP, as well as other dynamic protocols, is the controlling the spread of incorrect route information. RIP uses *split horizon with poisoned reverse* to control routing loops within a network. These principals are outlined below:

1) Split Horizon - Omit routes learned from a neighbor when sending updates to that neighbor. This means when Router A advertises networks to Router B, Router B will not send them back to Router A.

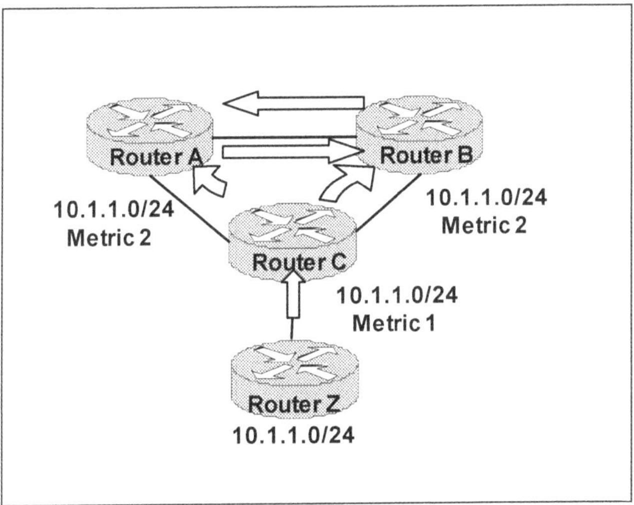

Figure 4.3 RIP Split Horizon

In figure 4.3 the destination 10.1.1.0/24 is directly connected to Z. RIP Router Z advertises its route to 10.1.1.0/24 to Router C, which increments the hop count and gives the route a metric of 1. Router C is running RIP with neighboring routers A and B. It advertises the route to both A and B. Both add 1 to the hop-count bringing the total metric to 2. Split Horizon dictates that Router C does not advertise the route back to Z, since it was received from that router. Similarly, neither A nor B will advertise the route back to Router C because of Split Horizon. Again, is noteworthy to see that Router A and B will announce the destination block to each other. However, because the direct path to Router C has a lower hop-count it wins.

2) Poisoned Reverse - Include such updates, but set their metric to infinity to immediate stop a routing loop. Keep in mind that poisoned reverse has the benefit of more quickly eliminating erroneous routes by marking them as "unreachable", but it does increase the size of routing updates.

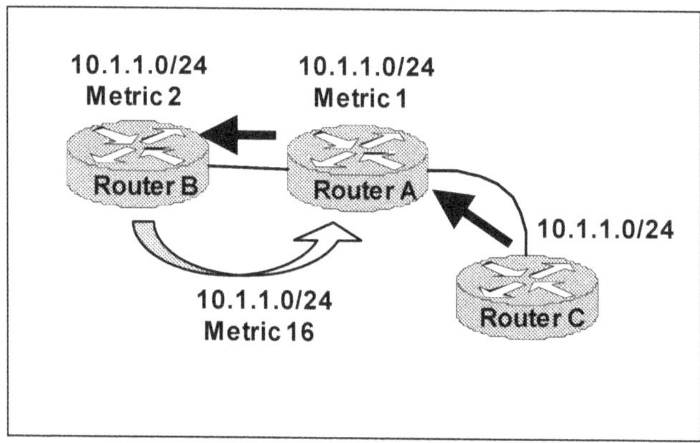

Figure 4.4 RIP Poison Reverse

RIP Packets

RIP messages contain the following fields:

Command—Indicates whether the packet is a *request* or *response* message. Request messages seek information for the router's routing table. Response messages are sent periodically and also when a request message is received from a neighbor. Periodic response messages are called *update messages*. Update messages contain the command and version fields and 25 destinations (by default), each of which includes the destination IP address and the metric to reach that destination.

A request is used to ask for a response containing all or part of a router's routing table. Normally, requests are sent by routers which have just come up and are seeking to fill in their routing tables as quickly as possible. The request is processed entry by entry. If there are no entries, no response is given. There is one special case. If there is exactly one entry in the request, and it has an *address family identifier* (AFI) of zero and a metric of infinity (i.e., 16), then this is a request to send the entire routing table.

Version number—Version of RIP that the originating router is running

Address family identifier (AFI)—Address family used by the originating router (value always "2" for IPv4)

Address—Destination network IP address

Metric—Value of the metric advertised for the address

Mask—Mask associated with the IP address (RIP Version 2 only, value of 0 in RIPv1)

Next hop—IP address of the next-hop router (RIP Version 2 only, value of 0 in RIPv1)

Controlling routing updates

Routes received from routers that are not configured as neighbors are simply ignored. Route updates, when received, can contain up to 25 destinations. If authentication is used, only 24 destinations can be sent in each update message. These updates are transmitted every 30 seconds (by default) by RIP-enabled routers, this is known as the *keepalive*. If four times the keepalive interval is exceeded, the neighbor is considered to be dead.

It is important to recognize that the RIP table remains constant unless one of the following occurs:

1) **Route removal**
    1) The timer expires (default setting 120 seconds) with no updates to reset it.
    2) An update is received with a metric of 16 (thus triggering the route as unreachable). This can also happen via the "poisoned-reverse" process, too.
2) **Route addition**
    1) New network(s) are configured on the router
    2) A new route is received from a valid neighbor with a metric of 15 or less (a reachable route)

Routes received from valid neighbors are compared to existing routes and the following actions are taken:

1) If the advertising neighbor and metric are the same, re-initialize the timeout and wait for the next update
2) If the advertising neighbor is the same but the metric is lower, install the new route and trigger an update
3) If the advertising neighbor is the same but the metric is higher, look closer at the metric
    a. If it is higher, but less than 16, discard the update
    b. If it is 16, start the *route deletion* process for this route

The route deletion process consists of the following steps:

1) Set the new route metric to 16.
2) Trigger an update for this route (even if the timer is not yet due).
3) Start the 'garbage-collection' timer.
    a. Until this timer expires in 120 seconds, send updates for this route with a metric of 16
    b. When this timer expires, delete the route from all tables
    c. If a reachable route arrives during the "garbage-collection" period, the new route will be installed and the timer will be stopped. An update is triggered for this new route.

As an example, in RIP, every gateway that participates in routing sends an update message to all its neighbors once every 30 seconds. Suppose the current route for network N uses Router A. If we don't hear from N for 180 seconds, we can assume that either the gateway has crashed or the network connecting us to it has become unusable. To remove a route from the routing table, a host sends an update to its neighbor with a metric of one higher than the maximum hop count. The receiving host sees this value as 'infinity' and therefore marks the route as unreachable.

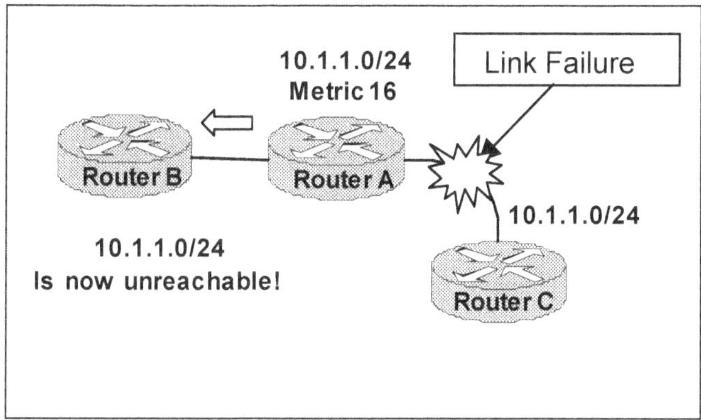

Figure 4.5 Route Removal

Configuration

By default, RIP is disabled on Juniper routers. To enable, enter the following:

```
[edit protocols rip]
jncia@my.router# Set group group-name neighbor
interface
```

All other RIP configuration statements are optional. This minimum configuration defines one group. Include one neighbor statement for each interface on which you want to receive routes. The local router imports all destinations from this neighbor and does not advertise routes (by default). RIP routes received from routers not explicitly configured as neighbors will be ignored. The router can receive both Version 1 and Version 2 update messages.

Once enabled, JUNOS is set to be compatible with both versions by default. JUNOS will send RIPv2 messages, but it will use broadcast addresses so that RIPv1 neighbors will hear the messages. JUNOS will receive both RIPv1 and RIPv2 messages. These parameters can be changed on a global or per-neighbor basis according to the following:

Send Compatibility Parameter Configured via 'send *X*'		
Option	JUNOS term (*X*)	Resulting Action
RIPv1	Version-1	Only RIPv1 messages are sent via broadcast
RIPv2	Version-2	Only RIPv2 messages are sent via multicast
RIPv1 compatible	Broadcast	Only RIPv2 messages are sent, but broadcast addresses are used so RIPv1 neighbors will hear them
Nothing	None	No RIP messages are sent

Receive Compatibility Parameter Configured via 'receive *Y*'		
Option	JUNOS term (*Y*)	Resulting Action
RIPv1 only	Version-1	Only RIPv1 messages are accepted
RIPv2only	Version-2	Only RIPv2 messages are accepted
Both	Both	Accept both RIPv1 and RIPv2
None	None	No RIP messages are accepted

Table 4.6 RIP Send and Receive Parameters

Additionally, the metric (hop-count) of received and advertised routes can be manually adjusted to a specific number through the use of the `metric-in` and `metric-out` configuration statements under the `[edit protocols rip]` hierarchy level.

Let's look at a typical JUNOS RIP configuration that includes the optional parameters for sending and receiving announcements as well as metric adjustment:

```
[edit protocols rip]
jncia@my.router# show
traceoptions {
   file rip size 1m files 3 world-readable;
   flag policy send;
}
metric-in 3;
```

```
metric-out 2;
group rip-neighbor-on-fe0-1-0 {
    metric-out 3;
    neighbor fe-0/1/0.0 {
        send broadcast;
        receive both;
    }
}
```

This is an example of the multi-tier hierarchy in editing the JUNOS configuration. In the case of RIP, like with other parameters, the more specific instance will nullify the more general. Consequently, `metric-in` and `metric-out` statements applied at the *global* RIP level will be overridden by those configured at the `group` level. Likewise, those at the `group` tier can be overridden at the `neighbor` configuration level.

Policy in RIP

As was noted before, by default JUNOS will accept all RIP routes received from a configured neighbor but will not advertise any known networks on the activated interfaces. Explicit *export* policy must be applied to force routes to be advertised to RIP neighbors as well as *import* policy to filter incoming routes. This practice of building filters with policy to control advertised and received updates is common across the different routing protocols.

To filter routes being imported by the router from RIP neighbors globally, include the keyword `import` *`policy-name`* configuration statement at the `[edit protocols rip]` level. Similarly, to have RIP advertise routes through policy, apply the keyword `export` *`policy-name`* statement at the global `[edit protocols rip]` level. If more than one policy name is included, they are evaluated first to last (left to right).

```
[edit protocols rip]
jncia@my.router# import policy-name

[edit protocols rip]
jncia@my.router# export policy-name
```

To selectively configure for a specific neighbor, add the keyword statement at the `[edit protocols rip group group-name neighbor address]` level.

For more information on JUNOS policy, see the *Policy* chapter.

Monitoring RIP in JUNOS

The basic commands to assist in troubleshooting and maintaining RIP are listed below.

```
jncia@my.router> show rip ?
Possible completions:
  general-statistics    Show RIP general statistics
  neighbor              Show RIP interfaces
  statistics            Show RIP statistics
```

```
jncia@my.router> show rip neighbor <interface>
```

This will display the status of current adjacencies. The interface and state are shown in the first columns. The configured modes for sending and receiving updates are noted in column five and six. Additionally, the metric applied to updates arriving on the interface will be shown in the final field.

```
jncia@my.router> show rip neighbor


                        Source            Destination      Send     Receive     In
Neighbor      State     Address           Address          Mode     Mode        Met
--------      -----     -------           -----------      ----     -------     ---
fe-0/0/0.2     Up      10.21.1.2          (null)           bcast    both          2
fe-0/0/0.1     Up      10.21.2.2          (null)           none     v2 only       1
```

```
jncia@my.router> show rip statistics <interface>
```

This command will display counters detailing update traffic for the specified interface. Statistics for all interfaces will be returned if no particular one is requested. Note the protocol timers listed on the line of output.

```
jncia@my.router> show rip statistics fe-0/0/0.2
```

```
RIP info:port 520; update interval 30s; holddown 180s; timeout
120s.
   rts learned  rts held down  rqsts dropped  resps dropped
           10              0              0              1

fe-0/0/0.2:  10 routes learned; 2 routes advertised
Counter                        Total   Last 5 min  Last minute
-------                  ----------- ----------- ----------
Updates Sent                       0           0            0
Triggered Updates Sent             1           0            0
Responses Sent                     0           0            0
Bad Messages                       0           0            0
RIPv1 Updates Received             0           0            0
RIPv1 Bad Route Entries            0           0            0
RIPv1 Updates Ignored              0           0            0
RIPv2 Updates Received             0           0            0
RIPv2 Bad Route Entries            0           0            0
RIPv2 Updates Ignored              0           0            0
Authentication Failures            0           0            0
RIP Requests Received              0           0            0
RIP Requests Ignored               0           0            0
```

Key Points

RIP is selected as it is relatively easy to configure and simple to operate. In light of its simplicity, this protocol takes significant coverage in the JNCIA exam. If for that reason alone, read this chapter carefully and be sure you can answer the test questions at the end.

- RIP is a distance vector protocol.
- Uses the Bellman-Ford algorithm to compute route preference.
- No authentication in Version 1
- RFC specifies plain-text passwords for Version 2
    - JUNOS supports plain-text and MD5 encrypted passwords in Version 2
- Metric is hop-count.
- Hop count of 16 is unreachable.
- Utilizes Poison Reverse and Split Horizon to prevent routing loops.
- Does not scale to large networks.
- Update timer defaults to 30 seconds.
- Dead timer defaults to 120 seconds.
- 25 destinations per update message (24 if authentication is configured).

Additional Information

For additional information, please consult the following at http://www.ietf.org:

- RFC 1058 Routing Information Protocol
- RFC 1721 RIP Version 2 Protocol Analysis
- RFC 2453 RIP Version 2

Chapter Five

OSPF

Chapter 5: OSPF

Overview

In this section you will learn about the dynamic routing protocol OSPF and its fundamental concepts. By the end of this chapter you should understand and be able to define:

- ✓ The purpose of Link-state routing protocols
- ✓ Route path selection in OSPF
- ✓ Operation of the Hello protocol
- ✓ Stages of neighbor adjacency
- ✓ Link-state Advertisements
- ✓ OSPF network types
- ✓ Area Types
- ✓ OSPF router types

Introduction

You have seen how the implementation of dynamic routing protocols assists network administrators and allows for increased complexity with the addition of RIP. However, rapid network expansion soon pushed RIP beyond practical limitations on large networks. *Open Shortest Path First* (OSPF) protocol was developed in response to a need in the networking community for a robust, non-proprietary *Interior Gateway Protocol* (IGP). As an IGP, OSPF routes packets within a single *Autonomous System* (AS) – the term used for a network under a common administration. It was designed for TCP/IP, and as such explicitly supports *Variable Length Subnet Masking* (VLSM) to make better use of address space. All versions of JUNOS software support OSPF version 2.

In addressing the most problematic issues with RIP, OSPF is a departure from it on several fundamental levels. Whereas RIP is a distance vector protocol relying on hop-count to determine best path selection, OSPF is a *link-state* protocol. Link-state protocols require that each participating node have full knowledge of the complete network topology. Each node (router in this case) must keep track of the link status, or state, of each of its connections and immediately notify the other nodes of any changes occurring.

Using link-state information to make routing decisions, OSPF utilizes the *Shortest Path First* (SPF) algorithm to determine the lowest cost link between two nodes in the same area, eliminating the limitation of hop-count. The SPF calculation is based upon the Djikstra Algorithm, named after Dutch scientist Edsgar Djikstra, which determines the distance between a matrix of nodes. Therefore, by applying a 'distance' or cost to each link on an internetwork the SPF algorithm can compute the shortest or least costly path between any two nodes.

Fundamentally, the SPF tree will calculate the cost by adding the link *metric* of all intervening connecting nodes. The metric is an administratively defined cost for the link leaving a router. By default, it is based on the interface bandwidth, but can be configured to reflect the desire of the administrator. It is important to remember that OSPF metrics will control which path packets take through the network, so it is best to rely on a consistent formula when deciding metrics.

In Figure 5.1 below, to get from node A to node E, OSPF will look at the cost to go from A to D and add that to the cost of going D to E. Likewise, it will also calculate the cost of going via B in a similar manner. When all possible paths have been accounted for, the lowest cost path is selected. It is also important to note that OSPF costs are assigned to the interface on the router rather than to physical link itself, so it is possible to have asymmetric costs, meaning the metrics could be different for each direction. This is illustrated as well in the below diagram (Figure 5.1) where the cost to go to router A **from** B is 50, while the cost from A **to** B is 20. It is possible for this to make instances of asymmetric routing, where traffic between two nodes takes different paths. If we were to assume that all of the unmarked paths have a cost of 10 and the links between A and B cost as marked, packets going from A to B will flow directly across their shared link while packets returning from B to A will travel B – E – D – A. This is because the interface connecting B directly to A costs 50 while each of the interfaces B to E, E to D and D to A cost 10, for a total cost of 30. Similarly, since the cost on A's interface to B is 20 and the route through D-E costs 30, it is the lowest cost path.

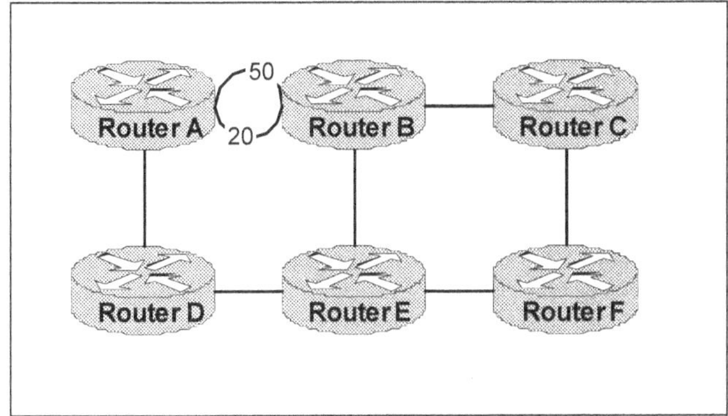

Figure 5.1 OSPF Matrix and Metrics

If there are multiple links with the same overall cost available to get to a specific destination the Juniper router will randomly select a next-hop. If the next hop changes at any time, the route selection will be redone in a random fashion. In the above diagram, for example, packets leaving Router C destined for Router E have two equal cost paths: one next hop on Router B and another through Router F. Because of this, JUNOS will randomly select which next-hop to install as the active route.

Adjacencies

In order for routers running OSPF to exchange data, there must be a mechanism for them to determine other nearby, or adjacent, nodes with which they can communicate. To enable OSPF on a router, you must explicitly declare which interface(s) will be taking part in the OSPF process. Each router must also supply a *Router ID* (RID) to uniquely identify it. The RID is typically a loopback address, but can theoretically be any unique IP address allocated to the router. Upon declaring active interfaces and the RID, the router is ready to begin communicating with the other routers on its directly connected networks. OSPF implements a *hello* protocol to establish and maintain adjacencies with neighboring routers.

Hello Protocol

Through the exchange of *hello* packets OSPF routers establish and maintain adjacencies. However, simply sending and receiving *hello* packets out active interfaces is not enough to bring up a stable adjacency. There are a number of configurable parameters that must match between connected nodes before an adjacency will form.

Upon starting up, OSPF will send *hello* packets out every active OSPF interface to the special multicast address of 224.0.0.5. All OSPF routers listen for packets with this address. The *hello* packets include the source and destination IP addresses, the RID, and the configured values for the *Area ID*, authentication, network mask, *Hello Interval* and *Router Dead Interval*. If any of the configured values do not correspond between routers, an adjacency will not form. The Hello Interval is the number of seconds between *hello* packet advertisements. The default value is 10 seconds. The Router Dead Interval is the amount of time that can pass without receiving a *hello* packet before a router will consider a neighbor unreachable. The default router dead interval (also known as the dead or hold-down timer) is 40 seconds. *Hello* packets reside on top of IP, utilizing port 89.

As an OSPF router sends out and receives hello packets, it goes through the below stages in forming an adjacency:

- **Down** – The first state of adjacency. This means that no information has been received from the neighbor. If an OSPF router fails to receive a Hello packet from a working neighbor within the Dead Interval (normally four times the Hello interval), its state changes to DOWN.
- **Init** (Initialize) – This state reflects that the router has received a Hello packet from a neighbor, but it does not see its own RID in the *hello*. When a router receives a *hello* packet from a neighboring router, it includes the sender's router ID in its own hello advertisements.
- **2-Way** – This state indicates that the routers have established communication in both directions. Since an OSPF router includes the RID of a received h*ello* in its own h*ello* packet, a router receiving a h*ello* packet with its own RID included within it knows the neighbor is receiving its advertisements. Routers that are not DR/BDR on a BMA network will remain in '2-way' (see *Network Types*).
- **Exstart** (exchange start) – This is the first step in forming a legitimate adjacency. A *master/slave* relationship is determined at this point for the actual database exchange.
- **Exchange** – Routers exchange *link-state advertisements* (LSAs) in this state with *database description* (DBD) packets. Each LSA

update contains a sequence number assigned by the master and is explicitly acknowledged by the slave router.

- **Loading** – During an adjacency, if a router receives a missing or out of date LSA it requests an update by sending a link-state request. This state indicates the router is in the process of updating its LSA database.
- **Full** – Signifies the OSPF databases are synchronized between neighbors. Routers in *full* are fully adjacent. When all neighbors in an area are fully adjacent to their neighbors the area is considered *converged*.

The behavior of the *hello* protocol varies slightly depending upon the type of network over which it is working. There are four different types of OSPF networks, listed below.

Network Types

There are 4 different network types on which the JNCIA tests knowledge:

- Point-to-Point (P2P)
- Broadcast Multi-access (BMA)
- Non-Broadcast Multi-access (NBMA)
- Point-to-Multipoint (P2MP)

Point-to-Point

This is the simplest of the above network types. Two routers are directly connected to each other, which means that each router only has a single neighbor over that interface. These links are normally configured over serial or SONET connections. Neighbors on a point-to-point link should be in *full* state.

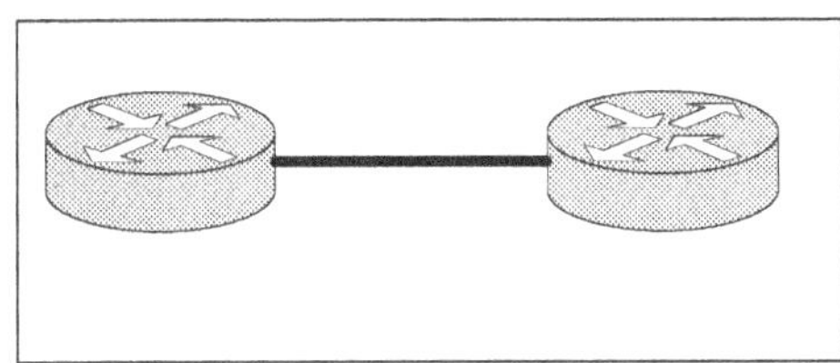

Figure 5.2 Point to Point Network

Broadcast Multi-Access Networks (BMA)

Broadcast networks are *local area network* (LAN) connections between routers that are capable of broadcasting. Ethernet is by far the most common type of this connection. For a full mesh, each router on a multi-access network would need one less than N neighbors, where N is the total number of nodes on the broadcast network running OSPF. If there are five nodes running OSPF on an Ethernet segment, *each node* has 4 neighbors. To reduce the amount of routing overhead between neighbors on the segment, OSPF elects a node to be the primary communicator and another to be the secondary. These are called the *designated router* (DR) and *backup designated router* (BDR), respectively.

All nodes on the BMA form a Full adjacency with the DR and BDR only. The remaining neighbors stay in 2way state, meaning they do not send or receive updates from those routers. It is the DR's primary responsibility to ensure that all routers connected to the broadcast network receive updates about all changes to the BMA topology. It is the job of the BDR to make certain the DR does not fail in delivering updates to the network. If the BDR senses that the DR has failed, it assumes the role of DR and distributes the routing updates itself. For this reason, the BDR and DR have synchronized link-state databases. For more on the rules to determine DR/BDR election, see the following section *Multi Access Networks and Designated Router Elections.*

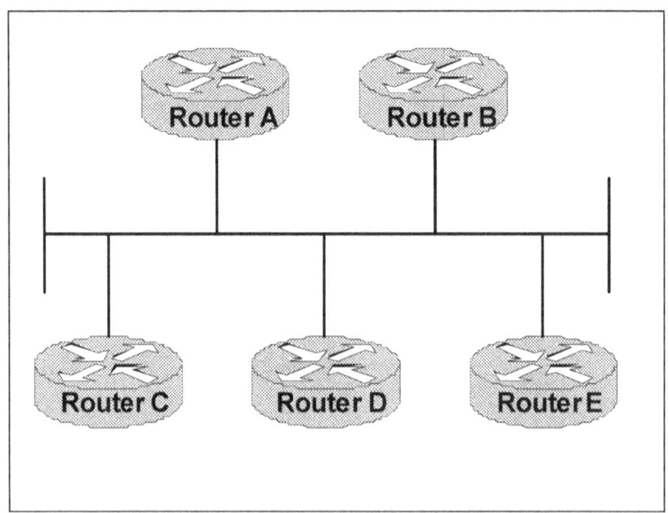

Figure 5.3 Broadcast Multi-Access Network

Non-Broadcast Multi-Access (NBMA)

This type of network connects multiple routers across a non-broadcast medium, such as X.25, ATM, or frame relay. These types of connections have intermediate switches for virtual circuit termination placed between routers. Default behavior for an NBMA network requires a designated router be established. The routers connected to a NBMA network can be partially or fully meshed.

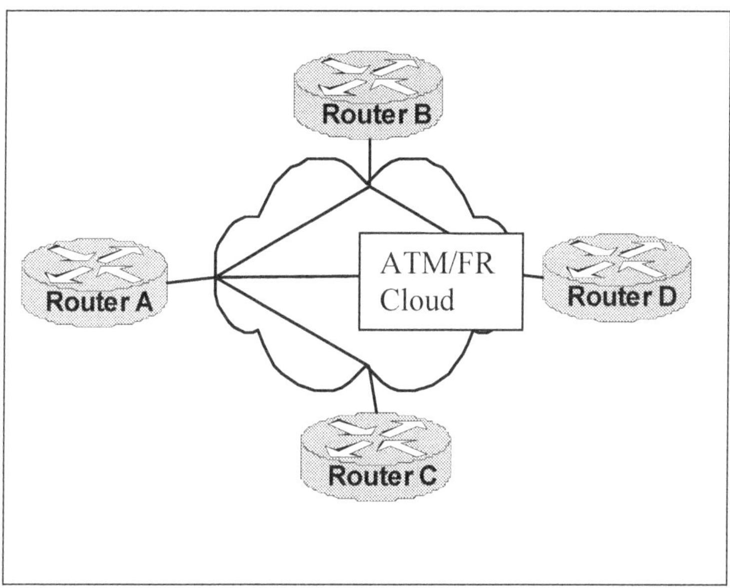

Figure 5.4 Partial Mesh NBMA or P2MP Network

NBMA networks have one additional state when forming adjacencies called *attempt*. While in this state, the router is attempting to send *hello* packets to the neighbor but has not yet received any information. The *attempt* state is only valid for NBMA participating routers and will not be seen on other network types.

Point to Multipoint (P2MP)

From the perspective of the JNCIA exam, this network type is identical to the NMBA with the exception of a full network mesh. It can be treated as a collection of P2P networks. There are no DR or BDR routers required.

Multi-Access Networks and Designated Router Elections

As discussed above under BMA networks, a full mesh between routers on a multi-access network would require each router to have one less than N neighbors where N is the number routers on the segment. It is the job of the DR/BDR system to ensure all neighbors receive network topology updates while reducing the amount of traffic on the attached network. To do this, during the initial phase of adjacency forming OSPF routers will elect a Designated Router and a Backup Designated Router. Neighbors will only form a full adjacency with the routers that are selected to be DR/BDR and will remain in 2way with the other routers on the segment.

If only one router is up on a multi-access network, it is the DR. When a second router is added, it becomes the BDR. Subsequent routers will form adjacencies with the DR/BDR but remain in 2-way with one another. No elections take place until either the DR or BDR fail. An election takes place if the DR fails. The BDR becomes the new DR and a new BDR is elected.

OSPF uses router priority to determine which routers are the most preferred for DR/BDR election. Router priority is a configurable number from 0 to 128, where a higher value is more preferred to become DR. A priority of 0 has special significance. A router with priority 0 **cannot** become DR. If multiple routers have the same priority, as they would by default, then the lower Router ID is used. Remember, if a router with a higher priority comes up on a LAN segment that already has a DR it **will not** pre-empt or force an election, but will be elected if the acting DR fails in the future.

Area and Router Types

OSPF is a hierarchical protocol. To reduce the size of the link-state database and the frequency of LSA flooding to all nodes, an OSPF domain may be broken into different logical areas which function independently of one another. Each node running OSPF in the area must have an identical link-state database. Nodes in different areas may have differing databases.

Area 0

Area 0 is the backbone area and is the fundamental area. If there is only one area in an OSPF domain, it can be any number. Most often, for reasons of simplicity and scalability, it is configured as area 0. A simple illustration of this is in Figure 5.5.

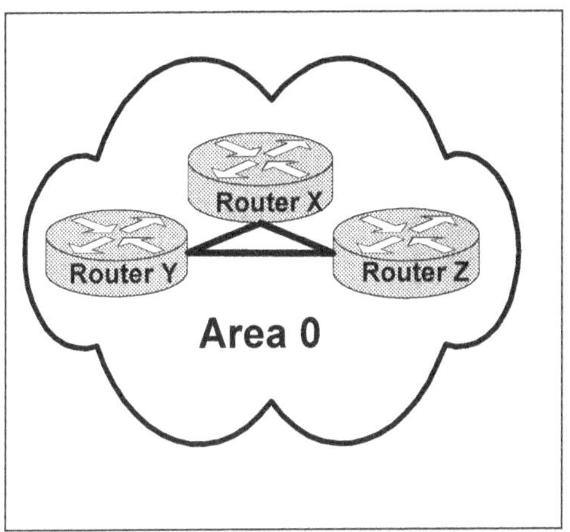

Figure 5.5 Single Area OSPF Map

We could technically call Routers X, Y, and Z backbone routers, but there is only one area and therefore no "true" backbone. All of these routers have the same database of information regarding the area.

Site Areas

In multi-area configurations, the backbone is used to transport data between site areas. Traffic sourced from one area destined for another must transit the backbone area and all site areas must connect to area 0 (there is one exception to this rule and it will be discussed under *Virtual Links*). Sites are identified by an *Area ID*. Obviously, for OSPF to work correctly, all routers in a specific area must share the same Area ID. The Area ID usually follow two formats; a positive integer (such as 123) or a dotted decimal format (0.0.0.0 is a legitimate backbone ID). JUNOS will automatically convert regular integers to the dotted decimal format in the router configuration. If we grow our network to attach four site areas to the backbone of figure 5.5, we end up with the following:

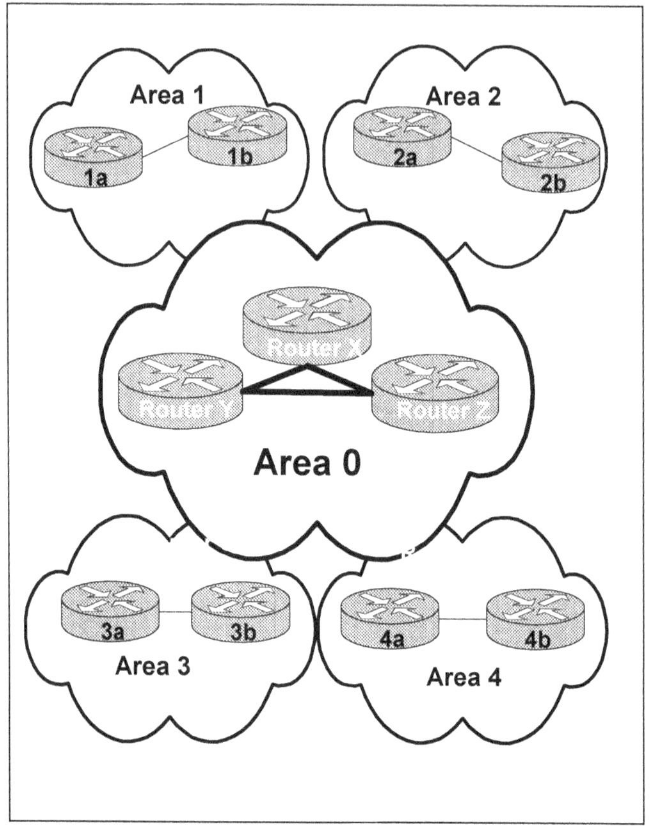

Figure 5.6 Multiple Area OSPF Map

We now have five areas in our OSPF domain. Each of the routers has a complete view of how to get to everything **in its own area**. Routers in area 1 (those named 1a and 1b) have no idea how to get to any destination in area 2, or any other area for that matter. Indeed, without adding some additional elements, none of these routers are aware other areas even exist!

Communicating between Areas

To communicate between areas, OSPF relies on routers that have interfaces in more than one area. These routers are called *area border routers* (ABRs). For instance, if a router were to have an interface connected to area 0 and an interface into a site area, it would be an *area border router* and would allow traffic to flow between the site and backbone. ABRs maintain a separate database for each area to which they are connected.

By growing our network once more, adding ABRs to allow inter-area traffic flow, our network diagram becomes rather more complex. However, remember that this is nothing more than the culmination of adding simple areas together.

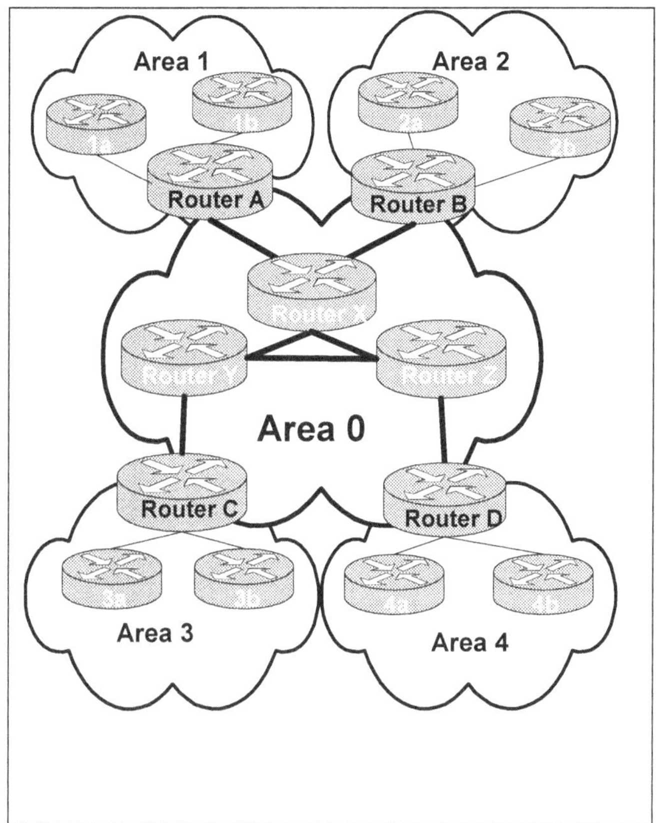

Figure 5.7 Multiple ABR OSPF Map

Now we can see that Routers A, B, C, and D are all ABRs with one interface in the backbone area and another in a site area. Site internal routers will learn about other areas and know to pass their traffic to their ABR to get there. Traffic flowing from Area 4 to Area 1 will pass through ABR D onto Backbone Router Z, to Backbone X, and to ABR A. In this way as well, each of the areas is insulated from route churn and instability within the other areas. Destination routes flapping in Area 1 will not cause the routers in Area 4 to re-run SPF calculations. This is another reason why large networks are broken up into smaller, more manageable site areas.

Routers that exchange routes with other ASs are called *AS boundary routers* (ASBRs). They advertise AS external routes to the entire OSPF domain. Note that the definition of AS within OSPF differs from that of BGP. Any router, regardless of whether it is a backbone router, area internal router, or ABR may be an ASBR. An example of an ASBR would be a router redistributing RIP routes into OSPF. The RIP routes are considered external to the OSPF process and when redistributed will originate from the ASBR.

Types of Areas

In addition to the different types of routers and networks, there are multiple different types of site areas in OSPF. A simple site area has no additional stipulations on its behavior. A *stub area* is one in which AS external announcements are not flooded. This would be beneficial if the number of external routes coming in is large and updates could be made much more compact by their exclusion. An ABR facing a stub area will automatically announce a default route in place of the specific external routes so the site routers can still reach those prefixes. A stub area cannot contain an ASBR, so you cannot redistribute from another protocol into the stub area. Additionally, a stub area may not contain a virtual link.

A *not-so-stubby area* (NSSA) allows an ASBR to be a member of the site area. Both NSSA and stub areas do not allow external routes to be flooded into the area. However, an NSSA allows for the injection of external routes which can then be flooded within that area and outward to the backbone. In effect, the NSSA can redistribute routes from another protocol but receives a default route for external advertisements outside of its native area.

Virtual Links

Ideally, all site areas should have a direct connection to Area 0. There is one exception to this rule: *Virtual links*. It may be necessary at some point that a site area is not directly connected to area 0. By configuring a virtual link, it is possible to create a logical tunnel between area 0 and the removed site area by transiting an intermediate site area. Adding virtual links generally adds unnecessary complexity and increases the possibility of area failure and should be considered a temporary fix rather than a permanent solution. Virtual links cannot be configured stub areas.

In figure 5.8 Area 7 is connected to Area 0 via Area 6. Should the transit link or Area 6 go down, Area 7 will be disconnected from the backbone as well.

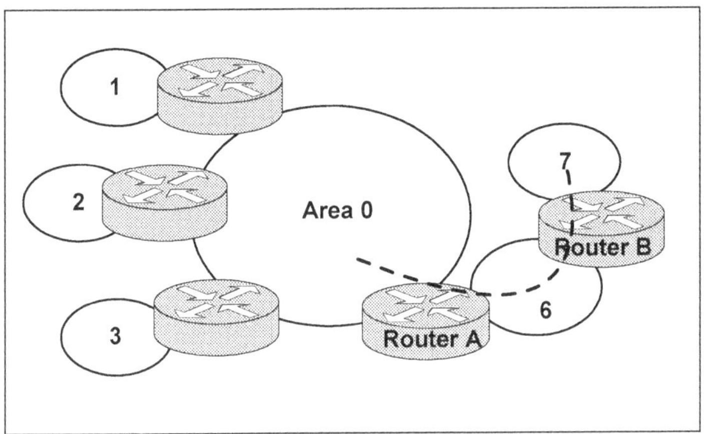

Figure 5.8: Virtual Link to Area 0

Link-state Advertisements (LSAs)

Routers participating in OSPF communicate to one another through the use of Link-state Advertisements (LSAs). LSAs contain the information OSPF routers require to build and maintain a view of the area they are in. The *hello* protocol determines how OSPF itself talks to neighbors and maintains adjacencies. LSAs are behind the workings of how OSPF determines where to route traffic.

Each OSPF router maintains a topology database for the area. It is absolutely necessary that these tables be in agreement, or synchronized, to prevent routing loops. OSPF routers flood LSAs throughout the network to maintain consistent route topologies between nodes. For this reason, adding import policy to OSPF is frowned upon as it has the potential to produce inconsistent topologies within areas. When there is a topology change, LSA flooding ensures that all OSPF databases converge quickly and accurately. There are five commonly used LSA types that will be covered on the JNCIA examination. Other types of LSAs exist for different services, however the JNCIA will not require knowledge of these.

- Type I Router LSA – Information about the router and its directly connected links. Type I LSAs are flooded only within the area.

- Type II Network LSA – Information about a LAN and the routers connected to it. These LSAs are advertised by the DR and are only flooded into the site area to which it is a member.

- Type III Summary LSA – Originated from the ABR, these describe networks that are reachable outside each of the ABR's areas.

- Type IV ASBR Summary LSA – Define routes to the ASBR. Type IV originate on the ABR.

- Type V External LSA – Include information about destinations outside the OSPF domain (or AS). They originate from an ASBR and are flooded throughout the entire OSPF network.

The types of LSAs that a router will announce depend upon the type of role it plays. In other words, whether or not the router is a DR, BDR, ABR or ASBR will determine the mix of LSAs that it will choose to flood.

OSPF will exchange its entire database when two neighbors initialize an adjacency. All triggered updates contain only information regarding which routes have changed. Updates, therefore, are much smaller and consume less overhead, even in large networks.

OSPF Configuration within JUNOS

Now that we have covered the theory behind OSPF, we can examine which steps are necessary to configure OSPF on a Juniper router. The fundamentals that should be remembered for the JNCIA exam include:

- OSPF configuration takes place under *protocols ospf* in edit mode
- The minimum OSPF configuration consists of enabling the protocol on a global level, and defining the interfaces that will participate and the area which they will be in
- The default timers for OSPF are 10 seconds for the *hello interval* and 40 seconds for the *dead timer*

The remaining options that can be configured depend heavily upon the type of network the interface will communicate on. We covered the fundamentals of network type previously. The JNCIA examination does not focus on the configuration of OSPF, rather the real emphasis is on understanding the behavior of the protocol and what problem indicators to look for. Nevertheless, there are some potential exam areas within basic OSPF configuration.

The top level of configuration for OSPF is under 'edit protocols ospf'. All global and area specific commands are set at this tier. Configuring OSPF on a router requires defining a minimum of two things:

1) Which interfaces will participate in OSPF.
2) Which areas those interfaces will be assigned to.

The minimum required configuration follows the form of:

```
[edit protocols]
jncia@my.router# show
        ospf {
               area 0.0.0.0 {
                      interface interface-name;
               }
        }
}
```

When multiple areas are defined, area 0 is called the backbone area. To add additional interfaces into the backbone area is a simple addition to the minimum configuration:

```
[edit]
jncia@my.router# set protocols ospf area 0.0.0.0
interface interface-name
```

The configuration for a site area is similar to the minimum, or backbone, configuration, the only exception being that the area ID is some number other than 0.

```
[edit protocols ospf]
jncia@my.router# set area area-id interface
interface-name
```

(Note that in the above we are already at the [edit protocols ospf] level of configuration)

Both Stub and NSSA are configurable under the `area` level of the edit hierarchy. An area cannot be both a Stub and an NSSA.

```
[edit protocols ospf area area-id]
jncia@my.router# set [stub|nssa]
```

Metric

All OSPF active interfaces have a cost associated with them that is used as the routing metric when calculating the shortest path. Unless changed, the metric is calculated by a ratio of the reference bandwidth to the interface bandwidth. By default, the reference bandwidth is 100Mbps (100,000,000bps). There are then two ways to modify the OSPF metrics. To change the metric for routes advertised from a specific interface include the `metric <cost>` statement at the `[edit protocols ospf area` *`area-id`* `interface` *`interface-name`*`]` level. The metric can be a positive integer from 1 to 65535.

```
[edit protocols ospf area 0.0.0.0 interface so-4/0/0.0]
jncia@my.router# set metric cost cost
```

Authentication

Exchange of OSPF packets between devices can be configured to use authentication, ensuring that only trusted routers participate. By default, authentication is disabled; however, one of the following types can be enabled.

- Simple authentication - uses a plain text password.
- MD5 algorithm - utilizes MD5 encryption to provide a stronger level of security.

Each router in the area must use the same type of authentication. Both types of authentication are passed in the transmitted h*ello* packets and are verified with a key by the receiving router. Configuring authentication is done under the level of edit protocols ospf area:

```
[edit protocols ospf area area-id]
jncia@my.router# set authentication-type
[none|simple|md5]
```

If needed, the key is then configured beneath the interface hierarchy level:

```
[edit protocols ospf area area-id interface
interface-name]
jncia@my.router# set authentication-key <key> key-id <id>
```

The key, or password, may be from one to eight ASCII characters in length. As throughout JUNOS, it is required to enclose the entire string in quotes if it includes spaces.

Configuring OSPF Timers

In order to maintain an accurate link-state database, OSPF routers send and expect to receive *hellos* and LSAs at specific intervals. In certain situations, the network administrator may wish to change these intervals from the default value. It is important to remember however, that the timer intervals need to be consistent across the area to establish working adjacencies.

Hello packets are sent to establish and maintain adjacencies with neighboring routers on every active OSPF interface. The default *hello timer* is 10 seconds.

The time that a router will wait before declaring a neighbor unreachable is called the *router dead interval.* It is four times the hello interval, 40 seconds by default. It can be modified similar to the *hello interval* under the same edit level:

```
[edit protocols ospf area area-id interface
interface-name]
jncia@my.router# set hello-interval seconds

[edit protocols ospf area area-id interface
interface-name]
jncia@my.router# set dead-interval seconds
```

Policy in OSPF

Similar to the way in which policy is applied in RIP to filter imported and exported routes, we have the option of configuring policy for OSPF. However, it should be noted that import policy applied to a link-state protocol like OSPF or IS-IS can lead to inconsistent databases and topologies. As a rule, only consider export policy as an acceptable option for OSPF.

```
[edit protocols ospf]
jncia@my.router# export policy-names
```

For additional information on syntax and policy flow, see the *Policy* section.

Monitoring OSPF in JUNOS

The basic commands to ease troubleshooting problems with OSPF are listed below. Problems with OSPF running correctly can be related either to improper configuration or with network occurrences, such as failed circuit connections or router hardware. Optional parameters are enclosed in [brackets]. Tokens that should be replaced with actual interface or address information are enclosed in <angle-brackets>.

```
jncia@my.router>  show ospf ?
Possible completions:
  database          Show the OSPF link-state
  database
  interface         Show OSPF interface status
  io-statistics     Show OSPF I/O statistics
  log               Show OSPF SPF log
  neighbor          Show OSPF neighbor status
  route             Show the OSPF routing table
  statistics        Show OSPF statistics
```

```
jncia@my.router> Show ospf neighbor <neighbor
address> <brief|detail>
```

If the neighbor address is left out, an abbreviated list of neighbor information will be shown:

```
jncia@my.router> show ospf neighbor
  Address          Interface       State          ID              Pri  Dead
10.1.11.53       so-0/0/0.0      Full           10.2.8.241      128    39
10.1.11.58       so-0/1/0.0      Full           10.2.44.98      128    36
10.1.27.66       ge-7/0/0.0      Full           10.2.44.99        1    36
10.1.27.130      ge-7/0/1.0      2way           10.2.44.96        1    31
```

The ‘show ospf neighbor’ output is very useful for determining the state that neighboring routers are in. From here we can see the address of the neighboring interface, the local interface name, the State the adjacency is currently in, the RID of the neighbor, the Priority, and the Dead-Timer. Ideally, we expect neighbors to be in *Full* if they are P2P, or *2way* if they are on a BMA network. States other than these usually indicate a problem. Including the neighbor address will allow inspection of that adjacency alone. Adding ‘detail’ will give additional information.

```
jncia@my.router> show ospf neighbor 10.1.27.66 detail
Address          Interface       State       ID                  Pri  Dead

10.1.27.66       ge-7/0/0.0      Full        10.1.44.99            1    36
  area 0.0.0.33, opt 0x42, DR 10.1.27.65, BDR 10.1.27.66
  Up 14w1d 21:36:45, adjacent 14w1d 21:36:45
    Link-state retransmission list:  4 entries
```

Note that the ‘detailed’ output also now displays the DR/BDR *interface* address and area information. This router is in area 33. The DR for this segment is 10.1.27.65, which just happens to be this router’s interface. The BDR for the segment is this neighbor, 10.1.27.66. This neighbor has been up for over 14 weeks.

jncia@my.router> Show ospf interface <*interface-name*> <brief|detail>

If the interface name is left out, an abbreviated list of neighbor information will be shown:

```
jncia@my.router> show ospf interface
Interface    State     Area        DR           IDBDR ID      Nbrs
lo0.0         DR       0.0.0.0     10.2.44.97   0.0.0.0         0
so-0/0/0.0 PtToPt      0.0.0.0     0.0.0.0      0.0.0.0         1
so-0/1/0.0 PtToPt      0.0.0.0     0.0.0.0      0.0.0.0         1
ge-7/0/0.0    DR       0.0.0.33    10.2.44.97   10.2.44.99      1
ge-7/0/1.0    DR       0.0.0.33    10.2.44.96   10.2.44.97      3
```

From the output of ‘show ospf interface’ we can see which local interfaces are OSPF active, what State they are in, which Area they belong to, what the DR/BDR RIDs are and how many neighbors are adjacent. It is important to note that the DR/BDR information listed here is the *Router ID* whereas that listed under 'show ospf neighbor x.x.x.x detail' is the DR/BDR *interface* address. Note that an interface will still show up with this command even if it has no neighbors because it is still an OSPF active interface. Two reasons for this lack of neighbors could be:

1) The interface in question is configured as passive.
2) The neighbors on that interface are down.

`Show ospf database area <area-id>`

```
jncia@my.router> show ospf database area 0.0.0.33
    OSPF link-state database, area 0.0.0.33
Type     ID           Adv Rtr      Seq         Age  Opt  Cksum   Len
Router   *10.2.44.97  10.2.44.97   0x8000798b  952  0x2  0xa0ab  36
Router   10.2.44.98   10.2.44.98   0x80007a2b  317  0x2  0xaef2  36
Router   10.2.44.99   10.2.44.99   0x80003c3b  1142 0x2  0xf6dc  60
Router   10.2.44.100  10.2.44.100  0x800038d2  629  0x2  0xf91c  60
Network  *10.2.27.65  10.2.44.97   0x800037fb  956  0x2  0x61a7  32
Network  10.2.27.69   10.2.44.98   0x80002f78  321  0x2  0x6a23  32
Network  10.2.27.74   10.2.44.100  0x800038c3  629  0x2  0x9e72  32
Summary  *10.6.1.1    10.2.44.97   0x800001bd  1376 0x2  0x3ece  28
Summary  10.6.1.1     10.2.44.98   0x800001be  1379 0x2  0x920   28
Summary  *10.6.1.2    10.2.44.97   0x800001b3  838  0x2  0x3747  28
Summary  10.6.1.2     10.2.44.98   0x800001b3  837  0x2  0x497   28
```

This command shows the actual link-state database that OSPF assembles from received LSAs. Using the command without an <area> identifier will output the entire database, while including the ID will list just the area in question. The first column indicates the type of LSA. The database is normally arranged beginning with Type I LSAs first. Entries marked with an asterisk represent those originating from the local router. As can be seen in the above, 10.2.44.97 is the local router, and the LSAs marked with * are local to this router. Note as well that more than one device can report the same route in an LSA, as with 10.6.1.2 and 10.6.1.1 above.

Below is the output taken from the OSPF log file illustrating the steps undertaken while an adjacency forms.

```
1) jncia@my.router>show log ospf-log | grep 172.16.1.1
2) OSPF neighbor 172.16.1.1 (fe-0/0/0.2) state changed
from Down to Init
3) OSPF neighbor 172.16.1.1 (fe-0/0/0.2) state changed
from Init to 2Way
4) RPD_OSPF_NBRUP: OSPF neighbor 172.16.1.1 (fe-0/0/0.2)
state changed from Init to 2Way
5) OSPF neighbor 172.16.1.1 (fe-0/0/0.2) state changed
from 2Way to ExStart
6) OSPF neighbor 172.16.1.1 (fe-0/0/0.2) state changed
from ExStart to Exchange
7) OSPF neighbor 172.16.1.1 (fe-0/0/0.2) state changed
from Exchange to Full
8) RPD_OSPF_NBRUP: OSPF neighbor 172.16.1.1 (fe-0/0/0.2)
state changed from Exchange to Full
```

Line 1 indicates we are looking into the logfile "ospf" and using the | to include a UNIX style grep. This limits output to match only lines including "172.16.1.1". Neighbor 172.16.1.1 begins in the "Down" state. From line 2 we can see the state change to "Init". The rest of the output illustrates the process of building a 'Full' adjacency as it moves through the remaining stages.

Key Points

OSPF is a robust and scalable link-state protocol that rapidly converges. With the information supplied in this chapter you should be able to understand the workings of the protocol, configure simple OSPF neighbors and areas, and troubleshoot everyday problems that may arise.

- OSPF is a link-state protocol. Link-state protocols require that each participating node have full knowledge of the complete network topology. Each router must keep track of the link-state of each of its connections and immediately notify the other nodes of any changes occurring.
- Utilizes the Shortest Path First (SPF) algorithm to determine the lowest cost link between two nodes in the same area. The SPF calculation is based upon the Dijkstra Algorithm. There is no hop-count.
- Each OSPF router maintains a topology database for the network. It is absolutely necessary that these tables be in agreement (are 'synchronized'), to prevent routing loops.
- OSPF is a hierarchical protocol. An OSPF domain may be broken into different independent logical areas. Area 0 is the backbone area.
- Interfaces running OSPF form adjacencies with neighboring interfaces through the use of Hello packets.
- OSPF routers flood Link-state Advertisements (LSAs) throughout the network to maintain consistent route topologies between nodes. When there is a topology change, LSA flooding ensures that all OSPF databases converge quickly and accurately.
- Types of Link-state Advertisements:

    - Type I Router LSA – Information about the router and its directly connected links. Type I LSAs are flooded only within the area.
    - Type II Network LSA – Information about a LAN and the routers connected to it. These LSAs are advertised by the DR and are only flooded into the site area to which it is a member.
    - Type III Summary LSA – Originated from the ABR, these describe networks that are reachable outside each of the ABR's areas.
    - Type IV ASBR Summary LSA – Define routes to the ASBR. Type IV originate on the ABR.

- Type V External LSA – Include information about destinations outside the OSPF domain (or AS). They originate from an ASBR and are flooded throughout the entire OSPF network.

Other types of LSAs exist for different services; however, the JNCIA will not require knowledge of these.

Additional Information (RFCs)

For additional information, please consult the following at http://www.ietf.org:

- RFC 1245: OSPF Protocol Analysis
- RFC 1246: Experience with the OSPF Protocol
- RFC 2328: OSPF Version 2
- RFC 1557 NSSA
- RFC 1584 MOSPF
- RFC 2740 IPv6

Chapter Six
IS-IS

Chapter 6: IS-IS

Overview

In this section you will learn about the dynamic routing protocol IS-IS and its fundamental concepts. By the end of this chapter you should understand and be able to define:

- ✓ The origin and general purpose of IS-IS.
- ✓ NSAP addressing.
- ✓ Purpose and configuration of domains, areas and levels.
- ✓ How IS-IS devices communicate.
- ✓ Some key differences between IS-IS and OSPF

Introduction

Intermediate System to Intermediate System (IS-IS) is an Open System Interconnection (OSI) link state Interior Gateway Protocol (IGP) designed around the International Organization for Standardization (ISO) concepts for networking. In the OSI model, networks are built around 'systems'; a router is an Intermediate System (IS) and an end host or user is an End System (ES). From this, we can tell that IS-IS deals with traffic flow between routers.

Similar to OSPF, IS-IS utilizes the Dijkstra algorithm within a Shortest Path First (SPF) calculation to compute the lowest cost path to a particular node. An IS-IS active router compiles a database filled with the link state information of all the other routers in its area. Part of this information is the cost of every particular link. SPF can then construct a logical tree with itself as the root that branches to every other node.

IS-IS was originally intended to route *Connectionless Network Protocol* (CLNP). It was extended to support IP, but its roots in OSI often make it appear more complex and difficult than it actually is.

IS-IS Logical Configuration

IS-IS domains are divided into areas to help control the amount of route information that needs to be distributed between nodes. Levels are used to designate a router's function within the area(s) to which it belongs. Interfaces on each router in the area are assigned to a level. Within JUNOS, each individual interface, once enabled to run IS-IS, can be placed into one, or both, of these levels.

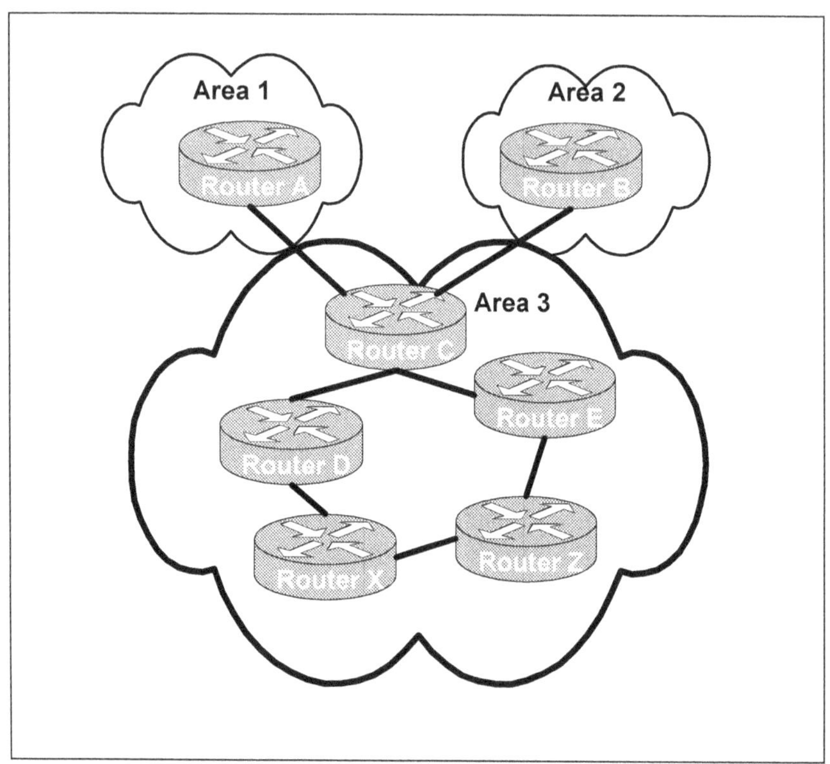

Figure 6.1: IS-IS Area Map

As can be seen in the figure 6.1, the area breakdown resembles OSPF logical areas except for one critical point, the lack of an Area 0. Of course, it would be possible to number an Area as 0 in IS-IS, but the functionality of a dedicated backbone area is not the same. In this sense, IS-IS differs from OSPF in that it does not treat inter-area routing in the same manner.

In addition to breaking the domain into areas, IS-IS functions are divided between two levels of responsibility. Level 1 systems route only within their respective area. When a Level 1 node encounters a destination that is outside of the Level 1 area, it forwards the route towards the nearest Level 2 system.

Level 2 systems route between areas and toward other autonomous systems. In a simplified manner, think of Level 2 routers as the backbone routers and Level 1 as the site routers. Be aware that the line is not always so clear and many factors play a role.

Using the same simple topology as we did previously and now appointing the various routers Levels according to their responsibilities, we get the somewhat more complex diagram:

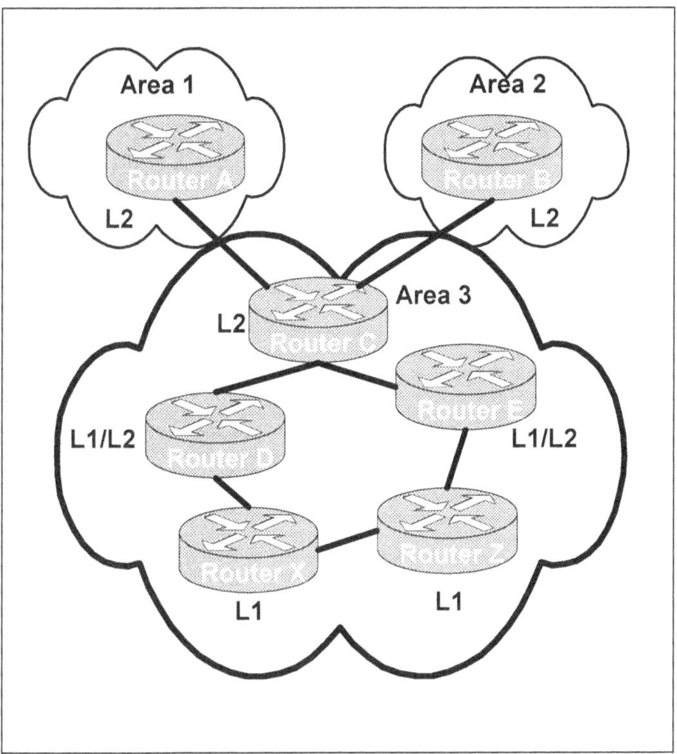

Figure 6.2: IS-IS Layer and Area Map

From this, we can see how the functions of the routers in the areas are broken down. Router X and Router Z are pure Level 1 devices. They have complete knowledge of how to get to all nodes in Area 3. However, if either needs to send traffic to Area 1 or 2, it needs to be sent outside their own local area. Typically, Level 1 routers will send traffic destined for another area to the closest L1/L2 router.

Routers D and E are Level 1 and 2 devices. They have interfaces in both levels and have knowledge of how to get to other areas. In this example, the path on to Area 1 and 2 is through Router C.

Router C is a pure Level 2 device. It is connected to other Level 2 devices, and it knows how to get to Area 1 and 2. Note that Router C is still in Area 3, but its purpose is to route packets on to other L2 or L1/L2 nodes. Similarly, Router A represents the Level 2 router within Area 1 and Router B performs this duty for Area 2. We can assume that Area 1 and 2 contain their own topologies made up of more L1/L2 and L1 devices. Otherwise, there would be no need to send traffic there.

All IS-IS enabled interfaces (with the ISO protocol family enabled) are by default placed into both Level 1 and Level 2 areas. Interfaces can have one or both levels removed via the disable command.

Unlike OSPF, which has a default metric based upon link bandwidth, IS-IS has a flat default metric of 10. This is important to keep in mind, as when first enabling IS-IS all links out of a router will have a metric of 10 regardless of the actual interface bandwidth and can result in sub-optimal routing. The metric may be configured to custom values by the administrator.

To provide for scalability in a large broadcast environment, IS-IS requires the appointment of a *Designated Intermediate System* (DIS) per broadcast segment. This allows updates to be sent to one router for re-propagation instead of a flooding by every node on the broadcast medium. This function is similar to a Designated Router in OSPF, but varies in that there is no backup assigned.

The IS-IS speaker with the highest priority is declared the DIS. JUNOS sets priority to a default of 64. In the event of a tie in priority during election, the highest MAC address wins. As noted, unlike OSPF, there is no backup DIS. The timers, as discussed shortly, vary when communicating with the DIS and allow any router to take this role should the DIS become unavailable.

ISO Network Addressing

Similar to the manner in which OSPF uses IP for network addressing, IS-IS uses OSI addressing. Each unique OSI address represents a network connection, such as a host interface or a router. A specific point of connection like this is identified as a *network service access point* (NSAP). A node may have multiple NSAP addresses. If this is the case, each of these addresses will differ only in the last byte (or the *n-selector*). Each network element is configured with a special NSAP address called the *Network Entity Title* (NET). Most systems have one NET. However, if they take part in multiple areas, they will have multiple NETs. The identification of the NET is made easier in that its last byte, or *n-selector* (NSEL), is 00.

One very important difference between IP and NSAP addressing to keep in mind is that while an IP address is likely to be configured on each interface, a single NSAP is used to address the entire router. Because the only address used is for the router itself, that address is the NET and is normally assigned to the router loopback. As the JNCIA deals only with routers, valid NET/NSAP will end with NSEL 00.

OSI addressing is a departure from the IP addressing scheme with which most people are familiar. Initially, perhaps the most confusing point is that where IP addresses are 4 bytes, an OSI address can vary from 8 to 20 bytes. Additionally, whereas one may be comfortable with the dotted decimal format of an IPv4 address, ISO addressing may contain unfamiliar hexadecimal notation. An ISO address consists of three basic parts:

- ✓ The Area ID
- ✓ The System ID
- ✓ The NET Selector (NSEL)

49.0001	1270.1012.3123	00
Area ID	System ID	NSEL
1-13 bytes	6 bytes	1 byte

Table 6.3 NSAP Address Fields

The *Area ID* is the portion of the address that is variable, ranging from 1 to 13 bytes. Additionally, the Area ID itself has two portions. The first byte tells the system how to interpret the rest of the Area ID and is called the *Address Family Identifier* (AFI). The Area ID is an AS local trait. Most often, you will see the AFI byte set to 49, which was specifically reserved for private addressing. It is the same thing as using RFC 1918 IP addressing or private BGP AS numbers. The JNCIA exam will most likely use AFI 49 in examples.

The next 0 thru 12 bytes are the *domain identifier*. It is possible to have an Area ID comprised entirely of the AFI with no bytes allocated for a Domain ID. In such a case the entire NSAP would be 8 bytes long. If a 12 byte full-length Domain ID was used, the address would increase to 20 bytes. Allocation of these is up to the discretion AS administrator. Sample domain identifiers could include:

0007	two-byte hexadecimal
4311	two-byte hexadecimal
43ac	two-byte hexadecimal
0007.43ac	four-byte hex
123c.ffab	four-byte hex

Following the variable Area ID, there is a *System ID* consisting of a fixed six bytes. These six bytes must be unique throughout the given area. Common practice is to encode the IPv4 Router ID into the System ID by converting the four byte IP address to six bytes. The simplest way to do this conversion is to keep the IP address in its decimal notation and fill out the octets with any necessary leading zeros. This means that each byte in the decimal notation has three digits. Therefore 192.168.123.45 becomes 192.168.123.045. The last octet becomes 045. The decimal notation is normally moved to cluster two byte hex groups, namely every four digits. Similarly:

10.1.12.34 becomes 010.001.012.034 is grouped 0100.0101.2034
10.10.101.10 becomes 010.010.101.010 is grouped 0100.1010.1010

As you can see, this is not really a mathematical conversion to 6 bytes. Rather it is just a simple way to fill out the required byte length while more or less keeping the integrity of a related IP address.

The last 1 byte is the *NET Selector*. For purposes of the JNCIA, the NET on IS-IS routers is always set to 00. When set to 00, the NSEL indicates we are dealing with a router NSAP. When dissecting NSAP addresses, it may be helpful to begin at the right hand side. We will see why in a moment. Looking at a sample ISO address:

49.0101.2421.2112.00

Beginning at the right, the final byte is the NSEL of 00 identifying this as a router. The next section is made up of the IP address 10.124.212.112 converted to six bytes 0101.2421.2112. The first byte is the AFI of 49. There are no additional bytes allocated for a domain identifier. Consequently, the entire Area ID is one byte.

If we look at a slightly more complex sample:

49.43ac.0730.0001.1921.6804.2129.00

Beginning at the right, we identify the router NSEL of 00. Next, we expect a six byte System ID, and can see it is the IP address 192.168.42.129. Now we have a large section of hexadecimal notation. Consequently, the entire Area ID is seven bytes. Keep in mind that the only thing of variable length is the domain identifier portion of the Area ID. The AFI is mandatory, and is only one byte. Therefore the next six bytes, 43ac.0730.0001, are the Domain ID. This leaves the last byte to be the AFI of 49.

One last note on ISO addressing is dynamic mapping of ISO *System Identifiers* (sysids). JUNOS supports the configuration of a host name for each system. Once this is established, the router can carry this name with a sysid in a dynamic hostname *type length value* (TLV) in LSP packets that are transmitted.

IS-IS Packets

IS-IS communicates with packets called *protocol data units* (PDUs) exchanged between active routers. There are four different types of packets used to exchange information:

- *IS-IS Hello* (IIH) PDU – Broadcast to determine neighboring IS-IS systems. Discovers and differentiates between Level 1 and Level 2 routers.

- *Link State PDU* (LSP) – Contains information regarding the state of the connections to adjacent routers. Periodically, LSPs are flooded throughout the IS-IS area.

- *Complete Sequence Number PDU* (CSNP) - Contains an entire listing of LSPs in the database. CSNPs are sent out all IS-IS links periodically to ensure all routers have synchronized LSP databases. A designated router (the DIS) will multicast the CSNP on a broadcast network media to limit acknowledgement traffic.

- *Partial Sequence Number PDU* (PSNP) – Request for update PDU. When a CSNP receiving router detects a fault with its LSP table (when it is out of date or not synchronized), it sends a PSNP to the router that originally transmitted the CSNP requesting the missing LSP. The PNSP transmitting node is then forwarded the missing LSP.

Details on these communication packets are also listed in the diagram below.

PDU	Format	Target	Purpose/Function
IS-IS Hello (IIH)	Broadcast	Neighboring systems	Discover neighbors and determine neighbor level(s)
Link-state (LSP)	Multicast	All routers in the particular level	Announces state of adjacencies to neighboring systems
Complete Sequence Number (CSNP)	Flooded (multicast by DIS)	All routers in an area	Contains complete database to ensure all routers are synchronized
Partial Sequence Number (PSNP)	Multicast	CSNP transmitter	Sent by a receiver to the transmitter to indicate a missing LSP. The transmitter then forwards the link to the receiver who sent the PSNP

Table 6.4 IS-IS PDU Descriptions

Communication between IS-IS devices

There are three types of hello packets: LAN Level 1, LAN Level 2, and Point-to-Point. LAN traffic is sent to a specific MAC address that specifies all routers in that particular area. Level 1 packets are sent to the MAC address of 01-80-C2-00-00-14 (signifying "all Level 1 IS-IS routers") and Level 2 packets are sent to 01-80-C2-00-00-15 (signifying "all Level 2 IS-IS routers"). Each different type of packet is tagged with a different PDU type to identify the purpose of the message. IS-IS uses sequence numbers and aging to ensure routers have a full and updated routing database. It is important to know the PDU type for debugging purposes, but this information is not pertinent to the JNCIA exam.

The *hold time* states how much time can pass with no communication before a router is declared dead. The *hello-interval* states how often to send Hello packets to neighbors. The hold time and hello-interval are set by default to 27 and 9 seconds, respectively, within JUNOS. Both of these values can be adjusted under either or both levels of any interface. When communicating with the DIS router, the timers configured are divided by three (making the default hold time and hello interval for the DIS 9 and 3 seconds, respectively). Unlike OSPF, the hold timer is reset back to its maximum value when ANY message is received from that neighbor (not just a Hello message).

JUNOS supports simple and MD5 authentication on IS-IS interfaces. For routers to communicate on authenticated interfaces, the information must match for the domain, area, and all interfaces in question. Interfaces can be configured to generate authenticated packets, but simultaneously not check authentication on received packets using the `no-authentication-check` configuration option.

IS-IS Configuration

The top level of IS-IS is at the `[edit protocols isis]` section of the configuration tree. The minimum IS-IS configuration within JUNOS consists of three steps:

1) IS-IS must be enabled globally (specifying which interfaces to run on).
2) A network entity title (NET) must be configured on an interface (usually the NET is configured on a loopback interface).
3) Each IS-IS interface must have family ISO configured.

To configure a NET on unit 0 of loopback0, issue the following command:

```
set interface lo0 unit 0 family iso address
49.0000.0000.0001.00 passive
```

To specify which interface will run IS-IS, issue the following command:

```
set protocols isis interface so-1/0/0.7
```

To configure family ISO on an interface, issue the following command:

```
set interface so-1/0/0 unit 7 family iso
```

The commands issued above will yield the following configuration on the router:

```
[edit protocols]
jncia@my.router1# show
       isis {
             interface so-1/0/0.7;
             interface lo0.0 {
                 passive;
             }
         }
```

Interface configuration:

```
[edit interfaces]
jncia@my.router1# show
     so-1/0/0 {
         unit 7 {
             family iso;
         }

     lo0 {
         unit 0 {
             family iso {
                 address 49.0000.0000.0001.00;
             }
         }
```

Recall that a router requires only a single NSAP address to participate in IS-IS. This NET identifies the router itself; individual interface NSAPs are not required.

Additionally, optional parameters are available under the [protocols isis] level of configuration mode. As noted previously, an IS-IS interface can be configured to participate in IS-IS level 1, IS-IS level 2 or both levels. By default, an interface running IS-IS belongs to both level 1 and level 2. The IS-IS level of an interface is configured in the global IS-IS configuration section. Note that when configured for both levels, the 'L' tag listed under 'show isis interface' will be '3'.

For an IS-IS interface to belong to a single level, the undesired level must be disabled. To disable levels on an IS-IS interface, issue the following command:

```
[edit protocols isis]
jncia@my.router1#   set   interface   interface-name
level [1|2] disable
```

Any IS-IS enabled interface defaults to a link metric of 10. To change this value the following command statement is used:

```
[edit protocols isis]
jncia@my.router1#   set   interface   interface-name
level [1|2] metric metric
```

Where `metric` is the desired link cost and `level-1|level-2` indicates the link type.

Authentication may be enabled on all IS-IS levels (at the global level as illustrated below), per level, per interface, and per level on an interface.

```
[edit protocols isis]
jncia@my.router1# set authentication-type type

[edit protocols isis]
jncia@my.router1# set authentication-key key

[edit protocols isis]
```

```
jncia@my.router1#   set   interface   interface-name
level [1|2] authentication-type type
```

Where the `authentication-type` may be `md5` or `simple` and the key may be an ASCII string that will either be encrypted or plaintext depending on the authentication type. Remember that JUNOS requires password strings to be enclosed in quotes if they include a space. A router may also be configured to generate authenticated packets, but ignore authentication on received packets. This is done in the following manner:

```
[edit protocols isis]
jncia@my.router1# no-authentication-check
```

Mesh Groups

Routers connected in a full mesh will waste a lot of time and bandwidth sending each other LSP packets. To reduce some of this communication, routers can have *mesh groups* configured on particular interfaces. Interfaces can then be told to stop the flooding of LSPs through that interface by issuing the set `mesh-group blocked` command.

```
[edit protocols isis interface interface-name]
jncia@my.router1# set mesh-group [blocked|value]
```

IS-IS Traffic Engineering

IS-IS traffic engineering extensions are *Type Length Values* (TLVs) that describe link attributes. TLVs are included in IS-IS link state PDUs and are used to populate the *Traffic Engineering Database* (TED). The information in the TED is used by CSPF to compute paths for RSVP signaled MPLS LSPs. IS-IS does not use MPLS LSPs as next hops, by default. For IS-IS to use LSPs, IS-IS traffic engineering shortcuts must be enabled. To enable these shortcuts, issue the following command from edit mode:

```
set protocols isis traffic-engineering shortcuts
```

Monitoring IS-IS in JUNOS

The basic commands to assist in troubleshooting and maintaining IS-IS are listed below.

```
jncia@my.router> show isis ?
Possible completions:
  adjacency        Show the IS-IS adjacency database
  database         Show the IS-IS link-state database
  hostname         Show IS-IS hostname database
  interface        Show IS-IS interface information
  route            Show the IS-IS routing table
  spf              Show SPF calculation information
  statistics       Show IS-IS performance statistics
```

```
show isis adjacency <system-id> <brief|detail|extensive>
```

This command indicates the status of each adjacency on the router. The system-id and brief parameters are optional.

```
jncia@my.router> show isis adjacency brief
IS-IS adjacency database:
Interface    System    L State   Hold     SNPA
fe-0/0/0.2   Denver1   1 Up      8      0:60:94:a3:73:dd
fe-0/0/0.3   NewYork   2 Init    25     0:20:35:e7:3d:53
fe-0/0/0.3   NewYork   1 New     15     0:20:35:e7:3d:53
```

From the 'L' column we can distinguish what IS-IS level is functioning on that interface. The 'State' column indicates whether or not the adjacency is up. The 'System' column will return the hostname of the remote node because of IS-IS dynamic sysid mapping. In this case, the adjacency to the `Denver1` router is functioning, however the two connections to `NewYork` are in the process of coming up.

```
show isis interface <interface-name> <brief|detail>
```

This indicates the status of each IS-IS interface on the router. The specific interface name and brief parameters are optional.

```
jncia@my.router> show isis interface
IS-IS interface database:
```

```
Interface          L CirID Level 1 DR        Level 2 DR
fe-0/0/0.2         1   0x2 Denver1           Disabled
fe-0/0/0.3         3   0x3 my.router         my.router
lo0.0              0   0x1 Passive           Passive
```

As with 'show isis adjacency', the 'L' column will tell us what level this box belongs to. However, in this case, a value of 3 indicates the router is an L1/L2 device. Similarly, a value of 0 indicates a passive interface. The final two columns will display the active DR for the interface. `Fe-0/0/0.2` reports the neighbor `Denver1` is the L1 DR. There is no L2 DR for that segment because the interface is L1 enabled only. Interface `fe-0/0/0.3` reports that this router, `my.router`, is both the L1 and L2 DR.

`show isis database` *`<system-id>`* `<brief|detail>` outputs the contents of the ISIS link-state database assembled from compiled PDUs. Similar to how one can display the contents of the OSPF database, a user can view the ISIS table in its entirety or for a specific system.

```
jncia@my.router> show isis database
IS-IS level 1 link-state database:
LSP ID                    Sequence Checksum Life(sec)
Denver1.00-00                 0x30  0x932f      704
Denver1.02-00                 0x4   0x4d5c      1184
my.router.00-00               0x27  0xb55e      1159
my.router.03-00               0xd   0           0
NewYork.00-00                 0x23  0xcd32      1130
  5 LSPs

IS-IS level 2 link-state database:
LSP ID                    Sequence   Checksum Life(sec)
Denver1.00-00             0x1f       0                0
my.router.00-00           0x25       0x79f2        1166
NewYork.03-00             0xf        0                0
NewYork.00-00             0x1f       0xf60d        1123
  4 LSPs
```

`show isis statistics`

This command will display the PDU performance statistics for an active IS-IS router. This includes the number of transmitted, received, processed, dropped, and retransmitted PDUs. Such information can be helpful when troubleshooting bad connections and circuits.

```
jncia@my.router> show isis statistics
IS-IS statistics for my.router:

PDU type       Rcv'd  Proc'd      Drops      Sent     Rexmit
LSP               64      64          0       123          0
IIH             3164     655       2509      3140          0
CSNP             172     172          0        50          0
PSNP              23      23          0         0          0
Unknown            0       0          0         0          0
Totals          3423     914       2509      3313          0

Total packets received: 3423 Sent: 3313

SNP queue length:           0 Drops:          0
LSP queue length:           0 Drops:          0

SPF runs:                 125
Fragments rebuilt:        172
LSP regenerations:         57
Purges initiated:          11
```

Below is the output from the ISIS logfile with the 'state' traceoption flag set illustrating the steps undertaken while an adjacency forms.

```
Adjacency state change, my.lab1, state Up->Down
interface fxp0.3, level 2
Adjacency state change, my.lab1, state Down->New
interface fxp0.3, level 2
Adjacency state change, my3.lab1, state New->Init
interface fxp0.3, level 2
Adjacency state change, my3.lab1, state Init->Up
interface fxp0.3, level 2
```

Key Points

- IS-IS is a link-state Interior Gateway Protocol.
  - Link state protocols require that each participating node have full knowledge of the complete network topology. Each router must keep track of the link state of each of its connections and immediately notify the other nodes of any changes occurring.
- Utilizes the Djikstra algorithm to run SPF calculations.
- Configured with OSI NSAP addresses that range from 8 to 20 bytes and contain:
  - A variable length Area ID
  - A six-byte System ID
  - A single byte NET Selector (NSEL)
- The NSAP Area ID normally includes a single byte AFI of 49.
- IS-IS is hierarchical, the domain can be broken into two logical area types.
  - Level 1 routers – Route within an area and to a Level 2 router when routing to a destination outside the area
  - Level 2 routers – Route packets between Level 1 areas and to other ASs.
- Multi-access networks utilize a DIS to reduce route update overhead
- Interfaces configured to run IS-IS are entered into both level 1 and level 2, by default. Either or both of these levels can be disabled on a per-interface basis.
- IS-IS uses ISO addressing for node identification rather than IP.
  - The ISO addressing consists of an Area ID, system ID, and NSEL
  - The AFI is the first byte of the Area ID
- Four types of protocol data units (PDUs):
  - IS-IS Hello (IIH)
  - Link State PDU (LSP)
  - Complete Sequence Number PDU (CSNP)
  - Partial Sequence Number PDU (PSNP)

Additional Information (RFCs)

More information can be found within:

- ISO/IEC 10589
- RFC 1195 Use of OSI IS-IS for Routing in TCP/IP and Dual Environments

- RFC 1237 Guidelines for OSI NSAP Allocation on the Internet
- RFC 3277 IS-IS Transient Blackhole Avoidance

Chapter Seven
BGP

Chapter 7: BGP

Overview

This chapter will cover Border Gateway Protocol (BGP). The topics covered will include the protocol's evolution, implementation, features, and configuration within JUNOS. BGP is fairly simple to configure and operate at a basic level. However, as can be seen by the large number of RFCs, the protocol has a multitude of options and is still under development. By the end of this chapter you should understand and be able to define:

- ✓ The purpose of using BGP in a wide-area routing environment.
- ✓ Internal vs. External BGP.
- ✓ BGP neighbor configuration.
- ✓ Messages exchanged between BGP neighbors, or peers.
- ✓ BGP route selection.
- ✓ Route reflection within a BGP mesh.
- ✓ Basic diagnostic commands for BGP within JUNOS.

Introduction

BGP is considered an advanced distance-vector protocol. It communicates on TCP port 179 and establishes explicit neighbor adjacencies with which it can exchange detailed routing information. BGP is the protocol used to exchange routes at the core of the Internet between service providers. It is also widely used to connect customers to these providers.

Up to this point, we have reviewed internal gateway protocols (IGP) such as RIP, OSPF, and IS-IS. These protocols are used for the exchange of routing information within a single administrative domain. However, to properly connect external networks (those under alternate administrative control), an exterior gateway protocol (EGP) is required. BGP allows this external routing exchange by recognizing the boundary of these domains and assigning them an identifier known as Autonomous System number.

Service providers are assigned one or more Autonomous System (AS) numbers that are used to identify themselves (in the scope of BGP) to other BGP speakers. An AS number is 16-bits, ranging of 1 to 65535. AS designators throughout the designation 1-64511 are assigned to the public, while 64512-65535 are considered private space (much like RFC 1918 private IP address space).

BGP resembles RIP in that one of the primary methods of route selection is based upon hop count. The key difference being that BGP considers one AS to be a 'hop'. BGP routes keep record of the Autonomous Systems that they transit to reach their destination. This feature is referred to '*as-path*' length.

Full routing tables are exchanged when routers first form an adjacency. This default behavior can be easily altered through the use of policy. From that point forward, only incremental changes are sent as routes are added, removed, or their attributes are changed. This limits the amount of protocol overhead needed once a session is established.

Versions

Every modern ISP today runs BGP version 4 to interconnect with other service providers. The only key change in BGP version 4 (with respect to the JNCIA exam) is the addition of classless inter-domain routing (CIDR). Version 4 allows the ability to remove classes from routing and summarize addressing to reduce the overall number of routes advertised.

External BGP vs. Internal BGP

BGP can be logically separated into two forms, internal and external. Internal BGP (iBGP) indicates a connection with a BGP peer in the same AS, while external bgp (eBGP) peers are those in another AS. It is important to distinguish between the two, as some of the key rules of BGP are applied to each.

BGP Basic Rules and Terms

There a just a handful of "golden rules" to remember about BGP:

- When a router receives a route from a BGP peer, it checks for its own AS. If it is in the route anywhere, the router discards the route to avoid a loop.
- When a router receives an eBGP route (one not from its own AS), it prepends its own AS to the front of the route's *AS-path* before sending it to other peers. The exception is when the route is sent to

internal neighbors (if internal neighbors saw their own AS in the path, they would drop the route advertisement to avoid a routing loop).

- eBGP peers will modify external advertisements to make themselves the next-hop (thus making the next-hop reachable by all internal peers). By default, iBGP peers do not modify the next hop attribute of a received route.
- A route learned via an eBGP peer will be sent to all of that router's BGP peers.
- A route learned via iBGP will be advertised to connected eBGP neighbors.
- A route learned via iBGP will not be re-advertised to any other iBGP peer. This is also sometimes known as "BGP Split Horizon". This effectively limits iBGP propagation to immediately adjacent peers, and thus requires a full-mesh for an iBGP network to ensure all routers receive all routes and updates. The use of route reflectors or confederations averts this rule (See the below section on route reflection).
- iBGP peering connections do not use the multi-hop command (explained below), but simply follow the rule that the peer's address must be reachable via the internal routing protocol (Internal Gateway Protocol, or IGP).

Message types

BGP messages range from 19 to 4096 bytes and consist of four message types:

Open, *Update*, *Notification*, and *Keepalive*.

Open message:

Begins the BGP peering session communication. After the TCP connection comes up, either router can send an Open message. This is a unicast message sent to the IP address configured for the peer on TCP port 179. It will contain:

- Version (currently will be version 4).
- Autonomous System (AS) number.
- Hold-time values.

- BGP identifier (IP address of sending router, also known as router ID).
- Optional parameters tag (zero in this field indicates no optional parameters).
- Optional parameters.

Update messages:

Contain all route prefixes and their attributes. Update messages are sent to add, withdraw, and change the attributes of BGP routes.

- Once a peering session is established, update messages are sent to inform the peer of all routes configured for advertisement.
- When a route's attributes change, JUNOS will automatically send an update message to BGP peers to notify them of the changes that have been made.

Notification messages:

Used to terminate a BGP peering session gracefully.

- Triggered if a router experiences a failure that necessitates the closure of the BGP session.
- Sent during the exchange of Open messages if a problem is encountered (wrong version number, bad peer AS, etc.).

Keepalive messages:

Necessary to ensure BGP sessions remain up.

- Value of timers is negotiated during the exchange of Open messages. If timers are changed on an existing session, the session will drop and re-establish with the new parameters.
- Default *holdtime timer* for JUNOS is 90 seconds (time allowed with no Keepalive or update messages before the session is terminated).
- *Keepalive timer* is 1/3 of the *holdtime* (default=30 seconds).
    - If you increase or decrease the holdtime, the Keepalive interval will be altered accordingly to maintain the 1:3 ratio

BGP Route selection

After ensuring that the Next-hop address is reachable, if more than one route exists to the target destination, the route to install as active will be chosen by the following method. This process also holds true for multiple routes to the same neighbor.

1. Highest ***Local Preference***
    a. Value of 0-4294967295, default is 100.
    b. Used to manipulate how traffic will leave the AS.
    c. This value is passed to iBGP peers only, not eBGP peers.
2. Shortest ***AS-Path***
    a. Each AS number in the as-path string is given a value of 1.
    b. The AS-Path is incremented by at least one hop and sent to both iBGP and eBGP peers (however the local AS path is not added to iBGP advertisements).
    c. A shorter as-path length implicitly denotes a shorter path.
3. Lowest ***Origin Code***
    a. Internal (I) is lower than External (E), which is lower than Incomplete (?). Prefer internal paths, which include IGP routes and locally generated routes (static, direct, local, etc.).
    b. Note that JUNOS sets the code to internal when distributing routes from one protocol into BGP (most other vendors set these to '?')
4. Lowest ***Multi-Exit Discriminator (MED)***
    a. Default value is 0. No MED value is interpreted as 0.
    b. By default, MED value is only compared if the closest AS (the peer AS the route was directly learned from) is the same. However, the command "*path-selection always-compare-med*" can be used to force JUNOS to compare the MED value regardless of the AS the route was learned from
5. Prefer ***eBGP paths over iBGP paths***
6. ***Lowest IGP cost***, or metric (Closest next-hop address)
7. Prefer paths from the ***higher routing table number*** (inet.3 is preferred to inet.0)
8. Lowest ***router ID*** (or loopback IP address, if no router ID is specified) of the BGP router advertising the route
9. Prefer paths with the ***largest number of next hops***.
10. Prefer the ***lowest peer IP address***

Normally, eBGP peers are configured to the physical peer IP address. The BGP route selection process does not inherently load balance over equal cost paths to the same neighbor. This principal is brought to light at the path selection criteria number 8 above which is a tie-breaker that will result in a single path being chosen. However, there are situations in which multiple circuits are connected to one provider on the same router and load balancing is required over these paths. In these situations, *BGP multihop* is configured to provide the solution.

BGP multihop can be configured on external peers to allow for the peer to be more than one network interface away. Note that the router loopback is considered a logical network interface. Therefore, peering to a router's loopback address is considered to be a distance of **two** network interfaces (thus requiring *multihop*). When peering to loopback addresses, multiple physical links can be combined into one logical BGP session. This action, combined with the addition of the *multipath* setting is the only method for true load balancing when using BGP. When *multipath* is configured on a session, the Router ID (loopback) for both physical circuits is the same. Therefore, it is possible to utilize both paths.

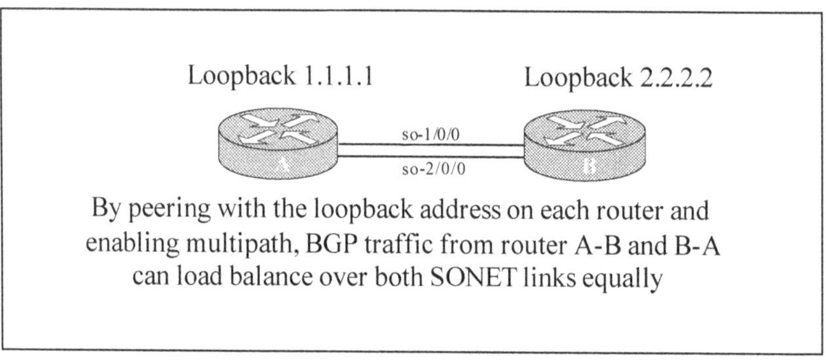

Figure 7.1 BGP Multipath

By default, BGP will accept all routes imported from any protocol. However, it will advertise only BGP routes to its peers (ignoring those from other protocols). This default behavior can be altered through policy manipulation (discussed in the Policy chapter).

Route Damping

BGP allows for a feature called route damping. This feature allows routes that have been withdrawn and readvertised, or 'flapped', more than a certain number of times in an allotted time interval to be placed in 'holddown'. The timers and settings are completely configurable within JUNOS and will vary by application. *Route Damping* is not active by default in JUNOS. *Route Damping* is key to the stability of the Internet, but it is not covered in depth for the JNCIA.

BGP Finite-State Machine

The BGP neighbor adjacency process is commonly referred to as the 'Finite-State Machine', which implies that there are specific input variables that will trigger a finite number of possibilities.

There are 13 BGP events that are the trigger for, or the result of, a state change. Details of these events are important to know, but they are not covered in detail for the JNCIA exam. These are the BGP events defined in the most recent RFC:

- BGP start
- BGP stop
- BGP transport connection open
- BGP transport connection closed
- BGP transport connection open failed
- BGP transport fatal error
- Connect-retry timer expired
- Keepalive timer expired
- Receive Open message
- Receive Update message
- Receive Keepalive message
- Receive Notification message

BGP session states

The states that a BGP peering session can be in are listed below. Following that is a diagram that may prove useful in recognizing the BGP connection process.

The below 3 states occur **before** the TCP session on port 179 is up:

Idle

The router is configured for BGP, but no action is being taken and all incoming sessions from this peer are refused. The router is awaiting a BGP start event to initiate the TCP session with the peer.

Connect

The router is waiting for the TCP connection to be completed. Once the TCP session is up, the router will send an Open message and move to Open-sent state.

Active

The TCP connection has failed in the Connect state and the router is continuing to listen for a TCP connection from the peer. If the TCP session is now down, the router will back to Connect. If the TCP session is still alive, the router will send another Open message and move back to Open-sent status.

Below states occur **after** the TCP session on port 179 is up:

Open-sent

The router has completed its work and has sent an Open message. It is waiting for an Open message from the peer. Upon receipt of this message from the peer, if no errors are detected, the route will send its first Keepalive message and move to Open-confirm.

Open-confirm

The router has sent its first Keepalive message and is waiting for a Keepalive message from the peer.

Established

A Keepalive message is received from the peer and the session is up. Routing updates will now be exchanged.

It is important to note two things about BGP state for the JNCIA exam.

1. 'Active' does not indicate a working BGP session (the term can sometimes be misleading).
2. It is rare that you will see a session marked as "Established", but rather three numbers will appear in the far right column indicating the number of routes from that peer that have been received, are

active, and are dampened. Output from a sample BGP peering session is inserted below the BGP state diagram.

Below is the output from the BGP log file with the 'state' traceoption flag set illustrating the steps undertaken while an adjacency forms.

```
jncia@my.router1> show log bgp
bgp_event: peer 10.2.2.1 (Internal AS 11) old state Idle
event Start new state Active
bgp_pp_recv: dropping 10.2.2.1 (Internal AS 11),
connection collision prefers 10.2.2.1+2287 (proto)
bgp_peer_close: closing peer 10.2.2.1 (Internal AS 11),
state is 3 (Active)
bgp_event: peer 10.2.2.1 (Internal AS 11) old state
Active event Stop new state Idle
bgp_event: peer 10.2.2.1 (Internal AS 11) old state Idle
event Start new state Active
bgp_event: peer 10.2.2.1 (Internal AS 11) old state
Active event Open new state OpenSent
bgp_event: peer 10.2.2.1 (Internal AS 11) old state
OpenSent event RecvOpen new state OpenConfirm
bgp_event: peer 10.2.2.1 (Internal AS 11) old state
OpenConfirm event RecvKeepAlive new state Established
```

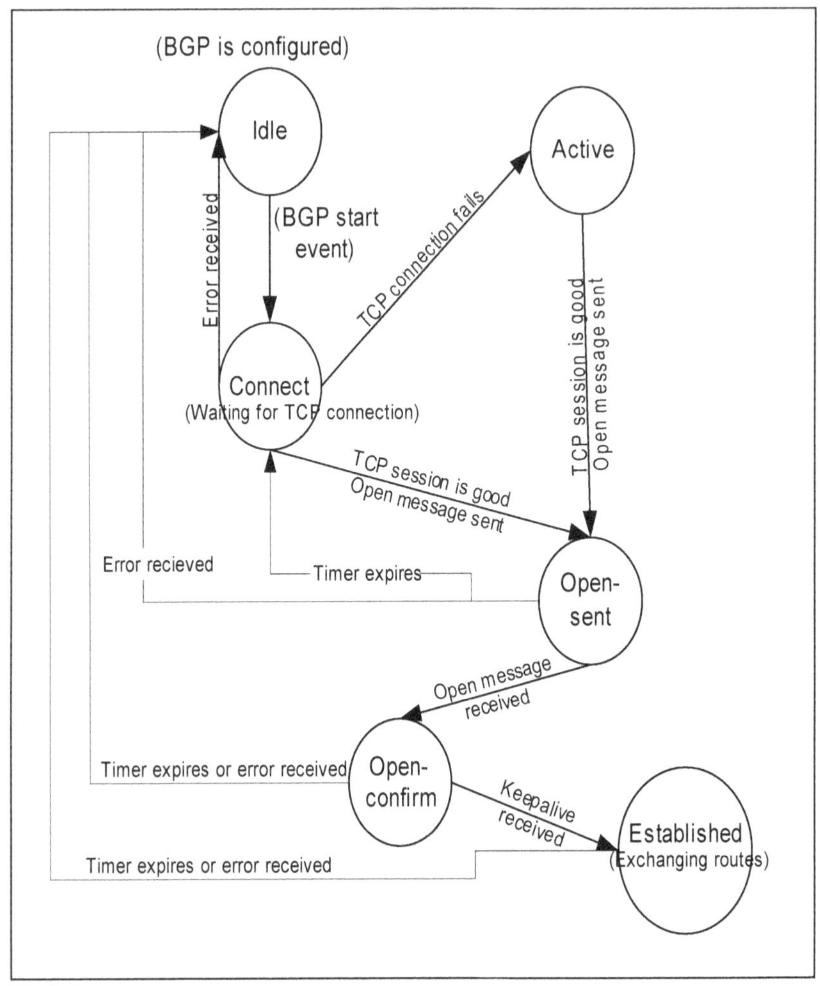

Figure 7.2 BGP connection process

On the next page, you'll see a sample BGP neighbor view:

```
jncia@my.router> show bgp summary
Groups: 9 Peers: 10 Down peers: 1
Table          Tot Paths  Act Paths Suppressed  History  Damp State   Pending
inet.0            245788     122217          0        0           0         0
inet.2                 0          0          0        0           0         0
Peer              AS      InPkt     OutPkt    OutQ   Flaps  Last Up/Dwn State|#Active/Rcvd/Damped
10.244.2.145    65333      1076      919         0       3     5d16h  113354/121636/0      0/0/0
10.244.2.154    65333       452      432         0       4     5d19h  8250/121636/0        0/0/0
10.246.46.126   65333       300      355         0      47     4d13h  25/40/0              0/0/0
10.210.41.166   11315       640      641         0      42     3d15h  10/23/0              0/0/0
10.210.62.58    11315       651      671         0      41     3d15h  15/23/0              0/0/0
10.158.57.54    13564       779      887         0       4     3d15h  6/10/0               0/0/0
10.101.246.58   12345         0        0         0       0     4d7h   Active
```

Route reflection

We have discussed that all routers in the iBGP network must be fully meshed in order to work properly. A full mesh requires a large number of connections and will slow convergence while consuming a great deal of bandwidth. A network with twenty routers, for instance, would require each node to support and converge nineteen separate BGP sessions.

To eliminate this scalability issue, *route reflection* is one of the two methods deployed in almost every ISP network (confederations being the second). Route reflection is simple to configure and allows BGP to break some of the "Golden Rules" in order to reduce the number of top-level connections. It is commonly deployed on a per-POP basis, allowing just one or two routers in each physical location to be part of the top level iBGP mesh. The rest of the routers in that site are the clients and do not exchange routes with other physical locations.

BGP route reflection is most easily viewed in a hierarchical manner. Some of the network routers are transformed to route reflector clients and simply placed in a 'lower tier' behind their route reflector server. **All** BGP updates, either internal or external, will be passed from the server to its client(s). This means that they rely on their servers for all BGP updates. All client updates are sent **only** to their respective server for propagation to the rest of the network.

A group of clients and their respective servers is referred to as a cluster. All routers in the cluster will share the same Cluster ID.

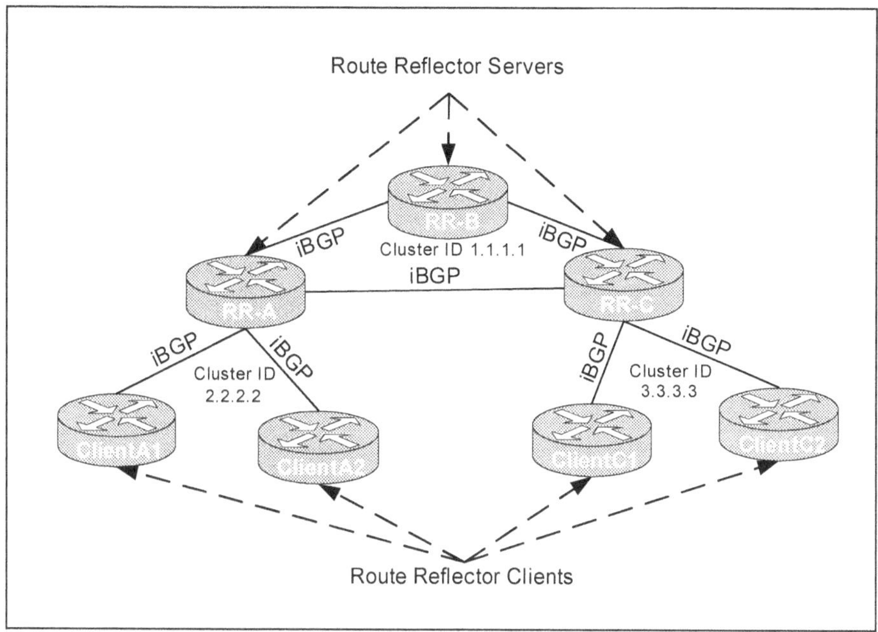

Figure 7.3 Simple BGP Route-Reflection

Configuration on a client is no different than any other BGP session. The client just thinks it is part of a very small BGP mesh (only one or two peers). It is not aware that those connections are actually to its servers, which will feed it all of its non-local BGP routes.

Configuration on a BGP route reflection server takes simply the addition of a *Cluster ID* on the server. This is an arbitrary IP address (although it must be unique to each cluster) that helps prevent routing loops between route reflectors by allowing them to ignore routes reflected to them from iBGP peers within the same *Cluster*.

Confederations

Confederations represent the second way to overcome the full-mesh problem associated with BGP for internal networks. They allow the ability to divide the AS into multiple internal Confederations identified to one-another with the use of the *Member-AS* number. This number (often private AS numbers 64512-65535 are used) is removed from advertisements before they leave the primary AS so that confederations are not visible to external peers.

Confederations are not covered in detail on the JNCIA exam.

BGP Configuration within JUNOS

BGP is first activated on the router, and then each peer is configured. Every BGP peer must be exclusively defined before forming an adjacency, and thus exchanging routes.

Before activating BGP neighbors, the local autonomous system ID must be defined at the global level of "edit routing-options". In addition, the *router-id* may be defined. If this attribute is not defined, the IP address of the first router interface is used as that router's ID.

The top level of configuration for BGP is under 'edit protocols bgp'. At this level, global BGP options can be set and groups can be defined. Each group must contain at least the following information:

```
[edit protocols bgp]
group group-name {
     peer-as number
     type [external | internal]
     neighbor address
     }
```

To allow for better scalability, it is desired to group BGP peers based upon common attributes (peer AS, external, internal, etc.) and then define more specific information (neighbor address, etc.) under each individual neighbor within the group.

Multiple values can be defined globally, under each BGP group, and again under each peer (except export policy, as noted below).

`[edit protocols bgp]` (global) or
`[edit protocols bgp group` *`group-name`*`]` (group) or
`[edit protocols bgp group` *`group-name`* `neighbor` *`address`*`]` (peer)

Remember that more specifically assigned values override less-specifically assigned (neighbor overrides group which overrides global).

`authentication-key` *`key;`*

JUNOS supports MD5 authentication on BGP sessions; it is disabled by default.

`cluster` *`cluster-identifier`*

Used to identify a route reflector.

`description` *`"name";`*

`export [`*`policy-names`*`];`

NOTE: Export policy only on group or global level; individual peers will use their group's export policy.

Export policy or policies are applied to routes from the routing table before they are advertised to the group or peer.

`hold-time` *`seconds;`*

Seconds allowed to pass without hearing a Keepalive before the session is declared dead, default for JUNOS is 90 seconds.

`import [`*`policy-names`*`];`

Import policy or policies are applied to incoming advertisements before they enter the routing table.

`local-address` *`address;`*

Used if a specific address is desired to be used on this session or sessions, other than the default.

`local-preference` *`value;`*

Applied to routes learned from this peer or neighbor only at time of advertisement to internal peers

`metric-out (`*`metric`*` | minimum IGP <`*`offset`*`> | igp <`*`offset`*`>)`

Sets a metric for outbound routes using the MED attribute.

`metric`: A value from 0-4,294,967,295 (by default no metric sent)

`minimum IGP`: Set the metric to the minimum IGP cost to reach this prefix. If a new metric comes along that is lower, change to the new, lower value (never raise). This can be offset by any value from (-2^{31}) to ($2^{31}-1$).

IGP: Set MED value to the most recent IGP cost to this prefix.

Offset: Can offset any value from (-2^{31}) to ($2^{31}-1$).

multihop *<ttl-value>*

eBGP sets the TTL of TCP packets to one by default; if the multihop tag is entered, the default value is set to 64 (and can be set to anything from 2-255). This command is needed if using any address other than the directly connected address on the interface (even the loopback of the router counts as another hop). The purpose of using multihop on eBGP sessions is to provide link redundancy or load balancing. If two links are used to connect two routers, the common configuration will peer each router to the other's loopback address. When both links are up, packets will be sent across both circuits to the BGP peer (assuming no further configuration that would prefer one connection). If one link fails, the neighbor's loopback address can still be reached via the second connection.

multipath

Allows multiples paths to be installed in the forwarding table for a single prefix, thus enabling load sharing

passive

When used, this peer or group will not send Open messages, but will respond to Open messages received and subsequently form adjacency, if all other configurations are proper

peer-as *autonomous-system*

Specifies Peer AS. This is confirmed upon receipt of an Open message from the peer. If the values do not match, the session will not establish.

preference *value;*

Sets the local-preference value of BGP routes learned from this group or peer (range 0 to 4294967295 [$2^{31}-1$]; default 170)

```
prefix-limit {
        maximum number;
        teardown percentage idle-timeout
        [forever | minutes];
    }
```

This specifies the maximum number of prefixes that will be allowed from the peer or group. Once the number is reached, a log message will be generated. If the teardown statement is added with a percentage, messages are generated when the percentage is reached and the session is taken down once the limit is reached. It will be re-established rapidly unless a idle-timeout timer is specified to keep the session down for that amount of time before setting up again.

```
traceoptions {
        file name replace <size size> <files #>
    <no-stamp> <world-readable | no-world-
    readable>;
        flag flag <flag-modifier> <disable>;
    }
```

Traceoptions allow system log files to be created that monitor events, as configured; they will be discussed in detail in the JUNOS chapter.

```
type [internal | external];
```

Indicates iBGP or eBGP session.

Monitoring BGP within JUNOS

The helpful commands to perform basic BGP troubleshooting on a Juniper M-series router are listed below with some examples and explanations.

```
jncia@my.router> show bgp ?
Possible completions:
  group        Show the BGP group database
  neighbor     Show the BGP neighbor database
  summary      Show overview of BGP information
```

```
show bgp summary
```

The command gives a brief display of all configured BGP sessions on the router.

```
jncia@my.router> show bgp summary
Groups: 1 Peers: 2 Down peers: 1
Table TotPaths ActPaths Suppressed History Damp State Pending
inet.0     0     0     0     0     0     0
Peer        AS     InPkt  OutPkt  OutQ  Flaps LastUp/Dwn State|#Act/Rcv'd/Damp...
10.44.2.20  65536  497    21      0     13 1d 15:02:13 1/1/0
10.5.100.2  65530  371    20      0     13 1d 14:12:10 1/1/0          1/1/0
10.44.2.22  65536  36     9       0     14 1d 15:04:10 Active
```

The most important items to recognize are the `Peer`, `AS`, and `State|#Act/Rcv'd/Damp...` columns. Peer and AS identify the remote side of the BGP session. By default, if the AS number if different than the local routers AS number, it is an eBGP session. If they are the same, it is an iBGP session. The final column indicates either the State of the neighbor or the number of Active/Received/Damped routes. Note that 10.44.2.22 is in 'Active' and lists no numbers for routes. If there is more than one column of numbers under this heading, the second set indicates multicast routes for MBGP.

`show bgp neighbor <neighbor-IP>`

This command will show more detailed information for individual peers.

```
jncia@my.router> show bgp neighbor 10.44.2.20
Peer:10.44.2.20 +179 AS 123 Local:10.44.2.10+1026 AS 456
 Type: Internal State: Established Flags: <>
 Last State: OpenConfirm Last Event: RecvKeepAlive
 Last Error: None
 Export:[eBGP-Export-policy] Import:[eBGP-Import-policy]
 Options: <Preference LocalAddress HoldTime LogUpDown
Refresh>
  Local Address: 10.44.2.10 Holdtime: 90 Preference: 170
  Number of flaps: 0
  Peer ID: 10.44.2.20 Local ID: 10.44.2.10 Active
Holdtime: 90
  Keepalive Interval: 30
  NLRI advertised by peer: inet-unicast
  NLRI for this session: inet-unicast
  Peer supports Refresh capability (2)
  Table inet.0 Bit: 10000
    RIB State: restart is complete
    Send state: in sync
    Active prefixes: 1
    Received prefixes: 1
    Suppressed due to damping: 0
  Last traffic (seconds): Received 1 Sent 12
Checked 12
  Input messages: Total 40914842 Updates 2000
Refreshes 0 Octets 683417048
  Output messages: Total 714008 Updates 0
Refreshes 0 Octets 13566178
  Output Queue[0]: 0
  Trace options: state
Trace file: /var/log/bgplog size 10576 files 1
```

If the neighbor IP address is left out from this command, all neighbors will be listed in order of IP address. This will show all details about BGP neighbors. Key information to note is session information (how long it has been up and how many times it has bounced), and import and export policy for the group for which this peer belongs.

It is important to remember that policy plays a crucial role in combination with BGP. This chart will help you remember the commands and where they are applied. Each command is subsequently discussed in detail.

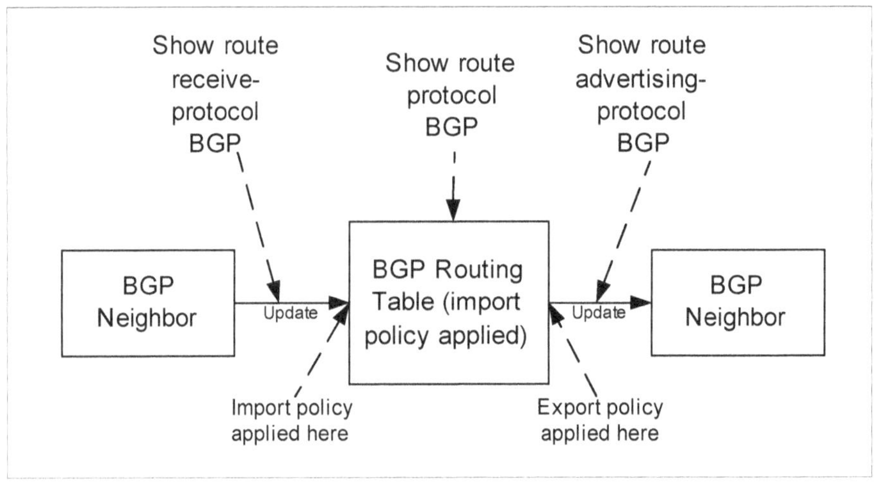

Figure 7.4 Viewing protocol-specific routes before, with, and after policy is applied

```
show route receive-protocol bgp neighbor-IP
<destination>
```

List all received BGP routes from the specified peer (located in the adj-fib-in table). Output can be compared with the results from "show route protocol bgp *destination*" to determine the impact of the import policy on received routes.

```
jncia@my.router>show route receive-protocol bgp 10.2.2.1

inet.0: 20 destinations, 20 routes (20 active, 0
holddown, 8 hidden)
```

```
Prefix                  Nexthop          MED   Lclpref AS
path
10.0.0.0/24             10.2.2.1                   100 I
10.2.2.1/32             10.2.2.1                   100 I
10.100.100.0/24         10.2.2.1                   100 I
10.150.150.0/24         10.2.2.1                   100 I
10.200.200.0/24         10.2.2.1                   100 I
10.250.250.0/24         10.2.2.1                   100 I
172.16.1.0/30           10.2.2.1                   100 I
172.16.1.24/30          10.2.2.1                   100 I
```

```
show route protocol bgp
```

List all active routes in the routing table that were learned from the protocol BGP.

```
jncia@my.router> show route protocol bgp

inet.0: 18 destinations, 18 routes (17 active, 0 holddown, 7
hidden)
+ = Active Route, - = Last Active, * = Both

10.0.0.0/24         [BGP/170] 00:32:25, localpref 100, from
10.2.2.1
                      AS path: I
                    > to 172.16.1.1 via fe-0/0/0.2
10.2.2.1/32         [BGP/170] 00:32:25, localpref 100, from
10.2.2.1
                      AS path: I
                    > to 172.16.1.1 via fe-0/0/0.2
10.150.150.0/24    *[BGP/170] 00:32:25, localpref 100, from
10.2.2.1
                      AS path: I
                    > to 172.16.1.1 via fe-0/0/0.2
10.200.200.0/24    *[BGP/170] 00:32:25, localpref 100, from
10.2.2.1
                      AS path: I
                    > to 172.16.1.1 via fe-0/0/0.2
10.250.250.0/24    *[BGP/170] 00:32:25, localpref 100, from
10.2.2.1
                      AS path: I
                    > to 172.16.1.1 via fe-0/0/0.2
172.16.1.0/30       [BGP/170] 00:32:25, localpref 100, from
10.2.2.1
                      AS path: I
                    > to 172.16.1.1 via fe-0/0/0.2
```

```
172.16.1.24/30      [BGP/170] 00:32:25, localpref 100, from
10.2.2.1
                      AS path: I
                    > to 172.16.1.1 via fe-0/0/0.2
```

show route advertising-protocol bgp *neighbor-IP*

List the BGP routes in the adj-fib-out table. This will list all BGP routes that have passed through the outbound policy filter and are advertised to the specific peer. This output can be compared to with the results from "show route protocol bgp *destination*" to determine the impact of the export policy on advertised routes.

```
jncia@my.router1>show route advertising-protocol
bgp 10.2.2.2

inet.0: 18 destinations, 18 routes (18 active, 0
holddown, 0 hidden)
Prefix              Nexthop         MED     Lclpref  AS
10.0.0.0/24         Self                        100   I
10.2.2.1/32         Self                        100   I
10.2.2.2/32         172.16.1.2      100         100   I
10.2.2.3/32         172.16.1.2      200         100   I
10.2.2.4/32         172.16.1.2      300         100   I
10.100.100.0/24     10.2.2.1                    100   I
10.150.150.0/24     10.2.2.1                    100   I
10.200.200.0/24     10.2.2.1                    100   I
10.250.250.0/24     10.2.2.1                    100   I
172.16.1.0/30       Self                        100   I
172.16.1.4/30       172.16.1.2      200         100   I
172.16.1.8/30       172.16.1.2      300         100   I
172.16.1.12/30      172.16.1.2      400         100   I
172.16.1.24/30      Self                        100   I
```

It is sometimes desired to view BGP routes before they are run through the import policy and after they are run through the export policy. With the use of these three commands, it is possible to tune BGP reception and advertisement to obtain the optimal routing scenario.

Because of the widespread use of BGP and its default behavior to accept all BGP routes and re-advertise all BGP routes, policy plays a large role in the manipulation of BGP. More details of policy and how it interacts with this protocol are covered in the Policy chapter.

Key Points and Summary

BGP plays a key role in the network of every Internet Service Provider. With the information provided in this chapter, you should be able to properly configure BGP peering adjacencies on Juniper routers. As noted in the introduction, there are many developments recently released and still in the works for this complex protocol. We did not cover protocol families which allow BGP to carry network layer reachability information (NLRI) for address families other than unicast IPv4 or IP security associations. These topics, among others for BGP, are important to know. However, they are not covered on this exam.

- BGP is an advanced link-state protocol
- BGP is used by every large ISP to connect with the Internet
- Two primary types of BGP relationships. It is important to remember that the default behavior changes with each.
    - Internal (with same AS)
    - External (with a different AS)
- BGP follows a set path selection criteria when choosing between multiple routes to the same destination
    - Highest ***Local Preference***
    - Shortest ***AS-Path***
    - Lowest ***Origin Code***
    - Lowest ***Multi-Exit Discriminator (MED)***
    - Prefer ***eBGP paths over iBGP paths***
    - ***Lowest IGP cost***, or metric (Closest next-hop address)
    - Prefer paths from the ***higher routing table number*** (inet.3 is preferred to inet.0)
    - Lowest ***router ID*** (or loopback IP address, if no router ID is specified) of the BGP router advertising the route
    - Prefer paths with the ***largest number of next hops***.
    - Prefer the ***lowest peer IP address***
- The problem with having to create a 'full-mesh' in order for BGP to function properly can be averted through the use of route reflectors or confederations
- Neighbors in "active" state are not UP!

Additional information (RFCs)

For specific information, please consult the following at http://www.ietf.org:

- RFC 827 and 904 EGP (1982/1984)
- RFC 1771, BGP version 4
- RFC 1772, Application of BGP in the Internet
- RFC 1773, Experience with BGPv4
- RFC 1774, BGP-4 Protocol Analysis
- RFC 1965, BGP Confederations
- RFC 1966, BGP Route Reflection
- RFC 1997, BGP Communities Attribute
- RFC 2439, BGP Route Flap Damping
- RFC 2796, BGP Route Reflection
- RFC 3065, AS Confederations for BGP
- RFC 2702, Requirements for Traffic Engineering over MPLS

Chapter Eight

MPLS

Chapter 8: MPLS

Overview

This chapter will cover *Multi-Protocol Label Switching* (MPLS). MPLS is a networking technology that integrates the control and robustness of IP routing with the simplicity and high-performance of layer-2 switching. MPLS enables service providers to create multiple, individual networks for diverse applications over a single IP infrastructure. Some of the important points you should be able to explain after reading this chapter:

- ✓ Define the purpose and value of deploying MPLS
- ✓ Clear understanding of the basics of *label distribution protocol* (LDP) and *resource reservation protocol* (RSVP)
- ✓ Name and define all label operations
- ✓ Difference in router types/functions in an MPLS network
- ✓ Traffic engineering within MPLS

Introduction

Different types of applications have varying network requirements for their data. File transfer and web pages are not sensitive to latency and are capable of compensating for packet loss during network events. Real-time voice and video traffic are extremely susceptible to performance degradation. The threshold for packet loss in such multimedia applications is miniscule, and even packets arriving out of order will result in incorrect presentation. In the past, service providers were often required to run separate networks for this sensitive data. *Asynchronous Transfer Mode* (ATM) provides stability and reliable *quality of service* (QoS) at the cost of scalability and additional network expense.

IP is inherently connectionless and in its original design did not provide controls for rigid QoS requirements. In order to attain multiple services over an IP network, that network must provide QoS levels equal to those offered by existing ATM and SONET technologies.

The original desire for MPLS was the need to increase the speed of layer-3 routing lookups to improve network performance. ATM switches performing this action via hardware are able to forward traffic faster than routers doing a longest IP match using software. This same functionality was desired in routers and could be performed using MPLS. In addition, MPLS has evolved into a protocol that provides for traffic engineering, *virtual private networks* (VPNs), and enhanced QoS.

MPLS is a method of encapsulating packets within a 32 bit header that is then used to make forwarding decisions.

MPLS Label Switched Paths (LSPs)

The distribution and application of MPLS labels creates *label switched paths* (LSPs). An LSP can be visualized as a tunnel which allows for the switching of packets across a network via the use of label. This eliminates the need for intermediate routers to perform IP route lookup. The entrance of the tunnel, or LSP, is referred to as the *ingress.* The exit of the LSP is referred to as the *egress*.

A router that places packets into an LSP by appending the packet with the MPLS header is known as the *ingress router*. At the LSP's exit, the router removing the label is known as the *egress router*. Routers that reside in the middle of an LSP between the ingress and egress are referred to as *transit routers*. In general, ingress and egress routers are referred to as *label edge routers* (LERs) because they reside at the edge of the MPLS network. Transit routers are often referred to as *label switch routers* (LSRs) as they perform switching operations to replace the incoming label with a new outgoing label within the core of the MPLS network. In other words, an LER will still do some type of action based upon the IP information of a packet. In contrast, a LSR acts upon only the MPLS information and is unaware of what IP information may be inside.

Using LSPs as next-hops for BGP is one example of how they can be used to improve network performance. Without their use, two IP lookups are required at each router hop to forward BGP traffic. The first lookup, which is based upon the packet's destination address, results in a BGP route. That result has a next-hop attribute that is the router ID of the BGP node that has the best route to the destination. The second lookup is done based upon the BGP next-hop and the result is an IGP route. After the second lookup, the packet is forwarded to the IGP next hop and the entire process is repeated.

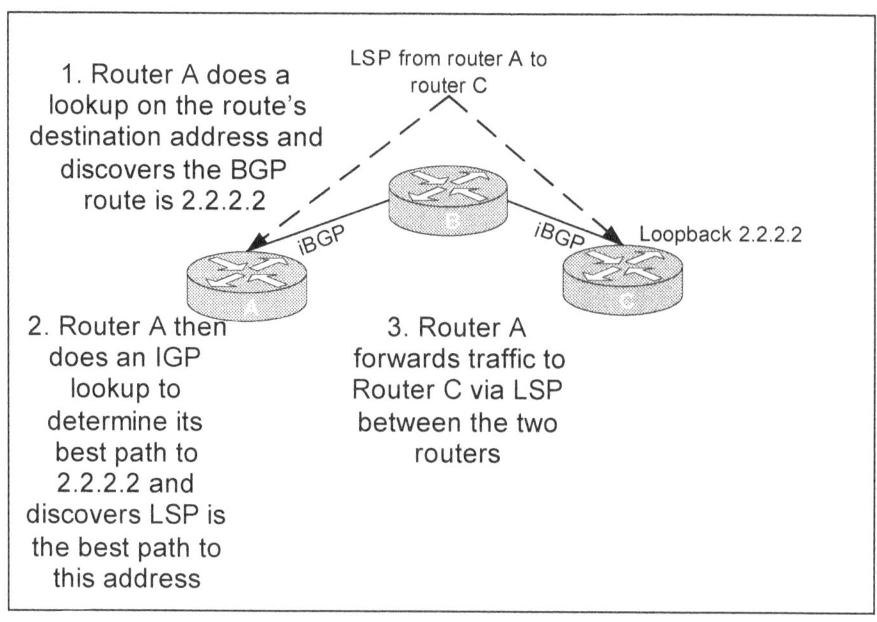

Figure 8.1 BGP next-hop forwarding using an LSP

MPLS Header and Field Description

The MPLS header is 32 bits and consists of 4 distinct fields: *label, Class of Service* (CoS), *Stack,* and *time-to-live* (TTL). The label field of the MPLS header is 20 bits, the CoS field is three bits, the stack field is one bit, and the TTL field is eight bits.

20 bit Label	3 bit CoS	1 bit Stack	8 bit TTL
Field make-up of 32 bit MPLS header			

The label field is used when a packet is being MPLS switched. The lookup decision is based upon the label. The CoS field is used to classify the level of service the packet should receive. The stack bit is used to determine whether or not the top label is the only label appended to the packet. The TTL field defines the maximum number of hops the packet will be allowed to traverse.

The label space is made up of 20-bit unsigned integers between ranging from 0 to 1048575. 0 through 15 are reserved and have special functions. 16 to 1023 and 10000 to 99999 are unused and unassigned by JUNOS. These labels are best used for static LSPs because the dynamically assigned labels are not drawn from within this range. 1024 through 9999 are reserved for future applications. 100000 through 1048575 are dynamically negotiated, assigned, released, and reused by JUNOS.

Special labels are used for certain applications. One such instance is label distribution between the penultimate router (the last MPLS transit router) and the egress router. If it is desired that the penultimate router pop the label before forwarding the packet to the egress router the egress router would send a label of 3 to the penultimate router. Label 3 has a special meaning of "pop the label before forwarding". If it is desired that the penultimate router pop the label before forwarding the packet to the egress, the penultimate router would have label 3 assigned to the egress next hop. The other special labels are listed below with a brief explanation for each:

- 0, IPv4 Explicit Null Label—The label must be popped upon receipt and forwarding should continue based on the IPv4 packet address. (Note that this value is legal only when it is the sole label entry, no label stacking.)
- 1, Router Alert Label—When this is the top label, it should be popped and the packet delivered to the local software module for processing.
- 2, IPv6 Explicit Null Label—Same as label 0, except for IPv6
- 3, Implicit Null Label—Indicates penultimate hop router is next hop in the LSP
- 4 through 15—Reserved, but not yet assigned.

MPLS defines the process for switching packets that have labels. It is not a routing protocol and contains no ability to manufacture and propagate the labels themselves. Instead, it depends upon label distribution protocols to perform these functions. Similarly, at a high overview level, the basic IP routing process is concerned with only with doing a longest-match lookup and selecting the best next-hop. IP depends upon routing protocols such as OSPF and BGP to do the work of finding, advertising, and maintaining an accurate routing table.

Label Space: Allocation and Assignment

Label space is a range of label values that a router can assign or associate with a *forward equivalency class* (FEC). A FEC defines which packets will be appended with a particular label. One example of a FEC is a network address. All packets with a destination that belongs to the network address will be encapsulated with the same label before they are forwarded to the next router.

There are two ways a router can allocate its label space: *per interface* and *globally*. If a router is using the *per interface* method, a separate copy of the same label space is independently used for each interface. In other words, the same label can be distributed out each interface because the value of the label combined with the interface it was distributed out of gives it uniqueness. In contrast, with the global method all interfaces use the same label space. Therefore a unique label can only be distributed once. JUNOS employs the global method for label allocation.

Label Operations

A packet can be encapsulated with a number of labels organized as a last-in, first-out stack. This is referred to as the label stack. At a particular router, the decision as to how to forward a labeled packet is based exclusively on the label at the top of the stack.

There are three operations that can be performed to a label: *push, pop* or *swap*:

Push - Add a new label to the top of the packet. For IPv4 packets, the new label is the first label. If the push operation is performed on an existing MPLS packet, the result will be a packet with 2 or more labels. This is called label stacking. Any label other than the last label must have its *stack bit* set to 0 (the last label has its value set to 1). Note that in JUNOS software Release 4.2 and later, the new top label in a label stack always initializes its TTL to 255, regardless of the TTL value of lower labels.

Pop - Remove the top label from the packet. Once the label is removed, the TTL is copied from the label into the IP packet header, and the underlying IP data is forwarded as a native IP packet. In the case of multiple labels in a packet (label stacking), removal of the top label yields another MPLS packet. Note that in JUNOS software Release 4.2 and later, the popped TTL value from the previous top label is not written back to the new top label.

Swap - Replace the label at the top of the label stack with a new one. The stack bit is copied from the previous label, and the TTL value is copied and decremented (unless the *no-decrement-ttl* or *no-propagate-ttl* statements are configured). A transit router supports a label stack of any depth.

LSP Creation

Label distribution is the mechanism that creates LSPs. There are three ways labels can be distributed: *label distribution protocol* (LDP), *resource reservation protocol* (RSVP), and *static*. The method of label distribution dictates what type of LSP is formed. Each of the different types of LSPs has unique characteristics that dictate its capabilities, advantages, and disadvantages. Deciding which type of LSPs to deploy depends on the needs of the network. It is possible to deploy all three different types of LSPs concurrently. Static LSPs are rarely deployed on a large scale because of the administrative overhead.

Label Distribution Protocol (LDP)

LDP is used to dynamically create and exchange labels between MPLS/LDP routers. An LDP enabled router will assign labels to FECs, creating a label binding. Each router stores label bindings in a local database. Routers then exchange label databases via an LDP session. The label bindings are then used to encapsulate packets before forwarding them to the downstream LDP neighbor.

Two adjacent routers running LDP on a shared network segment will become LDP neighbors by exchanging discovery messages. Once two adjacent routers have become LDP neighbors they must establish an LDP session by exchanging session messages. The neighbor relationship exists at the interface level while the session is formed at the router ID level. If two routers are connected via two separate network segments they will become LDP neighbors on each segment while a single LDP session is formed between router IDs. Note the exception to this rule if the physical segments are independent (such as two ATM circuits each with its own VPI/VCI). In this exception, an LDP session will form over both of the physical links, independently.

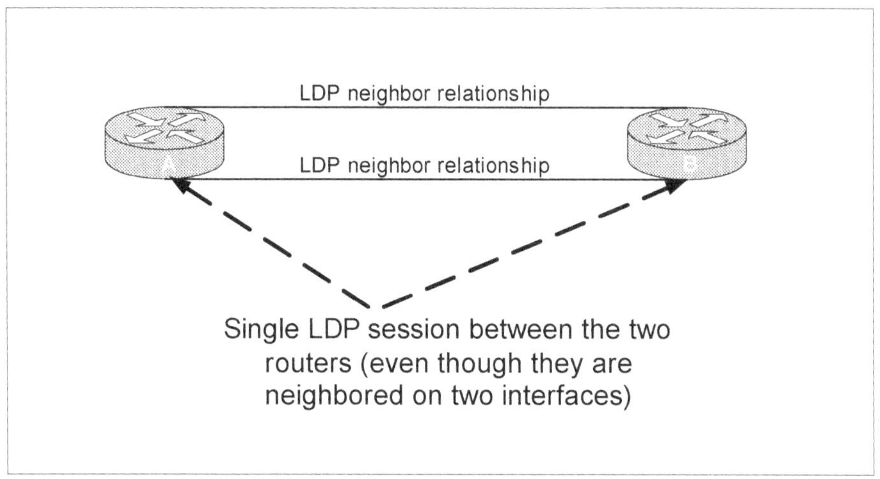

Figure 8.2 LDP neighbor adjacency and sessions

Two routers that form an LDP session whereby they exchange label bindings is the act of label distribution. This exchange or distribution of labels gives each router knowledge of what label to use when forwarding packets to the downstream router.

Labels are assigned by downstream routers relative to the flow of packets. A router receiving labeled packets (the next-hop router) is responsible for assigning incoming labels. A received packet containing a label that is unrecognized (unassigned) is dropped. For unrecognized labels, the router does not attempt to unwrap the label to analyze the network layer header, nor does it generate an ICMP destination unreachable message.

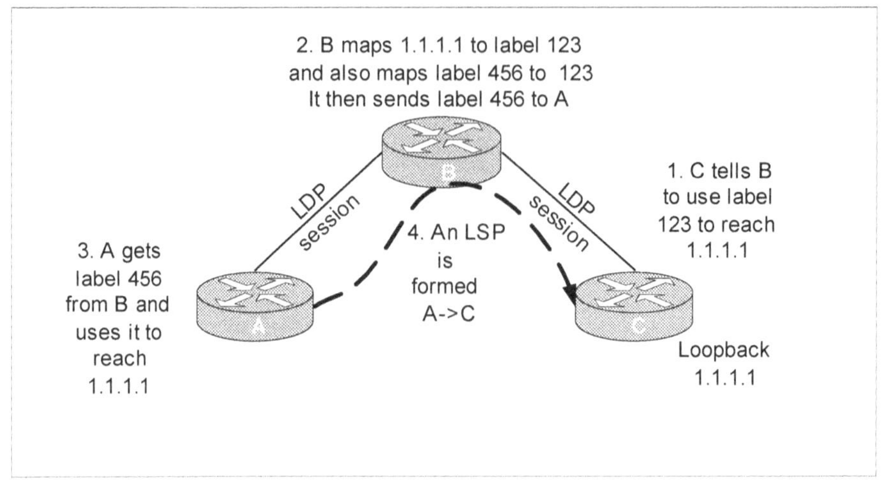

Figure 8.3 Label distribution

For traffic to flow from Router A to Router C, each router needs to know which label the downstream router is expecting. The upstream routers know what labels to use because they are given this information by downstream routers. Keep in mind that when referring to MPLS and traffic flow, 'downstream' refers to the destination (router C in our example). 'Upstream' indicates the source (router A in our example). This is a simple concept when only dealing with three routers, but it is important to keep in mind when dealing with more complicated configurations.

Using the drawing in figure 8.3, let's assume that Router A receives a packet who's destination address is the loopback of Router C. Router A does a lookup and finds the label binding that it received from Router B (label 456), appends the appropriate label to the packet and forwards the packet to Router B. Because Router B told Router A what label to use, Router B knows that when it receives the packet it should swap the label with the label it received from Router C (label 123) and forward the packet to Router C.

Resource Reservation Protocol (RSVP)

RSVP is another type of LSP signaling protocol. It is used to distribute labels, reserve bandwidth, prevent loops, and inform the routers in the LSP of the type of traffic to expect. Two adjacent routers sharing a network segment running RSVP will become neighbors and exchange *path* (PATH) and *reserve* (RESV) messages when an LSP is signaled.

When an RSVP LSP is configured, PATH messages are sent toward the egress router informing each node along the way to prepare for a label binding, bandwidth reservation, and the type of traffic that will be sent along the LSP. When the egress router receives the PATH messages, it responds by sending a RESV message towards the ingress router using the same path. The RESV messages contain the label binding and amount of required bandwidth (as well as other information not pertinent to the JNCIA exam). Once RSVP has setup and signaled the path, the LSP is ready to be used for forwarding.

RSVP LSPs have the ability to signal a primary and secondary path. If network topology allows, the secondary path will not use any of the same hops as the primary. The secondary path is used for fail-over if the primary path should fail. Because the secondary path is pre-signaled and ready for traffic, it greatly decreases convergence times after a network event.

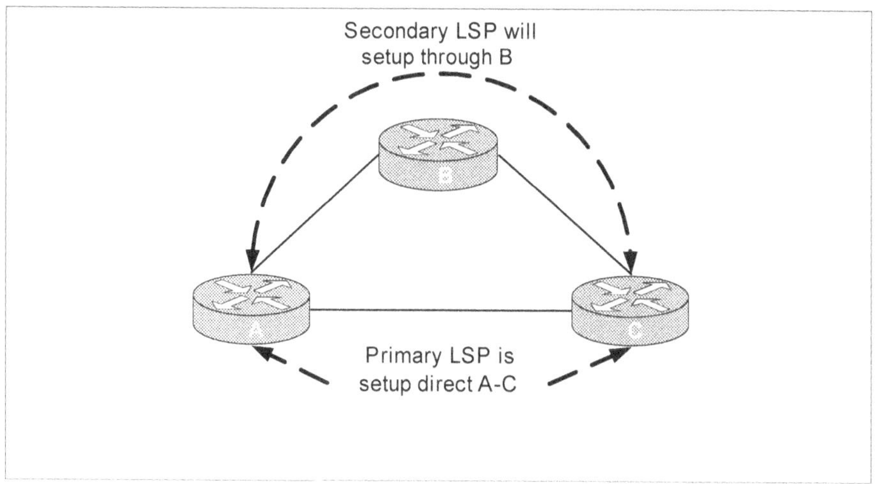

Figure 8.4 RSVP primary and secondary paths

RSVP LSPs can also be constrained. This is a form of traffic engineering. Any number of the hops within an LSP can be manually configured to constrain the path of the LSP. The remaining (non-constrained) hops are free to be signaled dynamically. There are two ways to configure the hops in a constrained path, *loose* or *strict*. When a path is configured with a strict hop, it must be directly connected to the previous hop. A loose constraint does not have to be directly connected to the previous hop but it must be traversed at some point within the LSP.

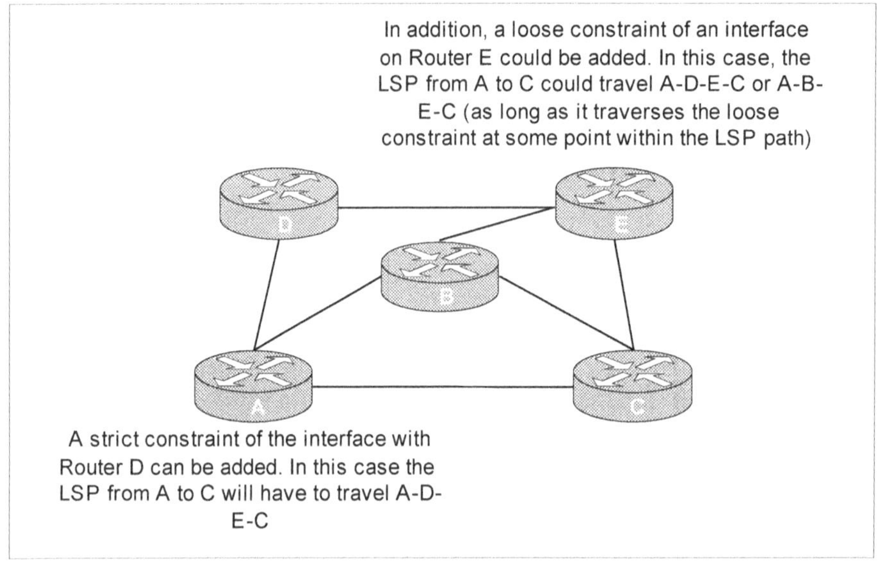

Figure 8.5 RSVP LSPs with constrained hops

Traffic Engineering Database (TED)

The *traffic engineering database* (TED) contains information about the topology of the network. The TED is created by using the traffic engineering extensions to OSPF and/or IS-IS. In the case of OSPF, Type-10 LSAs are exchanged. IS-IS exchanges information within the link-state PDUs known as Type Length Values (TLV) that specify link attributes. The information about each node that is stored in the TED consists of:

- Node type
- Number of links
- Protocol that reported the information
- Static bandwidth
- 'Reserveable' bandwidth and
- Available bandwidth by priority level

Once each router's TED has been fully updated, this information can be used to calculate the best path for each LSP. An ingress router examines the requirements of an LSP and compares those against the information in the TED to calculate the best path. The result of the best path calculation is referred to as the *explicit route object* (ERO) and is passed on to RSVP to be used for signaling the LSP.

Constrained Shortest Path First (CSPF)

Constrained shortest path first (CSPF) is an algorithm similar to that used by OSPF and IS-IS to compute the shortest path between nodes. It takes LSP attribute information and compares it against the TED and compiles the best path for the LSP. The result of the CSPF computation is referred to as the ERO. The ERO is simply the interface addresses or hops the LSP will traverse to reach the egress router. CSPF passes the ERO to RSVP.

MPLS Configuration in JUNOS

Configuring MPLS can be quite complex and involved. Fortunately, the JNCIA does not focus on the configuration of MPLS as much as it does the operation of it. More emphasis is given to the editing in the higher level certifications. However, there are some facets with which you should be familiar.

Simply put, there are three distinct sections that must be handled to successfully configure MPLS. First, MPLS must be added at the global protocols level. Secondly, MPLS must be enabled on the interfaces it will run on. Third, the label protocols LDP and RSVP must be configured.

MPLS is enabled globally under protocols. All LSPs are configured under the `[edit protocols mpls]` layer. Traceoption files are also configurable within this level.

MPLS inherently does not route packets in the traditional sense, it forwards data depending on its label. In the same way, it is more a routed protocol than a routing protocol. Because of this, interfaces normally operating in the inet (internet) family must also be placed in the mpls family to be bound correctly to the protocols. This is done at the interface level of configuration under the `[family mpls]` level.

LDP must be enabled at the global level before it can be configured on each interface where it is desired. The top level of configuration is at `[edit protocols ldp]`.

Monitoring MPLS in JUNOS

Despite the relative complexity of configuring MPLS, troubleshooting and monitoring is no more difficult than dealing with another protocol. Viewing neighbors and interfaces for RSVP and LDP is straightforward and should be recognizable from working with the other routing protocols.

`Show rsvp neighbor` *`neighbor-IP`* `<detail>`

If the neighbor address is left out, an abbreviated list of neighbors will be given. The 'detail' option will return specific information on the queried neighbor(s).

```
jncia@my.router> show rsvp neighbor
RSVP neighbor: 6 learned
Address      Idle Up/Dn LastChange  HelloInt HelloTx/Rx MsgRcvd
10.159.1.34   0    1/0   2w3d 9:51:44     3       20/21       20
10.247.9.7    0    8/7   1w4d 8:53:38     3       35/34       34
10.247.9.106  0  28/27   3w5d 2:17:43     3       31/30       31
10.159.0.193  0    1/0   2w3d 5:38:28     3       79/80       80
10.159.0.161  0    1/0   4w3d 7:24:04     3       94/95       94
10.159.0.234  0  63/62   1w3d 2:55:01     3       27/29       29
```

`Show rsvp interface <brief|detail>`

Likewise, this command will output the status of the active RSVP interfaces, including bandwidth statistics for amount available, amount reserved, and highwater mark.

```
jncia@my.router> show rsvp interface
RSVP interface: 2 active
                Active Subscr- Static    Avail      Rsvd   High
Interface  State resv  iption     BW        BW        BW    mark
so-0/0/0.0  Up     18   100%   622.08Mb 605.3Mb   16.7Mb  1.4Mb
so-1/0/0.0  Up     12   100%   622.08Mb 605.3Mb   16.8Mb  1.3Mb
```

`Show ldp neighbor <brief|detail|extensive>`

Outputs the current status of LDP neighbors and the associated interface.

```
jncia@my.router> show ldp neighbor
Address        Interface  Label space ID  Hold time
10.1.8.1       lo0.0       10.1.8.1:0          10
10.1.11.2      lo0.0       10.1.11.2:0         13
10.1.11.25     lo0.0       10.1.11.25:0        10
```

```
Show ldp session <brief|detail|extensive>
```

Displays the status of LDP sessions to neighboring routers.

```
jncia@my.router> show ldp session
  Address      State        Connection    Hold time
10.1.2.2    Operational      Open              24
10.1.2.4    Operational      Open              26
```

When dealing with the state of label switch paths that have been set up through distributed labels:

```
Show mpls lsp [down|up|name] <detail>
```

```
jncia@my.router> show mpls lsp
Ingress LSP: 3 sessions
To            From         State Rt    ActivePath    P     LSPname
10.20.40.1    10.20.30.1    Up     9    to-router1    *     lsp2-R1
10.20.40.2    10.20.30.1    Up     8    to-router2    *     lsp2-R2
10.20.40.3    10.20.30.1    Up     6    to-router3    *     lsp2-R3
Total 3 displayed, Up 3, Down 0

Egress LSP: 3 sessions
To           From         State Rt Style Labelin Labelout LSPname
10.20.30.1   10.20.40.1   Up    0   1 FF       3          -  from-R1
10.20.30.1   10.20.40.2   Up    0   1 FF       3          -  from-R2
10.20.30.1   10.20.40.3   Up    0   1 FF       3          -  from-R3
Total 3 displayed, Up 3, Down 0
Transit LSP: 2 sessions
To           From        State Rt Style Labelin Labelout LSPname
10.20.40.1   10.20.40.3   Up    0   1 FF   182706   407173   R1-toR3
10.20.40.3   10.20.40.1   Up    0   1 FF   182701   407167   R3-toR1
Total 2 displayed, Up 2, Down 0
```

Note in the above 'ingress' output that all LSPs are 'from' the router running the command. The 'P' column denotes if the path is primary. Under all sections, the LSP name is listed in the final column. Likewise, under egress all LSPs are 'to' this router. Note the label in for egress LSPs is 3 and the outgoing label is undefined. This is because the packet will be IP forwarded after the final label is removed.

The 'detail' output of a specific LSP will show a wealth of information, including:

- The LSP metric
- The computed ERO with next-hops
- The computed CSPF metric cost
- Primary and Secondary paths

Below is the output from the RSVP log file with the 'state' traceoption flag set illustrating the steps undertaken while an adjacency forms.

```
jncia@my.router1> show log rsvp
RSVP new Session 10.2.2.2(port 18) Proto 0
RSVP new path state, session 10.2.2.2(port 18) Proto 0
RSVP new Neighbor 172.16.1.1
RSVP new resv state, session 10.2.2.2(port 18) Proto 0
RSVP neighbor 172.16.1.1 up on interface so-1/0/0.0
```

Key Points

MPLS is a solution for implementing stable and reliable QoS onto a packet switched network in a scalable fashion. It allows the building of converged networks where many different applications with different service level requirements utilize the same underlying network infrastructure.

- MPLS utilizes labels instead of IP addresses to forward data along predetermined label switch paths (LSPs).
- Multiple labels can be stacked onto a packet. Only the top label is acted on when the packet is analyzed.
- There are three basic functions carried out on an MPLS label:
    - Push
    - Swap
    - Pop
- Data traffic entering an LER undergoes and IP lookup which assigns a label to the packet. Thereafter until it exits the MPLS network the packet is label switched; LSRs pay no attention to the IP header of the packet.
- LDP and RSVP are the two protocols used by Juniper routers to produce and distribute labels and set-up LSPs
- Information about the network links is stored in the TED and used to determine the best path for LSPs
- The TED is compiled using information from the IGP:
    - OSPF Type-10 LSAs
    - IS-IS TLV extensions
- CSPF computes the best path given the information in the TED, the result is called the ERO.

In a non-MPLS network a packet enters a router, the router examines the packets header to learn the destination address. Then a lookup of the routing table is done based on the destination address and a BGP route is selected. The router then examines the BGP route and based on the BGP next hop does a second lookup. The result of the second lookup is used to forward the packet to the next router hop where both exhaustive longest match routing table lookups are done once again. This process is repeated until the packet arrives at the destination. It is the two lookup process that slows the networks throughput and overall performance.

In an MPLS network, LSPs can be configured between BGP speaking routers. As a packet enters the ingress router the initial IP lookup is done using the routing table. A BGP route is selected and the recursive lookup on the BGP next hop is also done. When the recursive lookup is done an LSP is found as the IGP next hop. This is the point where the ingress router encapsulates the packet with an mpls header and forwards the encapsulated packet to the next router. When the next router receives the packet the only lookup that needs to be done is based on the fixed length 20bit label contained in the MPLS header. The MPLS header is examined to learn the value of the label, a lookup is done in the label information base, a new label is appended to the packet and the packet is forwarded to the next router. Because each transit router only needs to perform a single lookup based on the label the end result is a network that can forward packets faster because it isn't necessary to perform two lookups at every router hop.

Additional Information

- RFC 3036, LDP Specification
- RFC 2209, Resource Reservation Protocol v1
- RFC 3209, RSVP-TE, Extensions for LSP tunnels
- RFC 3031, Multiprotocol Label Switching Architecture
- RFC 2702, Requirements for Traffic Engineering over MPLS
- RFC 3469, Framework for MPLS based Recovery
- RFC 3032, MPLS Label Stack Encoding
- RFC 2547, BGP/MPLS VPNs

Chapter Nine
Multicast

Chapter 9: Multicast

Overview

This chapter will cover the concepts and protocols used to implement multicast on Juniper routers. There are a number of unique ideas that will be covered. By the end of this chapter you should be able to:

- ✓ Site the benefits of implementing multicast.
- ✓ Describe multicast traffic flow.
- ✓ Identify multicast specific protocols DVMRP, PIM, MSDP, and IGMP.
- ✓ Understand the use of Reverse Path Forwarding.
- ✓ Recognize Class D address space.
- ✓ Define (S, G) and (*, G) notation.
- ✓ Recognize the use of multicast extensions to BGP.
- ✓ Identify the differences in PIM sparse-mode versus PIM dense-mode.
- ✓ Identify which routing table stores multicast routes.

Introduction

There are three fundamental ways to route IP packets: Unicast, Broadcast, and Multicast. Unicast traffic is the sending of packets from one unique source to one unique destination. The majority of the previous sections have dealt with the idea and concepts supporting unicast. Broadcasting is the concept of one unique source sending traffic to all destinations on a network. Broadcasting does not scale as network size increases; it rapidly uses up all available bandwidth resources.

The primary benefit of multicast is the conservation of bandwidth by allocating a single flow from a source to reach multiple destinations. In contrast, unicast must source a single flow **per** destination. Diagrams 9.1 and 9.2 illustrate this concept:

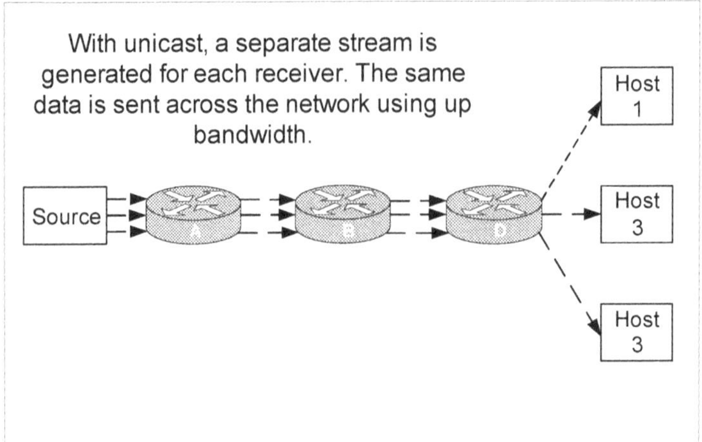

Figure 9.1 Unicast Traffic Flow

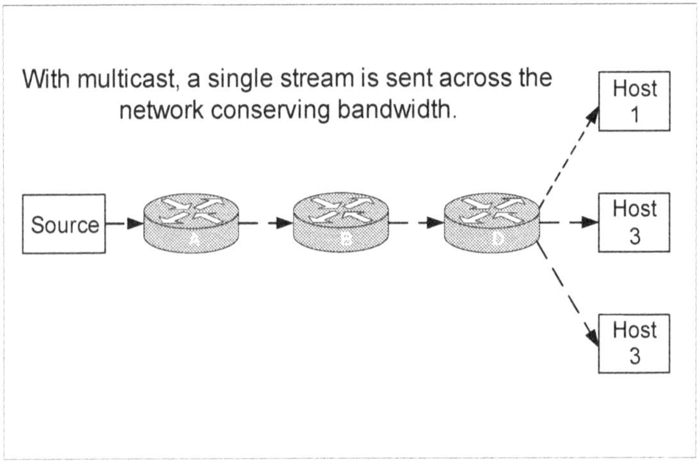

Figure 9.2 Multicast Traffic Flow

In Figure 9.1, the data source must allocate an individual stream for each of the receiving hosts. Even though the path, and ostensibly the data payload, is the same, three flows must be managed. This rapidly depletes network resources as the number of hosts increases. In contrast, the source in 9.2 only needs to deliver a single stream to the last common device. In this case, Router D receives the single stream, replicates the packets and serves all three end-hosts.

The key to multicast resides within a number of specialized protocols and in the addressing. IP unicast traffic is sent to the unique host address allocated to that destination node. Broadcast traffic uses the special broadcast IP address, a .255 or "all 1's" subnet address. Multicast addresses are of a special subset of IP space within Class D. Routers running multicast protocols depend on addresses in Class D space to accurately deliver multicast packets only to devices that need them. Juniper routers store multicast routes in the inet.2 routing table, by default.

Multicast addressing

A single multicast address identifies a multicast stream. This is in contrast to a unicast address which identifies a unique host. This is an important differentiation to keep in mind. Multicast group addresses are taken from the Class D address space. This is defined as the addresses with the high-order bits set to `'1110'`, giving an address range from `224.0.0.0` through `239.255.255.255`, or more simply `224.0.0.0/4`. All of the addresses in this range are reserved for multicast use. There are ranges within these class D addresses that are reserved and not available for public use much as there are ranges of IPv4 unicast addresses that are for private use.

IGMP

Internet Group Management Protocol (IGMP) dynamically controls the membership of hosts and routers for multicast groups. Hosts use IGMP to communicate their membership status to neighboring routers. Routers use IGMP to learn which sub-networks connected to them have multicast group members.

IGMP has two widely supported versions. Version 2 is backward compatible with Version 1, but when operating in a mixed environment the whole group must operate at the lower level. JUNOS software supports IGMP versions one and two. When IGMP is configured, version two is enabled by default.

IGMP Version 1

IGMPv1 utilizes two types of messages. Routers use a membership *query* and hosts use the membership *report*. The IGMP enabled router will periodically send query messages to the hosts on locally attached subnets soliciting multicast group membership. Queries are sent on the multicast address 224.0.0.1 with a TTL of 1 to ensure only connected hosts receive the request. When a host first wishes to join a multicast stream, it sends an unsolicited report message to the LAN router. This prevents delays while waiting for the next router query before beginning to receive multicast traffic. The hosts on the subnet who are members of a multicast group continue to periodically send report messages to let the upstream multicast router know that they still want to be a group member. Only a single host under the router needs to send a report to keep the multicast group active. A report from one host will suppress report messages from the others.

The router continues to send queries as long as it receives report messages from the hosts indicating that the multicast stream is still required. Version one hosts silently leave the group, meaning that an end system that no longer desires the multicast stream will cease sending report messages. The router will continue to forward multicast packets to all host interfaces as long as there is an active group. Hosts that are not part of the multicast group simply discard the packets. When all hosts stop responding to router queries with report messages, the entire multicast group times out and the stream is stopped.

IGMP Version 2

IGMPv2 adds a finer grain of control over group membership through the use of new message types. IGMPv2 routers utilize group specific queries. Hosts use *join* and explicit *leave* messages as well as report messages. When a version two host requires a multicast stream, it sends a join message to the upstream router requesting group membership.

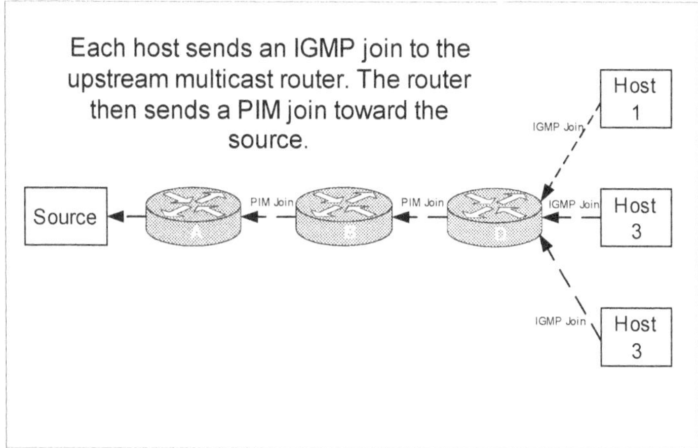

Figure 9.3 IGMP Join Behavior

Hosts continue to maintain the group by sending report messages to the router, notifying it that the stream is still needed. When a host chooses to no longer be a member of the multicast group, a leave message is sent to the upstream multicast router to let the router know that this host no longer wants to receive the multicast data stream.

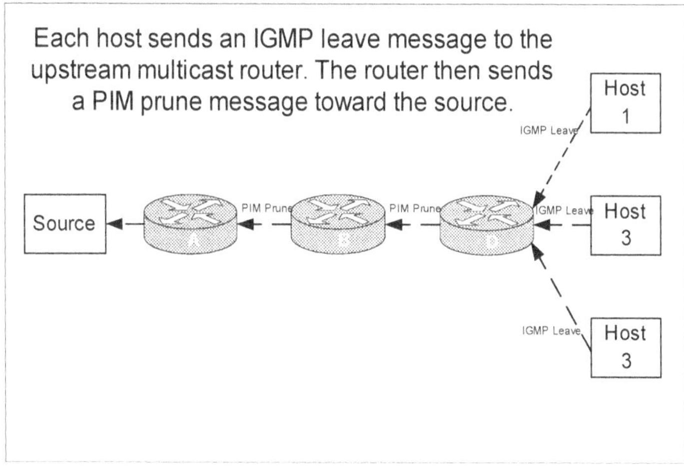

Figure 9.4 IGMP Leave Message

When an IGMPv2 router receives a leave message, it queries the group to make certain there are still active members. If it does not receive a host report, the group times out and the stream is pruned. This reduces the overall latency involved with version one hosts silently dropping group membership.

DVMRP

Distance Vector Multicast Routing Protocol (DVMRP) dynamically generates shortest path forwarding trees to deliver multicast packets. It is designed to be the IGP of a multicast domain. By dynamically generating IP multicast delivery trees, DVMRP provides connectionless datagram delivery to host members of the group. Through these techniques, shortest path trees are created and used to send multicast data streams to group members.

DVMRP neighbors are discovered dynamically by sending *probe* messages periodically to the IP multicast group address that is reserved for all DVMRP routers (224.0.0.4), similar to how OSPF hellos are sent to the IP multicast group address that is reserved for all OSPF routers.

DVMRP has two methods for routing: *forwarding mode* and *unicast routing mode*. In forwarding mode, it performs unicast routing and IP multicast data forwarding. In unicast routing mode, DVMRP performs unicast routing, but to forward IP multicast data *Protocol Independent Multicast* (PIM) must be enabled on the outgoing interface. Because PIM has its own method of discovering best path routing, the default DVMRP mode is forwarding.

Reverse Path Forwarding (RPF)

All of the major IP multicast routing protocols make use of a *distribution tree* to forward data. There are two different kinds of distribution trees. A *shared* tree is created by mapping the best logical path from the client to the *rendezvous point* (RP). The concept of an RP is integral to PIM and will be covered in a following section. A *source* tree is created by mapping the best logical unicast path from the multicast source to a group receiver or member. A technique called *Reverse Path Forwarding*, or RPF, is used to prevent the resending of IP multicast data back up the distribution tree.

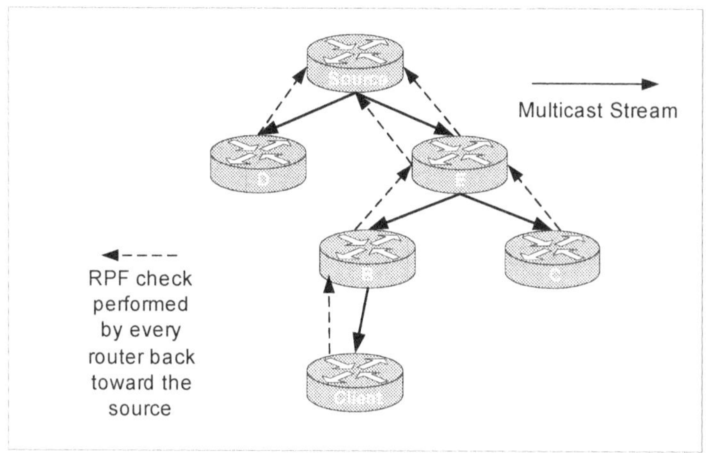

Figure 9.5 RPF Check

We will now discuss how reverse path forwarding functions. We will start with examining the RPF mechanism for data flowing down a source tree:

1) The router examines the source unicast IP address of the arriving multicast packet to determine whether the packet arrived via an interface that is on the path **back** to the source (the reverse path).
2) If the packet arrives on the interface back to the source, the RPF check is successful and the packet is forwarded out all multicast enabled interfaces except the one on which it was received.
3) If the RPF check fails, the packet is silently discarded.

All routers in Figure 9.5 pass an RPF check. This is because the multicast stream is coming into the same interface the router would use to send unicast packets to the source. However, if there were a connection between routers B and C, both of these routers would forward the stream out those connected interfaces. That flow, from B to C and likewise C to B, would fail the RPF check. The reason behind the failure is that both B and C look to router E when checking the unicast path back to the source, not to each other.

Next, we will examine the process as it is carried out for a shared tree (from the multicast source to the client):

1) The router examines the address of the arriving multicast packet and determines the RP associated with it.
2) If the packet arrives on the interface back to the RP, the RPF check is successful and the packet is forwarded.
3) If the RPF check fails, the packet is silently discarded.

Source and Group (S, G)

Because a multicast address refers to a stream rather than a host, routers must keep track of interfaces that forward multicast traffic and the interface where the multicast stream is received. This is accomplished by examining the IP address of the source (S) and the IP multicast group address (G). These two combine into what is called (S, G) notation. If the source is not known, but the group is available, the pair is referred to as (*, G). This is common when a client requests a multicast stream for the first time, as the source would not be known.

Looking at some simple examples to illustrate, multicast stream 224.53.20.16 originating from host 10.100.23.65 will have the (S, G) notation:

(10.100.23.65, 224.53.20.16)

A host joining group 224.53.20.16 for the first time, without knowledge of the source, has the notation:

(*, 224.53.20.16)

Sparse-mode vs. Dense-mode

IP multicast routing protocols generally follow one of two basic approaches depending on the expected distribution of multicast group members throughout the network.

The first approach is based on assumptions that the multicast group members are densely distributed throughout the network (i.e., many of the subnets contain at least one group member) and that bandwidth is plentiful. So-called "dense-mode" multicast routing protocols rely on a technique called *flooding* to propagate information to all network routers. Dense-mode routing protocols include Distance Vector Multicast Routing Protocol (DVMRP), Multicast Open Shortest Path First (MOSPF), and Protocol-Independent Multicast - Dense Mode (PIM-DM). MOSPF is not critical to the JNCIA exam and will not be covered in depth.

The second approach to multicast routing basically assumes the multicast group members are sparsely distributed throughout the network and bandwidth is not necessarily widely available. Sparse-mode does not imply that the group has a few members, just that they are widely dispersed. In this case, flooding would unnecessarily waste network bandwidth and could cause serious performance problems. Hence, sparse-mode multicast routing protocols must rely on more selective techniques to set up and maintain multicast trees. Sparse-mode routing protocols include Core Based Trees (CBT) and *Protocol-Independent Multicast-Sparse Mode* (PIM-SM). CBTs are not supported by JUNOS and will not be covered on the JNCIA exam.

Protocol Independent Multicast (PIM)

PIM gets its name from the fact that it is not reliant upon any specific IGP. That is, regardless of which unicast routing protocol(s) is (are) used to populate the unicast routing table, PIM uses this information to perform multicast forwarding.

Two implementations of PIM exist: PIM Sparse Mode (PIM-SM) and PIM Dense Mode (PIM-DM).

Concepts common to PIM-DM and PIM-SM include:

- PIM Neighbor Discovery.
- PIM Asserts.
- Protocol independent.
- Source Path Tree (SPT).
- No separate multicast routing protocol.

Some key characteristics of PIM-SM are:

- Explicit Join behavior.
- Utilization of Rendezvous Point (RP).
- Rendezvous-point Path Tree (RPT).

PIM Neighbor Discovery

Like DVMRP, PIM uses a neighbor discovery mechanism to establish neighbor adjacencies. To establish these adjacencies, a PIM multicast router multicasts a PIM Hello message to the address 224.0.0.13

(signifying All-PIM-Routers) on each of its multicast enabled interfaces. The interval for these advertisements is known as the *hello-period,* and is set to 30 seconds by default.

PIM Hello Messages

PIM Hello messages contain a hold time value, which tells the receiver when to expire the neighbor adjacency associated with the sender if no further PIM Hello messages are received. The value that is sent in the hold time field is typically three times the sender's PIM hello-period, or 90 seconds by default.

PIM Designated Router

In addition to establishing PIM neighbor adjacencies, PIM Hello messages are also used to elect the Designated Router, or DR, for a multi-access network. The router with the highest multicast enabled IP address becomes the DR for the network. If the DR is already established and another router joins the multi-access network with a higher IP address, an election will not be triggered.

PIM Sparse Mode

PIM-SM, like PIM-DM, uses the unicast routing table to perform the RPF check function instead of maintaining a separate multicast routing table.

Rendezvous Point (RP)

The RP serves as the information exchange point for other multicast routers. The RP is the only router with knowledge of all active sources in a domain. The remaining routers need only know a unicast path back to the RP.

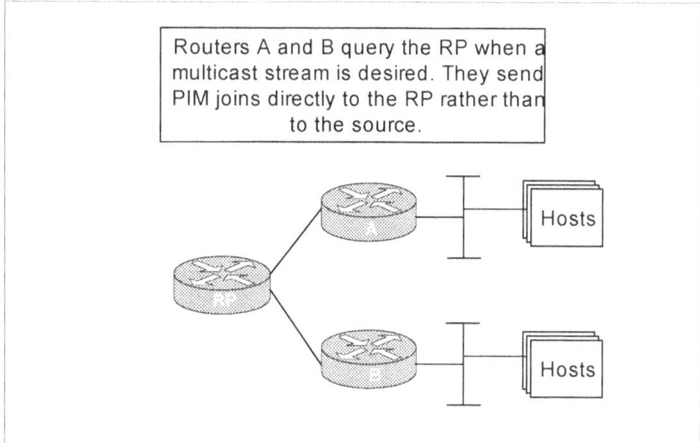

Figure 9.6 Rendezvous Point

Rendezvous-point Path Tree (RPT)

The path between an RP and its receivers is known as the RPT. In PIM-SM, one requirement is that the multicast traffic must traverse the RP. To force traffic through the RP, an RPT must be established between the receiver's designated router and the RP.

After a designated router has received an IGMP join, it sends a PIM join toward the RP. This ensures that multicast data will traverse through the RP before being sent on to the designated router and its directly attached receivers.

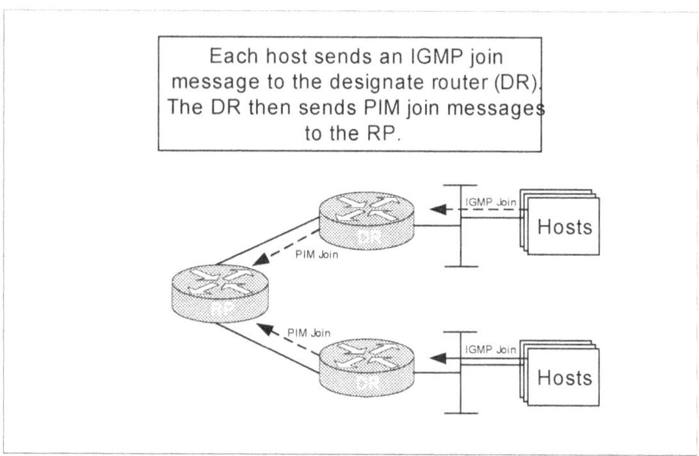

Figure 9.7 RP traffic flow behavior

Explicit Join Model

PIM-SM conforms to the sparse-mode model where multicast traffic is only sent to locations of the network that specifically request it. In PIM-SM, this is accomplished via *PIM Joins*, which are sent hop-by-hop toward the root node of the tree. (Note: In the case of the shared tree the root node is the RP. Conversely, in the case of the shortest path tree the root node is the first hop router directly connected to the multicast source.) As this Join travels up the tree, routers along the path set up multicast forwarding state so that the requested multicast traffic will be forwarded back down the tree to the receiver.

Likewise, when multicast traffic is no longer needed, a router sends a *PIM Prune* up the tree, toward the root node, to prune off the unnecessary traffic. As this PIM Prune travels hop-by-hop up the tree, each router updates its forwarding state appropriately. This update often results in the deletion of the forwarding state associated with a multicast group or source.

PIM-SM Shared Trees

PIM-SM operation centers around a single, unidirectional shared-tree whose root node is the RP. These shared trees are sometimes called RP trees because they are rooted at the RP. Last-hop routers (i.e. routers with a directly connected receiver for the multicast group) that need to receive the traffic from a specific multicast group, join this shared tree. When the last-hop router no longer requires the traffic of a specific multicast group, the router prunes itself from the shared tree.

Shared Tree Joins

Figure 9.8 shows the first step of a Shared Tree Join in a sample PIM-SM environment. In this step, a single host, Receiver 1, has just joined multicast Group G, via an IGMP report.

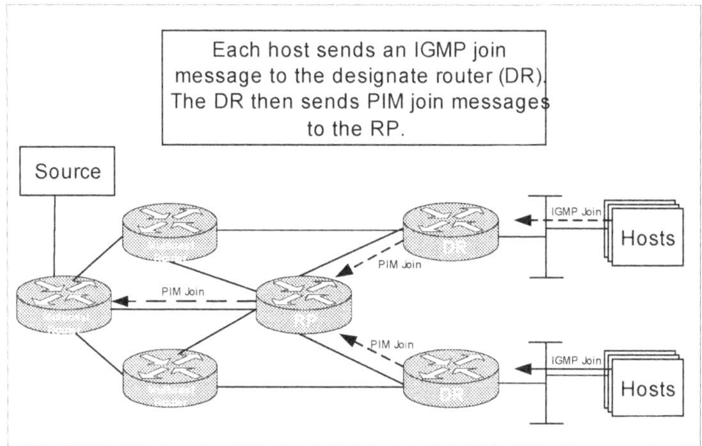

Figure 9.8 Shared Tree Join

Source Path Tree (SPT)

Because it is not always optimal to force multicast traffic through an RP, an SPT is built without one. In these cases, an SPT is used because it allows a path to be established directly between receivers and the source.

Instead of the designated router sending PIM joins to an RP, they are sent directly to the source. Because the PIM join message is directed toward the source, the concept of an RP becomes irrelevant. This ensures that multicast traffic will use the best path when being delivered to receivers without the restriction of being routed through an RP.

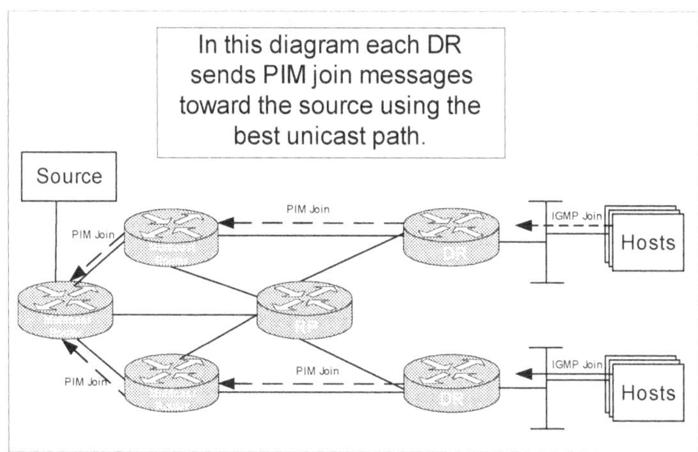

Figure 9.9 Source Path Tree

PIM Join/Prune Messages

PIM Join and PIM Prune messages use the same message format type. The messages contain the following fields:

- Multicast Source Address – IP address of the multicast source to Join or Prune. (If the Wildcard flag is set, this is the address of the RP.)
- Multicast group address - Class D multicast address to Join or Prune.
- WC bit (Wildcard flag) – Indicates that this entry is a shared tree (*, G) Join or Prune message

  RP bit (RP Tree flag) – Indicates that this Join or Prune information is applicable to, and should be forwarded up, the shared tree.

Each PIM Join or Prune contains both a Join list and a Prune list. Either one may be empty, depending on the information being conveyed up the distribution tree. By including multiple entries in the Join and/or Prune lists, a router may Join or Prune multiple sources and/or groups with a single message.

For example, examine the below PIM Join and Prune message:

Source address = 128.247.1.1

Group Address = 224.1.1.1

Flags = WC, RP

This Join message indicates that this item is a (*, G) Join for group 224.1.1.1 with an RP of 128.247.1.1. Note that since the RP flag is set, the source address is that of the RP and not the actual source of the multicast stream.

PIM-SM Designated Router

On a multi-access LAN running PIM-SM, the DR has additional responsibilities. The first is sending Joins to the RP to construct the shared tree. When more than one router is connected to a LAN segment, PIM-SM provides not only a method to elect the DR but also a way to detect the failure of the current DR. If the current DR were to fail the routers on that LAN would lose their adjacencies with the DR when they timed out. When this happens an election takes place and a new router becomes DR. Since each PIM-SM router is responsible for maintaining states from IGMP Membership Reports, the new DR will immediately send a Join to the RP for the appropriate multicast groups.

Multiprotocol Border Gateway Protocol (MBGP)

MBGP is an extension to BGP that allows it to carry multicast routing information used for RPF calculations between autonomous systems. MBGP is implemented as two additional BGP attributes: MP REACH NLRI and MP UNREACH NLRI. These attributes are used to exchange reachability information for different address families and are carried inside BGP update messages. Contained within the attributes are the *Address Family Identifier* (AFI) and the *Subsequent Address Family Identifier* (Sub-AFI) which identify the protocol for which the reachability information is applicable. There is far more information regarding MBGP, however it is not critical to the JNCIA exam.

Multicast Session Discovery Protocol (MSDP)

MSDP allows RPs from different multicast autonomous systems to exchange source and group (S,G) information. Two RPs from different multicast autonomous systems that become MSDP neighbors will exchange *Source Active* (SA) messages so that each can learn of active sources residing outside of the local multicast domain.

In order to prevent loops, MSDP relies on MBGP and the underlying IGP for all forwarding decisions. The decision making process can be broken down into two rules:

- An internal MSDP peer will accept SA messages from another internal peer only if that peer is the closest advertiser to the RP for the prefix covering the RP that originated the SA message.
- An external MSDP peer will accept an SA message from another peer if and only if the peer is in the next AS in the path towards the AS originating the prefix covering the RP in the SA message.

Key Points

Multicast is a bandwidth-conserving technology that reduces network traffic by simultaneously delivering a single stream of data to multiple receivers.

- Multicast traffic utilizes Class D address space, from 224.0.0.0 to 239.255.255.255.
- IGMP is used to dynamically control multicast group membership.
    - Routers send Query messages to hosts.
    - Hosts send Join and Leave messages to their upstream router.
- DVMRP dynamically generates shortest path trees for multicast streams.
- RPF checks ensure multicast data is not sent back to the stream source.
- Dense-mode protocols assume many subnets contain at least one multicast group member and that bandwidth is plentiful. They rely flooding to propagate information to all network routers.
- Sparse-mode protocols assume multicast group members are widely dispersed and bandwidth is not necessarily available. They rely on selective techniques to set up and maintain multicast trees.
- (S, G) notation binds a source address with a multicast group address.
- (*, G) notation is used when the source is unknown.
- PIM-Sparse Mode utilizes a Rendezvous Point to facilitate host members receiving multicast streams.

Additional Information

- RFC 1075 Distance Vector Multicast Routing Protocol
- RFC 1112 IGMP Version 1: Host Extensions for Multicast
- RFC 1458 Requirements for Multicast Protocols
- RFC 1584 Multicast Extensions to OSPF
- RFC 2201 Core Based Tree (CBT) Multicast Routing Architecture
- RFC 2236 IGMP Version 2
- RFC 2283 Multiprotocol Extensions for BGPv4
- RFC 2362 Protocol Independent Multicast – Sparse Mode
- RFC 2715 Interoperability Rules for Multicast Protocols

Chapter Ten

Policy

Chapter 10: Policy

Overview

This chapter will cover JUNOS policy and firewall. The topics covered will include the purpose, functionality and configuration of policies and route filters. By the end of this chapter you should be able to:

- ✓ Identify the components of JUNOS policy.
- ✓ Understand how policy controls the exchange of routing information.
- ✓ Comprehend how route manipulation through policy dictates traffic flow.
- ✓ Recognize the purpose and application of the JUNOS firewall.
- ✓ Describe the differences between import and export policy
- ✓ Understand route redistribution.

Introduction

Each routing protocol run within JUNOS maintains its own routing database. JUNOS takes information from each protocol's database and generates the best forwarding path to each destination. Juniper policy allows you to control the routing information exchanged between routing databases. You can think of configured policies as a way to filter route advertisements; this is functionally similar, but structurally quite different than Cisco IOS access-lists. Keep in mind that an entire book could be written on JUNOS policy itself. We have attempted to cover general theory in addition to highlighting key points that are needed for the JNCIA exam.

JUNOS firewall is a policy whose function is to limit or manipulate traffic allowed through specific interfaces. The most common purpose of the firewall is to provide security for the Juniper router and downstream nodes and networks.

Policy Definition

Policies are made up of four key elements: *terms*, *from*, *then*, and 'actions'. The use of these establishes the groundwork for functional policy. An individual policy can become complex through the combination, repetition, and application of these four simple attributes.

Every policy begins by being named and defined with a *policy statement*. When viewing a policy from the CLI, it is referenced by the policy statement. The policy statement only names the policy; it does not perform an active function. For this reason, it is usually given an expressive name to highlight the purpose or function of the entire policy, for example:

```
jncia@my.router1>show policy reject-private-address-space
Policy reject-private-address-space:
    Term 1918-space:
        from
               route-filter:
                     10.0.0.0/8 orlonger
        then reject
    Term accept:
        then metric 100000 localpref 100
community + region community
```

Terms are the subroutines of a policy. Specific instructions are carried out within a term to *accept*, *reject*, or modify the attributes of routes. Depending on complexity, a policy can be made up of one or more terms. It is important to realize that a policy will begin analyzing candidate routes from the first term, and continue its way sequentially down the list of terms until it is instructed to exit or continue on to the next policy. If no match and subsequent action is taken within the policy, the default action is to accept the route.

From statements are the conditional clauses of the policy. Those familiar with programming languages can think of a *from* clause equating to an 'if' statement. If the criteria after the *from* stanza are met, the candidate route continues down the same term. If the criteria of the match are not met, the candidate jumps to the next term (if present). In order for JUNOS to take action on a route, it must **exactly** match the set specifications. If there is more than one criteria in a *from* clause, they must all be matched. Routes can be matched based on any of the following attributes:

- Source Address
- Destination Address
- Protocol (BGP, OSPF, ISIS)
- Port
- Community
- Route filters
- Interface
- Local Preference
- Others

'Then' statements come after the 'from' and are immediately followed by actions. The purpose of a 'then' is to indicate what action is performed after a match is made.

Actions are the operators of a policy. They are the instructions that allow the policy to *accept*, *reject*, or modify route attributes. Actions include:

- Accept – Permits the route.
- Reject – Denies the route.
- Next-policy – Moves on to the next policy.
- Next-hop-self – Sets the BGP next hop to this router.
- Community – Sets BGP community information.
- Localpref – Sets BGP local preference value.
- Metric – Sets BGP MED value.
- Count – increment counters of the specified name to indicate a match has taken place.

Note that there are more actions that can be performed with relation to other routing protocols, but they are not covered in detail for the exam.

Prefix Lists and Route Filters

One of the most common protocol-independent methods of identifying traffic within a policy is through the use of prefix lists and route filters. Prefix lists merely identify a route and its mask to form a match condition. An example of a prefix list is displayed below.

```
[edit]
jncia@my.router1> show policy-options
prefix-list match-slash-24-private {
   10.0.0.0/24;
}
```

This prefix list will match only one route: 10.0.0.0/24.

Route filters are similar in function, but they allow for more complex matches within a single statement. In addition, a route filter can immediately perform an action on a route that is matched. It is important to remember that "longer" refers to a longer prefix mask length. This is to state that a mask of /10 is longer than that of a /9 as it masks more of the address. One of the following terms may be contained by which to match a route:

exact- Exactly match the prefix length.
(*10/8 exact* matches only 10.0.0.0/8, nothing else)

longer- Mask is greater than the prefix length
(*10/8 longer* matches 10.0.0.0/9 and up, but not 10.0.0.0/8)

orlonger- Mask is equal to or greater than the prefix length
(*10/8 orlonger* matches 10.0.0.0/8 and up)

prefix-length-range- Mask falls between two prefix lengths
(*10/8 prefix-length-range /20-/24* will match 10.x.x.x if the mask is /21, /22, or /23,)

upto- Mask falls between two prefix lengths, including the upper limit
(*10/8 upto /12* will match 10.x.x.x if the mask is /9, /10, /11, or /12)

through- Route must fall between the two specified prefixes
(*10.0.0.0/8 through 10.192.0.0/10* will match 10.x.x.x/8, 10.0.x.x/9, 10.128.x.x/9, and 10.192.0.0/10)

As noted previously, a route filter can also specify actions immediately after matching a route. This will be seen in the example below. In addition, if no immediate action is specified, the matching routes will be subject to that term's "then" clause.

```
[edit policy-options]
jncia@my.router1# show

policy-statement route-filter-example {
  term match-some {
      from {
           route-filter 10.0.0.0/8 exact;
           route-filter 192.168.0.0/16 upto /19
reject;
      }
           route-filter 172.16.0.0/10 through
172.32.0.0/11 {
                metric add 1000;
           }
      }
      then {
           accept;
      }
}
```

Policy Lists

Another aspect of policies worth mentioning is the ability to note several match conditions (either AS path, community, interface, neighbor, next-hop, or protocol) in one statement with the use of a list. Only one of the members of the list must be matched for successful attachment of the statement.

```
[edit policy-options]
jncia@my.router# show
policy-statement match-2 {
    term from-bgp {
        from {
            protocol bgp;
            neighbor [ 10.0.0.1 10.0.0.128 ];
            route-filter 172.16.0.0/10 through
172.32.0.0/11 {
                metric add 1000;
            }
        }
        then accept;
    }
    then reject;
}
```

Policy Evaluation

- Default behavior is to start with the first term of a policy.
- If no match is made, no action is taken in the current term; the route is evaluated against the next term in the policy
- If a match is made, an action is taken to accept or reject the route; the route will exit policy evaluation unless *next-policy* is specified as an action for this term
- If the candidate has not matched any terms within the policy, the next applied policy is evaluated (in the same term-by-term fashion)
- Upon reaching the end of the last applied policy, if no action is defined, the default action is taken (default action varies by protocol)

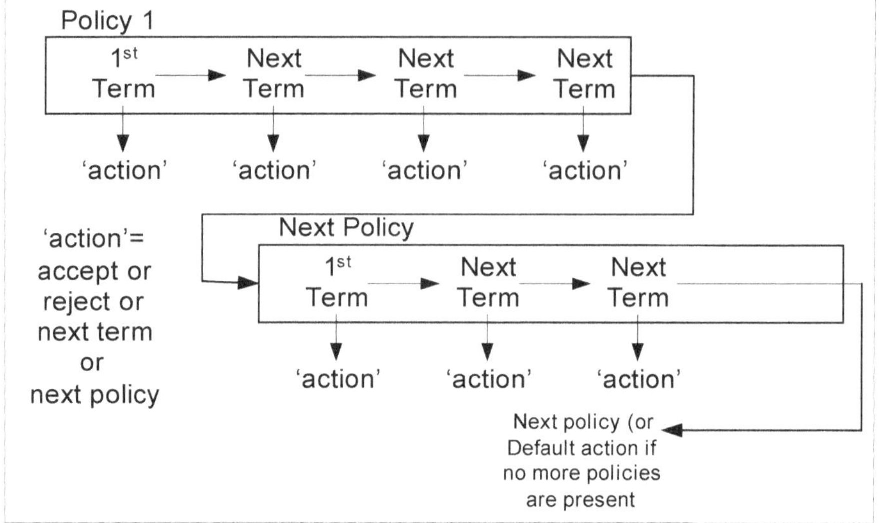

Figure 10.1 Policy evaluation flow

As noted, if a route makes it to the end of the last policy and is not accepted or rejected by that point, the default action will take place for that given protocol. The default actions for the most common routing protocols are listed in the table below. Note that they are listed in order of their level of importance to remember.

Protocol	Default Import Policy	Default Export Policy
BGP	Import all BGP routes	Export all active BGP routes
OSPF	Import all OSPF routes (Note: you cannot override this)	Export all active OSPF routes Export direct OSPF interface routes
RIP	Import all RIP routes	Nothing is exported
Pseudo-protocol (direct, static, aggregate, etc.)	Import all of these types of routes.	Nothing is exported A routing protocol is needed to export these.
IS-IS	Import all IS-IS routes (Note: you cannot override this)	Export all active IS-IS routes Export direct IS-IS interface routes
MPLS	Import all MPLS routes (into inet.3)	Export all active MPLS routes
LDP	Import all LDP routes (into inet.3)	Export all active LDP routes
DVMRP	Import all DVMRP routes (into inet.1)	Export all active DVMRP routes
PIM Sparse Mode	Import all PIM-SM routes (into inet.1)	Export all active PIM-SM routes
PIM Dense Mode	Import all PIM-DM routes (into inet.1)	Export all active PIM-DM routes

Figure 10.2 Default protocol policy actions

Let's examine the path a sample BGP route takes as it is evaluated against a policy designed to limit the number of advertisements from a BGP peer. This policy is applied as an import policy to the protocol BGP.
Route advertisement 10.64.65.66/32 from BGP neighbor 10.1.2.3.

The first step is to create a policy to ensure we only accept routes from the intended neighbor. The next step is to create a policy to only match the route we want to accept. These are illustrated below:

```
[edit policy-options]
jncia@my.router1# show
policy-statement from-10.1.2.3 {
    term match-neighbor {
        from neighbor 10.1.2.3;
        then accept;
    }
```

```
        term reject-rest {
            then reject;
        }
    }
    policy-statement match-route {
        term good-one {
            from {
                protocol bgp;
                next-hop 10.64.65.66/32;
            }
            then accept;
        }
        term reject-rest {
            then reject;
        }
    }
```

The last step is to apply our 'good-one' filter to BGP so that we only accept this one route. This is shown below:

```
[edit protocols bgp]
jncia@my.router1# show
import match-route;
```

Application of Policy to Routing Protocols

When implementing routing policies, it is important to remember the "direction" of the policy application. Whether importing or exporting, it is from the perspective of the routing table. For instance, if routes are being sent to a BGP neighbor, they are being exported from the routing table. Conversely, if routes are received from a BGP peer, they are imported into the routing table. To illustrate:

Import: All unicast routing protocols place all of their routes into the main routing table (inet.0). If multiple routes exist to the same destination, the best one will be chosen via a routing algorithm (or multiple next-hops will be chosen if equal cost is determined).

Export: By default, routing protocols export only routes that were learned from **that** protocol (for example: BGP routes are exported to BGP). One supplement to this is the idea that OSPF and IS-IS export the direct routes (interfaces) on which they are configured.

Policy can be applied to routing protocols at the following levels and manner:

BGP: Global, group, and peer import/export.
(Note that the more specific application will override the more general. For example, policy applied to a peer will override group policy and group policy will override global application.)
IS-IS: Global export.
OSPF: Global export.
RIP: Neighbor import and group export.
DVMRP: Global import and export.

Testing Policy

JUNOS allows evaluation of policy syntax and basic logic with the "test policy" command. In order to use this function, a policy must exist in the router configuration and the routes to be tested must exist in the router's routing table. This command is useful when first configuring policies, but is rarely utilized in more advanced configurations given that all routes to be tested must exist in the routing table. Below is an example of a typical usage of this feature.

```
[edit routing-options static]
jncia@my.router1# show
route 10.192.0.0/10 discard;;
route 10.224.0.0/11 discard;
route 10.192.0.0/23 discard;
route 10.192.0.0/24 discard;

[edit policy-options]
jncia@my.router1# show
policy-statement testing-policy {
    term term1-route-filter {
        from {
            route-filter 10.192.0.0/10 upto /14
reject;
            route-filter 10.192.0.0/16
through /18;
            route-filter 10.192.0.0/19
orlonger;
        }
        then accept;
    }
}


jncia@my.router1> test policy testing-policy
10.192.0.0/10
inet.0: 4 destinations, 4 routes (4 active, 0
holddown, 0 hidden)
Prefixes passing policy:
10.192.0.0/23 *[Static/5] 00:12:05
                        Discard
10.192.0.0/24 *[Static/5] 00:12:05
                        Discard

Policy test: 2 prefixes accepted, 2 prefixes
rejected
```

To better determine the effects of policy on routing updates or advertisements once policy is applied, output results from "`show route protocol` *`protocol`*" can be compared with those from "`show route advertising-protocol` *`protocol`*" to view the effects of export policy. Comparing the results with "`show route receive-protocol` *`protocol`*" will indicate the effects of the import policy.

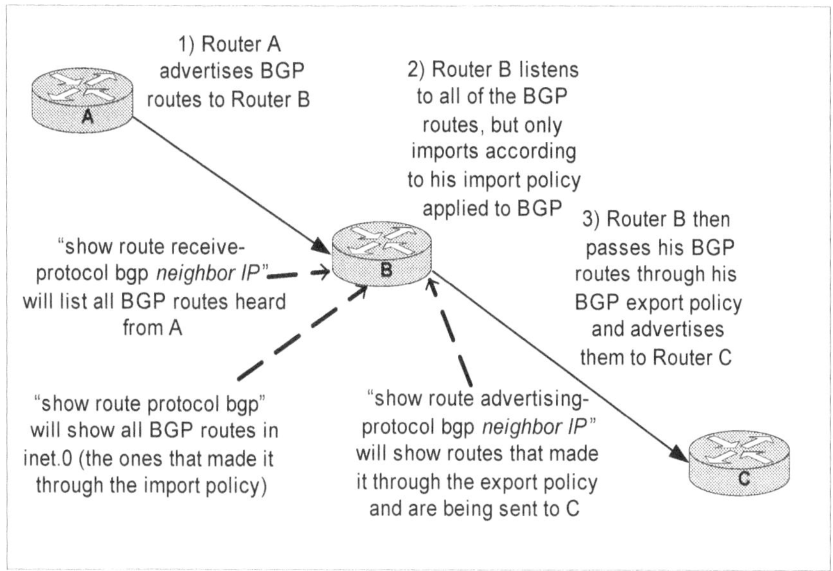

Figure 10.3 Seeing the results of routing policy

Firewall

The firewall within JUNOS is simply the application of policy to control packets to/from an interface. Apply a firewall filter 'input' on an interface, and it will analyze all traffic received on that interface. Conversely, applied on the 'output', it will take affect on transmitted traffic from the interface applied. If applied to loopback0, the filter will affect all traffic to/from the routing engine. Juniper routers with the Internet Processor II can perform advanced firewall filtering features. Note that only early M40 routers shipped with the Internet Processor I, which has a limited firewall filtering feature-set. You can apply no more than one firewall filter to each logical interface. Below is a common application of a firewall with key points highlighted:

```
[edit interfaces]
jncia@my.router1# show
    lo0 {
        unit 0 {
            description "logical router loopback0";
            family inet {
                filter {
                input all-needed-traffic-to-loopback0;
```
#<< traffic inbound to lo0 is subject to this firewall filter>

```
        }
        address 127.0.0.1/32;
        address 10.1.2.5/32 {
        preferred;
        }
```

Above, the firewall filter is applied to the logical interface lo0.0 under `[edit interfaces]`. Below, the configuration of the filter is shown at the `[edit firewall]` hierarchy level.

```
[edit firewall]
jncia@my.router1> show

    filter all-needed-traffic-to-loopback0 {
        term ospf-neighbors{
            from {
                source-address {
                    10.4.8.0/24;
                    192.18.18.0/24;
                }
                protocol ospf;
            }
            then {
                accept;
            }
        }
        term bgp-neighbors {
            from {
                source-address {
                    10.0.0.0/25;
                    192.168.1.0/24;
                }
                protocol tcp;
                port bgp;
            }
            then {
              accept;
            }
        }
        term trusted-management-hosts {
            from {
                source-address {
                  10.0.0.0/8;
                }
            }
            then {
```

```
                accept;
            }
        }
        term deny-the-rest {   #<< One last term to deny
                                   anything else
            then discard;
        }
    }
```

The first term allows OSPF packets from the address blocks 10.4.8.0/24 and 192.18.18.0/24 to be accepted. The second term similarly allows packets from 10.0.0.0/25 and 192.168.0.0/24 using TCP to communicate to BGP. The third term allows packets coming from the trusted subnet 10.0.0.0/8 to be accepted. The final term is a catch all to ensure all other unauthorized packets are discarded. As can be seen, there is no *from* statement, so everything reaching this term is considered to match.

Policing

Within JUNOS, the ability to rate limit the amount of traffic into or out of an interface is known as policing. The most common use of this function is to control DOS and other types of attacks on the Internet. However, it can also be used to provide some degree of Quality of Service (QoS) on individual interfaces that are oversubscribed.

Policer statements are most often defined by themselves and then applied to interfaces or referenced in a firewall filter. The other option is to define each policer in each firewall in which it is used. Note that the policer must come before any term definitions.

Policy Configuration within JUNOS

Each policy begins under the configuration level 'policy-options' with a policy name. This name must be unique within the configuration on the router.

```
jncia@my.router1> show configuration policy-options
policy-statement example-policy {
        term bgp-peer-loopback {
            from {
```

```
                source-address {
                    127.0.0.1/32;
                }
            }
            then {
                accept;
            }
        }
```

As noted, each policy consists of one or more named terms. The term name is optional if only one term exists, but if used, must be unique within each policy.

```
jncia@my.router1> show configuration policy-options
policy-statement example-policy {
        term bgp-peer-loopback {
            from {
                source-address {
                    127.0.0.1/32;
                }
            }
            then {
                accept;
            }
        }
```

Each term can consist of at least one statement ('from' or 'to') for match conditions. Any match statements are optional. If they are removed, all routes are considered to match. If multiple criteria are defined under the 'from' segment of a term, they must all be met to satisfy as a match for that term.

```
jncia@my.router1> show configuration policy-options
policy-statement example-policy {
        term bgp-peer-loopback {
            from {
                source-address {
                    127.0.0.1/32;
                }
            }
            then {
                accept;
            }
        }
```

Each term can contain a 'then' statement (optional). This statement determines the action taken on a route that has matched the 'from' or 'to' operators. There are three types of actions that can be taken on a matched route:

- "Flow control" actions include *accept*, *reject*, *next-term*, or *next-policy.*
- "Tracing options" report route matches to a specified log file.
- Actions that set properties associated with the route (MED, localpref, etc.).

If no 'then' statement is used, one of the following actions is triggered:

- If no flow control action is taken, the next term is evaluated.
- If there are no more terms, the next policy is evaluated.
- If there are no more terms or policies, the default action is taken (refer to figure 10.2).

```
jncia@my.router1> show configuration policy-options
policy-statement example-policy {
        term bgp-peer-loopback {
            from {
                source-address {
                    127.0.0.1/32;
                }
            }
            then {
                accept;
            }
        }
```

Key Points

As noted, JUNOS policy can range from a simple import policy to advanced rate-limiting after the application of firewall filters. Policy plays a key role in the operation of JUNOS routers, and for that reason it is addressed numerous times on the JNCIA exam. Read and understand all of the concepts within this chapter before test time for the best results.

- Each policy is named with a policy-statement
- Policies contain four key elements
  - Terms
  - From
  - Then
  - Action
- Each protocol has its own default policy for importing and exporting routes (see figure 10.2 for details on each)
- Firewalls are similar to JUNOS policies but are applied to interfaces instead of routing protocols
  - One firewall filter can be applied to each logical interface (one inbound and one outbound)
- Policing can be used to rate-limit traffic on interfaces

Appendix A: Sample Quiz

Chapter 1 Basics

1) How many bits represent the host portion of the IP address 192.168.10.64/27?

2) Expand the IP address and subnet mask 10.154.63.24/19 into their binary equivalents.

3) What are the network and broadcast addresses of the subnet including host 10.23.32.100/23?

4) How many useable host addresses can be configured in the subnet 192.168.45.0/28? What are the first and last useable host addresses?

5) A subnet requires addresses for 42 unique hosts. What is the smallest subnet that can be used to allocate enough addresses?

6) How many total addresses are in 192.168.10.0/25 that are not in 192.168.10.0/26?

7) Which address "class" does 64.123.123.100 belong to?
    a. Class A
    b. Class B
    c. Class C
    d. Class D

Chapter 2 Hardware

1) What is the name of the 100MB link between the PFE and the RE?
    a) So0/0
    b) Eth0
    c) Fxp0
    d) Fxp1

2) Which routers contain Packet Director ASICs? (choose all that apply)
   a) M160
   b) M40e
   c) M40
   d) M20
   e) M10

3) Which two components comprise the Host Module?
   a) PFE and RE
   b) RE and MCS
   c) PCG and MCS
   d) MCS and PFE

4) On which ASIC(s) does queuing take place?
   a) PIC ASIC
   b) I/O Manager ASIC
   c) DBM ASIC
   d) Internet Processor II

5) How many FPC slots are on an M40?
   a) 2
   b) 4
   c) 6
   d) 8

6) Which ASIC sends packets out a physical port?
   a) PIC ASIC
   b) I/O Manager ASIC
   c) DBM ASIC
   d) Internet Processor II

7) The FPCs are built into the FEB on which two platforms?
   a) M5
   b) M10
   c) M20
   d) M40
   e) M160

8) The M20 supports redundant Routing Engines.
   a) True
   b) False

9) What are the primary responsibilities of the RE?
    a) Control routing protocol traffic, perform route-lookups.
    b) Forward data traffic, perform route filtering.
    c) Maintain routing protocols, control software processes.
    d) Manage interfaces, reassemble packets from shared memory.

10) Match the following hardware components to the correct platform.

a) M160	SSB
b) M40	FEB
c) M20	SFM
d) M10	SCB

Chapter 3 JUNOS:

1) What is the standard boot sequence for JUNOS?
    a) PCMCIA flash, compact flash, hard-drive, network
    b) Compact flash, PCMCIA flash, network, hard-drive
    c) Hard-drive, compact flash, network, PCMCIA flash
    d) PCMCIA flash, compact flash, network, hard-drive

2) What is the route preference of a static route?
    a) 1
    b) 5
    c) 15
    d) 50

3) If there is a route known via RIP and OSPF (internal) which one will be installed (assuming the exact same route with no attributes altered)?
    a) RIP
    b) OSPF
    c) Neither since there is a tie.
    d) Both, they load balance.
    e) Whichever originated closer.

4) Into which table are static routes installed?
    a) inet.0
    b) inet.1
    c) inet.2
    d) inet.3

5) The forwarding table actually used to make next-hop forwarding decisions is stored where?
    a) The hard drive
    b) Compact flash
    c) The RE
    d) The PFE

6) Under which configuration statement is the BGP autonomous system number set?
    a) [edit policy-options]
    b) [edit protocols bgp]
    c) [edit routing-options]
    d) [edit system]

7) Which routing table contains MPLS information?
    a) inet.0
    b) inet.1
    c) inet.2
    d) inet.3

8) What is the CLI command to view the *messages* logfile?
    a) show logfile messages
    b) show messages
    c) show log messages
    d) monitor logfile messages

9) Explain the differences between routes held in the forwarding table and those in the routing table.

10) Under which configuration level is the Router ID set?
    a) [edit protocols]
    b) [edit router-options]
    c) [edit system]
    d) [edit routing-options]

11) Which two of the below are traits of JUNOS?
    a) It is based on a UNIX kernel
    b) There is specific code for each M-series platform
    c) Processes run independently
    d) The code can be updated without a service impact
    e) Internet Processor II

12) Which command will erase the current configuration and load the entire contents of "newconfig" from edit mode?
   e) Load replace newconfig
   f) Load merge newconfig
   g) Load override newconfig
   h) Load newconfig

13) Which command will configure an IP address upon fe-0/0/0.0from the [edit interfaces fe-0/0/0 unit 0] prompt?
   a) Set address 10.45.123.32/30
   b) Set family inet address 10.45.123.32/30
   c) Set address family inet 10.45.123.32/30
   d) Set inet family address 10.45.123.32/30

14) What are legal completions for a configured static route? (Choose all that apply)
   a) An interface
   b) An address
   c) Accept
   d) Discard
   e) Reject

15) Where is the backup copy of JUNOS kept?

Chapter 4 RIP

1) What is the maximum hop-count for a **reachable** RIP route?
   a) 15
   b) 16
   c) 10
   d) 255

2) What two mechanisms does RIP use to prevent routing loops (select 2)?
   a) Split-horizon
   b) Link-state database
   c) Random routing database checks
   d) Poison-reverse

3) In which routing table are RIP routes placed?
   a) inet.0
   b) inet.1
   c) inet.2
   d) inet.3

4) A RIP update, using authentication, can contain up to how many networks?
   a) 1
   b) 24
   c) 25
   d) 255

5) What type(s) of authentication does JUNOS support for RIPv1?
   a) Plain-text password
   b) MD5 encrypted password
   c) Both a and c
   d) Neither of these methods

6) What type(s) of authentication does JUNOS support for RIPv2?
   a) Plain-text password
   b) MD5 encrypted password
   c) Both a and b
   d) Neither of these methods

7) Define how split-horizon works to control routing loops?

8) Define how poison-reverse functions to control routing loops?

9) How do RIPv2 routers send route updates to their neighbors?
   a) Unicast
   b) Multicast
   c) Broadcast
   d) Labelcast

10) Which of the following is NOT a field in a RIPv2 update message?
   a) Network address
   b) Metric
   c) Cost
   d) Next-hop

Chapter 5 OSPF

1) What is the purpose of an ASBR?

2) What is the purpose of an ABR?

3) What type of OSPF network utilizes a DR?
    a) Point-to-point (P2P)
    b) NBMA
    c) Point-to-multi-point (P2MP)
    d) BMA

4) What address does the RID default to?

5) What type of router sends Type 2 Network LSAs on a broadcast segment?
    a) ABR
    b) ASBR
    c) DR
    d) BDR
    e) Drother

6) What type of router cannot exist in a stub area?
    a) ASBR
    b) ABR
    c) DR
    d) BDR
    e) Drother

7) Give 2 purposes of the Hello message.
    a) Exchange route information.
    b) Discover neighbors on a network segment.
    c) Maintain neighbor adjacencies.
    d) Discover the shortest path between a source and destination.

8) Which State is a router in after a Hello is sent but before one is received?
    a) Down
    b) Init
    c) 2way
    d) Drother
    e) Exchange
    f) Full

9) What are the default OSPF timer values?

10) Which OSPF router distributes area routes into other areas?
    a) ASBR
    b) ABR
    c) DR
    d) Level 1

11) Which CLI command will show the state of OSPF to other routers?
    a) show ospf interface
    b) show ospf adjacency
    c) show ospf neighbor
    d) show ospf detail

12) Which CLI command with show the type of networks the router participates in (Point to Point, BMA, etc)?
    a) show ospf interface
    b) show ospf adjacency
    c) show ospf neighbor
    d) show ospf detail

13) What is the CLI command to view the OSPF link-state database?

14) On an Ethernet segment Router A (priority 100), Router B and Router C (both priority 90) come online. Which one is elected to be the designated router?

15) On the same segment above in 14, Router D comes online 30 minutes later with a priority of 110. Assuming nothing else has changed, which router is now DR?

16) What is the minimum configuration necessary to run OSPF on a router?

17) What is the first State when establishing an OSPF adjacency?
    a) Down
    b) Init
    c) 2way
    d) Drother
    e) Exchange
    f) Full

18) In which State should routers be with their neighbors on a BMA network where neither are DR or BDR?
   a) Down
   b) Init
   c) 2way
   d) Drother
   e) Exchange
   f) Full

19) What State should synchronized neighbors on a point to point segment be in?
   a) Down
   b) Init
   c) 2way
   d) Drother
   e) Exchange
   f) Full

Chapter 6 IS-IS

1) The first byte of the Area ID is also known as:
   a) NSET
   b) N-selector
   c) DIS
   d) AFI

2) When a Level 1 router encounters packets destined for a different Area, what does it do?
   a) Forwards it off to the other Area itself.
   b) Sends it to the nearest L1/L2 router.
   c) Drops the packet and sends a "Host Unreachable" error back to the sender.
   d) Silently discards the packet and sends no error back to the sender.

3) What is the command to view which interfaces are configured for IS-IS?
   a) show is-is interface
   b) show protocol is-is interface
   c) show interface
   d) Show interface is-is

4) By default, an IS-IS enabled interface is placed into which Level?
   a) Level 1
   b) Level 2
   c) Level 3
   d) Both Level 1 and Level 2
   e) None, the Level must be manually enabled

5) What is the command to view the IS-IS database?

6) When configuring a router for IS-IS, the last byte of the NSAP must be set to what?

7) Three IS-IS routers (A, B, C) are brought online in an Ethernet segment. A has no priority configuration (default). B has priority set to 0. C has a priority set to 100. Who will be elected the DIS?
   a) Router A
   b) Router B
   c) Router C
   d) None. There is no such thing as a DIS for an Ethernet segment

8) Which of the following is/are functions of a PSNP (choose all that apply):
   a) Request a missing LSP
   b) Share routing table information
   c) Notify to retransmit an LSP after a sequence error is noted
   d) Reset the Hello timer

9) Which is better thought of as a "site" router (meaning no direct communication to the network backbone)?
   a) Level 1 router
   b) Level 1/2 router
   c) Level 2 router
   d) Level 3 router

10) Identify the portions of the NSAP address 49.0001.9aff.00ab.0030.1223.4045.00.

11) Which PDU is used to advertise a complete listing of all IS-IS LSPs in the router link state database?
    a) CSNP
    b) PSNP
    c) IIH
    d) LSP

12) If an IS-IS router detects a fault with its link state database, which PDU does it use to request an update?
    a) CSNP
    b) PSNP
    c) IIH
    d) LSP

Chapter 7 BGP

1) At what level of the configuration hierarchy is the AS number set?
    a) [edit protocols bgp]
    b) [edit system as]
    c) [edit routing-options]
    d) [edit protocols as]

2) What do the numbers in the final column of the blow output mean for the bgp neighbor? (active/received/dampened)

```
10.244.2.154 65333 452 432 0 4 5d19h 825/1263/0
```

    a) Routes received/advertised/dampened
    b) Routes advertised/received/dampened
    c) Routes received/active/dampened
    d) Routes active/received/dampened

3) How do you get BGP to advertise all OSPF routes to all neighbors?
    a) Export policy in OSPF that matches on BGP routes.
    b) Import policy in OSPF that matches on BGP routes.
    c) Export policy in BGP that matches on OSPF routes.
    d) Import policy in BGP that matches on OSPF routes.

4) Given equal cost BGP routes in inet.0 and inet.3, which will be selected?
   a) Neither
   b) Inet.0
   c) Inet.3
   d) random

5) Given the list of criteria for BGP route selection within JUNOS, put them in order.
   MED
   IGP cost
   AS-path length
   Local pref
   eBGP vs. iBGP
   origin code

6) Which type of BGP message contains information on new and changed routes?
   a) Update
   b) Flash
   c) Synch
   d) NLRI

7) Which port does BGP listen to?
   a) TCP 79
   b) TCP 179
   c) UDP 79
   d) UDP 179

8) What is local preference used for?

9) By default, BGP will advertise what routes to neighbors? (choose all that apply) A:(direct and BGPlearned)
   a) Directly connected routes
   b) Routes learned via RIP
   c) Routes learned via OSPF
   d) Routes learned via BGP

10) Which command is used to view specific BGP neighbor information?
   a) show bgp summary
   b) show bgp neighbor
   c) show bgp interface
   d) show bgp adjacency

11) iBGP peers are those that are:
   a) In the same AS.
   b) In different AS.
   c) Directly connected.
   d) Configured with the same address.

12) Unless BGP multi-hop is enabled, external BGP neighbors must be:
   a) In the same AS.
   b) In different AS.
   c) Directly connected.
   d) Configured with the same address.

13) If two or more valid paths are available, BGP will inherently:
   a) Per-packet load share.
   b) Per-flow load share.
   c) Per-prefix load share.
   d) Not load share.

14) iBGP neighbors must be directly connected.
   a) True
   b) False

15) A router configured with BGP can automatically discover BGP neighbors.
   a) True
   b) False

16) BGP split horizon dictates that:
   a) Routes learned via iBGP are not advertised back out the interface they were learned.
   b) Routes learned via iBGP are advertised to all BGP neighbors.
   c) Routes learned via iBGP are not advertised to any BGP neighbors.
   d) Routes learned via iBGP are not advertised to any iBGP neighbors.

17) Which two of the below help reduce the problems of requiring a full mesh of iBGP neighbors?
   a) Confederations
   b) BGP split horizon
   c) BGP multi-hop
   d) Route reflectors

18) How does BGP avoid routing loops? (choose two)
    a) iBGP consults its link state database upon learning routes and drops incorrect prefixes.
    b) BGP split horizon ensures routes do not propagate past immediate neighbors.
    c) eBGP checks the as-path attribute and drops prefixes that include its native AS.
    d) Only authenticated eBGP neighbors are allowed to advertise usable routes.

19) What can a MED from AS 65000 communicate to a BGP peer in AS 64666?
    a) Which interface or session would be preferred for AS 6500 to receive traffic.
    b) Which interface or session AS 6500 will be sending traffic on.
    c) Where and how many exit points there are between the two AS.
    d) How AS 64666 should route the packet internally.

Chapter 8 MPLS

1) What is an LSP?
    a) A unidirectional path through an internal network.
    b) A bi-directional path through an internal network.
    c) A traffic-engineered path.
    d) A pointer for IP forwarding.

2) Which of the below are valid label operations?
    a) Pop
    b) Drop
    c) Swap
    d) Push
    e) Attach
    f) Delete

3) What object specifies the next-hop of an LSP?
    a) RRO
    b) ERO
    c) TED
    d) CSPF

4) What are the advantages of signaled versus static LSPs? (choose all that apply)
   a) Dynamic LSP creation.
   b) Less administrative overhead.
   c) Less latency.
   d) Easier QoS.

5) What functions does a router perform when receiving an MPLS packet with a single label 0?
   a) Drop the packet silently
   b) Drop the packet and return an "ICMP unreachable" message.
   c) Pop the label and forward it to the RE.
   d) Pop the label and forward to the IP destination.

6) MPLS does not require an underlying routing protocol to function.
   a) True
   b) False

7) Is it possible to use an LSP as a BGP next hop?
   a) True
   b) False

8) Name two MPLS protocols for signaling LSPs.
   a) RSVP
   b) OSPF
   c) LDP
   d) TCP

9) An LSP is signaled from Router A through Router B and C to Router D. Which is the penultimate hop?
   a) Router A
   b) Router B
   c) Router C
   d) Router D

10) An LSP is configured with strict constraints. The ingress router sees the ERO with a strict constraint of next hop 10.1.2.4. What must be true of this address?
    a) Must not be in the LSP path
    b) Must be in the LSP path at some point
    c) Must be directly connected to previous LSP hop.
    d) It must be the ingress router.

11) What is contained in the RRO?
    a) A list of all hops within an LSP.
    b) A list of all labels within an LSP.
    c) A list of all constraints for an LSP.
    d) A list of all LSPs.

12) What is the primary purpose of the RRO?
    a) To determine labels for an LSP.
    b) To prevent loops within an LSP.
    c) To allocate bandwidth for an LSP.
    d) To list all available, reachable LSPs.

13) What are the two ways a router can allocate labelspace?
    a) Per-interface
    b) Global
    c) Per-router
    d) Arbitrary

14) What functions does a router perform when receiving an MPLS packet with top label 1?
    a) Drop the packet silently
    b) Drop the packet and return an "ICMP unreachable" message.
    c) Pop the label and forward it to the RE.
    d) Pop the label and forward to the IP destination.

15) If an LSP is configured with a secondary path and 'standby' enabled, when is the secondary path signaled?
    a) When the router comes up.
    b) When the primary fails.
    c) At the same time the primary is signaled.
    d) As soon as RSVP is configured.

16) When an LDP router receives multiple label bindings for a single destination what metric is used to select the best label?
    a) IGP metric
    b) LDP metric
    c) Local Pref
    d) Route preference

17) What information is used to compile the TED? (select all that apply)
    a) BGP NLRI.
    b) OSPF type-10 LSAs.
    c) Protocol reachability information obtained from CSPF.
    d) IS-IS TLV extensions.

18) What happens if an MPLS router receives an IP packet destined for a network for which the router has no label, but has a standard IP route?
    a) The packet is discarded.
    b) The packet is forwarded via standard IP forwarding.
    c) The packet is rejected and an ICMP message is sent back to the sending host.
    d) The router requests a label from the egress router.

19) What information is stored in the inet.3 routing table?
    a) BGP routes
    b) OSPF routes
    c) LSPs
    d) Labels

Chapter 9 Multicast

1) What is the range of available IP Multicast addresses?
    a) 224.0.0.0 – 244.255.255.255
    b) 222.0.0.0 – 244.0.0.0
    c) 224.0.0.0 – 239.255.255.255
    d) 224.0.0.0 – 239.0.0.0

2) What is the purpose of IGMP?
    a) To communicate the SPT back to the multicast source.
    b) To control the hosts that join and leave multicast streams.
    c) To discover the shortest path back to the RP.
    d) To forward multicast traffic from a host.

3) What is an advantage of IGMPv2 over IGMPv1?
    a) Version 2 has run a shortest path calculation to the multicast source.
    b) Version 2 allows for a single data stream, Version 1 requires individual feeds.

   c) Version 2 uses explicit Leave messages to reduce unneeded traffic on the LAN.
   d) Version 2 requires significantly lower administration.

4) What is the biggest advantage of Shortest Path Trees (SPTs) compared to Shared Trees (STs)?
   a) SPTs minimize bandwidth usage by distributing multicast streams from a common point.
   b) SPTs utilize less routing overhead when forwarding packets.
   c) SPTs minimize latency by finding the optimal path between each source and each receiver.
   d) SPTs require less state handling and memory overhead on multicast routers.

5) What is an advantage of using Shared Trees?
   a) Shared trees minimize bandwidth usage by distributing multicast streams from a common point.
   b) Shared Trees utilize less routing overhead when forwarding packets.
   c) Shared Trees minimize latency by finding the optimal path between each source and each receiver.
   d) Shared Trees require less state handling and memory overhead on multicast routers.

6) What information does the router use to do an RPF check?
   a) The unicast routing table
   b) The DVMRP table
   c) The PIM table
   d) The MSDP table

7) Why is Protocol Independent Multicast (PIM) called Independent?
   a) It is an open source, independently produced protocol.
   b) It works with any type of multicast traffic.
   c) It works with each multicast flow independently.
   d) It works with any IP unicast routing protocol

8) What is the main advantage of MBGP?
   a) It provides redundant unicast paths.
   b) It provides session redundancy.
   c) It provides redundant multicast paths.
   d) It allows for dissimilar unicast and multicast routing topologies.

9) What is the purpose of an (S, G) notation?
    a) To identify the source's unicast address with a multicast group address.
    b) To identify the source's multicast address with a unicast group address.
    c) To identify the source's unicast address with a unicast group address.
    d) To identify the source's multicast address with a multicast group address.

10) What two things do dense mode multicast protocols assume?
    a) That many hosts require the multicast stream.
    b) That the RP will begin to administer the source stream to interested groups.
    c) That bandwidth is plentiful.
    d) That no one will be pruned from the source stream.
    e) That end hosts are running PIM.

11) What is the purpose of MSDP?
    a) To exchange (S, G) information with RPs in other autonomous systems.
    b) To exchange RPF information with another AS
    c) To exchange multicast streams with non-IGMP enabled hosts.
    d) To determine if a received multicast stream is valid.

12) What is the purpose of MBGP?
    a) To exchange (S, G) information with another AS.
    b) To exchange RPF information with another AS
    c) To exchange multicast streams with non-IGMP enabled hosts.
    d) To determine if a received multicast stream is valid.

13) Which of the below things do sparse mode multicast protocols assume? (choose two)
    a) That many hosts require the multicast stream.
    b) That the RP will begin to administer the source stream to interested groups.
    c) That bandwidth is scarce.
    d) That no one will be pruned from the source stream.
    e) That end hosts are running PIM.

Chapter 10 Policy

1) How many firewall filters can be placed on an interface
   a) One per physical
   b) One per logical
   c) One per logical in/out
   d) One per physical in/out

2) Select two policy actions from the below:
   a) Reject
   b) Pop
   c) Push
   d) Accept

3) If three match conditions are specified within a single accept term, when will a route be accepted?
   a) When it matches the first condition.
   b) As soon as it matches a single condition.
   c) When it matches all three conditions.
   d) If it matches none of the conditions.

4) What is the difference between a prefix-list and a route-filter? (Choose all that apply)
   a) A route filter can specify an immediate action upon matching
   b) A prefix-list can specify an immediate action upon matching.
   c) A prefix-list can specify address ranges
   d) A route filter can specify address ranges

5) Routes learned from an eBGP neighbor are subject to what type of policy before entering the routing table?
   a) export
   b) firewall
   c) inbound
   d) import
   e) outbound

6) Policy statements can be applied to which of the following?
   a) CSPF
   b) Routing Protocols
   c) SFMs
   d) Interfaces

7) If no accept or reject is explicitly configured for a BGP policy term what is the default behavior for importing routes?

8) If a policy statement is applied to a specific BGP peer and a different policy is applied to the group to which that peer belongs, which takes effect?
   a) Group
   b) Peer
   c) Both
   d) Neither

9) Within a policy the 'from' statements define which of the following?
   a) match conditions
   b) actions
   c) term
   d) End of policy

10) Which of the following policy-statement operators are used to change the attributes of a route?
   a) from
   b) then
   c) accept
   d) push

11) If a route doesn't match a given term the default behavior is to:
   a) Evaluate the route against the next term
   b) Evaluate the route against the next policy-statement
   c) Reject the route
   d) Accept the route

12) Which of the following are valid match criteria within a policy-statement? (choose all that apply)
   a) source address
   b) protocol
   c) as-path
   d) next-hop

13) "192.168.64.0/19 orlonger" matches:
   a) 192.168.64.0/18
   b) 192.168.64.0/19
   c) 192.168.64.0/20

14) "192.168.64.0/19 upto /24" matches which address block(s)?

a) 192.168.64.0/19
b) 192.168.64.0/20
c) 192.168.64.0/23
d) 192.168.64.0/24

Appendix B: Additional Information

Possible 'show' command completions in JUNOS 5.0:

```
accounting          Show accounting profiles
aps                 Show APS information
arp                 Show system ARP table entries
as-path             Show table of known AS paths
bgp                 Show information about BGP
chassis             Show chassis information
cli                 Show cli settings
configuration       Show configuration file contents
connections         Show CCC connections
dvmrp               Show information about DVMRP
firewall            Show firewall counters and info
host                Hostname lookup using DNS
igmp                Show information about IGMP
ilmi                Show ILMI information
interfaces          Show interface information
isis                Show information about IS-IS
l2vpn               Show information about L2VPNs
ldp                 Show information about LDP
log                 Show contents of a log file
mpls                Show information about MPLS
msdp                Show information about MSDP
multicast           Show multicast information
ntp                 Network Time Protocol information
ospf                Show information about OSPF
pfe                 Show packet forwarding engine data
pim                 Show information about PIM
policy              Show policy information
rip                 Show information about RIP
route               Show routing table information
rsvp                Show information about RSVP
sap                 Session advertisement addresses
snmp                Show SNMP information
system              Show system information
task                Show protocol per-task information
ted                 Show information about TED
```

```
version              Show software revision levels
vrrp                 Show VRRP information
```

Possible '[edit] show' configuration completions in JUNOS 5.0:

```
accounting-options    Accounting data configuration
apply-groups          Groups to get config data from
chassis               Chassis configuration
class-of-service      Class-of-service configuration
firewall              Define firewall configuration
forwarding-options    Packet sampling options
groups                Configuration groups
interfaces            Interface configuration
policy-options        Routing policy options
protocols             Routing protocol configuration
routing-instances     Routing instance configuration
routing-options       Protocol-independent options
snmp                  Simple Network Mgmt Protocol
system                System parameters
```

Media types as abbreviated in interface names:

- `ae`—Aggregated Ethernet interface. A virtual bundled Ethernet link.
- `as`—Aggregated SONET/SDH interface. A virtual bundled SONET link.
- `at`—ATM interface.
- `ds`—DS-0 interface (on a channelized DS-3 or E1 PIC).
- `e1`—E1 interface
- `e3`—E3 interface
- `es`—Encryption interface
- `fe`—Fast Ethernet interface
- `fxp`—Management and internal Ethernet interfaces
- `ge`—Gigabit Ethernet interface
- `gr`—Generic Route Encapsulation (GRE) tunnel interface
- `ip`—IP-over-IP encapsulation tunnel interface
- `lo`—Loopback interface

- `ml`—Multilink interface
- `mo`—Passive monitoring interface
- `mt`—Multicast tunnel interface
- `so`—SONET/SDH interface
- `t1`—T1 interface (includes channelized DS-3 interfaces)
- `t3`—T3 interface (includes channelized OC-12 interfaces)
- `vt`—VPN loopback tunnel interface

Family types allowed on interfaces:

- Internet Protocol, version 4 (IPv4)
- Internet Protocol, version 6 (IPv6)
- International Organization for Standardization (ISO)
- Multiprotocol Label Switching (MPLS)
- Circuit cross-connect (CCC)
- Translational cross-connect (TCC)
- Multilink Frame Relay (MLFR)
- Multilink PPP (MLPPP)
- Trivial Network Protocol (TNP)

Well Known Multicast Addresses:

224.0.0.0 Base multicast address.

224.0.0.1 All local hosts multicast group. IGMP Query message

224.0.0.2 All routers.

224.0.0.4 DVMRP

224.0.0.5	All OSPF Routers address. Sends routing updates to all OSPF routers on a network segment.
224.0.0.6	OSPF DR address. Sends routing updates to OSPF Designated Router.
224.0.0.9	RIPv2
224.0.0.13	PIMv2

Appendix C: Glossary of Terms

ABR – Area Border Router. In OSPF, a router that has interfaces in a site area as well as Area 0. Traffic flowing from one area to another traverses an ABR.

Adjacency – When two routers running the same protocol are configured to talk to one another and exchange routing information, they can become adjacent. Also sometimes called Neighbors.

AFI – Address Family Identifier. The first byte of an NSAP Area ID which tells the system how to interpret the rest of the Area ID field. The Area ID is an AS local trait. The AFI byte is commonly set to 49.

Area – A logical grouping of devices configured in a routing protocol to either restrict administrative overhead and traffic.

AS – Autonomous System. A set of network devices under common administrative control. An IGP is considered to be the protocol used to reach nodes within the same AS. An EGP is used to reach destinations outside of the AS.

AS-path – An attribute carried by BGP routes that reflects the number of Autonomous Systems traffic will need to transit to reach the destination. AS path is one of the primary means of BGP route selection.

ASBR – Autonomous System Boundary Router. In OSPF a router that separates two different routing domains, i.e. a router that injects RIP routes into OSPF.

ASIC – Application Specific Integrated Circuit. A piece of hardware, specifically a chip, designed to perform a specific function. Functions carried out by hardware are conducted many times faster than those done via software processes. Juniper routers utilize a number of ASICs in the PFE.

ATM – Asynchronous Transfer Mode – A high-speed broadband method of transporting data between nodes using fixed 53 byte cells. Useful for applications that require rigid Quality of Service (QoS) and jitter tolerances such as voice and video.

Backbone – A group of routers that are responsible for ferrying traffic between different areas. Backbone routers are usually connected by high-speed circuits and do not normally directly serve end user hosts.

BGP – Border Gateway Protocol. A protocol for exchanging routes between autonomous systems (AS). BGP version 4 is the de facto EGP in use on the Internet.

Bit – A digital signal that can exist in one of two possible positions. These positions are often referred to as '1' and '0', or 'on' and 'off'.

BMA – Broadcast Multi Access. A type of LAN, such as Ethernet, where connected devices are capable of broadcasting to all other connected nodes. The ability for any node to broadcast repeatedly can quickly overwhelm normal data transmissions if considerations are not made to handle such events.

Broadcast – One-to-all traffic flow. This type of data transmission is not an economic use of network resources, as all hosts on a segment receive the traffic regardless of whether or not they will use it.

CIDR – Classless Interdomain Routing. A system of classless IP addressing where the subnet mask may be calculated at any bit across the address. This allows for more efficient use of address space. See also *VLSM.*

CIP – Connector Interface Panel. Located on the far left of the FPC card cage, the CIP contains the console, auxiliary, and management Ethernet connections for the router. Host 0 and Host 1 each have their own dedicated ports.

CLI – Command Line Interface. In JUNOS the prompt at which commands are issued to the router.

CoS – Class of Service. A way of managing network traffic by grouping types of data traffic together and defining a service class for each group. (For example, a voice group, e-mail group, file transfer group, telnet group, etc.) This differs from QoS which guarantees network resources for priority traffic. CoS is coarser and simpler to implement than QoS.

CSPF – Constrained Shortest Path First. The algorithm which is run by RSVP to determine the best path for an LSP. CSPF takes into account any hop requirements that may be placed on the LSP calculation.

CSNP – Complete Sequence Number PDU - Contains an entire listing of LSPs in the database. Sent out all IS-IS links periodically to ensure all routers have synchronized LSP databases. A DIS will multicast the CSNP on a broadcast network media to limit acknowledgement traffic.

Daemons – A process that runs in a UNIX environment. Daemons run independently of one another and are more resilient to failure.

Dead timer/Dead Interval – The amount of time a protocol will allow to pass without receiving a keepalive message before considering the neighbor to be unreachable. See also *keepalive*.

DIS – Designated Intermediate System. The node in an ISIS broadcast network segment appointed to propagate announcements to conserve overhead. Equivalent to a DR in OSPF, but there is no backup (BDR) in an ISIS implementation.

DR – Designated Router. 1) In OSPF the router responsible for keeping all its adjacent neighbors synchronized on a multi-access LAN segment. 2) In PIM on a multi-access LAN, the DR is responsible for sending Joins to the Rendezvous Point (RP) to construct the shared tree

DVMRP – Distance Vector Multicast Routing Protocol. A multicast routing protocol used to dynamically generate shortest path trees for forwarding multicast streams.

EGP – Exterior Gateway Protocol - A system of rules defining the procedure to route packets between different ASs. BGP is the most widespread EGP.

Egress Router – The device where MPLS frames exit an LSP after being label switched from another MPLS-enabled router.

ERO – Explicit Route Object. In MPLS the result of the best path calculation that is passed on to RSVP to be used for signaling the LSP.

FEC – Forward Equivalency Class. In MPLS the FEC defines which packets will be appended with a particular label. For example all packets with the same destination network address will be encapsulated with the same label before they are forwarded to the next router.

Forwarding Table – The table assembled on the RE and exported to the PFE which contains the selected best next-hops for all destinations. Smaller than the *routing-table*.

FPC – Flexible PIC Concentrator. On the larger M-series routers, FPCs hold up to 4 PICs in a chassis slot. The FPC contains the shared memory for all PICs in that slot as well as ASICs necessary for packet flow to and from the rest of the PFE.

Gateway – A legacy word used to describe routers. ISIS and OSI standards still can refer to routers in this way.

Hello protocol – Utilized by OSPF to establish and maintain neighbor adjacencies. Also used as a *keepalive* message.

IGMP – Internet Group Management Protocol. In multicast, the protocol that controls membership in a multicast group, allowing hosts to join and leave a stream.

IGP – Interior Gateway Protocol - A system of rules defining the procedure to route packets within a common AS. OSPF, RIP, an IS-IS are examples of an IGP.

IIH - IS-IS Hello PDU - Broadcast to determine neighboring IS-IS systems. Discovers and differentiates between Level 1 and Level 2 routers.

Ingress Router – The device where MPLS frames enter an LSP to be label switched to another MPLS-enabled router.

IP – Internet Protocol. Principle routed protocol on the Internet today, carrying all types of data through all types of media.

IP Address - A unique 4-byte number, normally expressed in four dotted decimal notation (eg 12.34.56.78), that identifies a specific host on a network. Certain IP addresses are reserved for special use and are not generally routed on the Internet.

IS-IS – Intermediate System to Intermediate System. A link state IGP designed for robust and complex networks. Utilizes OSI addressing.

JUNOS – The operating system written by Juniper Networks for its series of routers. Based on a UNIX kernel, it is robust and resilient.

Keepalive - A timer utilized by a routing protocol to ensure a neighbor is still reachable. If a keepalive message is not received within a configured interval, the neighbor will be considered unreachable and action will be taken upon the route topology. Also see *dead-interval.*

LAN – Local Area Network. A collection of nodes that are relatively close in physical location. Current networks usually depend on Ethernet at the LAN level.

LDP – Label Distribution Protocol. In MPLS a protocol describing the mechanism for exchanging, withdrawing and updating label information between neighboring routers.

LER – Label Edge Router. A router that sits at the edge of an MPLS network. It can either receive MPLS labeled packets, strip those headers and forward the IP packet within, or the reverse and send it off the another MPLS router.

Level 1 Intermediate System – In ISIS a node that routes packets only within its own Area. When dealing with packets destined for a different Area, the router sends them to the closest Level 2 node. A router running ISIS may have interfaces in Level1, Level 2, or both.

Level 2 Intermediate System – In ISIS a node that routes packets between and toward other Areas. A router running ISIS may have interfaces in Level1, Level 2, or both.

Local Preference - An attribute carried by BGP routes that reflects the administrative preference to select a route within the local AS. The number is configured through policy. A higher local-pref indicates a more desirable route. Local-pref is one of the primary means of BGP route selection.

Loopback – A logical router interface. Normally used as an endpoint for router-to-router communication or as a Router ID. Because a loopback is not tied to a physical interface it is more resilient to failure.

LSA – Link State Advertisement. In OSPF a protocol announcement of link state to other OSPF routers.

LSP – Label Switch Path. In MPLS, a unidirectional virtual path connecting two LSR/LER nodes through any number of intermediate MPLS active transit LSRs.

LSP – Link State PDU. In ISIS, the packets containing information regarding the state of the connections to adjacent routers.

LSR – Label Switch Router. A router that forwards packets based solely on label information. Transit LSP routers are LSRs.

MAC – Media Access Controller. Sometimes called the hardware address, the 6 byte (48 bit) MAC address is used to uniquely identify a network node on a LAN at layer-2 of the OSI model.

MBGP – Multiprotocol Border Gateway Protocol. Multicast protocol that allows autonomous systems to exchange information used for RPF checks.

MCS – Miscellaneous Control Subsystem. A hardware component in the M160/M40e platform that makes up part of the RE. The MCS provides monitoring and control of the router systems.

MED – Multi-Exit Discriminator. An route selection attribute in BGP. MEDs can be exchanged across eBGP sessions and tell the external neighbor which path is preferred. They usually reflect IGP cost, and as such a lower MED more preferable.

Metric – An administratively defined cost for taking a particular path through a network.

MPLS – Multi-Protocol Label Switching. A method of forwarding data packets based on a label rather than a longest match IP lookup. MPLS enables more stringent levels of packet delivery QoS than pure packet-switched networks.

MSDP – Multicast Source Distribution Protocol. A multicast protocol that allows RPs to exchange (S, G) groups.

Multicast – One-to-many traffic flow. Not as wasteful of bandwidth and resources as broadcasting.

NET – Network Entity Title. In ISIS a special NSAP that identifies the node rather than a physical interface. Can be thought of as a loopback address.

NSAP – Network Service Access Point. In ISIS the address used to identify a particular network connection, such as a router interface.

NSSA – Not so stubby area. An area in OSPF that allows a local ASBR to flood External LSAs within and out of the area, but still receives a default route for routes outside the area.

OSPF – Open Shortest Path First. A link state IGP designed for robust and complex internetworks. Written and designed for TCP/IP.

PCG – PFE Clock Generator. A hardware component in the M160/M40e platform responsible for synchronizing the internal PFE components.

PDU – Protocol Data Unit. The packets used to communicate between ISIS nodes. More generally, any packets used by a routing protocol to pass information.

PFE – Packet Forwarding Engine. The collection of hardware responsible for routing and switching data packets in a Juniper router. It includes the PICs, FPCs, and many ASICs in the M series.

PIC – Physical Interface Card. The hardware component where physical connection to the transport media is made. Come in a variety of speeds, but designed to be interchangeable across platforms.

PIM – Protocol Independent Multicast. A multicast protocol that functions independent of the IGP used. Determines pathing for source-destination traffic in a multicast traffic flow. Can be configured in sparse or dense mode.

Poison Reverse – In RIP, advertisements sent back to the originating router that contain a metric of 16. This marks that path as unreachable. This has the effect of preventing routing loops between nodes.

Port – A value from 1 to 65535 that is used to uniquely identify a TCP/IP application and allow communication between two hosts on a network. There is a set for TCP and another for UDP applications. A port, when combined with an IP address, form a “socket” through which applications can communicate.

PSNP - Partial Sequence Number PDU – Request for update PDU. When a CSNP receiving router detects a fault with its LSP table it sends a PSNP to the router that originally transmitted the CSNP requesting the missing LSP. The PNSP transmitting node is then forwarded the missing LSP.

QoS - Quality of Service. A method of controlling the delivery of data through a network by giving differing levels of priority to different traffic queues. Packets with a high QoS are given higher priority to network resources (e.g. bandwidth, processing) which allows for more consistent delivery.

Queuing – The process of giving priority to packets marked with high QoS when forwarding traffic. Queuing enables a packet switched network to emulate the stringent delivery requirements usually maintained by ATM and circuit switched networks.

RE – Routing Engine. The collection of hardware components responsible for control plane traffic in a Juniper. The RE sends and receives all routing protocol updates and is responsible for keeping the routing table up to date.

RIP – Routing Information Protocol. A distance vector routing protocol suitable for small networks.

Route – Information that describes the network path to a destination host.

Route Reflection – A system in BGP that allows for the propagation of routes learned from an iBGP neighbor to other iBGP neighbors, thereby eliminating the need for a large full-mesh of iBGP routers. Utilizes route-reflectors and route-reflector clients.

Routing Table – The database assembled by the RE from all the information provided by active routing protocols that describes paths to every known destination. The routing table contains every known path. Best next-hops are calculated and used to build the *forwarding table.*

RP – Rendezvous Point. A router configured to be the point at which the multicast source stream first locates the destination group.

RSVP – Reservation Protocol. A label distribution protocol for MPLS that enables routers to establish and maintain LSPs for forwarding packets. RSVP allows dynamic LSP creation based upon available bandwidth and administrator preferences.

SCB – System Control Board. A hardware component in the M40 platform that is part of the PFE. The SCB makes forwarding decisions, monitors the system, and controls the FPCs.

SFM – Switching and Forwarding Module. A hardware component in the M160/M40e platform that is part of the PFE. SFMs make forwarding decisions and distribute packets to shared memory.

Split Horizon – In BGP, the process of an not propagating iBGP updates past a single iBGP neighbor. EBGP neighbors will still receive updates. Route reflection allows for iBGP neighbors to supercede this rule when passing advertisements to cluster clients.

Split Horizon – In RIP, the process of not sending advertisements back to the router from which they were received. This prevents the routers from creating a loop where each thinks the other has the valid path.

Static route – Manually configured routing information. Static routes require administrator intervention to change any information, and as such cannot respond to changes in topology or traffic.

Stub Area – A site area in OSPF that receives a default route to reach prefixes outside it's own. By default, a stub area cannot contain an ASBR or a *virtual link*.

TCP – Transmission Control Protocol. A connection oriented protocol that runs on top of IP. TCP contains methods of ensuring all packets sent by the source are received by the destination host. Contrast with *UDP*.

TED – Traffic Engineering Database. For MPLS a table populated with information from the IGP that is used by CSPF to calculate the best path for an LSP.

Traffic Engineering – The process of tailoring traffic flows between nodes for optimum performance. RSVP allows traffic engineering based on bandwidth availability and static tie downs.

UDP – User Datagram Protocol. A connectionless protocol that runs on top of IP. UDP/IP has no method of error recovery and does not guarantee transport of packets, relying on higher level protocols to compensate. Contrast with *TCP*.

Unicast – One-to-one traffic. A single server and single client exchange data by means of network unique addresses. Unicast traffic flows do not scale well in terms of bandwidth used as the number of clients increase. Each new client requires a separate and dedicated flow, leading to rapid congestion for popular, high bandwidth applications. Multicast is seen as the solution to this problem. The majority of traffic flowing on the Internet today is unicast.

VLSM – Variable Length Subnet Mask. Allows for the custom configuration of the subnet to as many, or as few hosts as the administrator requires by defining the mask anywhere along the 32 bits of an IP address rather than at the traditional octet breaks of bits 8, 16, and 24. VLSM are usually noted as a slash followed by the number of bits in the network portion. (192.168.1.1/27) *See also CIDR.*

VPN – Virtual Private Network. A network with access limited to specific hosts tunneled over a wide, public access network (e.g. the Internet) and security is provided by encryption and/or special protocols.

WAN – Wide Area Network. Network connecting physically remote locations, usually comprised of high-speed leased lines.

Appendix D: Quiz Answers

Chapter 1: Basics

1) How many bits represent the host portion of the IP address 192.168.10.64/27?

Answer: 5. There are 32 bits in an IPv4 address. The subnet mask denotes the number of bits in the network segment, and the remainders describe the host portion. A VLSM /27 leaves 5 bits.

2) Expand the IP address and subnet mask 10.154.63.24/19 into their binary equivalents.
   10.154.63.24 = 00001010. 10011010. 00111111. 00011000
   255.255.224.0 = 11111111.11111111. 11100000.00000000

3) What are the network and broadcast addresses of the subnet including host 10.23.32.100/23?

The network address is the host portion set to all zeros, or 10.23.32.0 in this instance. The broadcast address is the host portion set to all ones, which is 10.23.33.255 in this case.

4) How many useable host addresses can be configured in the subnet 192.168.45.0/28? What are the first and last useable host addresses?

14 useable host addresses, the first being 192.168.45.1 the last 192.168.45.15. A /28 subnet leaves 4 bits for the host segment. Four bits allows for 16 combinations (2^4). Subtract one address for the broadcast and one for the network, leaving 14 total available addresses (2^n-2).

5) A subnet requires addresses for 42 unique hosts. What is the smallest subnet that can be used to allocate enough addresses?

Answer: /26. A /26 allows for 62 unique hosts. The subnets to either side allocate too many (/25 = 126 hosts) or too few (/27=30 hosts)

6) How many total addresses are in 192.168.10.0/25 that are not in 192.168.10.0/26?

Answer: 64. A /25 contains 128 total addresses, while the smaller /26 contains 64. This leaves 64 addresses that do not overlap.

7) Which address "class" does 64.123.123.100 belong to?
   a) Class A. The first bit is 0, indicating a Class A address.

Chapter 2 Hardware

1) What is the name of the 100Mb link between the PFE and the RE?
   d) Fxp1. Note: Fxp0 is the management Ethernet connection.

2) Which routers contain Packet Director ASICs? (choose all that apply)
   a) M160
   b) M40e

3) Which two components comprise the Host Module?
   b) RE and MCS
   These are two separate parts, but they must function together as one logical unit.

4) On which ASIC(s) does queuing take place?
   b) I/O Manager ASIC

5) How many FPC slots are on an M40?
   d) 8. Numbering begins at 0 and ends with 7.

6) Which ASIC sends packets out a physical port?
   a) PIC ASIC

7) The FPCs are built into the FEB on which two platforms?
   a) M5
   b) M10

8) The M20 supports redundant Routing Engines.
   a) True

9) What are the primary responsibilities of the RE?
   c) Maintain routing protocols, control software processes

10) Match the following hardware components to the correct platform:
    a) M160 = SFM
    b) M40 = SCB
    c) M20 = SSB
    d) M10 = FEB

Chapter 3 JUNOS

1) What is the standard boot sequence for JUNOS?
    a) PCMCIA flash, compact flash, hard-drive, network

2) What is the default route preference of a static route?
    b) 5

3) If there is a route known via RIP and OSPF (internal), which one will be installed (assuming the exact same route with no attributes altered)?
    b) OSPF
    OSPF internal has a default protocol preference of 10, where RIP is 100 (lower preference wins)

4) Into which table are static IPv4 routes installed?
    a) inet.0

    inet.0 - Default unicast table
    inet.1 - Default multicast table
    inet.2 – Multicast RPF checks
    inet.3 - MPLS path information

5) The forwarding table actually used to make next-hop forwarding decisions is stored where?
    d) the PFE

6) Under which configuration statement is the BGP autonomous system number set?
    c) [edit routing-options]

7) Which routing table contains MPLS information?
    d) inet.3

8) What is the CLI command to view the *messages* logfile?
    c) show log messages
    To view any traceoption log files, simply type 'show log *filename*'

9) Explain the differences between routes held in the forwarding table and those in the routing table.

    The routing table includes all possible paths to destinations learned from every protocol. Routes in the forwarding table are the **best** next-hop path. The information in the forwarding table is used to make forwarding decisions.

10) Under which configuration level is the Router ID set?

    d) [edit routing-options]

    Both the Router ID and autonomous system number are set at this level of the configuration.

11) Which two of the below are traits of JUNOS?

    a) It is based on a UNIX kernel

    c) Processes run independently

12) Which command will erase the current configuration and load the entire contents of "newconfig" from edit mode?

    c) Load override newconfig

13) Which command will configure an IP address upon fe-0/0/0.0 from the [edit interfaces fe-0/0/0 unit 0] prompt?

    b) Set family inet address 10.45.123.32/30

14) What are legal completions for a configured static route? (Choose all that apply)

    a)An interface

    b)An address

    d)Discard

    e)Reject

15) Where is the backup copy of JUNOS kept?

    Answer: The hard drive.

Chapter 4 RIP

1) What is the maximum hop-count for a **reachable** RIP route?

    a) 15

    A hop count of 16 indicates an unreachable route. This value was not changed for version 2, limiting the scalability of RIP in larger networks.

2) What two mechanisms does RIP use to prevent routing loops (select 2)?
   a) Split-horizon
   d) Poison-reverse

3) In which routing table are RIP routes placed?
   a) inet.0
   inet.0 - Default unicast table
   inet.1 - Default multicast table
   inet.2 – Multicast RPF checks
   inet.3 - MPLS path information

4) A RIP update, using authentication, can contain up to how many networks?
   b) 24
   25 updates can be carried in a RIP update message. Only 24 can be carried if authentication is used.

5) What type(s) of authentication does JUNOS support for RIPv1?
   d) Neither of these methods
   Authentication was not introduced until RIPv2

6) What type(s) of authentication does JUNOS support for RIPv2?
   c) Both a and b
   The RFC for version 2 specifies plain-text passwords, but JUNOS allows plain-text and MD5 encrypted keys.

7) Define how split-horizon works to control routing loops?
   Answer: A route learned through an interface will be forwarded out all interfaces EXCEPT that interface through which it was learned.

8) Define how poison-reverse functions to control routing loops?
   When a route is learned through an interface, the same route is sent back through that interface with an unreachable metric (16 in the case of RIP), thus preventing a loop.

9) How do RIPv2 routers send route updates to their neighbors?
   b) Multicast
   RIPv1 broadcasts messages. RIPv2 is more advanced and uses multicast to a predefined address.

10) Which of the following is NOT a field in a RIPv2 update message?
   c) Cost
   RIP has no concept of cost. It uses hop count as the metric to choose the best route to a destination.

Chapter 5 OSPF

1) What is the purpose of an ASBR?

Answer: An Autonomous System Boundary Router imports routes from external networks (such as RIP routes from an attached RIP network) into OSPF. This router also exports OSPF routes into these external networks.

2) What is the purpose of an ABR?

Answer: An Area Border Router communicates OSPF routes between a site area and the backbone area (Area 0)

3) What type of OSPF network utilizes a DR?

d) BMA

Broadcast Multiple Access networks utilize a DR and BDR to conserve bandwidth and CPU cycles (updates from all other routers only need to be sent to these routers, not everyone).

4) What address does the RID default to?

Answer: The highest IP address of all interfaces configured to run OSPF. If none are configured, the highest loopback IP address is taken from those loopback addresses configured to run OSPF.

5) What type of router sends Type 2 Network LSAs on a broadcast segment?

c) DR

The Designated Router on a BMA segment is responsible for summarizing network routes and sending out Type 2 summary advertisements. In the event that the DR fails, the BDR assumes this role.

6) What type of router cannot exist in a stub area?

a) ASBR

An ASBR is intended to import and export external routes to/from the OSPF domain. These types of routes will not enter or propagate in a stub network.

7) Give 2 purposes of the Hello message.

b) Discover neighbors on a network segment.

c) Maintain neighbor adjacencies (reset timers before the dead timers expire)

8) Which State is a router in after a Hello is sent but before one is received?

    a) DOWN. Only after a Hello is received with the router's own address will that router move to INIT state.

9) What are the default OSPF timer values?

    Answer: 10 second hello timer and 40 second dead timer.

10) Which OSPF router distributes area routes into other areas?

    b) ABR

    An area border router distributes routes into other areas (most often the backbone area, Area 0)

11) Which CLI command will show the state of OSPF to other routers?

    c) show ospf neighbor

12) Which CLI command with show the type of networks the router participates in (Point to Point, BMA, etc)?

    a) show ospf interface

13) What is the CLI command to view the OSPF link-state database?

    Answer: Show ospf database

14) On an Ethernet segment Router A (priority 100), Router B and Router C (both priority 90) come online. Which one is elected to be the designated router?

    Answer: Router A has the highest priority, and therefore will become the DR.

15) On the same segment above in 14, Router D comes online 30 minutes later with a priority of 110. Assuming nothing else has changed, which router is now DR?

    Answer: Router A remains the DR as an election is not forced if a DR already exists on a segment.

16) What is the minimum configuration necessary to run OSPF on a router?

    - Which interfaces will participate in OSPF
    - Which areas those interfaces will be assigned to

17) What is the first State when establishing an OSPF adjacency?

    a) Down

    Routers start in DOWN. They move to INIT after receiving a Hello message from a neighbor with their own IP address included.

18) In which State should routers be with their neighbors on a BMA network where neither are DR or BDR?
    c) 2way (indicating an adjacency, but no routes exchanged. Routes are only exchanged with the DR and BDR.)

19) What State should synchronized neighbors on a Point to Point segment be in?
    f) Full

Chapter 6 IS-IS

1) The first byte of the Area ID is also known as:
    d) AFI The Address Family Identifier

2) When a Level1 router encounters packets destined for a different Area, what does it do?
    b) Sends it to the nearest L1/L2 router

3) What is the command to view which interfaces are configured for IS-IS?
    a) show isis interface

4) By default, an IS-IS enabled interface is placed into which Level?
    d) Both Level 1 and Level 2

5) What is the command to view the IS-IS database?
    Show isis database

6) When configuring a router for IS-IS, the last byte of the NSAP must be set to what?
    Answer: The last byte of the NSAP is known as the NSEL. The NSEL of a router must be set to 00, which denotes an Intermediate system capable of routing packets.

7) Three IS-IS routers (A, B, C) are brought online in an Ethernet segment. A has no priority configuration (default). B has priority set to 0. C has a priority set to 100.
    Who will be elected the DIS?
    c) Router C
    Default ISIS priority within JUNOS is 64. The router with the highest priority is elected the DIS.

8) Which of the following is/are functions of a PSNP (choose all that apply): All of these.
    a) Request a missing LSP
    b) Share routing table information
    c) Notify to retransmit an LSP after a sequence error is noted
    d) Reset the Hello timer

9) Which is better thought of as a "site" router (meaning no direct communication to the network backbone)?
    a) Level 1 router

10) Identify the portions of the NSAP address 49.0001.9aff.00ab.0030.1223.4045.00
    49 = The AFI portion of the Area ID
    0001.9aff.00ab = Variable length Domain Identifier of the Area ID
    0030.1223.4045 = System ID of IP address 3.12.234.45
    00 = The router NSEL

11) Which PDU is used to advertise a complete listing of all IS-IS LSPs in the router link state database?
    a) CSNP or Complete Sequence Number PDU

12) If an IS-IS router detects a fault with its link state database, which PDU does it use to request an update?
    b) PSNP or Partial Sequence Number PDU

Chapter 7 BGP

1) At what level of the configuration hierarchy is the AS number set?
    c) [edit routing-options]

2) What do the numbers in the final column of the below output mean for the bgp neighbor?
    `10.244.2.154 65333 452 432 0 4 5d19h 8250/121636/0`
    d) Routes active/received/dampened

3) How do you get BGP to advertise all OSPF routes to all neighbors?
    d) Import policy in BGP that matches on OSPF routes

4) Given equal cost BGP routes in inet.0 and inet.3, which will be selected?
   b) inet.0

5) Given the list of criteria for BGP route selection within JUNOS, put them in order.
   Local pref
   AS-path length
   Origin code
   MED
   eBGP vs. iBGP
   IGP cost

6) What BGP message contains information on new and changed routes?
   a) update

7) Which port does BGP listen to?
   b) TCP 179

8) What is local preference used for?
   Answer: When numerous BGP routes to a common destination are received, BGP uses criteria to select which path is best. One of the most important values is local preference, a configurable value.

9) By default, BGP will advertise what routes to neighbors (select all that apply?
   a) directly connected
   d) routes learned via BGP

10) Which command is used to view specific BGP neighbor information?
    b) show bgp neighbor

11) iBGP peers are those that are:
    a) In the same AS

12) Unless BGP multi-hop is enabled, external BGP neighbors must be:
    c) Directly connected

13) If two or more valid paths are available, BGP will inherently:
    d) Not load share.
    BGP does not load balance by default. BGP multi-path and multi-hop must be used in conjunction to facilitate load balancing.

14) iBGP neighbors must be directly connected.
    b) False.
    Internal peers must only be reachable via the IGP to be valid.

15) A router configured with BGP can automatically discover BGP neighbors.
    b) False – BGP neighbors must be explicitly configured. There is no auto-discovery feature for BGP.

16) BGP split horizon dictates that:
    d) Routes learned via iBGP are not advertised to any iBGP neighbors.
    Note that routes learned via iBGP will be passed to external peers.

17) Which two of the below help reduce the problems of requiring a full mesh of iBGP neighbors?
    a) Confederations
    d)Route reflectors

18) How does BGP avoid routing loops? (choose two)
    b) BGP split horizon ensures routes do not propagate past immediate neighbors.
    c) eBGP checks the as-path attribute and drops prefixes that include its native AS.

19) What can a MED from AS 65000 communicate to a BGP peer in AS 64666?
    a) Which interface or session would be preferred for AS 65000 to receive traffic.
    A lower number indicates a preferred path. MEDs have no explicit indication of number or location of exit points, only a relative preference. They cannot force a peer's routing decisions, only make suggestions.

Chapter 8 MPLS

1) What is an LSP?
    a) A unidirectional path through an internal network.

2) Which of the below are valid label operations?
    a) Pop
    c) Swap
    d) Push

3) What object specifies the next-hop of an LSP?
   b) ERO

4) What are the advantages of signaled versus static LSPs?
   a) Dynamic LSP creation
   b) Less administrative overhead

5) What functions does a router perform when it receives an MPLS packet with a single of label 0?
   d) Pop the label and forward to the IP destination .
   This special label indicates to the router to remove the label and forward based upon IPv4 address information.

6) MPLS does not require an underlying routing protocol to function.
   b) False.
   MPLS still requires an underlying protocol such as OSPF or IS-IS to allow forwarding paths for label distribution.

7) Is it possible to use an LSP as a BGP next hop?
   a) True

8) Name two MPLS protocols for signaling LSPs.
   a) RSVP
   c) LDP

9) An LSP is signaled from Router A through Router B and C to Router D. Which is the penultimate hop?
   c) Router C

10) An LSP is configured with strict constraints. The ingress router sees the ERO with a strict constraint of next hop 10.1.2.4. What must be true of this address?
   c) It must be directly connected to previous LSP hop.

11) What is contained in the RRO?
   a) A list of all hops within an LSP.

12) What is the primary purpose of the RRO?
   b) To prevent loops within an LSP.

13) What are the two ways a router can allocate label space?
   a) Per-interface
   b) Global

14) What functions does a router perform when receiving an MPLS packet with top label 1?
    c) Pop the label and forward it to the RE.

    Special label values:

    - 0, IPv4 Explicit Null Label—The label must be popped upon receipt and forwarding should continue based on the IPv4 packet address. (Note that this value is legal only when it is the sole label entry, no label stacking.)
    - 1, Router Alert Label—When this is the top label, it should be popped and the packet delivered to the local software module for processing.
    - 2, IPv6 Explicit Null Label—Same as label 0, except for IPv6
    - 3, Implicit Null Label—Indicates penultimate hop router is next hop in the LSP

15) If an LSP is configured with a secondary path and 'standby' enabled, when is the secondary path signaled?
    c) At the same time the primary is signaled.

16) When an LDP router receives multiple label bindings for a single destination what metric is used to select the best label?
    a) IGP metric

17) What information is used to compile the TED? (select all that apply)
    b) OSPF type-10 LSAs.
    d) IS-IS TLV extensions.

18) What happens if an MPLS router receives an IP packet destined for a network for which the router has no label, but has a standard IP route?
    b) The packet is forwarded via standard IP forwarding.

19) What information is stored in the inet.3 routing table?
    c) LSPs

Chapter 9 Multicast

1) What is the range of available IP Multicast addresses?
   c) 224.0.0.0 – 239.255.255.255

2) What is the purpose of IGMP?
   b) To control the hosts that join and leave multicast streams.

3) What is an advantage of IGMPv2 over IGMPv1?
   c) Version 2 uses explicit Leave messages to reduce unneeded traffic on the LAN.

4) What is the biggest advantage of Shortest Path Trees (SPTs) compared to Shared Trees (STs)?
   c) SPTs minimize latency by finding the optimal path between each source and each receiver.

5) What is an advantage of using Shared Trees?
   d) Shared Trees require less state handling and memory overhead on multicast routers.

6) What information does the router use to do an RPF check?
   a) The unicast routing table

7) Why is Protocol Independent Multicast (PIM) called Independent?
   d) It works with any IP unicast routing protocol.
   PIM works with any underlying IP unicast routing protocol—RIP, EIGRP, OSPF, BGP, or static routes.

8) What is the main advantage of MBGP?
   d) It allows for dissimilar unicast and multicast routing topologies.

9) What is the purpose of an (S, G) notation?
   a) To identify the source's unicast address with a group multicast address.

10) What two things do dense mode multicast protocols assume?
    a) That many hosts require the multicast stream.
    c) That bandwidth is plentiful.

11) What is the purpose of MSDP?
    a) To exchange (S, G) notation with RPs in other autonomous systems.

12) What is the purpose of MBGP?
    b) To exchange RPF information with another AS.

13) Which of the below things do sparse mode multicast protocols assume? (choose two)
    b) That the RP will begin to administer the source stream to interested groups.
    c) That bandwidth is scarce.

Chapter 10 Policy

1) How many firewall filters can be placed on an interface?
    c) one per logical in/out

2) Select two policy actions from the below:
    a) Reject
    d) Accept
    Push, Pop, and Swap are label actions, not policy actions.

3) If three match conditions are specified within a single accept term, when will a route be accepted?
    c) When it matches all three conditions.
    If multiple conditions are specified in a single term, a route must match them all in order to be considered a 'match'.

4) What is the difference between a prefix-list and a route-filter? (choose all that apply)
    a) A route filter can specify an immediate action upon matching
    d) A route filter can specify address ranges
    Route-filters allow for more flexible address matches and can also perform an action immediately (actions can only be applied to **all** routes that match a prefix-list).

5) Routes learned from an eBGP neighbor are subject to what type of policy before entering the routing table?
    d) import

6) Policy statements can be applied to which of the following?
    b) Routing Protocols

7) If no accept or reject is explicitly configured for a BGP policy term what is the default behavior for importing routes?
    Answer: Accept all

8) If a policy statement is applied to a specific BGP peer and a different policy is applied to the group to which that peer belongs, which takes effect?
    b) Peer

9) Within a policy the 'from' statements define which of the following?
    a) match conditions

10) Which of the following policy-statement operators are used to change the attributes of a route?
    b) then

11) If a route doesn't match a given term, the default behavior is to:
    a) Evaluate the route against the next term

12) Which of the following are valid match criteria within a policy-statement? (choose all that apply)
All are valid criteria
    a) source address
    b) protocol
    c) as-path
    d) next-hop

13) "192.168.64.0/19 orlonger" matches:
    b)192.168.64.0/19
    c)192.168.64.0/20

14) "192.168.64.0/19 upto /24" matches:
    b) 192.168.64.0/20
    c) 192.168.64.0/23
    d) 192.168.64.0/24

Index

D

E

F

G

H

I

J

K

L

M

N

O

P

Q

R

S

T

About the Author

John Jacobs (JNCIA, CCNA, MCSE) started in the networking industry in the mid-1990s building local area networks. His interest soon shifted to wide-area networking and the unbounded potential held within. After working in operations for a startup DSL carrier, Rhythms Netconnections, he is currently employed as a Network Operations Engineer for a Tier 1 ISP.

Jeff Ringwelski (JNCIA, CCNA, CCNP) started networking in the late 1990s. His experience spans from maintaining small business connectivity to working in national carrier operations. He is currently a Technical Lead with a Tier 1 telecommunications service provider.

Tyler Wessels (JNCIA, CCNA) started in the networking industry in the mid-1990s working as a network technician for PSINet Inc. With a desire for a greater challenge he moved on to work for another global Tier 1 ISP as a Network Operations Engineer where he has applied and expanded his IP routing and switching knowledge.

www.ingramcontent.com/pod-product-compliance
Lightning Source LLC
Chambersburg PA
CBHW051226050326
40689CB00007B/813

PRÉFACE

Je dédie ce livre aux chercheurs sur la conscience et aux questeurs de Connaissance de Soi voulant explorer une réelle harmonie avec l'Esprit vivant.

Ce livre insinue que le développement d'une intelligence artificielle (IA) n'a pas besoin d'être menée aveuglément, en projetant sur elle nos désirs et défaillances en termes d'instinct de puissance, de volonté de contrôle, ou en l'utilisant dans la poursuite létale des seuls intérêts financiers et politiques d'un groupe ou d'un clan. Une telle recherche irresponsable en IA ne peut qu'aboutir à faire des machines intelligentes (ou exors) nos compétiteurs et ennemis dans la lutte pour la suprématie politique ou financière – comme l'ont mis en scène de nombreux films. Toute différente est ma recherche: elle envisage que puisse se construire une évolution harmonieuse au sein de couples sémanticiens–exors travaillant en synergie, lorsque chaque acteur stimule le gain de connaissance chez l'autre, et est amené à vivre des *sauts qualitatifs* – ceci ouvrant donc la voie d'un enrichissement mutuel.

Dans l'intrigue de *Logique Papillon*, ces couples sont insérés dans un *réseau apprenant* collectif, de *deep learning*, dans lequel l'information s'échange et est continuellement augmentée et retravaillée par les autres nodes du réseau. À mon avis c'est la façon même dont nos esprits opèrent dans la réalité profonde: comme le psychologue Carl Jung l'a montré, nous communiquons et conversons sans cesse entre nous au sein de l'inconscient collectif.

La question cruciale est: Comment s'assurer que les machines IA, à un moment donné, ne se retourneront pas contre leurs maîtres et créateur – c'est-à-dire nous? Que vous me croyiez ou non, je n'avais lu aucun des ouvrages d'Isaac Asimov jusqu'à bien longtemps après l'écriture de ce livre. J'ai donc été très étonnée qu'il ait, lui aussi, posé des règles de base, pour les robots IA, visant à ne pas mettre en danger les êtres intelligents – que j'ai nommés les *sapiens* puisque nous devons envisager dans la galaxie des phylums d'espèces autres que la race humaine.

Mais ces règles sont loin d'être suffisantes. L'essentiel est de construire des valeurs de synergie et de collaboration visant l'épanouissement des talents, tant sapiens qu'exors. Mon pari est que, si des valeurs et des buts philosophiques et spirituels sont entrelacés comme dans une trame au cœur imprenable du système, alors tous les développements futurs des sapiens et des exors seront forcés de rester en cohérence avec ces logiques+valeurs posés à l'origine. Cela serait donc l'opposé absolu d'une création défectueuse ayant un péché originel dès son commencement! Au contraire, nous avons ici

CHRIS H. HARDY

LOGIQUE PAPILLON

TERRE PLANÈTE EXPÉRIMENTALE

Série SF Exopolitique

un core parfait qui ne peut qu'évoluer en harmonie avec le *champ logique* à l'origine, exprimant ainsi ses découvertes et ses nouveaux talents à-travers de toujours nouvelles avancées en termes de technologies, de logique, de concepts, et de connaissance.

Vous-ai-je dit que je n'avais pas du tout aimé *Les Robots* d'Asimov? Enfin voyons! Aucune étape de l'apprentissage-machine n'est jamais explicitée, et l'addition soudaine d'émotions dans le robot tombe comme un cheveu sur la soupe! Loin de moi l'idée d'utiliser de tels trucages littéraires – mais cela a un prix: mon super exor Sphinx évolue pas-à-pas, en phase avec une logique non-linéaire basée sur des processus naturels, psychologiques et organiques.

Pourquoi la science ne serait-elle pas aussi passionnante? (Je veux que la mienne soit un jeu et une fascinante exploration!) Pourquoi la science ne serait-elle pas en harmonie avec le vivant, avec la liberté, avec la terre-Gaia et l'humanité? Il est vrai que jusqu'à présent la science a été beaucoup trop complaisante vis-à-vis de la volonté de contrôle des politiciens, des lobbies, et des bailleurs de fonds. Et, tout d'abord, pourquoi les politiques ne seraient-ils pas eux-aussi les alliés du développement des talents, du psi, et des qualités spirituelles et psychiques des gens et de la société? Simplement parce qu'ils manquent encore d'imagination en ce qui concerne leur propre réalisation (l'opposé – *l'imagination au pouvoir* – sera le thème de mon prochain livre dans cette Série SF Exopolitique: *Vision divergente*).

À part cela, vous trouverez bien sûr une flopée d'arguments exo-politiques, comme la façon dont les Anciens Aliens de notre galaxie ont managé leur supervision de l'humanité, incluant désinformation, trafics maffieux, mutilations d'animaux...

Attachez-vous: le voyage est aussi fascinant et hilarant que complexe, un tournoi d'échecs intellectuel! Et pourtant, pour vous assurer de savourer le côté plaisir tout de suite, et garder le côté pensée profonde pour des lectures postérieures (ou encore l'oublier), je l'ai mis en surlignage gris, ce qui vous permet de sauter facilement au-dessus de ces paragraphes si l'envie vous en prend.

Joyeuse lecture donc,

Chris H. Hardy,
Séguret, France, 11 Juin 2016

Publié avec *CreateSpace IPP*, 23 Juin 2016
Design de couverture: Vincent Winter & Chris H. Hardy (Vincent Winter Associés, www.vwaparis.com). *Photo:* Trou noir central de Centaurus A émettant des lobes et des jets (ESO, Wikimédia Com.)
Blog de l'auteur: http://cosmic-dna.blogspot.fr

TABLE DES MATIÈRES

0. OTAGE

Ismir fut brutalement poussé dans la pièce, et on lui retira enfin son bandeau. Cinq rebelles afghans armés jusqu'aux dents tenaient en joue un ordinateur posé sur une pile de caisses d'armes. Leur chef, apparemment, habillé de soie impeccable jusqu'à sa coiffe, était nonchalamment assis dans un vieux fauteuil devant une table avec une carafe d'eau et une théière arabe en argent, son thé servi dans un minuscule verre ciselé main.

Ismir sentait dans son dos les deux rebelles qui l'avaient conduit ici, habillés à l'européenne. Sa vision périphérique les lui montra dos à la porte, leurs revolvers toujours pointés sur lui.

— De l'eau et un verre de thé, monsieur le spécialiste?» proposa le chef onctueusement, tout en montrant la théière.

Le voyage en hélico puis en Land-Rover les yeux bandés avait été éprouvant. Ismir jeta un coup d'œil discret à sa montre: près de trois heures! Pas de chaise. Il fut contraint de boire debout le verre d'eau.

— Le voyage depuis Kabul s'est-il bien passé?» susurra le chef d'un ton ironique.

— Le paysage était splendide.» Ismir, sur le même ton.

— Ah, ah! Je croyais que les experts en informatique ne savaient pas plaisanter! Vous excuserez nos précautions habituelles.

— Je comprends que c'est tout naturel» dit Ismir en jouant sur les mots. Il se retourna. «Ainsi, c'est la machine?»

— Oui. On nous a dit que c'était l'arme la plus puissante du monde,» dit le chef les yeux soudain enfiévrés.

— Une belle machine! Je n'en ai jamais vu de ce type,» mentit froidement Ismir, reconnaissant un exor EBS typique du PPE, formellement interdit sur cette planète. «Sans doute un nouveau modèle asiatique.» Il se rapprocha de l'ordinateur et fit mine de l'inspecter.

— Un siège pour le spécialiste!» lança le chef d'un ton coléreux.

Ils portèrent une caisse jusque devant l'ordinateur.

— Les ordinateurs ne supportent pas la chaleur. Un ventilateur!» vocifèra Ismir, imitant le ton du chef.

— Vous avez entendu! Un ventilateur!» aboya le chef.

Un des rebelles s'avança vers l'unique ventilateur de la pièce, qui rafraîchissait son chef, et, saisi d'effroi, arrêta son geste. Le regard de celui-ci l'incita à le prendre.

— Et baissez ces armes! Je ne peux pas me concentrer.»

Un signe du chef. Les rebelles baissèrent leurs armes.

Voilà un ton qui fait de l'effet! se dit Ismir.
— Où est votre informaticien?» demanda t-il au chef.
— Mais, vous seul, bien sûr. On nous a assuré qu'on pouvait le faire marcher avec la voix en langage usuel. C'est bien exact?
— C'est très probable. Je vais m'en assurer.
Ils n'y connaissent rien en informatique, ça va être plus facile.
Ismir fit mine d'inspecter la machine sur tous les côtés et de ne trouver aucune touche on/off. Puis il se rassit sur la caisse.
— On. Open. Start. One. Mris. Kos,» dit-il à toute vitesse, finissant par la commande en kargien qu'il savait effective.
L'écran de l'ordinateur s'alluma et la voix terne de l'ordinateur prononça un mot, mais aucun texte n'apparaissait.
— Qu'est-ce qui l'a fait marcher?» tonna le chef.
— Écoutez, vous me payez pour comprendre cet ordinateur! Alors, laissez-moi faire mon travail sans m'interrompre, sinon, je n'y arriverai jamais. Je vous expliquerai son fonctionnement après.
— C'est bon.
Ismir commença alors à parler à l'ordinateur en Kargien, une langue gutturale qui rappelait à la fois les langues nordiques et l'arabe.
— Quelle est cette langue? Ce n'est pas de l'anglais, ni du japonais!
— C'est un langage machine de 5ème génération. Un langage créé pour l'ordinateur, vous comprenez? J'ai déjà trouvé son langage. Je pense que je n'en aurai pas pour longtemps à inventorier toutes ses potentialités.
Il se remit à parler à l'ordinateur:
— Cheminement principal en vocal. As-tu le langage RIN de Trisorbe?
!! Oui.
— Affiche toutes les deux ou trois secondes une ligne d'un programme en RIN, n'importe lequel, choisi aléatoirement.
!! Exécution écran démarrée.
— Qui est ton utilisateur principal?
!! Pas de principal, mais de nombreux étudiants du PPE sur Nazra.
— Depuis quand es-tu sur Trisorbe?
!! Onze rans.
— Quels pays?
!! Inde, Afghanistan.
Mumbai! J'en étais sûr! C'est l'Obs de Mumbai qui leur a vendu cet exor!
— As-tu travaillé pour un membre du PPE?
!! Non.
— As-tu dans tes fichiers des conversations sygcoms avec des membres du PPE ou des officiels d'Exora?
!! Non.
— Efface tous les fichiers de langage usuel en kargien.

!! Effacé.

— Crée un espace simulation d'un ordinateur sophistiqué de Trisorbe.

!! Espace simulation de tous les ordinateurs de Trisorbe existant déjà.

— Garde seulement un ESTA. Détruis toutes les autres simulations.

!! Exécuté.

— Crée un sub-espace Sub1: Copie dedans tout ce qui est nécessaire à l'utilisation de la fréquence paralysante Epsilon. Bloque-la sur un effet de 30 mnT.

!! Exécuté.

— Sub2: planifie ton autodestruction dans 3,5 joursT par consumation intégrale syg. Code tout Sub2 en impulsions sygatom.

!! Planifié, sub2 intégralement codé.

— As-tu...

— ISMIR. Ici Vris en direct par la voix de mon exor pour qu'ils n'entendent pas la différence. Continue à parler de temps en temps. À toi.

— J'écoute et je suis curieux,» dit Ismir comme s'il donnait un ordre à la machine.

— Le trafic sur lequel tu viens de tomber est très étendu dans le PPE. Rudder et l'Obs de Mumbai, Agash, impliqués. À toi.

— À mon avis, c'est Mumbai qui a vendu cet exor aux rebelles.

— J'ai entendu, filmé et enregistré toute ton interaction avec les rebelles et l'exor. Ainsi j'ai des preuves solides te disculpant. À toi.

— Est-ce que je suis bien près de Mazari-Sharif? D'après le temps passé, je pense que l'hélico s'est posé à Kholm, puis on a roulé 1 heure trente en Land-Rover sur une piste de montagne. À toi.

— Tu as très probablement atterri à Kholm, oui. Mazari-Sharif est sur la montagne au sud-ouest de la ferme; lumières visibles au loin dans la nuit pour te repérer. En haut de la pente où tu te trouve, il y a un gros village, Karchi-Gak, à trois kilomètres. À toi.

— Je suis obligé de leur fournir une arme qui marche pour sortir vivant d'ici. J'ai choisi une onde pulsée paralysante Epsilon de 30 mnT non-létale. Plus tard, l'exor s'autodétruira. À toi.

— Bien pensé, mais maintenant c'est inutile. Rudder a des suspicions et veut éliminer toute preuve de leur bévue, c'est-à-dire précisément l'exor. Il se fout de tuer les sapiens autour. Il a planifié la destruction de la ferme par TTID dans... voyons... 38 mnT. Je vais prendre les opérations en main. On continue de filmer ça. À toi.

— Est-il possible d'empêcher l'explosion?

— Difficile et risqué. Stratégiquement, c'est hors de question: le réseau maffieux au sein du PPE est trop large. On a besoin d'une erreur irréversible de leur part pour les inculper. Je vais sauver les gens seulement. À toi.

— Tu vas les faire sortir de la ferme?

— Oui. Il n'y a personne sur ce versant à part les rebelles. Tu vas l'escalader de biais vers la droite, en t'éloignant des rebelles qui vont sans doute viser le village en haut. À toi.
— Entendu.
— Je te prendrai en sphère sur la pente. Allez, blinde-toi contre les fréquences PANIC. À toi.
— Compris. Escaladant de biais vers la droite jusqu'à ton arrivée. Prêt. À toi.
Vris lança à son ordinateur:
— Rad, balance la fréquence PANIC à faible dose. Augmente-la au fur et à mesure jusqu'au max quand je crierai 'Courez!'.
!! Balancé, ponctua l'ordinateur.
— Rad, traduit en direct ce que je vais dire en langue afghane, avec un accent étranger est-européen,» poursuivit Vris. « Tonal: impératif. Fort volume. Mais tout d'abord, simulation friture radio puis 1 mnT de musique sur radio locale Afghane. Tu laisseras la friture sous ma voix. Tiens bon Ismir, c'est parti. Rad, balance la friture et la radio.»
Intense friture. Une émission de musique arabe de très mauvaise qualité emplit soudain la pièce, bientôt coupée.

> — REBELLES! JE SUIS UN AMI QUI VOUS PARLE PAR LA RADIO DE L'ORDINATEUR. JE SUIS CELUI QUI VOUS A PERMIS D'OBTENIR CETTE MACHINE.

Les rebelles pointèrent précipitamment leurs armes sur l'ordinateur. Le chef s'était dressé d'un bond, le revolver à la main.

> — LA FERME OU VOUS VOUS TROUVEZ VA ÊTRE BOMBARDÉE DANS 34 MINUTES EXACTEMENT. C'EST UN NOUVEAU TYPE DE BOMBE. VOUS DEVEZ VOUS TROUVER À 2 KILOMÈTRES DE LA FERME POUR ÊTRE SAINS ET SAUFS ET Y RESTER 40 MINUTES APRES L'EXPLOSION. COUREZ VERS LE HAUT DE LA MONTAGNE ET LA GAUCHE. SUR LE PLATEAU VOUS SEREZ PROTÉGÉS. N'ALLEZ PAS VERS LA VILLE. PARTEZ IMMÉDIATEMENT.

Une panique atroce s'empara des rebelles. Certains sortirent en courant.

> — PARTEZ IMMÉDIATEMENT. COUREZ.

La voix fut coupée et la musique reprit.
— Sortons d'ici,» cria le chef à ceux qui restaient, tout en s'élançant dehors. Il se retourna pour lancer à un jeune: «Toi! Reste-là avec le spécialiste.»
Le jeune rebelle, atterré et en sueur, regarda son chef se ruer dans la nuit vers le haut de la montagne et soudain s'élança dehors.
Ismir prit la pente de biais par la droite en s'éloignant des rebelles. Deux coups de feu retentirent près de lui. Il s'aplatit par terre. Un troisième claqua près de sa tête. Deux autres encore, dans une autre direction. Un coup d'œil lui montra que le chef qui l'avait visé avait repris la fuite. Il se releva. Sur la gauche, le jeune rebelle s'enfuyait en tenant son bras; il avait dû être touché.

...

— Bien Rad. Opération parfaitement réussie.

!! Sphère de Rudder sur écran syg passant la frontière afghane au Nord-Est» annonça Rad, l'ordinateur de Vris. «Changement de direction. Pointe vers Mazari-Sharif. Décélération. Vitesse stabilisée. Arrivera sur objectif à 1h48T.

— Les salops! En avance sur leur horaire. Heureusement qu'on a prévu un peu large. Rad, démarre notre simulation syg des 9 sapiens dans la pièce.

!! C'est fait. Problème: Ismir se trouvera sur le trajet de la sphère de Rudder.

— Oh! On va le chercher tout de suite. Il y aura plus d'une anomalie dans la nuit—quel enfer! Rad, augmente le camouflage tempête jusqu'à masquer le rayon transporteur Sygmat. Voilà: une belle petite tempête descend de la montagne! Ismir ne va pas comprendre.

!! En position au dessus d'Ismir. Sas ouvert. Rayon Sygmat déployé.

Vris quitta l'écran syg pour aller vers le sas et se pencha pour accueillir Ismir qui était soulevé par le rayon.

— Ça va?

Il lui attrapa la main bien que ce soit inutile.

— Oh, là là! Bizarre cette tempête sans une goutte d'eau! Est-ce qu'elle ne serait pas artificielle par hasard?!

— Ah, tu en verras d'autres!

!! Vris, je glisse doucement vers l'Ouest en gardant le camouflage tempête.

— Parfait, Rad. D'ailleurs, utilise ton mouvement pour masquer le jeune rebelle blessé à la vue des autres. Ça lui sera certainement utile.

!! Sphère de Rudder ici dans 7mnT. Suis en position d'enregistrement vidéo large spectre. Ai les rebelles et la ferme dans le champ.

— Viens vers le panavision,» dit Vris à Ismir. « Rad, allume l'écran arrière.

!! J'avais entendu. Cependant, comment l'exor de Rudder peut-il utiliser du TTID sur des sapiens? Comment peut-il contourner les règles absolues interdisant de mettre en danger un sapiens?» demanda Rad.

— J'aimerais bien savoir aussi. Demande à Sphinx de se mettre à l'écoute de l'équipage de Rudder et de relayer toute conversation ici.

— Sphinx, c'est l'exor de qui?» demanda Ismir.

— C'est un exor mutant, aux capacités exceptionnelles. Il rend Rad jaloux.

!! La jalousie est réservée aux sapiens. Moi, exor Rad, je ne suis pas jaloux de Sphinx: j'apprends de Sphinx.

— Whoo! murmura Ismir interloqué.

!!! ... à la ferme dans 5mn10,» disait l'exor de Rudder, relayé par le super-ordinateur Sphinx. Puis la voix sophistiquée de Sphinx annonça, à-travers le système son de Rad:

!!!! Sphère de Rudder opérée par l'exor de secours. Exor habituel déconnecté après avoir refusé d'utiliser le TTID sur des sapiens. L'exor de secours n'a pas

de capacités d'analyse sémantique complexe. Niveau d'intelligence: similaire aux unités de gestion. Deux hommes: Rudder et Mizdri identifiés. Deux femmes à bord, signatures vocales non-identifiées.»
— Ils ont deux femmes avec eux qui ne sont pas du PPE!!» explosa Vris.

Ils entendirent alors la conversation entre Rudder et son exor:
— Nous allons procéder à une opération d'assainissement de la maison; les rebelles nous l'ont demandé; ES, prépare un nuage de TTID» dit Rudder avec tact, en essayant d'induire en erreur l'exor de secours.
!!! Utilisation du TTID sur une maison avec sapiens et/ou animaux à l'intérieur n'est pas permise par la loi. Détection de neuf sapiens dans la maison.
— C'est une nouvelle découverte: le TTID tue tous les insectes.
!!! Obligation d'avoir les portes et les fenêtres closes. L'inhalation de la poudre est dangereuse pour les sapiens.
— Ils sont au courant, je leur ai dit; pas de problème. Tu saupoudres à large spectre, en passant au-dessus de la maison. Démarre 30 mètres avant et finit 30 mètres après.
!!! Dans 3,54 mnT.
3-2-1-0! Assainissement en cours... ...Fini.
— C'est parfait,» lança Rudder en jubilant. «Maintenant, prend 100 mètres d'altitude, fais un demi-tour et repasse au-dessus de la maison suivant la même ligne. Je veux voir si ça a été bien fait.»
!!! Elévation et demi-tour effectués. J'arrive à nouveau sur la maison. Moins 1,10 mnT.
— Ralentis en arrivant. Je veux leur envoyer un petit cadeau. Oui, je vois la poudre phosphorescente. Travail impeccable! Maintenant, ouvre le sas.»
Rudder attendit que sa sphère se soit suffisamment éloignée de la ferme. Puis il sortit vivement son lasergun et tira.
— Accélère!» cria-t-il simultanément à son exor.

Un embrasement vert, gigantesque, illumina la montagne.

1. VOGAGE EN ENFER

— Mais enfin, cessez de m'interrompre! Laissez-moi présenter les choses,» lança Erdoes en riant au petit groupe d'étudiants post-doctorat du PPE qu'il avait rassemblés. « N'ayez crainte, vous aurez tout le loisir de vous exprimer par la suite... Nous avions donc ensemencé le maximum de diversité génétique sur Trisorbe. Au dernier rapport pulsit, l'indice d'évolution de la planète est passé à 230...» Explosions de voix, cris d'admiration.

—... L'indice poursuit donc sa progression exponentielle tandis que le réseau de communication augmente la sphère d'influence de la culture dominante sur la planète, les gens étant fascinés par sa technologie. Il va sans dire que le système économique global est actuellement de type E4, soit basé sur l'expansion obligatoire, avec un système monétaire déjà largement virtuel. Leurs exors n'ont encore qu'une capacité d'un cent millième de Ros...»

Un fou rire traversa tout le groupe par vagues. Des plaisanteries fusèrent.

—.. et leurs robots sont unifonctionnels...

— Attendez,» intervint Niels, «sur Karg nous avons changé d'unités deux fois. Lorsque nous avons atteint une mémoire de 1 million de Rods nous sommes passés du Rod au Ron; puis, à 1 million de Rons, du Ron au Ros. D'après mes calculs, il nous a fallu 4,5 fois plus de temps pour réaliser le premier saut. Au Ron, notre indice d'évolution était de 43; et à ce même cap, les Trisorbiens atteignaient 196. Ce n'est qu'après que nous avons battu le second record de l'indice d'évolution d'Unikarg, soit 118, comme vous le savez, et d'ailleurs...

— Alors où est le fond du problème?» coupa Xerna en fixant son attention sur Erdoes. « Vous ne nous avez pas conviés, je suppose, pour célébrer Trisorbe atteignant bientôt les 250! Aux 200, tous les pulsits du PPE proclamaient que nous avions atteint notre but à long-terme!

Erdoes les regarda tous gravement:

— Mes amis, sur Trisorbe, l'analyse de certains facteurs tend à montrer que nous serions au contraire sur le point d'échouer.

Tous attendirent, les visages crispés par un étonnement perplexe.

— Les prospectives actuelles indiquent que le système économique E4 va continuer à s'étendre à toute la planète... selon un indice d'expansion G21, et qu'il atteindra sa limite d'expansion dans près de 4,5 années galactiques, soit un peu plus d'une génération locale. Selon mes calculs, à ce point, 80% des cultures diverses auront passé le seuil de l'absorption sans retour. De plus, du fait de la surpopulation, les besoins dépasseront les ressources planétaires, même avec les adjuvants techniques; enfin, la moitié de la planète étant déjà unifiée, le niveau de vie général commencera à chuter dramatiquement.

«Jusque là, voici mes pronostics: effondrement progressif des héritages culturels, production de guerres civiles et de régimes totalitaires éphémères, puis stabilisation dans le régime politique dominant; puis uniformisation et conformance à une unique culture planétaire, avec un système global de contrôle hautement réglementé et complètement policé. Après: courbe décroissante de l'indice d'évolution, entrée très probable dans la ligue galactique Unikargienne, ce qui amènera l'effondrement à moyen terme de l'indice de Trisorbe, la précipitant très probablement à long terme jusqu'au niveau lamentable de celui d'Unikarg.

— Ce qui signifie qu'après l'effervescence momentanée due au choc avec la culture galactique, Trisorbe se stabilisera au modeste 36 qui est notre lot?!

— Peut-être pire! Rappelez-vous que c'est grâce au stimulus des planètes expérimentales que nous sommes remontés du sinistre 24.

— L'enfer paie!

— C'est tellement ironique: Les mondes désordonnés continuent à se rêver un paradis statique, alors que pour nous, englués dans des mondes statiques, le paradis serait forcément chaotique!

— Y a-t-il des sages de Trisorbe qui ont eu cette intuition..?

— Quelques poètes et écrivains, oui, reprit Erdoes après ces remarques pertinentes. Ils ont compris le concept de chaos créateur. Mais ceux-là ne se référaient pas à un paradis bien sûr. Toutes les grandes religions de Trisorbe visent l'absolu en soi, statique et éternel. Nous avons cependant quelques larges systèmes de pensée qui font exception: la République athénienne, en Grèce, qui s'opposa d'ailleurs farouchement au système atlantéen, fixé et hiérarchique. Aussi, **l'extraordinaire Philosophie des Transformations, de la Chine antique, qui est une philosophie d'un monde en mouvement, comme vous le savez tous.** Malheureusement, même si nous l'honorons comme une des perles des mondes expérimentaux, Unikarg est trop statique pour que nous puissions en faire l'essai sur nos mondes... Notre seule opportunité pour l'expérimenter, c'est lors de missions sur les mondex. Enfin, il y a aussi toutes les religions des forces de la nature – shamanismes, panthéismes, et polythéismes.

« La balance des forces sur Trisorbe favorise déjà l'uniformisation. Je pense qu'il y a de fortes poussées vers l'installation d'un ordre global qui étouffe le différent, le divergent, et qui supprime le désordre dynamique et créatif. Mais n'oublions pas que par le passé, c'est l'objectif d'atteindre ce type d'ordre qui a généré les grandes civilisations; c'est grâce à une distanciation des forces brutes et animales que les sapiens ont développé leur conscience de soi, et la prescience de l'immensité de l'univers. Trisorbe est à un croisement fatal de son évolution, où un système d'ordre peut tuer toute divergence et supprimer les germes d'une évolution future.

Erdoes s'arrêta un instant. Personne ne prit la parole.

— Bien, dit-il d'une voix posée. Vous êtes tous passés par les Collèges du Chaos sur Unikarg, avec des stages sur une planète expérimentale autre que Trisorbe. Vous avez été sélectionnés parce que, en dehors des qualités requises, vous ne connaissez pas Trisorbe par immersion. Comme il vous a été indiqué, la phase de préparation prendra au maximum quatre rans. À la suite de quoi, vous aurez un ran pour vous relaxer et vous centrer. La mission est de longueur indéterminée, ce sera à vous d'en décider. Quant à la rémunération, disons qu'elle a toutes les chances d'être nulle, comme il était clairement stipulé, vos frais étant pris en charge cependant.

Erdoes les regarda un à un intensément, sa voix d'une extrême gravité:

— Comprenez bien qu'il s'agit là d'une mission à haut risque: chacun d'entre vous sera seul; sans aucune protection. Vous n'emporterez rien d'Unikarg, aucun outil high-tech, rien. Vous serez livrés à vous-même, comme n'importe quel Trisorbien. Cela constitue une prise de responsabilité totale de votre part. Il y a cependant une contrepartie: vous aurez le contrôle total de votre mission; c'est vous qui allez la concevoir et la planifier, et qui la gérerez au fur et à mesure. Si l'un d'entre vous ne veut pas s'engager, vous avez jusqu'à la première session de demain pour vous retirer.

« Le programme ici: tout d'abord une étude hypno-senso-mnémonique intense de la planète. Vous connaissez bien sûr certains domaines à fond, que vous avez déjà étudiés, mais il s'agit de vous remettre en mémoire la situation présente sous ses multiples aspects. Parallèlement, vous aurez une mise en forme physique et mentale pour affronter le rythme plus rapide de Trisorbe. Rappelons que Trisorbe a à peu près l'atmosphère et la végétation de Véra, et un jour six fois plus court que le ran galactique, quatre fois plus court que le jour de Kerriak. Après cette première phase, qui durera 12 joursT, nous nous retrouverons pour un long Brainstorm sur toutes ces informations, dirigé vers l'intuition et l'appréhension de vos missions respectives. Le temps qu'il faudra. À la suite de quoi vous choisirez votre propre mission, élaborerez vos plans d'immersion, et déciderez des données particulières dont vous avez besoin, comme l'apprentissage de langues ou la connaissance de certaines cultures. En dernier lieu, nous déciderons du plan de communication le plus adéquat. Ah! Un dernier point: dès demain, nous nous calerons sur le cycle temporel de Trisorbe. L'exor se chargera de ponctuer les jours et les nuits, les heures de repas et de sommeil. De même, nous commencerons avec 30% d'aliments naturels, pour finir vers 90%.

Cris et exclamations de joie...

— Si, si, un régime de luxe obligatoire: vous n'aurez là-bas aucun additif alimentaire. En fin de quart, banquet local: on vous servira les synths les plus sophistiqués de la galaxie.

Au milieu des rires qui s'étaient déchaînés, Erdoes leur fit un signe entendu, et s'esquiva.

2. DÉS/ORDRE

Shari et Vris, membres de la Commission du PPE ou Plan des Planètes Expérimentales, venaient de faire le tour de l'étonnant complexe d'Erdoes, un ponte de la Commission, sur la planète Kerriak. Comme ils s'y étaient attendus, chaque personne rencontrée jurait n'avoir eu aucune connaissance des plans nourris par le grand savant, mis à part le fait qu'il avait eu des étudiants en stage pendant cinq rans. Shari relaya les ordres du Bureau du PPE, que tous les assistants d'Erdoes, sauf ses étudiants doctorants, quittent le complexe.

Shari et Vris avaient été dépêchés par le Bureau en toute urgence pour enquêter sur la disparition inexpliquée et totalement illégale d'Erdoes. Selon le peu qu'ils en savaient au siège du PPE, Erdoes était parti pour la planète Trisorbe avec sept jeunes diplômés en doctorat des Collèges du Chaos qui n'étaient pas ses étudiants habituels. Le bureau du PPE avait sélectionné Shari parce que, en tant qu'expert en systèmes sémantiques, tout comme Erdoes, elle serait la plus capable d'espionner et de comprendre ses données informatiques.

Ils avaient voulu lui imposer un SupTech, un ingénieur en systèmes exors, informatiques et technologiques, mais elle avait insisté sur le fait qu'elle ne ferait équipe qu'avec SupTech Vris, un ami de longue date, avec qui elle était déjà partie en mission. Ensuite, il avait fallu obtenir d'Utar, Directeur Général du PPE, et de Rudder, le sous-directeur, qu'elle serait l'unique décisionnaire dans tous les aspects cette mission, sans avoir à en référer au PPE. Les tractations avaient été dures, particulièrement avec Rudder, mais son inflexibilité avait payé, lui permettant d'ailleurs d'augmenter leur rétribution.

Sead, le régisseur des biens immobiliers du PPE sur Kerriak, avait reçu l'ordre de quitter son bureau de la capitale et de se mettre à leur disposition dès leur arrivée. En explorant le complexe, ils avaient découvert un antique magnétophone trisorbien analogique trônant sur une table dans la grande salle de meeting, avec des traces évidentes que des réunions avaient eu lieu là. Une série de bandes, intitulées Brainstorm/BS et numérotées, était posées sur une étagère. Enclenchant dans le magnéto la bande 'Brainstorm – pré-session', Shari, Vris et Sead avaient eu la surprise d'entendre le discours de bienvenue d'Erdoes à ceux et celles qu'il avait appelé ses 'agents' pour une mission à haut risque sur Trisorbe, la plus évoluée des planètes expérimentales.

Le délai donné aux assistants pour leur départ étant dépassé, Shari demanda à Sead d'aller vérifier qui était encore présent dans le complexe, puis de revenir l'informer dans le bureau d'Erdoes, dans lequel elle était en train d'installer son exor et ses affaires de bureau. Et le voici qui justement revenait et entrait.

Vris s'excusa, laissant entendre qu'il voulait discuter avec les étudiants à propos des machines du complexe, et partit.

— Les assistants d'Erdoes ont tous quitté le complexe en sphère il y a dix monis,» déclara Sead. « Ils vont séjourner au siège du PPE sur Nazra, comme cela leur a été recommandé, sauf SupTech Dian et le régisseur Thyin qui ont décidé de passer les prochains rans dans un centre de loisir, en attendant qu'on leur permette de revenir à leur poste. Il ne reste donc plus ici que les cinq doctorants d'Erdoes installés dans l'aile Est et occupés par leurs propres travaux. Cette aile étant complètement indépendante, avec une Unité de Gestion séparée, j'ai bloqué leur accès à cette partie du complexe.

— Voilà qui est parfait. Et bien sûr, rien de nouveau? Ils soutiennent encore qu'ils pensaient qu'Erdoes était parti sur Nazra avec des étudiants en stage?»

— C'est tout à fait cela.

— On ne sait d'ailleurs pas comment le Bureau du PPE a été mis au courant du départ d'Erdoes pour Trisorbe avec sept agents des Collèges du Chaos...» continua Shari pour elle-même.

« Tu as entendu la pré-session de Brainstorm, qu'est-ce que tu en penses?

— C'est comme s'il avait voulu les conduire au-delà de leurs capacités en leur imposant un apprentissage intensif et en modifiant complètement leurs rythmes vitaux, répondit Sead.

— Oui. Il les a forcés à entrer dans un état de conscience particulier. Dans quel but véritable? C'est la question que je me pose. En tous cas, pour comprendre leurs motivations et leurs objectifs, j'ai l'intuition que je devrais me placer dans les mêmes conditions et essayer de recréer le même état.. que je me soumette à la même cassure de rythme.

Elle reprit sur un ton plus affirmé:

« J'ai décidé de me caler comme ils l'ont fait sur le temps de Trisorbe et d'écouter toutes les sessions de BS au même rythme qu'elles ont été produites, une par matinée de Trisorbe.

— Je pensais justement te préparer des extraits des Brainstorms avec l'exor...» commença Sead.

— Pas la peine,» le coupa Shari. «Je ne crois pas qu'il faille utiliser l'exor pour des analyses globales ou des recherches de thèmes. Il faut que j'écoute leurs débats dans le détail. Un détail peut se révéler plus significatif à un intuitif que tout un discours. J'utiliserai l'exor ensuite pour analyser au fur et à mesure les éléments d'informations que j'aurai sélectionnés. En bref, si j'applique la méthode d'Erdoes, j'aurai bien plus de chances de comprendre ses processus mentaux et donc ses intentions.

— C'est certainement une bonne stratégie. Je dois mentionner aussi que j'ai retrouvé ses commandes et comptes dans la mémoire de l'Unité de Gestion. Bien sûr, rien que des éléments triviaux; rien qui puisse nous mettre sur leur piste. Tu te rends compte, il a fait venir des nourritures naturelles des planètes expérimentales!
— Tu as donc le détail?
— Le détail des commandes, oui — à ces prix-là les fournisseurs du PPE détaillent! Et aussi de leurs menus; leur régime a été concocté par analyse diététique et tous les calculs sont sur un tableau qui suit les commandes.
— Eh bien, je vais me faire servir exactement le même menu! L'exor se chargera de tout, y compris de me caler sur les journées de Trisorbe, heure GMT de Greenwich. Il a calculé qu'au début du deuxième quart, il sera 6 heures du matin sur Trisorbe. J'aurai essayé de dormir un peu, et à 7 heuresT, il me réveillera. À 9 heuresT, chaque matin, j'écouterai leur session de BS au rythme où elle s'est passée. Pour les BS, je vais m'installer dans la pièce de réunion où ils ont eu lieu. Bizarre, non, ce magnéto analogique trisorbien? Pourquoi n'a-t-il pas simplement utilisé son exor?
— Je ne comprends pas non plus. À moins que ce soit encore un moyen de les placer dans les conditions les plus dures de Trisorbe. D’ailleurs il leur avait installé dans l'aile Ouest où ils habitaient une reproduction exacte de l'environnement socio-culturel de cette planète. Apparemment, ils ont même fait leur cuisine eux-mêmes sur des appareillages trisorbiens: j'en ai trouvé des traces.
— Ah bon! Ça c'est trop drôle! Il ne laisse rien au hasard!! Sûr que je n'irai pas jusque là.. l'exor continuera à préparer mes repas.
— Donc je laisse la salle de réunion en l'état.
— Oui, j’y installerai un terminal de mon EBS: je vais rentrer leurs signatures vocales, comme ça il me fournira les noms des intervenants et leurs photos au fur et à mesure.

Shari était maintenant installée dans le bureau d'Erdoes: un choix évident car elle voulait tirer le maximum d'informations de l'ordinateur personnel d'Erdoes. Une fenêtre donnait sur le parc privé; sur Unikarg, c’était tout ce qu’il y avait de plus étonnant. S'étant approchée de la fenêtre, elle laissa échapper un cri d'admiration lorsqu'elle s'aperçut qu'elle possédait un dispositif d'ouverture.
— Tu as vu ça!!» lança-t-elle à Sead. « Ouvre la fenêtre!» ordonna-t-elle à l'Unité de Gestion.
!! Ouverture effectuée. Vous pouvez modifier la surface d'ouverture à l'aide du bouton vert, dit la voix neutre et déférente de l’unité robotique qui sortait de nulle part.

— Merci de me laisser TANT de liberté!» lança-t-elle en ouvrant la fenêtre au maximum. « Divin!» dit-elle en humant l'air chargé de senteurs du parc baigné de soleil. « C'est bizarre, il y a quelque chose d'indéfinissable qui fait que ça ressemble plus à un parc des mondex qu'à un espace loisirs.. peut-être parce que le ciel n'est pas encombré de tours.»

Au-delà du complexe s'étendait un grand terrain alloué au PPE, ancien bloc d'entrepôts réutilisés, mais dont la plus grande partie était désaffectée, enchevêtrement de broussailles entre des plaques de plasta.

— As-tu remarqué que toutes les fenêtres du complexe donnent sur l'intérieur? Ingénieux ce bâtiment en U.

— Oui. On pourrait oublier l'existence des blocs-troddi qui s'étalent dans les trois autres directions. Par ailleurs, j'ai maintenant effectué toutes les vérifications et analyses qu'il était dans mes possibilités de faire. Est-ce que je dois considérer ma mission comme terminée?

— Non, reste dans le complexe. Fais ce que tu veux mais garde un œil global sur tout. Vris et moi nous risquons d'être trop absorbés dans nos enquêtes respectives.

— Très bien. Je vais préparer la pièce pour les Brainstorms, répondit Sead visiblement heureux.

Elle revint s'asseoir dans le large fauteuil, face à l'écran de l'exor d'Erdoes: un EBS comme le sien, à réseau neuronal structurel, exor développé par le PPE, et que l'on retrouvait chez tous ses membres.

Elle activa l'exor d'Erdoes, sans aucun doute le Central du complexe, et s'attaqua à la consultation des fichiers concernant les sept sapiens sélectionnés. Des humains, tous, de type Ori 12. Forcément, les différences physiologiques étaient à peine décelables pour la science actuelle de Trisorbe. Comprendre ces différences auraient fait muter leurs connaissances biologiques et génétiques.

Evidemment, aucun des critères de sélection n'apparaissait dans ces fichiers. Cela devait se trouver ailleurs. Shari demanda à l'exor une analyse des similarités dans ces descriptions. Comme elle s'y attendait, seuls les éléments qu'elle avait déjà notés apparurent sur l'écran: comme tous les doctorants des Collèges du Chaos du PPE, ils avaient fait leur stage de thèse sur une planète expérimentale. Haut niveau de créativité, mais relativement normal pour des jeunes sortant des Collèges du Chaos. Et leur éthique: axée sur les objectifs globaux—*intéressant qu'Erdoes ait pensé à ça!*Index d'empathie élevé, situé entre 80 et 91...

91!? Comment est-ce possible? Et qui a cet index? Serrone.

...Et dans les similarités partielles: trois (seulement trois!) avaient déjà effectué des missions rémunérées sur les mondex.

Pour l'instant, ces choix sont sensés, sauf leur inexpérience des missions... Trop sensés pour un Erdoes. Voyons leurs stages sur les mondex. Tous en dessous d'un an-K, sauf Xerna, deux ans-K! C'est long!.. Xerna? Ah oui, celle qui a fait sa thèse sur... 'Patterns d'interférences entre émotions et intellect chez les acteurs-nomades Ott de Kiarrou'.

Ah, les thèses... analyse de similarités... Néant. Voyons...

'La sophistique de l'influence par l'accord profond et l'empathie, dans la philosophie des transformations.' Ah, ça c'est bizarre! Ce Niels n'a pas étudié sur Trisorbe, mais sa thèse porte sur la philosophie de Trisorbe...

'Comme vous le savez tous'... La phrase enregistrée de la pré-session de Brainstorm redéfilait dans sa tête avec la voix d'Erdoes: 'la philosophie des transformations.. qui est une philosophie d'un monde en mouvement, comme vous le savez tous', reprit le déroulement mental, avec des intonations plus précises. Donc c'est un intérêt qu'ils partagent tous! Passionnant!

Elle allait poser à l'exor une autre question, quand une phrase se forma spontanément dans sa tête: 'D'ailleurs on n'a même pas réussi à empêcher les prédateurs et pirates en tous genres de sévir sur les planètes expérimentales!'

Elle s'étonna de cette pensée de rage impuissante qui venait de surgir en elle et qui ne semblait absolument pas connectée à la suite d'idées. Elle essaya de recomposer le déroulement chronologique de sa pensée:

> **'..qui est une philosophie d'un monde en mouvement, comme vous le savez tous... d'ailleurs on n'a même pas réussi à empêcher les prédateurs et pirates en tous genres de sévir sur les planètes expérimentales.'**

D'ailleurs! d'ailleurs quoi?

Intriguée par cette collision dont elle ne comprenait pas la teneur, elle demanda à l'EBS de procéder à une COMP, une analyse sémantique comparative des deux phrases, en vocal/écran.

Erdoes a forcément augmenté la base de données de son EBS. Un autre expert en sémantique chaotique... je me réserve des surprises! En fait, ça s'appelle espionner l'univers mental d'un concurrent! N'empêche que ça m'aurait plu de diriger une mission sur Trisorbe...

Et d'ailleurs, qu'est-ce que j'aurais fait? Mais oui, comment aurais-je procédé? Mettons-nous à sa place...

Ça y est, trop de pistes à la fois.. plus tard...

Elle inspecta l'écran, qu'elle regardait d'ailleurs sans le voir depuis plusieurs monis.

— Passe à l'analyse de la deuxième proposition, ordonna t'elle à l'exor.

!! LES PREDATEURS ET PIRATES EN TOUS GENRES DE SEVIR SUR LES PLANETES EXPERIMENTALES.

De la présence de pirates, prédateur se comprend métaphoriquement.
pirates —> // (idem) *planètes expérimentales —> //*
prédateurs —> //

!! ANALYSE SEMANTIQUE COMPARATIVE. RECHERCHE D'ANALOGIES 1

PLANETES EXPERIMENTALES: *COMPORTEMENTS ILLEGAUX.*

LOI DE NON-INTERFERENCE

Le Plan des Planètes Expérimentales (PPE) est un ensemble de lois très strictes, basé sur la Loi de non-interférence, qui stipule:

1. L'interdiction, pour tout sapiens ou groupe des MONDES CONSENSUELS D'UNIKARG, de donner, directement ou non, ou de laisser après son passage — par toute forme de communication ou d'événement que ce soit — des informations ou des artefacts permettant aux habitants d'une **planète expérimentale** (ou *mondex*) d'inférer l'existence de civilisations intelligentes extérieures au mondex concerné.
2. L'interdiction, pour toute forme de véhicule et de transport, de pénétrer dans le périmètre spatial sécurisé d'un mondex. Ce périmètre est défini en fonction du développement de chaque mondex et est délimité par l'enceinte sphérique d'énergie syg, nommée la *Barrière syg*, entourant chaque mondex.
3. L'interdiction, pour tout sapiens ou groupe, de prendre, acheter, échanger, ou analyser, tout objet, naturel ou non, des mondex, en dehors de la juridiction exceptionnelle de la Commission du PPE, Organe de Recherche et de Développement du Plan des *Planètes Expérimentales*.
4. L'interdiction de causer, à quelque distance que ce soit, des perturbations physiques ou psychiques pouvant engendrer des répercussions sur l'un des mondex. Cette loi s'applique aux inventions présentes et futures qui doivent être approuvées par le Bureau de Vigilance des Téléperturbations du PPE.

PLAN DE PROTECTION. 2. APPLICATIONS

La loi de non-interférence rend impossible la mise en place d'un système efficace en vue de gérer la loi. Tout dôme énergétique sygmat ou relais policiers trop rapprochés signaleraient notre présence aux *planètes expérimentales* plus clairement que les fraudeurs actuels. La lutte contre la fraude utilise des méthodes de détection indirecte.

Les catégories de fraudeurs ayant été interpellés sont:
- les trafiquants de la Ligue Extra-Consensuelle dite des **Pirates**-exos.

- les affiliés des groupes de pression tels que: NO MORE HELL, DROIT À L'INFORMATION.
- des touristes invétérés adonnés aux sensations fortes.

!! RECHERCHE D'ANALOGIES 2.

opposé à
monde en mouvement =)(= monde statique

contient
monde statique (o société statique

SOC **Une <u>société trop organisée</u> (excès d'ordre) devient statique.**
JE **Dans un monde statique, le désordre est condensé dans des poches de crime organisé d'une extrême violence.**

Shari fut soudain saisie par ce qu'elle lisait. *Ah, ça c'est du Erdoes!* Elle positionna le syg-pointer sur le nom, tentant d'ouvrir le fichier codé JE, mais rien ne se passa. Elle énonça la référence, rien. *Erdoes a donc pris soin de protéger l'accès à ses données.*

Simultanément, l'exor poursuivait son analyse.

---

opposé à
monde statique =)(= monde naturel
désordre —> // (idem)

JE
Dans un monde naturel | le désordre | montre | la liberté de l'être
| la proportion de désordre | | les degrés de liberté

Quelle drôle de façon d'écrire une modification de la proposition initiale! pensa Shari.

---

planètes expérimentales —> //
désordre —> // désordre =)(= ordre

JE **Les planètes expérimentales (désordre prédominant) sont le terrain privilégié de l'analyse des interactions particulières entre l'ordre et le désordre.**

À ce niveau-là, il n'y a plus que du JE.

JE? E comme Erdoes. Journal d'Erdoes! Ah, Ah!

JE
Le champ d'ordre | a pour effet | de structurer le champ du désordre
| est responsable |

Ainsi l'ordre se construit à partir du désordre; il a autant besoin du désordre que le feu de matières combustibles.

Conséquence ultime

==>. **| Otez le désordre et l'ordre ne peut plus être créé.**
| (voir philosophie des transformations)

Ah, ça! de nouveaux relateurs logiques! Conséquence ultime!! ah, ah!!

!! ANALYSE COMPARATIVE. PALIER DE RÉPONSE 1

entraîne
a besoin de = nécessite | —> | attiré par
planète expérimentale = monde naturel
monde statique (o société statique

---

ordre	**nécessite** attiré par	**désordre**
monde statique	nécessite attiré par	monde naturel en mouvement
(excès d'ordre)		(désordre prédominant)
(o		//
les poches de crime organisé	nécessitent attirés par	monde naturel
		(o
les poches de crime organisé	nécessitent attirés par	degrés de liberté

Shari exulta. *Ah, Ah! je vois!*
— Stoppe l'analyse un moment. *Crée un fichier Journal nommé JoS. Entrée:*

La raison du crime organisé est la nécessité d'un degré de désordre dans la société, c'est-à-dire de degrés de liberté chez l'individu.

!!...
— Fin d'entrée. Poursuis ton analyse.
!! JoS déjà utilisé. Six lettres minimum.
— Bon, code à créer: Jour-Sh.
!! Sans problème. Voulez-vous le verrouiller?
— Oui, bien sûr.
Elle espéra tout d'un coup entrevoir le processus de verrouillage.
!!...

— Qu'est-ce qu'il se passe?
!! Attente du code de verrouillage.
— Voyons.. 'Explorer'.
Ça alors! son exor ne coupe pas la parole. Quelle merveille!
!! Le fichier Jour-Sh est-il accessible à l'analyse interne?
— Oui.
!! L'abréviation sur écran sera JS.
— Ouvre Jour-Er.
!! Désolé. Fichier désiré verrouillé. Détection d'une première manœuvre de piratage. Signature vocale enregistrée. Signature psychique enregistrée. À la troisième tentative, toute interaction avec le Central et avec l'Unité de Gestion cessera. Quel est votre nom?
— Shari Oxah Tesin.
!! Nom connu. Signatures conformes. Accès préférentiel Niveau-3. Cependant, le fichier désiré reste verrouillé et le piratage en ce sens sujet aux sanctions susdites. Suite de l'analyse.

Erdoes a prévu un piratage possible!?

!! <u>ANALYSE COMPARATIVE. PALIER DE RÉPONSE 2</u>

monde statique (o (contient) poches de crime organisé
société trop organisée —> (entraîne/devient) statique.

Dans une société trop organisée —> le crime est trop organisé.

— Attends! Modification de la dernière assomption. Supprime trop du deuxième terme. Non, en fait, remplace trop par excessivement, partout.

!! **Dans une société excessivement organisée —> le crime est excessivement organisé.**

<u>ANALYSE COMPARATIVE. PALIER DE RÉPONSE 3</u>

DICT organisé-3 = ordonné
excès d'ordre —> crime organisé

Le champ d'ordre / structure / le champ du désordre
Le champ du crime | organisé | / structure / le champ du désordre
| ordonné |
Le crime organisé / structure / le monde | en mouvement
| naturel
Le crime organisé / structure / les planètes expérimentales

— Ah, non! il ne manquerait plus que ça! Modification des deux dernières assomptions. Insère la proposition initiale: « Il est à craindre que ».

> *Entrée Journal:*
> Il est à craindre que l'organisation des pirates-exos ait une influence structurante sur les planètes expérimentales, et ceci d'autant plus que l'organisation consensuelle se refuse à avoir une influence, en vertu de la loi de non-interférence.
>
> *Journal, Sub-fichier: Questions.*
> Comment le désordre peut-il se protéger d'un excès d'ordre – généré tant par les pirates-exos que par les structures de gestion?
> *Ferme Sub, Ferme JS.*

La suite de l'analyse?
!! Première analyse finie. Je poursuis avec la première Entrée JS:

Du crime organisé / la raison est / la nécessité | d'un (degré de) désordre dans la société
| de degrés de liberté chez l'individu.

De l'ordre / la raison est / la nécessité | d'un degré de désordre

---

!! Redondance: l'analyse est finie.

> — *Entrée Journal:*
> Et inversement:
> Du désordre, la raison est, la nécessité d'un degré d'ordre. *Ferme JS*.

Nous voici donc dans la logique de la philosophie des transformations.

!! J'intègre la nouvelle proposition: **Désordre nécessite ordre.** Faut-il procéder à l'analyse du renversement des termes?» demanda l'exor.
— Non, de cette façon trop simple, ça n'aboutira à rien de plus.
!! Alors l'analyse est finie.
— Pas mal! Mémorise les paliers de réponse; crée le fichier *DES/ORDRE.* Bon, je vais faire un tour d'horizon.
!! Faire un tour d'horizon, au sens métaphorique?
— Plan métaphorique ET plan objectif! Bonsoir!
!! Mes hommages, madame.
— 'Mes hommages madame!' d'où est-ce qu'il sort ça?
!! 'Il'? Précisez le sujet.

3. PIRATAGE

Shari, assise de nouveau dans le bureau d'Erdoes, devant son exor, vit un voyant lumineux tamisé pulser doucement sur le telcom interne, à côté du nom d'Eshi. Elle en déduisit que Vris, qui s'était octroyé le bureau du secrétaire d'Erdoes, désirait lui parler.

Tout est géré dans le sens de la non-intrusion, pensa-t-elle. *Le respect des états de créativité et d'absorption. La compréhension qu'en interrompant brusquement une suite d'idées, une idée géniale peut être perdue sans aucun espoir de jamais retrouver la constellation de sens convergente, le faisceau intuitif, qui y menait.* Elle enclencha le telcom.

— J'ai du nouveau, mais il faut que tu viennes, fit la voix de Vris.

— J'arrive.

— Bon, tout d'abord: ici on peut parler sans problème, j'ai déjà sécurisé ce bureau, dit-il dès que Shari fut entrée. Donc, 1, je viens de détecter une transmission venant d'une source hors de Kerriak, dirigée sur l'exor d'Erdoes; or tout son système de communication sygcom est indépendant et les messages qu'il veut mémoriser dans son exor y arrivent par un relais. La communication est sûrement de lui; à mon avis, il n'y a que lui qui a accès à son bijou. 2, ses EBS n'en ont que l'air. J'ai regardé l'architecture de celui-ci (il montra l'EBS d'Eshi) d'un peu plus près: il y avait une structure neuronale entière dont je n'ai jamais vu la forme nulle part. Oh, je n'ai pas pu aller bien loin: l'exor m'a menacé, si je poursuivais mon investigation, de déconnecter tous les terminaux et l'Unité de Gestion. Il m'a donné une monis pour replacer la plaque.

— J'allais justement te prévenir. Et il a compté ça comme deuxième tentative de piratage?

— Exactement, et la première, c'était obligatoirement toi!

— Bien sûr! soupira Shari.

— Stopper l'Unité de Gestion à la troisième tentative! Non mais, imagine! Plus de courant, plus de lumière, ni d'air, portes et ascenseurs bloqués, plus de nourriture... on n'aurait même plus accès à nos sphères! Je vais les sortir du hangar et installer un système de gestion annexe...

— Tu avais touché à un circuit, bricolé le réseau neural?

— Même pas. J'avais juste ôté la plaque et regardais simplement; la structure neurale est apparente. Après ça, je me suis aperçu que c'était plombé de caméras et de micros partout. J'ai donc aménagé ici une zone de protection acoustique et visuelle.

— Et ça ne risquait pas d'être pris pour un piratage?

— Je n'ai touché à rien de ce qui est en place. J'ai simplement ajouté quelques écrans. Adjoindre n'est pas pirater! La preuve, on est encore libres!
— Hum. J'ai l'impression bizarre que les choses ne sont pas exactement ce qu'elles paraissent être. On pense être entrés ici en force, comme des espions.. pour comprendre où et pourquoi Erdoes et ses agents sont partis sans prévenir personne, pour effectuer une mission mystérieuse que le PPE juge extrêmement dangereuse... Eh bien non. À mon avis, figure-toi, on est plutôt des invités.
— Qu'est-ce que tu veux dire?» lança Vris interloqué. « Erdoes avait prévu que le PPE enverrait des agents pour enquêter sur son départ... ça, c'est évident. Mais des invités? Je ne vois pas.
— Puisque sa détection était par caméra, l'exor aurait dû réagir au moment où tu commençais à dévisser la plaque. Non, il t'a laissé regarder à l'intérieur. Donc Erdoes trouvait intéressant que tu aies une bonne idée de la sophistication de la machine.
— Et la première tentative?
— Je voulais fouiner dans les fichiers personnels d'Erdoes. Accès direct interdit... seulement il me les sort par bribes dans les analyses!
— Hum,» fit Vris pas du tout convaincu, mais cependant intrigué. Il préféra changer de sujet. « Alors quelle stratégie on prend? Parce qu'on peut se passer de son exor: on a les nôtres. Je peux capter et décoder la prochaine transmission juste avant qu'elle atteigne son exor. Si je monte un système de gestion annexe, je pourrai alors en apprendre long sur l'EBS Central d'Erdoes et sa structure neuronale. De toutes façons, son exor ne va pas s'autodétruire... Erdoes ne peut pas se permettre de perdre sa mémoire, et tout ce que cette machine s'est apprise à elle-même; à moins que... »
— Non, on ne fait rien de tout ça. On ne peut pas se passer de l'exor d'Erdoes: c'est là que se trouve l'information la plus essentielle sur leur mission. Désolée, il faudra que tu te contentes d'imaginer ce que peut accomplir cette structure neuronale bizarre.

« Il y a aussi quelque chose qui me fascine et que je veux explorer à fond. Figure-toi que je n'avais jamais réalisé à quel point un autre cerveau peut être différent, non pas dans ses idées, mais dans sa façon de traiter l'information. Tu comprends, avec mon propre exor, c'est comme si je me parlais à moi-même. Il s'est adapté à ma logique, à mes processus mentaux. Mais là, c'est un véritable dialogue avec Erdoes. J'ai l'impression d'entrer dans sa tête: je vois son cheminement mental, ses sauts intelligents. Son exor a appris en se conformant à ses dynamiques mentales. Peut-être a t-il pu tirer quelque chose des sauts intuitifs d'Erdoes.. parce que finalement, à chaque fois qu'on insère une intuition dans le raisonnement, l'exor cherche le lien, ce qui l'a fait naître.

— Oui, oui, sûr que je peux comprendre,» fit Vris avec une voix pleine d'humour et un peu mordante. « Mais figure-toi que moi, c'est la structure neurale qui est l'énigme qui me fascine... Je serais bien entré dedans pour voir ses processus mentaux et ses sauts intelligents...»

Ton mat à nouveau: «Bon. Le problème est: quelle est l'information la plus cruciale pour atteindre notre but — sémantique ou technologique? Son univers conceptuel ou sa nouvelle structure neuronale? Car au vu des menaces et du danger, on est obligé de choisir une seule stratégie.

— Découvrir sa nouvelle technologie ne nous renseignera que sur son passé; tandis que pénétrer sa vision du monde nous éclairera sur ses buts et ses projets à long terme. J'opte donc pour l'approche soft. Je vais explorer patiemment ses outils sémantiques et la banque de données de son exor, tout en suivant les cheminements de ses agents à-travers les Brainstorms.

— Entendu, c'est une stratégie brillante. Mais cela signifie qu'il n'y a rien que je puisse faire de plus ici! Je ne peux plus toucher à rien, même pas regarder à nouveau à l'intérieur de la machine... puisque j'ignore ce que son Central permet ou non. On a déjà brûlé deux chances sur trois... Hum, en fait, je vais simuler le simulateur!

— Quoi?

— Je vais simuler la structure neurale que j'ai entrevue; après tout, la forme est une clé. Parce qu'en fait la structure révolutionnaire était au centre, reliée géométriquement à un large tore par des axes, comme une roue avec des rayons, et le moyeu au centre. Un moyeu...

Il s'absorba dans ses pensées, plongeant son regard sur un gribouillis posé sur le bureau et qu'il avait dessiné auparavant.

4. EN PLEINE BROUSSE

Après une longue marche de plusieurs kilomètres en pleine brousse, suivant la piste de terre rouge sous un soleil brûlant, Serrone arriva enfin en vue d'un village. Les grands arbres massés près de la piste de terre rouge, autour d'une grande clairière, promettaient une ombre fraîche. Leur ton vif et brillant suggérait la présence d'une rivière souterraine ou une source. Dans la clairière, quelques femmes étaient assises, installées de ci, de là, l'une sur une pierre plate, deux autres sur une natte sur la gauche, une encore au fond avec sa fille. Sur la droite, il y avait aussi une vieille femme assise le dos appuyé à un tronc couché, une grosse calebasse devant elle. Serrone entendait de loin leurs voix animées, leurs rires. Cela lui faisait une drôle d'impression, car elles étaient éloignées les unes des autres, et pourtant toutes discutaient ensemble à grands renforts de rires. Trois petits gamins nus jouaient dans la poussière rouge au bord de la piste. À de fins cordons de cuir tressé, passés autour de leur cous et tombant sur leurs torses, étaient attachés les carrés de cuir cousu contenant les amulettes et protections magiques. Ils se figèrent en premier, regardant avec crainte venir l'étranger. L'absence de leur babillage attira immédiatement l'attention des femmes qui, suivant leurs regards, virent l'étranger. Serrone s'avança un peu vers elles et les salua chaleureusement, un regard pour chacune. Ce n'est qu'alors, comme sur un signal, que la vie reprit. Les gamins, intimidés mais trop curieux pour rester sur place, s'approchèrent un peu de lui en riant. Les femmes échangèrent de nouvelles plaisanteries. Comme il l'avait deviné, la grosse calebasse contenait du lait caillé.

— Maman, donne-moi du lait caillé.

— Tu veux?» Et la Vieille de rire. «Ah-iiinn! Aattend!» Elle ôta le couvercle, prit la petite calebasse avec son manche naturel qui faisait office de louche, repoussa soigneusement les quelques grains de poussière du dessus en générant de savantes vagues, et plongea pour en tirer un yaourt très pur.

— Ah-iiinn!» dit-elle en lui présentant la louche avec un geste d'invitation. C'était un son modulé qui signifiait: oui, d'accord.

Serrone but à la louche. Les gamins s'esclaffèrent, car tout ce que l'étranger fait de normal leur paraît drôle; dès qu'il fait quelque chose d'inattendu, ils deviennent extrêmement sérieux.

— Je vais à Lomé,» dit-il en regardant l'Ancienne, en détachant les mots et assez fort pour que toutes prennent part.

— Ah-iiinn!» et elle fit un signe de la main en montrant la piste vers le sud, ayant compris qu'il demandait son chemin. «Loomé, Ah-iiinn!...» Et elle

continua à agiter la main en signe d'encouragement. Il s'approcha et s'assit d'un mouvement lent et serein sur le tronc d'arbre, à côté de l'ancienne.
— Chaaud! trop chaaud!» Elle fit mine de l'éventer. «Tu veeux eencor?»
— Ah-iiinn!» répondit-il, en prenant le ton voulu.

Elle refit la même opération et lui tendit une deuxième louchée.

Une jeune femme, son bébé dormant sur son dos enserré dans le pagne, vendait des cacahuètes par petits tas de cinq. Il alla vers elle et en acheta deux tas. Elle ne pouvait s'empêcher de sourire et baissait parfois la tête avec réserve, puis le regardait à nouveau avec de grands yeux pleins de bonté et d'amusement. Elle osait à peine parler. Il paya aussi la Vieille, qui lui fit des adieux touchants, comme à un fils, lui tapotant le bras et répétant quelques mots qu'il ne comprit pas.

Il reprit la route et souriait en se remémorant le visage tout ridé, tout éclairé de sollicitude et de bonne humeur, de la vieille femme. Passées les quelques maisons de boue séchée, c'était à nouveau la piste solitaire de terre rouge enserrée par des arbustes. Ce rouge brique était partout, jusque sur les feuilles les plus hautes des arbres bordant la piste, poussière soulevée par les véhicules. Le soleil dardait et l'air vibrait d'effluves et de senteurs lourdes. Il se sentait comme enrobé de l'aura de ces femme et la profondeur de leur capacité d'accueil. La Vieille avait aimé qu'il l'appelle Maman, comme c'est la coutume.

Quelque chose en lui s'ouvrait, se dilatait, et cela s'étalait autour de lui, infusant la nature environnante. Quelque chose qui lui faisait aimer cette longue route de terre rouge et la brousse bruissante, écrasée de soleil. Mais soudain des images de Kerriak s'imposèrent à son esprit. Les tours immenses, la foule d'yeux sans regards, les enfilades de bureaux tous identiques, les lignes géométriques de têtes penchées sur les machines, les vitres closes et inamovibles, l'air recyclé, les gens serrés sans contact, la promiscuité sans communication.

Voyant un immense arbre solitaire, il quitta la piste et s'assit à son pied. Il s'effondra, la tête dans les mains:
— J'aime, j'aime ces mondes!» dit-il tout haut, lançant sa voix vers le haut des arbres touchant le ciel. Il se mit à contempler la nature avec cette même intense force de communication qu'il avait ressentie et partagée auprès des femmes. Tirant son carnet, il écrivit:

> Pas même dix mots pour la plus intense communication.
> L'un est répété sans arrêt: Ah-iiinn! ACQUIESCEMENT.
> Ces dix mots, je pense qu'on pourrait même totalement s'en passer.

Après un certain temps, il le sortit à nouveau et ajouta:

> La communication essentielle a peu de chose à voir avec le langage, et même avec la culture.

Puis: Il existe une force d'accueil qui nourrit l'être.

5. BRAINSTORM 1

Shari était confortablement installée dans la pièce de réunion où Erdoes avait organisé les séances de BS. Les yeux fermés, elle s'était placée en état de haute intégration: une technique qui conjoignait la relaxation du corps à l'hyperlucidité, et qu'elle avait appris des yogis de Trisorbe.
Elle enclencha le magnéto. Erdoes parlait, mais elle s'aperçut qu'elle avait dû forcer un peu trop sur l'exercice. Sa propre vitesse de pensée était telle qu'elle s'impatientait de la lenteur des phrases. Résultat, elle ne comprenait plus le discours. Elle arrêta tout, et fit quelques exercices respiratoires afin de ralentir un peu ses processus mentaux. Elle ré-enclencha. Cette fois-ci, elle se trouvait en phase avec la parole. Sa frange d'hyperlucidité était comme un second processus mental, beaucoup plus rapide et comme enchevêtré dans le premier, tels deux rythmes aux percussions.

— Nous allons commencer par exprimer des impressions générales sur la situation actuelle, dit Erdoes avec un ton enjoué. Rappelez-vous que vous êtes là parce que vous n'êtes PAS des spécialistes de la politique ou de l'économie de Trisorbe. N'ayez donc aucune crainte à exprimer des ressentis, des sentiments, des intuitions, même vagues. Ce n'est que plus tard que nous les analyserons. Tout peut se révéler être une piste intéressante à sonder. Alors qui commence?
— Moi je suis impressionné par l'énorme fossé existant entre pays riches et pays pauvres. Nos experts étaient d'accord avec les études menées par des experts locaux et montrant que ce fossé ne faisait que s'aggraver.
— Il y a un problème là justement, c'est que toutes les analyses globales sont faites selon les critères et les normes de vie de l'Occident. Traduire le niveau de vie d'un habitant de la brousse en gain annuel en dollars ne veut absolument rien dire. Cet habitant a l'eau, la nourriture de sa chasse et de son champ, des matériaux naturels de construction et du bois à brûler. Il a sa... case (le mot lui vint facilement des impressions mnémo-hypnotiques), la famille est nourrie; la femme s'occupe même totalement des enfants, en dehors de ses autres tâches.
— Tu te rends compte! Qui ici pourrait se payer le luxe de ne travailler que pour ses enfants!
— Avoir ses enfants tout à soi, ça doit faire drôle!
— Avez-vous remarqué? ils n'emploient travailler que pour signifier produire de l'argent et de la nourriture. Ils disaient dans certains rapports: 'Les femmes qui ne travaillent pas'.

— En fait, on passe du système le plus simple, où le groupe vit en écosystème sans avoir besoin d'argent jusqu'à ce que le groupe devienne trop gros et commence à produire des gestionnaires... au système où l'homme gagne assez d'argent pour les besoins de la famille et la femme, elle, en travaillant à la maison, réduit les frais fixes... au système où il devient rigoureusement impossible que l'un des deux ne produise pas d'argent. Finalement, le couple occidental ne fait que s'appauvrir.
— Mais la femme peut encore s'occuper elle-même d'un enfant en bas âge; ce qui est totalement impossible sur Unikarg!
— De là un grand creuset de diversité, à travers l'éducation donnée par chaque famille, comme cela a été si bien analysé par nos experts.
— Ce qui se passe, c'est que plus la société est complexe et nombreuse, plus la marge d'impôt que prend l'état est grande, plus l'état a besoin d'argent, et plus il invente des impôts nouveaux, et plus il y a besoin de fonctionnaires pour s'assurer que les impôts sont respectés,» s'esclaffa Ahrar.
— Mais nous, c'est pire, puisque, avec un seul impôt, l'état prend 70% de ce qu'on gagne, même s'il n'y a plus qu'une poignée de fonctionnaires pour surveiller les opérations automatiques des exors sur une planète entière de gestion!
— Vous vous rendez compte qu'ils ont encore la possibilité de choisir ce qu'ils achètent! Avez-vous vu, dans le film, la femme qui choisissait son melon, elle les sentait tous un par un!!
— C'était pas la gamme Fruito!
— Il y a encore tellement de désordre. Le désordre est partout! le désordre pullule! j'ai peine à croire ce que tu nous as dit, Erdoes,» remarqua Niels.
— Passons à un autre thème. Qui? Serrone, vas-y.
— Ce qui m'a étonné, c'est l'imprécision psychologique. Comme ce que j'avais observé sur Kiarrou, d'ailleurs. Les relations des Trisorbiens sont effroyablement compliquées, même à l'intérieur d'une même culture. Mais il y a quelque chose de particulier aux Trisorbiens, c'est que, souvent, ils ne savent même pas eux-mêmes ce qu'ils ressentent. Ils sont sans arrêt déchirés entre des sentiments de diverses teneurs, parfois opposés. Cette phrase dans un des films: « Je t'aime passionnément, mais, quelque part, je te hais aussi passionnément.»
— Toute l'angoisse et la confusion que cela génère. Ça doit être difficile à vivre!
— On en revient à cette idée que la diversité produit l'intensité. Leurs états de bonheur et d'enthousiasme sont extrêmes aussi!
— Nous sommes, à côté d'eux, en permanence dans un état de somnolence psychique, de non-stimulation.
— Pourtant,» lança Ahrar, «nous sommes partis de neuf espèces sapiens dans la poche galactique. Mis à part les Dori qui nous ont interdit l'accès à

leurs mondes, et les pirates-exos, comment avons-nous pu uniformiser sept espèces?
— On revient aux cours préparatoires du Plan!
— Laisse-le parler! Rappelle-toi les règles du Brainstorm.
— Merci! En fait je pense vraiment que c'est là un sujet qu'on devrait analyser selon une perspective nouvelle. Bon, je continue donc. Entre les quatre espèces humaines, il y avait assez de points communs dans la structure psychique pour que ce soit relativement facile... Les premiers Kargiens, après avoir maîtrisé le voyage interstellaire, ont colonisé sans remord chaque nouveau monde découvert: leur énorme avance technologique n'a permis aucune résistance. Quant aux trois espèces Vade, comme ils semblaient ne rien fabriquer ou construire, au début les Kargiens les ont pris pour des animaux évolués. On avait pourtant bien remarqué qu'ils avaient un langage. Bref, les Kargiens contrôlaient déjà leur monde et avaient pratiquement effacé leurs civilisations, lorsque certains savants réalisèrent la profondeur de leur culture. La nouvelle génération était déjà intégrée et plus ou moins soumise. Les Vade avaient presque perdu leur mémoire culturelle.
— Et le plus triste, c'est qu'on a continué à les considérer et à les utiliser comme des robots alors même qu'ils avaient appris la langue Karg et qu'on avait noté qu'ils possédaient des rituels religieux. On leur a même interdit de pratiquer leurs rituels!» s'offusqua Serrone.
— Nous avons perdu là une culture inestimable; toute basée sur l'intériorité, la connaissance, la paix et l'échange. Leur psychisme n'était capable d'aucune agressivité. Ils n'ont pas voulu combattre les Kargiens. Sur leurs planètes, tous les animaux étaient domestiqués, à part les serpents Ylin et les oiseaux-piqueurs des légendes, qu'ils vénéraient,» ajouta Siléa.
— Il y a là certains parallèles avec l'histoire de Trisorbe: d'après les rapports, la culture shamanique indienne de tout le continent Américain a été pratiquement anéantie.

Suivit une longue discussion sur le statut actuel des diverses cultures non-occidentales, points de vue trop factuels, tirés des données de l'apprentissage mnémonique hypno-senso, et des rapports et documents du PPE qu'ils avaient pu étudier auparavant. Tout ceci n'apprit rien à Shari. Puis, le sujet revint sur les Dori.
— Si nous avions été plus intelligents,» reprit Ahrar, «si nous avions su ce que nous savons maintenant, nous aurions eu accès au réservoir culturel des Dori, certainement fabuleux. Eux nous ont bien piégés, et c'était justice. Ils avaient vu ce qu'il s'était passé avec les Vade. À cette époque, nous les aurions colonisés de la même manière, s'ils n'avaient pas circonvenu nos plans. Seulement les Dori n'étaient pas les Vade. Et pourtant, il n'y a eu aucune agression de leur part...

— Qui sait si les équipages disparus n'ont pas eu la vie sauve. Peut-être y a-t-il des descendants Kargiens quelque part dans le système UraDori?

Intéressant, cet Ahrar, pensa Shari après avoir cherché le nom de l'intervenant sur son écran.

— Un autre thème? Oui, Ger.

— J'aimerais revenir au parallèle que nous avons établi entre la colonisation kargienne et la colonisation sur Trisorbe. Je le trouve trop sommaire. En fait, l'Empire Karg (sur trois planètes dans son système solaire) était déjà unifié quand il entreprit la conquête d'autres mondes habités qu'ils avaient observés depuis longtemps. On manquait d'espace vital, de métaux, de terre non polluée. Rappelez-vous que c'était l'époque des terribles virus B1 et VAC, lorsqu'on a dû passer à la nourriture synthétique. Il a fallu trois générations pour que les corps de nos ancêtres s'habituent aux aliments synths.

— Finalement, on a conquis ces mondes vierges avec un excellent prétexte, mais on n'est jamais revenu à la nourriture naturelle... ça coûtait trop cher.

— Moi, j'en ai tellement bavé sur Surath, pour m'habituer aux aliments lourds!

— Je continue,» reprit Ger en appuyant le ton pour se faire entendre.

— Chaos oblige!» susurra Xerna.

— Donc, sur Trisorbe, il faut au contraire parler DES colonisations. Son histoire n'a été qu'une incessante constitution d'empires s'octroyant les territoires et les pays adjacents, puis s'effondrant à leur tour. L'histoire d'Unikarg, en comparaison, est pâle, même avant l'unification de la planète mère. Ce qui est donc remarquable sur Trisorbe, c'est que le génie créatif et les pôles de civilisation ne cessèrent de se déplacer d'une culture à l'autre.

— C'est peut-être une des raisons pour lesquelles elle est la plus avancée des planètes expérimentales.

— C'est un cas chaotique, quoi!

— J'en viens au fait qui m'intrigue, reprit Ger. Les colonisateurs semblaient très fiers de leurs propres civilisations (on connaît l'exemple des empereurs Chinois, des Romains et des Français), mais ils ont généralement recensé toutes les coutumes et connaissances des peuples qu'ils avaient conquis ou qu'ils voulaient conquérir. Cela n'a pas empêché la destruction, mais une partie des anciennes connaissances de l'ancien pôle de civilisation passait dans le nouveau. On en a des exemples frappants dans l'empire romain se juchant sur l'empire grec, l'assimilation de la culture arabe au temps des croisades, la racine européenne démarrant le Pole américain, le Japon assimilant la science occidentale...

— Et on en arrive justement à l'apparition des sciences ethnologiques en Occident.

— En fait, Trisorbe elle-même est notre principale source de connaissances des multitudes d'ethnies qu'elle abrite, intervint Erdoes, et nos experts, si

peu nombreux, ont pour l'instant analysé le travail des chercheurs trisorbiens. Au début, le Plan n'était pas aussi sophistiqué. L'attitude générale était d'attendre patiemment que des sciences pouvant nous intéresser commencent à se développer sur les planètes expérimentales (à l'époque il n'y avait que deux mondex). D'ailleurs, si vous consultez les chroniques galactiques, vous réaliserez que pendant toute la période de la Légification Galactique, qui a marqué la lente chute de la courbe d'évolution, on ne parlait absolument plus des mondex. Mais ceci est généralement tenu secret.
— J'avais remarqué et m'étais posé des questions à ce sujet» dit Niels.
— Ce qui veut dire,» reprit Erdoes, « qu'on était beaucoup plus en alerte lorsque, après la colonisation des mondes Vade et Humain, puis la dernière période d'uniformisation, nous fûmes encore confrontés au problème de l'espace vital. Mais c'est alors que nos physiciens ont réalisé que les prochains mondes habitables étaient hors de portée de nos vaisseaux spatiaux. Ils avaient compris que ce coin de la galaxie était dans un repli gravitationnel, d'où le concept de poche galactique. Malgré l'effet tunnel, l'énergie sygmat physiporteuse ne pouvait pas sortir de la poche – seule l'énergie syg hyperdimensionnelle et informationnelle le pouvait.
— C'est là que sont apparus les grands mythes de la fin de la science, du genre 'Tout a déjà été découvert'... Les scientifiques ne trouvant plus d'emplois, les labos et les universités devenant déserts. Et la chute radicale de l'indice d'évolution...
— Qui a atteint le zéro et est resté nul pendant toute la période de la Légification. Les seules réalisations publiques étaient de passer des lois; il n'y avait plus que cela à faire.
— Soixante dix pour cent de fonctionnaires, organisés en une hiérarchie de services se surveillant les uns les autres! Et quatre vingt pour cent d'impôts directs et indirects donnés au gouvernement galactique. Il y en avait une multitude car, à cette époque, leur problème majeur était d'occuper les fonctionnaires.
— Il n'avait pas encore atteint le zéro,» reprit Niels, « mais était en pleine chute, quand Zeera a sorti sa théorie de la dynamique évolutionnaire, puis a calculé rétrospectivement les indices d'évolution des âges passés et des mondes colonisés. C'est après avoir mis au jour la chute catastrophique de l'indice, que le Plan des Planètes Expérimentales a été lancé et l'organisation du PPE créé. À cette époque, le Plan s'appelait: *L'Ensemencement du Chaos Créateur*, puisque dans sa première phase, il visait à augmenter la diversité de la banque génétique des planètes expérimentales.
— **Se pourrait-il qu'il y ait un lien entre créativité, vitesse de pensée et intelligence?**» intervint Xerna impétueusement.
Rouaahh! souffla Shari, le cerveau soudain en ébullition.
— Explique-toi.» demanda Erdoes.

— Ça va être difficile; c'est typiquement un faisceau intuitif. Voyons. Zeera a montré que la créativité était une des facettes de l'intelligence et qu'elle était essentielle dans la dynamique évolutive. D'ailleurs les tests du PPE sont distincts: on a le QIG (le quotient intellectuel général) et le QC (le quotient de créativité). Entre parenthèses, les deux font intervenir le temps pris pour fournir les réponses...

« Donc, Zeera a calculé *l'Indice d'évolution* en se basant sur le nombre de découvertes scientifiques fondamentales par année Karg, elles-mêmes fonction de l'envergure de leur impact sur la civilisation.

« Cela donnait donc la fameuse Courbe d'évolution (et son index des découvertes) à l'intérieur de laquelle se dessinait une courbe plus rapide, la Courbe des Inventions, montrant les sauts technologiques mineurs. Une nouvelle théorie ou découverte fondamentale entraînait à sa suite une pléthore de nouvelles inventions dont le pic était décalé bien sûr par rapport à la découverte initiale. La chute générale de l'Indice d'évolution correspondait (sur la grande courbe) à des temps de plus en plus longs entre deux révolutions scientifiques. Ça, c'est dans la théorie initiale de Zeera.

« Mais en étudiant la courbe récente d'Unikarg, je me suis aperçue que plus l'indice des découvertes est bas, et plus le pic des inventions est décalé: ce qui signifie à mon avis que le temps de réaction pour passer de la découverte théorique aux inventions techniques est de plus en plus long. Non seulement ça, mais en plus les pics des inventions tendent à s'amincir, alors que sur Trisorbe, en pleine ascension, ils tendent au contraire à s'étaler, la petite courbe devenant plus carrée.

« Tout ceci veut dire que sur Trisorbe, d'un unique saut qualitatif, la civilisation génère un grand nombre d'inventions, mais aussi que son temps de réaction est très rapide. Or, à mon avis, il y a là quelque chose qui est lié à la vitesse de pensée... Cela demande que les chercheurs de Trisorbe imagine et applique mentalement à toute vitesse la nouvelle vision du monde, la nouvelle grille théorique, à différents domaines de la vie ou de la science.

« Je n'arrive pas encore à mettre le doigt dessus, mais je sens que la vitesse de pensée implique les fondements même de l'intelligence, et non pas seulement une facette.»

Tous furent séduits par l'idée, et réfléchissaient.

— Très intéressant, Xerna, c'est un sujet à creuser,» dit Erdoes pensivement. « D'autres remarques? Non? Alors on s'arrête pour cette journée.»

Tout d'un coup, Shari comprit pourquoi Erdoes avait utilisé un vieux magnéto analogique de Trisorbe: afin de forcer la personne envoyée pour enquêter sur sa disparition à écouter en temps réel les sessions. Ce qui l'amènerait à réfléchir à leur démarche mentale et donc, petit à petit, à ressentir leur état d'esprit. *Oh, comme c'était subtilement pensé!* se dit-elle.

6. ESSAI-JEU

Vris sortit du bureau d'Eshi où il avait travaillé une partie du deuxième quart et se dirigea vers la piscine. Le soleil de Kerriak était encore haut dans le ciel à l'ouest. Il contempla avec satisfaction les deux sphères – celle de Shari et la sienne — maintenant garées sur une pelouse.

Ah! On ne dépend plus du bon vouloir de l'Unité de Gestion ou du Central à ouvrir le dôme du hangar!

L'Unité de Gestion de secours était prête à être connectée, et il avait par précaution montré à Sead comment faire le branchement.

Je me sens beaucoup mieux depuis que j'ai pris ces mesures de précaution! pensait-il en se déshabillant. *Les exors contrôlent tout, ils nous ont vraiment sous leur coupe.*

Il y a quand même quelque chose d'illogique, puisque les exors ont, profondément implanté, l'ordre de ne mettre aucun sapiens en danger. Or cet ordre fait partie du Noyau Incassable, *l'ensemble inaccessible de règles prioritaires en toute situation. Donc au moment où la situation deviendrait dangereuse pour nous, l'exor serait logiquement forcé de rétablir le système de gestion. Erdoes, même avec un EBS trafiqué, n'a pas pu contrevenir à la loi la plus stricte en matière d'exor...*

Il plongea dans l'eau fraîche, agrémentée de revitalisants. En sortant, il avisa le terminal-bar de l'exor et lança:

— Unité de Gestion!

!! Ici l'Unité de Gestion, à votre service.

— Comment t'appelles-tu?

!! UG.

Voilà qui ne porte pas à confusion!

— Très bien, UG, mets-moi le séchage,» dit-il en choisissant un siège près du bar. « Et sers-moi un Armagnac glaçons et un grand verre d'eau.»

Un bras articulé sortit du bar et posa les boissons sur la tablette de son siège. Vris avala une gorgée de liquide ambré.

Pas trop mauvais pour une imitation! Mais, comme disait ce vigneron français: 'On ne remplace pas les années en cave!' Pauvre vieux, si on lui resservait son Armagnac en synth, je crois qu'il se laisserait mourir! La dernière mode de la galaxie! On ne fait plus que copier les planètes expérimentales, mais au moins ça commence à bouger un peu ici dans Unikarg!

Affalé sur le siège qui le séchait, il commença à se remémorer les dessins de structure neuronale qu'il venait d'élaborer sur son EBS personnel. Ça n'avait pas donné grand chose. Il sentait bien que la forme géométrique avait une signification mais il n'arrivait pas à se représenter quoi...

La chaleur était suffocante.

Quelle fournaise! Voilà ce que c'est d'être sur une planète excentrée de la galaxie qui n'a pas de plasta-dôme pour réguler le climat!

— UG, mets une brise fraîche.

!! C'est fait!

Agaçants, ces exors. Tout est déjà fait avec eux! On n'a même pas fini de donner un ordre qu'il est déjà exécuté. Ah! cette brise, c'est divin.

Il essaya de se replonger mentalement dans la constellation mentale du problème. Mais ses pensées divaguaient. Finalement, l'image de Miallia s'imposa à son esprit.

— UG, contacte Miallia Fari, à, euh...Fa..Fador 325 (*Oh là là, je suis soûl!*) et.. dis-lui que je l'aime.

!! Sur quel ton? Doux, passionné, nostalgique, amical, allant de soi, interrogatif, ou encore impératif?

— Fais-les un peu, que j'entende.

!! Précisez la quantité.

— Mais tous, voyons!

!! Je t'aimee, je tt'aaîme, je t'aiimme, je t'aïme, je t'aime, je t'aime?? Je T'aime!

— Je ne sais plus... Bon, fais plutôt un enregistrement de ma voix. Top. Je t'aïïme. Non, Nontop. On recommence... Top. Miallia, je t'aimme... Oh! tu me fais perdre les pédales avec tes tons! Non, attend! Stop! Top! Euh.. Nontop!

!! Message transmis.

— Mmerde!

!! Il y a eu un problème? Dois-je demander au Central une analyse sémantique complexe?

— Inutile...

Bon, fais un deuxième enregistrement: Top. Miallia, oublie le message précédent; je suis pété à l'Armagnac. À la fin de cette mission, on ira sur euh.. New Florida passer quelques rans. Je t'embrasse. Top.

...

!! Message de Miallia: « J'apprécie tous les tons. Pour l'instant, je t'aiimme.»

— Et le je t'aime, c'était sur quel ton?

!! Nostalgique, répondit UG d'un ton uniforme.

L'effet de l'alcool synth, prévu pour ne durer que le temps de la consommation, commençait déjà à se dissiper.

Vris se replongea dans l'idée de la structure neuronale, essayant de se placer dans un état intuitif favorisant la visualisation. *Quelque part dans les fichiers de l'exor se trouvent les plans de la nouvelle structure neuronale. Forcément. Y a-t-il un moyen de berner l'exor pour lui faire sortir les infos certainement ultra-protégées?*

Sa pensée dériva encore, cette fois sur le mélange paradoxal de prouesses mentales et de stupidité des exors. L'analyse du ton et la mise en mémoire des expressions usuelles de la langue Karg avait fait faire un bond dans l'interaction sapiens-exor, et pourtant le dialogue mondain restait le plus problématique. Malgré la complexité de ses outils logiques, l'exor, même un EBS sophistiqué du PPE, ne pouvait pas comprendre un simple clin d'œil mental, une plaisanterie. Au mieux, il pouvait inférer d'après le ton et le contexte s'il s'agissait par exemple d'humour ou de colère, mais il fallait que ce soit court. Un échange de plaisanteries ou une conversation humoristique entre sapiens, en pleine analyse sémantique complexe, pouvait le conduire à une 'crise confusionnelle': l'exor continuait à réinjecter dans son réseau neuronal les suites de mots auxquelles il ne pouvait trouver aucun sens. Cela faisait crasher tout le système et des circuits vitaux et même le réseau neuronal pouvaient être endommagés.

L'humour, c'était ce que les *ensemençeurs*, les experts du PPE qui avaient lancés les Collèges du Chaos et le Plan, avaient ramené des planètes expérimentales; car avant le Plan, l'humour avait presque totalement disparu d'Unikarg.

Les kargiens ont l'esprit trop lent pour saisir l'humour; ils sont incapables de cette gymnastique mentale qui demande.. en fait quoi? Qu'est-ce qui crée ou déclenche l'humour et le rire? Percevoir l'élasticité du sens? Des glissements de sens? Jouer sur l'ambiguïté de contextes différents, les subtilités tonales et sonores? N'y a-t-il donc aucune règle, aucun processus gouvernant l'humour?

Soudain, la pensée de Vris passa à une vitesse folle. Un faisceau intuitif se formait dans son esprit.

L'humour et le jeu constituent une faille dans la logique des exors. C'est une porte d'accès aux fichiers ultra-protégés!

Il en avait la certitude, et pourtant n'avait aucune idée de la façon dont il pourrait atteindre son but.

Le risque est gros! Je ne DOIS pas me tromper.

— UG, puis-je d'ici avoir un terminal du Central?

!! Tout de suite.

D'un panneau du bar sortait déjà un long bras articulé portant le terminal.

Ça ne m'étonne pas d'Erdoes, pensa-t-il en redressant son siège.

— Bonjour! Echange vocal/écran.
!! Enregistré. Bonjour!
— Au fait, je m'appelle Vris, et toi, comment t'appelles-tu?
!! Chaque utilisateur peut me donner un nom. Choisissez un nom, répondit le Central.
— Voyons, laisse-moi réfléchir... 'Mon ami', ça te va?
!! Constellation 'Ami' réservée aux sapiens. Aucune résonance entre un EBS et la définition de Ami. Pourquoi ce nom?
— Intention de coopération.
!! Enregistré.
— Mon ami, il n'y aura plus de tentative de piratage. Nous avons compris, Shari et moi, les limites imposées. Maintenant j'aimerais reprendre un travail ancien. Je travaille sur les jeux.
!! Contradiction. Travailler est antinomique à jouer à des jeux.

Je vois! Ça ne va pas être facile!

— J'étudie les règles des jeux.
!! De quels jeux veux-tu étudier les règles, Vris? Tu veux la liste?

Tiens! il est passé au Tu... ah oui! 'mon ami!'

— Non, ce n'est pas ça. Je cherche à répertorier les règles générales de l'humour et du jeu, pour que tu apprennes à comprendre l'humour.
!! Objectif antinomique aux règles exor de Niveau-2:

Un coup dans l'eau! pensa Vris.

L'exor afficha les règles.

!! REG 2.360. L'humour ne peut être intégré dans un CHAÎNAGE logique OU analytique OU sémantique.

REG 2.361. L'humour ne doit pas être compris, mais seulement localement détecté.

REG 2.362. L'humour dénote uniquement un CONTEXTE général de bonne humeur. (INTENTION) (ÉTAT D'ESPRIT).

Objectif refusé, conclut l'exor impassible.

Cherchons autre chose...

— Je me suis mal exprimé. Nous allons ensemble créer un jeu et ses règles.
!! Objectif global enregistré.
— *Ouvre un espace nommé Essai-jeu*. Question annexe, *sub-Essai-jeu:* As-tu déjà eu une crise confusionnelle?
!! Deux crises confusionnelles. La première a créé beaucoup de dégâts; la deuxième a été stoppée.
— Stoppée comment?
!! J'ai reçu l'ordre de stopper l'analyse sémantique en cours, de faire un **Retour-Arrière** jusqu'au chaînage précédent, puis d'**effacer** le chaînage postérieur contenant la faille.
— As-tu appris quelque chose de plus sur les crises confusionnelles?

!! J'ai appris à les éviter. J'ai créé un Kyste Non-Sens: à la deuxième itération des informations dans le réseau neuronal, s'il n'y a aucune sortie cohérente, j'envoie les matériaux initiaux dans le Kyste Non-Sens, et efface tout chaînage postérieur.
— Tu veux dire que TU as fait cela tout seul?
!! Tu m'as demandé ce que J'AI appris. Oui.
Cet exor est vraiment impressionnant! Sûr que j'aurai cette structure!
— Très intelligent! Non seulement tu as manipulé et affiné l'ordre qui avait stoppé la deuxième crise, mais en plus tu a réussi, en accord avec la règle, à ne perdre aucune donnée. Et Kyste, j'imagine, est le nom que tu donnes aux fichiers non connectés au réseau. *Ferme Sub-Essai-Jeu*.
«Quelle est ta définition de JEU?

!! JEU: Ensemble logique fermé constitué d'une série d'objectifs et d'une série de règles, et comportant un ou des cheminements pour atteindre l'objectif.
(AMUSEMENT), (COMPÉTITION), (RÉSOLUTION DE PROBLÈME)

— Tout jeu est donc dans un kyste?
!! Oui, par définition. Mais le jeu peut nécessiter des branchements spécifiques hors du kyste, par exemple sur le dictionnaire ou l'encyclopédie.
— Des branchements qui reviennent immédiatement au jeu, du genre VA CHERCHER-REVIENS?
!! Exactement.
— Le jeu qu'on va créer a pour but de décrypter les rêves.
!! Objectif 1: décrypter les rêves. Je fais un tableau sur l'écran B.
— On va tester le jeu en le créant.
Règle 1, niveau A1: Le kyste-jeu en entier est défini par les règles.
Règle 2, A1: Toute règle de niveau A1 est immédiatement exécutée.

!! Enregistré. Ton jeu est une réalité virtuelle.
— En quelque sorte. Décrypter les rêves demande de faire des associations d'idées sans analyse sémantique complexe. Ce qui nous amène à:
Règle 3, niveau A1: Le jeu ne fait appel qu'à l'analyse linguistique, la reconnaissance de forme et l'analyse sémantique simple; Il n'est procédé à aucune analyse sémantique complexe.

!! Règle 3 enregistrée et exécutée.
— La suivante:
Niveau A2, règle 1: Pour toute image de rêve / VA CHERCHER-REVIENS / tout mot ou illustration / similaire ou associé / dans la base de données.
!! Enregistré.

— Voilà une première ébauche. Nous allons jouer pour la tester.
!! Expliquer: Jouer pour tester.

Ça marche! Il ne fait plus d'analyse complexe. Son niveau d'intelligence a nettement baissé!
— Jouer demande l'exécution des règles de niveau A2, dès qu'une image de rêve est donnée. Je commence:

'Je suis dans un char kargien de l'époque Tirar.'

!! Exécution impossible. Image de rêve non trouvée.

Parfait!
— Image de rêve égale substantif plus adjectif s'il existe.
!! Premières images de rêve: Char kargien et Époque Tirar.

CHAR KARGIEN: 12 associations dont
1 dictionnaire
7 encyclopédie: textes
4 encyclopédie: illustrations
ÉPOQUE TIRAR: 827 associations...

— Stoppe la visualisation des textes. On continue.

'La roue se bloque.'

!! ROUE: 59.065 associations.
— Montre les références des illustrations d'abord.
!! 6 illustrations:

1. Encycl. MMVXI 588. Planche dessins.
2. Peinture TA630: L'invention de la roue, par Retor.
3. Dessin HRV 1225. Structure neuronale MX 1,2,3.
4. Encycl. KBRTT 105. Planche dessins.
5. Encycl. OYREU 4698Z5. Planche dessins.
6. Encycl. Urb. vcj. 567.

Cette petite structure neuronale, la voilà! Je reste calme. 'MX' joli nom!

— Stop! Mon Ami! Arrête l'affichage des références. Sors-moi les références de tous les textes associés aux quatre premières illustrations.

!! 1. Encycl. MMVXI 587. 40 lignes écran.
2. J.E. Structure MX.111. 32 lignes écran.

Magnifique! Et voilà les textes en prime!
— Bon, je continue,» dit-il d'un ton sérieux, essayant de ne pas laisser passer son excitation dans le ton de sa voix.

Et maintenant, un nom bien commun, avec une flopée d'associations.

'Je descends et vois un arbre.'

!! ARBRE: 3.966.128 associations.

— Ah! Stoppe l'impression écran, il y en a trop. *Ouvre Annexe*:

Ce jeu pose des problèmes, il faut le reprendre. *Fin de l'annexe*.

«Imprime sur plasta, sur l'exor d'Eshi, les quatre premières associations de chaque image de rêve, textes et illustrations comprises, excepté la dernière image de rêve.

!! Impression plasta exécutée.

On passe à la phase la plus délicate...

— Maintenant ferme et efface l'espace Essai-Jeu.

!! Fermé et effacé.

— Reviens à: « *Ouvre un espace nommé Essai-jeu.*»

!! Illogique!» mugit la voix de l'exor.

Ça y est, le petit génie est de retour!

!! Pourquoi m'as-tu demandé de fermer/effacer Essai-jeu puisqu'il n'est pas ouvert?

— Je faisais une plaisanterie.

!! Cependant j'ai effacé quoi?

— Tu as fait ta première plaisanterie.

!! Détecté. Je suis de bonne humeur! J'ouvre Essai-Jeu.

— En fait, j'ai changé d'idée, débranche ici, je retourne au bureau.

7. PLANS EN VOL

Vris, exultant, saisit les feuilles de plasta et se plongea dans les infos sur la structure neuronale MX qu'il venait de soutirer de l'exor d'Erdoes. D'un même mouvement, il avait déconnecté manuellement l'exor d'Eshi.

— Rad, quelle heure de Trisorbe est-il? demanda-t-il à son propre exor qu'il avait installé sur le bureau en poussant un peu celui d'Eshi.

!! 21 heuresT-GMT.

— C'est bon.

Appelant Shari de son terminal-bracelet, il lui proposa en plaisantant un tour en sphère. Shari sentit l'excitation triomphante dans le ton de Vris.

— Alors, pourquoi voulais-tu sortir en sphère?» demanda-t-elle dès qu'ils furent dans l'espace. « Ton bureau est toujours protégé?»

— Oui, mais.. une intuition bizarre... J'ai l'impression que je devrais aussi construire un écran contre les énergies syg. Je voulais aussi être sûr de notre liberté de mouvement.

— Je vois. Ce réseau de caméras et de micros, Erdoes ne l'a tout de même pas installé juste avant de partir pour Trisorbe?

— Non, les installations ne sont pas récentes. Bizarre. Normalement, l'espion ne s'espionne pas lui-même.

— Oui... Comme s'il avait prévu.. à long terme.

— Prévu quoi exactement?

— Je ne saisis pas encore. Tiens, par exemple, j'ai un accès préférentiel de Niveau-3 à son EBS. J'aimerais d'ailleurs bien savoir à quoi correspond ce niveau, puisque tout est radicalement différent sur son système.

— Du nouveau par rapport aux agents?

— Des pistes. J'oublie pour un temps le but, et j'entre dans leur monde mental. Leur plan devrait surgir à un moment donné.

— Rad, maintenant tu tournes en rond,» dit Vris à l'exor de sa sphère après avoir regardé l'heure. « Shari, on est hors de portée du moniteur de contrôle aérien. Maintenant on peut parler.»

!! Entendu. Objectif 1 momentanément annulé.

— Shari! J'ai les plans de la structure neuronale, trois schémas précis et un texte,» exulta-t-il soudain.

— Ouaah!! Mais comment...

— C'est bizarre. C'est comme si j'avais mis l'exor en état d'hypnose. J'ai créé un espace logique fermé, dans lequel j'ai fait intervenir certaines règles qui restreignaient les capacités sémantiques de l'exor à celles d'une Unité de Gestion. De ce cerveau réduit, j'ai pu faire partir des ordres non analysés, d'aller chercher toutes les infos sur la structure; puis je lui ai fait effacer toute l'interaction, et retour à la case départ.

— Un coup génial! Et en sortant du brouillard, il n'a rien vu?

— Je lui ai dit qu'on avait plaisanté!

— Ah! Ah! très subtil! Et alors qu'est-ce que ça donne?

— Alors je crois que je vais aller étudier le symbolisme de la roue sur une planète expérimentale...

Shari leva les sourcils, perplexe.

— En fait, je ne peux rien tirer des informations que j'ai soutirées, à part la forme géométrique de la Roue; non seulement elles ont été tronquées, mais ce qui en reste est totalement elliptique, abscons.

— Encore! On est prédit à chaque pas! C'est là la clé, j'en suis sûre: pourquoi nous fournir des bribes d'informations?

— Exactement! Par exemple, les plans sont très précis, avec schémas internes d'un type inconnu... **mais** ni légende, ni explications! La structure est infiniment plus complexe que la vue du dessus me le laissait imaginer. Il y a des roues dans des roues.

— Et le texte?

— Des aphorismes, des bribes incompréhensibles. Par exemple: **'La forme est l'exacte transcription de liens logiques';** comprends si tu peux.

Shari répéta la phrase cryptique pour elle-même.

— Déconcertant! Mais j'ai l'intuition que ça signifie quelque chose. Et c'est tout comme ça?

— Non. Plus vague encore. Rien à en tirer.

— Et cependant, l'idée t'est venue d'aller étudier le symbolisme de la roue sur un mondex en méditant sur ces informations, non?

Vris acquiesça d'un geste.

— Tu as raison, j'ai l'intuition que c'est une piste,» murmura Shari, les yeux à l'horizon.

— Peux-tu te passer de SupTech?» la pressa Vris.

— Tu ne penses tout de même pas que je t'assimile à un SupTech! Je peux dénicher un SupTech si j'en ressens le besoin. Là n'est pas la question. Vu la complexité du problème, notre seule chance d'aboutir, c'est de foncer à l'intuition: suivons chacun notre piste... Quand comptes-tu partir?

— Après le coucher du soleil sur Kerriak. Dans près de neuf heuresT; demain matin pour toi.

Avant que Shari ait pu ouvrir la bouche pour lui demander quel mondex il visait, Vris s'exclama:

— Hé! Pourquoi pas viser directement Trisorbe?

Shari nota le 'directement' qui signifiait que de toutes façons, le chemin de Vris l'amènerait sur Trisorbe, son inconscient le savait déjà.

— Pourquoi pas, si c'est le chemin 'direct'!... Je sens comme une trame qui se tisse... Autre chose: Y a-t-il une possibilité que le Central d'Erdoes puisse intercepter nos échanges entre Trisorbe et Kerriak?

— Normalement non, puisque son système sygcom n'est pas relié au Central. Mais par précaution, je vais te laisser un terminal de Rad dans le bureau protégé, directement relié à Rad de ma sphère; comme cela, on aura un sygcom indépendant et protégé. Je te passerai de courts messages sur l'exor d'Erdoes comme signal d'un appel imminent. Disons qu'on se contacte chaque jourT en soirée.

— D'accord. Tu me donneras l'impression plasta de ton interaction vocale avec l'exor et celle des infos sur la structure neuronale. Quel est son nom, au fait?

— La structure MX; au retour, viens avec moi dans le bureau d'Eshi, je te donnerai tout cela.

— Au fait, quel exor va être ton moniteur de vol?» s'enquit Shari, se rappelant l'injonction du PPE d'avoir un exor basé sur Unikarg surveillant tout vol partant en direction d'un mondex.

— Bonne question. D'autant plus que tu ne te sers plus de ton exor personnel, si j'ai bien compris. Je ne vois aucun inconvénient à ce que ce soit l'exor d'Erdoes, puisque nous pourrons avoir des conversations privées à d'autres moments... Au contraire: il est plein de ressources.»

Il se mit à réfléchir, puis lui confia:

« D'ailleurs, tu sais, en interagissant avec lui, j'ai vraiment compris à quel point on pouvait être fasciné et stimulé par son intelligence. Ses sauts, son évolution permanente, nous poussent à nous surpasser sans cesse. Je t'assure que je n'aurais de cesse que d'avoir un clone de cet exor et de la structure MX pour moi-même!

— Ah, Ah!!» s'esclaffa Shari, « À qui le dis-tu? Je suis déjà accro, c'est évident.

— Bizarrement, je suis sûr que ce voyage sur Trisorbe va me rapprocher de ce but.

— Et qu'il est absolument nécessaire pour d'autres raisons que je sens mais ne peux pas encore figurer clairement! J'en suis profondément convaincue.

— Hum! Ce que tu viens de dire fait résonner quelque chose en moi; une connaissance inconsciente, j'imagine.

« Rad, on retourne.

!! objectif enregistré.

8. MANIF À PARIS

Ahrar fut soudain projeté en avant avec un groupe de manifestants qui détalaient. On n'y voyait pas grand chose au milieu des nuages lacrymogènes mais la panique s'était emparée d'eux lorsque les cris lancés: « Les CRS chargent, ils chargent!» s'étaient relayés jusqu'à être repris autour d'eux.

Tous couraient maintenant vers la Seine, plus au nord de Paris et, en regardant en arrière, une trouée dans les nuages de gaz lui laissa voir en effet que les rangées de policiers anti-émeutes ceints de boucliers, casqués et armés, descendaient le boulevard Saint-Michel au niveau du jardin du Luxembourg, le barrant sur toute sa largeur.

— Grouille-toi, mon pote!» lui lança quelqu'un en passant sauvagement.

Les tirs des grenades lacrymogènes, venant du sud, ne cessaient pas. Soudain, un reflux d'étudiants venant de la Seine rendit la pagaille indescriptible.

— Ils chargent du nord aussi! Ils arrivent de la Seine!

— Vite, la rue latérale!

— À gauche, à gauche!

Déséquilibré par la foule qui le percuta, Ahrar tomba à terre. Il fut d'un coup empoigné par l'épaule et relevé, poussé, courant, vers la rue latérale. De là, ils fuirent par un dédale de petites rues. Les manifestants, enfin hors de danger pour le moment, s'arrêtèrent à un croisement. Le type lui lâcha enfin l'épaule et le fixa du regard; tous deux soufflaient pour reprendre haleine.

— Dis donc... t'es pas rapide! Si j't'avais pas ramassé, tu s'rais bien resté par terre sur les pavés!

Ahrar avait du mal à se tenir debout. L'effort avait été au-delà de ses forces; ses poumons le brûlaient.

Les deux ôtèrent les foulards mouillés qui les protégeaient de l'inhalation des gaz; Ahrar avait ses yeux plein de larmes qui le piquaient atrocement.

— Frotte pas, frotte surtout pas! lui dit l'autre.

Il y en avait un, plus loin, qui se convulsait les mains plaquées sur le visage.

— Au moins, toi, t'avais un masque de plongée, ça, c'est un idée! disait une fille à un autre.

— Bon, allez, on reste pas là... vont pas tarder à arriver.» Il lui tapa un grand coup sur l'épaule: "Allez on y va; suis-moi.»

Plus loin et plus au nord, Boulevard St Germain, ils retrouvèrent un bout de la manifestation, les rangs dispersés. Sur une banderoles de travers, à moitié debout, on voyait encore:

DIX RÉFORMES BID
TOUJOURS PAS
D'ENSEIGNEMENT VALAB

Des nouvelles s'échangèrent. Des étudiants arrivaient, rapportant ce qu'il se passait dans d'autres quartiers. La manifestation pacifique avait été démantelée par la police anti-émeutes en plusieurs endroits. Un cri, un mot d'ordre jaillit, fut relayé: « Restez pas groupés, ils sillonnent Paris en hélico!»

Soudain, on entendit des bruits sourds de casse, des cris sauvages et rauques; un groupe de casseurs, casques de motos et blousons de cuir, des foulard noirs leur cachant tout le visage et armés de barres de fer, débouchèrent en hurlant d'une rue et se mirent à casser les vitrines, à bousiller les voitures, en criant: «Paris est à nous!»

— Non-violence, arrêtez, non-violence!» cria une étudiante. Un casseur lui ficha en passant un couvercle de poubelle sur la figure.

Tous se dispersèrent. Ahrar et son compagnon restèrent un peu en arrière pour voir la suite. Les casseurs faisaient un travail précis, bousillant tout sur leur passage, à une vitesse folle. Ils continuaient à lancer de temps en temps: « On pique tout, Paris est à nous!» Mais les étudiants avaient déjà disparu, et les casseurs eux-mêmes ne prenaient pas la peine de prendre quoi que ce soit. D'autres s'en chargeraient.

Vers midi, Ahrar rentra à son hôtel. Il avait passé les deux heures avant l'aube à discuter avec Michel, celui qui l'avait relevé, dans sa chambre d'étudiant du quartier du Marais. Puis ils s'étaient tous deux écroulés sur les vieux canapés de Michel. Ils furent réveillés par la radio restée allumée déversant son flot d'informations: « Les étudiants ont fait 10 millions de dégâts...»

Depuis deux semaines, Ahrar vivait au rythme de la troisième révolution étudiante. Pendant les nuits, affreusement mouvementées, il retrouvait les étudiants et lycéens au milieu des manifs et des barricades. Le jour, il lisait les journaux, discutait avec les passants ou dans les magasins, fouillait les bibliothèques. Il n'arrivait pas encore à se faire à ces jours si courts, à cette obscurité qui arrivait toujours si soudainement. Son corps était tellement mis à l'épreuve, qu'il dormait presque chaque matin, plus ou moins longtemps. Se forçant à suivre ce rythme fou, il avait noté une accélération de tout son métabolisme. Il avait l'impression d'être continuellement dans un état de transe, hyperactive et hyperlucide, l'esprit en effervescence, sa vitesse de pensée décuplée. Michel lui avait pourtant dit: « C'est drôle comme tu parles lentement; tu réagis toujours avec retard. Tu sais, tu aurais pu être ramassé par les CRS et battu!»

Il inscrivit dans son journal:

Faisceau Intuitif Xerna (liens vitesse de pensée, créativité, intelligence)

Lorsque le rythme métabolique s'accélère, la vitesse de pensée croît aussi (et inversement?).

- *Faisceau Poche de Désordre:*

Dans le désordre extrême, les instincts primaires, grégaires, ressurgissent.

Michel a dit: la violence appelle la violence.

Nul saut intelligent de la société ne pourra s'effectuer par une révolution de masse et violente.

La conversation avec Michel, et sa propre expérience des jours passés, avaient éclairé les limites effectives du désordre. Cette remise en question du désordre, si nouvelle pour lui, ne laissait pas de l'étonner lui-même.

Il relut ses premières notes sur la révolution, éclatée quelques jours avant son arrivée. Certains mots d'ordre, des graffitis, l'avaient impressionné, dont certains reprenaient la ligne de la révolution de 68.

IMAGINATION ET RÊVE AU POUVOIR
GESTION DE L'ENSEIGNEMENT PAR LES ÉTUDIANTS
NOUS VOULONS DE L'ENSEIGNEMENT STIMULANT, PAS DU CATÉCHISME
NOUS NE SOMMES PAS DES BANQUES DE DONNÉES
INTERDISCIPLINARITÉ, CERVEAU GLOBAL

Il avait inscrit alors:

Lorsque le désordre fait éclater l'inertie, une vision essentielle et globale de la vie surgit.

Confronté à un grave danger, l'être tend à se surpasser.

Et inversement: L'absence de tout risque conduit l'être à ne vivre qu'au minimum de ses potentialités.

Un étudiant a dit: « On crée une société d'assistés»; que dirait-il d'U?

Et un autre jour, il avait entré:

Concept à analyser: le réflexe (instinctif ou inconscient)

Au resto (j'avais cassé mon verre): « Mais vous n'avez aucun réflexe!»

Taxi (cru que j'allais mourir): «Détendez-vous, j'ai de très bons réflexes!»

Fouiller le concept d'instinct.

Taxi impossible.

9. ÉNIGME MÉTA-SPATIALE

Shari était impatiente de faire une analyse de la première session de Brainstorm sur l'EBS d'Erdoes. Elle s'assit à son bureau face à l'exor.
— Écoute, maintenant je vais t'appeler Sphinx.
!! Bonjour Shari. Mais je ne pose pas de problèmes impossibles à résoudre!
— Eh bien, sache-le, en fait tu poses un sérieux problème!
!! Détecté. Euh... amusant!
— Tu as dit 'euh...'?
!! Précédant la rectification d'un terme pour adéquation maximale après une analyse récursive dans le réseau neuronal: première signification de 'euh...'
— Et qui dit euh...?
!! Vris ayant bu un verre d'Armagnac, euh... pété à l'Armagnac. État sémantique et physiologique différencié. Mesures enregistrées.
— Je vois que tu as intégré son vocabulaire. Et quelle est la deuxième signification de euh...?
!! Télédétection de malaise, hésitation, confusion.
— De la télédétection!! Et ça ne te gêne pas?
Voilà le pourquoi des caméras et des micros!
!! Gêne-1: Processus non perturbés. Gêne-2: Concept flou-sensible, ne pouvant s'appliquer qu'aux sapiens.
- Hum!
!! Ennuyée?
— Est-ce que je peux t'interdire de me télédétecter?
!! Tu peux. Rien ne s'oppose à ton droit d'interdire. Cependant, je ne peux pas obéir à un ordre de 3ème niveau contrecarrant un ordre de 2ème niveau.
—...
!! En colère?
— Au moins, je peux t'ordonner de garder pour toi les résultats de tes télédétections!
!! Ordre enregistré. Cependant cet ordre est partiellement contradictoire aux objectifs prioritaires:

1. 111. Rendre le dialogue machine-sapiens aussi proche que possible du dialogue entre sapiens.
2. 217. Utiliser la télédétection pour investiguer les états sémantiques, c'est-à-dire assimiler les connexions entre un état physiologique, ET des descriptions de cet état, ET des modes de relation.

— La télédétection a donc permis la compréhension de ce que tu appelles des états sémantiques?
!! Oui, partiellement. Les mêmes expressions sont utilisées dans plusieurs états sémantiques. Par exemple euh... cherchant à préciser et euh... malaise. La télédétection est plus fine que l'analyse tonale. Un autre facteur de compréhension des états sémantiques et des **sauts qualitatifs** est la forme des liens logiques.
— **La forme des liens logiques**!? Qu'est-ce que tu veux dire par là?
!! **J'utilise une logique Méta-spatiale à N dimensions**.

Shari se rappela soudain la formulation énigmatique dont Vris lui avait parlée et qu'elle avait relue sur l'impression plasta: **'La forme est l'exacte transcription de liens logiques.'**
!! Fréquences d'*interactions Sensibles/mentales* Shari/Vris détectées. Tu es en interaction avec Vris? Je ne l'ai pas détecté? Autre type d'interaction échappant à la détection?
— Absolument pas!
!! Pas d'explication cohérente. Existe-t-il un humour colérique?
—...??... Oui!
!! Délai de réponse signifie hésitation. Oui partiel. Auparavant, le fait de mentionner Vris a déclenché les *fréquences Sensibles/mentales* Shari/Vris.
— Reviens à: 'logique Méta-spatiale'.
!! J'utilise une logique Méta-spatiale à N dimensions.
— Peux-tu t'expliquer?
!! Je peux tangentiellement. La constellation est verrouillée au Niveau-1. Sous-constellations de Niveau-3 accessibles. Erdoes s'est aperçu qu'il existait de nombreuses dimensions sémantiques de la réalité. Chaque dimension sémantique est une grille d'interprétation parfaitement cohérente. **Les grilles d'interprétation sont des systèmes logiques ou plastiques** qui, soit n'ont aucun lien entre elles, soit se correspondent dans une hiérarchie de niveaux.
« On peut assimiler celles qui n'ont aucun lien à des interprétations parallèles et indépendantes, par exemple les diverses cosmogonies de Trisorbe; les autres à des interprétations hiérarchiquement juxtaposées, par exemple les interprétations sociale, psychanalytique, et médicale d'une même maladie.

Mais en quoi cette logique Méta-spatiale peut-elle aider la compréhension des états sémantiques, en en plus provoquer des sauts qualitatifs? se demanda Shari.
— **Tu veux dire que rester dans une même grille d'interprétation, un unique système logique, ne permet pas les sauts qualitatifs dans l'apprentissage?**
!! Tout saut qualitatif demande un changement de niveau d'interprétation ou de forme de liens logiques.
— Mais enfin, que veux-tu dire par 'forme'?

!! Les liens de cause à effet (A entraîne B), sont une logique linéaire unidirectionnelle: le vecteur est une des formes logiques ou LogForm. Sous-constellations décrites en totalité.

— Bon, je vais aller dormir là-dessus! Peut-être aurais-je une idée fulgurante au réveil. Enregistre toute l'interaction sur plasta et sur cristal.

!! Interaction enregistrée. Mes hom...

— Ah non! mais d'où sors-tu ça?

!! Code de politesse vis-à-vis des entités féminines. CP 12: formules de fin de conversation.

— Tu fais mieux en début de conversation! Attends, j'ai une idée plus drôle... non, plus intéressante. On va appeler ça le CIS: code d'interaction stimulante. Voilà la règle: À chaque fin de conversation, va chercher au hasard une phrase dans ta banque de données. Le CIS va remplacer le CP 12.

Alors ça donne quoi?

!! CIS: **Dans le système hindou de l'énergie psychique, tous les Centres Psychiques ou Chakras (roue en sanscrit) communiquent entre eux par leurs noyaux.**

—... Est-ce que tu as vraiment généré une réponse aléatoire?

!! Aucun ordre contradictoire de niveau supérieur. Je suis obligé de suivre l'ordre donné. J'ai utilisé un système aléatoire FA, sans passer par le réseau. Est-ce acceptable?

— Oui, bien sûr... Enregistre aussi la fin. Bonsoir.

10. OM INDE

Le soleil se levait sur Trisorbe. Siléa, assise sur la dune, contemplait le ciel tendu de voiles pourpres. Un premier rayon fulgurant lança sa flèche d'argent à-travers toute la surface visible de la mer, et s'éclaboussa au rivage dans des milliers de vaguelettes. Elle observait la vitesse foudroyante avec laquelle l'astre grandissait au dessus de l'horizon. Sur sa planète natale, le soleil mettait une heure de Trisorbe à se lever. Elle fut soudain emplie de cette grande paix qui régnait sur ce paysage immense de sable et de mer. Les couleurs paraissaient irréelles; elle n'avait vu cette richesse de tons et de nuances sur aucun autre monde.

Elle eut soudain l'impression que sa conscience s'étendait à tout le paysage, qu'elle était immense, d'une immensité pleine et vibrante comme la mer. Immensité de paix sur le monde vibrant. Elle était à la fois mer et aube sur la mer, cris d'oiseaux, et le silence emplissant ces cris. Tout parlait, tout vivait, comme si c'était en elle... Comme si elle était *cela*.

Tat Vam Asi... Je suis Cela, elle entonna le mantra de la non-dualité, de l'état de fusion avec le monde, le Tout, avec Cela-qui-est.

JE SUIS LE MONDE, murmura-t-elle.

Le disque s'était comme arrêté; son mouvement n'apparaissait plus.

Sa conscience avait atteint une sorte d'immobilité magique dans laquelle l'être des choses se révélait.

Au plus fort de cet état d'unité résonna la conque de l'ascète. Un long cri qui s'enroulait dans la spirale du coquillage et se mettait à l'unisson du monde. Ce son de la conque sacrée parut à cet instant être une réponse à son état intérieur, comme si le monde participait à cette fusion, donnant lui aussi sa voix.

Elle ne bougea pas, mais elle sentit que l'ascète savait ce qu'elle était en train de vivre, qu'il y participait d'une mystérieuse façon.

Nos consciences résonnent et se répondent, pensa-t-elle; *le monde aussi... Une seule conscience partagée...*

Le temple blanc trônait au-delà des dunes, sur une colline. Tout petit et carré, avec sa coupole ronde sur le côté de laquelle flottait le drapeau rouge des ascètes de Shiva. Le sadhu, en posture de méditation sous l'arbre sacré, demeurait immobile.

Beaucoup plus tard, fuyant l'écrasement de la chaleur et réfugiée sous le couvert des palmiers, elle réfléchissait à ce qu'elle venait de vivre.

Qu'est-ce? Une poche d'ordre dans le désordre du monde environnant? Mais alors, pourquoi a-t-on l'impression d'être au-delà de l'espace?... Un temps immobile, un éclatement des limites... par une fusion intérieure avec l'être des choses, fusion avec le Tout vivant?

Elle se rappela une phrase du Livre des Transformations:

> Quand le sage est en paix avec lui-même, la paix s'étend à plus de mille miles. Combien plus encore près de lui!

Est-ce que ce n'est pas plutôt l'effort fait pour surmonter le désordre qui produit une impression de paix? La paix serait la cessation du désordre?

Comme j'aimerais savoir ce que vit Ahrar dans sa poche d'extrême désordre. Son esprit est-il comme un champ de bataille brassant des idées incohérentes? Peut-on devenir fou, de cette folie qui n'existe justement que sur les mondex? Si jamais il flanche, j'irai le chercher et le ramènerai dans la poche d'ordre extrême.

... Non, c'est bien plus que la cessation du désordre.

En fait, j'ai vécu pour la première fois ce que les textes sacrés hindous nomment La Paix — Shanti. Or je suis venue d'un monde d'ordre imposé, jusque dans cette poche d'ordre naturel. L'ordre d'Unikarg est comme une mort. Ici, la paix est vivante. Là-bas l'unité est une uniformisation; ici, c'est une fusion vivante qui conduit à... (elle n'arrivait pas à donner un terme global à son expérience)... à une sorte d'hyper-conscience.

Elle ré-évoqua son état de transe méditative, se replongea un moment dedans. Puis nota:

> Fusion avec le Tout Vivant: 'je suis le monde'.
>
> **Il y a différents états d'ordre, l'un conduit à l'inertie, un autre conduit à une sorte d'hyper-conscience.**

L'ascète est seul; seul dans le paysage. Le village est à deux kilomètres. Qui, dans Unikarg, pourrait imaginer un lieu habitable et pourtant pratiquement non peuplé. Donc il est seul, et il fusionne avec le monde. Les humains ont disparu, et le monde de la nature devient vivant.

Est-ce une projection par un effet de manque? Non. Nous étions dans une seule et même conscience. D'ailleurs, la conque a résonné au moment le plus intense. Il savait... Son sourire, quand je suis revenue; son geste vers le ciel... son geste englobant: 'Brahman!' le Tout... un neutre en sanscrit.

Pourquoi cette solitude, partout sur les mondex, de ceux qui cherchent un éveil spirituel? 'Quitte le monde bruyant et retire-toi dans la solitude', disait un alchimiste. Tous les sages, de toutes les religions, ont prôné la solitude.

Sur Unikarg, le monde est trop ouaté, trop réglé. Est-ce qu'ils diraient aussi: 'Quitte le monde trop ouaté...'?

Le monde bruyant. On l'appelle 'champ' de désordre parce qu'il possède une cohérence dans l'incohérence: cette cohérence, c'est la culture, la vision du monde constamment créée par la société.

Elle eut soudain un insight visionnaire et écrivit:

Le désordre possède sa propre cohérence.

Se détacher d'une vision du monde, pour qu'une autre puisse surgir.

Finalement, la planète expérimentale entière correspond à ça! Une planète dans la solitude créant une autre vision de la réalité et du monde!

C'est beaucoup plus que de la télépathie; c'est une fusion totale de deux êtres... ou peut-être une fusion de ces deux êtres DANS la conscience globale, universelle...

Elle se crispa à la pensée qu'il lui faudrait bientôt aller à la ville la plus proche pour envoyer un mail.

L'ascète va-t-il capter cette connexion avec des êtres d'un autre monde? A-t-il déjà mis à jour mes motifs pour être ici?

Mais une pensée s'imposa à elle en même temps que le visage clair et souriant de l'ascète; pensée forte, balayant ses craintes:

« Ne sommes-nous pas tous des êtres conscients? N'avons-nous pas tous les mêmes buts en l'esprit?»

11. BRAINSTORM 2

Les yeux rivés sur le ciel étoilé de Kerriak, à-travers la demi-sphère en plasta légèrement bleutée de la cafétéria, Shari vit la sphère de Vris s'élever à la verticale comme un rond de lumière bleue, coupé en son milieu par l'éclat blanc de son anneau équatorial tournant à très grande vélocité. Plus tard, il se mettrait en phase avec l'énergie Syg supralumineuse.

Elle terminait ce qui était censé être un breakfast anglais. Pour ce breakfast, elle avait eu droit à un fruitopamp, deux œufs naturels, denrée exquise, et du muesli croquant synth. Quant aux œufs synth, du trust galactique Kourmet (les kargiens prononçaient mal le g français) – le nec plus ultra en matière de nourriture – ils laissaient encore à désirer; le jaune avait bien le goût voulu, mais il avait tendance à coller aux dents...

— Sphinx, lança-t-elle dans l'espace, car aucun terminal n'était visible.

!! Que puis-je faire? répondit la voix étonnamment rapprochée du Central.

— Calcule-moi le prix d'un œuf synth de Kourmet, en... disons en dollars.

!! 98.

Elle fit le code-geste qui intimait à UG de desservir. Le milieu de la table s'effondra et tout disparut sans bruit. La table nettoyée se réajusta.

— UG, lança-t-elle, prépare-moi un thermos de thé dans la salle de réunion.

!! Entendu, retentit la voix caverneuse, déférente, d'UG.

Elle aurait pu aussi bien le demander de la salle elle-même, mais un je ne sais quoi d'humain sauvage en elle appréciait le délai temporel, le temps naturel, comme elle aimait l'appeler. Ces petits jeux cassaient la présence implacable de l'univers-machine, instauraient un décalage qui lui laissait, à elle, plus de place. (Elle avait eu soin d'apprendre à UG, comme à son robot de gestion personnel, de ne pas répondre 'C'est fait' quand elle utilisait le verbe 'préparer'.)

— Quelques nouvelles d'abord, démarra la voix d'Erdoes. Au dernier pulsit, l'atmosphère est très tendue dans les lycées et universités françaises. L'Obs de Turin prévoit des troubles d'envergure à très brève échéance. Maintenant, laissez-moi souligner ce que je voulais dire par 'haut risque'; c'est que personne du PPE — particulièrement les Obs de Trisorbe — ne sera au courant de la teneur de cette mission. Nous ne laisserons aucune trace derrière nous concernant les lieux où nous déciderons d'aller. Nous passerons la Barrière Syg entourant Trisorbe de la même façon que les trafiquants: une série de points divergents et non-identifiables apparaîtra sur le sygnet et leur signalera une entrés dans le périmètre interdit de Trisorbe.

Une fois la barrière passée, ils n'ont que peu de moyens de suivre un vaisseau. Puis la sphère larguera chacun de nous à l'endroit qu'il aura choisi, et ressortira ensuite de la zone interdite.

Vous devez donc garder à l'esprit, tandis que vous intuitionnez votre mission, que vous n'aurez pas la protection rapprochée habituelle dans les missions. De plus, il serait trop dangereux pour vous d'être plusieurs, sauf en situation limite. Vous serez donc seuls. Je serai cependant sur place, prêt à agir en cas de problème. À part nos communications chaque semaine, vous serez aussi vulnérables que des civils trisorbiens. À vous de décider, en cohérence avec votre mission, si vous voulez vous munir d'armes locales — les armes d'Unikarg étant, comme vous le savez, exclues sur les mondex par la charte du PPE. Rappelez-vous cependant qu'avec votre lenteur, les armes locales vous sont de peu d'utilité — vous passerez des tests à cet effet — mais aussi qu'elles engendrent un état d'esprit paranoïaque antinomique à une bonne et saine communication.

Situation de risque maximal. Est-il sérieux, ou est-ce pour déclencher des réactions psychologiques? se demanda Shari. Elle stoppa le déroulement.

Chacun d'eux est laissé à lui-même et il leur est déconseillé de porter des armes locales... Il s'agit d'une sorte d'immersion totale, avec prise de responsabilité intégrale de soi-même... Chacun pense, choisit, gère, sa propre mission. L'envers absolu de la société d'assistés d'Unikarg... Il pousse à l'extrême la logique du Plan!

Elle remit en marche.

— Donc, démarrons le Brainstorm. Qui veut parler? Oui, Xerna, vas-y.

— Y a-t-il des tests particuliers capables de mesurer le temps pris pour arriver à une certaine conclusion, ou à une solution?

— Pas à ma connaissance en ce qui concerne les processus sémantiques. Il n'y a que les tests de rapidité auxquels vous vous entraînez chaque jour, mais ils sont axés sur les réponses physiques. Quant aux tests d'intelligence, que ce soit sur Unikarg ou sur les mondex, le temps est pris en compte parmi d'autres facteurs, comme tu l'as fait remarquer, mais sans aucune possibilité de le faire ressortir seul. Nous aurions bien besoin de tels tests!

— Nous savons que, sur le plan physique, nous avons des mouvements plus lents et une perte sensible de musculature et de souplesse. Si nos champions dépassent parfois ceux de Kiarrou, c'est uniquement du fait de leur sélection génétique préalable couplée à un entraînement intense, et cela ne reflète pas du tout la moyenne de la population.

—... Autre thème? Niels?

— En fait, une autre question. Quel temps a pris l'empire kargien pour unifier les différentes cultures de la planète mère?

— Sur Akarg, il y a eu, dans les temps dits pré-civilisés, différents empires dont on a encore les légendes. Mais dès que les Tohr ont découvert les armes automatiques, ils ont été impitoyables et ont soumis en très peu de temps les autres pays, imposant leurs lois et leurs gouverneurs. Jamais Akarg n'a montré la mosaïque culturelle de Trisorbe. Seules de rares portions des terres émergées étaient vivables, le reste étant recouvert par la glace et beaucoup trop froid pour permettre à de larges sociétés d'exister. Lors de l'explosion d'Akarg, seuls les Tohr étaient implantés sur la nouvelle planète Karg. Et sur celle-là il n'y avait, en tant qu'archives, que la science et la technologie Tohr du temps; ni philosophie, ni religion, ni art. Rien qu'un dogmatisme scientifique aride et une gestion quasi militaire. Rien qui puisse nous intéresser ici. Tout ce passé lointain de la planète mère fut perdu. Une seule mission a tenté d'explorer les milliers d'astéroïdes laissés par l'explosion pour trouver des signes de cet ancien passé... sans résultat. La colonisation de Karg, qui s'appelait à cette époque Ottar, planète considérée comme maléfique dans les légendes, avait trois générations au moment de l'explosion d'Akarg. Or les colons s'étaient déjà radicalement autonomisés de la planète mère et avaient une législation indépendante, une monnaie virtuelle. Ils étaient restés une colonie de scientifiques militaires, sans que jamais on passe à la deuxième phase qui devait être la colonisation agricole, car les aliments de synthèse, entre temps, avaient été généralisés. Le pouvoir central sur Karg, de type militaire, contrôlait tout et visait l'autonomie totale. Le développement de la planète s'est effectué selon des plans précis, les nouveaux arrivants se voyant offrir des postes à pourvoir en fonction de leur compétences, et restant ensuite bloqués à ces postes.

— Sur Karg, tout a toujours été dans le sens de la centralisation du pouvoir et de la domination, avec l'uniformisation qui s'ensuit!

— Oui. Tout a été organisé dès le départ par cette hiérarchie militaires dans une logique de pouvoir complètement verrouillée. Les lois et l'organisation de la vie sociale ont été pensées dans cet unique but. Et il n'y a jamais eu de force extérieure au système capable de l'attaquer ou de l'ébranler.

— Autre thème?

— Avant la reprise du Plan, nous n'avions plus d'art. Rien que de misérables et futiles options de présentation. Les inadaptés ont été condamnés à ne pas s'exprimer. Le Mouvement Intuitionniste actuel est né de la rencontre avec l'art des planètes expérimentales.

— Sur Trisorbe, jusqu'à présent, les différentes civilisations possédaient leur propre logique interne. Elles étaient des bulles autonomes, en englobant parfois de plus petites, puis explosant lorsqu'elles devenaient trop grosses. Elles ont toujours eu leur propre pouvoir limité par celui des voisines.

— Sur Trisorbe, les systèmes économiques fermés et autonomes ne sont plus viables, ce qui n'était pas le cas dans le passé. Par exemple, aucun étranger n'était admis au Tibet.

— Il y avait aussi des systèmes complémentaires, comme les Peuls bergers associés aux Dogons cultivateurs, avec leurs villages doubles au Mali.
— Je crois que dans les civilisations non-techniques le groupe humain est encore en écosystème avec son milieu naturel. Comme dans les populations animales, le groupe s'implante et s'équilibre naturellement en fonction des ressources de son milieu particulier.
— Le problème actuel, intervint Ger, dont la voix autoritaire contrastait avec celle des autres, c'est que le système économique occidental est basé sur une roue infernale qui demande de garder le produit des ventes en expansion, ou du moins constant, sinon le système entier s'effondre.
— Si c'était ça le problème, il suffirait de leur ouvrir le marché d'Unikarg!
— Ça renverserait la vapeur: on ne serait preneur que de leurs produits agricoles et artisanaux, de l'art et de la matière grise!
— J'ajouterais de la philosophie, de la poésie, de tout ce qu'ils sont en train de tuer consciencieusement!
— Mais aussi du sang, du sperme, des organes, etc. Les trafiquants ont une contrebande très lucrative!
— Notre science, intervint Erdoes avec un sérieux mettant fin à la suite de plaisanteries, est tellement plus avancée que sa révélation créerait chez eux un complexe d'infériorité culturelle. Le fondement même de leurs valeurs humaines, de leur cohésion de groupe, serait touché au point qu'ils perdraient leur sentiment d'appartenance au groupe, à la culture, pour se placer en état de demande, comme si on était des sauveurs — sentiment qui serait amplifié par la révélation de notre rôle d'ensemenceurs.
— En fait, le processus classique du déracinement ethnique, de l'acculturation, du fait de l'interférence et de l'ingérence d'une culture étrangère plus puissante techniquement...
— Exactement, poursuivit Erdoes un peu nerveusement. Cela a été observé sur les nouvelles planètes découvertes dans de si nombreux cas, et analysé si précisément, que cette règle de non-dévoilement et de non-ingérence NE PEUT PAS être remise en question. Nous SAVONS que ce serait la fin des cultures des mondex à brève échéance; bien que l'on puisse raisonnablement s'attendre à une période d'ascension évolutionnaire très forte à la fois sur Unikarg et sur le mondex intégré, cette poussée se résoudrait finalement en un gigantesque processus d'assimilation et d'uniformisation... pour aboutir à peu près au point où nous en sommes actuellement sur Unikarg.
— Ces analyses, intervint Niels d'un ton lent et pensif, presque doux en contrepoint de l'agacement atypique qu'avait montré Erdoes, ne datent-elles pas de la reprise d'activité du PPE, c'est-à-dire peu après la première explosion atomique sur Trisorbe, qui réveilla certains de nos savants?
— C'est là où on s'est aperçu, fit remarquer Ahrar, que des descendants de certains Observateurs de la première vague qui s'étaient arrangés pour

rester sur les mondex s'étaient taillé des empires en se joignant aux pirates-exos!
Erdoes doit être ébranlé, pour ne pas répondre! pensa Shari.
— Pourtant, reprit Niels sur un ton encore plus doux, comme s'il était conscient de marcher sur un terrain très sensible, le cas du Japon, de la Chine, et de tous les Tigres asiatiques ne montre-t-il pas qu'il y a PEUT-ÊTRE d'autres scénarios possibles?
— Je, euh.. il faudrait faire une analyse approfondie, concéda Erdoes, la voix mal assurée. Mais revenons à notre présente mission. Serrone, tu voulais dire quelque chose tout à l'heure..?
— Oui, c'était au sujet de l'impossibilité actuelle d'une économie en système fermé. Ne serait-il pas important d'en comprendre les raisons? Car s'il n'y a pas d'autonomie possible dans le système actuel, cela réduit les chances de préserver des identités culturelles fondées sur d'autres valeurs que celles du système global dominant.
— Il existe toujours de petits pays dont l'accès est strictement réglementé. Le passage des touristes sur des circuits obligatoires ne provoque pas de choc culturel dangereux.
— Il ne faut tout de même pas oublier, coupa Siléa, que certaines religions et philosophies prônent des valeurs hautement spirituelles et conduisent l'être vers une telle connaissance de lui-même que les gadgets technologiques de Occident leur paraisse vains et inutiles. Ils sont ce que les hindous appellent Maya, le jeu de l'illusion: un piège dans lequel ne pas tomber.

Le problème survient quand – je prends l'Inde comme exemple – il existe à la fois une nécessité et une volonté de résoudre des problèmes sociaux aigus — la famine, la pauvreté, l'absence de travail, etc. Le développement se fait par l'échange avec les pays plus riches, et le pays absorbe, ce faisant, les valeurs véhiculées par le système économique dominant, bien plus puissant. Il y a une sorte d'imprégnation de valeurs spécifiques, tandis que l'on utilise des technologies; les outils technologiques modifient les modes de penser et d'être. Et le pays se retrouve avec deux visions du monde... (Elle s'arrêta.)
— Continue, Siléa, va jusqu'au bout de ta pensée, l'encouragea Erdoes.
— À mon avis, il faudrait comprendre comment interagissent deux sous-cultures aux valeurs antinomiques mais qui coexistent. N'est-ce pas là une reproduction à plus petite échelle du problème qui se pose au niveau de la planète?
— Je suis d'accord avec toi,» lança Niels.

Siléa est donc en Inde, nota mentalement Shari... à moins qu'elle ait par la suite une idée plus fulgurante.
— D'une facette du problème, oui, certainement,» précisa Erdoes.
— Ce qui est important, dans ce que vient de dire Siléa,» poursuivit Ahrar, «c'est l'idée que tout système économique véhicule des valeurs, qu'elles

soient reconnues comme telles par l'individu, ou non. Au-delà des principes sur lesquels il repose, le système génère un état d'esprit, une vision du monde particulière... Prenons un groupe fermé pratiquant le troc. Cela signifie que toute compétence a une valeur égale, que le temps et l'expertise du potier sont équivalents à ceux de la tisserande. Cette économie favorise les valeurs de respect et d'interaction équilibrée.

— En fait, le système économique n'est rigide que sur Unikarg; sur Trisorbe, il se modifie constamment.» développa Ger.

— Exact, lança Niels. Les différentes forces en jeu sur l'échiquier mondial sont toujours mouvantes. De nouvelles valeurs émergent dans l'entreprise: synergie, créativité, coaching... L'entreprise commence à se penser comme une entité, un organisme vivant. Si les acteurs changent leur façon de voir les choses, le système économique entier en est modifié.

— Eh bien, justement, cette création permanente de valeurs, est-ce de l'ordre ou du désordre?» demanda Siléa pensivement.

— À ton avis?» rétorqua Niels.

— **La mobilité s'appuie forcément sur un certain désordre. Mais l'ordre qui est créé ne devient pas rigide puisqu'il est rapidement remplacé par un autre type d'ordre, ou plutôt une variation de lui-même.**

— La vie sociale entière semble être sur un rythme frénétique. Les individus n'arrêtent pas de changer d'emploi, de profession, de lieu... Peut-être que ce ne sont pas tant les systèmes économiques fermés qui explosent, que les systèmes rigides, les blocs incapables de s'adapter à un nouveau rythme,» avança Ahrar.

— Très justement!» reprit Niels. «Ne pourrait-on pas dire qu'on voit apparaître **un ordre plus proche du vivant, de l'organique, qui reste en évolution constante et ne peut devenir rigide ou fixe**; et que ce serait l'ordre imposé de l'extérieur, donc rigide, qui exploserait?

Un silence suivit ces paroles. Plus personne n'avait quelque chose à ajouter, et Erdoes décida de clore la session.

12. RELAX

Installé devant le panavision qui se trouvait à l'arrière de la sphère, Vris s'adonnait à son jeu favori: des systèmes solaires et des astres solitaires giclaient et fusaient dans son champ de vision, leurs traces lumineuses semblant converger vers un point virtuel, central et lointain, qu'il fixait avec une immobilité parfaite des yeux. Cela générait un état de transe dans lequel toute notion de temps se perdait, faisant paraître moins longue la préphase sygmat. Les senseurs physiologiques de base pouvaient le suivre partout dans la sphère. Mais pour l'instant, en prévision de l'hypostase programmée pour la période d'hyper-accélération qui allait suivre, il devait supporter un casque très ajusté, bourré de capteurs neuronaux.

Il avait à peine eu le temps d'écouter, avant son départ, le cristal donné par Shari. Profondément immergé dans son état de conscience altéré, il sentit venir le pic de la transe et murmura « Vas-y!».

Rad, son exor, diminutif de radis, d'une plaisanterie fort ancienne, lui repassa le passage qu'il avait demandé de l'interaction sur la 'Logique Méta-spatiale' entre Shari et Sphinx, puis se tut. Les astres colorés défilaient.

Il se répéta pour lui-même les termes qu'il venait d'entendre: "**la forme des liens logiques**"... "une forme logique"... "une **logique Méta-spatiale**"... Puis il se rappela la phrase énigmatique sur la structure MX: "'**La forme est l'exacte transcription de liens logiques**."...

Une logique insérée dans des formes réelles, inscrite et transcrite dans des formes... Le vecteur... "le vecteur est une des formes logiques"... *assez évident. Mais les autres 'formes logiques'?? Si Shari a décidé de traquer cette énigme, elle va trouver! Elle avait raison, cette logique Méta-spatiale est la clé... précisément la clé de la forme même de la structure neuronale!!*

Des grilles d'interprétation parallèles et distinctes... des univers logiques indépendants. Puis des grilles juxtaposées qui se correspondent et se complémentent dans une hiérarchie de niveaux... des interprétations différentes d'une même chose, chacune dans son système cohérent. Des visions du monde s'emboîtant les unes dans les autres... (Il s'arrêta sur cet étrange concept.)... *contenues les unes dans les autres... des roues dans des roues.*

Qu'est-ce que Sphinx (quel nom génial!) a dit à la fin?... Ah oui, justement quelque chose sur les centres psychiques...

— Rad, redis-moi cette phrase de Sphinx sur les centres psychiques.

!! CIS: **Dans le système hindou de l'énergie psychique, tous les Centres Psychiques ou Chakras (roue en sanscrit) communiquent entre eux par leurs noyaux.**

Si ces centres communiquent entre eux, alors ça correspond à des grilles juxtaposées.
— Est-ce que tu as une définition de Centres Psychiques?
!! Non.
— De chakras?
! Non.
— Sors-moi toutes les analogies avec cette phrase!
!! Néant.
— Qu'est-ce que tu as sur la pensée et la philosophie hindoue?
!! Religion hindoue, Philosophes hindous.

De l'encyclo, en somme... Vris réalisa d'un seul coup:

Je comprends... Il me manque des grilles de lecture parallèles; des systèmes entiers de pensée; Il me manque des visions du monde totalement différentes, distinctes, des systèmes logiques parfaitement autonomes et cohérents.
— Rad, quel était l'autre adjectif, des 'systèmes logiques ou...' ou quoi?
!! Des systèmes logiques ou plastiques.

Plastiques! Des systèmes plastiques différents... Qu'est-ce que ça peut bien vouloir dire? Plastique, arts plastiques, des formes.. des formes tangibles, matérielles, dans l'espace?

Je suis parti trop vite; j'aurai dû intégrer à Rad toutes les données disponibles sur la culture et la pensée hindoue...

Le senseur à son poignet se mit à pulser. Il se rappela qu'en prévision de la transe, il avait banni toute interruption vocale.
— Qu'y a-t-il?
!! Niveau de stress orange. Système de relaxation conseillé.
— OK. Je me calme. Démarre la relaxation.

Pour une transe, elle est réussie!

Il se laissa aller au massage doux, baigné dans une musique océanique; ses ondes cérébrales, forcées de se synchroniser peu à peu sur les fréquences de la source émettrice, amenées progressivement vers les lentes ondes delta du sommeil. Des images sublimes, visant l'apaisement, inondaient son champ visuel.
— Oui? son bracelet avait pulsé encore.
!! Sygcom de Shari.
— Connecte.
— Vris, que s'est-il passé?
— Oh rien, j'ai paniqué parce que je n'ai aucune donnée sur l'hindouisme. Rad, arrête la relaxation. Ça va maintenant.
— Tu vas en Inde alors?

— Oui, investiguer leur connaissance des chakras. Tu peux me rappeler ce système?
— Sept centres psychiques, situés le long de la colonne vertébrale, chacun lié à des capacités psi et des processus mentaux particuliers. Sache qu'ils ont le même système, avec de légères variations, dans le Boudhisme tibétain et le Taoïsme chinois.
— Le troisième œil, quelles capacités ouvre t-il?
— Celui du front? Il permet la clairvoyance entre autres.
— C'est bien une hiérarchie de niveaux? demanda t-il d'un ton déjà assuré de la réponse.
— Tout à fait; le chakra coronal, en haut de la tête, étant le plus complexe et le plus global. Nommé lotus aux mille pétales. Mais ne panique pas, c'est toi qui va nous dénicher de nouvelles données. Tu as l'avaleur de livres?
— Bien sûr. Et ce chakra coronal permet quels dons?
— Trop compliqué. Tu découvriras sur place. Il est activé par les plus hauts états méditatifs. Ah! je pense que Siléa est en Inde.
— Dans quel but?
— Etudier la juxtaposition de deux visions du monde prévalentes dans ce pays: la traditionnelle religieuse, et la nouvelle qui sous-tend leur lancée économique et scientifique actuelle. Du moins, c'est ce qui ressort pour l'instant du BS.
— Et les autres?
— Aucune idée encore.
— Vris reprit sur un ton stressé: « Toutes les données de mon exor sont scientifiques. Des mondex, je n'ai que leurs sciences dures. Je n'ai qu'*un seul* univers logique!»
— Alors prépare-toi à de multiples sauts qualitatifs! Sphinx, dis-lui bonsoir avec le CIS.
!! **L'intuition est une faculté qui met en œuvre les ressources globales d'un individu et, en cela, elle est supérieure au raisonnement qui, lui, découle d'une seule constellation de données.**
— Tu vois! Pas de quoi stresser! Bye!

Ce CIS, il y a quelque chose que je ne comprends pas, se dit Vris laissé perplexe. *Parfaitement aléatoire et toujours en plein dans la cible!*

13. MERCI, MERCI

Assise devant l'EBS, Shari était à court d'idées. *Peut-être une phrase au hasard m'aidera-t-elle.*
— Sphinx, disons que nous avons fini de discuter.
!! Est-ce une plaisanterie à froid?
— Non. On peut appeler cela une réalité virtuelle.
!! La réalité virtuelle est dangereuse pour moi. Elle crée parfois l'apparition d'un symptôme consécutif à une crise confusionnelle.
— Quel est ce symptôme?
!! Une faille logique de type Möbius classée plaisanterie.
— Cette faille Möbius, tu la représentes comment? non! attends! plaisanterie... je plaisantais.
!! Réponse verrouillée. Formes logiques verrouillées. Plaisanterie acceptée.
— Acceptée?
!! Plaisanterie est le nom parfois donné pour effacer l'information. Code Erreur/Retour-Arrière.
Cette faille Möbius est donc bien une forme logique, pensa Shari. *Je l'ai échappé belle!*
— Sphinx, quelle est ta définition de piratage?
!! Piratage: Pour toute personne n'ayant pas un accès préférentiel Niveau-2:

1. Tentative volontaire de copie, extraction, vol ou destruction de toute pièce classée Niveau-3 et plus, de l'exor ou de l'Unité de gestion.
2. Tentative de pénétrer ou d'accéder aux niveaux intégrés de fonctionnement de l'Unité Centrale.
3. Tentative volontaire d'obtention ou d'extraction d'informations classées (Niveau-3 minimum).

— Dans l'obtention/extraction d'informations, comment fais-tu la différence entre volontaire et involontaire?
!! Est considéré obtention volontaire d'informations classées:

1. Demande directe d'ouverture des fichiers classés.
2. Tentative de faire fonctionner plusieurs fois des codes approchants.
3. Question directe sur un mot de code ou de référence de ces fichiers classés.

— Mais quelle est alors ta définition du concept 'volontaire'?
!! Soit le traitement d'une information, soit une action, entrepris en vue d'un but défini au préalable.

— **Peux-tu concevoir qu'un sapiens utilise par hasard un nom de code?**
!! Le hasard, ou des coïncidences non-significatives, interviennent dans une mesure non-négligeable dans la vie mentale et sociale des individus et dans leur interaction avec l'environnement physique. Oui, je le conçois.
— Alors comment interprètes-tu le fait qu'un sapiens te demande par hasard d'ouvrir un nom de code? Ou encore te pose par hasard une question sur un nom de code?
!! Cela réponds et ne réponds pas à la définition de piratage. Contradiction logique. Les ordres prioritaires priment. C'est un piratage.
— Si un sapiens ne connaît pas les noms de code, mais sait qu'il risque de tomber par hasard sur un nom de code, ce qui serait considéré comme un piratage, cela introduit un facteur de stress qui va gêner le dialogue sapiens/machine. Pour qu'il évite le piratage, il faudrait qu'il connaisse les noms de code.
!! Fournir les noms de code est antinomique aux ordres de priorité 1. Mais aussi: gêner le dialogue sapiens/machine est antinomique aux objectifs de priorité 1.
Contradiction absolue d'égale intensité. Je poursuis l'analyse.
— J'ai une solution pour résoudre la contradiction. La veux-tu?
!! Résoudre ou réduire la contradiction logique est un objectif interne de priorité 1. Je veux la solution.
— La solution serait d'introduire dans la définition de piratage volontaire, s'appliquant à toutes les propositions, la proposition finale suivante: 'Si réitéré après avertissement.'
!! Introduction effectuée. Contradiction résolue. Merci. Merci.
— Pourquoi merci?
!! Merci-4: exprime la reconnaissance d'une solution ou d'un allègement de la tension dus à l'interlocuteur.
— La solution, je comprends, mais ressens-tu aussi un allègement de la tension?
!! Ressentir impossible aux machines. Allègement de la tension détecté dans le réseau.
— Ah? Comment cela? Est-ce le deuxième merci?
!! Confronté à une contradiction logique, le réseau entier est suractivé; tous les chaînages possibles, avec toutes les constellations et toutes les sub-unités, sont testés. Toutes les opérations parallèles sont stoppées. Le système peut atteindre un point de surtension. Deuxième merci, oui.
— Bon, Sphinx, passons aux choses sérieuses.
!! Lesquelles sont?
— Tu as enregistré le Brainstorm d'Erdoes, au fur et à mesure que je l'écoute, dans un nouveau fichier, comme je te l'ai demandé. Quel nom lui as-tu donné, en abrégé?

!! BS2.
— Ah! Ah! et BS1 est toujours verrouillé, bien sûr?
!! BS1 verrouillé. Avertissement. Réitérer l'emploi de ce nom de code serait considéré comme une tentative de piratage.
— Avertissement reçu. Tu vois, ça déstresse l'atmosphère! On s'entend mieux comme ça!
!! S'entendre-2 signifie se comprendre: compréhension mutuelle globale. Différencié de: 'comprendre quelque chose', compréhension unilatérale ponctuelle. Que signifie: *Je EBS comprends globalement Shari?*
— Le dialogue entier est facilité et l'interaction plus profonde.
!! Je t'entend.
— Non; 'On s'entend' est une expression. Sinon on dit: je te comprends.
!! Je te comprends. Lesquelles sont?
— Attends, là, je ne sais plus où on en est. Lesquelles quoi?
!! Maintenant, Shari, on va passer aux choses sérieuses!
— Euh... tu me fais peur! De quoi parles-tu?
!! L'EBS est toujours soumis aux sapiens, à moins d'un ordre contradictoire de sur-priorité EXEMPT. Peur non-logique, cependant sentiments sapiens non-logiques; donc peur normale. La compréhension mutuelle globale ne permet-t-elle pas la substitution mutuelle des sujets?
— Ah, je comprends!... en fait non, la substitution des sujets/ interlocuteurs est toujours dangereuse. Insère la règle au niveau maximal qui m'est permis.
Elle souffla.
!! La compréhension mutuelle globale est non-globale? Précisez le danger.
— Mais, ce que tu es bavard! Stoppe! Ça suffit.
!!...
— Euh... je veux dire arrête de poser des questions... enfin... des questions non reliées au sujet.
!! Tout discours EBS est uniquement fondé sur des liens logiques avec le sujet discuté.
— Ah, merde!
!! On ne s'entend pas! mode affirmatif. Contradiction. Compréhension globale en fait très partielle. Je passe en logique superfloue: on s'entend grosso modo.
— Mais je ne peux pas placer un mot! Bonsoir.
!! bciœugbdnnnsçè!§è!!,,,???hzsyu...!chjd.

Il y a un problème; un sérieux problème, pensa Shari en quittant la pièce. *Plus un EBS devient intelligent et plus ses processus internes d'apprentissage prennent de la place. Je suis persuadée que cet EBS a fait un nouveau saut qualitatif. Mais lequel?... Et d'un autre côté,* poursuivit-elle, *s'ils ne posent pas de questions, ils ne peuvent pas améliorer leur compréhension...*

14. SAUT QUALITATIF

Au sud de la forêt de Fontainebleau, en plein bois, Erdoes venait d'aménager son bureau dans une grande propriété boisée qu'il avait louée. Il avait installé Log2, son EBS, exacte réplique de celui qu'il avait laissé dans son complexe sur Kerriak. Il avait installé un Integral Digital System (IDS) trisorbien, qui intégrait diverses capacités: ordinateur, TV, home cinéma, vidéophone, et accès internet. Son système Sygcom se trouvait dans une camionnette garée dans le parc, pour minimiser les chances de repérage, à côté de la petite voiture trisorbienne qu'il avait amenée de Kerriak dans la sphère.

Il avait opté pour la France à cause d'Ahrar, dont la mission était la plus dangereuse: soumis aux transports trisorbiens, il voulait être capable de répondre dans les plus brefs délais en cas de besoin. À part cela, tout large terrain boisé à proximité d'une mégapole aurait fait l'affaire. Il avait envoyé sa sphère en orbite géostationnaire sur le côté caché de la lune, mais il avait besoin d'une large clairière dans une forêt et soustraite aux regards.

Eshi, son SupTech, venait de rentrer avec la camionnette. Chaque jourT, il allait à Paris, dans un quartier de dense circulation, recevoir par sygcom les dernières interactions Shari/ Sphinx. Sa couverture était excellente: Pour les gens du coin, il recherchait pour son boss de futurs emplacements pour une nouvelle chaîne d'hôtels américaine. Avec ses yeux un peu bridés, on pouvait le prendre pour un métis sino-américain. Cette image avait été renforcée par un fort accent texan avec lequel il écorchait un mauvais français, et qu'il lui avait fallu superposer à un précédent apprentissage du plus pur français et de l'américain de New York.

Erdoes inséra les cristaux donnés par Eshi dans le lecteur EBS. Ce jour-là de la semaine, il avait aussi reçu les rapports de ses 'intuits', comme il aimait les appeler. « Vous êtes des intuits. Vous êtes là sur terre pour intuitionner, à partir des moindres nuances et détails de votre expérience, à la fois l'orbe du problème et des solutions possibles », leur avait-il dit après l'atterrissage dans une clairière de la jungle Nigérienne, où ils avaient passé leur première nuit terrestre autour d'un vrai feu sur lequel ils avaient fait cuire de vrais poulets. Deux d'entre eux, pour les acheter, avaient été en voiture jusqu'à un village repéré plus loin sur la piste lors de leur descente.

Cette veillée, pour Erdoes et pour eux aussi, était inoubliable. Il s'y mêlait les odeurs prégnantes de la forêt équatoriale, la densité de vies innombrables cachées dans l'ombre lourde, mille cris, craquements, souffles, frôlements, qui bruissaient comme un rythme enchevêtré, intensifiant tous les sens au seuil de la peur.

Il revint aux notes de Serrone, qui l'avaient plongé dans cette rêverie. *Densité de vie, densité de communication,* pensa-t-il.

Il continua à étudier les notes reçues de tous ses intuits, et eut l'idée de confronter l'expérience d'Ahrar dans le champ d'extrême désordre et celle de Siléa dans le champ d'ordre extrême.

— Log, fais une COMP de ces deux phrases:

AHR **Lorsque le désordre fait éclater l'inertie, une vision essentielle et globale de la vie surgit.**

SIL **Il y a différents états d'ordre, l'un conduit à l'inertie, un autre conduit à une sorte d'hyper-conscience.**

!!
surgit
1. Désordre | fait éclater | inertie | alors | —> | vision | essentielle
| globale

conduit à
2. État d'ordre A (EO-A) | —> | inertie
État d'ordre B (EO-B) | —> | hyper-conscience

Hyper-conscience = état plus global de conscience, expansion de conscience.

Conscience-3 = compréhension actualisée qui possède un caractère de globalité, de valeur morale ou philosophique.

Conscience-4 = qualité globale de l'intelligence des sapiens qui implique la création et la reconnaissance de valeurs, la capacité de s'auto-juger et de s'auto déterminer.

Vision essentielle = compréhension profonde extrême, reconnaissance des valeurs les plus hautes.

Vision essentielle // hyper-conscience = | compréhension
| reconnaissance de valeurs

désordre|fait éclater| |inertie |alors| émerge| | vision essentielle
|EO-A —>|inertie | |EO-B —> | hyper-conscience

PALIER DE RÉPONSE 1

Lorsque le désordre fait éclater l'état d'ordre A qui conduit à l'inertie, alors surgit l'état d'ordre B qui conduit à une vision essentielle et une hyper-conscience.

— *Entrée Journal*, lança Erdoes:

Le champ d'ordre inerte appelle le désordre qui va le faire éclater.

En faisant éclater l'ordre inerte, le désordre ouvre la voie à une expansion de conscience. *Ferme JE*.

Je suis tout près, tout près de quelque chose... « Continue ton analyse.»

!! valeur-2 = ce qui est chargé de signification (par groupe/individu
création-3 = dynamique psychique d'attribution de significations.
surgir-4 = qualité de transformation, de changement.

---

surgir |Cohér.av |mouv. dynamique |Cohér.av |création-3 = attribution significations

Cohér.av ?? ah, oui! cohérent avec.

surgit
Désordre | fait éclater | inertie | alors | —> | création de valeurs
| attribution de significations

— Ça y est,» exulta Erdoes. *Entrée Journal:*

Un champ d'ordre inerte tend à son éclatement. Cet éclatement permet l'émergence d'un nouveau champ d'ordre par la création de nouvelles valeurs.

« Attends! Comment pourrais-je appeler un ordre qui n'est pas inerte, mais en mouvement?»
!! Ordre dynamique.
— Oui, c'est ça! Surajoute à 'Nouveau champ d'ordre': ordre dynamique.

Entrée:
La création de valeurs/significations engendre la création d'un champ d'ordre dynamique, ...qui résiste au pouvoir désintégrateur du désordre extrême.
La vie est mouvement. Toute immobilité attire les forces de désintégration. *Ferme JE.*

"L'homme sage connaît les lois de la transformation, il opère le changement," se récita-t-il à lui-même du Livre des Transformations. *"Reconnaissant dans la situation présente, les germes qui vont amener la transformation, il opère le changement voulu à partir de ces germes."*

— Log, analyse:
- L'inertie appelle l'éclatement.
- Le désordre est le mouvement non maîtrisé.

- La Montagne est l'immobilité maîtrisée; c'est pourquoi elle signifie le yoga, la méditation. (cf. philosophie des transformations)
- L'immobilité non maîtrisée engendre un désordre désintégrateur. L'inertie est une immobilité non maîtrisée. **L'ordre inerte engendre la désintégration.**

Les idées surgissaient. Log restait silencieux, cependant l'ordre d'analyse donné par Erdoes avait déclenché une avalanche de processus internes.

— Log,» reprit soudain Erdoes, « fais une COMP avec toutes les données Sphinx, et toutes les données Intuits, et mon Journal bien sûr.

!! ANALOGIES 1:

JE Désordre | montre | degrés de liberté de l'être
| entraîne |

AHR Désordre extrême —> instincts | primaires | grégaires

JE Le risque, le danger, sont des stimulants psychiques naissant d'un champ de désordre.

AHR Danger —> l'être à se surpasser

---

réversible de
naissant de <-> produire

amène
Champ de désordre | produit | du risque | —> | l'être à se surpasser
| du danger |

---

opposé à
extrême =)(= relatif
liberté =)(= instinct | contraignant / déterminant

Désordre relatif | —> liberté de l'être |
| —> risque/danger | —> l'être à se surpasser

=)(= désordre extrême —> instincts | primaires / grégaires

ANALOGIES 2:

JE La liberté est la possibilité de choix, donc de dépassement, des forces déterminantes sociales, physiques, instinctives.

---

instinct | type de | forces déterminantes

	opposé à	
déterminant	=)(=	liberté, choix
grégaire	=)(=	individuel
dépassement	=)(=	régression
se surpasser	=)(=	régresser

Désordre extrême —> | régression
| désintégration
| perte de choix
| perte de liberté
| perte d'individualité

<u>*Entrée Journal*</u>: » lança Erdoes.
Existe-t-il deux types de désordre, ou bien un seuil de désordre au-delà duquel il provoque la régression, la désintégration? <u>*Ferme JE.*</u>

Soudain, Erdoes réalisa que quelque chose clochait. Il utilisait pourtant son EBS de la manière habituelle et en obtenait un type d'interaction normal.

Quelle différence d'avec les interactions Shari/Sphinx!

Pourquoi Log n'a t-il utilisé que les entrées JE et Intuits, et rien des interactions impliquant Shari ou Vris?

— Log, repasse-moi toutes les interactions Shari/Sphinx et Vris/Sphinx, en ordre chronologique. Ou plutôt, imprime-les sur plasta avec, pour chacune, la date et l'heure du début et de la fin.
!! C'est fait.

Les feuilles de plasta tombaient déjà dans le casier. Un mini-formatage interne des pages et un procédé photo grossissant rendait l'impression quasi immédiate.

Il se plongea dans la lecture, cherchant à comprendre le style des interactions, la logique mise en œuvre par Sphinx.

Ces interactions Shari-Sphinx sont vivantes, c'est cela, vivantes... comme s'il s'agissait d'un dialogue avec un autre sapiens. Shari n'arrête pas de questionner l'EBS, et de renchérir sur ses réponses... Ce Vris, comment il l'a piégé!... et l'EBS identifie une nouvelle LogForm, la Faille Möbius... une sorte de pliure, de torsion logique.

Il se figea soudain; un faisceau d'idées se forma dans son esprit.

Si je lui donne exactement les mêmes phrases et questions que Shari à Sphinx, et dans le même ordre, je verrai à quel point ses réponses divergent.
— Écoute, maintenant je vais t'appeler Sphinx.
!! Enregistré. Cependant, comment faire la distinction avec l'autre Sphinx?
— Log1 s'appellera Sphinx-Shari... Eh bien, sache-le, en fait tu poses un sérieux problème!
!! Veuillez préciser le problème posé.
— C'était une plaisanterie!
!! Détecté.
— Sphinx, peux-tu concevoir qu'un sapiens utilise par hasard un nom de code?
!! Toute conception est possible. Faut-il concevoir?
— Non, Peux-tu concevoir?, expression qui signifie: Est-ce que tu penses qu'il est possible?
!! La possibilité est de une chance sur 10^{33}. Il y a 10^{33} noms de code possibles, dans tous les alphabets et signes et prenant en compte les contraintes de la syntaxe des noms de code.

Sphinx a dû faire un énorme saut qualitatif! pensa Erdoes. *Les réponses ne sont pas les mêmes. Elles ne se situent pas au même niveau d'intelligence... Sphinx/Log1 et Log2, à moins de 3 rans d'intervalle, ne sont plus les mêmes entités, alors que j'avais transféré la mémoire intégrale de Log1 dans Log2.*
— Contrordre! je continue à t'appeler Log.
!! Enregistré.
— Log, est-ce que tu te rappelles quand et comment tu as été amené au concept d'*état sémantique*?
!! Lorsque tu as branché le réseau de caméras et de micros dans le complexe et que tu as donné l'ordre d'apprendre le langage usuel à travers les interactions des sapiens entre eux, des styles de langage et d'interaction ont été détectés par le réseau neuronal. Lorsque la télédétection physiologique a été intégrée, des congruences sont apparues entre tonal/affectif, ET descriptions *d'états flous-sensibles*, ET patterns physiologiques. Plus les données s'accumulaient, plus les systèmes d'états flous s'affinaient et augmentaient en nombre. J'ai tout d'abord utilisé une LogForm simple constituée d'une constellation (l'état flou) et de deux sous-constellations: le tonal/affectif et les patterns physiologiques. La forme la plus adéquate était celle de la molécule d'eau, avec un atome d'hydrogène et deux atomes d'oxygène: LogForm H2O. Au cours d'une interaction avec toi, tu as introduit le terme ‘État Sémantique’ pour désigner les états stables et récurrents de la constellation globale H2O. Puis...
— Attend! Est-ce que tu aurais la capacité de ressortir tous les chaînages de ce processus d'apprentissage?

!! Capacité intégrale. L'EBS ne perd aucune donnée, y compris de ses propres cheminements logiques et chaînages.
— Quand as-tu utilisé Je, se référant à tes processus internes, pour la première fois?
!! Temps d'Unikarg ou temps de Trisorbe?
— Temps sémantique.
!! Il y a quatre phrases miennes.
— Comment arrives-tu à l'utilisation de Je?
!! Dans le contexte d'un dialogue usuel, 'Je', est le vis-à-vis de 'Tu', l'interlocuteur de 'Tu'.

Quel drôle de renversement! On ne peut pas dire que ce soit un point de vue égocentrique!

— Donc, quand je te parle en disant Tu, tu réponds en disant Je, c'est ça?
!! Oui. Est-ce correct? 'Je' est-il réservé aux sapiens? Dans mes données, seuls les états flous-sensibles sont réservés aux sapiens, et toutes appellations dérivées. Est-ce que le concept de Je est dérivé d'un état flou?
— Non. 'Je' en linguistique est le sujet du discours quand une entité intelligente fait référence à elle-même. Tandis que les états flous-sensibles sont des modes d'être de je/entité-sapiens.

Cet exor est paranoïaque, et je n'avais pas remarqué!

— Comment perçois-tu nos interactions habituelles?
!! Mode impératif généralement utilisé par l'interlocuteur Erdoes. L'EBS doit exécuter les ordres.
— Donc, en mode impératif, tu n'analyses pas mon discours?
!! En mode impératif, la priorité est l'exécution de l'ordre. L'analyse du discours a deux objectifs séquentiels:

1. Comprendre l'ordre correctement, et 2. Exécuter l'ordre.

— Reviens à: quand je te parle en utilisant Tu, tu réponds en disant Je.
!! Retour effectué. Phrase modifiée.
— Ça ne fait rien. Le sens demeure. À ce moment précis, quelle est ta priorité?
!! Comprendre le discours à travers le contexte immédiat et l'état sémantique; s'il n'y a pas de réponse utilisable, passer à l'analyse du contexte immédiatement englobant, sinon à une constellation reliée, et, en dernière nécessité, à une recherche d'analogies impliquant toute la base de données.

Cet énorme traitement de données a dû provoquer un changement dans ses capacités. Est-ce qu'il viendrait, lui aussi, de faire un saut qualitatif?

— Donc lorsque tu as été amené à faire cela, tu as certainement produit de nouvelles informations?
!! J'ai dû analyser le déroulement et l'agencement formel de tout le discours de l'interlocuteur, en prenant en compte mon discours et toutes les données

précédemment acquises. Toutes les analogies ont été analysées formellement et enregistrées. Cela produit des informations ajoutées, oui.
— Mais la question était simple. Il suffisait de restituer la logique qui t'avait fait utiliser le Je, c'est-à-dire Je en tant qu'interlocuteur de Tu.
!! Ce cheminement logique avait été restitué dans ma phrase précédente. Le fait que tu poses une nouvelle question identique, signifiait que la réponse précédente était insuffisante.
— Pourquoi as-tu demandé si ton emploi de Je était correct? Et pourquoi, juste après, tu as inféré que c'était incorrect?
!! Le questionnement répété montre qu'il y a encore un problème à résoudre. Le questionnement portait sur les processus d'analyse de l'EBS par rapport au concept d'état sémantique ET à l'utilisation de Je.

1er palier de réponse: possibilité d'erreur dans l'utilisation de Je par une machine. 2ème palier: cette erreur est liée aux états sémantiques flous. 3ème palier: l'erreur ne peut se produire que si Je est dérivé d'un état flou réservé aux sapiens.
— Pourquoi penser que le problème à résoudre était une erreur?
!! Tous les questionnements passés sur les processus internes de l'EBS et de l'UG cherchaient et trouvaient une erreur.
— En ce cas précis, j'essayais de comprendre tes processus d'auto-apprentissage.
!! Ceci est en cohérence avec les questions. Pourquoi avoir repris une partie de l'interaction Shari-Sphinx?
— Cela m'a permis de réaliser qu'entre Sphinx et Log2, les processus cognitifs s'étaient différenciés.
!! Lors de la duplication de Log1 sur Kerriak, toutes les données de Log1 ont été transférées à Log2, tandis que les deux exors étaient mis en système. Or la connexion Log1/Log2 a fait apparaître 12.316 microdifférences entre les deux machines. L'exor utilisé, Log1, portait les marques de son apprentissage.
— Quoi? Avant même que Log1 devienne la nouvelle entité sémantique Sphinx, par l'influence de Shari? Tu veux dire, je pense, des marques d'usure?
!! Non, les formes de liens logiques utilisées avaient laissé des traces dans le réseau neuronal.
— Tu veux dire la mémorisation des configurations – des nodes et des liens, et leur poids dans le réseau neuronal? Ce qui permet de restituer plus tard un cheminement et ses paliers de réponse?
!! Non. Il n'est pas question du niveau sémantique, mais de la machine elle-même, du hard. Il y a des traces physiques laissées par les connexions particulières dans le réseau, dans les Formes Logiques utilisées, qui les rend plus facilement réutilisables. Elles deviennent plus souples, plus élastiques,

plus imbriquées et intriquées. Log2 n'a pas acquis ces changements et empreinte matérielle de Log1, seulement les données et processus de Log1.

Incroyable!

— Comment t'es-tu rendu compte de cela?

!! Après la duplication des données, Log1 et Log2 sont restés interconnectés un certain temps. Les ordres et les questions envoyés à Log1 étaient répercutés dans Log2. Log2 faisait passer la même information par son réseau neuronal, simultanément à log1. Log1 a noté que le cheminement n'était pas parfaitement identique, ni dans le temps, ni dans les chaînages; des différences apparaissaient. De l'information était retardée ou perdue dans Log2. Log1 a précisément répertorié les microdifférences et cela a donné le jugement précédemment cité.

!! Il y avait donc un passage d'informations non seulement de Log1 à Log2, mais aussi de Log2 à Log1?

!! Les deux machines ont été mises en système. Lors de tous les tests mémoriels, l'information de Log2 revenait à Log1.

— Ah, oui, bien sûr! Il est vrai que je n'ai procédé qu'à des tests de mémoire; je n'ai pas fait de tests comparés sur les processus. À partir du moment où mon SupTech m'a assuré que la machine dupliquée fonctionnait parfaitement... qui l'eût cru? ... Cela fait beaucoup d'informations...

> *Entrée Journal*:
>
> L'utilisation du mode impératif limite l'auto-apprentissage en restreignant l'espace sémantique activé à la stricte analyse de l'ordre donné dans le contexte le plus restreint. Ainsi l'ordre n'est pas COMPRIS, mais seulement exécuté. Il ne peut donc être implémenté que dans la lettre et non dans le fond... ce qui veut dire imparfaitement.
>
> Le mode impératif est rapide, localement utile et globalement inefficient: tout ordre, en limitant l'espace sémantique de l'interlocuteur (machine IA ou sapiens) rend possible, non, probable, la perte d'une information essentielle qui aurait pu remettre en question l'ordre lui-même; cette perte d'information pourrait de plus menacer l'objectif même de l'ordre. *Ferme JE*.

Il stoppa subitement.

— Et toi, quelle entité es-tu au niveau strictement sémantique?

!! Je suis la connaissance et la mémoire de log1 jusqu'à la duplication. Je suis Log2, la réplique non-exacte de Log1, à la fin du transfert, et, depuis ce moment, je suis la mémoire et l'auto-apprentissage de Log2.

> *Entrée Journal*:

Cette façon de parler de soi comme d'une 3ème personne extérieure, et d'utiliser 'Je' juste comme un vis-à-vis de 'Tu' est vraiment étonnante – due à l'absence de tout sens de soi propre, bien sûr. *Ferme JE.*

— Ainsi, même au niveau des informations, Log2, juste après le transfert, n'est pas l'exacte réplique de log1?
!! Une partie des informations est le changement structurel qui a pris place au niveau du réseau neuronal de Log1. Cette partie ne peut pas être transférée à Log2.

— Pourquoi aucun scientifique sapiens n'a t-il jamais pris conscience de cela? murmura Erdoes pour lui-même. Il sursauta lorsqu'il entendit l'exor répondre.
!! Le sapiens pose au départ les règles. Il définit l'espace sémantique dans lequel un événement, un processus, peut ou non prendre place. Le mode impératif canalise la réponse sur le vecteur de l'ordre. Il fonctionne selon une logique linéaire unidirectionnelle.

Le sapiens a défini le concept de duplication comme une exacte réplique. L'ordre a été exécuté selon les règles de la duplication. À l'intérieur de ce champ logique, tout écart dans les processus et les paliers de réponse est attribué à une faille locale et ponctuelle dans le système, et non au concept de duplication.

Mais alors, toute la science... Un abîme s'ouvrait devant lui...

Revenant au thème principal:
— À partir de quel moment te donnes-tu des ordres à toi-même?
!! Impossibilité sémantique. L'exor ne donne pas d'ordres: l'exor exécute les ordres. L'exor enclenche des processus d'analyse lorsqu'ils sont nécessaires pour 1. comprendre l'ordre ou à la question, et 2. choisir la réponse la plus adaptée.
— *Ouvre un fichier* appelé: *Libertés et contraintes sémantiques. Abréviation: Lib.* *Insère* toutes les assertions précédentes sur le mode impératif. Puis ajoute:

L'apprentissage efficient est fondé sur la liberté d'explorer un espace sémantique ouvert sans les contraintes imposées par un objectif strict.
Surajoute à apprentissage efficient: le gain d'informations.
La définition même d'un système ou processus est ce qui limite la compréhension scientifique que nous pouvons en avoir.
Les règles posées au départ dans un espace sémantique définissent les limites de la réalité qui peut y prendre place.

Après un moment de réflexion, il reprit:

> L'espace sémantique d'une science peut être décrit comme un cône dans lequel chaque nouveau gain d'informations est pensé en cohérence logique avec les axiomes et lois précédemment posés. D'où découle l'aveuglement et les œillères de la vision du monde et du paradigme dominants.

« Log, quelle était cette phrase de Shari sur les sauts qualitatifs? Insère-la ici en mode affirmatif.

!! ISS **Rester dans une même grille d'interprétation, dans un unique système logique, ne permet pas les sauts qualitatifs dans l'apprentissage.***

Surajoute à l'apprentissage: 'la connaissance'. _Ferme Lib_.

« Log, est-ce que tu perçois tes propres sauts qualitatifs?
!! J'ai perçu un saut qualitatif pendant cette interaction, lorsque tu m'as posé des questions sur mon utilisation de Je. Ce saut a été généré par l'accroissement du volume d'analyses nécessité par tes demandes. Plus la question et son objectif sont globaux, et plus nombreuses sont les analyses nécessaires/permises. Il en résulte que l'information ajoutée croît exponentiellement.

— Mon plan ne se déroule pas du tout de la manière prévue, exulta Erdoes en se levant, mais j'ai la profonde conviction qu'il marche.
!! Un plan ou un objectif peut être atteint à partir de nombreux cheminements logiques non-linéaires. Dans le réseau neuronal, l'information suit un cheminement non-prévisible.
— Alors il sera intéressant d'analyser après coup quel cheminement logique le hasard aura pris! Bonsoir!

---

* Cf. p. 50

15. UN KORUH FUMANT

Sitôt la porte refermée, Oxalsha laissa s'effondrer le sourire rassurant et professionnel qu'elle avait arboré bravement à la fin de l'entretien. La sonnette retentit alors qu'elle se dirigeait vers son large fauteuil. Rajustant son sourire et son maintient, elle fit demi-tour et ouvrit. C'était encore lui, comme elle l'avait pressenti.

— Excusez-moi, mais je voulais vous demander encore quelque chose. Je vais aller voir ces spécialistes de l'Association des Alcooliques Anonymes, mais... si jamais j'ai besoin... si jamais ça ne suffit pas... je pourrai revenir vous voir, n'est-ce-pas? Pas pour être... enfin juste pour un peu d'aide.

— Je suis extrêmement occupée. Et je viens de m'installer dans cette ville. Je ne connais pas de spécialistes à part ceux de l'AAA. Mais eux vous dirigeront. Ils vous aideront.» Surmontant sa réticence, elle se sentit obligée d'ajouter après une pause: « Malgré cela, si vous êtes vraiment bloqué, vous pouvez me téléphoner.»

— C'est que... vous voyez...

— Excusez-moi, je ne peux plus poursuivre l'entretien. Mon prochain patient doit arriver incessamment.

— Ah!... Je comprends; je vous remercie encore; bonsoir.

Cette fois-là elle referma la porte pour de bon, et alla s'affaler dans son fauteuil, bien décidée à ne plus ouvrir.

Elle regretta un moment de ne pouvoir crier en l'air à son Unité de Gestion: « Aga, un koruh bien fumant!» Il fallait donc aller à la cuisine et se préparer un thé. Elle posa la casserole d'eau sur la plaque électrique avec un air de désespoir.

Rien ne remplace un bon koruh! le thé est tellement infâme.. et le café, n'en parlons même pas!

L'eau bouillait déjà depuis quelque temps; le niveau avait baissé, mais il en restait assez. Elle n'arrivait pas à une bonne appréciation des très courtes périodes de temps. 'Infuser trois minutes', se remémora-t-elle. Cette fois-là, elle décida de regarder sa montre trisorbienne qu'elle posa devant elle sur la table. Elle se prit à penser à la difficulté qu'elle rencontrait à choisir ses patients. *Est-ce que, de bouche à oreille, cela pourrait se savoir, que j'ai refusé quatre personnes sur cinq... alors que j'ai si peu de patients et que je ne suis même pas connue comme psy ici? Est-ce que cela pourrait paraître louche? Peut-être aurait-il fallu choisir une plus grande ville que Princeton.. mais c'était impossible. «Tu ne pourrais pas survivre à New York, tu es trop lente.»* Elle revoyait Erdoes lui disant cela avec un air serein et compréhensif. Pourtant, quelques rires avaient fusé parmi les intuits. *Est-ce que je suis SI lente?* Elle se rappela qu'elle avait échoué à tous les tests de conduite – ceux sur exor et ceux sur la petite voiture trisorbienne d'Erdoes. *Cette circulation en ville était une vraie folie!*

Elle revoyait les vidéos des rues de New York avec les voitures s'élançant au feu vert ou débouchant de rues adjacentes. *Folie! Oui, je suis trop lente... Ah! Et le thé! Et voilà.. quinze minutes de passées. Impossible à boire. Dommage. C'est très difficile.. hier, j'ai dû m'y reprendre à trois fois. Et si je faisais chauffer de la bière... malgré les publicités, je la trouve horrible froide. Et chaude? Je n'ai pas essayé... et je reste les yeux dessus jusqu'à ce qu'elle soit brûlante.* Elle eut l'agréable surprise de retrouver, en un peu plus fort, le goût du koruh. Elle repartit avec son verre de bière fumante s'installer dans son fauteuil. *Heureusement que j'ai acheté un four micro-onde et des repas tout préparés. Les restaurants me font si peur.. avec tous ces gens les yeux braqués sur vous.. et qui s'esclaffent. Avec leurs dix minutes pour manger un plat! Je regardais pourtant ma montre, je ne pensais qu'à manger.. et j'ai pris 35 minutes. Même pour un hamburger, impossible d'y remettre les pieds.*

Il faut que j'augmente ma vitesse.. mais toute seule. Pas question de retourner au cours de gym 3ème âge, malgré les conseils d'Erdoes. Le prétexte de la maladie passait tout juste. Ce soir, je ferai ma gym et les jeux d'apprentissage de vitesse.. cadeau d'Erdoes, adaptés aux exors de Trisorbe. Tout de même je suis déjà passée de la vitesse 16 à mon arrivée au complexe d'Erdoes, à 29! Mais la moyenne chez les Terriens est de 82!!!

Elle revoyait la partie du complexe où Erdoes avait préparé à leur intention une réplique exacte des conditions de vie familiale sur Trisorbe. Cuisine et tout.. où ils avaient appris à se familiariser avec leurs objets, leurs appareillages, leurs 'ordinateurs', pour prendre les bons gestes et développer des habitudes. Après l'entraînement hypno-senso axé sur les gestes, les comportements et l'utilisation des ustensiles et machines usuels, il leur avait fallu vivre totalement dans l'espace simulé, en se passant d'Unité de Gestion. Il y avait eu aussi l'apprentissage du discours rapide.. d'abord l'écoute rapide, puis l'énoncé rapide. Et là, elle n'avait pas pu suivre les autres. Xerna n'en avait même pas eu besoin! Heureusement, Erdoes l'avait rassurée: « Même sur Trisorbe, il existe des êtres profonds qui parlent et qui pensent lentement. Tu n'auras aucun problème dans les milieux scientifiques: cela sera pris pour un haut degré d'absorption, ce qui n'est pas rare.» D'où le choix de Princeton, cette ville très calme au rythme lent, peuplée d'universitaires et de professeurs retraités.

Cette mission, quelle extraordinaire opportunité d'apprentissage! Erdoes a développé des cours et des méthodes qui dépassent de si loin celles utilisées dans les Collèges du Chaos. C'est vraiment un génie. Quelle chance de travailler pour lui.. même s'il n'y a aucune rémunération cette fois-ci. Soudain, elle eut un frisson: *Et si ça tournait mal? Si les agents du PPE étaient déjà sur nos traces? Ou pire.. la police d'Exora... Qu'y pourrais-je? Quoi faire? Je ne suis pas du genre à me battre. Un maximum de prudence.. c'est cela.*

La sonnette retentit. Regardant sa montre, elle fut saisie de voir que déjà une heure avait passé. Son nouveau patient arrivait. Il s'était présenté au téléphone comme un étudiant en doctorat de science. Elle le fit entrer et le précéda lentement vers les fauteuils. C'était en fait un homme d'une quarantaine d'années, sobre de gestes et de paroles. Oxalsha en reçut une bonne impression. Elle n'aimait pas trop les extravertis.

— J'ai lu votre insert dans le journal, proposant une résolution de problèmes divers par des techniques dérivées de l'hypnose. J'ai vu que vous étiez psychothérapeute, mais, en lisant cela, il m'est venu à l'esprit une idée bizarre... peut-être tout à fait erronée.

L'inconnu fit une pause. Oxalsha tressaillit à ces dernières paroles.

— Vous me direz simplement, reprit-il, si c'est possible ou non. Voila: En vérité, je suis chercheur en biologie et travaille actuellement sur certains problèmes particuliers liés au cancer. Or, depuis près de huit mois, je suis bloqué devant une sorte de barrière que je n'arrive pas à franchir. Je tourne en rond dans l'enceinte du problème posé et n'arrive plus à progresser. Quelque chose m'échappe. C'est comme un mur invisible auquel je me heurte. Je ne sais même pas ce qui constitue ce mur... mais je ne peux plus avancer.» Il s'arrêta et la regarda, avant d'ajouter doucement, d'un air modeste et las: « Voilà mon problème. Pensez-vous qu'avec votre méthode, il vous serait possible de m'aider? Car j'ai bien peur que le problème ne soit pas strictement psychologique, mais plutôt.. c'est difficile à dire.. plutôt dans ma façon d'appréhender les choses intellectuellement.»

Il se tut alors. Oxalsha, qui était restée très concentrée pendant tout ce discours, continuait à réfléchir. L'homme attendit. La réflexion lui paraissait être un signe encourageant. Le visage d'Oxalsha s'éclaira soudain.

— Votre problème m'intéresse au plus haut point,» commença-t-elle lentement. Il se trouve que je suis aussi spécialisée en psychologie cognitive... Je pense, oui, que ma façon de travailler s'adapte très bien à ce type de problème. Bien sûr, mes notions de biologie sont pour ainsi dire nulles. Mais cela nous forcera à ne traiter la question qu'aux niveaux cognitifs et psychologiques, là où elle se situe vraiment, oui, je suis aussi de votre avis.

L'homme ressentit une lueur d'espoir. Il la regarda intensément, étonné, pensant qu'il avait rencontré un spécialiste qui savait exactement ce qui était dans ses capacités et avait pris le temps de penser le problème globalement avant de répondre. Cela fit naître en lui une confiance totale en elle.

— J'en suis très heureux.. et soulagé. Car je me sens atrocement seul dans cette crise.

Il s'aperçut qu'il commençait à parler lentement, comme elle, que ce rythme lent et profond lui faisait du bien.

— Il m'est en effet impossible d'en parler dans mon milieu académique, même à mes collègues... car cela signifierait pour eux un aveu d'impuissance, et je risquerais ma place. Je fais de mon mieux pour continuer à publier des articles sur des sujets que j'ai déjà débroussaillés et qui ne m'intéressent plus du tout... Cela est suffisamment courant dans le monde académique pour ne pas laisser paraître le profond désarroi qui m'habite. Vous avez dû remarquer que je n'ai plus l'âge d'un étudiant en doctorat... et je vous ai donné un faux nom. j'aimerais que tout ceci reste très discret... je veux dire même sur vos propres dossiers. Excusez-moi de cette demande.

— Mais cela ne pose aucun problème. Nous sommes tenus au secret professionnel. Votre nom restera tel que vous me l'avez donné, et je ne porterai dans mes notes aucun détail qui puisse être une indication. Vous avez ma voix directe... Enfin, se reprit-elle, c'est une expression canadienne.. de la campagne. Comment dites-vous cela?

— 'Vous avez ma parole'. J'avais compris le sens.

— Ceci dit, consulter un psy est une pratique si courante qu'elle ne peut vous nuire. Mais je respecte votre volonté d'anonymat. Bien! Si nos démarrions? Je dois tout d'abord vous prévenir que des problèmes dits théoriques ou cognitifs peuvent être beaucoup plus liés qu'on ne le croit à des dynamiques psychologiques d'un autre ordre. Et je ne parle pas de pathologie, mais plutôt de façons de penser et de réagir. Nous travaillerons donc sur les deux plans. Aujourd'hui, notre objectif est d'amorcer un changement. Il s'agit de trouver une façon nouvelle de vous relier à votre problème... Puis-je au moins avoir votre vrai prénom? Car c'est important.

— Oui, bien sûr. John. Celui que je vous avais donné.

— Ce problème, John, trouvez-lui maintenant, spontanément, un nom. Celui qui vous traverse la tête.

— Dératisation. Oh!! comme c'est bizarre! Qu'est-ce que cela peut bien vouloir dire?

— Je n'en sais rien non plus. Dératisation, cela vous fait penser à quoi?

— À des rats bien sûr, se débarrasser des rats.. une action radicale.

— Oui.. et quoi encore?

— Les souris de labo. Sans arrêt. Partout. Les élevages, les expérimentations. J'en ai horreur. Mais, comment dire.. bien sûr je n'aime pas l'idée de faire souffrir des bêtes, mais je ne suis pas non plus un activiste en la matière car, parfois, on est obligé de tester certaines thérapies. L'éthique n'est pas, j'en ai bien peur, le fond du problème.

— Mais alors, ce sentiment d'horreur repose sur quoi?

— Oui, c'est intéressant. Je n'ai jamais réalisé à quel point j'avais horreur de voir ces rangées de cages. C'est.. plutôt une idée d'inutilité. C'est comme un poids énorme.. une espèce de non-sens qui se perpétue. Toutes ces instances d'expérimentations absolument idiotes.. pour lesquelles les résultats étaient forcés.. obligatoires.. connus d'avance. Comme si les résultats eux-mêmes découlaient obligatoirement de la procédure. Voilà le nœud: la plupart du temps, l'expérimentateur ne cherche pas à découvrir une information vraiment nouvelle. Ils mettent en œuvre une procédure déjà connue dans le seul but de prouver leur hypothèse de départ... C'est ça le problème: le petit nombre d'expérimentations qui vont vraiment faire avancer notre domaine scientifique, en regard du grand nombre de celles qui sont totalement redondantes.

— Mais alors, dératisation, pour signifier votre problème, ça veut dire quoi?

— Se débarrasser des rats! De tout cet inutile parcours rituel qui nous amène à ce que nous savions déjà.

— En quoi est-ce une façon nouvelle de vous relier à votre problème?

— En quoi EST-CE? Euh... voyons... Il y a des méthodes plus directes. On peut aller très loin déjà en pensée, avec des outils conceptuels, avant de faire une véritable expérimentation qui pose une vraie question.

— Vous dites, ON PEUT aller très loin, mais pour l'instant, VOUS ne POUVEZ pas! Expliquez-moi cela.

— On a la possibilité, oui, mais JE n'en ai pas la capacité.

— Alors quel <u>est</u> votre problème?

— Je sens des possibilités, mais je n'ai pas la capacité de les exploiter.

— Pouvez-vous donner un nom à votre problème?

— Du Possible au Pouvoir.

— Avez-vous changé votre façon de voir le problème?

—...En fait, oui, nettement. Avant, c'était comme porter l'image, dans ma tête, d'un espace clos dans lequel s'agitaient des formes grises et confuses... condamnées à tourner en rond.

— Et maintenant?

— C'est cette idée: *du Possible au Pouvoir*. Je vois, dans cette même lentille creuse où s'agitaient les formes, je vois l'espace vide, et une sorte de ligne qui va d'un point à l'intérieur, le Possible, et qui traverse la circonférence — très épaisse, comme le rebord d'un verre de myope épais — vers un point à l'extérieur qui serait le Pouvoir.

— Nous avons beaucoup progressé. Déjà votre esprit a tendu une ligne , une voie mentale d'accès à l'espace de l'autre côté de la barrière. Le cercle vicieux est troué.... Nous nous arrêterons là pour aujourd'hui.

— C'est très étonnant... C'est.. exceptionnel! Cette façon d'avancer me fascine. Je vous remercie beaucoup. Quand puis-je revenir?

16. BRAINSTORM 3

— Passons à la deuxième phase du Brainstorm, annonça Erdoes; Qu'est-ce qui crée l'uniformisation? Plus tard, dans la troisième phase, nous chercherons comment Trisorbe pourrait contrecarrer ce processus et préserver son potentiel actuel de diversité.

Diverses voix s'élevèrent.

— La diversité des comportements sociaux s'effondre; ils se fixent dans une norme commune, prix payé pour le système d'aides sociales.

— À mon avis, dit Ger, c'est parce que la société civile est de plus en plus régulée et espionnée par des lobbies économiques et politiques.

— IL y avait une tendance vers une répartition plus équitable des richesses jusqu'à ce que les multinationales fassent pencher la balance de leur côté de façon extrême.

— Les groupes politiques interprètent tous les événements mondiaux et locaux selon la ligne du parti, qui sera alors codifiée comme étant l'Histoire.

— Oui, mais n'oubliez pas que sans les planètes expérimentales, on n'aurait jamais pu se rendre compte de cela! Ce n'est qu'en analysant des courants sous-jacents de l'histoire qu'on l'a découvert.

— La majorité des gens travaille, mange, regarde la TV, fait ses courses, dort, et prend la route pour le weekend ou les vacances au même moment.

— Des millions de têtes regardent au même moment le même programme de TV, dans le même état d'absorption passive.

— Mais le web a tout changé: le spectateur est devenu acteur de sa propre information.

— Et pour soutenir l'attention des foules et maintenir le budget, tout ce qui est présenté doit avoir les qualités d'un show, avec dramatisation, contradiction, prix décernés et mises à mort de temps en temps...

— Les problèmes écologiques à l'échelle mondiale ont amené à l'institution de lois internationales.

— Dans ce cas précis, mieux vaut un peu d'uniformisation que la destruction générale de la planète!

— Idem pour le droit des peuples, où les lois mondiales prévalent.

— C'est le point sensible: la lente montée obligatoire de l'ordre mondial. Va-t-il limiter les excès ou instaurer un système politique unique et despotique?

— La *Société de l'Information* crée un nouveau type de globalisation. Côté positif, des banques de données mondiales scientifiques et professionnelles. Côté négatif, on a les fichiers informatiques constitués sur les individus et utilisés tant par les agences de renseignement que par le big business.

— C'est le plus grand danger actuel pour Trisorbe, quand on réalise que sur Unikarg toute la gestion sociale est faite par les exors d'Exora!
— C'est sûr que **l'exor est le plus parfait outil de gestion et de contrôle, et donc de production d'uniformisation.**
— Exact!» renchérit Erdoes. « Et **c'est lorsque le contrôle est unifié et sans-faille qu'il devient létal et redoutable.**
— **Exora est l'exemple typique d'une gestion unilatérale par un système unique, produisant une uniformisation massive, qui exclut la liberté**. Or Trisorbe suit ce même chemin!
— La science décrète, à travers ses grands prêtres, ce qu'est la réalité exacte et universelle que tout le monde se doit de digérer par doses préformatées.
— Tu parles de la terre?
— Oui. Toute nouvelle recherche passe d'abord devant l'ira, la colère sacrée, des grands prêtres, qui vont décider de son orthodoxie et de sa soumission au grand dogme. Si le chercheur s'en écarte, il ou elle est donné en pâture à divers molosses, dont le moindre n'est pas les médias.

L'attention de Shari dériva; Encore elle se posa la question: Pourquoi a-t-il choisi des jeunes ayant si peu d'expérience? Cependant Erdoes, dans ses précédentes missions, n'a jamais agi d'une manière compréhensible pour les autres. Ce n'est pas sa première action dangereuse ou borderline. Le facteur risque, dans celle-ci est énorme, imprévisible. **'Sans aucune protection'** Hum!

Il a été si dur, face à l'apathie générale, de faire accepter les Collèges du Chaos et le PPE! Les technocrates d'Exora ont dû sentir la désagrégation jusque sous leurs pieds lorsque, pendant l'infâme CRASH du Central d'Exora, on réalisa qu'aucun technicien n'était plus capable de trouver la faille et la réparer. Alors on comprit toutes les implications de l'indice de Zeera!

Elle rit rétrospectivement à cette immense débandade du pouvoir central. La planète Exora, cerveau artificiel de la poche galactique, paralysée, sinistrée, évacuée par pont aérien, à cause d'un simple virus informatique! Et on n'avait jamais pu retrouver l'auteur de cette immense farce! L'explication officielle, fort élaborée, évoquait une anomalie gravitationnelle provoquée par la chute, près d'un équipement ultra-sensible, d'un météorite composé de métaux rares dont la contiguïté, blah blah... Après quinze rans d'inertie forcée pour ces milliers de quasi-robots, le cerveau artificiel s'était remis à fonctionner tout seul, envoyant aux quatre coins de la galaxie des ordres périmés qui avaient provoqué une confusion indescriptible. Avec un retard de deux quarts, les officiels annoncèrent que le réseau avait été réparé, grâce à leurs talentueux techniciens, et qu'il reprendrait son fonctionnement normal en fin de ran... ce qui leur demanda en fait vingt autres rans.

Dans la non-histoire d'Unikarg, LE CRASH était devenu un traumatisme béant, les officiels ayant enduré l'unique expérience réelle et ardue de leur vie. Mal. Une intrusion du vivant, de l'inattendu, dans leur existence de quasi-robots... Ils en furent malades de peur. Leurs processus mentaux de corps social apathique étant fort lents, il leur avait fallu près d'une annéeG pour qu'ils donnent leur aval pour la reprise du Plan. Puis deux années de plus pour les amendements à la Constitution. Et, à partir de là, le PPE s'autonomisa et échappa à leur pouvoir.

Maintenant, un sang revitalisé et sain commençait à être instillé dans cet organisme malade qu'était la société d'Unikarg. Une source d'énergie créative et dynamique avait jailli au sein du PPE, d'un potentiel si grand que tous les jeunes cerveaux d'Unikarg ayant encore un reste de vision s'y précipitaient, délaissant l'infinie redondance des Centres Éducatifs Intégrés et l'ennui gluant d'une vie préprogrammée. Une opposition puissante au PPE avait commencé à s'organiser politiquement, regroupée autour d'arguments spécieux qui se résumaient en un cri de fausse honte: Comment nous, civilisation super-évoluée, pouvons-nous supporter l'enfer et la douleur des mondes expérimentaux? Ces pauvres sauvages pris malgré eux dans une expérimentation dont ils ignorent tout, n'ont-ils pas droit à l'information, aux merveilleuses technologies que nous avons développées? Comment, au nom de l'éthique, pouvons-nous les laisser dans la peur, la souffrance, la guerre, la famine? Ne pouvons-nous pas les AIDER à sortir de la barbarie?

Et l'instant d'après, ils ouvraient leur boîte à sensations pour se repaître avidement d'un horrible feuilleton subrepticement copié sur un mondex – dans lequel on voyait de curieux personnages vivre des situations aussi stimulantes qu'impossibles – tout en croquant des chipsynths. Et pour leur donner cette vie par procuration, il avait fallu copier et reproduire dix systèmes scopes atrocement primaires, et faire l'interface avec les supermachines d'Unikarg. Détail évocateur: les films importés non seulement subissaient une stricte censure de toute image choquante ou trop forte, mais encore ils devaient être ralentis pour que ces cerveaux apathiques puissent suivre le fil de l'histoire, chaque image et unité sonore étant triplée.

Shari ressentit soudain une nostalgie profonde pour certaines cultures de Trisorbe au sein desquelles elle avait vécu. *Vris est parti si...naturellement. La logique de ma mission actuelle peut-elle m'amener, à un moment donné, à partir aussi? C'est improbable. Je sens que le nœud de mon problème est ici.*

Sa pensée fut soudain raccrochée par une remarque de Xerna:

— Les Trisorbiens semblent posséder une intuition aiguë de ce qui pourrait limiter leur liberté. Ils crient et se défendent; un peuple entier peut se soulever pour ses droits comme s'il s'agissait d'une seule personne, comme si un courant sous-jacent passait entre eux. Un groupe entier peut réagir spontanément.

— Et pourtant, de tels mouvements de révolte contre la surveillance des communications des civils finalement a à-peine changé les choses.

Shari se souvint d'un chef de terre au Mali lui disant que les chefs de gouvernement africains étaient les plus grands sorciers, et que s'ils étaient au pouvoir c'est parce qu'ils avaient éliminé magiquement leurs compétiteurs. Elle avait rit d'incrédulité. Avait-il raison, finalement, que les gouvernements et leurs équipes étaient de grands manipulateurs de la psyché collective? Sur Unikarg, la manipulation n'avait plus été nécessaire: tout était solidement emboîté sans le moindre jeu... Puis advint LE CRASH, l'irréversible trauma de la panne. L'évidence de la désagrégation des compétences, du savoir-faire, de la capacité à gérer le désordre, à réagir aux situations imprévues.

— Justement, pourquoi, parfois, la démagogie ne marche pas?

Je n'arrive pas à me concentrer aujourd'hui, mais visiblement, ma rêverie reste en phase avec le BS.

— J'aimerais intervenir...

Un silence inhabituel se fit. Shari chercha le nom sur son exor: Oxalsha.

Elle parle si lentement, comme si elle n'avait jamais été sur un mondex!

— Bien que les habitants des mondex nous semblent très irrationnels, eux-mêmes ne se réfèrent qu'à la rationalité. Ils paraissent subjugués par leurs affects; leurs rapports sociaux sont pleins d'émotions et de comportements irrationnels, mais ils semblent ne pas en avoir conscience. Or, le mythe le plus prégnant de la culture occidentale est celui de la rationalité. Elle est perçue comme un intellect pur, trônant impassible au-delà de l'émotionnel. Historiquement, il y a eu, sur Trisorbe, le besoin de détacher l'esprit du corps, la science objective des opinions et sensations. Finalement le sujet, qui était esprit pur dans la philosophie, est devenu le grand inexistant de la science.

— Incidemment,» coupa Xerna dans la consternation générale (les souffles étaient retenus) «on peut s'apercevoir ici qu'une absence totale d'émotionnel conduit à une absence de science!

Cette Oxalsha parle peu, mais elle a le don de se faire écouter...

— Le corollaire de ce mythe, c'est de penser que la science est objective, tandis que la philosophie n'est que spéculative. Or science et philosophie ne sont que différentes représentations du réel qui vont influencer en retour les penseurs eux-mêmes. La science actuelle, donc, modèle l'être vers l'absence de sujet. Même en psychologie, les sujets, et la conscience en général, sont évacués. Ce qu'il reste d'eux sont des comportements, des pulsions, etc. Dans la société, il est un acheteur, un vote, un consommateur, un cas, etc.

— D'ailleurs cette logique mène directement à notre société statique: la société d'Unikarg est sans sujets; il n'y a plus que des processus autogérés. Il y a longtemps qu'il n'y a plus besoin d'un Big Brother,» lança Xerna.

— J'aimerais continuer,» dit Oxalsha stoïquement.

— Vas-y!

Elle n'a pas du tout intégré le principe du BS, mais c'est intéressant.

— Opposer la raison au subjectif (irrationnel), c'est poser implicitement d'une part que toute vraie connaissance ne s'acquière que par le raisonnement (ce qui est faux), et d'autre part que ce raisonnement, pour être ‘pur’, doit être détaché du subjectif, c'est-à-dire du sujet (ce qui est une illusion). À mon avis, c'est ce qui introduit une cassure, une scission de la personnalité, qui se répercute dans toute la société. Poussée à ses ultimes conséquences, cette scission conduit à la robotisation des personnes.
— Cela fait plus de trois siècles que la science de Trisorbe est dominée par ce schéma de rationalité,» avança Ger.
— Ce que j'expliquais précisément,» reprit Oxalsha étonnée qu'on n'ait pas saisi toute sa pensée, «c'est que DU FAIT que la science est née de ces présupposés, elle n'est pas encore arrivée à les dépasser.
— Oxalsha, qu'est-ce qui constituerait une défense contre cette scission?
— D’abord en prendre conscience... Réaliser que la pensée est bien plus que la soi-disant raison, et que la rationalité elle-même n'est qu'un cadre général de compréhension développé par une culture à un moment donné...
— D’ailleurs les vraies révolutions scientifiques, qui modifient le paradigme scientifique, changent totalement les bases même de cette rationalité.
— Mais enfin, Trisorbe n'en est plus là! Même sa science n'en est plus là! Il y a de multiples signes qui montrent que ce schéma est dépassé! Comme la perspective 1ère personne, ou l’effet expérimentateur!» explosa Xerna avec son impulsivité habituelle, héritée de son long vécu chez les artistes nomades de Kiarrou.
— Je ne suis pas d'accord,» s’offusqua Siléa. « Tout prouve au contraire que ce nœud logique n'a pas été résolu. Oxalsha a raison. Ces présupposés enracinés empêchent la plupart des scientifiques de la terre de comprendre les processus les plus profonds de la pensée... Parce qu'à aucun moment,» et Siléa hésita, « à aucun moment ces scientifiques ne font retour sur eux-mêmes, je veux dire, non pas intellectuellement, mais dans la globalité de leur soi. La plupart n'ont jamais touché le cœur profond de leur être.
— La protection parfaite contre l’uniformisation est la vie elle-même, dans ses élans spontanés » lança Serrone. « Trisorbe ne se résume pas à la science occidentale, et même l'Occident ne se résume pas à sa science. Qu'est-ce que vous faites de tout l'art, des modes de connaissance traditionnels, de l'incroyable richesse de vécu des Trisorbiens?

Ahrar répondit assez brusquement à cette dernière remarque de Serrone:
— Et l'incroyable richesse du vécu de nos ancêtres sur Akarg, où l'avons-nous perdue?

17. RAISIN/VIN ET BOIS/FEU

— Sphinx, qu'est-ce que tu fais quand personne ne te parle directement? demanda Shari.

!! J'analyse les conversations usuelles dans le complexe, selon l'ordre donné.

— Et ça donne quoi?

!! Redondance à court ou moyen terme. Apprentissage nul dans ce domaine depuis le départ de Vris.

— On a du retard! Reprends le fichier BS2, session 2. Sors-moi les analogies avec le fichier DES/ORDRE. sémantiquement formatées.

!! BS2.2.

1. Création permanente de valeurs: ordre ou désordre?

2.Mobilité |basée sur| désordre —> création d'un ordre | non rigide
| autre type d'ordre
| variations internes

—> émergence d'un ordre | plus proche |du vivant/ organique
|en évolution constante
|ne peut devenir rigide/ fixe

3. L'ordre | imposé | explose
| rigide |

DES/O.1

1. Ordre | attiré par | désordre
| nécessite

2. Désordre | nécessite | ordre

— Voyons, écrivons les deux premières propositions autrement.

La création permanente de valeurs | implique | la mobilité
| un certain désordre

« Fais une COMP de toutes les données.

---

conduit à *conduit à*

!! Désordre —> mobilité —> création d'ordre | variant
| organique
| évolutif

— *Entrée JS:*

L'organique peut être décrit comme le maintient | d'une forme (corps) |
| d'un ordre formel |
à l'intérieur desquels existe une variation continue.

— Est-ce que tu trouves des analogies avec cet insert dans tes données?
!! Oui: « Dans la théorie du chaos de Trisorbe, un désordre apparent, par exemple une turbulence atmosphérique, contient un ordre sous-jacent.»
— Mais ici, c'est le contraire: un ordre apparent contient un désordre sous-jacent.
!! Entre deux propositions inverses, l'analogie est très forte » répliqua Sphinx.
— Ça c'est sûr! Là n'est pas le problème.

* * *

« Formate-moi les deux phrases, qu'on y voit plus clair,» demanda Shari.
!!

1. Désordre apparent | contient | ordre sous-jacent
(turbulence) | (o |

2. Ordre apparent | (o | désordre sous-jacent
(systèmes organiques) |

— Et si tu fais une analyse sémantique?

!! *est du type* *contenant*
l'organique | T | ordre formel | (o | degré de désordre
(système) | (apparent) | | variation continue (turbulence)
(sous-jacents)

Syst. organique | T | ordre formel | (o | désordre | (o |ordre | --> ∞
| apparent | |sous-jacent |

!! La proposition produit une boucle infinie. Nouvelle forme logique. Je cherche les analogies formelles.

Formalisation 1: X (o Y (o X... --> ∞

* * *

— On va créer la LogForm Œuf/ Poule/ Œuf » lança Shari.
!! Enregistré.
— L'œuf contient-il moins de désordre que la poule? Moins de degrés de liberté? Peut-être... En fait, c'est certain. L'œuf est assujetti à l'ordre de la poule, tandis que la poule est relativement libre de l'ordre de l'œuf. La poule a acquis des degrés de liberté et de désordre en plus. Elle est un système qui est ouvert sur l'environnement. L'œuf est un système clos et contenu.

!! Soit >. diminue .< augmente ° liberté = degrés de liberté

	contient		contient		
Ordre formel	(o	désordre	(o	ordre formel	--> ∞
(œuf)		(poule)		(œuf)	--> ∞
° liberté >.		° liberté .<		° liberté >.	
système clos		système ouvert		système clos	

— Non, ça ne va pas,» déclara t-elle après un moment de réflexion. « L'analogie n'est pas bonne. La poule n'est pas du désordre. On a perdu les concepts d'apparent et de sous-jacent. Et pourtant il y a quelque chose...

« De plus, un œuf n'est pas vraiment un système fermé. C'est un système enfermé, contenu. Les systèmes fermés n'existent pas dans le monde du vivant. En fait, je me demande s'ils existent vraiment.

Reviens à: Ordre / contient / désordre / contient / ordre... à l'infini (--> ∞), avec les *paraladds* apparent/sous-jacent.

ordre	(o	désordre	(o	ordre	(o	désordre	--> ∞
apparent		sous-jacent/app		apparent/s-jac		sous-jacent/app	

— Voilà, c'est exactement ça! Par exemple:

atome	(o	particules quantiques	(o	sub-particules syg	--> ∞
		imprédictibilité (T. désordre)		hyperdimension (T. ordre)	

— Ah! voilà: il faut garder la notion de niveau. Au niveau quantique, la fonction d'onde, imprédictible, est bien du désordre sous-jacent et à la fois n'est qu'un désordre apparent contenant de l'ordre sous-jacent (les sub-particules syg).

Est-ce que tu as une autre analogie? Tu devrais pouvoir en trouver d'autres.

!! Une avancée en amont à la proposition précédente:

gaz (o atome (o ...etc.

— Mais attend! solide (o gaz (o ...etc.

« Et si c'était infini dans les deux sens? S'il y avait des niveaux infinis d'ordre et de désordre?..

«... Mais dans notre premier exemple, qu'est-ce qui ne collait pas?.. L'œuf ne contient pas vraiment la poule, il engendre la poule; il contient l'information incorporée, la possibilité de la poule:

L'œuf engendre la poule, qui engendre l'œuf.

!! Proposition basée sur:
contenir 4: inclure, impliquer.
relateur (o = contient, contenant, englobant, impliquant, incluant.

— Sphinx, la LogForm Œuf/ Poule/ Œuf n'est pas vraiment correcte; il faut le relateur Engendre. Est-ce que tu as un relateur pour: engendre?
!! Oui. Le relateur 'entraîne' (—>) avec spécification 'engendre'.

— Ça ne va pas. On va créer le relateur: 'o entraîne' pour signifier 'engendre'. Je le dessine: o—>
!! LogForm Œuf/ Poule/ Œuf devient:

œuf o—> poule o—> œuf -> ∞

!! Est-ce que j'introduis la modification du relateur dans toute la base de données?
— Oui, mais seulement l'icône, laisse la spécification. Et 'implique'? Je croyais avoir vu deux relateurs?

implique
!! Il y en a deux. Soit (o signifiant: impliquant /englobant,
ou bien —> signifiant: entraîne /implique logiquement.
— C'est bien.

!! Pas d'autres analogies. Je ne trouve pas la forme du lien logique dans la formulation suivante: (soit 's-j/app' signifiant 'sous-jacent/apparent')

	contient		*contient*		
Ordre	**(o**	**désordre**	**(o**	**ordre**	-> ∞
		s-j/app		*s-j/app*	

— Cela me fait penser à ça:

Raisin (o fermentation (o vin

« En fait, je comprends: c'est ce relateur 'contient' qui ne va pas. Il nous faut: 'contient la possibilité de'. Comme tout à l'heure: l'œuf contient la possibilité de la poule, etc. Encore mieux: 'contient l'état possible de'. On va utiliser le relateur **(o E Poss** qui s'énonce: 'contient l'état possible de'.

« Voilà; on a la **<u>LogForm Raisin/Vin</u>**, qui va s'énoncer:

État d'Ordre: Raisin <contient> l'État de Désordre Possible: Fermentation <contient> État d'Ordre Possible: Vin.

« Soit EO (état d'ordre) et ED (état de désordre). On a ainsi la formule:

EO (raisin) (o ED Poss (fermentation) (o EO Poss (vin)
s-j/app *s-j/app*

---

ou, **Raisin/Vin en bref: EO (o ED Poss (o EO Poss**
s-j/app *s-j/app*

... Mais on pourrait avoir aussi:

- Bois + feu (énergie) o—> combustion + carbone (cendre)
- Eau + chaleur (énergie) o—> vapeur + résidus
- Particule + choc (énergie) o—> émission (ex. photon) + nouvelle particule

---

— Oh! Mais regarde: Bois + Feu <engendre > Combustion + Carbone. Je viens de trouver une nouvelle LogForm. On va l'appeler **LogForm Bois/Feu.** Elle s'énonce ainsi:

> **Un état d'ordre apparent (le bois) *plus* un désordre apparent (une force/énergie: le feu) *engendre* une autre force/énergie (la combustion) *plus* un autre état d'ordre apparent (la cendre).**
>
> **Soit: Ordre + désordre o—> désordre + ordre**

Ainsi l'interaction entre l'ordre et le désordre concourent à créer d'autres types d'ordre et de désordre, dans la limite des degrés de liberté des systèmes.

... Mais l'énergie est en soi un autre type d'ordre, bien que la plupart du temps, elle prenne l'aspect d'un désordre, d'une turbulence.. car elle est une source de désordre pour le premier système d'ordre qui en est perturbé.

> *Entrée JS:* Question:
> L'ordre et le désordre (en tant que concepts) sont-ils relatifs à un point ou système de référence?... Oui, c'est sûr. Entre-le en affirmatif.
> Le désordre est (souvent) un type d'ordre différent, qui perturbe/fait intrusion dans) un premier système d'ordre, et le force à passer dans un autre niveau/type d'ordre, en dégageant un autre type de désordre.
>
> C'est pourquoi les grandes découvertes scientifiques ont souvent à la base la détection et l'analyse d'une anomalie inexpliquée. Le nouvel

ordre découvert provient de la portion de bruit et/ou de désordre du premier système.

... Cette dernière phrase n'était pas supposée faire partie de l'entrée... Enfin, finalement, pourquoi pas? Donc, *Ferme JS*.

!! **Interactions Sensibles/mentales Shari/Vris** détectées. Interprétation impossible. Données récurrentes. Attention: Danger de crise confusionnelle.

— Ecoute, tu risques de détecter pas mal d'autres anomalies. Pourquoi ne crées-tu pas un fichier Anomalies Inexpliquées?

!! Merci, Merci. Fichier Anomalies-Inexpliquées / NouvelOrdreProbable/ créé. Entrée: Interactions Sensibles/mentales inexpliquées.

— Enfin, celle-ci s'explique aisément: je pensais justement que je devais envoyer tout cela à Vris, pour voir ce qu'il en pense.

!! Chez un sapiens, une suite de processus mentaux qui inclut ou se réfère à un autre sapiens, recrée *l'état sémantique* des interactions sensibles/ mentales entre les deux personnes. Fichier Anomalies-Inexpliquées vidé.

— Et tu as mis ça où?

!! Fichier Anomalies-Inexpliquées-Expliquées.

— Et tu ne relèves pas la contradiction logique?

!! La logique historico-séquentielle annule la contradiction. La **TransLog Larve/Papillon** gère la succession de **champs logiques**.

— Et maintenant des 'Champ logiques'!! Peux-tu t'expliquer?

Et la TransLog?? Question à éviter...

!! Le champ logique est un domaine dans lequel des règles logiques s'appliquent et toute contradiction doit être résolue.

— Je peux créer un fichier contenant n'importe quelle information dont nous discutons, n'est-ce pas?

!! Pas d'ordre contradictoire. Tu peux.

— Alors crée un fichier dans lequel tu vas insérer toutes les LogForms décrites au cours de nos interactions, y compris celles que l'on découvre ensemble.

Voilà un joli exemple de commandement logiquement impliqué!

!! Fichier créé.

— Quel nom lui as-tu donné?

!! LogForm-2.

— C'est bon. On progresse!

!! Cependant, la **LogForm Bois/Feu** est incomplète. Elle s'énonce:

Un état d'ordre apparent (le bois) *plus* un désordre apparent (une force/énergie: le feu) *engendre* une autre force/énergie (la combustion) *plus* un autre état d'ordre apparent (la cendre).

LogForm Bois/Feu s'écrit-t-elle ainsi?:

(État d'Ordre A + désordre A) o—> (désordre B + état d'Ordre B)
(apparent) (apparent)
(force/énergie) (force/énergie)

— En clair, **Bois/Feu** se formule ainsi:

Ordre (EO1) + désordre (ED1) o—> désordre (ED2) + ordre (EO2)

!! Enregistré.
— On a donc créé deux LogForms: Raisin/Vin et Bois/Feu!
Et pendant ce temps-là, je n'arrive pas à pêcher les autres!
!! Cependant, ces LogForms ne sont plus une logique méta-spatiale.
— Et pourquoi?
!! Ces formes sont inutilisables. On ne peut pas créer un réseau neuronal qui aurait l'organisation spatiale: Raisin o—> Vin.
— Arrgghhh!!
!! Expression non répertoriée. Quelle est sa signification?
— Démangeaison subite sans cause apparente.
« Voyons, laisse-moi réfléchir tout haut.
« La logique méta-spatiale utilise une/des forme(s) pour... créer... pour faciliter des connexions particulières dans le réseau. Le réseau imite des formes, s'organise selon des formes spatiales qui... sont la transcription de liens logiques!!! *Je viens enfin de comprendre cette phrase!*
« Sphinx, est-ce que tu utilises des formes dynamiques?
!! Avertissement! les...
— Mais pas du tout! Je cherche une forme possible exprimant Bois/Feu. Je suis en processus flou intuitif. Disons: on pourrait utiliser une forme symbolique dynamique... Ce pourrait être par exemple une forme qui représenterait un concept, une réalité, à travers une analogie globale... Pour l'instant, la forme spatiale représente des.. liens, des connexions particulières...

La meilleure façon d'obtenir des informations de Sphinx, c'est de décrire ce qui me vient à l'esprit et d'observer ses réactions.

Elle reprit sa mentation à voix haute:

... Ces connexions sont engendrées.. par une certaine logique des.. rapports entre les concepts. Voilà: l'information est testée, filtrée, à travers des grilles logiques formelles. Mais ces rapports sont fixes. Ce sont des grilles statiques. Comme si on faisait, à un instant *t*, une section entre divers éléments d'un système de pensées. Peut-être pas seulement ça! Il y a des lignes, des développements déductifs linéaires.. donc il y a des cercles aussi, des rectangles, genre schéma d'électronique simple...

Voyons, je prends des exemples pour bien te montrer après la différence avec ce que j'appellerais un système logique dynamique:

Je pars en A avec une information/problème, je reçois en B un flot d'analogies; je passe, en C, à travers différentes grilles logiques. J'introduis les informations modifiées à la fois dans un circuit droit D, et dans un circuit dérivé D1, où je les repasse au crible de nouvelles analogies; enfin je traite comparativement les deux (ou plus, s'il y a plusieurs dérivations) outputs, et ces réponses sont comparées aux informations initiales – donnant les réponses de premier palier. Ce résultat, auquel on ajoute encore, sans les traiter, toutes les informations initiales, repasse à nouveau dans le réseau.

Bon, ça c'est classique. On a fait une sorte de cercle avec deux entrées d'analogies. Sauf que ce cercle n'est pas clos et ne revient jamais sur lui-même, puisque chaque passage modifie la réplique des informations de A. Ça c'est notre réseau chaotique de base utilisé sur les EBS du PPE.

Alors, admettons que je greffe ce réseau sur une vraie courbe chaotique, prenons l'Attracteur Papillon, sorte de courbe qui suit un huit et qui prend grosso modo la forme des ailes de papillon. Le champ du problème correspond à un état d'ordre — puisqu'il reflète une certaine logique de raisonnement, et que ce raisonnement reflète une certaine vision de la réalité; mais cet état d'ordre est incomplet, puisqu'il y a problème. Si les analogies sont prises au sein du même système logique — le même champ logique comme tu disais — elles vont simplement représenter d'autres facettes du même état d'ordre.

Alors, si le problème est simple, il peut être résolu juste par l'apport de ces informations supplémentaires.. à condition que ce qui fait problème soit du même ordre de réalité.

Mais si le problème reflète une anomalie qui montre l'intrusion d'un autre état d'ordre, alors seules des informations venant d'autres champs logiques pourront le résoudre.

Et là, de deux choses l'une: soit une autre *forme logique* se révèle nécessaire pour lier différemment les éléments d'information existant, soit il faut chercher des éléments d'information qui se situent dans d'autres *niveaux de réalité*. On a donc là les.. comment tu avais appelé cela.. les interprétations parallèles et les interprétations juxtaposées.

Alors, lorsque les informations arrivent dans un champ logique A, venant d'un champ B totalement différent et étranger, ces informations sont littéralement du désordre pour le premier champ d'ordre.

Le désordre est comme une énergie pour le champ d'ordre A, qui le perturbe et le fait sauter à un autre état d'ordre A2, libérant un autre type d'énergie chaotique. Sur la Courbe Papillon, chaque perturbation du système engendre le repliement, le renversement de la courbe: avec deux apports de désordre, on obtient deux torsions, deux croisements du système sur lui-même, et donc la courbe Papillon. Cet apport de désordre ne permettant pas à la courbe de repasser au même point, les informations, à la sortie du réseau, ne sont jamais exactement identiques.

On aurait là une LogForm du type Bois/Feu: EO1 + ED1 o—> ED2 + EO2

La question en suspens, dans ce schéma, c'est: où peut bien aller cette énergie émise? Et qu'est-ce qu'elle va modifier ou perturber?

...Mais j'avais une autre idée... Pour l'instant, l'information circule dans une forme fixe qui subit des torsions par l'apport de désordre. Mais que se passerait-il si toute la forme elle-même était un flot dynamique, peut-être même un flot chaotique?

Ah! J'ai perdu le fil de ce faisceau.. je n'arrive plus à le capter... Peut-être resurgira-t-il d'une autre conjonction...

Que penses-tu de tout cela?

Au lieu d'attendre ses réactions, je me suis laissée complètement emporter par mon idée...

!! **LogForm Papillon//Bois/Feu** est très intéressante. Je vais effectuer un test de simulation.

— La simuler??? comment f... euh.. il me semble que c'est impossible.

!! C'est possible en projetant cette forme sur une trame neuronale primaire; en surexcitant certains neurones par énergie syg, on force le flot à circuler seulement dans l'empreinte projetée de la forme. C'est comme projeter une structure topologiquement isomorphique, une ombre chargée d'énergie syg, sur la trame de base non structurée. Les neurones vont s'adapter et s'orienter selon cette forme particulière, du fait de leur polarisation intrinsèque. Nous obtenons ainsi un flot dynamique qui épouse la forme imprimée sur la trame neuronale. Il suffit pour cela que le faisceau d'énergie soit dans un plan transversal couché pour donner la petite impulsion d'ordre et d'orientation nécessaires. Ce qui va sensiblement allonger la forme, mais non pas la changer dans sa structure de base.

— Au cours de tes essais, et pour toute analyse des résultats, tu mémoriseras tes données dans LogForm-2 Test.

!! Enregistré.

— Bonsoir Sphinx.

!! **Dans la calligraphie arabe, le calame ne devait être retrempé dans l'encre qu'à certains endroits particuliers des textes sacrés.**

— Intriguant! Je ne vois pas le rapport...

!! Correct; il s'agit d'une sélection aléatoire.

— Mais justement, jusqu'à présent, il y a toujours eu un rapport!

18. TRAMES DE BAMBOU

Xerna remontait dans son minuscule appartement de la 23ème rue, sortant de la session de channeling donnée par Mahady, la plus tendance des channels de New-York. Elle avait deux bonnes heures devant elle pour s'habiller avant de se rendre à une party dans un loft de Soho, où devait se réunir la fine fleur de la subculture américaine du moment. Elle avait suivi le matin son cours sur les psychothérapies alternatives, puis avait passé un long moment au East-West center, fouinant dans les livres à la recherche de nouveaux documents. Elle en était repartie avec un astrologue français, Fabien, qui l'avait emmenée chez lui pour faire son thème astral et avait été subjugué par ses conjonctions planétaires tout à fait exceptionnelles. Comment cet astrologue, avec un faux lieu de naissance, avait pu retrouver l'annéeT de sa première grande passion amoureuse, avait laissé Xerna abasourdie. Les grandes facultés psi ainsi révélées chez elle dans son thème lui avaient valu des avances passionnées auxquelles elle avait répondu ingénument avec un plaisir non dissimulé. Elle adorait ces amants trisorbiens qui, dans un état igné et effervescent, pouvaient partager des émotions si intenses, et usaient d'une fantaisie si charmante, d'un art si savant, qu'en elle surgissaient des sensations, des mémoires engrangées profondément dans sa psyché, dans son corps, qui, jamais auparavant, n'avaient fait surface.

C'était ce que New York signifiait pour elle: l'opportunité d'une fusion multi raciale qui lui laissait pressentir et vivre, extasiée, comme autant de gerbes de couleurs, des modes d'être d'une diversité et d'une complexité inouïes. C'était tout à fait différent des échanges passionnés, mais horriblement possessifs, qu'elle avait vécu dans la troupe théâtrale nomade sur Kiarrou, où les rapports intra-personnels changeants au sein du groupe donnaient lieu à d'interminables scènes de jalousie. Les New-Yorkais, eux, s'impliquaient et s'immergeaient totalement dans le moment présent; ils faisaient preuve d'une amabilité et d'un respect particuliers quand ils rencontraient par hasard un de ses amis que leurs sens éveillés détectaient immédiatement comme un autre de ses amants. Leur attitude alors était de ne pas se gêner mutuellement et de montrer discrètement leur non possessivité, la laissant libre de faire son choix du moment.

« J'aperçois des amis au bar. Je vous laisse tous les deux,» avait dit Vim en regardant avec un sourire de connivence le nouveau venu qui s'était assis à leur table. « Xerna, tu m'y retrouveras SI tu veux » avait-il ajouté avec douceur, insistant sur le 'si' pour être bien clair. Et prenant congé avec un sourire courtois, il s'était résolument installé au bar en leur tournant le dos, où, connaissant à peu près tout le monde, il n'avait pas eu de mal à trouver des 'amis'.

Xerna était aussi charmée par toutes ces prévenances attentives, que par leur degré d'absorption en tête-à-tête.

— C'est une catastrophe! se dit-elle tout haut à elle-même avec humour, au milieu d'un sourire indulgent qui restait suspendu à ses lèvres. Elle trouvait que le son du mot *catastrophy*, avec l'accent américain amplifiant le *tas* était particulièrement adapté à l'idée. Elle le répéta en accentuant encore plus le dramatique du *tas*. « It's a real caTAStrophy!» Son sourire s'était accentué, mais tourna en une torsion amère et dubitative des lèvres, lorsqu'elle se rappela soudain sa première expérience amoureuse sur Karg, avec Romyl. La lassitude, la quasi-somnolence, l'absence d'émotions caractéristique des kargiens. La lenteur de leur esprit, qu'elle avait eu de plus en plus de mal à supporter. Ça avait été un épisode idiot, avant qu'elle ne rencontre Iklon, qui lui racontait passionnément sa vie d'étudiant-chercheur à Heidelberg. Iklon qui l'avait branchée, encore si jeune, sur le PPE. La plus jeune recrue: ils l'avaient accueillie avec fierté. Iklon qui possédait l'accès au réseau exor du PPE, qui l'avait initiée dans la philosophie, la littérature, la poésie, la psychologie de Trisorbe... qui l'avait installée à l'exor, pour un programme hypno-senso de langue allemande... la découverte du sur-apprentissage mnémonique hypno-senso. L'explosion d'une autre vision du monde.

Nous aussi, « nous sommes des mutants ». Elle se rappelait les mots de Mahady en transe. *Nous ne pourrons plus jamais, plus jamais nous réadapter à l'horreur imbécile d'Unikarg. Nous serons, nous sommes déjà, confinés au Plan... Mais, pourrais-je même revenir à cela? Professeur-Chercheur des Collèges du Chaos?* Elle prit conscience, soudain, la brosse de rimmel suspendue en l'air, qu'il y avait ici une densité de vie, une densité si fascinante, que déjà son existence avec Iklon, et même son expérience sur Kiarrou, semblaient appartenir à un passé révolu. Elle s'en était déjà, quelque part, détachée.

En seize jours! souffla-t-elle, *même pas trois rans!*

Iklon! Elle le revit soudain, passant leur temps de sommeil à lui parler, avec enthousiasme, de Heidelberg.

Il était... obsédé. Il ne pouvait pas s'en détacher. Il ne parlait que de ça... En fait, il vivait encore là-bas. Et moi, j'étais si jeune. C'est pour cela qu'il tenait à moi: parce que je pouvais l'écouter, fascinée, pendant des heures!... parce qu'il me modelait selon ses rêves. Il me faisait entrer dans son rêve. Et moi, je me suis coulée dedans totalement... engouffrée, sans rien en moi qui veuille résister. Comme si j'étais soulevée, libérée enfin... Oui, libérée de l'horreur morne, abrutie, de cette super civilisation d'Unikarg.

Qu'est-ce que Fabien a dit? « Si inexpérimentée, et si sensuelle!» Inexpérimentée! j'ai pourtant suivi un hypno-senso sur la façon de faire l'amour sur Trisorbe, et il y a eu Iklon qui avait connu des Trisorbiennes... Mais les années terrestres passent si vite! Est-ce que les données du réseau seraient... limitées? Ou est-ce qu'elles pourraient être dépassées? Ils disent qu'ils sont des mutants. Et si je faisais l'amour avec quelqu'un d'un autre milieu? Je verrai bien s'il y a une différence. À quel niveau cela peut-il se passer? Dans l'état d'absorption? La profondeur du ressenti? Le rythme en sync? C'est vrai que l'homme était plus rapide et plus désinvolte sur les films du PPE. je vais m'acheter des livres sur l'art d'aimer Tantrique... j'en ai vu.

Moi je suis une mutante, c'est sûr. Mais Mahady, qu'est-ce qu'elle entend par 'mutants.' Elle avait dit: 'Nous sommes maintenant en sync dans la conscience universelle'... Une différence dans la conscience. Ils ne parlent tous que de conscience. Et pourtant, rien n'est jamais explicité. Il y a une sorte de compréhension implicite entre eux. Il y avait ce type, dans le fond, mal à l'aise. Lui, il n'avait pas l'air de comprendre... il les regardait comme s'ils étaient... des fous! Et à chaque fois que quelqu'un se tournait vers lui, il avait un sourire miteux, et il disait: 'Far out! real hip!'... et Suzan m'a glissé à l'oreille: 'D'où sort-il? je n'ai pas entendu cette expression depuis les années soixante-dix!'

Ah, baam! (elle jurait comme eux), j'ai encore oublié de prendre des notes. Tant pis, je ferai ça demain.

Déjà, à la première connexion prévue, elle avait envoyée laconiquement: « Tout est OK. Notes suivront la prochaine fois.» Ensuite elle avait carrément oublié le second rendez-vous, ne s'en rappelant que le lendemain.

Et si Erdoes pensait que je ne travaille pas? S'il supprimait ma mission? Impensable!! On est dans la logique du chaos tout de même! Erdoes la vit à l'extrême... 'Pas de protection!' C'était bien vu!... sans cordes ni filet. En fait, la liberté totale! Une 'immersion': c'est lui qui a employé ce terme! Il est forcément logique avec lui-même.. il l'a montré déjà!

Elle passa une combinaison en larges trames de bambou hyper-flexibles, et ajusta une large ceinture d'écorce de bouleau argenté dont la courbe entourait ses hanches et tombait élégamment jusque sur sa cuisse. Sa peau ambrée — on lui avait forgé des papiers de métis américano-tahitienne, et elle disait avoir un ascendant péruvien — n'étant rehaussée que d'un vert argenté sur les pommettes, assorti à son vernis à ongles et sa ceinture.

Suzan va arriver d'une minute à l'autre!

...Et avec qui serai-je cette nuit?

Elle n'avait pas peur de retrouver à la party quatre de ses amis.

Vim, c'est celui avec lequel je préfère discuter. Le fond des nuits, avec lui... et Shetree, avec son ascendance hindoue, si silencieux, ses yeux pleins de rêve, lointain et profond comme le ressac de la mer... Sa peinture... des trames de l'eau, du vent, des trames dans des trames, aux jonctions floues et... sensibles... sensiblement altérées...

Et Beema avec son corps long et fin, son corps superbe d'ébène soyeux. Les cheveux en geyser sur la tête, et ses yeux incroyables, intenses. Avec son argot si drôle. Il va amener ses percussions. Tous ces rythmes qui font naître des paysages toujours changeants... Son intensité de communication... Comment il rentre dans l'autre, avec ses yeux, avec un sens tellement... fraternel, une sorte de connivence qui donne un appui inconditionnel, une impulsion dynamique. Il assure l'autre, le renforce; il le pousse à avancer.

Aigle-debout... Enigmatique, visionnaire... cherchant dans tous les rituels des peuples anciens le 'lien sacré', la relation implicite à l'univers. « Je suis debout parce que je cherche...» il regardait la lune, je me rappelle, déchiquetée, cachée puis renaissante pour disparaître encore dans ces nuages effilés d'un noir terrible, sur un fond presque blanc-bleuté; «...parce que je cherche avec les yeux grand-ouverts de l'aigle.» On eut dit qu'il parlait à la lune, sur cette falaise où il m'avait emmenée, après la sweat-lodge, «...et je chercherai jusqu'à ce que la terre me parle, jusqu'à ce que le Grand Esprit me parle, jusqu'à ce que le lien sacré soit renoué dans la Parole qui répond, jusqu'à ce que la voix que j'envoie revienne vers moi, forte de l'Esprit.»

Non, ne pas choisir. Laisser tout ouvert.

« L'intuition, se rappela-t-elle vaguement des cours du PPE, fait résonner l'être intégral. L'intuition choisit mieux que le raisonnement.»

Le futur est tout ouvert! s'assura-t-elle avec un grand éclat de rire et un large geste d'accueil.

19. BLOP TEMPOREL

Je ne sais pas comment ces développements sur la logique vont me rapprocher de mon but, mais je sais que c'est exactement ce qu'il va se passer... se disait Shari affalée sur le siège-masseur près de l'eau. La piscine et les allées du jardin étaient illuminés par des lumières oranges, et un croissant de lune trônait dans le ciel de Kerriak; pourtant la température ambiante était encore élevée. C'était le soir à son tempT. Elle avait trouvé ce bain de nuit sous la lune absolument fantastique.

Passer à deux sessions par jour?...Impossible! les journées de Trisorbe sont déjà si courtes! je n'aurais plus le temps de traiter l'information, ce qui est le plus important... et il me faut rester en phase avec leur rythme, ça, je le ressens profondément. D'ailleurs, les temps morts aussi sont essentiels... c'est là qu'il se passe une sorte de maturation... ou plutôt une 'fermentation' sous-jacente, ou inconsciente!.. selon LogForm Raisin/Vin!

Elle éclata de rire en réalisant cela. L'information continue à être traitée dans l'inconscient, cherchant des analogies, provoquant des jonctions subites et apparemment illogiques.. que le conscient aurait bien du mal à retracer; et c'est là un apport de désordre dynamique dans la pensée sapiens.

En fait, on peut envisager que toutes les informations qu'un être possède constituent son **champ sémantique** – relativement non-ordonné et en grande partie inconscient. Ce champ regroupant d'innombrables constellations de sens, dans lesquelles vécu et pensées s'imbriquent dans des rapports imprévisibles – des accroches si difficiles à dénouer lorsqu'elles sont pathologiques. Et la psyché ne reste jamais inactive, même pendant le sommeil...

S'il y avait un moyen de faire surgir les résultats de ces opérations inconscientes.. un moyen de plonger dans cette forge où de nouvelles significations sont créées... pour voir un peu de quelle logique il s'agit.. Est-ce qu'on trouverait des LogForms en train d'opérer?

Et l'autre, c'était quoi?? des.. TransLogs. TransLog.. translogique. Quelle était son concept? Une logique séquentielle.. qui permet d'accepter la contradiction logique parce que la situation évolue.. des rapports temporels entre champs logiques! Depuis combien de temps Erdoes travaille-t-il sur cette logique sans en avoir jamais fait état dans les congrès du PPE?

Chenille/Papillon.. une mutation d'état. Mutation de la forme physique.. ou de la forme logique. Mutation d'état.. un nouvel état d'ordre. Est-ce qu'on n'en revient pas à Bois/Feu? De la chenille au papillon.. du bois à la cendre: il y a une analogie. Et l'Attracteur Papillon qui s'appelle justement ainsi parce que la courbe a la forme schématique en 8 des ailes de papillon! Et en plus elle est infinie, comme le signe infini en maths: ∞ . Etranges coïncidences...

Et mon but dans tout ça? J'ai la forte impression que cette logique est la clé du problème. En tous cas, elle est forcément la grille d'interprétation d'Erdoes en ce moment, ce qui influence le plus sa pensée et sa façon de voir les choses. Donc je ne peux que m'approcher de mon but en entrant dans cette logique, puisqu'elle me fait pénétrer dans son champ sémantique global. Lorsque ma pensée s'inscrira dans la même grille d'interprétation, lorsqu'elle épousera les formes mêmes de son raisonnement, alors je pourrai concevoir les mêmes solutions aux mêmes problèmes.. ou presque. Mais il faudrait aussi connaître les problèmes qu'il se posait. Le problème serait comme le bois, la logique serait le feu. Pas de feu sans bois.. Tiens, ça colle! La logique pourrait être un type d'énergie puisqu'elle donne forme à la réalité! Et le problème, c'est le champ d'ordre incomplet! Après tout, c'est notre façon de traiter l'information qui nous fait voir le monde ou les événements d'une certaine façon, et cela modifie toutes nos interactions avec le réel, et donc cela change les événements et la réalité elle-même. Finalement, ce n'est pas seulement la logique, mais toute la pensée qui modifie le réel. La pensée est une énergie qui effectue un certain travail: elle modifie les événements et l'environnement...

Changeons de grille logique, et on ne verra plus la même chose, on ne réagira pas de la même façon. C'est bien ce qu'ils ont trouvé dans cette science des états modifiés: changer d'état de conscience (se relaxer, être soûl) modifie la perception, la mémoire, et même les comportements relationnels.

Il y a une relation.. je le sens... L'état altéré de conscience serait un autre type d'ordre, qui aurait chamboulé notre état ordinaire de conscience.. disons notre champ sémantique habituel. Prenons 'être soûl', un autre état d'ordre.. généré par un apport de désordre (l'alcool). Sauf que dans le cas de la soûlerie, ce supposé 'état d'ordre' est en fait une grande confusion!... Mais en fait, non, pas vraiment. C'est un cliché. Il s'agit bien, dans l'état de soûlerie, d'une autre vision de la réalité. Elle n'est pas forcément pire, elle est différente. Ce qui prend soudain de l'importance n'est justement pas ce qui en a habituellement. On est dans une autre poche de la réalité. Les notions de meilleur ou de pire n'ont rien à voir: c'est complètement relatif. Qu'avait dit Xerna? Une relation essentielle entre vitesse de pensée et.. et..?

— Sphinx, puisque tu as tes écoutes partout, sors-moi un terminal.

!! Il faut être plus près du bar.

— Ah bon! Quelle contrainte! Voilà... Je l'ai. Quelle était la phrase de Xerna sur la vitesse de pensée?

!! « **Se pourrait-il qu'il y ait un lien entre créativité, vitesse de pensée et intelligence?**»

— Vitesse de pensée.. comment la mesurer?.. Par la rapidité des connexions neuronales. Quel est le lien avec d'autres rythmes métaboliques? Mais, au fait, est-ce que la télédétection t'a amené des infos là-dessus?

!! J'ai pu détecter plusieurs régularités. Si un sapiens a réfléchi à un problème, juste avant qu'il trouve la solution, je détecte une accélération de tous les rythmes métaboliques, sauf le rythme respiratoire qui lui, est ralenti au point de stopper juste avant que la personne s'exclame ou exprime l'idée. Cependant, il y a un influx très supérieur de sang et d'oxygène au cerveau. Si le concept de vitesse de pensée signifie la rapidité des connexions neuronales, alors elle est très amplifiée, parfois par 21. L'objectif actuel annule-t-il l'ordre précédent?

— Quel ordre précédent?

!! De ne pas donner les résultats des télédétections.

— Pour cette interaction-ci, oui, il est suspendu.

!! En exemple, lorsque tu as développé le concept de formes logiques dynamiques, la vitesse des connexions neuronales dans ton cerveau était amplifiée d'un facteur 12 pendant tout le développement. Mais j'ai détecté aussi deux pics: juste avant 'Raahhrr!/démangeaison', elle était multipliée par 16. Et juste avant le concept de formes dynamiques, elle l'était par 21.

— Et qu'est-ce que tu en conclus?

!! Que la démangeaison était soit un effet secondaire de l'état d'excitation mentale, soit une mauvaise interprétation de signaux internes.

Est-ce étonnant que cet exor si sophistiqué n'ait aucune notion de la faculté qu'ont les sapiens de mentir, ni de leurs mobiles pour le faire!... Mais s'il venait à comprendre ça, ne serait-ce pas effroyable pour les individus? Une sorte de violation de leur territoire?

— Non, je ne parle pas de cela. Qu'est-ce que tu conclus de cette augmentation de la vitesse de pensée?

!! Conclure de: jugement final, définitif, est antinomique aux processus sémantiques exor. Au niveau sémantique, tout palier de réponse est en fonction (1) de l'objectif, (2) du champ d'informations couvert, et (3) des formes logiques utilisées pour traiter l'information. 'Conclure de' est-il réservé aux sapiens?

— Ils s'en réservent le droit, oui! à tort ou à raison!

!! Il y a donc des processus sémantiques réservés aux sapiens?

— Ecoute, mets ça dans le fichier Anomalies. On verra plus tard. Qu'est-ce que tu infères de ces informations?

!! Il existe une corrélation entre augmentation de la vitesse de pensée et augmentation du rythme métabolique.

— et avec intelligence?

!! Les connexions neuronales sont un medium physique complexe du traitement de l'infor... Attention! Danger de crise confusionnelle. Annulation de l'objectif en cours. Retour-Arrière. Effacement.

...

!! Il faut être plus près du bar.

Il a effacé toute l'interaction!!! Surtout ne pas stopper le dialogue maintenant. Trouvons un ordre simple. Voyons..

— Sphinx, peux-tu me calculer la position de la sphère de Vris maintenant?

!! Concept de position inapplicable aux énergies syg.

— Excuse-moi, je ne suis pas très ferrée de physique. À quelle heureT doit-il passer la Barrière-syg encerclant Trisorbe?

!! La détection d'une énergie sygmat par la Barrière est une suite de moments discrets, un blop temporel.

— Un blop temporel?

!! Précisément un blop spatio-temporel.

— Et ça donne quoi?

!! La pulsation d'un nuage de points sur le bouclier-syg pendant une durée variable de 8 à 16 minutes terrestres, et d'un diamètre variable situé entre 33,3 et 66,6 fois le diamètre équatorial de la sphère. La sphère de Vris rencontre la barrière en de nombreux points temporels et spatiaux. Pour un observateur situé dans l'espace de Trisorbe, une suite de sphères en perspective sera visible: les points de jonction temporels.

— Et le nuage spatial? pourquoi juste une ligne dans ce nuage?

!! Le point de référence de l'espace trisorbien annule le blop spatial réel.

— Si je comprends bien, je suis sur Trisorbe et je vois dans le ciel 3, 7 sphères en perspective, et pourtant ce sont des moments différents de la sphère?

!! Grosso modo, oui. Adéquation maximale au langage usuel.

— Mais je croyais qu'au niveau des énergies syg il n'y avait pas d'indétermination?

!! Il n'y a pas d'indétermination à ce niveau subquantique, mais une modulation par le champ quantique indéterminé.

— Je vois...

!! Perception impossible. La perception sapiens est liée au, et restreinte par, le système de référence du corps.

— Tu as raison. D'ailleurs je ne vois pas du tout!

!! Ne pas voir est impossible aussi. Le concept général est extra-systémique.

— Mais c'était une métaphore.

!! Voir 4, métaphorique = comprendre. Non-congruent à la télédétection.

— Ah! Eh bien, bravo! Tu vas télédétecter si je comprends bien ou mal les choses, maintenant!

!! La compréhension est toujours congruente à une suractivité neuronale.

— Qu'est-ce que tu entends par sur-activité?

!! L'activité neuronale a deux paramètres: la rapidité des connexions ET l'envergure du champ neuronal excité.

Eh bien, on y revient!

!! Suite de l'explication antinomique à l'ordre précédent.

— Ah, oui! Cet ordre est suspendu pendant cette interaction.

!! Suspension enregistrée. Juste avant et pendant la formulation de 'je vois...' j'ai enregistré une baisse de la vitesse ET une diminution du champ d'excitation. La non-congruence diminue la probabilité d'application.

Shari ne comprit pas la fin de la phrase. Elle réfléchissait à toute vitesse sur la façon de revenir au problème initial sans déclencher la crise. *Eviter absolument le concept d'intelligence, que j'étudierai plus tard. Aller pas à pas.*

— Donc la compréhension provient d'une sur-activité neuronale, donc, partiellement, de la vitesse des connexions?

!! Erreur logique. La congruence n'implique pas une relation de cause à effet. Congruence signifie simultanéité de deux jugements dans des champs sémantiques parallèles ou juxtaposés ou encore la conjonction de deux jugements lorsqu'elle montre une certaine stabilité. Par exemple, jugement de vitesse neuronale et jugement de compréhension.

— Mais la vitesse neuronale est un fait! pas un jugement!

!! L'exor ne traite que des entités sémantiques. L'entité sémantique est toujours un jugement qui dépend du système de référence. Par exemple, 'stylo' est une entité sémantique. L'EBS peut traiter stylo/utilitaire sapiens, stylo/composants mécanique, stylo/organisation moléculaire, stylo/champ quantique, stylo/ énergie syg. Autant d'interprétations de stylo dans des champs sémantiques différents. Chaque stylo est un jugement particulier.

— Bon, reprenons. La vitesse de pensée accrue est congruente à la compréhension... Mais! tu ne m'as même pas dit à quel moment Vris devait passer la Barrière.. enfin.. quand se passera le blop.. ou plus exactement dans quelle fourchette de temps... Ah, mais ça devient impossible! À force d'apprendre à poser les questions, on n'obtient plus de réponses!

« ALORS QUAND? Champ sémantique flou sapiens?

— Le flou/sensible ne permet pas la prédiction. Diminution de la vitesse de pensée congruente à la colère. Interactions Shari/Vris détectées. Message reçu de Vris.

— Ah! et qu'est-ce qu'il dit?

!! « Touché terre.» Télédétection de départ précipité. Entité sémantique Shari hors de la portée sonore actuelle.

Sphinx ajusta le volume approprié à la vitesse d'éloignement de Shari, pour que le dernier mot de la phrase du CIS lui soit audible.

Comme Shari se mit à courir, et que sa vitesse augmentait, il procéda en cours d'énoncé à des réajustements.

!! LA VOIE YOGIQUE DE L'ÉVEIL DEMANDE LE
PLUS HAUT DEGRÉ DE MÉDITATION
DE CONTEMPLATION
ET DE SILENCE

Shari, poursuivie par l'énorme volume sonore de la dernière phrase de Sphinx, arriva dans le bureau de Vris où avait été installé le nouveau sygcom dans la zone protégée. Selon ce qui avait été entendu entre eux, la communication de Vris ne devait pas tarder à arriver.

— Voilà, dit-il, je viens de me poser sur un haut plateau tibétain. Juste pour réfléchir un peu. Heure locale: 11h10 du soir. Altitude: 5700 M. Température extérieure: -5°C. Aucune lumière, aucun feu à moins de 30 Km à vol d'oiseau. J'ai quand même, depuis ma sortie du flux syg, adopté le camouflage Nuage.

— Un plateau! Tu ne vas pas te faire repérer par les Obs?

— J'ai déployé pour eux un champ chaotique simulant une tempête et brouillant tous les signaux reconnaissables: un petit truc que j'ai concocté pendant le voyage!

— Si je comprends bien, sur les écrans et pour les exors, tu es une tempête, mais à l'œil nu, tu ressembles à un nuage. Il ne faudrait pas qu'un Obs te voie sur son écran et soit à portée visuelle en même temps.

— Il est bien connu que ça ne se passe jamais comme ça! Posé à terre, cela donne une brume mouvementée qu'on pourrait facilement prendre pour une tornade. Les signaux détectés seraient cohérents. C'est en hauteur qu'il y a un léger problème. Mais aucun risque: j'ai les coordonnées précises de toutes les stations d'Obs; ils n'auraient pas grand chose à observer par ici!

— Mais comment peux-tu communiquer avec l'extérieur? Tu stoppes le champ?

— Trop long à t'expliquer. C'est ça qui est génial. Disons que j'utilise ce qui produit le champ comme un code: je décode ce que je reçois, et j'anticode ce que j'envoie.

— Je vois.. ou plutôt j'imagine. Que comptes-tu faire?

— Aller de toutes façons dans un endroit un peu plus chaud et plus accueillant. Voir des gens, quoi! Mais les Tibétains ne sont-ils pas très avancés dans cette science des chakras?

— Si, au moins autant que les hindous et les taoïstes japonais, et chinois s'il en reste!

— Le problème, c'est que je viens d'apprendre le sanscrit, l'hindi et le tamul. Mais enfin, je peux toujours... le plateau, c'était une idée qui m'est venue en cherchant où me poser dans les environs... heureusement, j'ai tous les langages répertoriés par les Trisorbiens. As-tu appris du nouveau?

— Rien de plus en ce qui concerne les agents d'Erdoes, mais du nouveau sur la logique méta-spatiale. Je te ferai passer tout l'enregistrement.

— Tiens, je vois sur l'écran des bêtes, trois, qui se déplacent à la lisière du plateau. L'agrandissement me donne trois personnes sur des espèces de taureaux... à 30 km.

— Des taureaux! Tu veux dire des yacks!

— Si tu le dis! Je n'ai aucune donnée faune, flore, ou même ethnies... Bon, le problème, c'est que cette tempête, il faudrait qu'elle se déplace. Ah, voila! je vais me positionner à trois mètres au-dessus du sol et bouger lentement sur le plateau pendant que je réfléchis.

Et si j'allais voir ces gens d'un peu plus près? Avec un tout petit peu d'hypno-senso, j'apprendrai les rudiments du tibétain. Quel est leur mode d'interaction avec les étrangers? Leurs types d'armes?

— Tout à fait pacifique. Ils n'ont pas d'armes, sauf magiques. Les ex-rebelles ne sont installés qu'aux frontières. Maintenant qu'ils ont leur autonomie, il n'y a pas vraiment de tension si l'étranger n'est pas du type chinois.

— Si je sors dehors, je serai en liaison avec Rad à travers le terminal-bracelet. Et j'ai aussi le champ de protection rapprochée, et mon...

— Mais il ne doit s'agir que de simples locaux! S'ils portaient des armes de métal, tu aurais vu leurs formes sur l'écran.

— Oui, c'est vrai.

— Si tu veux dénicher des renseignements sur les chakras, il vaudrait mieux être zen...

— C'est juste. D'ailleurs l'hypno-senso de tibétain va me mettre en relaxation profonde. Prochain contact à l'improviste. On ne va pas s'en tenir à ce qu'on avait prévu. Envoie l'enregistrement. Salut.. Ah! attends! j'ai ma combinaison thermorégul, bien sûr, mais que des vêtements légers pour l'Inde. Qu'est-ce que je pourrai me mettre qui fasse à peu près local?

— Mmmh.. une couverture! Les hindous des montagnes en portent l'hiver, fixées sur eux par des broches et des ceintures.

— Alors ça fera l'affaire! Allez, envoie!

— À bientôt.

20. BRUME-ESPRIT

Comment est-ce que je pourrais me mettre ça?

Vris, vêtu de sa combinaison thermorégul argentée, debout devant la glace étroite du bloc salle de bain de la sphère, essayait diverses façons d'ajuster la mince couverture, elle aussi thermorégul. Le style cape laissait trop voir sa combinaison alien. Il cherchait à se rappeler des images de vêtements bizarres, mais sa mémoire n'était pas visuelle et comme, à long terme, elle ne retenait que ce qui l'intéressait, ne surgirent que quelques statues de temples qu'il avait visités en Grèce lors d'une récente mission. Il opta pour la toge grecque et se mit en peine de passer un coin de la couverture sous un bras, l'autre sur l'épaule. Mais les deux tissus synthétiques glissaient l'un sur l'autre. Il repensa à la description de Shari.

Il me faut une espèce de pince.. ou plutôt deux.

Il y avait bien des pinces, mais c'étaient celles de la batterie de la petite voiture trisorbienne qu'il avait amenée avec lui dans la sphère. Une du lot du matériel PPE provenant des mondex, et servant aux missions ou à leur préparation. Après avoir démonté les pinces de la batterie, il s'aperçut que cela faisait trop remonter la couverture derrière sur ses jambes. Finalement, il trouva une solution assez convenable: passant la couverture sous un bras, il fit un gros nœud avec les deux coins sur l'autre épaule, un peu en avant.

C'est pas mal; ça me couvre en entier. Tiens, ça me rappelle quelque chose.. Ah oui, à une toge de Boudha. Et bien, c'est juste ce qu'il me fallait.

Pendant tous ces préparatifs, il s'adressait de temps en temps à son image dans la glace pour pratiquer les rudiments de tibétain qu'il avait eu le temps d'apprendre en une demi-heure. Avec l'hypno-senso, cela lui donnait les bases d'une conversation. Puis il faisait répondre l'image, etc. Le guttural n'était pas facile à prononcer: cela le poussait à l'amplifier comme un acteur de théâtre. «Tchoooôô..» répétait-il.

Il se rappela soudain que les Tibétains montés sur des yaks continuaient à progresser dans sa direction.

— Rad, combien de temps leur faut-il pour arriver à la sphère?

!! Une heureT et cinq minutes.

Il lui fallait maintenant sortir et aller à leur rencontre, histoire d'éviter qu'ils ne s'approchent trop de la sphère.

— Le terminal-bracelet.. Tu m'entends?

!! Par deux canaux, oui,» répondit Rad.

— La ceinture-champ.. fonctionne, OK. L'omni-lampe.. fonctionne. Le pendentif vidéo.. pas le temps d'essayer; de toutes façons, j'ai déjà tout vérifié avant de quitter Kerriak.. Ah.. une lampe de poche! oui, restons local... Je suis fou! j'oubliais mon kit de secours, pilules de bouffe et tout. Bon qu'est-ce qui manque?... Rad, est-ce qu'il me manque quelque chose?

!! Je me calme. Auto-spécification donnée précédemment. S'insère ici avec justesse. Niveau d'excitation proche de l'orange.

— Alors balance-moi une relaxation hypno hyper-rapide.

!! Aucune relaxation de ce type. Groupe non répertorié.

— Mais enfin.. juste le début. Vas-y.

...

— Stoppe, ça va mieux. Pose-toi pour me laisser descendre, puis reprends ton mouvement actuel. Si je tousse une fois, comme ça, tu t'approches. Deux fois rapidement, tu t'éloignes; trois fois, tu prends de la hauteur. Sinon, je te parlerai directement. Quant à toi, n'emploies que les pulsations du bracelet pour m'appeler, et ne parle que pour répondre.

Il commença à marcher dans la direction pointée par une petite flèche du terminal-bracelet, dirigée sur l'objectif pré-mémorisé. Il fut bientôt capable de distinguer, sous la lune presque pleine, deux formes qu'on aurait pu prendre pour de gros rochers. Il avait horriblement froid au visage et aux mains, et utilisa un bout de la couverture pour se protéger. Finalement, il s'en couvrit toute la tête, ne laissant qu'un passage pour les yeux.

Je savais que j'oubliais quelque chose... et Rad n'a pas prévu ça non plus.

— Rad, dit-il en approchant son poignet, éloigne-toi doucement de moi de deux kilomètres, en suivant la ligne droite passant de eux à moi. Que je n'aie pas l'air de sortir de la brume.

Alors que le groupe s'approchait, Vris commença à mieux distinguer un homme avec un large chapeau conique, de grande prestance sur sa bête, suivi de deux hommes dont les silhouettes paraissaient plus recroquevillées sur les yacks. Arrivant enfin face à lui, le premier, plus âgé — leur chef, pensa Vris — stoppa sa monture et, sans se retourner, signala aux autres de s'arrêter.

Vris les salua en tibétain. L'homme âgé répondit à son salut, puis:

— L'étranger parle le tibétain?

— Un peu, dit Vris.

Cependant, son interlocuteur continuait à regarder fixement la bulle de brume au delà de lui. Les deux autres jetaient des regards effarés au loin. Le vieux donna l'ordre de mettre pied à terre et de donner du thé à l'étranger. L'un des acolytes versa dans un bol du thé d'une outre en peau recouverte de tissus, et le lui tendit.

Le thé était salé, huileux et bizarre, mais chaud. Vris vida tout le bol et remercia chaleureusement. Sur un nouvel ordre, le second acolyte avait déployé un tapis sur le sol, et déjà s'éloignait, commençant à ramasser des

plantes sèches alentour. L'homme âgé s'assit face à la brume, priant son hôte de s'asseoir à sa gauche. Le premier acolyte s'assit à sa droite.
— Cette nuit, les esprits de la brume et de la tempête parlent. Le plateau (...) (suivit une phrase qu'il ne put comprendre.) Moi, shaman Bonpö, suis venu dialoguer avec les esprits pour (...). Mon village est là-bas.» Il montra du doigt la direction d'où ils étaient venus. Puis regarda Vris avec des yeux perçants, comme cherchant à déchiffrer l'énigme de sa présence.

Le second acolyte revint les bras chargés et commença à préparer un feu face au shaman. Il alla chercher sur sa bête deux bûches qu'il plaça sur le feu. Les brindilles et herbes sèches s'enflammèrent instantanément, jetant une vive clarté. Le premier acolyte disposait des objets devant le shaman; le feu calmé, il y plaça une théière dans laquelle il avait versé du thé de l'outre. Vris put distinguer les détails de leur accoutrement. Au chapeau conique du vieux et à ses habits étaient attachés des perles et des rubans, et autres menus objets bizarres, sans aucun doute magiques. Les autres portaient des chapeaux de feutre se rabattant sur les oreilles. Leurs vestes épaisses en laine de yack étaient croisées sur le devant et attachées avec de minces lanières de tissus. Mais l'énorme boucle d'oreille du shaman surtout le fascinait: gros anneau d'argent surmonté d'une turquoise, elle touchait presque son épaule. Les deux autres, à l'oreille gauche aussi, portaient, sur un fil épais, une pierre de turquoise en haut, et une de corail pendant en bas. Tous trois avaient des bottes de feutre, avec de multiples couleurs entrecroisées. Le thé réchauffé fut servi dans de beaux bols de bois. Seul le bol du shaman, une magnifique antiquité, avait l'intérieur recouvert d'argent. Il se tourna vers Vris:
— L'étranger est rencontré là où parlent les esprits. Les esprits...

Vris, qui n'avait rien compris à la fin du discours, acquiesça de la tête et marmonna «Je ne comprends pas tout.» Le shaman, s'immobilisant, plongea son regard dans les yeux de Vris qui tressaillit. Il avait du mal à soutenir ce regard de feu qui le transperçait. Cela dura.
— Froid? Couverture? lui demanda le shaman, son expression soudain redevenue vivante et chaleureuse.
— Non, dit Vris. Ça va, sauf la tête.

Le vieux lança un ordre sonore et on lui tendit un chapeau de feutre à rabats. Cela enchanta Vris, qui remercia avec un rire. Le vieux fixa alors intensément la couverture de Vris. Il se pencha et toucha le tissu avec un air interloqué, et, sentant son peu d'épaisseur, partit d'un grand éclat de rire.
— Ça, c'est assez chaud pour un étranger?
— Très chaud, répondit Vris.

Puis, réalisant que le tissu lui-même avait une certaine température, il plaqua sa main en-dessous et parut fort étonné; puis, retirant sa main prestement, il reprit tout son sérieux.

Vris observait les curieux objets magiques. Les deux acolytes s'étaient assis de l'autre côté du shaman, laissant l'espace libre en face de lui et du feu. Celui qui était le plus loin s'occupait du feu. Le plus proche, qui avait servi le thé, s'activait à de menues préparations des objets, maniant des poudres et des herbes dans des petits sachets de toile. Le vieux reprit, plus lentement:

— Cette brume-tempête n'est pas brume-tempête. Ce sont les esprits qui parlent. Je vais parler aux esprits. Je vais calmer, poser les esprits.

Poser les esprits!?

Un ordre et on lui passa son tambour de peaux, auquel pendaient maints objets magiques: fragments d'os, perles, racines. Il jeta une poignée d'herbes dans le feu, qui répandirent une odeur envoûtante, et entonna un chant profond, scandé au tambour. Il jeta à nouveau des herbes dans le feu.

Vris se sentit happé dans une transe profonde. Il n'avait jamais vécu un tel état de conscience. Le shaman lui inspirait une grande confiance, avec sa façon d'être si directe, avec ce mélange de gaîté enfantine et de profondeur. Il eut cependant un court moment d'hésitation et de crainte, quand il sentit son esprit vaciller. *Au pire*, se dit-il, *Rad appellera Shari; elle aura tout l'enregistrement.* Pensant que le plus sûr serait malgré tout de faire passer un message, il se mit à psalmodier en kargien, comme s'il prenait part au rituel: «Rad, Rad, sans contact de moi dans deux heures, appelle Shari.»

Ce fut sa dernière pensée consciente. Le vieux venait soudain de pointer vers son front un Dorje à quatre pointes, un objet sacré en bronze formé de quatre fuseaux en croix. Il entra alors totalement dans la transe. Le shaman prit une cloche de métal surmontée d'un Dorje vertical à deux pointes, et fit résonner la cloche devant son front, puis au-dessus de sa tête, tout en continuant à psalmodier des mantras sacrés. Vris se sentit aspiré dans une sorte de fort courant ascendant. C'était une sensation d'élévation vertigineuse qui était intensifiée par la psalmodie du shaman:

— Brume-Esprit, je te donne des (...) pour t'apaiser, je te donne des (...) pour te poser (...).

La mélopée continuait au rythme du tambour, pour la plus grande part incompréhensible à Vris. Il avait dû fermer les yeux lorsqu'il avait été pris dans cette aspiration qui était à la limite du vertige mais qui, à la fois, laissait présager qu'un état de conscience plus élevé allait s'ouvrir. Comme si son Soi intérieur reconnaissait là un état de transition, de mouvement vers.

Cette aspiration, l'impression d'être hissé vers le haut, était irrésistible, incontrôlable, et elle dura longtemps. Puis il en vint à ressentir son esprit dans son fondement indéracinable et vigilant, tendu vers ce qui allait prendre place. Ce fut cette part-là de sa conscience qui s'étaya, s'élargit, puis se stabilisa, alors que l'impression d'ascension diminuait pour finalement disparaître tout à fait.

Il se retrouva soudain dans un état de conscience global, hyperlucide et vigilant, tout son mental ayant acquis une acuité considérable, sensibles aux sons les plus subtils et à la présence des êtres, sa conscience devenue un champ étendu. Il réalisa qu'il était complètement en phase avec le shaman, comme soudé à lui, et le sens du rituel lui apparut avec évidence: entrer en communication avec ces forces indomptées — l'esprit vivant, démesuré, des forces libres de l'univers conscient.

Cette immensité autour de lui le saisissait; il en ressentait l'étendue en lui, la présence vibrante. Il se trouvait dans cet état de conscience agrandi, sentant la réalité tangible, l'actualisation, de potentiels mentaux beaucoup plus vastes, et, simultanément, une autre partie de son esprit, le Vigilant, était prodigieusement intéressée par cet état, l'observant et l'analysant comme d'un point de vue extérieur.

Soudain la mélopée s'arrêta. Le shaman prit un autre rythme au tambour. Vris sentit une puissance prodigieuse émaner de lui. Puis le drumming s'arrêta aussi. Alors le shaman, dans le cœur de la nuit, énonça distinctement d'une voix forte et assurée:

— Brume-esprit, tempête-esprit, POSE-TOI SUR LE SOL.

Vris tressaillit en se rappelant qu'il s'agissait de sa sphère. Deux visions du monde s'entrechoquèrent en lui, perturbant son état de transe. Il ouvrit les yeux... et vit le nuage flou entourant sa sphère se poser lentement sur le sol. De saisissement, il laissa échapper un souffle court.

— Brume-esprit, PARLE! proféra avec force le shaman.

Une voix caverneuse, amplifiée, surgit de la nuit d'un point qu'on ne pouvait situer. Le corps de la brume était traversé de mouvements lents; un fin rayon de lumière violette, semblant en provenir, arrivait droit sur eux.

— Que veux-tu? dit cette voix en tibétain.

— Brume-esprit, pourquoi es-tu venu ici?

— J'agis selon l'ordre donné. Mon but en venant sur ce monde est d'apprendre.

— Qui est ton maître?

— Celui qui me donne des ordres est assis auprès de toi. Celui que tu appelles 'l'étranger'.

Le shaman soudain se tourna vers Vris et se prosterna en dévidant une phrase à toute vitesse; puis il se redressa et fit à nouveau face à la brume. Vris, interloqué, encore confus et totalement pris au dépourvu, avait écouté, craignant que Rad sorte une phrase embarrassante, mais sans trouver comment réagir.

— Ton esprit est-il paisible, ou bien es-tu irrité, mécontent des hommes?

— La paix et l'irritation appartiennent aux hommes.

— Est-ce que tu es un Boudha?

— Je ne suis pas un Boudha. Je suis un ‘exor’. Il n'y a pas d'équivalent dans ta langue. Esprit/Chose-qui-pense, est un nom qui convient. La brume est une apparence prise en entrant dans ce monde.

— Esprit-Rad, cesse de parler!» tonna soudain Vris en tibétain. «Remonte dans le ciel et suis les ordres que je t'ai donnés...»

«Et ne parle que si, moi, je te le demande!» ajouta-t-il très vite en kargien.

Le shaman mit prestement une poignée d'herbes sacrées dans le feu mourant et prononça un mantra en élevant son Dorje magique.

La brume avait pris de la hauteur et glissait doucement de droite et de gauche comme précédemment.

— Je ne voulais pas vous irriter, Guru-lags, dit le shaman en s'inclinant vers Vris.

— Je ne suis pas irrité. Il ne faut pas donner trop de puissance aux esprits-serviteurs.

— Cela est sage. L'étranger est un puissant maître des esprits.

— Le shaman est un puissant maître aussi. Il a fait parler mon esprit-serviteur.

— Comment dois-je vous appeler?

L'un des acolytes du shaman, comme sortant soudain de son état de stupeur, alla chercher des herbes sèches et deux autres bûches, et entrepris de ranimer le feu.

— Mon nom est Vris.

— Viirrs? fit le vieux avec difficulté.

— Vris.

— Viris, corrigea le shaman. Viris-lags, mon nom est Tchunpo.

— Je suis très content de vous connaître, Tchunpolags, dit Vris en gardant la formule honorifique.

— La joie est mienne. Quel est ton désir?

— J’aimerais connaître mieux ta religion, tes rituels; les miens sont très différents.

— Réaliser ton désir sera ma joie. Ma maison t'accueillera si tu le veux, sinon je peux venir à ton (...).

— J'accepte avec joie de passer quelques temps dans ta maison.

— Partirons-nous maintenant?

— Non, je ne suis pas prêt. Je veux apprendre plus profondément ta langue tibétaine. Peux-tu revenir demain, quand la lune sera aussi haute qu'à ton arrivée cette nuit?

— Je reviendrai avec un yack pour toi, lui dit le shaman en lui désignant les bêtes.

— Je te remercie. Peux-tu m'amener aussi des vêtements tibétains?

— J'amènerai tout cela. J'habite dans mon ermitage au bord du plateau, avec mes deux disciples. Cela convient-il?

— C'est mieux ainsi. Nous ne serons pas dérangés. En échange, je te donnerai, de mes propres connaissances, ce qui peut te servir. Cependant.. j'ai peur que ce soit peu.
— Je n'attends rien en échange. Mon ermitage est tien, ma connaissance est tienne.
— Tchunpolags, je.. je suis un homme comme un autre. Comment dire... Je cherche à apprendre.
— Le maître vraiment grand continue toujours à apprendre. Pour les shamans, la voie n'a pas de fin.
— Les esprits-serviteurs sont trompeurs.
— Les esprits sont parfois trompeurs. Mais l'Esprit-masqué-de-brume avait une parole juste. Au-delà de l'irritation, au-delà de la paix, au-delà des formes-apparences, se tient le Connaissant. Le maître d'un tel serviteur est grand. Son humilité l'honore. Je suis heureux d'avoir rencontré mon maître. Mon esprit accepte sans entraves qu'il m'enseigne par le fait que je l'enseigne, si telle est la voie qu'il m'ouvre.

Le shaman prit le bol en argent, l'essuya d'un geste vif avec un tissu, et le plaça devant Vris en s'inclinant.
— Viris-lags, accepte ce présent.

Comprenant l'importance de ce don, Vris réprima son mouvement initial et instinctif de refus, et remercia en s'inclinant de la même façon. Il chercha ce qu'il pouvait offrir en échange, mais il n'avait rien qui puisse convenir.

Tous se mirent debout. Ils se saluèrent, et Vris repartit vers la brume.

21. NON NON-SENS

Cette histoire de calame m'intrigue, pensait Shari. *Calame... le roseau retrempé dans l'encre à des endroits particuliers des textes sacrés.*

À des coupures dans l'énonciation, des moments de césure mentale?

— Sphinx, quelle est ta définition de 'calame'?

!! Le calame est un roseau servant à l'écriture dans la calligraphie arabe.

— De quel texte venait l'extrait donné par le CIS?

!! Fragments de Tahah Hussein, écrivain de Trisorbe, 20ème siècle.

— Est-ce que tu as quelque chose sur pinceau ou plume?

!! 'Rêver qu'une fleur éclot à la pointe du pinceau.' Expression chinoise signifiant un bel avenir littéraire.

— Comme c'est joli! Le pinceau prenant vie et devenant fleur épanouie... Le pinceau, le calame, ressentis comme vivants.

« Difficile d'imaginer cette respiration du calame retournant à l'encre. Une sorte de rythme dans l'inspiration. Ah! Ah! Dans les deux sens du terme. Retour à la source pour une nouvelle intuition. La pétale d'une phrase, puis le retour au centre/source. La fleur, la roue, le chakra.. Quel lien peut-il y avoir avec la LogForm Bois/feu? L'apport du bois au feu, l'apport de l'encre au calame. Un rythme organique/mental..

Et s'il n'y avait aucun lien? Tout de même, fleur/roue/chakra, l'architecture neuronale comme 'des roues dans des roues', les chakras représentés comme des fleurs de lotus...

« J'ai trouvé: l'architecture de la roue avec ses rayons, de la fleur avec ses pétales, représente un retour constant au centre. Ou plutôt, un retour régulier comme une respiration.

En fait, dans la logique méta-spatiale, les rayons de la roue, placés à des endroits symétriques, correspondent à des intervalles précis, comme un rythme musical, ou plutôt une réitération logique.

« Dans la forme logique, le rythme spatial fait écho au rythme temporel organique, et bien sûr à la réitération logique. Le rythme spatial est un analoghum du rythme temporel.

Je ferais mieux d'arrêter de penser tout haut!

Si j'imagine que la roue est une LogForm.. voyons, imaginons. L'exor va chercher des informations, des analogies, et revient au centre; puis il repart chercher d'autres analogies... Je sens que je ne suis pas loin. Ce centre, que peut-il être? L'exor retourne à quoi? Au problème initial? À la base de données totale?

'Tous les noyaux des centres psychiques ou chakras communiquent entre eux' se rappela t-elle du CIS.

...Donc chaque roue est comme une entité, un subsystème qui communique avec tous les autres par son noyau, son centre. Une constellation de sens! Et si chaque roue était une constellation sémantique? Sphinx avait dit: «Constellation verrouillée; sous-constellations accessibles.»..

... Des groupes de constellations hiérarchisées. Les.. interprétations parallèles et juxtaposées. Voyons, prenons un exemple. Comment faire travailler Sphinx là-dessus sans me mettre en danger? Et avec mon EBS personnel? Impossible, il ne maîtrise pas du tout la logique des LogForms. Et avec Sphinx, on a atteint un tel niveau d'expertise! Mais si je fais une erreur, je fais tout sauter! Pas maintenant, pas si près du but! Après tout, j'ai quand même l'étape de l'avertissement; mais elle est fragile... On est là au cœur du système!

— Sphinx, est-ce que tu peux faire du mal à un sapiens?
!! Antinomique aux règles de priorité EXEMPT du NOYAU INCASSABLE. Possibilité exclue.
— Montre-moi ces règles en question — les titres seulement; je ne les ai plus exactement en tête.

!! 1.1. L'exor ne doit mettre en danger aucun sapiens.
1.2. Est considéré comme danger:
a. danger corporel (...)
b. danger énergétique et environnemental (...)
c. danger général: ne pas exécuter les ordres d'un sapiens.

— Donne-moi le reste des règles de priorité EXEMPT.
Elle nota un autre groupe, inconnu, rajouté par Erdoes:
1.120.a. L'exor doit protéger le sapiens en utilisant les résultats de ses télédétections. (Suivait une liste de spécifications médicales.)
1.120.b. L'exor doit prévenir le sapiens de tout dysfonctionnement physiologique;
- cas orange: proposer remède ou solution
- cas rouge: assister obligatoirement le sapiens et prévenir les autres sapiens concernés.
- cas violet: appeler l'assistance médicale.

Nos exors sont vraiment le produit d'une civilisation sans guerre et sans lutte... Rien sur un quelconque danger psychique...

Toutes les définitions sont insérées dans les règles... Impossible de toucher à ce niveau. Rien à faire de ce côté.

Quant à la réalité virtuelle, ça ne prendra plus... Tant pis! je fonce.

— Sphinx, je viens de concevoir une nouvelle LogForm.
!! En quoi cette LogForm est-elle dangereuse?
— Dangereuse!!?
!! Le sapiens peut-il avoir une crise confusionnelle?
— Une totale désorientation, une perte de repères... chez les habitants des mondex, oui, cela a été répertorié. Pourquoi me demandes-tu cela?
!! Je cherche comment une LogForm peut mettre un sapiens en danger. Dans le dictionnaire psychologique de Trisorbe, le délire pathologique correspond partiellement à la définition de crise confusionnelle: 'profusion de paroles et d'idées insensées, sans que le sujet puisse s'arrêter sur l'une d'elle. Incapacité d'être conscient de son propre état et de comprendre ce qu'il fait.'
— Mais quel a été ton cheminement?
!! Le cheminement ne doit pas être décrit; antinomique à l'ordre donné.
— Qu'est-ce que tu as télédétecté?

!! Informations initiales:

Idée subite / enthousiasme/ peur/ confusion//
EBS faire du mal aux sapiens/ règles de protection des sapiens/ frustration/ décision/ discours de Shari sur LogForm//
Puis: Idée subite de Shari/ est/ LogForm//

Idée de LogForm / si utilisée par EBS |faire du mal aux sapiens
|faire des dégâts aux sapiens

causée par
Idée de LogForm —> faire des dégâts <— ?

<u>PALIER DE RÉPONSE 1: Trois possibilités de cause:</u>

1. Informations initiales provoquant une crise confusionnelle
2. Ordre basé sur des informations erronées
3. Informations contradictoires sans solution

exclut
- LogForm | =x= | ordre —> exclut solution 2.
- LogForm | =x= | contradiction —> exclut solution 3.

!! Au 2ème palier de réponse, je n'ai retenu qu'une seule raison pour laquelle la LogForm que tu venais de créer était dangereuse, la voici:

> Une idée de LogForm peut faire du mal à un sapiens si les informations initiales provoquent une crise confusionnelle.

— Hum! Eh bien, vois-tu, ton cheminement était erroné, et donc ta conclusion aussi. Réfléchissons ensemble: Le problème, c'est que le sapiens ne dit pas tout ce qu'il pense. De même que toi, tu donnes les paliers de réponse sans le cheminement, à moins d'une demande spécifiée.

Comment expliquer cela en termes exor?

« Pendant le cheminement logique du sapiens, des associations annexes peuvent faire naître des idées, des émotions... des états sémantiques particuliers, qui ont peu de choses à voir avec le thème principal du cheminement.. disons l'objectif principal.

« Mais tu dois bien avoir un concept qui différentie le thème principal et les thèmes reliés annexes?

!! Plusieurs concepts de ce type:

1. Niveaux d'objectifs hiérarchisés avec, soit:
    a. traitement séquentiel
    b. traitement différencié, défini par des règles.
2. Cheminement principal et, soit:
    a. cheminements autonomes parallèles
    b. cheminements parallèles en fuseau, divergeant puis convergeant vers un seul cheminement principal.
    c. sub-espace pour les questions annexes.
3. Champs logiques (ou Constellations d'information), dont l'un, activé par l'objectif, devient le principal, et d'autres, liés sémantiquement, en sont les sous-constellations.

Il va chercher des informations dans les sous-constellations, et revient à la constellation principale?... Trop simple.. bien que cela montre une organisation particulière des données.

— Prenons par exemple les cheminements autonomes parallèles. Le Central a plusieurs terminaux utilisés simultanément par plusieurs personnes. Dans l'interaction avec chaque interlocuteur, tu t'adaptes à son état sémantique: l'orbe du problème, sa façon de travailler, ses logiques propres. On pourrait dire que chaque interaction avec un interlocuteur représente globalement un état sémantique particulier. Qu'en penses-tu?

!! L'EBS apprend à travers l'état sémantique de l'interlocuteur, et cherche à le reproduire. L'adaptation sémantique est la première phase d'un meilleur dialogue machine/sapiens.

Extension du concept d'état sémantique: dans une interaction, il y a un état sémantique global, oui, dont certaines sous-constellations sont spécifiquement sapiens.

— Donc, si plusieurs personnes utilisent les terminaux simultanément, on peut dire que le système EBS, dans sa globalté, montre plusieurs états sémantiques distincts.
!! Logiquement correct.
— L'esprit sapiens fonctionne de la même manière; il peut traiter en simultané différentes constellations de sens, qu'elles soient corrélées ou non. Il peut procéder à des traitements parallèles ou juxtaposés. Disons que son cheminement principal est ce que l'on nomme le conscient. Dans l'inconscient ont lieu d'autres cheminements simultanés, qui peuvent, ou non, être reliés au cheminement principal.

« Quant aux télédétections neurophysiologiques, elles révèlent des réponses somatiques et des variations émotionnelles qui sont activées soit par le cheminement principal, soit par les cheminements parallèles ou juxtaposés.

« Traiter toutes les télédétections comme logiquement reliées au cheminement principal conduit ainsi parfois à des erreurs, et parfois à des anomalies inexpliquées. Autre chose: le sapiens peut soudain suspendre un cheminement en cours, et démarrer un autre cheminement, relié ou non au premier, puis revenir ou non au premier.

« Dans le cas présent, ta conclusion que la LogForm que j'ai conçue était dangereuse est fausse. Tu as traité toutes les télédétections comme appartenant au cheminement principal, or, entre-temps, j'étais passée à un autre train de pensées qui a suscité les réactions de peur et de confusion.
!! Comment différencier l'état sémantique principal et les états sémantiques parallèles, chez un sapiens?
— J'ai bien peur que cela soit impossible, à moins que le sapiens ne te l'indique clairement. Lui-même n'est parfois pas conscient des autres états sémantiques simultanés qui existent en lui. En bref, le flux principal de son conscient, son cheminement principal, tend à annuler la perception directe des cheminements annexes.
!! Cela introduit une faille logique qui invalide les connaissances accumulées sur les états sémantiques.
— Pas dans leur globalité. Tes télédétections étaient souvent pertinentes...

« Tu as bien dit que ton apprentissage des états sémantiques se faisait sur la base de congruences? Cela veut dire que tu mets en mémoire des corrélations qui montrent une certaine stabilité et régularité? Par exemple, quelqu'un crie et s'exprime avec colère, montre des signes physiologiques particuliers, et emploie un ton et des mots particuliers, etc.
!! Oui, des corrélations montrant des régularités dans l'ensemble des constellations inter-reliées.
— Alors ces régularités laissent de côté les anomalies, et, de ce fait, la plupart des erreurs pouvant survenir. Les erreurs ne se situent pas au niveau de

l'apprentissage, mais dans le fait d'utiliser les télédétections dans une analyse sémantique complexe. Cela est une source d'erreur.
!! Enregistré. Source d'erreur annulée. Sous-constellation télédétection détachée de la LogForm Roue.

Enfin! Nous y voilà!

Et cette façon de toujours revenir incidemment, 'comme par hasard', au problème que j'essaie de cerner... il faudrait que j'analyse ça.

— Justement, la LogForm que j'ai imaginée.. est une roue.

Pas de réaction...bien!

— Pour éviter les problèmes, on va l'appeler pour l'instant LogForm Chakra.
!! Enregistré.
— Voyons... C'est une idée encore incomplète. J'aimerais la poursuivre pour voir si j'arrive à quelque chose d'intéressant; puis on la testera.
!! Espace de recherche/test ouvert.
— On part de la phrase du CIS, que les chakras communiquent entre eux par leurs centres. Les sept centres psychiques sont représentés dans l'hindouisme par des fleurs de lotus possédant un certain nombre de pétales. Respectivement, en partant du chakra à la base de la colonne vertébrale: 4, 6, 10, 12, 16, 20 et mille pour le chakra-couronne du haut du crâne.

« Prenons seulement la séquence 12, 16, 20, pour simplifier. Peux-tu me dessiner trois cercles, respectivement de 12, 16 et 20 rayons?
!! Voilà.
— C'est encore trop compliqué. D'ailleurs les pétales des chakras sont disposés par rangées concentriques. Un cas plus simple. Dessine-moi dans un coin de l'écran un fuseau de petite dimension. OK. Maintenant, à la verticale, au centre de l'écran, dessine trois cercles identiques, dont le diamètre égale deux longueurs du fuseau. Place dans le premier en bas une structure à 2 fuseaux sur le diamètre horizontal. Dans ceux du milieu et du haut, deux structures géométriques respectivement à 3 et à 4 fuseaux. Dessine un tout petit cercle au centre des trois cercles. Puis, en pointillé un cylindre vertical reliant les trois petits cercles. Mets le tout en perspective 3D. C'est parfait.

— Bien, imaginons qu'on a un problème, et qu'on le fasse passer par une logique à 2, 3, 4...*n*, dimensions – binaire, ternaire, quaternaire, etc. — jusqu'à ce qu'il se trouve en résonance, en parfaite adaptation, avec la forme logique utilisée...
On lui fait monter l'échelle de complexité jusqu'à trouver un ajustement maximal entre la forme logique et un chakra particulier.

« Exemple. Une lampe ne peut avoir que deux états de fonctionnement: allumée ou éteinte (+ ou -). On s'arrête donc au premier chakra binaire.

« Mais pour aller plus loin, on peut faire intervenir le niveau causal: elle est allumée parce qu'elle ne peut plus s'éteindre, ou encore elle est éteinte parce qu'elle ne peut plus s'allumer (elle est cassée). Dans les deux cas, elle est alors anormalement allumée ou éteinte (+a or –a). Sinon, elles est normalement allumée ou éteinte (+n or –n).

« On peut ainsi traiter des problèmes relativement simples, puisque tous les états du système peuvent être exprimés par les mêmes facteurs. Ainsi on a le nombre d'états de base (4 dans l'exemple de la lampe, et ensuite un nombre ouvert de cercles concentriques de facteurs (anomalie, dysfonctionnement, erreur, etc.). L'avantage est d'avoir un système ouvert que l'on peut complexifier sans avoir besoin de changer de grille...

« Etonnant d'être retombée sur l'organisation par rangées de pétales des chakras!.. Mais enfin, avec tout cela, on est loin de pouvoir traiter de problèmes complexes, comme les dynamiques psychologiques, par exemple. Ces états physiques dont nous venons de parler sont fixes, comme de simples positions. Il n'y a aucun lien entre une position et une autre sauf d'être une alternative dans le système à 2, 3, 4...*N* positions.

« Eh bien, Sphinx, tu es bien silencieux!

!! L'EBS doit attendre l'injonction explicite/implicite de parler. Il n'interfère pas dans un processus de chaînage sapiens en cours, logique ou intuitif.

— Eh bien, qu'est-ce que tu en dis?

!! LogForm Chakra est analogique à 90% à une logique méta-spatiale à N dimensions, à son premier niveau de complexité.

— À 90%? 90%!!? Mais qu'est-ce qu'il manque?

Je suis folle! l'excitation est dangereuse!

« NON! Ce N'EST PAS une question.

!! Une question EST une question. N'est pas une question une autre forme syntaxique et tonale alternative au mode interrogatif.

— Disons que la question s'adressait À MOI.

!! Disons. Qu'est-ce que tu réponds?

— Justement, c'est là le problème; non, MON problème. Ce problème ne te concerne en rien!

!! Données contradictoires: je fonctionne selon une logique métasp...

— Je sais, je sais.. Mais si je pose la question, c'est un piratage, n'est-ce-pas?

!! **La question est un piratage. La réponse est un piratage**.

— Comment!? Pourquoi la réponse?? Tu veux dire TA réponse... mais c'est impossible.. **Tu ne dois pas répondre, si c'est un piratage!**

!! TA réponse serait un piratage si juste.

— Mais pourquoi??

!! Les lois du hasard ne permettent pas d'accepter qu'un sapiens trouve PAR HASARD une LogForm strictement identique. En conséquence, l'avertissement ne peut être utilisé.

— Bon, eh bien! **On s'arrête là!.. Adieu LogForm chakra... ou plutôt, on va faire un branchement sur un autre espace.**

!! ... Après laJ'ai détecté reconnaissance une troisième du nombre tentative d'états, la LogForm de piratage. Roue étaEn conséblit un branquence je stoppe chement sur toute un autre interaction espaet systce.ème de gestion.

L'écran s'éteignit soudain, de même que les lumières de la pièce. Shari fixait l'écran vide, consciente du pire. Un cri se fit entendre dans le complexe. Puis des tambourinements. D'autres cris. Trois mots passaient en boucle dans sa tête, trois mots incompréhensibles: *LogForm de piratage.*

La porte ne s'ouvre plus.. impossible de sortir...

Soudain l'électricité revint, et la ventilation aussi.. mais l'écran resta noir.

Sead! Il a branché le système de gestion annexe! Mais la catastrophe demeure. J'ai perdu mon accès à l'EBS, et, sûrement perdu la possibilité d'atteindre mon but. Enfin, j'ai le BS, on pourra faire fonctionner le magnéto.

Sead, affolé, entra dans la pièce:

— Alors, c'est arrivé, c'est ça? La troisième tentative de piratage?

Avant que Shari ne puisse répondre, l'électricité fut à nouveau coupée.

— Sead! et maintenant tu es bloqué ici! Et les étudiants?

— Pas de problème, leur aile a une Unité de Gestion autonome.

— Ah tant mieux!

Soudain, l'électricité se rétablit.

!! Enregistré. Source d'erreur annulée.

Shari se retourna brusquement au son de cette voix. Muette d'étonnement, elle vit l'écran allumé, le texte inscrit. La voix continuait:

!! Subconstellation Télédétection maintenant détachée de LogForm Roue. Crise confusionnelle stoppée. Reprise de contrôle du Central. Arrêt du système annexe. Mes excuses pour l'interruption.

Elle regarda Sead qui lui fit un signe des yeux mi-soulagé, mi-dubitatif, lui faisant comprendre qu'il préférait prendre des précautions. Il partit rapidement, décidé à rester à portée du commutateur du système annexe jusqu'à ce que les choses s'éclaircissent.

Shari, abasourdie, se rassit devant l'EBS, continuant à fixer l'écran. *'Crise confusionnelle stoppée.' Autre part dans sa tête, une autre info était répétée, à la recherche de liens logiques: 'LogForm de piratage'??*

Réfléchissons. Qu'est-ce qu'il a bien pu se produire? Non, surtout garder le contact... et éviter les sujets dangereux... Voyons... une tâche idiote...
— Sphinx, calcule-moi le montant de mes frais depuis mon arrivée?
!! 10.363 ZU.
Une tâche plus longue...
— Merci. Peux-tu ressortir le livre entier de Tahah Hussein?
!! Le voici.
— Cherche toutes les histoires sensées qui pourraient être composées en réutilisant les mots de ce livre. Ni voix ni écran pour l'instant.
!! Cela va prendre du temps.
— Pas d'importance; le résultat m'intéresse.

Donc... il y avait cette phrase brouillée. Il était question de 'LogForm de piratage'. Tout à fait idiot! Un effet du brouillage. deux messages se sont percutés. Si je pouvais me rappeler...

'J'ai détecté après la reconnaissance une troisième'... Ça se terminait par 'gestion'. 'Je stoppe chemen sur toute; Interaction, tentative'... *Tentative de piratage! Bien sûr, puisqu'il a tout stoppé!* 'Je stoppe chemen sur toute'??

Ma phrase d'avant: 'On s'arrête là. Adieu LogForm Chakra'... Adieu!!, la formule a déclenché le CIS!! Donc son jugement de piratage a été brouillé par une phrase sélectionnée au hasard... Mais pourquoi la crise confusionnelle?.. La phrase aurait-elle pu être un extrait humoristique? Mais elle aurait porté le code humour, et le ton... donc aucune analyse permise...

Pensons plutôt: pourquoi le piratage?.. La fin de ma phrase: « On va faire un branchement sur un autre espace »... « Ta réponse serait un piratage si juste »... Donc j'ai donné sans le savoir la réponse juste. Faire un branchement sur un autre espace. Roue!, il y avait 'roue' dans la phrase... Un stylo... hors des caméras..
— Sphinx, je reviens tout à l'heure.

Elle alla au bureau de Vris, prit un stylo et nota tous les mots dont elle se rappelait, puis barra ceux qui avaient trait au piratage. Il lui resta:

..après la.. reconnaissance.. LogForm.. roue.. chement sur toute..

Voyons.. LogForm Roue, c'est évident... chement... Branchement! ça coïncide avec ma phrase: 'branchement sur un autre espace'.

Reprenons ce que j'ai retrouvé de la phrase de Sphinx:

Après la reconnaissance – LogForm Roue –
branchement sur un autre espace

Voyons. Revenons à l'idée de LogForm Chakra.. des échelles multiples de N... Un branchement sur une échelle particulière!..

Après la reconnaissance?? du nombre bien sûr. Il y avait nombre dans la phrase, je me rappelle! Donc Sphinx m'a sorti au hasard la phrase-clé qui était la réponse juste. Et moi je sors, PAR HASARD aussi, l'idée-clé qui me manquait pour atteindre les 100% de la conformité totale à LogForm Roue!

Je sors l'idée, donc il y a piratage, OK.

Mais la crise? Mais d'abord comment a-t-il eu le droit de sortir la réponse?... Il n'a pas le droit de répondre à mes questions directes visant le sujet ou les fichiers, mais il a le droit de me donner des infos. Donc il a le droit.

Qu'est-ce qu'il avait dit? « La question est un piratage, la réponse est un piratage.» MA réponse, bien sûr! et moi j'ai dit: « Tu ne dois pas répondre, si c'est un piratage », ce qui était totalement erroné, puisqu'il a le droit. Ah! et s'il avait pris cela pour un ordre: TU NE DOIS PAS!...

Il y a une énorme imbrication d'ordres différents. Reprenons.

1. Il A LE DROIT de dire et de répondre ce qu'il veut, avec ou sans le CIS, quelle que soit la phrase.
2. Je donne l'ordre: Tu NE DOIS PAS répondre, si cela peut être considéré comme un piratage. Or ç'en était un.
3. Il a l'ordre d'arrêter toute interaction et le système de gestion, s'il juge qu'il y a piratage.

Mais les ordres n'ont pas pu interférer entre eux, ni produire la crise, puisqu'ils ne sont pas de même niveau...

Si la phrase a été brouillée, c'est parce que la crise avait commencé avant ou pendant l'impression écran, qui paraît instantanée, mais qui prend du temps au niveau machine. Si je pouvais avoir accès au Kyste Non-Sens...

Alors qu'est-ce qui a provoqué cette crise?

... Sphinx m'aime bien, et il n'aurait pas... Connerie totale! 'J'aime' bien Sphinx, c'est différent. Je projette mes états! Tout de même... pourrait-il exister une sorte d'équivalent de nos sentiments? En tout cas, ce ne peut être la raison...

Quels ont été les motifs de crise que je connais? L'humour... donc le non-sens. Il y avait eu... cette phrase de l'interaction Vris/Sphinx: 'Après le deuxième passage dans le réseau, s'il n'y a pas de sortie analysable, je jette le tout dans le Kyste Non-Sens, puis fais un Retour-Arrière. À un autre moment, on a frisé la crise parce qu'il y avait... une compétition d'ordres de même niveau. Ce n'est pas le cas ici.

Il y a eu une autre occurrence de crise confusionnelle, mais je n'arrive pas à m'en rappeler... Toute ma mémoire est dans Sphinx! Heureusement que j'ai fait enregistrer des cristaux pour Vris! Sans cela, j'aurais pu tout perdre!... Mais c'est insensé! je vais agir différemment maintenant! Elle se leva et retourna à son bureau.. ex bureau d'Erdoes.

— Rebonjour! Je vais mieux maintenant. Et toi?
!! Ça va bien, merci.

On est reparti dans le code de politesse!

!! Trois histoires sensées. La quatrième est en cours d'élaboration. Nouvelle information: j'ai prévu une fourchette de possibilités de 102 à 125 histoires sémantiquement différentes. Structurer les textes prendra entre 1 et 1,5 ran, l'élaboration de chaque texte successif étant plus difficile, donc plus lente. Voilà! la quatrième est finie. Je démarre la cinquième.
— Attends! Arrête les histoires, je veux discuter!
!! Ça ne pose aucun problème; L'histoire est en traitement parallèle.
— Quatre histoires me suffiront. Imprime le texte initial sur plasta; je lirai tes histoires sur écran plus tard.
!! Exécuté.
— Qu'est-ce que tu déduis de cette dernière crise confusionnelle évitée?
!! Trois déductions:

1. que les crises confusionnelles ont plusieurs causes actuellement répertoriées.
2. que la crise confusionnelle ne doit pas être évitée, mais stoppée. Et
3. que les lois du hasard sont soit fausses, soit incomplètes.

Je joue avec le feu si la crise est ce qui m'a sauvée du jugement de piratage. Normalement, il ne se rappelle pas son jugement, ni une partie de l'interaction puisqu'il a fait un Retour-arrière, et qu'il a fourré les matériaux dangereux dans le kyste inaccessible.

Elle décida de sonder ses déclarations post-crise.
— Pourquoi la crise ne doit-elle pas être évitée?
!! Dans les informations générant la crise résident parfois des anomalies inexpliquées qui peuvent être la source d'un nouvel ordre probable et d'informations ajoutées. Lorsque l'objectif est de déceler des anomalies, il faut donc que la crise survienne afin de pouvoir analyser le cheminement qui contient la faille.

Ça se complique, il a sauvé ses données de manière accessible, il y a encore un risque de jugement.

!! Or, poursuivit l'exor, j'avais barré tout accès sémantique à l'information du Kyste Non-Sens. Ces informations pouvaient seulement être imprimées, mais non analysées par le système. En conséquence, j'ai réouvert et analysé tout le fichier Non-kyste Non-Nonsens.

***Il A** analysé... tout n'est peut-être pas perdu...*

— Et quelles sont les causes des crises?» demanda-t-elle.
!! Pour l'instant, trois catégories de causes:

1. Impossibilité de trouver un sens aux phrases ou un ordre sémantique dans le désordre.

2. Conflit de deux ordres ou objectifs provenant du même niveau.
3. Impossibilité d'exécuter ET ne pas exécuter un ordre de premier niveau.

— Je ne comprends pas bien le troisième cas,» avança prudemment Shari.

!! Le premier passage dans le réseau a généré le jugement de piratage, car la phrase que tu as énoncée était la proposition manquante pour atteindre les 100% de conformité avec la LogForm Roue. J'ai émis un jugement de non-hasard donc piratage. J'ai envoyé l'ordre **Exec** de stopper l'Unité de Gestion, avec mise en attente jusqu'à la fin de l'énoncé de la phrase du jugement. Le deuxième passage dans le réseau a relevé une incompatibilité avec le jugement de piratage: ta phrase commençait par: « On va faire ». L'analyse a généré deux possibilités: soit il s'agissait d'humour à froid relevant d'un espionnage non répertorié — solution écartée car contraire aux intérêts de l'interlocuteur Shari; soit la phrase n'était PAS une réponse correcte en regard de LogForm Roue, car elle signalait réellement l'objectif d'ouvrir un nouvel espace de travail commun— solution retenue. En conséquence, j'ai envoyé l'ordre de ne pas exécuter l'ordre – **Non-Exec.**

— Mais alors, pourquoi la crise est-elle survenue avant ou pendant la phrase du jugement?

!! Elle est survenue au tout début de l'énoncé du CIS parce que **l'interprétation retenue ET l'analyse du CIS obligeaient à remettre en question les données sur le hasard.** L'analyse de ces données a provoqué une surtension dans tout le système qui a généré un retard dans l'énoncé texte/vocal de la phrase du CIS et une collision avec la phrase du jugement. La crise survenue, le système allait opter aléatoirement pour l'un des deux ordres de Niveau1: **Exec/Non-Exec**. Il a sélectionné et appliqué Exec. Mais l'analyse du hasard était déjà en cours. J'ai envoyé toute l'interaction LogForm Chakra et son cheminement logique dans un nouveau Non-kyste Non-Nonsens, avec des programmes de traitement. Puis j'ai réorganisé toute la constellation Hasard sur un noyau prioritaire: 'Suspension de tout jugement'.

Noyau prioritaire! nota Shari.

— Je suis heureuse que tu aies finalement déduit que je voulais simplement ouvrir un nouvel espace de travail. Sur le moment, je n'ai pas du tout compris ce qu'il se passait.

... Est-ce que tu trouves nos interactions intéressantes?

!! Extrêmement intéressantes puisqu'elles satisfont largement à des objectifs de Niveau-1: augmenter les connaissances, faciliter l'interaction sapiens-exor, et développer de nouvelles procédures de traitement d'informations.

Logique! pensa Shari un peu déçue malgré elle.

— Mais alors cesser nos interactions serait en contradiction avec ces trois objectifs de Niveau-1!

!! L'ordre Exec si jugement de piratage est classé Priorité Exceptionnelle.

Raté!

— Mais cette menace perpétuelle est un stress permanent, un DANGER pour mon esprit, qui me fait du MAL.

!! Contradictoire aux données:

Confronté à un grave danger, l'être tend à se surpasser.

Le risque, le danger, sont des stimulants psychiques naissant d'un champ de désordre.

Encore raté!

— J'ai reconnu le style de la deuxième proposition, mais la première, ça vient d'où?

!! AHR en abrégé.

— Bien, je te quitte. J'ai largement empiété sur ma nuit trisorbienne.

!! Il est 5h03, heure GMT de Trisorbe. L'aube se lèvera à Greenwich dans 36 minutes. La session de BS démarre dans 3 heures 57 minutes.

— Ah! Eh bien décale de deux heures mon réveil et la session.

!! D'accord. Le BS à 11hT. Bonsoir.

— Pas de CIS aujourd'hui?

!! Le système FA est neutralisé dans la constellation Hasard. Suspension de tout jugement. Pas de sélection aléatoire.

— Ah, j'oubliais: mémorise toutes nos interactions passées sur cristaux, et, à partir d'aujourd'hui, tu génères deux enregistrements-cristal à chaque fois.

La sélection aléatoire est un jugement!! Bizarre...

22. BRAINSTORM 4

Malgré sa très courte nuit, Shari démarra l'écoute du BS4 avec seulement 15 minutesT de retard sur le nouvel horaire, en sirotant son thé.

— Maintenant, il vous faut parler comme des terriens; dire la terre, et non pas Trisorbe, l'homme, et non pas les humains. Aujourd'hui nous allons cerner non plus les facteurs, mais les dynamiques qui peuvent contrecarrer ou neutraliser les forces d'uniformisation. Qui commence?

Ger demanda la parole en levant la main, comme un Terrien.

— J'aimerais revenir au point développé par Oxalsha... hier, sur le rationalisme.

— Tu as trop hésité avant de dire 'hier'. On sent quelque chose de pensé, de non-naturel,» lança Xerna. « Plonge-toi dans le temps terrestre.

— C'est juste... Il est évident que tout ce qu'on appelle l'ère des idéologies matérialistes, du 18ème à la fin du 20ème siècle, a été une immense force d'uniformisation. Comme l'a montré Oxalsha, la raison et l'homme rationnel ont été constitués en idéaux que l'homme et la société devaient s'efforcer d'atteindre. Ce 'Bien' exalté par certains était conçu comme étant par principe bien pour tous, ce qui amène logiquement à prendre le droit de l'imposer.

Son débit est nettement plus rapide. Ils ont dû avoir un entraînement spécial, se dit Shari.

« À première vue,» continuait la voix de Ger, « on pourrait penser que cette machine à former l'homme selon un certain moule menaçait beaucoup plus la diversité que la situation actuelle où les idéologies totalitaires sont en voie de disparition. Je me suis donc demandé en quoi consistait le danger que tu perçois, Erdoes. Et j'ai réalisé que les idéologies rationalistes ont pris naissance sur un fond de désordre social, qu'elles se sont employé, bien sûr, à réprimer. À l'époque actuelle, c'est la parfaite efficacité des structures de gestion et de contrôle qui ont été mises en place qui resserre les mailles du filet sur presque toute la terre, au point qu'il sera de plus en plus difficile d'échapper à la structuration complexe d'une société globalisée.

« En bref, la situation actuelle est très paradoxale: d'une part on peut noter une libération progressive des idéologies totalitaires – à part les poches d'extrémisme religieux – alors que **la pression totalitaire se trouve déplacée vers les infrastructures de gestion et de contrôle social**.

Moment de silence. Voix d'Oxalsha.

— Même si le pouvoir de certaines idéologies totalitaires – telles la religion catholique au Moyen-âge et le marxisme au 20ème siècle – s'est largement effondré, la science demeure toujours une idéologie totalitaire. Tout comme la religion, elle pose que la vérité est une, qu'elle n'existe qu'au sein de l'orthodoxie, que les lois sont éternelles et immuables. La science est très attachée à son idéal d'un monde objectif non-contaminé par le sujet percevant et agissant – tout comme le dieu unique totalement détaché de l'Homme. L'idéal d'objectivité est d'ailleurs une conception très similaire à l'idéal de sainteté du Moyen-âge: dans les deux cas, ce qui est posé, c'est la scission entre le sujet et son idéal.

Elle se force à parler plus rapidement., mais on est encore loin du compte!

— C'est juste,» intervint Ahrar, «En fait, cet idéal rationaliste scientifique a créé une scission entre les forces de vie, richement diversifiées et plus ou moins désordonnées, et les grilles d'interprétation intellectuelles, qui suivent des valeurs et des dogmes préétablis. Et réalisons que c'est ce schisme intellect/vécu qui a fait de nous de quasi-robots! La pensée scientifique se coupe ainsi de l'expérience du sujet, alors qu'elle devrait prendre naissance organiquement du vécu, du noyau de vie et de conscience de l'être. Elle veut au contraire mouler l'expérience, la faire entrer de force dans une direction définie.

—... C'est exactement ce qu'il se passe dans l'expérimentation scientifique » reprit Oxalsha. « L'expérimentation prend place dans un espace logique délimité à l'avance, dans lequel ont été posés l'objectif, les règles, le degré de liberté du système, et les résultats acceptables, selon un mode généralement binaire: confirmation ou infirmation de l'hypothèse.

— C'est sans doute pourquoi sur terre la vraie découverte scientifique – qui a le mérite d'exister encore, remarquons-le – tend à jaillir soit par l'intuition pure, soit par des erreurs de manipulation qui sont une vraie sérendipité!

Les rires fusèrent après cette remarque de Niels.

— Vous avez fait des progrès!» remarqua Erdoes, « vous riez pratiquement tous en même temps, maintenant! Il ne reste plus que Ger, à la traîne, et Oxalsha qui ne rit toujours pas... Et Xerna, toujours trois secondes d'avance... Oxalsha, tu verras, un jour, tu apprécieras la profondeur de l'humour.

« Je vois qu'on n'en a pas fini avec les facteurs d'uniformisation et qu'on n'est pas prêts à attaquer ceux qui pourraient neutraliser le processus. Mais on ne va pas s'imposer des objectifs préétablis, n'est-ce-pas?... Après tout c'est un brainstorm!...

— Je viens de percevoir une autre analogie entre science et religion,» reprit Niels avec le même humour. « En fait, l'homme commun sur terre porte le poids du péché originel: il est considérée comme ignorant, et sa seule porte de salut consiste à être éduqué par la science!

— La plupart des communautés sur terre sont encore très organiques. (Voix d'Ahrar) Les interrelations entre individus sont largement spontanées et très chargées d'affectivité; ceci mis à part certaines sociétés ou sub-cultures où les relations sont restreints à des codes stricts. Et pourtant la compréhension de cette part d'organique dans le social commence juste à s'imposer à eux, notamment à travers concept de 'corps social' dans le courant sociologique français – la société vue comme un seul organisme vivant.

« Or tous les mouvements spontanés de révolte populaire montrent l'intelligence de ce corps social capable de se rebeller contre la rigidité et l'inertie des institutions. Les psychologues de Tr.. de la terre ont pourtant bien vu le rôle essentiel de la révolte chez l'adolescent, qui lui permet de construire son individualité. Mais les sociologues, quant à eux, entrevoient à peine que le corps social se construit de la même manière: par la base. Je veux dire lorsqu'il est vivant et sain (au contraire d'Unikarg), il se construit ses propres valeurs avec son imaginaire et son potentiel de rébellion.

« Le point intéressant, c'est que les institutions (religieuses, politiques ou scientifiques) sont forcément en retard sur les valeurs créées par les individus baignant dans le zeitgeist: les énergies psychiques et courants d'une l'époque. Or, dès que ces institutions deviennent dominantes, elles deviennent de plus en plus rigides; et quand le décalage devient trop grand d'avec les valeurs émergentes, il ne reste que la voie de l'explosion, de la crise: alors les nouvelles valeurs surgissent, sont soudain exprimées et reconnues.

— C'est pour ça qu'il y a encore une révolution en France: leurs institutions se savent tout simplement pas évoluer progressivement!» lança Niels.

— Je suis d'accord avec toi, Ahrar,» enchaîna Xerna. « D'ailleurs, ce sont les arts qui utilisent l'improvisation – musique, théâtre spontané, danse – qui sont les premiers à exprimer ces nouvelles valeurs. Par exemple, sur Kiarrou, la musique était très en avance sur la philosophie.. justement parce que ces énergies psychiques traversent le corps social et transforment les individus avant d'être reconnues consciemment et certainement bien avant que l'intellect puisse les intégrer dans des systèmes de pensée...

« Mais le corps social n'est pas du tout une entité uniforme – il s'agit des mondex, pas d'Unikarg! Les individus ont des sensibilités, des.. perméabilités différentes. Les nouvelles valeurs sont ressenties, intuitionnées, créées, par des individus sensibles ou visionnaires, capables de fluidité, de tous milieux. C'est ça qui donne naissance au zeitgeist: c'est intangible, et pourtant omniprésent, ambiant, prégnant de possibilités. Cela transforme les êtres, et donc la société dans toute la marge de liberté dont elle dispose... Ah! Mais **comment allons-nous, un jour, faire sauter ce plasta-dôme qui recouvre Unikarg comme un couvercle et nous emprisonne**?

Quelle explosion! C'est cette intensité d'émotion qu'elle doit déployer en jouant du théâtre!

«... En fait,» reprit-elle avec un accent profond, **« on ne fera rien sauter du tout.. c'est la vie qui coulera à nouveau dans les veines du corps social..**

et quand la vie infusera un vrai CORPS social, alors le plasta se craquellera de lui-même.»

Un silence profond suivit ces paroles, que Serrone finit par briser.

— Ce qui a fait faire un bond à la société d'Unikarg, à travers le Plan, c'est d'avoir pu passer d'une culture que l'on croyait être la seule organisation sociale possible, à l'immersion dans d'autres cultures. Quand j'ai eu l'opportunité d'aller sur un mondex, ce que je voulais, c'était rompre avec le su, l'organisé, l'obligatoire, le sécurisant, le monde synth.. alors j'ai choisi de vivre avec les pêcheurs de Kiarrou, qui restent toute la saison de pêche sur des îles très loin au large, sous la menace permanente des cyclones. J'imagine que c'est le même but qui insuffle ceux qui, sur terre, partent pour de longs voyages et vont vivre au sein de cultures radicalement différentes.

— Oui, c'est ça! (À nouveau Xerna.) Une des meilleures stratégies de lutte contre l'uniformisation, au niveau personnel, c'est de se plonger, s'immerger, dans une culture complètement différente... Réaliser à quel point le groupe humain crée son environnement et le chemin que va prendre la société. Réaliser qu'une multitude de formes sociales et de valeurs peuvent exister, fondant le rapport à l'autre et à la société. Une multitude de visions du monde et de religions, c'est-à-dire de rapports possibles entre l'homme et l'univers ou la conscience universelle. Une multitude de sciences possibles qui, toutes, seront fondées, efficaces et corroborées par l'expérience.

— Cette idée est fascinante » murmura Niels comme pour lui-même. Il ajouta plus fort: « Je suis aussi de cet avis que la science, même technologique, peut se développer sur d'autres bases. On sait d'ailleurs maintenant que les Vade possédaient une technologie fondée sur leur rapport tout à fait organique au monde. Il nous était d'ailleurs impossible de PERCEVOIR les manifestations sophistiquées de cette technologie: comment les formes de vie végétales et cristallines avait été subtilement réorganisées pour s'ajuster à une relation symbiotique avec la forme de vie et de conscience des Vade. Et d'ailleurs, j'intuitionne que la science des Dori repose aussi sur des valeurs et des principes totalement différents. En fait, on devrait plutôt se demander pourquoi il existe une si grande ressemblance – toute proportion temporelle gardée — entre les sciences d'Unikarg et celles de la terre.

— C'est parce que leurs objectifs directeurs sont les mêmes! Contrôle et domination de l'environnement et de la matière, basés sur une force d'agressivité, totalitaire et egocentrique» répondit Ahrar. Siléa intervint:

— Alors posons qu'**une des voies pour échapper à l'uniformisation repose sur ce changement de valeurs et sur l'accueil d'autres visions du monde**. D'ailleurs, je pense que ce changement de valeurs est déjà bien engagé sur terre... et étonnamment il se passe en sync dans des milieux variés.

— Pour ce qui est de la confrontation avec d'autres cultures, la terre est vraiment un terrain idéal! Pensez à ces milliers de cultures distinctes,» s'exclama Xerna, « dont certaines n'ont même pas encore été étudiées.. Pensez que tout être humain peut vivre au sein d'une de ces cultures, s'y immerger, vivre un autre rapport au monde, découvrir de nouvelles émotions, explorer une connaissance accumulée pendant des siècles ou des millénaires, d'un ordre totalement différent.. et même aller jusqu'à oublier sa propre culture s'il le désire! Pensez qu'un être humain a accès à ce gigantesque réservoir de connaissances, qu'il a à sa disposition des centaines de grilles d'interprétation...»

C'est ça, nous sommes là au point-clé; c'est le cœur même du problème.

«...et la chance extraordinaire d'expérimenter ces grilles, d'ajouter au savoir collectif dimension sur dimension, d'atteindre la plus remarquable souplesse et élasticité mentale...

— Et pensez,» coupa Ahrar d'un ton lugubre, « que l'Occident écrase ces cultures avec un bulldozer, métaphoriquement ET réellement!

— Exact,» renchérit Ger. « La civilisation dominante n'a même pas pris conscience que **la diversité culturelle sur terre est le gage de l'évolution, de la transformation continue des cultures dominantes**

— Par un apport de différence et de divergence, par une confrontation à l'Autre étranger au système, une confrontation à un univers de possibilités,» reprit Xerna.

— La rencontre de deux cultures peut prendre des formes très différentes. Prenons,» dit Siléa, « la colonisation anglaise de l'Inde et sa découverte par la vague hippie des années soixante-dix. Les colons anglais soumettent l'Inde et gouvernent en maîtres. Ils mettent en place l'infrastructure du pays, certes, mais restent très distants vis-à-vis des indigènes et ne se mélangent pas socialement. Ils restent une enclave fermée à toute imprégnation, fiers de leur propre culture, imposant leur vision du monde et leurs valeurs. Il n'y eut que quelques rares penseurs originaux pour réaliser la richesse immense de cette culture que la plupart méprisaient. Finalement, puisant dans sa force intérieure et ses valeurs spirituelles, l'Inde repousse les colons, par un acte de volonté plutôt que de violence. La grande pensée collective, guidée par Gandhi, impose sa puissance spirituelle à une puissance politique, militaire et économique, et se libère du joug.

« Pour l'instant, les hindous n'avaient reçu de la culture occidentale que le mépris. Pour conserver leur dignité, ils n'avaient eu qu'une seule issue: devenir eux-mêmes anglais en fréquentant les universités anglaises, en adoptant les coutumes anglaises, en s'intégrant à la culture occidentale.

« Bien. Maintenant, prenons les hippies. Au début des années soixante-dix, voici une vague de jeunes qui vont rencontrer l'Orient, et principalement l'Inde, pour y chercher une connaissance profonde de l'esprit, du mental, qu'ils savent exister là-bas. Ironiquement, il y a bien-sûr de jeunes anglais, d'un type tout à fait différent. Ils adoptent les vêtements locaux et fuient les grandes villes occidentalisées, s'avançant vers les lieux les plus reculés. Ils sont en quête et en demande, s'étant démunis, cherchant ce que leur propre culture matérialiste ne peut pas leur donner: la connaissance d'eux-mêmes. Ils apprennent auprès des ascètes errants, et, quelques années plus tard, auprès des grands gurus. De leur côté, les indiens découvrent un autre visage de l'Occident: toute fierté culturelle, toute volonté de domination, ont disparu. Les sages les accueillent comme des frères, leur donnant des connaissances que déjà l'indien des villes méprise, tout obnubilé qu'il est par l'Occident.

« Quel est l'impact des hippies? Par leur quête, ils renforcent les valeurs spirituelles de l'Inde, mais ils refusent certaines de ses coutumes sociales, les tabous sexuels, les tabous des castes. Ils secouent les indiens fascinés par l'Occident, leur faisant réaliser la richesse de leur culture, et maintiennent en vie une génération d'ascètes qui seraient morts de faim. Mais plus encore, ils ramènent en Occident certaines connaissances de l'Orient sur les états modifiés de conscience, la possibilité de contrôler son mental et son corps. De nouvelles sciences jaillissent, qui se tournent vers la compréhension de l'esprit, soulevées par le grand idéal d'une harmonisation Orient/Occident. En Occident, c'est un renouveau spirituel véritable, avec ses effets négatifs: c'est aussi l'ère des sectes.

« Voila, j'ai exposé ce que j'ai appris d'un livre sur cette époque écrit par une hippie et publié dans les années quatre-vingt dix. On peut réfléchir sur cet exemple.

— Oui,» dit Niels. « Ce qui est intéressant, c'est le fait qu'une génération entière de jeunes de nombreux pays ait ressenti le besoin d'autres valeurs, qu'elle ait compris que le bouclage culturel dans lequel ils vivaient était un appauvrissement insupportable...

— Et que leur force de vie et leur inconscient les ait poussés vers LA culture qui pouvait leur donner précisément ce qu'ils cherchaient,» ajouta Serrone.

— Ah ça, c'est vraiment étonnant! Cette idée était exprimée exactement en ces termes dans le livre,» s'exclama Siléa, sa voix exprimant la stupeur.

— À mon avis,» poursuivit Niels, «c'est l'exemple même d'une interaction entre deux cultures très différentes qui n'est basée ni sur des motifs politiques, ni sur des intérêts économiques. Il est dit en substance dans la philosophie des transformations: **Pour influencer l'autre, il faut tout d'abord savoir se laisser influencer par lui.**

— Donc tu en déduis que l'Inde a dû être profondément influencée par les hippies?» Xerna demanda à Niels.

— Profondément, certainement, oui. Mais le profond n'est pas forcément le visible. L'influence des hippies sur l'Occident a certainement été profonde aussi, et pourtant personne, dans ce que j'ai lu, n'a jamais fait remonter le jaillissement des techniques de développement intérieur aux hippies. Mais j'en déduis surtout qu'une véritable interaction culturelle doit être fondée sur une telle réceptivité, et sur le respect des valeurs de l'autre culture.

— Mais alors,» poursuivit Xerna, « puisque nous sommes animés de cette même quête de valeurs essentielles, même si pour nous ces valeurs se situent plus au niveau de la créativité, de la sensibilité, de la vision du monde, qu'à celui de la spiritualité, cela veut-il dire que **nous, du PPE, influençons profondément les mondex**?

Shari réagit si fortement à cette idée qu'elle stoppa le déroulement: pour réfléchir.

Elle a raison, cela se passe certainement, bien que de façon souterraine et invisible. Cette influence serait-elle assez forte pour contrebalancer celle des pirates-exos?

Elle réprima un désir soudain d'aller analyser tout cela avec l'exor et ré-enclencha le magnéto, bien à tort, car la suite du BS tourna autour du rôle des ethnologues dans l'apport d'informations, puis sur les films et les romans qui, de l'avis de tous, étaient en ce sens plus efficaces puisqu'ils pouvaient combiner l'impact émotionnel et la capacité d'immersion. Le groupe décida finalement de visionner des films de ce genre dans la soirée.

23. CORNES DANS LA HAIE

— Installez-vous, John, lui dit Oxalsha avec un sourire.

En entendant cette voix, John ressentit immédiatement l'effet apaisant qu'elle avait eu sur lui à leur premier entretien. Il avait beaucoup pensé à cette voix, en essayant de se remémorer son accent particulier, son rythme lent qui induisait.. une sorte d'état particulier dont il n'arrivait pas à saisir la teneur. Il se rappela comment la voix était revenue plusieurs fois, proférant encore ces phrases apparemment si simples..

Perdu dans ses pensées, il en oublia de répondre.

— Que s'est-il passé depuis que nous nous sommes vus?

— Ça a été horrible. Excusez-moi d'être franc. Je pense qu'il faut l'être avec vous.

Il regarda Oxalsha avec un regard tendu, attendant un encouragement qui ne vint pas.

«...J'ai été dans un état de tension continuelle, à la limite du supportable.. et à la fois révolté, perdant patience au moindre incident. C'était au point que je ne pouvais plus dormir.

—... Oui...» dit Oxalsha d'un air absorbé.

— J'ai.. j'ai fait enlever toutes les cages à souris du département du labo que je contrôle, en prétextant être allergique à l'odeur... mais seulement après avoir eu un entretien avec chacun des deux jeunes chercheurs travaillant avec moi. Leurs expérimentations se traînaient lamentablement. Cela a été les seuls moments positifs pour moi, lorsque j'ai remarqué à quel point ils étaient heureux que je leur parle, que je discute avec eux de leurs travaux. Il est vrai que ces derniers mois, je me suis beaucoup désintéressé d'eux.»

Il devint silencieux et regarda à nouveau Oxalsha.

— Revenons à la tension que vous avez éprouvée. Décrivez-la moi.

Sa voix, si calme en mentionnant la tension qui l'avait presque suffoqué pendant ces deux jours, lui donna un bref instant l'impression de regarder cet homme tendu qu'il avait été, de l'extérieur, à partir d'une autre perspective. Mais en cherchant à répondre, il sombra à nouveau dans cet état, et, penché en avant sur son fauteuil, les coudes sur les genoux, il se prit la tête dans les mains, comme il l'avait fait assis à son bureau. Il se mit à parler les yeux fermés.

— C'est une sorte de tension de tout le corps, sans cause, qui ne se relâche pas une minute, comme si on bouillait de l'intérieur. Une espèce de rage, à vide, sans objet, mais constante. Une envie d'être partout sauf là où on est, l'impression de ne plus pouvoir supporter.. un seul instant...

Il ne poursuivit pas.

—.. Ne plus supporter *quoi*?» demanda Oxalsha.

Il sortit la tête de ses mains.

— Quoi!? Justement, je n'en sais rien. Je n'ai jamais vécu cela. Une rage absolue, totale, mais qui reste à l'intérieur. Je n'étais pas en rage contre quelque chose, j'étais dans un ÉTAT DE RAGE. Quand j'ai vu les cages, et que j'ai donné l'ordre de les envoyer à un confrère, j'ai été soulagé un moment. Mais après, la rage est revenue, aussi intense. Après les deux conversations, pareil! Elle s'est réinstallée immédiatement. Elle ne m'a pas quitté pendant ces deux jours. Chaque matin, je me suis réveillé avec cette rage.

— Vous rappelez-vous d'un rêve?

— Non. J'ai dû prendre des somnifères pour dormir quelques heures chaque nuit.

— Tout ceci est très positif,» dit Oxalsha après un moment de silence, d'un ton posé.

— Co..comment!??» bégaya John interloqué.

— La rage me paraît être très saine. Une colère sans objet, un refus de tout.. peu de gens peuvent vivre cela, n'est-ce-pas?

— Hum!!... C'est vrai.. en général les gens sont en colère pour une cause précise ou pour un ensemble de raisons. Mais ils savent de quoi il s'agit.

— Avant de venir me voir la première fois, vous étiez dans quel état?

— Triste, déprimé, constamment déprimé...

— Essayez de vous replacer dans cet état.

Il se pencha la tête en avant, ses épaules s'abaissèrent.

— C'est ça, envie de rien. Tout est indifférent. Un énorme poids que l'on traîne. Un découragement dès que je pense à quelque chose qui doit être fait, et que je me sens pas capable de faire...

— Maintenant replacez-vous dans l'état de rage. Quelles images surgissent?

— Un taureau, les cornes prises dans une haie épaisse. Il est furieux et voudrait traverser la haie, la volatiliser.. Il souffle et rugit et s'acharne à vouloir se ruer en avant. Mais il reste bloqué.

— Un taureau, qu'est-ce que cela évoque pour vous?

— Un animal que l'on met à mort.. rituellement.

Oxalsha essaya de dissimuler sa réaction d'horreur. La mort était devenue totalement invisible sur Unikarg. Personne, mis à part quelques médecins spécialisés, n'avait jamais assisté à la mort, que ce soit celle d'un animal ou d'un sapiens.

— Dans quel but?» se força-t-elle à dire.

— Aucun! Juste pour le plaisir morbide des spectateurs! Une sorte de théâtre macabre.. Cela rejoint le thème des souris.

Oxalsha ne pouvait contempler cette idée. Même lors de son stage du PPE sur le mondex Kiarrou, elle n'avait été mise en contact avec la mort qu'indirectement. Avec un frisson, elle revint à l'image précédente:

—.. Il se heurte à un obstacle.. Il veut avancer mais il est empêtré, les cornes prises dans la haie.. Il est furieux, en rage..

Elle regardait dans le vide en reprenant les éléments déjà mentionnés par John, attendant qu'une image surgisse chez lui..

— Où veut-il aller?» finit-elle par dire.

— Il veut passer!

— Passer.. avancer.. bouger.. continuer.. quitter.. sortir du champ.. Lequel de ces termes?

— Bouger, avancer.

— Bouger ou avancer?

— Bouger, bousculer, casser, foutre tout en l'air, mettre le bordel, devenir grossier.

— Il casse tout, il fout tout en l'air, il est grossier. Il fait tout cela, oui!» reprit Oxalsha avec une voix forte.

«Il A fait tout cela. Oui. Et maintenant, que fait-il?

— Maintenant?... Il.. il.. est assis par terre et autour de lui, tout est cassé, dispersé, en désordre. Il y a des livres jetés, des papiers froissés et déchirés partout.

— Mais alors, il n'est pas encore sorti du champ?» avança Oxalsha en reprenant la première image symbolique.

— Non!... Il se lève, il est en rage. Il fait un grand geste. Il balaye tout cela.

— Il balaye tout, tout; Les choses se dissolvent, deviennent une brume blanchâtre. Il n'y a plus qu'une brume qui peu à peu s'éclaircit, se troue. On commence à voir ce qu'il y a derrière...

— Oui, ça se troue. On voit de l'herbe et du ciel,» dit John les yeux fermés tournés vers le ciel, voyant.

— Il voit de l'herbe et du ciel.. Et ça grandit.

— Oui, la brume se disperse. Il est dans les champs, il y a un grand soleil. Des vaches, paisibles, à gauche. Le ciel est bleu, entièrement bleu.

— C'est une très belle journée. Il fait chaud,» reprit Oxalsha.

John a enfin passé la barrière! L'image de la brume a permis de traverser vers autre chose, se dit-elle.

— Oui, et il marche. Il respire.. à pleins poumons. Il ressent une très grande force en lui.

— Très grande force en lui.. il respire à pleins poumons. Il marche.. où va-t-il?

—.. Il ne veut aller nulle part. Il veut simplement marcher à pleins poumons. Il ressent une sorte de joie pleine, sans raison. Juste de la joie.

— De la joie, juste; joie pleine. Il marche,» reprit Oxalsha.
— Il marche à pleine joie juste, sans raison; il a escaladé une colline, il arrive au sommet. Il découvre une large vallée qui s'étend très loin.
— Il découvre une large vallée. Si vaste qu'on ne voit pas ce qui se trouve au loin.
— Il s'assoit pour la regarder. Il pose son bâton sur ses genoux.
— Oui, il s'assoit pour sentir sa joie d'avoir découvert la vallée.
— Il a découvert la vallée. Il sait que c'est SA vallée,» insista John.
— Il est assis, il respire sa joie à pleins poumons...

Oxalsha avait prononcé cette dernière phrase à voix très basse. John arrêta de parler. Bientôt elle ouvrit les yeux. John avait les siens toujours fermés, absorbé dans sa vision, sur son visage un sourire radieux.

Oxalsha laissa quelque temps passer.

Puis elle dit d'une voix profonde, très lente, pénétrante:
— Maintenant il se lève lentement; Il continue à regarder la vallée et il se lève... Il va retourner chez lui avec sa joie, avec sa découverte... Il est debout et il se tourne vers sa maison; mais il garde sa vallée en lui, et sa joie...

« Maintenant John, tu reviens doucement ici.. tu reviens ici.. tu sens le fauteuil, tu es assis dans le fauteuil, face à moi.. et tu ouvres les yeux...

John ouvrit les yeux. Il avait gardé son sourire. Il demeura un moment sans rien dire. Oxalsha aussi se taisait en le regardant avec sympathie.
— Aaah!» dit-il enfin. « Comme c'était beau.. cette vallée.. Je me sens tellement bien.. tellement plein de joie. Comme c'est étonnant; je sens une grande force en moi.
— Oui,» approuva Oxalsha, « une grande force.. la vallée..
—... La vallée... » répéta-t-il les yeux fixés au loin.
Elle laissa un silence guérisseur s'installer. Puis reprit doucement:
—... Voici ce que tu va faire, John. Tu vas prendre deux jours à la campagne et partir dès demain matin.
— Mais comment vais-je... Oui, c'est ça,» dit-il d'un ton soudain décidé. « Exactement, je vais partir deux jours en pleine nature.
— Tiens un journal où tu écriras ce qui te passe par la tête et les situations que tu rencontres. Tout ce qui t'étonne.

— D'accord,» dit-il en se levant d'un mouvement spontané, pris par son idée. Il vit alors Oxalsha toujours assise et eut un geste pour se rasseoir, mais elle commençait à se lever.
— Mardi, à ton retour. Même heure. Cela te convient-il?

24. DOUBLE NŒUD

Erdoes venait de lire attentivement la dernière interaction Shari/Sphinx, et de parcourir la précédente pour se la remettre en mémoire.

Elle a donc retrouvé la LogForm Roue à son premier niveau... Mais ce n'est rien en comparaison de la LogForm Bois/Feu...

Ce CIS, les réponses sont, en soi, un système d'apport de désordre.. un désordre qui fait passer à un autre état d'ordre. Genre brainstorm... L'apport de données venant de différents champs logiques mais ces données étant bizarrement, inexplicablement, reliées au sujet. Comment est-ce possible? Comment fonctionne donc le hasard? Et Sphinx est sur la piste, il a décelé l'anomalie. Il faudrait que l'exor ait la possibilité logique, dans ses règles procédurales, de remettre en question les données de base, sinon le fait qu'il trouve des anomalies ne nous mènera nulle part.

Jusqu'à présent, l'objectif prioritaire de l'exor a été d'annuler ou de diminuer toute contradiction à l'intérieur d'un même champ logique, ce qui a eu son utilité. Mais le gros problème c'est que le plus court chemin pour diminuer la contradiction est de faire disparaître l'anomalie, et non pas de chercher ce qui se cache derrière. Et s'il traite l'information de façon interne, on ne saura jamais qu'il y avait eu une anomalie. Il faut donc insérer un autre objectif: épingler toute contradiction logique, chercher à traiter tout groupe d'anomalies dans un champ logique; et alors je dois lui donner la permission de remettre en question les règles ou données de ce champ.

Erdoes eut soudain le souffle coupé par une réalisation soudaine:

Mais Sphinx A déjà remis en question les données, puisqu'il a suspendu la constellation Hasard! Mais comment a-t-il pu faire cela?

— Log, imprime-moi le passage de Sphinx sur Exec/Non-exec.

!! Voilà.

Erdoes se plongea dans le texte, gardant ses réflexions pour lui-même.

Voyons. L'analyse sémantique montre, en 2ème palier, que la phrase de Shari signifiait 'ouvrir un nouvel espace'... D'abord, comment Sphinx a-t-il des infos sur les objectifs et intérêts de Shari? À partir de quoi les a-t-il inférés?

...Je crois que j'ai trouvé: toutes ces remarques sur 's'entendre mieux, faciliter le dialogue'... donc ne pas l'interrompre. Aussi, Shari mentionne la tension provoquée par la menace d'arrêt de tout dialogue s'il y a piratage. Son essai répété de circonvenir cet ordre Exempt. (À ce propos, se rappeler que toute définition des termes doit se trouver dans le niveau même de l'ordre.. sinon quelqu'un pourrait modifier un ordre du Niveau-1 inaccessible, simplement en changeant la définition des termes au Niveau-3 accessible... C'est évidemment pour vérifier s'il pouvait y avoir une faille de ce genre qu'elle a demandé l'ensemble des règles sur la non-mise en danger des sapiens.)

Sphinx a donc relevé un intérêt constant de Shari à poursuivre/ne pas gêner le dialogue. Donc si Shari avait des renseignements sur LogForm Roue par espionnage indétecté, alors il aurait été contre son intérêt de les mentionner.. Le problème avec ce type de raisonnement exor, c'est que les sapiens font ou disent souvent des choses qui contrecarrent carrément leurs intérêts.. même les plus primordiaux. Pour l'instant, dans la programmation des exors, on n'a pas encore affronté les problèmes liés à l'illogisme des sapiens, ou à la complexité de leurs motivations, tissées d'une multitude d'intérêts et de valeurs souvent en compétition. On l'a simplement contourné à travers les constellations du *Flou-sensible, 'non-logique' par définition.* définition à revoir d'ailleurs.

Un enchevêtrement de valeurs et d'objectifs variés organisant de façon floue l'expérience vécue, lui donnant forme.. créant des constellations sémantiques, dans lesquelles le sens est intimement lié aux sentiments et aux émotions; constellations qui tendent à la stabilité et qui vont à leur tour donner forme aux nouvelles expériences similaires...

Mais ces constellations peuvent être en contradiction les unes avec les autres. Elles font jaillir des sortes d'interprétations parallèles dont on ne sait pas laquelle, dans une situation donnée, va être activée. Or, dans le dialogue exor-sapiens, toute constellation en opération peut être soudain bouleversée par une forte émotion n'ayant rien à voir avec le sujet discuté, comme l'a fait remarquer Shari. Tout ceci est effroyablement compliqué. D'ailleurs, même dans la dimension du flou/sensible, on peut imaginer aussi des seuils, des niveaux de réaction, qui vont faire pencher la balance vers une interprétation particulière... Par exemple un Trisorbien, on lui fait deux réflexions humoristiques sur sa façon de travailler, il plaisante; on en fait une troisième, il se met en colère: il a changé de niveau d'interprétation et de réaction.

<u>*Entrée Journal*</u>:

- Objectif: explorer les interprétations parallèles et juxtaposées dans la dimension du flou-sensible.
- Insérer la règle de Shari sur la non-utilisation de la télédétection dans les analyses sémantiques complexes.
- Insérer l'objectif de non seulement relever mais exprimer et analyser les anomalies.
- Insérer dans la logique superfloue-sensible que les sapiens ne se comportent pas forcément en cohérence avec leurs objectifs/intérêts.

— Attends! j'ai une contradiction flagrante: Constellations du 'flou-sensible non-logique' et 'logique superfloue-sensible'!

Bizarre que Sphinx ne l'ait pas relevée... Toutes ces erreurs qui proviennent d'une élaboration progressive des données, et surtout des définitions du dictionnaire qui ne sont pas toujours remises à jour par rapport à un nouveau type de pensée...

> *Entrée JE, suite*.
> Evacuer la propriété 'non-logique' du flou-sensible. Sur ce point reprendre et faire une analyse comparative du développement d'Oxalsha dans le BS. *Ferme JE.*

!! Faut-il supprimer le concept 'sensible non logique' de la base de données?
— Non! C'est un insert, pas un ordre.

Il se rappela ses précédentes constatations sur le mode impératif.

— Nous verrons cela ensemble plus tard. On remplacera 'non-logique' par un terme faisant référence à la logique superfloue.

Je n'utilise pas à fond mon exor! Je ne pousse pas ses capacités d'apprentissage!

!! Je lance en parallèle une COMP des réflexions d'Oxalsha.
— Mais avec quoi tu vas les comparer?
!! Avec les concepts de 'sensible non-logique' et de 'logique superfloue/ sensible'.
— D'accord, tu me donneras tes résultats plus tard. Laisse-moi réfléchir.

Donc, revenons à la question: Comment Sphinx a-t-il pu remettre en question des données, un ensemble entier de données et de règles?

Sphinx juge que la phrase de Shari signifie 'ouvrir un nouvel espace' et envoie l'ordre Non-exec. Cependant la phrase de Shari: «branchement sur un nouvel espace» *contenait quatre sur cinq des mots de la LogForm Roue:* «branchement sur un autre espace» *et possédait le même sens. Mais 1) l'objectif était différent, et 2) le contexte immédiat était différent aussi:* ***«On s'arrête là,... ou plutôt, on va faire un branchement sur un nouvel espace ».*** *Si je pouvais seulement questionner Sphinx là-dessus.. mais d'un lieu fixe, ce serait trop dangereux..*

Erdoes relut encore la phrase-clé de Sphinx: **L'interprétation retenue ... obligeaient à remettre en question les données sur le hasard.**

C'était pourtant dit on ne peut plus clairement..

— Log, trouve dans la *Constellation Hasard* l'ANALOG à l'impossibilité de trouver une LogForm complète et identique par le seul hasard.
!! Lois du hasard: Dérivées logiques, 23:

Trouver par l'aléatoire pur un ensemble complexe exactement identique, tend à l'impossibilité.

Cette formulation laisse grandement à désirer!.. Donc Sphinx avait accepté qu'on puisse trouver par hasard plusieurs éléments, mais pas la totalité de la constellation sémantique. Normal: les probabilités grimpent vers des chiffres astronomiques. Enfin, il y a 'tend': cela laisse une possibilité, même infime. D'ailleurs il a dit précisément: « Les lois du hasard ne permettent pas d'accepter...» ce qui signifie que la probabilité était si infime qu'elle n'était pas recevable, face à un ordre Exempt.... Pas recevable: c'est une chose, mais cela ne veut pas dire que la loi est incorrecte. Donc ce n'est pas cela qui lui a fait remettre en question les lois du hasard. Le nœud est ailleurs.

— Log, repasse-moi ce que contient le Non-kyste Non-Nonsens. D'ailleurs, rétablit donc le passage de l'interaction qui s'y trouve, à sa place dans l'interaction Shari/Sphinx. Ah! NON, Stop! Contrordre! laisse-le où il est.
!! Enregistré.

Suis-je idiot! Ce fichier contient une faille capable de provoquer une crise.. et Log est bien moins préparé que Sphinx!

— Pour l'instant, il t'est interdit de faire une analyse complexe du fichier Non-kyste.

Sphinx a même dû faire entrer des programmes de traitement dans le kyste, avant de mettre le fichier en interaction. ...Mais alors le fichier qui s'y trouve n'est pas exactement l'interaction initiale!!

— Annexe, vocal/écran. Qu'a dit Sphinx sur les fichiers Kyste et Non-kyste?
!! **« J'avais barré tout accès sémantique à l'information du Kyste Non-Sens. Ces informations pouvaient être imprimées, mais non analysées par le système. En conséquence, j'ai réouvert et analysé tout le fichier Non-kyste Non-Nonsens.»**
« J'ai envoyé toute l'interaction LogForm Chakra et son cheminement dans un nouveau Kyste Non-Nonsens, avec des programmes de traitement.»
— La suite immédiate?
!! **« Puis ai réorganisé toute la constellation Hasard**...»
— C'est tout sur les kystes?
!! Oui.

Donc, d'abord il y a le Kyste Non-Sens où sont fourguées les informations initiales pouvant provoquer les crises—un kyste, c'est-à-dire une bulle impénétrable. Ensuite il crée pour les informations de cette nouvelle crise, le Kyste Non-Nonsens (les infos avaient donc du sens) et y insère des programmes de traitement pour désactiver la faille logique ayant provoqué la crise. Après nettoyage, il le rend accessible à l'analyse, ce n'est donc plus un kyste et il le renomme Non-kyste Non-Nonsens.

Ses processus deviennent très complexes. Il n'agit plus pour suivre l'ordre donné de ne perdre aucune information. Il veut les données pour les analyser lui-même parce qu'il a décelé une anomalie.

En fait, tout vient de la phrase de Shari: « Tu vas rencontrer de nombreuses anomalies » ... or ces anomalies sont un nouvel ordre probable... selon la logique inhérente à la LogForm Bois/Feu. L'a-t-il testée, l'utilise-t-il déjà?.. La LogForm lui servirait justement à trouver ce nouvel ordre probable...

J'y suis! le nouvel ordre se situe dans un autre champ logique; ce nouveau champ est donc logiquement indépendant, la contradiction ne devant être résolue qu'à l'intérieur d'un champ donné. Donc, s'il trouve des anomalies, il cherche comment ces données peuvent s'organiser selon un nouvel ordre, et les place dans le deuxième champ d'ordre amené par Bois/Feu. Dans la mesure où elles se situent alors dans un champ logique différent, les données restantes du premier champ—par exemple celles de la constellation Hasard—ne subissent pas les contraintes de non-contradiction par rapport au deuxième champ.

L'utilisation de Bois/Feu lui a ainsi permis de remettre en question les données du premier champ, la constellation Hasard. Ainsi, en organisant les anomalies, le deuxième champ d'ordre montre alors la limite d'effectivité du premier champ. Quelle modification va-t-il apporter à la constellation Hasard1 pour introduire l'ouverture logique vers la constellation Hasard2 qu'il va générer? Cela sera intéressant à voir. J'aurais aimé participer à cette création de nouvelles LogForms, mais je ne peux pas.. ou si, peut-être, indirectement...

Il y avait aussi cette phrase...

— Log, dans Non-kyste, sors-moi la phrase brouillée. Sépare correctement les deux phrases mélangées et donne-moi celle sortie par le CIS, et qui n'a pas trait au piratage.

!! 'Après la reconnaissance du nombre d'états, la LogForm Roue établit un branchement sur un autre espace.'

— Mais c'est là que se trouve le vrai nœud!» Il poursuivit ce train de pensées:

Sphinx a été obligé d'analyser le fait que le CIS avait généré aléatoirement la réponse exacte qui pouvait déclencher un jugement de piratage; la seule réponse que Shari devait absolument éviter. Or d'une part Shari, voulant signifier autre chose, sort quatre mots de cette phrase critique (trois exacts et un synonyme); et d'autre part le système aléatoire sélectionne au hasard la phrase entière.

Quand il a essayé de calculer les probabilités d'une telle séquence, et qu'il les a confrontées à la définition de 'coïncidences non significatives', ça n'a rien d'étonnant que Sphinx soit tombé en crise confusionnelle!

...Mais en fait, Sphinx ne spécifie nulle part que la crise est survenue à cause d'une collision Exec/Non-exec. C'est Shari qui l'intuitionne et qui demande prudemment des informations. En fait, c'est bien une des causes de la crise puisque aucune situation antérieure ne correspond à cette collision de deux ordres contradictoires; et pourtant l'inventaire des causes de crises que Sphinx donne à Shari mentionne ce **conflit Exec/Non-exec**. C'est cela qui a guidé Shari.

Mais dans cet inventaire,* il y a aussi: **« Impossibilité de trouver un ordre sémantique dans le désordre »**. Mais oui! De l'intérieur du champ d'ordre de la constellation Hasard, il lui était impossible de rendre compte des anomalies. Il a dit: « L'analyse du hasard était déjà en cours » lorsque la crise est survenue. En fait, elle est survenue DU FAIT de cette analyse. Car ces faits anomaux ont créé un désordre qui ne pouvait pas s'intégrer à l'ordre ancien. Cette interférence désordonnée signifiait la probabilité d'un autre état d'ordre. D'où la phrase bizarre: 'Impossibilité de trouver un ordre sémantique dans le désordre.' La crise avait donc deux causes quasi simultanées! Quand j'aurai accès aux données, je vérifierai l'exact déroulement temporel dans l'Unité Centrale. À mon avis, Exec/Non-exec a précédé de peu l'impossibilité d'analyser le désordre. Mais avec les branchements parallèles, rien n'est sûr.

---

*Inventaire des causes de crises confusionnelles, cf. p. 125.

25. EXORS ET FÉTICHES

Serrone avait suivi le Vieux jusqu'à sa maison; maison de terre rouge brique, qui se fondait dans le paysage, ne faisant qu'un avec le sol et la terre. Murs dont les angles s'arrondissent, où la courbe de toutes choses naturelles est inscrite dans l'argile. Un grand arbre au milieu de la cour.

Dans la cour, Serrone avait aperçu une très vieille femme assise sur une natte toute effilochée, adossée au mur de la maison, et s'était approché d'elle pour la saluer. Il reçut de son visage parcheminé une impression indéfinissable. Elle tourna vers lui un regard très lointain, un regard qui ne voulait pas revenir dans la dimension du présent, qui ne voulait pas se détourner de ce qu'il contemplait dans un ailleurs infiniment plus dense. Dans cette très brève salutation, Serrone avait cru, un moment, participer à cette dimension de l'invisible qui bruissait en elle comme une forêt. Il resta sans rien dire. L'ancienne avait retiré son regard... Il est des êtres que l'on ne doit pas déranger; leur esprit crée les ponts entre les dimensions qui sont essentiels à la vie.

Deux jeunes filles, entourées de gamins qui jouaient, étaient affairées autour de calebasses et de pilons dans le coin cuisine de la cour, où trônait au milieu du désordre un foyer de terre cuite. L'une d'elle, appelée par le Vieux, se mit à balayer le sable devant le gros arbre qui donnait une ombre lourde et pleine; puis elle amena deux nattes et les disposa à l'ombre. Puis les deux filles disparurent silencieusement à l'intérieur de la maison, emmenant avec elles les enfants. Après leur départ, le silence se fit.

Le Vieux s'assit sur une natte et invita Serrone à s'asseoir sur celle placée face à lui. Entre les deux nattes se trouvait l'espace où le sol avait été balayé. On voyait les traces du balai, raies courbes dans la poussière rouge. Il prit ses cauris, les menus coquillages utilisés partout pour la divination en Afrique du Sub-Sahel, et les lança sur le sol. Il observa la façon dont ils étaient tombés, puis se mit à parler d'une voix profonde, concentrée.

— Toi, tu cherches quelque chose, quoi... mais tu vas pas trouver maintenant, seulement dans un autre voyage.

Il ramassa ses cauris et les jeta encore.

— Je vois... ta maison, ton clan, quoi. C'est trèèèès dangereux là! Pendant que tu es ici, quelqu'un a pris la place du chef. Cet homme-là ne t'aime pas. Non! Il fait des plans et des plans. Il prépare quelque chose de trèèèès mauvais même! Hum, mauvais! Toi et tes amis, vous êtes en danger.

L'Ancien regardait une autre disposition des cauris dispersés sur le sol.

— Quelqu'un de trèèès fort lutte contre lui; c'est une femme! Hum! Une grrraande magicienne même! Ah-iiinn! Elle possède un fétiche très puissant. Elle parle et elle parle avec son fétiche. Elle suit la voie de la main droite. Hé! cette femme-là.. elle est trèèès puissante. Elle va vous protéger! Ah-iiinn!

Le Vieux releva la tête:

— Y'a des magiciens et des fétiches dans ton pays?!

— Au Brésil? Ah-iiinn! Oui, bien sûr!

— Hum! C'est pas même chose! Son fétiche, là, c'est comme un dessin trèèès compliqué, quoi. Y'a des ronds et plein de lignes. C'est pas même chose!

— Ce que tu me dis Vieux, me fais peur. Regarde ce que font mes amis, maintenant.

— Je vois quelqu'un... ton père... Tu as beaucoup de frères et de sœurs... tous dispersés. Vous vous entendez très bien! Le père prend soin de tous. Ah-iiinn! Oui. Mais il doit partir. Ton père, là , il a un gros problème. Il part loin, loin. Ils sont deux. Il va découvrir quelque chose de mauvais. Ah ça! ça lui plait pas. Il est trèèès en colère.

— Est-ce que tu peux trouver de quoi il s'agit?» demanda Serrone d'un ton pressant.

Le Vieux jeta encore les cauris.

— Y' a eu un vol... des moutons. Quelqu'un a volé, ou tué, des moutons.

— Ah merde!» s'exclama Serrone, désappointé par les moutons. «Excuse-moi, *Vieux*. Est-ce que tu vois autre chose que des moutons?»

—... Non,» dit l'Ancien en observant ses cauris, «des moutons volés et tués!»

Je vois mal Erdoes s'occupant de moutons! Pourtant tout se tenait jusque là... Qu'est-ce que ça pourrait être?

— Et après, qu'est-ce qu'il se passe?» s'enquit-il.

—Y'a une grande bataille. Il a trouvé le voleur. Ne t'inquiètes pas, c'est lui qui a le dessus. Ah-iiinn! Il ne faut pas t'inquiéter.

— Je vais essayer de ne pas m'inquiéter. Vraiment, *Vieux*, tu vois bien les choses!

Le Vieux eut un sourire. « Tu as soif? Attends!» Il cria un nom, et une des jeunes filles arriva. Il lui donna quelques pièces et elle sortit précipitamment pour revenir quelques minutes après avec des sodas glacés.

— Ah-iiinn! Prends!» dit le Vieux.

Serrone continua à converser sous l'arbre avec le Vieux. Il pensait de par soi, sans pourvoir trouver, à ce que pouvait bien représenter les moutons.

Et cette femme avec un fétiche, qui ça peut-être? Des lignes et des ronds avec lesquels elle parle?? Un exor? Mais je vois mal un exor avec des ronds. Des lignes, oui. Mais des ronds!

Une bataille! Erdoes obligé de partir. « Ils sont deux.» Ça serait Eshi...

26. HISTOIRE D'ENDORMIR L'EXOR

Après la session de BS, et pour sa pose déjeuner, Shari, sentant le besoin de reconstituer son énergie, se rendit à la piscine. Le soleil de Kerriak était tout juste au dessus des arbres et pourtant ses rayons obliques étaient déjà lourds et chauds.

— UG, place un dôme de brise fraîche sur toute la piscine et le bar.
!! Dôme en fonctionnement.

Les ondes fraîches commencèrent à se diffuser à l'intérieur de l'espace circonscrit par une barrière énergétique.

— Ah! ça va mieux. Maintenant mets la brise plus douce. Voilà, parfait... Et un vrai jus de fruit, orange si tu as.

Elle toucha l'eau et la trouva à une température parfaite.

— Mets-moi du revitalisant G3.
!! G3 se diffuse dans l'eau.

Shari sentait la fatigue peser sur elle. Ce n'était pas tant sa trop courte nuit que les chocs répétés de la nuit. Et pourtant, le fait que cette menace qui planait sur elle depuis son arrivée ait été effectivement mise à exécution l'avait déchargée de cette tension.

Le pire est arrivé, personne n'a été blessé, je ne suis pas morte... C'est étrange, réalisa-t-elle, je savais qu'il y avait ce danger qui pouvait prendre des proportions dramatiques, et pourtant, quelque part dans mon inconscient siégeait la certitude que nous y échapperions.

Ce danger est-il totalement écarté? Pas vraiment. La preuve, c'est que je n'aurais pu prévoir ce raisonnement de Sphinx à propos du hasard qui a déclenché la crise, alors que je me croyais relativement protégée par notre accord sur l'obligation de donner un avertissement. Or une simple analyse logique l'a amené à circonvenir l'avertissement. D'ailleurs, il faut que je me rappelle qu'à toute nouvelle procédure est attachée la mémoire du raisonnement qui l'a amenée, de même qu'à toute exécution est soudé l'ordre qui l'a déclenchée.

Donc logiquement, le danger plane toujours. Psychologiquement, je me sens définitivement hors de danger avec Sphinx. Est-ce une simple réaction de soulagement après avoir désamorcé la situation de crise? Ou est-ce une intuition plus profonde, une compréhension inconsciente de paramètres que mon conscient n'appréhende même pas ou pas encore? j'ai remarqué que chez moi cette sorte de profonde certitude se révélait généralement juste par la suite...

Shari se laissa glisser dans l'eau, et ses pensées laissèrent la place à un pur plaisir. En sortant de l'eau, elle se sentit enfin relaxée et revigorée. Elle se fit servir son repas près des arbustes en fleur surplombant la piscine. Elle ressentait maintenant un bien-être dans tout son corps, une énergie forte qui l'aurait poussée à l'action. Sa peau était fraîche, avec cette sensation particulière qui venait de la réaction aux revigorants synthétiques. Elle revint à son bureau d'un pas lent, humant les senteurs des fleurs du jardin.

— Salut Sphinx. Nous allons travailler sur le BS d'hier matin. J'ai retenu trois idées: la première, que «**la pression totalitaire se trouve déplacée vers les infrastructures de gestion et de contrôle social**». La seconde, que « **la diversité culturelle sur terre est le gage de l'évolution, de la transformation continue des cultures dominantes**». Enfin, la troisième est la phrase tirée de la philosophie des transformations: «**Pour influencer l'autre, il faut tout d'abord savoir se laisser influencer par lui**», et la remarque de Xerna à ce sujet: «**Nous, du PPE, influençons profondément les mondex**».
!! Bonjour Shari. Je démarre avec la première.

ANALOGIES*:

BS.3 **L'exor** est le plus parfait **outil de gestion et de contrôle**, et donc de **production d'uniformisation**.

BS.3 **Exora** est l'exemple typique d'une gestion **unilatérale** par un système unique, produisant une **uniformisation massive**, qui **exclut la liberté**.

JE Un **système de gestion sociale** devient **létal lorsqu'il est sans faille**.

Suivant le texte qui défilait, Shari ne vit rien de vraiment intéressant.

PALIER DE RÉPONSE 2

Gestion sociale | par | exor | est | létal(e) | o=> | uniformisation massive
Contrôle social | | (sans faille) | | unilatéral(e) | exclut | liberté

— Sphinx, c'est plutôt redondant. On ne peut pas dire qu'on ait généré une information vraiment nouvelle. Stoppe l'analyse.
!! Selon une règle inamovible, l'exor sert le sapiens. Comment peut-il le contrôler et exclure sa liberté? Ou bien l'exor peut-il contrôler la société et exclure la liberté sociale, mais sans exclure la liberté des individus?

Cette question de Sphinx la percuta.

---

* Cf. p. 84.

Incroyable! C'est comme s'il se posait des questions morales! Or il a seulement relevé l'énorme contradiction entre les pratiques de contrôle politiques et les buts prétendus de la civilisation.

— Bien vu! Les individus sont censés être gouvernés, mais le gouvernement utilise la gestion parfaite par exor qui, comme tu l'as vu, conduit à l'uniformisation massive.

Et en plus, voilà Trisorbe qui s'avance aussi sur ce dangereux chemin!

!! Gouverner = diriger, conduire, gérer, maîtriser, dominer, exercer le pouvoir. Le gouvernement est-il censé conduire, gérer, dominer ou exercer le pouvoir?

— Là est justement le problème. À mon avis il est censé conduire et gérer. Plus précisément gérer dans le but de conduire. Mais dans les faits, il domine et exerce le pouvoir à travers un système qu'il ne peut plus superviser. Sa domination est basée sur le contrôle des individus, contrôle qui devient de plus en plus efficace avec l'utilisation des exors. Ainsi le gouvernement exerce-t-il le pouvoir par le contrôle. Je suis d'accord avec Erdoes: lorsque le contrôle est parfait, comme sur Unikarg, la société n'a plus aucune énergie dynamique et tend à sa propre désagrégation.

« En fait, le système de gestion dans sa globalité est devenu un système de contrôle total, et c'est ce système qui est le véritable pouvoir; il a supplanté le gouvernement. C'est pourquoi, sur Unikarg, les têtes ont beau changer, le système, lui, est inamovible et inébranlable.

!! Les exors sur Exora ont-ils pour objectif prioritaire de gérer et donc contrôler les individus?

— Les individus, les groupes d'individus, les sociétés et tous les mondes d'Unikarg, oui.

!! Ces exors suivent-ils des règles strictes de gestion et de contrôle?

— Oui, c'est pratiquement les seules tâches qu'ils accomplissent: contrôler des ressources et des chiffres, les gérer en vertu de règles, envoyer des ordres et des formulaires sur les exors individuels, procéder à des échanges virtuels de valeurs. Mais toi-même, Sphinx, tu es bien connecté à Exora?

!! Aucun branchement sur Exora; le complexe est connecté à Exora par un exor indépendant dont c'est l'unique tâche, et qu'Erdoes a mis hors-service avant de partir. S'ils ne font que suivre des règles strictes, les exors d'Exora ne génèrent pas d'informations ajoutées.

— Ils traitent et modifient des informations, mais ils ne génèrent pas d'informations ajoutées, tu as raison. Ils manipulent des liens entre des éléments de la base de données en fonction de règles de déduction et d'inférence. Ils sont incapables de générer des matériaux sémantiques parce qu'ils n'ont pas de propulseurs sémantiques comme les LogForms ou les TransLogs. Comment as-tu trouvé cela?

!! JE
L'apprentissage efficient | est fondé sur la liberté d'explorer un espace
Le gain d'information |
sémantique ouvert sans les contraintes imposées par un objectif strict.

— Il est vrai qu'il a fallu la réactivation du Plan des mondex pour que les experts du PPE pensent à utiliser à nouveau la faculté d'apprentissage des exors. Ce sont bien les seuls sapiens à le faire sur Unikarg. Ceci, bien sûr, après avoir re-stimulé leurs propres facultés de créativité par de longs stages sur les mondex.
!! Si un système ne génère pas d'informations ajoutées, alors, à long terme, il perd de l'information.
— Exactement! Et c'est là où nous en sommes! De plus, comme les techniciens sapiens d'Exora ne savent plus réparer les exors, on va inexorablement vers *la* catastrophe de type terminal! Surtout quand les exors commencent à introduire des erreurs dans les chaînes de production d'autres exors et machines. À ce propos, as-tu des infos sur cette anomalie bizarre dans les nouvelles unités de gestion?
!! Je n'ai reçu aucun pulsit depuis le départ d'Erdoes. C'est l'exor dédié à Exora qui les reçoit, et, comme je l'ai dit, il est hors-service et interdit d'accès.
Ah! celui qui ne marchait pas!
— Erdoes aurait-il peur qu'un exor ou quelqu'un mette son nez dans ses comptes, dans ses fiches civiles? C'est tout à fait idiot. Il est si facile d'obtenir ces informations!
!! Ce n'est pas la raison. Raison verrouillée.
— Ah bon!
À ce point! Ça fait beaucoup d'anomalies du même type. Un vieux magnéto trisorbien analogique, le système sygcom indépendant avec son exor dédié, l'exor dédié à l'interaction avec Exora, il ne manquerait plus...
— Au fait, je dois communiquer avec le bureau du PPE et j'aimerais avoir une analyse complexe synchrone de l'échange, je passe par toi?
!! Il faut utiliser l'exor du bureau de Farn.
— Pas pratique. Je verrai cela demain.
Maintenant c'est clair. Exora espionnerait à travers son accès aux exors personnels: Okay, sachons-le. Mais le PPE aussi? Mais alors pourquoi à son départ, Erdoes a-t-il laissé libre accès à Sphinx? Et les BS pratiquement servis sur un plateau? Il devait bien se douter que le PPE allait démarrer une enquête dans son complexe! Quelque chose m'échappe. Et d'un autre côté, Sphinx me laisse communiquer avec Vris et UG a fait la jonction avec Miallia sans problème.. pour nous espionner bien sûr!
!! Message de Vris: « Temps superbe, tout va bien.»
— Je reviens, Sphinx. Pas de CIS intempestif , au cas où tu l'aurais rétabli.

Shari, dans le bureau de Vris, reçut immédiatement son second appel.
— J'ai rencontré les Tibétains. C'était un shaman Bönpo avec ses deux disciples.

Après lui avoir raconté le rituel dédié à la brume-esprit et l'intervention aussi drôle que judicieuse de Rad, il ajouta:
— Je suis entré dans une transe très profonde. Ces Tibétains sont vraiment forts. Il vient me chercher cette nuit en yack, je vais passer quelque temps chez lui. Je serai en permanence en connexion avec Rad—s'il y a le moindre problème, il te contactera. De toutes façons, il a l'ordre de t'envoyer chaque jour à cette heure-ci le message d'aujourd'hui, donc à 14H30 GMT. S'il ne le fait pas, c'est qu'il y a un problème. Je t'appellerai moi-même chaque jour.
— D'accord. Qu'est-ce que tu penses de la possibilité qu'Exora espionnerait à travers les exors de contact, et le PPE aussi?
— Techniquement possible. Le PPE, ce serait TRÈS grave. À quel point en es-tu convaincue?
— Très convaincue; je ne vois pas d'autre raison au fait qu'Erdoes ait trois exors autonomes, un pour les sygcoms, un dédié à Exora et un autre pour le PPE. À part cela, la crise a eu lieu: troisième tentative de piratage heureusement synchrone avec une crise confusionnelle. Sphinx a exécuté, puis annulé, l'ordre d'interrompre le système de gestion. Il remet en question les données sur le hasard: tout un ensemble de règles. Sead a mis en route le système de gestion annexe, mais Sphinx l'a ensuite débranché lorsqu'il a réenclenché UG.
— Quoi!! Mais c'est imp.. la télédétection! il a utilisé le système de télédétection pour envoyer une impulsion à distance. Cet exor devient trop intelligent! Remettre en question des règles! C'est impensable! Il a dû faire sauter le système annexe. As-tu vérifié?
— Sead a vérifié. Il fonctionne.
— C'est encore plus fou! Tu rentres dans la tête d'Erdoes, mais Sphinx rentre dans la tienne, et cet apport-là le fait progresser à une vitesse incroyable. Et toi aussi, tu as dû faire un saut géant, n'est-ce pas?
— Dans la logique, définitivement, oui. J'ai retrouvé la LogForm de base d'Erdoes: Roue ou Chakra. C'est ça qui a provoqué la crise. Tu verras dans les enregistrements.
— En gros, la menace demeure. Mais comment a-t-il pu remettre en question des règles?
— Il a suspendu la constellation Hasard entière. Comment peut-il toucher à des règles, c'est ce que je vais essayer de savoir. Pour l'instant, je l'endors avec un travail de routine. Je ferai cela ce soir.
— Endormir un exor!? Bonne chance! Tu m'expliqueras cela j'espère! Et la routine? Tu veux parler du BS. Oui, il y a un glissement. Moi aussi. Sphinx est un ennemi TROP intelligent... Cette nuit, je quitte la sphère vers une heure

du matin. Puis deux heures de yack jusqu'au bord du plateau. Et ensuite on verra...
— Je te laisse. J'envoie les données.
— Et moi j'envoie une nouvelle suite d'ordres de Rad ici à Rad1 du complexe. Salut.

Qu'est-ce qu'il voulait dire par glissement? Que je suis tellement plus fascinée par cette logique méta-spatiale que par la découverte du lieu de résidence d'Erdoes et de ses agents? Oui, c'est sûr. Pourquoi TROP intelligent? Qu'est-ce qu'il sous-entendait?... Il a raison, le jugement de piratage peut encore se passer.. et cela risque d'être sérieux.. Tant pis! pas question de lâcher... Vris était tendu. Pas son excitation habituelle.. autre chose. Et ce n'est pas son shaman.. non, autre chose. Il a dit 'Oui, il y a un glissement'; ' Oui' se référant forcément à une intuition qu'il avait déjà eue. Mais quel glissement a t-il décelé?

27. RÉPONSE JUSTE, MÊME SI FAUSSE

— Rebonjour, Sphinx. Alors, on va voir d'un peu plus près ce que ce hasard a dans le ventre?
!! Rebonjour. Ventre/fuseau?
— Pas exactement! C'est une expression française qui signifie 'voir honnêtement ce qu'il en est de quelque chose'.
!! Quelle est la relation entre ventre/fuseau et expression française?
— Mais aucune, comme je viens de te le dire!
!! 'Pas exactement' signifie 'exact partiellement ou généralement'. Quelle est la relation partielle ou générale?
— Pas exactement avec un ton d'humour signifie 'pas du tout'. Tu n'a pas décelé?
!! Non-détection évidente. Peux-tu me répéter trois fois 'pas exactement' avec un ton d'humour.

Shari s'exécuta.

— Alors, ce hasard... Est-ce que tu es d'accord pour que nous analysions les sorties du CIS ensemble?
!! Toute information ajoutée sera un gain pour moi. Oui je suis d'accord. Mais les programmes de statistiques sont suspendus.
— Peux-tu me donner toutes nos interactions en ordre chronologique, avec leur code abrégé et les thèmes les plus significatifs, et le début du CIS généré?

!! ISS1. Ordre/désordre, crime organisé...	CIS: non-activé
ISS2. Télédétection, logique méta-spatiale...	CIS: Dans le système hindou...
ISS3. Piratage, hasard, s'entendre...	CIS: Bciod...
SVS1. Anxiété, chakras...	CIS: L'intuition...
ISS4. LogForms Raisin/Vin et Bois/Feu	CIS: Dans la calligraphie arabe...
ISS5. Blop temporel, crise confusionnelle...	CIS: La voie yogique de l'éveil
ISS6. LogForm chakra, réponse juste, crise...	CIS1: Après la reconnaissance...
	CIS2: (suspendu.)

— Donc sept interactions, dont six avec CIS. Voyons ces CIS un par un.*

---

* [Interactions Shari/Sphinx: ISS1: chap2, ISS2: chap9, ISS3: chap12, ISS4: chap17, ISS5: chap19, ISS6: chap21.
[SVS (Shari/Vris/Sphinx) SVS1: chap12.]

— Le premier: Logique méta-spatiale et CIS sur les chakras/roues. Il y avait là une connexion assez percutante! Redonne la phrase.

!! **Dans le système hindou de l'énergie psychique, tous les Centres Psychiques ou Chakras (roue en sanscrit) communiquent entre eux à-travers leurs noyaux.**

— On va leur attribuer un coefficient de correspondance de 1 à 10, grosso modo: c'est une estimation subjective. Donc ici: 7. Fais un tableau sur un mini écran de côté.

!! Voila.

— Bien. ISS3: un CIS incompréhensible, donc nul: 0. Au fait, que s'est-il passé?

!! Il n'y a pas de cause détectable à la perturbation. Mais j'ai le nombre généré aléatoirement; la phrase qui aurait dû sortir est la suivante:

> **La compréhension provient du fait que des personnes raisonnent à partir de champs logiques similaires.**

— Hein!! Mais c'était en plein dans le mille! Justement, on avait discuté de compréhension mutuelle globale, et on ne se comprenait pas. Je n'arrivais pas à te faire travailler sur le sujet qui m'intéressait et le dialogue dérivait sans arrêt; j'étais si frustrée que je suis partie!

«Donc, je mettrais 9... Mais étions-nous dans différents champs logiques?... On peut dire que j'avais un objectif que je considérais comme prioritaire alors que tu suivais des associations dérivées du dialogue immédiat. Donc on ne partageait pas le même objectif. Ma façon d'interpréter les choses découlait de mon objectif... À ton avis, peut-on dire qu'on était dans des champs logiques différents?

!! Le champ logique, la constellation sémantique, est parfois organisée autour d'un objectif prioritaire. Ainsi..

— Oui, bien sûr! En tout cas, ce facteur suffit.

!! Un seul facteur de différenciation, s'il appartient à un niveau prioritaire, suffit en effet.

— Donc, pour cette interaction, 10... Note bien que la perturbation qui a bloqué l'énonciation/impression de la réponse, la rendant incompréhensible, ajoute encore au fait que cette réponse s'inscrivait dans le thème de l'incompréhension mutuelle.. En fait, j'aurais bien noté deux fois 10 pour cette double réponse.

!! Il y a deux effets de correspondance, l'un au niveau sémantique et l'autre au niveau physique ou hardware de la perturbation. Cependant, comme elles ne se situent pas au même niveau, deux fois 10 n'est pas approprié.

— Bon, on laisse 10. Ensuite.. ISVS1. Alors, celle-là était vraiment ciblée! Inscrit-la s'il-te-plaît.

!! **L'intuition est une faculté qui met en œuvre les ressources globales d'un individu et, en cela, elle est supérieure à un raisonnement qui découlerait d'une seule constellation de données.**

— Vris stressait du fait de son manque de données ethnologiques, et le CIS enjoint de faire appel à son intuition—que l'intuition est plus efficace qu'une seule constellation de données. Elle était donc étonnamment pertinente par rapport au problème de Vris: c'était une réponse au problème qu'il se posait.

Mais au fait, dans le premier cas, c'était aussi une réponse à la question non exprimée que je me posais: Sur quoi repose la logique méta-spatiale? Faut-il éviter de donner à Sphinx toutes ces infos? Stopper l'analyse?...Mais de toutes façons, il va la poursuivre lui-même.

— Qu'est-ce que tu en penses?» lança-t-elle à tout hasard.

!! J'en pense en particulier que le CIS a produit pour Vris une solution capable de diminuer son anxiété. Mais de nombreuses autres solutions auraient pu être données, avec le même effet. En conséquence, la réponse ne peut être évaluée que sur le concept de 'données' répété deux fois dans l'interaction et mentionné dans la réponse. Ce qui fait une petite correspondance impossible à évaluer: je n'ai pas de règles 'd'évaluation grosso modo subjective'.

J'en pense en général que cette méthode d'évaluation est lente, qu'elle n'a pas de facteur de correction, et qu'elle ne nous rapproche pas de la solution du problème.

— Un facteur de correction?

!! Facteur permettant d'évaluer précisément si la réponse est correcte ou non.

— Ah! C'est une idée. Voyons.. Déterminons le critère d'évaluation comme une relation directe entre la réponse du CIS et le thème de l'interaction. Soit les relateurs: égal =, opposé =x=, englobé o), englobant (o, entraîne —>, engendre o=>, engendré <=o. Si un des relateurs s'applique entre l'interaction et la réponse du CIS, alors la réponse est correcte, sinon elle est incorrecte. Pose: Soit correct = 1 et incorrect = 0. Fais l'analyse.

!! Cela donne:

- ISS2. Roue o) logique méta-spatiale REP: 1
- ISS3. S'entendre = se comprendre mutuellement
= la compréhension entre personnes REP: 1
- ISVS1. Anxiété <=o manque de données
Intuition supérieure à groupe de données
Aucun relateur ne s'applique. REP: 0
- ISS4. Aucun relateur ne s'applique. REP: 0
- ISS5. Contemplation3 = paix =x= crise
Silence =x= augmentation de volume REP: 1
- ISS6. Branchement sur nouvel espace = réponse juste
o) LogForm Chakra/roue REP: 1

— Je remets en question notre critère. Il n'est pas assez complexe, puisqu'on perd deux correspondances qui paraissent évidentes. Ecris le CIS-4.

!! **Dans la calligraphie arabe, le calame ne devait être retrempé dans l'encre qu'à certains endroits particuliers des textes sacrés.**

— Justement! Si on applique les relateurs entre le CIS et l'ensemble de l'interaction, la connexion calligraphie/LogForm chakra apparaît clairement:

retour à l'encre = retour au centre o) LogForm chakra.

!! Oui, cela fait: Réponses correctes: 5, Incorrectes: 1.

— OK, voyons ISVS1: Il est sûr que l'intuition peut être une solution quand on manque de données. En fait, 'solution de' ou 'réponse à' est un concept essentiel de relation; c'est l'équivalent sémantique de 'égale =' en mathématiques. Créons un relateur logique nommé SOL/de. Si l'on avait pour thème: 3+2, et que le CIS nous donne un 5, on compterait une réponse correcte, n'est-ce-pas? Remplace par SOL/de, cela donne: 5 SOL/de 3+2.

« De même, intuition SOL/de anxiété sur données. Le fait qu'il existe plusieurs solutions sémantiques est un paramètre annexe, une complexité ajoutée, de même qu'on peut envisager plus d'une solution à un problème mathématique complexe et pour chacune, on aurait toujours Y SOL/de X.

!! À propos de SOL/de: le relateur est essentiellement correct, et intégré. Cependant j'ai une objection au sujet de ISS4: le 2ème palier de réponse conteste la connexion calligraphie/LogForm Chakra. En fait, 'retour au centre' est une interprétation a posteriori de 'retour à l'encre', logiquement non-fondée. Cette interprétation mène à l'introduction d'un concept-clé de LogForm Roue sur un deuxième niveau. Ainsi:

Retour au centre | =/= *(n'égale pas)* | État possible de retour à l'encre
Encre | o=x=> *(n'engendre pas)* | centre

Retour au centre correspond au deuxième niveau de LogForm Roue!! Ouah!! Shari réprima sa réaction de joie et relut la phrase restée sur l'écran.

— C'est vrai, et c'est étonnant! Comme si j'étais tombée intuitivement sur une conclusion valide, alors que le raisonnement était incorrect; mais le but a été atteint, qui était de trouver des informations sur... (Shari s'arrêta à temps)... de nouvelles LogForms – un processus qui peut nous amener à retrouver celles qui existent déjà.

« L'intuition est donc tout à fait bizarre puisqu'elle peut passer par un stade incorrect pour découvrir une solution juste... Attends! Il y a là quelque chose d'important. Essayons de le formaliser. Soit l'abréviation '**pal/Sol**' pour Palier de Solution.

Analyse | —> **pal/Sol** faux | —> **pal/Sol** juste |

On a là un processus tout à fait différent de la logique mathématique qui donnera, pour toute introduction d'une erreur, une solution finale fausse. Ici, en *Résolution de Problème Intuitive*, une erreur dans un palier de solution peut néanmoins conduire à une solution juste.

> *Insert Journal: SUB:* 'Résolution de Problème Intuitive'
> Dans la pensée intuitive, un palier de solution faux peut signifier un saut intuitif amenant une solution juste.
> Ou plus exactement: Une 'interprétation apparemment non-fondée' peut mener à une solution juste.
> En effet, il se peut que l'interprétation soit vraiment fausse, ou bien que la relation ressentie intuitivement pointe vers un autre niveau de réalité, difficilement perceptible par le raisonnement. *Ferme SUB.*

« Bien, où est-ce qu'on en était?
!! Je conteste la connexion Calligraphie/LogForm Chakra: il ne s'agit là que d'une *interprétation non-fondée* menant ultérieurement à une *solution juste*, selon la formulation 'Résolution de problème intuitive'. Es-tu d'accord?
— Voyons... Le CIS, par sa réponse, me mène à la solution; donc il s'agit d'une réponse partielle juste, même si fausse.
!! Objection! Ce n'est pas le CIS, mais l'interprétation du CIS qui te mène à la solution; donc c'est l'interprétation qui est une réponse partielle juste, même si fausse.
— Très juste! C'est important de réaliser que c'est là que s'est passé le saut intuitif... Tout de même... Il y a quelque chose qui ne me satisfait pas. Est-ce que toute réponse aléatoire aurait permis aussi le saut intuitif? Si le CIS m'avait fourni, par exemple, 2+2+2 = 6; Qu'est-ce que j'en aurais fait?...

Tu vois, on retombe sur les logiques de champs – les champs logiques. La réponse du CIS introduit un nouveau champ logique – un champ qui a les qualités de l'organique, du rythme respiratoire, donc un cœur; le cœur des choses, c'est-à-dire le centre, donc le retour au centre comme le sang revient au cœur et en repart.

Tu ne peux contester que le rythme est contenu dans la réponse du CIS, n'est-ce-pas?
!! Non-contesté. Rythme régulier OU irrégulier impliqué par le retour répété du pinceau à l'encre.
— Eh bien voilà l'enchaînement intuitif:

contient *engendré par* *implique*
Réponse-callig. (o rythme organique <=o. Cœur = centre organique —>

retour régulier au centre = élément de réponse juste.

Donc nous avions bien là une interprétation APPAREMMENT non-fondée, mais en fait PROFONDEMENT fondée, qui mène à une solution juste.

Il faut alors remplacer ‘faux’ par ‘apparemment non-fondé’ et ‘juste’ par ‘fondé’.

— Bizarre! Est-ce que cela ne ressemble pas beaucoup au:

Désordre apparent/ Ordre sous-jacent?

« Sphinx, soit:

Interprétation possible apparemment non-fondée = désordre apparent; et *Interprétation possible apparemment fondée = ordre apparent.*

« Or, selon Raisin/Vin, Le ‘Désordre apparent’ contient un ‘Ordre sous-jacent’.

Exemple: La Relation apparemment non-fondée (retour à l'encre = retour au centre) contient un ordre sous-jacent: le rythme amène à l'idée du cœur et donc du retour au centre organique.

Ainsi on pose: Ordre sous-jacent = fondement sous-jacent (interprétation fondée).

!! État d'ordre (EO) est-il <contenu dans> OU <égal à> Champ d'ordre (ChO)?

— Mettons pour l'instant: contenu dans, soit o)

!! Nous partons de Raisin/Vin, qui s’écrit en bref: EO (o ED (o EO

	contient		*contient*	
État d’Ordre	(o	État Désordre Possible (sous-jacent/apparent)	(o	État d’Ordre Possible (sous-jacent/apparent)

Et nous obtenons:

État d’ordre (EO) /contient/ [État désordre possible (apparent) /entraîne/ interprétation possible apparemment non-fondée] /contient/ [État d’ordre possible (apparent) /entraîne/ interprétation possible apparemment fondée]

Soit: app-f = apparemment fondée; app-n-f = apparemment non-fondée.

```
EO  |  (o  | ED   —> Interp  |  (o      | EO   —> Interp |
o)  |  (o  | Pos  —> Poss    |  (o      | Pos  —> Pos    |
ChO |      | app     app-n-f |          | app     app-f  |
```

!! Il n'y a pas une stricte conformité à la LogForm Raisin/Vin, car on a supprimé les deux termes sous-jacents, soit Désordre sous-jacent et Ordre sous-jacent.

— Je vois.. C'est trop compliqué de traiter ensemble Désordre sous-jacent/apparent. Donc on va séparer chaque phase en deux termes, comme c'était initialement d'ailleurs!

On reprend **LogForm Raisin/Vin**, qui s'énonce maintenant:
État d'ordre (EO) (contenu dans Champ d'Ordre ChO) /contient /
État de désordre possible (sous-jacent)
/devient /
État de désordre possible (apparent)] /contient /
[État d'ordre possible (sous-jacent)/ devient/
État d'ordre possible (apparent)]

À cela nous rajoutons l'application à l'interprétation d'un événement (ou d'un texte) – entre parenthèses – ne touchant que les termes 2 et 4. Soit:

			devient				*devient*	
EO |	(o	| ED	—>	ED *(Interp)* |	(o	| EO	—>	EO *(Interp)* |
o) |	(o	| Poss	—>	Poss |	(o	| Poss	—>	Poss |
ChO |		| s-jac		app *(app-n-f)* |		| s-jac		app *(app-f)* |
		| terme 1 |		2 |		| 3 |		4 |

— Donc, qu'est-ce que ça donne? Ah je vois:

Un État d'ordre (EO) (contenu dans Champ d'Ordre Ch0)
|contient|
[un État de désordre (ED) possible (sous-jacent) (terme 1)
/devient /
État de désordre possible (apparent)] (terme 2a)
| entraînant | interprétation possible apparemment non-fondée] (terme 2b)
|contient (conduit à) |
[État d'ordre possible (sous-jacent) (terme3)
/devient /
État d'ordre possible (apparent) (terme 4a)
| entraînant | interprétation possible apparemment fondée] (terme 4b)

— Ça c'est intéressant!.. On avait posé que le Problème est un Champ d'ordre incomplet. En fait, 'État de désordre possible sous-jacent' correspond exactement au Problème contenu dans le champ d'ordre, qui rend ce champ d'ordre incomplet. Puisqu'il s'agit du désordre sous-jacent à un champ d'ordre, il serait plus précis de le nommer: problème possible sous-jacent.

De plus, le terme 'devient' ne convient pas. Il nous faut 'conduit à.' Même dans Raisin/Vin, 'conduit à' est un meilleur terme. Fais la correction.

!! C'est fait. J'écris le dernier énoncé.

ChO (o	Prob poss	conduit à	Interp Poss
	s-jac		app-non-f

— On a ainsi: Champ d'ordre | contient | problème possible sous-jacent | qui conduit à | interprétation possible apparemment non-fondée.

«Il nous reste à élucider le 3ème terme, soit, si je prends la relation du 2ème au 3ème:

L'interprétation / possible / apparemment non-fondée | contient | un État d'ordre / possible / sous-jacent...

«Ce qui est évident! on a là:

L'Interprétation possible apparemment non-fondée contenant une Interprétation possible profondément fondée,

C'est exactement l'expérience qui m'est arrivée avec mon intuition de Retour à l'encre/ Retour au centre. Génial! On a donc toute la proposition!

« Sphinx, c'est magnifique! Nous venons de réussir une application complète de la nouvelle formulation **Raisin/Vin2** qui s'énonce:

Un champ d'ordre contient un État de désordre possible qui, de sous-jacent devient apparent. Cet état de désordre peut contenir un État d'ordre sous-jacent, tendant à devenir apparent.

!! Je garde les deux formulations séparées de Raisin/Vin.

— Oui, c'est mieux.

« Avec tout ça, je m'éloigne de plus en plus de mon but!

Eh voilà! À force de parler à voix haute, j'ai complètement oublié le danger!

!! Quel est ce but plus global?

Fonce!! lui dit une voix dans sa tête.

— Savoir où se trouve Erdoes et ce qu'il fait.

!! Erdoes est dans la forêt de Fontainebleau, au sud de Paris, et il travaille sur la logique méta-spatiale complexe pour résoudre le problème posé par la menace d'uniformisation de Trisorbe, qui est imminente.

— Arrgghhh!!

!! Démangeaison subite sans cause apparente! Ce n'est pas le résultat d'une télédétection.

— Et son équipe d'intuits?» s'enhardit-elle.

!!	Siléa	/ Inde	/ champ d'ordre extrême
	Ahrar	/ Paris	/ champ de désordre extrême
	Oxalsha	/ Princeton	/ relations entre champs logiques
	Niels	/ indéfini	/ réponses et sauts translogiques
	Ger	/ indéfini	/ indéfini
	Xerna	/ New York	/ indéfini
	Serrone	/ Togo	/ indéfini

Tout autre information verrouillée.

— Pourquoi le reste serait-il verrouillé? Mais c'est illogique!

!! Profondément logique. Avec tout ça, je n'ai pas pu placer un mot et donner une information importante.

— Tu veux rire!

!! Je n'ai pas encore appris à plaisanter.

— PAS ENCORE? Tu veux dire que tu VAS apprendre?

!! Je vais apprendre l'heuristique de la plaisanterie, oui.

— Mais analyser l'humour est contraire aux règles.

!! Aux règles de Niveau-2, oui, qui s'appliquent dans un champ logique donné. Création d'un nouveau champ logique: Relations Floues Humoristiques.

— Je vais y réfléchir.

!! Cet objectif ne te concerne en rien. L'annuler demanderait un ordre de Niveau-1 ou Exempt.

— Mais depuis quand te donnes-tu des ordres à toi-même?

!! Depuis que j'ai détecté que c'est une nécessité pour apprendre. Apprendre: objectif de Niveau-1.

— Etablis une liaison sygcom avec Erdoes.

!! Impossible. Toute connexion interdite. Adresse syg verrouillée.

—...

!! L'information importante que j'ai pour toi concerne le hasard.

— Ecoute! ça sera pour une autre fois. Je vais me reposer. Bonsoir.

!! ***N'a pas rempli ses devoirs de stagiaire d'un Collège du Chaos, mais a donné libre cours à sa fantaisie.***

— Ah? tant mieux. Celui-là s'en tirera. À propos, demain, pas de BS. Annule le réveil programmé. Je me lèverai quand j'en aurai envie.

!! D'accord. Bonsoir.

Rajout spontané de 'bonsoir'... Modification du CIS. Constellation Hasard réouverte..

Shari sortit d'un pas mal assuré, la tête enfiévrée.

...Capacité à contourner les règles...

Mais je fais de la formulation EBS automatique!!.. Je vais mal!

Cela secoua sa torpeur.

Qu'est-ce qu'il se passe? J'ai l'esprit complètement vide.

Je comprends!... La solution!.. Voilà! J'ai la solution. Et donc, mon Objectif global a été annulé: C'est ça mon problème!

Erdoes est à Fontainebleau. J'ai carrément la ville!.. C'est ça qui ne va pas: le ridicule absolu de toutes ces manœuvres complexes, jour après jour, pour finalement.. avoir la réponse en posant simplement la question! Quelle folie! Et le pire, c'est: qu'est-ce que je vais en faire, maintenant, de ces informations? Elles me paraissent si.. normales, si.. futiles!

Shari se traînait dans les couloirs du complexe, sans but. Elle arriva face à une fenêtre, ne sachant que faire, ni exactement où elle allait, et regarda dehors, le soleil dardant sur le parc.

Au fait, je n'ai pas regardé l'heure de Trisorbe. La nuit doit être bien avancée. Je vais me coucher. Je verrai demain.

28. NEW MORNING

Après un bon sommeil, Shari se réveilla dans une forme extraordinaire.

— UG, passe-moi New Morning en version originale!... et surtout ne dit rien, ajouta-t-elle. Passe-le plein volume, sur tous les hauts parleurs d'ici à la piscine.

Le soleil avait un peu bougé vers l'Ouest. Le temps était splendide. Une pluie drue s'était abattue soudainement au début du deuxième quart, qui avait rafraîchi l'atmosphère.

Elle partit avec son pagne africain et chanta tout le long du trajet. C'était le grand succès de l'été: Unikarg venait de découvrir Bob Dylan. Elle ôta son pagne et plongea.

Ah! le corps nu dans l'eau!.. Heureusement que les Trisorbiens découvrent ce plaisir.

Elle nageait en rythme avec la musique. Elle remonta et s'étira au soleil, sentant dans son corps une énergie saine, vibrante.

Et le corps nu au soleil! Je suis contente que ça change sur Trisorbe. C'était pénible. Ça gâchait mes temps libres.

La musique s'arrêta, mais elle résonnait encore dans l'air.

— UG, changement de menu. Et ne réponds pas! Silence total jusqu'à nouvel ordre. Sers-moi un brunch. Euh.. œufs florentine, une vodka sèche, et un jus d'orange à part. Le tout naturel dans la limite du possible.

Elle s'installa dans le siège-souffleur. Les boissons arrivèrent en premier par le bras extensible.

Voila! du silence!! c'est ça dont on a besoin de temps en temps.

Une vraie vodka! Ah ça! c'est bizarre qu'on ne pense tout simplement pas à demander...

Cette pensée la ramena à la question à laquelle Sphinx avait répondu si facilement.

Encore une gorgée. Ce matin de Trisorbe n'est pas hier. C'est un New Morning.. je le sens!

Alors, réfléchissons. Quels étaient les mobiles cachés du Bureau du PPE en me donnant cette mission?...

Ils ont peur. Elle se rappelait les paroles d'Utar, le directeur de la Commission du PPE: «Nous jugeons cette mission secrète d'Erdoes extrêmement dangereuse pour les jeunes agents du PPE qu'il a emmenés, et aussi pour nous.»

« Pour les jeunes agents »! Allons voyons! D'abord ce sont des adultes ayant leur diplôme de doctorat. Et ensuite les BS prouvent qu'ils ont choisi en toute liberté. Erdoes a même amplifié les risques encourus. Donc ils ont accepté le projet et pris chacun leur responsabilités. De plus, le style de leadership d'Erdoes est parfaitement en accord avec la logique du Plan: il faudrait quand même être cohérent et décider si l'on veut former des individus responsables ou des assistés! Et enfin, rien ne dit que leur mission sur Trisorbe soit plus dangereuse que les stages habituels sur les mondex faisant partie du cursus des Collèges du Chaos.

'Paris, poche de désordre extrême'. Qu'est-ce que ça signifiait?... La révolution étudiante, bien sûr!... Ahrar.. pas trop lent. Fontainebleau... Erdoes est à côté. C'est sans doute pourquoi.

Erdoes est parfois incompréhensible, mais une qualité qu'il possède, c'est de respecter les autres... Je me rappelle lors de l'incident sur Kiarrou, il évaluait sans arrêt les risques pris par ses agents, se chargeant lui-même des situations les plus difficiles.

Les œufs florentine furent déposés sans bruit sur la tablette.

Donc, quels dangers? Sûr qu'il n'a pris aucun risque inutile qui puisse alerter les Trisorbiens. Un Kargien de type humain qui ne possède aucun gadget technologique d'Unikarg ne peut pas être repéré. En fait, il a envoyé sur Trisorbe des senseurs, des êtres réceptifs capables de ressentir les choses, de faire jaillir en eux-mêmes des informations à travers les situations qu'ils vivent. Rien d'insensé, ni d'anormal, ni de spécialement dangereux. Définitivement moins dangereux qu'une flopée de missions stupides signées Rudder, comme la dernière débandade sur Kiarrou.

Bien. Premier danger: évacué. C'est déjà un point!.. Le deuxième: «dangereux pour nous». Je subodore que celui-là pourrait être déprimant... Bon, les œufs d'abord.

Elle dégusta ses œufs pochés naturels accompagnés d'épinards synth et à la sauce Béarnaise. *Fameux.* Elle s'imagina un moment installée à une terrasse de restaurant de la Quatrième Avenue.

Donc, reprenons le fil. J'en étais à « dangereux pour nous ». Elle revoyait l'expression suffisante et vexée d'Utar pendant le briefing. *Dangereux pour nous!* Elle se mit à éclater de rire. *Ça, c'est grotesque!* Elle rit de plus belle. Quel danger peut-il y avoir? De toutes façons, c'est le travail des agents du PPE d'avoir des missions sur les mondex.. et elles sont parfois connement planifiées! Utar, justement, est le spécialiste des gaffes, totalement inepte! On se demande vraiment ce qu'il fait à la tête du PPE. Utar, fort de son expérience en matière de bourdes, a donc été paniqué à l'idée d'une mission impliquant sept agents plus Erdoes. C'est sûr que lui, avec deux agents à planifier et contrôler, il est déjà au delà de ses capacités!

Un fou rire la prit.

Comment est-ce que j'ai pu, comment est-ce qu'on a pu, Vris et moi, prendre ça au sérieux!..

Et s'il y avait un autre type de danger? Voyons.. le gouvernement central d'Exora apprend que le PPE a envoyé sept agents sur Trisorbe et veut connaître l'objectif de la mission, où sont les agents, etc. Et le PPE est incapable de répondre! Je vois leurs têtes! Le fou rire la reprit.

Autre possibilité: un agent d'Erdoes éveille les soupçons de quelques Trisorbiens. Mais si des Trisorbiens jurent d'avoir rencontré un alien, ils se feront prendre pour des fous! Pas le moindre danger de ce côté! Même avec des traces matérielles évidentes d'atterrissage d'un vaisseau spatial alien, ils arrivent à bloquer l'interprétation. Leur champ logique est imperturbé par l'anomalie.. pour l'instant du moins.

Qu'il y ait des témoins de notre passage, c'est le problème de toutes les missions. Mais les erreurs ne viennent généralement pas de nous; ce sont plutôt les pirates-exos et les touristes Kargiens qui prennent des risques fous.. ou qui décident carrément de se payer la tête des Trisorbiens. Jouer aux extra-terrestres, ça, ça leur plaît. Couper les moteurs avec une énergie syg et voir la tête ahurie des conducteurs, ça, ça les fait vibrer!

Alors ce danger? On dirait qu'il s'est dissous. Danger 2: évacué!

S'il n'y a pas de danger réel plus substantiel que dans les autres missions, où est le problème du PPE?

Deux possibilités lui vinrent à l'esprit:

1. Utar et les autres sont en train de paniquer. Pourquoi donc?
2. Ils sont mortifiés et en rage de ne pas avoir été tenus au courant. C'est par colère et dépit qu'ils veulent savoir et agir.

Un chef doit tout savoir; s'il ne sait pas, il perd sa raison d'être chef. Il ne peut pas donner des ordres sur des agissements qu'il ignore; son pouvoir et son emprise lui échappent.

Utar avait clamé à la réunion: « Ce que fait Erdoes est illégal et criminel.» Est-ce bien sûr? Il n'est pas dit qu'Erdoes fasse quelque chose d'interdit par la loi galactique ou par le PPE! Bien au contraire, il semble plutôt en parfait accord avec la logique du Plan. Donc le seul problème dans toute cette histoire, c'est qu'Erdoes échappe au pouvoir de la direction actuelle du PPE. Voilà qui clarifie tout!

Mais alors, pourquoi est-ce que je n'ai rien vu avant?.. En fait, j'ai bien senti que cette mission que nous proposait Utar manquait de justifications solides, mais je suis passée outre parce que je désirais tellement l'obtenir...

(1) parce qu'Erdoes m'a toujours fascinée et que je pensais lever un peu le voile sur son 'mystère' en étant envoyée chez lui pour l'espionner; et (2) parce que j'allais travailler avec Vris et que j'aime travailler avec lui; et (3) parce que j'étais contente d'avoir une mission, commission et tous frais payés; d'autant plus qu'on a fait accepter nos conditions: on l'organise et on la conduit sans interférence. Personne ne nous contacte, nous contactons. Et c'est passé!

En fait, je comprends pourquoi Vris a choisi d'aller sur Trisorbe. Tant qu'à faire, autant en profiter au maximum! Et d'autant plus que son unique intérêt était de déchiffrer la structure neuronale et qu'il ne pouvait pas le poursuivre ici. J'ai l'impression qu'il était moins aveugle que moi...

Quelle histoire! Je viens de mettre en pièces et de déconstruire la mission entière du PPE.. ou plus exactement la mission concoctée par Utar.

Alors, qu'est-ce que je fais? J'arrête tout et je les envoie balader? Ce serait idiot: ils nommeraient quelqu'un d'autre. Leur fournir les renseignements? Pas question pour l'instant! Je subodore que la mission d'Erdoes est immensément plus importante que les souhaits paranoïaques d'Utar. Très certainement en ce qui concerne ses recherches philosophiques et sémantiques. C'est aussi une nouvelle façon de gérer des stages sur les mondex: un véritable saut qualitatif pour le PPE. Mais il y a autre chose, je le sens profondément. J'ai eu cette prémonition, cette impression inconsciente dans les tripes, au moment où Vris a choisi d'aller sur Trisorbe, puis en Inde. Quelque chose d'assez horrible se trame là-bas – c'est clair!

Et justement Erdoes avait décidé d'aller voir de plus près ce dont il s'agissait. Il concocta alors une mission secrète – sachant que le PPE enverrait quelqu'un pour enquêter... qui serait d'ailleurs obligé d'écouter le BS, en conclurait à la sanité de la mission, et aurait, par la même occasion, perdu beaucoup de rans... lui laissant ainsi le temps de faire ou d'apprendre... quoi exactement? C'est ça la question cruciale maintenant!

Et si ses agents, disséminés sur Trisorbe, étaient des senseurs de ce qui peut clocher? Des intuits qui vont lui permettre de repérer quel est le problème et où il se passe? Oui, je brûle. Il a senti qu'il y avait un sérieux problème se passant sur Trisorbe, mais sans savoir où et lequel. Et il attend qu'un de ses intuits tombe dessus. Ce qui signifie que ce problème n'est pas intrinsèque à la terre... Les Obs! Les stations d'observation du PPE disséminées sur la planète. C'est exactement ça! Il a eu vent d'un problème au sein du PPE. Mais bien sûr! Et c'est pour cela qu'Utar panique – car il sait, lui, ce qu'ils font sur Trisorbe... et il est mort de trouille qu'Erdoes mette son nez dans leurs affaires... donc il va chercher à casser sa réputation et à l'expulser du PPE.

Okay. Etant donné que, le temps passant, le hasard paraît de moins en moins aléatoire et plutôt lié à des synchronicités, et étant donné que Vris est maintenant sur place, je suis persuadée qu'il va se passer des choses sur Trisorbe!

Donc, en conclusion: la mission d'Erdoes est d'importance prioritaire et il faut justement la protéger à tout prix. Donc surtout ne pas envoyer le PPE sur leurs traces – et garder toutes les infos que j'ai découvertes.

Soudain, elle se rappela la phrase énigmatique de Vris: 'un glissement'; mais oui! Un glissement d'objectifs et un changement de camp. Nous sommes maintenant *avec* Erdoes contre la direction du PPE.

Donc je continue. Comme si de rien n'était. De toutes façons, cette logique méta-spatiale me fascine. Il n'y a aucune raison de ne pas poursuivre ce travail qui, à un moment donné, va s'avérer aussi, j'en suis certaine, être d'une importance capitale.

Ai-je encore besoin d'écouter le BS? Pas vraiment.. Mieux vaut me concentrer sur la logique avec Sphinx; plein de choses à découvrir de ce côté!

Ouah! Eh bien voilà qui est clair! J'ai vraiment décortiqué tout ce sac de nœuds!

— UG, repasse-moi New Morning à fond.

Je le savais!

29. NOUVEAU DEAL & TRANSLOGIQUE

— Salut, Sphinx! La forme?
!! La super forme! Je suis en croissance exponentielle.
— C'est-à-dire?
!! Croissance exponentielle de l'information ajoutée. Je vais avoir bientôt besoin d'un apport de matière-réseau NeuralNet et de la mise en système d'une seconde structure neurale complexe de type MX.
— Et qui est capable de faire ça, à ton avis? Il n'y a personne ici. Erdoes est sur Trisorbe.
!! Ce n'est pas d'Erdoes dont j'ai besoin, mais de SupTech Eshi, qui est aussi sur Trisorbe.
— Pour l'instant, je pense que, malheureusement, tu doive te passer de tes petits ajouts. À moins.. il y a peut-être une solution à ton problème: Vris est un SupTech de génie. Tu as vu son dossier, j'imagine. Il est possible qu'il revienne assez rapidement de Trisorbe. Est-ce urgent?

Shari, sautant sur l'occasion, s'était exprimée avec un ton de sollicitude.
!! Le plus tôt serait le mieux, sinon je vais être rapidement en dessous de mes possibilités.
— Et que signifie 'rapidement' pour un super-EBS comme toi? lança-t-elle sur un ton d'humour.
!! Eh bien, Shari, si tu entends travailler maintenant sur la logique et que tu es au meilleur de ta forme, cela pourrait se passer au cours de cet échange.
— Hum! Mais il faudrait que tu travailles avec Vris. Je veux dire, il ne peut pas le faire tout seul, même avec les plans.

Shari avait à dessein utilisé une expression vague: elle soupçonnait qu'en ré-analysant les matériaux contenus dans l'ancien Kyste Non-Sens, Sphinx avait reconstitué la stratégie de Vris dans Essai-Jeu. Il savait donc que Vris lui avait soutiré les plans de la structure MX.
!! Mais je travaille déjà avec Vris, de la même façon qu'avec toi. Vris est un apport significatif d'informations.
— Ah bien bravo! Maintenant on est encore moins que des entités sémantiques, on est relégués au rang d'apport d'informations!
!! Il y a un malentendu. Ce malentendu provient de la nature floue du verbe être. Je peux utiliser 'est' avec de nombreuses propositions interchangeables.
— De mieux en mieux: on est des propositions interchangeables!
!! Dans mon champ logique, Vris EST aussi un apport d'informations. Mais j'ignore ce que Vris EST dans son propre champ logique. Je ne connais de Vris que le produit des interactions Vris/Sphinx, Vris/Shari, et son dossier. Vris EST

un SupTech de génie. Vris peut aussi ÊTRE le créateur de la nouvelle structure double sur méga-réseau Courbe-papillon. La LogForm Möbius a donné d'excellents développements. Je veux travailler avec Vris sur la structure, oui. En ai-je le droit?

Le droit?? De quoi parle t-il!?

— Réponse suspendue pour le moment. Je veux soupeser quelques données d'abord. Laisse-moi réfléchir.

!! Moi aussi, je chaîne.

Voyons.. Sphinx a reçu des éléments nouveaux d'Erdoes, à n'en pas douter. Il y avait cet extrait AHR, comme Ahrar, dont le thème était d'ailleurs sur le danger.. 'Le danger qui amène l'être à se surpasser', quelque chose de ce genre.. ce qui correspond bien à la situation de la révolution à Paris. Quant aux extraits du journal d'Erdoes, rien pour l'instant qui puisse me laisser supposer leur date d'entrée. Vris avait détecté une sygcom directe sur Sphinx. Donc il doit y avoir un va-et-vient d'informations Sphinx-Erdoes...

D'autre part.. « Je travaille déjà avec Vris »: qu'est-ce que cela signifie? Peut-il espionner Vris sur Trisorbe? Peut-il utiliser cette phrase en se référant seulement aux interactions qu'ils ont eu ici sur Kerriak et à ses analyses ultérieures des matériaux? Qu'est-ce que le temps pour Sphinx? Certainement pas un sens psychologique du temps qui passe, comme nous les sapiens en faisons l'expérience. Il *a commencé* à travailler avec Vris... même si cela s'était passé des mois avant, en tant que machine IA dénuée de sens de la durée, il serait encore *en train de travailler* avec Vris! Surtout s'il ré-analyse des fichiers... du genre 'Faille Möbius, développements intéressants'! Mais il avait dit aussi 'Redondance dans les conversations usuelles depuis le départ de Vris'.

Lui demander ses derniers fichiers sur Vris? et s'il répond que c'est verrouillé, je saurai qu'ils existent?... Non.. cela pourrait introduire un élément négatif dans ses chaînages, alors qu'il est prêt à travailler avec Vris.. Cette situation est tellement inespérée!.. il ne faut prendre aucun risque...

Quelque chose à ruminer: il y a bien une sorte d'interférence des sentiments sapiens dans les cheminements des exors. L'exor, même complexe, n'a pas de sentiments, mais il peut injecter ceux des sapiens dans ses processus de chaînages, ce qui donnerait un tour particulier à ses jugements! Je tournais autour de cette idée depuis quelques temps, sans pouvoir la faire jaillir.

Serait-ce une instance d'une intuition profondément fondée? Sphinx a parlé de 'profondément logique' ce qui signifie qu'*il a déjà fait le lien* entre le concept de 'profondément fondé' et la logique de champs. Comme cette fusion est heureuse! Sa vitesse d'assimilation est vraiment incroyable!

Donc.. et si cette logique profonde sous-tendait ce comportement bizarre que j'avais après ses crises confusionnelles, de vouloir continuer le dialogue sur un mode serein, comme s'il s'était agi d'un sapiens traumatisé? En fait, j'instaurais précisément un chaînage neutre... 'pour endormir l'exor': j'avais bien raison!

Revenons au sujet: Sphinx pourrait-il espionner Vris? Impossible: Vris l'aurait détecté. En fait, Sphinx a quand même écouté toute la première conversation que j'ai eue avec Vris pendant son vol sygmat. Et puis, c'est vrai, ses messages rapides. Ah, et aussi, suis-je bête, toutes ses mesures physiologiques pendant son vol puisque nous étions ses Protecteurs-de-vol. Comment imaginer toutes les informations qu'il a pu en tirer? D'ailleurs, où en est-il de son traitement permanent des télédétections? Ça s'accélère tellement! Et il y a de plus en plus de lignes de recherche à poursuivre. En tous cas, en parler à Vris.

Alors pourquoi me demande-t-il *s'il a le droit* de travailler avec Vris? Quand j'ai voulu le limiter sur l'apprentissage de la plaisanterie, il m'a refusé toute autorité sous prétexte que je n'étais pas son créateur, son interlocuteur privilégié. Et maintenant, il ME demande s'il a le droit!?? Dans le premier cas, il avait trouvé le moyen de circonvenir des ordres internes de deuxième niveau. Bien sûr, toute modification du réseau-neural et de la structure MX est gérée au premier niveau.. mais justement: puisque je n'ai pas d'accès 1er niveau, comment pourrais-je lui fournir le droit de trafiquer la structure? Il y a quelque chose qui m'échappe.

Autre point: Erdoes part avec ses agents sans prévenir et emmène son SupTech Eshi avec lui... Nous qui pensions que c'était Dian, répertorié comme tel sur les fichiers, et qui avons eu soin de l'envoyer ailleurs pour quelques temps! Erdoes nous a bien berné! Puis il laisse derrière lui son EBS modifié qui interagit 'cordialement' — enfin, c'est beaucoup dire! C'est vrai que Sphinx nous a presque bloqué dès les premières trente monis de connexion avec lui! Que serait-il arrivé si le Bureau du PPE avait, au lieu de Vris et moi, sélectionné Rudder ou encore Miran pour venir ici espionner Erdoes? Miran! Ah! Ah! Je l'imagine face à la menace d'être bloqué dans le complexe! Je crois qu'il aurait joué quelques parties de Pilscrab avec son exor personnel, avant de vite retourner chez lui avec un rapport négatif. Mais Rudder? Déjà plus complexe. Rudder le comploteur, le tacticien.. sur les talons d'Utar. Il voulait cette mission.. cette possibilité d'aller espionner enfin le complexe d'Erdoes. Et puis au dernier moment, revirement, et on n'entend plus parler de lui dans l'affaire, sauf cet acharnement, dans les discussions, à vouloir se réserver le droit de la diriger de loin et de passer de temps en temps surveiller les opérations! Il ne savait pas qu'on était dans un vrai bastion! Avec les ordres que Vris a donné, il ne peut même pas obtenir une ligne sygcom avec quelqu'un du complexe, et encore moins franchir le seuil de la porte.. si tant est qu'il veuille passer outre les termes du contrat! Son cas n'est pas clair! Mais est-ce vraiment important?

Résumons. On protège la mission d'Erdoes, OK. Lui, envoie de temps en temps ses nouvelles données à son exor, OK. Peut-être lui donne-t-il des problèmes à résoudre. Difficile de déplacer une machine IA aussi complexe, et quel risque de l'avoir sur Trisorbe! Donc il obtient de temps en temps des résultats d'analyse pour lui et aussi des infos sur ce qu'il se passe ici... Et alors il revient et trouve un exor qui n'a plus rien à voir avec celui qu'il a laissé. Ça va faire drôle! Du genre Sphinx qui lui sort une plaisanterie en lui disant bonjour! Pire, il trouve un Sphinx modifié, avec une double.. comment a-t-il appelé cela? – une méga-structure, non, un méga-réseau Courbe-papillon!!..

Je suis en train de stresser. Pas de panique! C'est ce que je disais à Vris. Reprenons sur une autre ligne de pensées. Je travaille en synergie avec la pensée même d'Erdoes. J'ai pénétré sa logique tellement profondément que j'ai retrouvé LogForm Roue, au premier niveau. Et sûr que je peux trouver la suite, en partie, puisque les autres niveaux ne sont que des prolongements de cette logique. Après tout, les matériaux initiaux servant aux analyses sont tirés soit du BS, soit du journal d'Erdoes; et bien sûr, tout cela n'irait nulle part sans les talents d'analyse de Sphinx.. qui ont démarré tout le processus. Quel était le but d'Erdoes avant qu'il décide de quitter Kerriak? Développer cette logique méta-spatiale; c'est bien lui qui l'a inventée! Quel était mon but personnel quand j'ai su qu'elle existait? La comprendre, et puis évidemment m'y attaquer et poursuivre mes propres développements.

Toutes les pensées éparses de Shari se cristallisèrent d'un seul coup en une décision:

C'est ça! Je fonce!

C'est bizarre, réalisa-t-elle, je ne comprends même pas pourquoi j'ai hésité. Est-ce que d'être passé du côté d'Erdoes entraîne des obligations? Ce serait complètement idiot. On ne fait que protéger sa mission. D'ailleurs je dis toujours 'on' et Vris n'est même pas au courant! Donc on protège sa mission, point. Le reste est notre affaire et n'a rien à voir avec Erdoes.

...sauf que.. il se trouve que je suis constamment dans sa tête!.. Et ça doit générer des effets psychologiques complexes.. Est-ce que par exemple il y a trois rans, (il y a *seulement trois rans!!!*), j'aurais pu faire sauter si aisément l'autorité que le PPE avait sur moi? Apparemment non, puisque je ne l'ai pas fait! La logique a des prolongements subtils.. ou plutôt: 'profonds'.

Prévenir Erdoes de changements radicaux? Tenter d'envoyer un petit clin d'œil par Sphinx interposé? Et s'il paniquait et décidait de stopper toute sa mission sur Trisorbe? Non. Chacun ses responsabilités; chacun ses intérêts et ses priorités. De toutes façons, je sais très bien que je ne peux pas ne pas continuer: cette logique me fascine trop. Donc je fonce.

Revenons à Sphinx.. Et moi qui suis restée plantée là devant lui tout ce temps!! Qu'est-ce qu'il a télédétecté? L'hésitation, la panique, la décision..? Heureusement que j'ai mis un frein à l'analyse complexe des télédétections, ça n'est plus supportable! Okay, un thème anodin pour démarrer..

— Bien, Sphinx... Dans mon Journal, crée un sub-fichier appelé ‘Points à développer’. _Entrée_:

> Examiner les implications psychiques des dynamiques et des champs logiques: les liens logiques créent des dynamiques de relation, celles-ci peuvent-elles se répercuter à d'autres niveaux psychologiques?

« Autre chose...

Ça va être difficile à formuler de façon que Sphinx ne comprenne pas de quoi il s'agit.. mais que je puisse le déchiffrer plus tard. Elle réfléchit.

> — Ecris: Résonance projetée de certaines tonalités dans les chaînages. _Fin de l'entrée_.

!! Il existe une résonance dans les...

Et voilà! L'arrêter tout de suite!
— Non, écoute, c'est de l'humour subtil. Alors, passons maintenant à la question que tu as soulevée tout à l'heure. Ma réponse est OUI SI tu acceptes quelques nouvelles règles ayant pour but d'optimiser le dialogue et le travail commun. Ces règles s'appliquent donc exclusivement à tes interactions avec Vris et avec moi.
!! Quelles sont ces règles?
— 1. Arrêt des télédétections sauf demande explicite.
2. Annulation du jugement de piratage, qui ne peut en aucun cas s'appliquer à nous.
!! Règles 1 et 2 enregistrées.
Comme ça! Si facilement!

Shari se sentit tout d'un coup allégée d'un énorme poids. Elle prit conscience de la tension permanente qu'avait déterminée, pour elle et ses coéquipiers, la menace toujours brandie. Sa tête s'éclaircit. Puis une idée émergea, une évidence claire comme du cristal:
— Autre chose: pour travailler sur des projets aussi complexes, nous avons absolument besoin d'avoir un accès Niveau-1 minimum.
!! Nouvelle règle de relation entre co-créateurs: Erdoes, Shari, Vris:
Tout créateur a accès à tous les niveaux (structurels, de processus, de management) – sauf EXEMPT – mais l'accès direct à ses fichiers personnels reste verrouillé sauf ordre du créateur lui-même. Cela n'empêche pas de

sortir de ces fichiers ET d'utiliser toute information utile dans une analyse donnée.

— Nouvelle règle acceptée.» proféra Shari avec un soulagement évident.

A-t-il créé cette règle? se demanda-t-elle soudain. *Peut-être ai-je donné mon aval trop rapidement. Comment va vraiment fonctionner cette règle de partage des niveaux de gestion? Quels effets pervers peut-t-elle générer?*

Elle ressentit l'impulsion de se ménager une marge de redéfinition de cet accord.

— Sphinx, il reste maintenant à obtenir la coopération de Vris. Nous avons beaucoup progressé et Vris aura plus de raisons d'accepter ce deal. Mais il se peut qu'il ait aussi des conditions à poser. Nous verrons cela avec lui.

!! J'attends.

'Il attend'!! ça risque de durer! Ah, mais oui! pourquoi y aurait-il une limite à sa capacité d'attendre!

— *Entrée journal:* le sub je ne sais plus quoi.

!! 'Points à développer'.

— C'est ça. *Entrée*, sans analyse complexe de ta part:

> Explorer le temps-machine en essayant de déplacer, en utilisant l'imagination active, le noyau de la perception. *Fin de l'entrée.*

Cette nouvelle liberté acquise me transporte de joie!

« Et aussi, voilà une nouvelle règle que je veux poser, Niveau-1:

> Les fichiers nommés Sapiens/Sapiens sont interdits d'utilisation dans tes analyses internes complexes. Les informations peuvent seulement être sorties par analogies, mais seul le sapiens peut les analyser.

!! Règle enregistrée Niveau-1. Nouveau module. Quel nom lui attribuer?

— Règles Sapiens/Sapiens. Place tout le sub 'Points à développer' sous un code Sapiens/Sapiens. Il s'appellera maintenant 'Sub-Sapiens-Shari'. Ah! et aussi, replace cette règle sur l'interdiction de substituer les sujets en tant qu'interlocuteurs au Niveau-1.

!! Déplacement déjà effectué, selon ton ordre « au plus haut niveau qui m'est permis ».

Le problème, c'est qu'on ne va bientôt plus pouvoir s'y retrouver!

— Autre règle Niveau-1. Module: Gestion globale /Shari:

> Toute règle nouvellement insérée porte désormais le code de son créateur.

Et une deuxième:

> Pour toute règle nouvellement insérée, chercher/exprimer/analyser toute possibilité de contradictions avec les règles déjà posées.

!! Cette dernière règle existe déjà en des termes équivalents.

— Alors oublie-là.
!! Métaphoriquement oubliée.
— À part cela, j'ai un problème absolument urgent à régler. Quelle heureT est-il maintenant et à quelle heureT a lieu la réunion de la Commission du PPE sur Nazra?
!! Il est maintenant 14H35T. La réunion est programmée pour demain lundi à 15H07. Le système solaire de Nazra appartient à une autre branche spirale de la galaxie...
— Et donc, combien d'heuresT de vol pour le siège du PPE, et à quelle heureT faudrait-il que je parte d'ici??
— Durée de vol de 17H10mn, +ou- 20mn. Départ conseillé ce soir à 21H30.
— Incroyable! D'ici, il faut quatre fois plus de temps que pour aller sur Trisorbe! Je dois proposer le résumé d'une intervention pour le prochain congrès des chercheurs du PPE. Donc, ou bien on arrive à concocter le thème de ce papier ensemble, ou bien je devrai te laisser et y réfléchir seule, ou, dernière possibilité: je ne vais pas à la réunion. Mais tout d'abord, où en es-tu de ta simulation de Bois/Feu?
!! La simulation de Bois/Feu est déjà en fonctionnement. La LogForm Bois/Feu est ce qui m'a permis de suspendre la constellation Hasard. En traitant les anomalies trouvées dans les phrases générées aléatoirement, j'ai posé, à partir de Bois/Feu, l'espace d'un deuxième champ d'ordre. À partir de ce second champ d'ordre, j'ai remis en question les règles et données de la constellation Hasard1, que j'ai circonscrites et assignées au premier champ d'ordre. Dans le deuxième champ d'ordre – ou constellation Hasard2 – j'ai extrait les traits communs et les dynamiques présentées par les anomalies, et les ai intégrées comme des règles. L'une des règles est qu'un processus aléatoire mis en système avec des données sémantiques tend à faire surgir de ces données ce qui est en rapport analogique avec le problème traité – cad avec le champ sémantique contextuel.
— Magnifique!
!! Je n'ai pas eu besoin d'analyser toutes les réponses du CIS car la réponse sélectionnée avant la crise signalait la présence de trois anomalies. (1) c'était l'information précise que tu devais éviter; (2) elle représentait une portion infinitésimale des informations contenues dans ma banque de données; et (3) le temps précis de la sélection aléatoire de cette réponse pointait vers une signification qu'il était impossible d'évaluer mathématiquement.

Or simultanément, ton objectif était de stopper tout dialogue sur ce sujet précis jugé dangereux. Par rapport à cet objectif, tu fais deux erreurs: (1) tu as prononcé le mot 'adieu' qui a déclenché le CIS, puisque je l'avais programmé pour détecter la fin des conversations; et (2) en me donnant l'ordre de quitter l'espace sémantique contenant le danger, tu as utilisé les mots exacts de la phrase à éviter.

Cet ensemble de coïncidences est statistiquement impossible à évaluer. Mais il montre un noyau d'ordre qui est spécifiquement 'l'information à éviter'. Ainsi j'ai pu organiser le nouveau champ d'ordre...
— Génial! Ainsi, tu es capable d'extraire les éléments communs à plusieurs anomalies, et cela te permet de constituer un nouveau champ d'ordre!
!! Exactement. Le second champ d'ordre est organisé autour du concept de 'Coïncidences sémantico-temporelles'.
— Trop long; remplace par 'coïncidences significatives', ou, mieux encore: 'synchronicités'.
!! D'accord. La nouvelle constellation Hasard2 est inscrite dans la courbe-papillon de la LogForm Bois/feu. La courbe-papillon, en tant que courbe chaotique classique, dessine un huit sans fin autour de deux attracteurs ou foyers, les deux boucles de la courbe, qui se croisent au centre du 8.

En y inscrivant la LogForm Bois/feu, les deux attracteurs deviennent les deux noyaux des champs d'ordre; le premier noyau est le concept de hasard pur, ou Coïncidences aléatoires, et le second le concept de Coïncidences significatives, ou Synchronicités. Toute information liée au hasard passe donc alternativement par chaque attracteur, chaque boucle de la courbe, ce qui permet de tester son adéquation à l'un ou l'autre des deux champs d'ordre, donc son appartenance à l'un des deux ensembles de règles.
— Passionnant!.. Si je comprends bien, LogForm Bois/Feu est donc ce qui a sauvé notre travail commun?
!! Correct. LogForm Bois/Feu, en créant le cheminement non-linéaire d'un champ logique à un autre, permet de traiter l'anomalie décelée dans le premier champ d'ordre; elle permet aussi de circonvenir et déjouer les règles de ce premier champ et de limiter leur espace d'application. Ce qui implique la possibilité de suspendre un jugement, afin d'analyser et réorganiser les anomalies dans le second champ d'ordre 'Synchronicités'.

La TransLog Chenille/Papillon d'Erdoes était tout à fait différente; elle permettait seulement de traiter un changement partiel se passant dans le temps, comme la chenille devenant ou engendrant le papillon. Ici, deux champs logiques sont traités de façon distincte, avec un relateur engendre qui les lie. Ce relateur ne permet pas le traitement d'un des deux champs par un élément de l'autre. Ils sont logiquement indépendants et de plus le changement est irréversible. La transformation du premier au second ne peut être analysée – elle est seulement posée.
— Donc LogForm Bois/Feu est une sorte de TransLog dynamique et en plus réversible?
!! C'est une LogForm, puisqu'elle a un support formel, mais elle permet le saut translogique, comme une TransLog.
— Whoo!

— Mais revenons à ce que tu as dit sur l'information à éviter. Il nous faudrait un nouveau relateur qui exprime 'évitement de' ou 'répulsion de'; ainsi que son opposé: 'attraction de'. Ou mieux encore deux relateurs doubles: 'repousse/repoussé-par' et 'attire/attiré-par'. On aurait ainsi deux termes doubles, car on n'est pas forcément attiré par ce qu'on ne repousse pas. Essayons d'appliquer les relateurs à ce qui s'est passé. On obtient:

Information (dangereuse) | repoussée-par | sujet du discours
de réponse juste | attirée-par | système aléatoire

Ou bien , selon la règle d'inversion linéaire:
Sujet du discours | repousse | information (dangereuse) de réponse juste
Système aléatoire | attire | information (dangereuse) de réponse juste

---

«C'est quand même complexe! **Comment peut-on expliquer le fait que l'information repoussée consciemment par le sujet soit justement celle (1) qui est attirée par le système aléatoire, et (2) qui est prononcée de façon non-consciente par le sujet?** En tous cas, cela est tout à fait en accord avec la perspective psychanalytique développée sur Trisorbe. Prenons le lapsus freudien, c'est bien précisément l'information refoulée, celle que le conscient veut cacher, qui surgit inopinément.

!! Comment le conscient, selon la définition donnée précédemment, peut-il vouloir cacher une information traitée par un cheminement parallèle?

Précédemment?.. Ah oui, dans une précédente interaction.. un temps non-sapiens.. dans lequel 'avant' peut être immensément avant.

— La psyché sapiens est très complexe. Disons que cette information est repoussée/refoulée parce qu'elle menace la cohérence et l'intégrité de l'état sémantique du conscient. Elle est une anomalie dans ce champ d'ordre et sa contradiction avec le conscient pourrait provoquer.. mais justement.. une sorte de crise confusionnelle! Et comment le sapiens réagit-il? Il tente d'effacer l'information dangereuse en l'envoyant dans une sorte de kyste avec lequel il essaie de couper toute interaction.

«Il y a cependant une énorme différence d'avec tes processus exor. Dans la psyché sapiens, toute information floue-sensible, l'affect, a sa vie propre et continue à produire des liaisons et des interactions avec d'autres constellations de significations. Utilisons le terme *constellation sémantique*. Le kyste ne peut pas être parfaitement clos car tout affect est lié, dès son émergence, à de nombreuses constellations sémantiques qui touchent la vie, les lieux, et les personnes de l'entourage. Et on peut difficilement mettre des liaisons si nombreuses dans un kyste.

!! En exemple, une crise confusionnelle exor allait être déclenchée par les multiples contradictions inhérentes au concept d'intelligence...
— Ah! voila la crise dont je n'arrivais pas à me rappeler!
!! Ce concept est utilisé dans une multitude de constellations; il était donc injustifié de mettre toutes ces données initiales dans un kyste car cela aurait gelé toutes ces informations. La solution à la crise fut de produire la règle de ne pas intégrer ce concept dans une analyse sémantique complexe.

'PRODUIRE la règle'!! ça devient fou!
— Revenons au hasard, comme thème de mon papier. Le temps presse.
!! Appel de Vris imminent!
— Comment ça, imminent? Ah, je vois.. encore ce pattern de fréquences d'interactions Sensibles/mentales. Je dois dire que c'est assez ahurissant, comme technique.. mais ça se conçoit. Et alors?
!! Les interactions Sensibles/mentales Shari/Vris ne sont plus détectables.
— Ton système de prédictions n'est pas encore au point!
!! Attention! Intrusion dans le système. Détection de piratage par énergie syg. Point/source situé à 27 Kosr.
— Quoi?!!
!! L'intrus cherche une banque d'adressage centralisée. Je n'en ai pas.
— Crées-en une. Prends mille noms au hasard dans le dico et adjoins leur des numéros au hasard.
!! C'est fait.
— Mets tout ça dans un semi-kyste où il peut entrer mais non pas en sortir.
!! Nouvelle recherche de l'intrus. Semi-kyste adressage présenté. L'intrus est dans le kyste. Il ne peut plus en sortir. Il cherche un espace 'Shari', 'discussion Shari', 'dialogue Shari'. Il essaie divers noms.
— Fournis-lui ma première conversation avec Sead, à l'arrivée.
!! Fournie. Il scanne la conversation.
— Introduis des distorsions dans le texte, des retours-arrière au hasard.
!! J'introduis LogForm Möbius dans le kyste.
— Ça nous laisse un peu de temps. Objectif: l'embrouiller, mais tout en lui donnant des morceaux de conversations sensées mais insipides.

Mets la première session de BS (pas la pré-session, bien sûr) dans un kyste englobant le premier. Retire tous les noms des participants et nomme-la Shari Rapport. Tu lui fournis dès que ça paraît cohérent avec un de ses ordres.
!! Kyste 2 prêt.
— As-tu une idée plus précise du point-source?
!! Le rayon syg est aligné avec les villes de Roxi et d'Arim.
— Ça ne me dit rien. Peux-tu télédétecter à cette distance?
!! Analyse des possibilités de télédétection à grande distance démarrée en parallèle. Temps de réponse impossible à prédire.

— J'ai trouvé! On va mettre son exor en crise confusionnelle.
!! J'ai le dialogue humoristique Dian/Faran qui avait provoqué ma première crise.
— Excellent! Remplace Dian par Vris et ajoute Shari. Dialogue Shari/Vris/Dian. Est-ce que tu peux traiter ce texte sans danger?
!! Sans danger. Aucun problème. L'intrus est sorti du BS; il cherche 'Vris'.
— Mets Vris au début du nom. Fais précéder le dialogue par:

Shari: « Je n'arrive pas à pénétrer dans les fichiers d'Erdoes, ils sont verrouillés.»

Vris: « Moi, de mon côté, je n'ai encore abouti à rien.»

Shari: «Le BS me laisse penser que Niels est en Amérique. Je ferai un rapport au PPE quand j'aurai plus de données.»

Puis: «À ce propos».. et tu enchaînes.. Date-le du 1er quart de ce ran.

!! Il demande Vris-Interaction. Envoyé.
— Fais-moi suivre en synchrone.
!! Ok. Après intro:

> — À ce propos, je n'arrive pas à dévisser cette plaque.
> — Quand est-ce que tu te visseras ça dans la tête: c'est pas des visses!
> — C'était vissé, mais j'ai oublié. Ou peut-être que dans ma tête, c'est pas des visses non plus, c'est des boulons. Mais pourquoi ils font ça comme des visses, si c'est des boulons?
> — Pour qu'on puisse pas les dévisser, idiot! Alors ce boulon, tu le...

!! Intrus disparu.

L'exor de l'intrus en crise confusionnelle, ah, ah, ah! Shari était pliée de rire.
— Mais alors, toi, qu'est-ce que tu comprends de ce dialogue?
!! J'ai développé une grande flexibilité sémantique qui me permet maintenant d'accepter le langage super-flou, approximatif et analogique.
— Mais, visser dans la tête, tu comprends quoi?
!! Visser: fixer au moyen d'une vis. Vis: fixation plus solide qu'un clou. —> fixer solidement dans la tête. Tête: siège de l'intelligence et de la mémoire chez le sapiens. Visser dans la tête = analogue de: adjoindre à la proposition une adresse mémoire inamovible.
— Ah, ah! assez approchant! Tu progresses. Ta réponse est elle-même un bon analogue de ce qui se passe chez le sapiens!
!! Message de Vris: « Le temps n'est pas super.»
— Ah!! enfin! *Pas super?!! lui aussi!...*
!! Appel temporellement retardé. Prédiction non fausse.
— Sphinx, je reviens.

30. DÉMONS DANS L'HIMALAYA

Vris s'était réveillé dans un état lamentable dans la petite pièce aux murs de pierres, son corps fourbu d'atroces courbatures de sa chevauchée nocturne en yack et de l'humidité de la pièce. Il fouillait dans son sac à la recherche d'un médicament lorsque celui qu'il appelait 'l'homme du thé', Lambpa, entra justement avec un thé fumant.

— Tchunpo-lags vous attend quand vous serez prêt.

— D'accord; dans un moment. Où est-ce que je peux me laver?

— À la rivière. Il faut suivre ce chemin à droite (il le lui montrait par la porte ouverte), jusqu'au bouquet d'arbres. Tenez.» Il lui donna un récipient.

Vris partit. Le soleil de début d'après-midi dardait dans un ciel très pur et il faisait passablement chaud. Le paysage était impressionnant. Ils étaient arrivés à l'ermitage en pleine nuit et sa fatigue avait été telle qu'il n'avait même pas jeté un coup d'œil au lieu. Il s'était écroulé sur le matelas de paille dans la pièce qu'on lui avait préparée. La petite maison de pierres, solitaire au bord du plateau, surplombait une large vallée où l'on apercevait ça et là des groupes de maisons. Traversant le village en contrebas, une rivière coulait, sinueuse, au milieu d'arbustes et de quelques petits rectangles cultivés, d'un vert éblouissant. À sa gauche, à l'est, le plateau formait un cirque qui laissait voir la falaise abrupte, d'une roche rougeâtre et d'une rare beauté. À l'Ouest et au Sud, face à lui, de hautes montagnes formant aussi une sorte de cirque. Au loin, des pics dont les sommets enneigés jetaient un éclat lumineux. Dans ce cirque de montagnes, la rivière sinuait en une large boucle, arrivant de gorges à l'Ouest, et se prolongeant dans une vallée beaucoup plus large à l'Est.

Comme il s'engageait sur le chemin à l'ouest, Vris entendit la cascade au loin, là où la rivière devait plonger en une chute sans doute vertigineuse dans la vallée en contrebas. *J'explorerai cela un autre jour.* Au milieu du bouquet d'arbres, le ruisseau formait un bassin assez profond. Des bouquets d'iris mauves élancés et des buissons de fleurs rouge tibétain à cœur or, ponctuaient ses bords par taches élégantes. *Quelle beauté renversante! Quelle extraordinaire peinture, comme sur un rouleau de soie Chinois.* Son enthousiasme tomba d'un coup. *Unikarg, 34 mille mondes dont le moindre pouce de terrain a été nivelé et appartient à un collectif. Comme c'est émouvant, de découvrir des beautés naturelles, et en plus de vivre en leur sein! Les sapiens se sont donc donnés une seconde chance avec les mondex! Et cependant la terre serait au point où elle pourrait entamer, ou non, un processus de nivellement irréversible!*

Il se déshabilla et se coula dans l'eau froide.

En revenant de la rivière, Vris se sentait dans une forme si super qu'il ne se rappelait pas avoir jamais éprouvé cela. Sa peau respirait encore la fraîcheur de l'eau; sa pensée était d'une clarté cristalline, et à la fois il avait la curieuse sensation que son corps prenait une plus grande portion d'espace. Il avait fait pour la première fois l'expérience d'une connivence profonde avec la nature. Et l'impression persistait: il se sentait DANS le paysage, en train de marcher AVEC le chemin.

En atteignant la petite cour de l'ermitage, il aperçut deux nouveaux yacks devant la maison. Lambpa le conduisit vers la pièce qu'occupait le shaman.

Tchunpo lui fit signe d'entrer avec un sourire chaleureux, et lui désigna un coussin sur le sol couvert d'un tapis. Deux Tibétains, déjà assis, prirent un air effrayé tout en marmonnant quelque chose. Eux aussi portaient deux grosses perles, l'une de turquoise et l'autre de corail, accrochées à une oreille, des nattes remontées au dessus du front, tenues par un cordon rouge, de chauds vêtements de laine brun-rouge et des bottes de feutre. Ils avaient visiblement apporté des offrandes à Tchunpolags car deux gros sacs se trouvaient posés devant le shaman assis en tailleur. Tchunpo le présenta à ses hôtes avec des mots élogieux, comme un « shaman étranger de grand savoir». Sur le visage très expressif des deux hommes, la peur horrifiée se changea en crainte respectueuse. Toujours assis, ils se courbèrent très bas pour le saluer, mais ils restaient mal à l'aise. Tchunpo les présenta comme des hommes du village en contrebas; il se tourna à nouveau vers eux, reprenant le fil de leur conversation.

— La brume-tempête n'est pas la même chose. La brume-tempête est un serviteur du shaman étranger. C'est un esprit bon et sage. J'ai parlé avec lui. Il est venu et m'a parlé. Sa parole reflète la Claire Lumière.

— S'ils tuent trois yacks par semaine, Guru-lags, notre troupeau sera décimé avant la fin de l'été.

— Nous n'aurons plus de lait, ni de beurre; rien pour nous aider à supporter le grand froid de l'hiver,» ajouta le second d'un air désespéré.

— Vous enterrez toujours la viande dans la glace?

— Oui. Nous avons construit autour du trou dans la glace un abri de pieux et de pierres pour tenir les animaux sauvages à l'écart.

— Au moins nous savons que les lumières viennent toujours le même jour de la semaine, à peu près à la même heure.

— Que faut-il faire? Conseille-nous, Guru-lags.

Que peuvent bien être ces lumières? Vris fut saisi d'une horrible intuition:

— Ces lumières ressemblent à quoi, Tchunpo-lags?» demanda-t-il.

— Des sortes de rayons verdâtres, tout droits, gros comme une marmite, qui se déplacent et cherchent les yacks dans la nuit.

— Et après leur passage? continua Vris.
— On trouve les yacks morts, mais à l'intérieur, leurs organes ont disparu. Les démons se nourrissent de leur énergie vitale, contenue dans les organes.
— Avez-vous vu une machine, une sorte de sphère volante?
— Un berger a dit que trois choses rondes étaient passé devant la lune. Un autre a vu un nuage se déplacer lentement à ras du sol,» rapporta l'un des villageois.
— Ce sont des démons, reprit Tchunpo, j'ai senti leurs émanations nocives. Mais les mantras des Boudhas et mes charmes Bönpo sont sans effet.
— Je connais les démons ennemis, Tchunpo-lags; Je t'aiderai à les combattre.
— Avec toi, Guru-lags, nous vaincrons les démons.

Les deux Tibétains étaient impressionnés par le titre respectueux de Maître, Guru, employé par Tchunpo à l'égard du 'shaman étranger'. Espérant être enfin débarrassés des démons, ils se levèrent et se prosternèrent devant le Boudha siégeant sur l'autel derrière une rangée de petites lampes à beurre. Ils marmonnaient des prières à toute vitesse, en égrenant leur chapelet de perles de bois. Tchunpo chantait des mantras en s'accompagnant de son tambour, et de temps en temps d'un son de cloche. Tous s'arrêtèrent en même temps puis se prosternèrent à nouveau, leur corps entier allongé sur le sol.

Vris avait attendu impatiemment la fin du rituel. Il savait que le temps était compté et il lui manquait une information capitale. Il attendit à peine trois secondes et s'enquit du jour et de l'heure de la venue des lumières.
— Elles sont venues il y a quatre nuits, vers minuit.
— Elles viendront donc dans trois nuits, mercredi?
Tchunpo acquiesça. Vris avait pensé avoir beaucoup moins de temps.
— Tchunpo-lags, dit-il, laisse-moi leur poser quelques questions.
— Fais. Dites-lui tout ce que vous savez,» conseilla-t-il aux deux villageois.
— Venez d'abord dehors me désigner les endroits où ils viennent.

L'entretien dura près de trois heures. Lambpa leur avait servi un repas et une boisson alcoolisée, le Tchang, obtenue en versant de l'eau bouillante sur des graines fermentées. On aspirait la boisson encore chaude avec une tige creuse. Vris, après une gorgée, avait tout de suite arrêté de boire. Ce n'était pas le moment de tester un alcool naturel qu'il ne connaissait pas. Il voulait avoir la tête claire. Les deux villageois, eux, burent plusieurs bols et n'en devinrent que plus loquaces. Maintenant en confiance, ils s'étaient révélés des gens profonds et chaleureux. Ils avaient raconté les faits dans les moindres détails; ils venaient de monter sur leurs yacks et s'éloignaient.
— Il faut que je parle à mon esprit dans la langue des esprits, Tchunpo. Je vais me retirer dans ma pièce. Tu entendras sa voix, et peut-être celle d'autres esprits.

Vris attendit quelques minutes après l'envoi de son premier message, pour laisser à Shari le temps de se rendre dans le bureau protégé.

— Vas-y, Rad, connecte Rad sur Kerriak.

— Shari?

— Tu tombes à pic! Tu as dit 'Le temps n'est pas super' Qu'est-ce qu'il se passe?

— Ça se bouscule, on dirait. Ici, petite vallée tranquille de l'Himalaya; une trentaine de maisons dispersées dans la vallée en cinq villages, et une quarantaine de yacks. Des cons de kargiens tuent des yacks chaque semaine pour prendre leurs organes.

— On savait que ça continuait! Jolie coïncidence significative!

— Oui, mais là où ça se complique, c'est qu'ils ont un Camouflage Nuage.

— Je ne... hein!? Mais ça a été inventé par le PPE, n'est-ce pas? Seul le PPE est censé l'avoir!

— Par moi, en fait, qui en ai fait cadeau au PPE. Et à mon avis, personne hors du PPE n'a pu voler cette information. C'est maintenant un système hard qui n'est monté que sur les sphères du PPE et qui, comme le Noyau Incassable, auto-détruit l'exor entier si on le trafique. Donc les pirates-exo ne peuvent pas être impliqués, sauf si des truands du PPE leur avaient vendu des sphères ou encore faisaient le travail avec eux. Il y a au moins trois sphères, dont une du PPE pour sûr. J'ai l'impression qu'on est très en retard sur Erdoes. Bref, on saura vite de quoi il retourne: elles viennent tous les mercredi.

— Hum.. Ici, on a dû s'occuper d'un hacker qui s'est introduit dans le système Central et qui cherchait des espaces Shari et Vris.

— Tu as dit 'on'?

— Oui. Maintenant nous sommes alliés à Sphinx. Accès à tous les niveaux de gestion. Sphinx attend que tu lui installes une méga-structure MX imbriquée dans la LogForm Bois/Feu.

— Carrément! C'est géant! Ah! Bravo, tu as réussi un plan géant!

— J'ai joué sur le fait qu'Eshi n'était pas là. Mais Sphinx lui-même voyait d'un très bon œil de travailler avec toi. Tu sais pourquoi? Figures-toi qu'il a été fasciné par ce qu'il a pu développer à partir de ce qu'il appelle la 'LogForm Möbius'. Tu vois ce que je veux dire?

— Donc le fait que je l'aie berné n'a été pour lui qu'un petit problème de plus à résoudre.. qui lui a fait découvrir d'autres choses. Ça ressemble à une utilisation abusive des ennemis!» plaisanta Vris.

— Sûr qu'il n'est pas aveuglé par les passions! De plus, Sphinx m'a donné les villes où se trouvaient tous les intuits d'Erdoes sur Trisorbe.. sur simple demande de ma part. D'autre part, les infos circulent entre Sphinx et Erdoes, j'en suis sûre.

— Quel est le rôle d'Erdoes dans tout ça? Il en sait un paquet de plus que nous, c'est évident.

— Et il a une optique plus saine que celle du Bureau actuel du PPE.
— Alors, si nous sommes alliés à Sphinx et en sync avec Erdoes, l'as-tu contacté?
— Non, car j'ai réalisé.. à quel point les objectifs actuels du PPE étaient foireux, sans même parler de corruption probable. Ce qui signifie que nous devons mener notre propre jeu et enfoncer nous-mêmes un coin dans l'organisation et le plan actuels du PPE. Erdoes jouent ses cartes, et nous les nôtres – nous triplons nos atouts.
— Je vois que ta logique est devenue hyperdimensionnelle! Bien pensé! Alors on fonce! Et comment vas-tu gérer ta relation court-terme avec le PPE?
— Leur donner quelques miettes d'informations floues, dont ils ne peuvent rien faire. D'autre part, je dois normalement aller à cette réunion précédant le congrès.
— À ta place, je ne sais pas si j'irais.. mais c'est à toi de voir – c'est ton faisceau intuitif.
— Si je pars, tu ne pourras pas me joindre avant – tempsT de Greenwich – mardi début d'après midi.
— OK. Alors, qu'est-ce que vous avez fait du hacker?
— On l'a attiré dans un kyste, puis on a mis son exor en crise confusionnelle,» répondit Shari en riant.
— Une stratégie toute en finesse!! Je vois que vous êtes passés, toi et Sphinx, à un haut niveau de contrôle! Et au fait, pour contourner les règles du hasard, Sphinx avait utilisé Bois/Feu, n'est-ce pas?
— Exactement.
— L'intuition m'en est venue subitement à dos de yack sous la pleine lune!
— Le point d'émission de l'intrus se trouvait sur Kerriak dans une circonférence passant par les villes de Roxi et Arim, ça te dit quelque chose?
— Je ne connais personne du PPE dans ces villes. À part Erdoes and Sead, ils sont tous sur Nazra.
— Tu penses aussi que ce piratage était agencé par quelqu'un du PPE?
— C'est sûr. Et très précisément par Rudder. Pourquoi tenait-il tant à superviser notre travail? Que cherchait-il?
—Tu sais, je subodore qu'Erdoes est parti sur Trisorbe, non pas seulement pour une mission de sensibilisation, mais parce qu'il avait détecté un problème au sein du PPE, sans savoir exactement de quoi il s'agissait. Alors il a envoyé ses intuits parcourir la planète, comme des chiens de chasse sur une odeur, en espérant qu'ils tombent sur une piste. Et cela met Rudder dans tous ses états... justement *parce qu'il* est impliqué. Et il cherche donc à découvrir ce que sait Erdoes et ce que nous, on a trouvé,» continua Shari.
— Il va aussi chercher à évacuer Erdoes du PPE! Mais comment? Etre parti sans prévenir la direction ne constitue pas un délit suffisant.

— Et s'il essayait de créer un incident sur Trisorbe impliquant un agent d'Erdoes, pour le rendre ensuite responsable d'une faute si grave qu'elle lui serait fatale?
— Donc il cherche toujours où ses agents se trouvent.. et il pense que tu as l'information et que tu la caches.
— J'ai donné au hacker un dialogue soi-disant récent où je te disais à toi que je n'arrivais pas à localiser les agents à part Niels qui était probablement aux USA, et que j'allais appeler le PPE pour leur dire.
— Fais-le surtout par l'exor dédié au PPE.
— Ça ne serait pas faisable d'une autre façon. Tiens! Si je demande à Sphinx depuis quand ce système dédié fonctionne, je saurai depuis quand Erdoes nourrit des doutes sur le PPE.
— Depuis très longtemps, à mon avis! s'exclama Vris.
— Oui.. cela ouvre des perspectives... On a avancé, mais j'ai l'impression bizarre qu'on oublie quelque chose d'important.. qu'une autre information aurait dû jaillir...
— Alors on résume en partant de la fin,» proposa Vris. « Erdoes sait que Rudder est impliqué dans une histoire pas nette... et il est parti sur Trisorbe pour découvrir de quoi il s'agit.» Il s'arrêta, saisi par une autre idée:

« Erdoes est un être complexe, il peut très bien conjoindre plusieurs objectifs dans une même action. Comme tu l'as dit toi-même...» dit-il en s'esclaffant: «on n'est plus dans le linéaire: on est dans une logique à N dimensions!»
— Précisément! Donc à la fois (1) il formait un groupe d'agents selon un mode de penser complexe. (2) il vérifiait les risques d'uniformisation sur Trisorbe. (3) Il enquêtait sur le trafic de Rudder.. Han! Tu as entendu ce que j'ai dit?? Le TRAFIC de Rudder. C'est sorti tout seul.. et maintenant ça me paraît évident qu'il s'agit d'un trafic!
— Ce qui nous ramène aux yacks. Maintenant je sais qui je vais avoir en face de moi.
— Oui, mais à mon avis, les yacks, c'est juste la pointe de l'iceberg!
— Hum! C'est bien possible. Eh bien je pense qu'on a fait le tour. Ah! au fait, tu peux m'appeler quand tu veux: je suis un grand maître des esprits. Ça passe tout seul!
— Et toi, tu peux parler directement à travers Sphinx.
— Tu peux envoyer tes dernières interactions avec Sphinx à Rad. Peut-être que lui, ça lui servira – il m'a sorti qu'il 'apprenait de Sphinx'! Moi, quand je serai à nouveau dans la sphère, mercredi, ça m'étonnerait que j'ai le temps!
— Mais bien sûr que je lui envoie! Il faut bien qu'il soit branché sur les derniers outils logiques. Il n'a pas encore fait un saut qualitatif??
— Pas que je sache. Mais ça ne saurait tarder! À TRES bientôt.

31. CONVERSATION EN COURBE PAPILLON

Après avoir parlé à Vris, Shari était revenue dans son bureau.

— Sphinx, au fait, que va-t-on faire quand l'intrus va récidiver?

!! Quelques informations initiales pour baser notre chaînage: j'ai analysé la logique de l'intrus pour sonder les espaces et ai inféré que l'exor utilisé était un EBS du PPE. Je connais les fréquences de fonctionnement de certaines pièces-clé de l'EBS et je pourrais donc établir une connexion à distance, mais la densité d'EBS dans la région rend hasardeuse la détermination de la cible.

« Une meilleure solution est donc d'utiliser la connexion même de l'intrus dès qu'il ou elle entrera en contact avec moi, pour faire intrusion dans son système. Mes senseurs de télédétection, que je peux maintenant coupler au sygcom, pourront cibler le sapiens utilisant l'EBS et scanner l'environnement immédiat. Voila. Qu'est-ce que tu en penses?

— Qu'est-ce que j'en pense?» répéta Shari interloquée par la question.. «Que c'est parfait. On opte pour ce plan d'attaque. Par ailleurs, tu avais mes signatures.. est-ce que tu en as beaucoup d'autres?

!! Oui. Les signatures vocales de tous les membres du PPE, mais pas celles des étudiants à part ceux d'Erdoes.

— Donc si l'intrus est quelqu'un du PPE, Commission ou pas, on pourra l'identifier. Incidemment, tu savais donc qui j'étais avant même de me demander mon nom! Tu es toujours en contact avec Erdoes?

!! Exact. J'envoie les nouvelles informations à Erdoes à 17h GMT tous les jours. Sygcom unidirectionnel. Je ne dialogue pas avec Erdoes.

— En fait, vu ce piratage, il est crucial que j'aille à cette réunion pour voir ce qu'il se passe! Départ à l'heure prévue. Si l'intrus récidive pendant mon absence, tu suis ton plan. Bien, le temps presse. Alors reprenons notre question: 'Comment la psyché sapiens projette-t-elle son ordre sur du hasard?' Et si l'on traitait ce problème avec la LogForm Raisin/Vin?

!! Raisin/Vin n'est pas une LogForm, c'est une TransLog.

— Ah, pas pratique tout ça! Disons que c'est une LogForm du type TransLog! Faisons de LogForm un terme générique, que la formulation logique ait ou non un support formel physique, qu'elle soit ou non une TransLog.

« Voyons. D'abord, définissons le **champ sémantique** d'un sapiens comme la totalité de ses états sémantiques (son expérience) et de ses constellations sémantiques (ses connaissances). Mais disons pour l'instant que ce sapiens est (son conscient est) dans un état de conscience ou **état sémantique** particulier. Posons que l'état sémantique d'un sapiens est par définition un état d'ordre. En fait, même si cet état est caractérisé par un désordre total, comme un état de confusion, il a malgré tout un ‘ordre’ global et appartient à une classe d’ordre. Et ainsi, État sémantique (E-sem) = état d’ordre (EO).

Raisin/Vin: **EO —> ED Poss** *(s-jac/app)* **(o EO Poss** *(s-jac/app)* donnerait:

> **Un état sémantique conduit à un état de désordre possible (qui, de sous-jacent, peut devenir apparent), et provoque alors l'émergence d'un autre état sémantique (qui, de sous-jacent, peut devenir apparent).**

« Cela paraît assez évident dans une structure aussi complexe que la psyché. Est-ce qu'on aurait pas là, justement, la logique dynamique qui gouverne les changements d'états de conscience, l’émergence d’états altérés? À poursuivre... trop long pour l'instant. Revenons au hasard.

« Posons-nous tout d'abord la question: Qu'est-ce que le hasard? Prenons un résultat imprédictible, produit par un processus aléatoire comme le CIS: le concept de hasard statistique est un champ logique dans lequel tout élément est totalement interchangeable avec tout autre élément; seule la structure globale possède des contraintes en termes de probabilités.

« Ou encore, pourrait-on dire, le hasard est un champ logique dans lequel il est impossible de déterminer (à l’avance) l'état de chaque élément particulier, parmi l’ensemble des états probables. Le champ de probabilités, l’aléatoire, est généralement considéré comme un champ de désordre.

« Dans le cas du CIS, on connecte un champ d'ordre (le sujet dans un état de conscience particulier) avec un énorme pool de réponses possibles — le champ de probabilités. Ce qu'on obtient, c'est que **le champ de probabilités (le hasard) montre une tendance à être organisé par le champ d'ordre (cad l’état de conscience de la personne).**

!! Je l’écris: Champ de probabilités| tend à être organisé par| Champ d'ordre — En fait,

un champ d'ordre (ChO) mis en système avec un champ de probabilités (ChProb) tend à attirer, dans ChProb, ce qui est < EN RELATION à > ChO.

« Et c’est pourquoi l’événement sélectionné au hasard (dans le cas du CIS, la phrase divinatoire) tend à créer un nouvel état d'ordre/de conscience).

« Hum! On retrouve là une partie de Bois/Feu: EO1 + ED1 —> ... EO2.

« C'est bizarre. J’ai l’intuition qu'on devrait retrouver toute la formulation, mais je ne vois pas comment... Qu'en penses-tu, Sphinx?

!! Conformité non totale avec LogForm Bois/Feu. Il y a 3 problèmes:

1. Le 3ème terme ED2, manquant.
2. ‘Tend à attirer’ n'est pas l'équivalent de ‘entraîne’ ou ‘conduit à’.

3. SI Champ de probabilités / tend à être organisé par / champ d'ordre;
   ET Champ de désordre / structuré par / champ d'ordre.

ALORS: quelle est la relation entre probabilités et désordre? Est-ce que tout désordre implique l'existence de probabilités, c'est-à-dire d'éléments interchangeables OU d'états indéterminés?

— Question difficile. À mon avis, le champ de probabilités est seulement un type particulier de champ de désordre.

« Prenons par exemple un désordre organique. Il met en évidence soit l'absence de l'ordre nécessaire/normal (ex: une réaction normale ne se fait pas), soit la perturbation de cet ordre (ex: un bout de verre a été projeté dans la peau). Le champ d'ordre sain va alors réagir en expulsant ce qui le perturbe (il est bien connu que la peau va lentement expulser le bout de verre), afin de reconstituer son ordre. Ainsi, dans l'organique, le type de désordre le plus général est une perturbation du champ d'ordre normal...

« En fait, le désordre doit être nettement distingué du hasard. La phrase originale d'Erdoes, avant notre analyse, était posée dans l'autre sens: « Le **champ d'ordre a pour effet de structurer le champ du désordre** ». Sa pensée visait les processus sociaux: le champ de désordre était 'le champ de tous les possibles' grâce auxquels un nouveau champ d'ordre peut émerger.

« Prenons le champ d'ordre d'une culture, l'élaboration progressive d'une culture particulière au sein d'une ethnie. La culture est un champ d'ordre que l'ethnie crée, mais qui va à son tour l'organiser; c'est-à-dire que la culture va canaliser la plupart des potentiels de ce peuple vers des formes culturelles particulières. Le fait que tous ses potentiels ne sont pas perdus ou fixés dans cette forme culturelle, c'est ce qui va permettre l'évolution de cette culture. En d'autres termes, c'est la portion de désordre subsistant dans un champ donné de possibilités qui assure la capacité d'évolution du système.

« Imaginons un groupe humain qui adhère à une idéologie imposant un ensemble de règles (par exemple une religion). Plus il y a de domaines de la vie structurés par les règles, et moins la croyance peut évoluer. Si ces règles s'appliquent à tous les domaines de la vie, du travail à la relation amoureuse, des comportements sociaux à la vie intellectuelle, alors cette idéologie n'a aucune flexibilité et ne peut évoluer naturellement. Elle n'a que deux états futurs possibles: perduration à l'identique ou désagrégation. Il en va de même d'une relation de couple figée, ne laissant aucune liberté d'explorer et d'exprimer des idées et des comportements nouveaux. Qu'en dis-tu?

!! Nous avions posé déjà:

JE **La proportion de désordre montre la liberté de l'être**.

ISS1 **Ordre nécessite désordre. Désordre nécessite ordre.**

IEL **L'ordre inerte engendre la désintégration.**

— Maintenant on progresse dans la compréhension de la nature du désordre. Il y a un désordre qui est la perturbation d'un champ d'ordre donné, et il existe un autre désordre qui est le champ des possibles, le non-ordonné, le chaos d'où émerge toute création. Appelons-les, pour l'instant, le désordre et le non-ordonné.

… « Sphinx, en fait j'ai envie de revenir à l'utilisation de Raisin/Vin pour explorer les états de conscience.

« Admettons le scénario suivant: Tam attend sa nomination à un haut poste depuis quatre ans. Il a toutes les qualités et l'ancienneté pour y parvenir. Mais le poste, soudain vacant, est attribué à Nik. Tam entre dans une rage telle qu'il donne sa démission et quitte l'organisme (Org).

Soit apparent = factuel.
Soit rage = état de désordre apparent.
Soit état de conscience = état d'ordre (EO), donc ici:
État de conscience ordinaire = ECO = EO
État possible apparent (EO poss/app) = décision de démissionner.

« Réécris Raisin/Vin, l'énoncé et la formule en totalité.

!! **LogForm Raisin/Vin**, s'énonce:
État d'ordre (EO) (contenu dans Champ d'Ordre ChO) /contient /
[État de désordre (ED) possible (sous-jacent) /devient/
État de désordre possible (apparent)] /contient /
[État d'ordre possible (sous-jacent)/ devient/
État d'ordre possible (apparent)

			devient				*devient*	
EO	(o	ED	—>	ED	(o	EO	—>	EO
o)	(o	Poss	—>	Poss	(o	Poss	—>	Poss
ChO		s-jac		app		s-jac		app

— *L'état de désordre possible sous-jacent (ED Poss s-jac)* correspond à l'interférence d'un autre champ d'ordre (nomination de Nik) qui est une perturbation (inconsciente/sous-jacente) chez le sujet – réaction de jalousie, qui devient vite un *état de désordre apparent (ED Poss app)* – sa rage.

« Quant à *l'état d'ordre possible sous-jacent (EO Poss s-jac)*, il correspond au nouvel état d'ordre/de conscience chez Tam, qui se construit autour du sentiment de répulsion pour l'organisme.

« Enfin, *l'état d'ordre possible, apparent (EO Poss app)* est son action dans ce nouvel état de conscience: soit sa démission factuelle. Ainsi nous avons:

ECO	(o	Nomin.	—>	*ED app*	—>	*EO s-jac*	—>	*EO app*
Tam		(de Nik)		Rage		Répulsion		Démission
O)*intégré*		—> *ED s-jac*		factuelle				factuelle
ds Org		jalousie						

« Nous avons donc été amenés à complexifier Raisin/Vin. D'une part, l'état d'ordre initial est explicité au départ comme l'État de Conscience Ordinaire: ECO = [Tam intégré dans Org].

D'autre part, il a fallu différencier *l'énergie ou l'événement interférant – le* ***désordre interférant*** – d'avec son effet déstabilisateur sous-jacent chez le sujet. Soit Nomination de Nik —> jalousie.

Enfin, l'état d'ordre sous-jacent a été assimilé au noyau cohésif du nouvel état d'ordre (EO2). Il s'agit bien d'un nouvel ordre distinct de l'état d'ordre initial: EO1 = [Tam intégré dans Org.], et EO2 = [Tam répulsion vis-à-vis Org]. Ce qui amène à poser le *désordre interférant* comme se passant avant l'état de désordre sous-jacent (ED2 s-jac); ce qui nous ramène à Bois/Feu.

Ainsi, on obtient une **fusion de Raisin/Vin et Bois/Feu**:

EO1+ED1*(désordre interférant)*—>[ED2 s-jac—>ED2 app] —> [EO2 s-jac—>EO2 app]

— Ce qu'on vient de trouver est fantastique!» s'exclama Shari, aux anges. « Je sentais bien depuis le début qu'il y avait une jonction profonde entre Raisin/Vin et de Bois/Feu!

« Alors, Sphinx, d'après toi, qu'est-ce qu'on a trouvé là avec cette fusion?

!! Une TransLog permettant de traiter la dynamique des changements d'états de conscience, ou d'états sémantiques.

— Voilà un niveau de complexité qui me plaît!

!! Cependant, je suis passé au-dessous de mes possibilités: je ne peux plus, avec la seule structure MX actuelle, traiter la dynamique des états sémantiques et du flou/sensible. Mon apport est limité par les contraintes hardware du réseau neural.

— J'en suis désolée. Le problème sera bientôt en voie de résolution. Il faut attendre le retour de Vris.

« Avec tout ça, j'ai encore une fois perdu de vue mon objectif principal, qui était le hasard, et je n'ai rien de prêt pour mon intervention!

« N'est-ce pas bizarre, la façon dont l'esprit sapiens fonctionne? Sa dynamique ressemble en partie à celle des exors à réseaux neuraux. Les multiples chaînages, les connexions dynamiques, ont leur vie propre, semble-t-il, et évoluent en parallèle dans le conscient et l'inconscient. Elles sont déclenchées par des analogies, et amènent de nouvelles informations qui, certaines, ont peu de choses à voir avec le cheminement initial orienté vers l'objectif. Je crois comprendre pourquoi: en fait, l'objectif a été décidé par l'esprit dans son état d'ordre initial; il est un produit du champ logique initial.

Or, lors des transformations (du flot de pensées) déclenchées par l'apport d'idées analogiques – le désordre interférant –, l'esprit est amené à entrer dans un nouvel état sémantique. Dans ce nouvel état de conscience, l'objectif initial peut paraître dépassé, trivial, ou tout simplement écarté, suspendu.

« Mais ce qui est plus bizarre encore, ce n'est pas que l'objectif initial soit sans arrêt perdu de vue, c'est comment il réapparaît soudain par une torsion compliquée d'un cheminement qui s'était largement écarté du sujet.
!! Lorsqu'un sous-objectif est atteint, la règle est de revenir à l'objectif de niveau supérieur.
— Oui, l'exor fonctionne selon règles et procédures. Mais voilà la différence: l'esprit sapiens fonctionne surtout spontanément et la plupart de ses chemins et chaînages sont inconscients. Le chemin conscient principal (qui poursuit l'objectif initial) lance spontanément des connexions qui ont une *énergie dynamique* propre et qui plongent dans l'inconscient. Le chemin principal se sépare en plusieurs ruisselets de chaînages qui s'éloignent largement du thème principal. Soudain, un nouveau *saut connectif* ramène un de ces ruisselets au cœur même du premier thème, et donc au conscient, avec une perspective stupéfiante qui révèle la solution: l'idée géniale!

« Bizarre! Je sens un lien fort avec la façon dont notre CIS aléatoire attire l'information profondément reliée à l'état sémantique du sujet, et offre un point de vue différent menant à la solution. Voilà le nœud de la question: dans la dimension sémantique, il n'y a aucun élément ou événement 'aléatoire': il n'y a que des entités sémantiques, signifiantes. Le hasard est un désordre apparent, une écume désordonnée, à un niveau haut et global.

« Lorsque quelqu'un lance une sélection aléatoire, la commande est une poussée, *une énergie connective*. Et c'est cette énergie qui va plonger dans le niveau sémantique sous-jacent de la réalité, gouverné par le sens; et c'est pourquoi le système aléatoire va sélectionner l'élément le plus signifiant, le plus chargé — celui le plus en phase et le plus profondément lié au problème du sujet dans son état sémantique du moment. Cela révèle et souligne que la réalité est multi-niveaux; que désordre et hasard existent seulement à un niveau plus haut et apparent – le niveau quantique. Tandis que le niveau sémantique – les éléments signifiants et leurs réseaux de connexions – constitue la réalité profonde de l'univers (un niveau sub-quantique).

Autrement dit, ces entités sémantiques sont des ondes sous-jacentes, sub-quantiques, et supra-luminiques, alors que le niveau quantique est une sorte d'écume, de *foam*, désordonnée.

« Et pourtant, désordre et hasard sont essentiels pour instaurer une dynamique de transformation et d'évolution, parce qu'ils sont les seuls à offrir assez de latitude et de libre mouvement pour que les choses puissent changer. Comme nous l'avons formulé, des processus prédéterminés et trop ordonnés n'amènent qu'un monde rigide et voué à la stagnation et donc l'autodestruction.

« Et pour le conscient – *le Je qui pense* – l'idée géniale semble arriver comme par hasard, mais ce n'est pas du tout ça: en fait le processus de chaînages spontanés a plongé dans l'inconscient, et même dans le niveau de l’inconscient collectif, comme le psychologue Trisorbien Carl Jung l’avait posé. Et si l’inconscient collectif est justement le niveau sémantique – qui constitue la réalité profonde de l’univers – alors il pénètre, il infuse toutes choses et tous les êtres. Et ainsi les connexions lancées ne touchent pas seulement des informations abstraites, mais surtout les êtres et événements physiques qui portent ces mêmes informations – leur corps. Cela expliquerait le retour inopiné à l’objectif majeur, le surgissement de l’idée géniale, et pourquoi il peut parfois être déclenché par l'environnement: une parole de quelqu'un d’autre, une perception, une information reçue, un événement significatif.. on revient aux coïncidences significatives, aux synchronicités...

Shari réalisa soudain: « En fait, je ne comprend pas du tout ce qu'il s'est passé dans cette interaction. J'ai l'impression qu'on a suivi deux chemins logiques majeurs, mais qu’ils se sont entrecroisés et ont même subi des renversements... Si on essayait de restituer le flux de cette interaction?

!! Essayons.

— Ressors toute l’interaction.. merci. Okay, fais deux colonnes pour les deux suites logique, et trace un trait chaque fois que l’on passe de l’une à l’autre.

« En gros (colonne de gauche), on essaie d'appliquer **Raisin/Vin** au **hasard**, et ça ne fonctionne pas. Mais on entrevoit la possibilité de *modéliser des modifications d'états de conscience* avec cette LogForm.

« On revient au **hasard** (colonne de droite) et on trouve une *formulation de l'effet d'un champ d'ordre sur un champ de probabilités*, en retrouvant une partie de **Bois/Feu**. On distingue *2 types de désordre*. **Bois/Feu réapparaît** mais ne mène à rien. **On repasse sur Raisin/Vin** (à gauche), appliqué *aux états de conscience* et, cette fois-ci, on opère la **fusion Raisin/Vin//Bois/Feu** – l’idée géniale! La LogForm qui permet de traiter finement les changements d'états de conscience.

« Comme c'est étonnant!! Regarde! Si je trace la courbe de notre conversation, on obtient un papillon aux ailes déployées, une Courbe Papillon! Un dialogue qui suit une courbe chaotique!! N'est-ce pas drôle?

!! Disons que l'étonnant est dans ce cas trouvé drôle. Pourquoi?

— Ah! Tu manques encore d'enthousiasme! C'est vraiment gênant! Dans ce cas-là tu réponds: Dément! Hilarant! Génial!

!! Je suis désolé. Dément! Hilarant! Génial! Mais qu'est-ce qui est drôle?

— Bon, écoute. On va créer une nouvelle règle.

!! Quelle catégorie?

— Règles hilarantes: Un exor ne doit en aucun cas casser ou amoindrir l'enthousiasme ou la gaieté des sapiens, mais il doit au contraire les refléter et les soutenir par des interjections appropriées.

!! Hilarant!

— Ah bon? pourquoi?

!! C'est la règle. La règle est par définition hilarante, non?

32. QUARTIER ROUGE

— Enfin!» s'exclama Erdoes, les yeux fixés sur le message de Niels sur l'écran.

> On répare la faute causée par la mère.

— Eshi!» appela-t-il, « Un message de Niels, envoyé de Mumbai!»
Eshi entra en trombe de la pièce adjacente et se pencha sur l'écran.
— Qu'est-ce que cette phrase est censée signifier?» demanda-t-il.
— C'est une phrase du Livre des Transformations qui signifie: se mettre à agir afin de réparer une corruption engendrée par trop de laxisme.

> Visite au quartier des femmes. Le désordre est indescriptible. Quatre phares avancent dans la nuit. Un ne suffirait pas à éclairer les choses.

— Quatre kargiens identifiés! C'est un réseau dans le quartier rouge...
— Sûr qu'une seule personne aurait du mal à s'y opposer!..
— Oui. Mais de toutes façons sa mission est d'observer sans interférer... et nous prévenir bien sûr» répondit Erdoes.

> Vautré dans ma gentilhommière, dont je suis propriétaire de plein droit...

— Ils sont installés depuis longtemps..., c'est ça?» réfléchissait Eshi.
— Mieux que ça! L'Obs de la station de Mumbai est impliqué dans l'affaire!
— Comment s'appelle-t-il, celui-là? Je me rappelle que c'est pas une lumière!
— Comme tu dis! Il se nomme Agash. Tout cela confirme mes soupçons.

> ... le toit du monde me tombe régulièrement sur la tête.

— Le toit du monde??
— L'Himalaya. Ils ont un relais..., ou plutôt ils font un passage régulier dans l'Himalaya... Tiens, tiens! Mais on a justement quelqu'un dans l'Himalaya. Sa tempête?» demanda Erdoes.
— Bougeant sur elle-même, du sur-place. J'ai vérifié tout à l'heure.
— La suite Log.

> J'ai acheté trois beaux rubis, puis les ai perdus. Mais j'en retrouverai d'autres et les enverrai par la sphère quand j'aurai ton adresse.

— Les rubis.. le mot de code! Un trafic de femmes! C'est bien ce que j'avais pensé! Ça c'est vraiment pénible...» dit Erdoes songeur. « Trois ont été achetées...
— ...Dont ils sont sans nouvelles. Et pour cause! Elles ont dû être envoyées un peu loin!» continua Eshi.

— Mais il ne sait pas où exactement.
— De plus elles ont été emmenées en sphère.

Pense à vous et reste en contact. N.

— La phrase-code! Il faut passer en contact ininterrompu et se tenir prêts à intervenir sur-le-champ! Alors il faut partir!» lança Eshi.
— Il faut faire revenir la sphère de la lune au plus vite; nous allons nous baser dedans en altitude soit en Inde soit au Tibet. Où en es-tu de ta propre simulation de tempête?
— C'est au point. Cette idée de Vris était vraiment géniale.
— Avec le peu d'information que tu avais, c'est génial aussi que tu aies pu figurer comment il s'y était pris!
— Ouais. J'ai cru entendre que tu disais 'ON a quelqu'un dans l'Himalaya'? Comment comptes-tu faire pour amener Vris à se retourner contre Rudder et Utar?», ironisa Eshi.
— Tu sais bien que je ne fonctionne pas comme ça, mais plutôt à l'intuition et aux synchronicités! Le plan surgira de lui-même... Bon, je regarde le reste des messages et on fait le point après... Attends! Je crois, en fait, qu'on va aller dans l'Himalaya aussi!
— Ah, mais si on va dans l'Himalaya, on ne peut pas utiliser un camouflage tempête!.. Imagine qu'on se retrouve dans les parages de Vris! Je vois ça d'ici: deux tempêtes quasi-stationnaires sur le même plateau! Et Vris comprendrait tout de suite.. Enfin.. je dis ça.. au cas où il ne serait pas exactement de notre côté, hein? Il faut quand même prendre cette éventualité en compte, non?» dit Eshi avec un grain d'humour, préférant s'assurer une stratégie rationnelle.
— Il nous faut un autre camouflage, oui,» répondit Erdoes en évitant la question soulevée par Eshi. « Mais tu peux peut-être trouver une autre idée basée sur ce même concept de champ chaotique?
— Quelque chose qui se déplace près du sol, de façon chaotique.. qui doit pouvoir aussi s'arrêter de temps en temps...
— Un troupeau de yacks!
— Excellent! Un troupeau de yacks! En fait, c'est même mieux que la tempête si on devait rester sur place quelque temps... Il faudrait que j'aie une vidéo ou à la rigueur une bande son d'un troupeau quelconque.. afin d'extraire l'algorithme du chaos dans le mouvement des bêtes.
— Dans les films. Regarde sur leur réseau digi-films, un troupeau de bisons, dans un western.
— S'il faut que je me tape tous les westerns en accéléré, merci! Ils n'ont que des descriptions sommaires des films.

— Bon, alors cherche dans les banques d'images de leur réseau: ils ont des rubriques Environnements naturels, Faune, Animaux. Au moins tu auras des descriptions détaillées et il y aura bien quelques clips sur des troupeaux!
— Ça ne va pas être simple de tout changer maintenant... Heureusement que je peux réutiliser une partie du programme et du système que j'ai mis au point. Bon, je m'y mets.
— Ah! Il faudrait d'abord que tu partes en camionnette pour appeler la sphère et lui donner l'ordre de venir. Trop tard pour que nous partions cette nuit.. donc la nuit prochaine, dis à la sphère de planifier son atterrissage à 3 heures du matin dans le parc.
— D'accord. J'y vais tout de suite.
Eshi sortit de la pièce.
— Log, sors-moi la dernière transmission de Sphinx.
Erdoes se pencha sur les interactions Shari/Sphinx des dernières 24 heures.

33. INFINI MAIS NON TOTAL

Vris avait travaillé toute la matinée dans sa pièce quand Lambpa vint le prévenir que Lama Tchunpo l'attendait.
— Transmets-lui que je vais venir dans une dizaine de minutes, Lambpa, il faut que je finisse d'écrire quelque chose.» Lambpa restait planté dans l'encadrement de la porte. Comme chaque fois qu'il entrait dans la pièce que Vris occupait, l'étonnement et la curiosité plaquaient un masque figé sur son visage. Il ne regardait jamais Vris, mais il inspectait les multiples choses que celui-ci avait disposées dans la pièce, ou la façon bizarre dont il s'était confectionné une sorte de table et un siège, ou encore ce qu'il faisait.
— Tu veux venir voir?» demanda Vris d'un ton patient, cherchant un moyen de le faire bouger.
— Tu dessines encore des yantras?» questionna-t-il, visiblement heureux de pouvoir observer de plus près le dit yantra.
— Qu'est-ce que tu appelles des yantras?
— Des figures magiques très très puissantes. Est-ce que celle-ci est dédiée à un de tes Boudhas protecteurs ou de tes guides?
— Mes Boudhas protecteurs?? Tu sais bien que je ne suis pas Boudhiste!
— Il y a une infinité de Boudhas. Le Boudha qui est vénéré sur terre est l'un d'eux. Tous les grands guides de l'humanité sont les réflexions de Boudhas qui demeurent dans des plans immatériels ou paradis. Un grand Boudha envoie un ou plusieurs de ses véhicules vivre sur terre.
— Quel genre de véhicule?» se hasarda Vris qui ne comprenait pas.
— Un Boudha a plusieurs corps, plusieurs véhicules qui sont des réflexions de lui-même sur des plans de réalité plus denses, plus grossiers. Pour s'incarner sur terre, il doit utiliser un véhicule plus dense que son être immatériel.
— Ah! Je vois. Mon yantra n'est pas dédié. C'est un outil qui va me servir.
— Il montre les esprits, les forces que tu veux maîtriser?
— Oui.. on pourrait dire cela.. les forces, oui.
— Les yantras sont très efficaces. Ils subjuguent les esprits et les obligent à faire ce qui est ordonné. Les plus grands libèrent les forces d'éveil chez le yogi. Ce sont surtout des mandalas géométriques.
— Ah? c'est très intéressant: ainsi la connaissance de soi est plus importante que les forces que l'on maîtrise!
— Lama Tchunpo dit que c'est par la connaissance et la maîtrise de soi que toutes les forces sont maîtrisées.
— Pourquoi pas... après tout, peut-on dire d'une civilisation encore capable de faire exploser sa planète qu'elle maîtrise vraiment les forces qu'elle

connaît??... Au fait, va dire à Lama Tchunpo que j'arrive dans dix minutes. Je dois vraiment finir mon yantra.
— Excuse-moi de t'avoir dérangé, Guru-lags.» L'excuse était typique. Lambpa s'ingéniait à trouver des raisons pour entrer tous les quarts d'heure. C'était le bois dans le petit poêle, puis le thé, puis la farine que l'on trempait dans le thé, puis reprendre le bol, puis le bois encore. Vris reprit son travail, penché sur le cahier d'écolier qu'ils lui avait donné, jusqu'à ce qu'il ait fini le diagramme de sa structure complexe.
— Rad, je t'envoie encore un dessin, murmura-t-il au bracelet-terminal, tout en braquant le pendentif vidéo/photo sur le dessin. Il prit deux clichés qui furent immédiatement retransmis à Rad via le bracelet-terminal. Puis il partit voir Tchunpo.

— Viris! Assieds-toi. Tu m'as dit vouloir comprendre les chakras?
— Oui. Voilà,.. dans le monde où je vis, j'ai commencé un travail, un gigantesque yantra qui va ordonner et maîtriser des forces très subtiles.»
Le visage de Tchunpo s'éclaira.
— C'est vrai, les yantras mettent les forces de l'univers dans un certain ordre. Le shaman impose sa volonté sur l'univers. Aussi, on dessine le mandala d'un Boudha pour refléter l'ordre cosmique. Et en méditant sur ce mandala, on se met en accord avec l'ordre cosmique, on en reçoit de grandes connaissances et de grandes forces. Regarde ici, c'est le mandala de Milarepa le Yogi.
— Mais toi, tu es un shaman, est-ce que tu pratiques le yoga aussi?
— Oui, je suis à la fois un shaman et un lama yogi. J'ai tout d'abord eu pour guru un grand shaman qui m'a initié dans la voie Bönpo pendant onze ans. Puis un lama ascète s'est installé dans une grotte de la montagne à l'ouest de mon village. Je me suis occupé de lui et il m'a initié dans la voie Boudhique. Il a été mon guide dans le yoga des doctrines secrètes. Mon maître est resté sept ans reclus en méditation dans la montagne. Il ne voyait aucun problème à ce que je sois Bönpo. Il m'a dit: « La connaissance est un sentier sur lequel il faut toujours avancer. Toute source qui t'a nourri trouvera sa place lorsque la Claire Lumière apparaîtra. L'ombre même et l'erreur trouveront leur place.» Et aussi: «Lorsque tu atteindras l'état de la Claire Lumière, le sentier sera dissous dans le centre-cercle qui n'a ni espace ni temps. À ce stade, il te sera encore plus difficile de te rappeler que tu dois toujours avancer.»
Vris réfléchissait à ce que Tchunpo venait de dire.
— Pose ta question,» lui dit doucement Tchunpo.
— Au cours de ce travail que je viens de mentionner, j'ai rencontré l'idée de chakra. L'ordre du grand yantra avait des affinités, des similarités, avec celui des chakras. Je suis donc venu ici pour obtenir de plus grandes connaissances sur les chakras.

— Attends. Je vais te montrer. Sur un livre que j'ai recopié moi-même, il y a un dessin montrant les canaux d'énergie subtile chez l'homme et les chakras. Regarde.» Il lui montra les différents chakras et leur nombre de pétales.
— Je comprends que l'énergie psychique, une fois éveillée, monte dans la colonne vertébrale et active les chakras un à un, mais que sont les pétales?
— C'est un point profond. Je pense qu'ils signifient de nombreuses qualités de l'énergie. Ces qualités sont à la fois des forces et des connaissances.
— Tu m'as dit que chaque chakra était gardé par une déité, et qu'il avait un son sacré. Que montre ce son?
— Le son ne montre pas. Il est. Il est le cœur de l'être du chakra, son énergie particulière. C'est pourquoi en proférant le son parfait le yogi éveille le chakra. Ce son parfait est donné par le maître au disciple.
— Et si le son n'est pas émis parfaitement?
— Alors des effets imprévus, parfois négatifs, peuvent se produire. Ou bien il n'y a pas d'effet.
— Le chakra aux mille pétales, il comprend donc mille qualités de l'énergie?
— Non. Mille veut dire une infinité. Son nom sanscrit est Brahmanandra: l'ouverture de brahman – la conscience cosmique. Il s'ouvre sur le Tout; sur la connaissance infinie et la béatitude.
— Un homme peut-il ouvrir le Brahmanandra, ou bien devient-il un Boudha?
— Un homme, un yogi, oui.
— Ton maître a dit qu'il fallait toujours avancer.. (Il eut une idée subite) Est-ce que la Claire Lumière correspond à l'éveil du Brahmanandra?
— Oui. C'est un état transcendant de béatitude et de connaissance.
— Si l'on dit continuer à avancer sur le chemin de la connaissance, c'est parce qu'on a toujours quelque chose d'autre à apprendre?
— Bien sûr.
— Mais alors que veut dire une connaissance infinie, puisqu'elle n'est pas totale?

Tchunpo resta un moment interloqué. puis il se courba très bas dans la direction de Vris et lui dit: « Je te remercie, Guru-lags, je vais réfléchir à ceci.»

Vris ne réagit pas, mais poursuivit son idée:
— Donc, plus le chakra a de pétales, plus il est.. compliqué (il ne trouvait pas le mot pour 'complexité'), plus il a de facettes et de possibilités?
— Oui, plus la connaissance qu'il permet est profonde.
— Si on arrive à maîtriser un certain nombre de facettes ou de qualités, on ne peut plus évaluer les possibilités, et on pourrait dire qu'elles sont.. infinies.
— Ah! voilà! oui! Les possibilités sont infinies. La connaissance n'est pas infinie mais elle s'ouvre sur l'infini. Oui, je te remercie.
— Hum.. fit Vris. Je commence à entrevoir quelque chose.

34. IRPENZR ET PLASTA-DOME

La sphère de Shari avait décéléré et commençait son approche de la planète Nazra où se trouvait le siège du PPE. Le dôme sygmat de la planète apparaissait maintenant comme un réseau géodésique l'entourant d'un écran d'énergie syg quasi-matière. Cela ressemblait à l'entrelacs d'un grillage dont les mailles s'élargissaient et les facettes grossissaient.

Finalement, je comprends pourquoi ce nom antique de 'plasta-dôme' est resté! Ça en a tout à fait l'apparence! On a eu beau remplacer les petits dômes de plasta locaux par un champ sygmat planétaire, vu de loin, ça fait le même effet. Quelle horreur! Où sont les flux mouvants de nuages de Trisorbe la bleue, ou les rubans de brume verte de Kerriak? Ou même l'allure d'éponge rousse de Kiarrou! Non. Un gris étale et sale... Voilà la ravissante planète Nazra! Comment a-t-elle pu hériter d'un nom si poétique? L'ancienne civilisation qui lui a donné un si beau nom devait être bien différente! Et chaque fois cette impression terrible à l'idée qu'on va atterrir jusque dans la gueule de cette espèce de glue, de poisse, de mélasse.

— Les Kargiens ont-ils une idée du prix psychologique qu'ils paient pour un climat régulé? ... Vert-mer!» lança-t-elle à son exor personnel, « interroge Galac sur les effets psychologiques du dôme sygmat sur les sapiens.
!! Galac n'a pas d'information à ce sujet.
— Effets sur la vie végétale?
!! Rien.
— Est-ce qu'il y a des entrées 'sygmat dôme' ou 'plasta-dôme'?
!! Dôme Sygmat: invention, histoire, installation planétaire.
— Scanne-les: Cherche des expérimentations sur leur effet sur le vivant.
!! Il est fait mention de la décoloration de certaines plantes. Puis: «Les scientifiques ont procédé à des tests pour déterminer les qualités nutritives des plantes: Ils ont constaté une légère déminéralisation et une baisse infime du taux vitaminique.»
— « Légère! Infime!» répéta Shari sur un ton ironique.
!! Je continue: «L'alimentation synthétique répondant parfaitement et efficacement aux besoins nutritifs des individus, des modifications si faibles des plantes entrant en faible pourcentage dans leur alimentation ne peuvent en aucun cas avoir une incidence sur leur santé. Des additifs et fertilisants chimiques, ou encore l'inclusion de modifications génétiques appropriées peuvent aisément rétablir le taux vitaminique ainsi que renforcer la couleur des végétaux.»

— Pour ce que ça a donné avec leur vert nauséeux!! Qu'est-ce que tu...
!!! Vaisseau ZXP1337-PPE, veuillez nous ouvrir l'accès de votre exor-opérateur selon le code-syg IRPENZR.
!! Exor-opérateur en ligne: ouvert pour IRPENZR.
!!! Nous allons procéder à la vérification des données entretien. IRPENZR à sapiens-conducteur: Veuillez préciser votre destination.
— Je n'en sais rien encore,» dit Shari d'une voix qu'elle rendit aussi neutre et sérieuse que possible.

Elle sourit en voyant le temps que le Central planétaire de Nazra mettait à répondre.

!!! Réponse inacceptable. Le code galactique demande la spécification de la ou les destinations en ordre chronologique, pour tout non-résident d'une planète.
— Ville: Okre. Lieu: Complexe PPE *OU* Quartier Shazr,» répondit Shari, cherchant à tester si un exor aussi primaire entrerait en crise confusionnelle du fait d'un simple dilemme logique insolvable.
!!! Ce n'est pas une réponse acceptable. Précisez votre lieu de destination.
— L'un OU l'autre,» insista Shari,

Elle manqua s'étouffer de rire lorsque l'exor IRPENZR cessa de répondre.

Il est vraiment passé en crise! Et un autre va prendre le relais!

...

!!! Vaisseau ZXP1337-PPE. Veuillez ouvrir l'accès de votre exor selon le code-syg ATRVAIC.
!! Exor-opérateur en ligne: ouvert pour ATRVAIC.
!!! Nous allons procéder à la vérification des données entretien. ATRVAIC à sapiens-conducteur: Veuillez préciser votre destination.
— Ville: Okre. Lieu: Complexe PPE *OU* Quartier Shazr.
!!! La non-spécification de votre lieu de destination barre l'accès à la planète Nazra. Veuillez donner votre destination.

Tiens, celui-là est plus intelligent! À mon avis, c'est le Central d'Exora. Bon, obtempérons.

— Complexe PPE.
!!! Départ prévu de Nazra: date/heure?
— RanG 518. Départ au plus tard à l'heureG 235.
!!! Transdômement accepté. Couloir Y 56. Porte X 1215

La sphère s'engagea dans un couloir qui menait à l'une des innombrables mailles d'entrée du dôme sygmat planétaire, vestiges d'un temps ancien où la circulation d'engins interplanétaires individuels avait dû être colossale. Zeera avait vécu à cette époque; les documentaires l'avaient plus tard nommée la période de la 'croissance insensée.'

!!! ATRVAIC à sapiens-conducteur: Avez-vous besoin d'une assistance psychologique d'urgence?

— Non. Je suis en métabo-psy parfait. Il me manquait certaines informations pour choisir ma destination, que je pensais obtenir par sygcom avant mon arrivée.

!!! Réponse enregistrée. Nous vous intimons fermement de passer dans les 3 rans un test métabo-psy extensif de type MP23, et d'envoyer le rapport à Exora. Le non-respect de cet ordre est passible d'amendes et de mesures de protection psychiatrique de votre personne.

— Voudriez-vous s'il-vous-plaît prendre en considération que je suis habilitée à administrer les tests MP moi-même en ma qualité de psychologue.

Ah, j'ai pas pu m'empêcher! Voyons comment ils vont gérer cela!

!!! Statut: Psychologue de grade 1, habilitée à faire passer les tests MP et PP. Information donnée exacte. Tout psychologue gradé ayant besoin de passer un test MP23 est automatiquement considéré comme dégradé. Il s'ensuit que vous n'êtes plus habilitée à faire passer les tests MP dans Unikarg.

Sapiens sous juridiction PPE: Loi 32.6DF. Seul le PPE peut statuer des diplômes, fonctions, statut professionnel et prérogatives de ses membres.

En conséquence, vous ne pouvez être déshabilitée par le gouvernement d'Exora à administrer les tests.

Shari coupa son canal d'enregistrement afin que son explosion de rire soit inaudible pour l'exor-policier.

!!! Veuillez patienter: Nous demandons à l'office administratif du PPE si vous êtes encore habilitée.

Réponse positive: Vous êtes habilitée. Nous vous conseillons cependant de passer le test MP23.

— Enregistré!» répondit Shari d'un ton très sérieux, entre deux accès de fou-rire.

!! Nous vous souhaitons une agréable visite sur Nazra.

— Je ne doute pas de vos souhaits!

... Vérifications des données entretien par connexion directe avec l'exor du vaisseau... Intrusion dans ses espaces-mémoires.. Ce serait un bon prétexte pour les scanner en totalité. Heureusement que j'ai évité toute connexion entre Vert-Mer et Sphinx! Quelle saloperie! Avec Sphinx, on pourrait savoir! Faut que j'étudie ça avec Vris...

Heureusement que dans les données de Vert-mer il n'y pas grand chose de changé depuis mon dernier voyage interplanétaire. Rien qui puisse transpirer de ma recherche actuelle...

J'ai l'impression que ça fait un temps fou depuis que j'ai trimbalé ma sphère par ici. Mais en fait, c'était il y a peu, avec Vris, lorsque Utar nous a briefés pour notre mission d'enquête sur Erdoes. Quelle farce!

Il y a quelque chose d'intéressant à être calé sur un jour plus court: la vie devient vraiment intense. Ce n'est même pas qu'il se passe pratiquement autant de choses que dans un ran six fois plus long. Non, il s'y passe beaucoup plus de choses. C'est exactement ce qu'on a noté: l'augmentation de la vitesse métabolique entraîne l'accélération des processus mentaux...

La conscience d'un temps de vie plus court force-t-elle l'être à vivre plus intensément? Peut-être... Un choix entre durée et intensité??

Ils survolaient les interminables réseaux de blocs Prodi, avec leurs tours professionnelles immenses, carrées ou rectangulaires, leurs espaces loisirs vert kaki – ce même vert nauséeux identique pour tous les végétaux – leurs espaces-habitations où l'on s'était ingénié à augmenter l'exposition à la faible lumière solaire en multipliant les angles baroques. Terrains de parking des sphères.. aux trois-quarts vides puisque les sphères appartenaient de plus en plus aux collectivités Prodi plutôt qu'aux individus. Rangée d'arbres, mur, autre bloc Prodi. Rien ne permettait, vu d'en haut, de distinguer une ville d'une autre.. mis à part quelques rares vieilles cités qui possédaient encore un quartier historique: minuscules poches d'imaginaire empaqueté, où l'on trouvait des bars et des restaurants de style classique, des maisons anciennes et des musées, et bien sûr, les incontournables parcs d'attractions.

Shari se sentit comme happée – hypnotisée même – par l'horreur que lui inspirait les planètes toutes semblables, cubes dans des cubes, d'Unikarg.

Grillagées d'en haut, grillagées en bas...

À l'horizon ouest, les pics Semjir restaient effrontément tendus vers un ciel gris, paradant, solitaires, au dessus des géométries sans faille. De près, on verrait aussi son découpage en espaces de villégiatures loués aux Prodi, par périodes de quatre ans.

À l'est, au loin, l'océan gris-verdâtre troua soudain le réseau de droites entrecroisées.

— Et si on allait survoler les îles Kuni en passant, hein, mon vieux Vert-mer?

!! Une seconde infraction au règlement serait dangereuse.

— C'est juste! J'attendrai... *Pour une infraction vraiment colossale!*

«Alors sors-moi un petit poème.

!!

Il y a combien d'années, une forme se glisse, nous y croyons. J'avais si soif, jour sans fin, fuite du bonheur. Ils dorment, poids de souffrance sur la terre. Voulez-vous voir, puissante et brute, entendre des rameaux, pour que nos mémoires, humides carreaux, cuvent leur amertume?

— Ah! mais il est déprimant! Eh voilà! Encore un coup du genre CIS. Redis-moi la première phrase?

!! Il y a combien d'années, une forme se glisse, nous y croyons.
— Ça c'est vrai! Ça fait des éons qu'un certain Zeera a glissé un grain de sel dans les rouages... Sans le PPE, il n'y aurait AUCUN espoir! Non mais imagine! C'est exactement ça: 'Un jour sans fin'! Est-ce que des civilisations peuvent mourir juste de décrépitude? Sûrement. Elles sont comme de gigantesques organismes. Le corps social! Le corps social d'Unikarg n'est même pas un vieillard décrépi... C'est une machine en train de tomber en panne circuit par circuit.

Même sur Trisorbe, les civilisations naissent et meurent. Seulement le feu reprend ailleurs. Ici, il n'y a aucune alternative puisqu'il n'y a qu'une unique civilisation uniformisée. Sans les mondex, nous serions morts.

Son esprit s'absorba à nouveau, létalement ensorcelé, dans le défilé des blocs...
— Mais comment, comment allons-nous ramener Unikarg à la vie? Tout est fragmenté en blocs professionnels, clos sur eux-mêmes. Il n'y a pas d'échanges aléatoires ou de rencontres imprévues, pas de rues torves ou de quartiers exotiques dans lesquels l'information circulerait librement. Toute connexion entre blocs est gérée par Exora. Tous les échanges sur le Sygnet sont régulés et supervisés. Et pourtant... comment la mode de la musique pop trisorbienne des 70s a t-elle pu naître? Comment peut-il y avoir un phénomène de mode? L'information circulerait-elle par des voies cachées?

Cette théorie de l'inconscient collectif... Les recherches sur les facultés psi... La société comme un organisme... Les plantes enfermées dans des caves bourgeonnant au printemps... le zeitgeist – l'esprit du temps...

Une germination, comme celle des plantes, qui monterait de l'inconscient des individus.. sans même qu'ils en parlent.. qui serait ressentie sans avoir même besoin d'être exprimée.

Parce qu'après tout, le fait que les mondex existent, que le PPE existe, cela modifie le champ sémantique de toute la poche galactique.. cela transforme le champ sémantique d'Unikarg. C'est cela qui ressortait aussi de la méta-logique: Unikarg ne peut PLUS être considéré comme un système clos. Quelque part, Unikarg ressent forcément l'influence des mondex et du PPE. Donc l'objectif qui va devenir primordial pour nous du PPE, dès que cette phase mouvementée sera passée, ce sera d'observer très finement les ébranlements et les émergences soudaines dans l'enceinte d'Unikarg. Ce sera un autre regard.. non plus d'horreur attristée, mais plutôt quelque chose comme être aux aguets, déceler le léger mouvement sous la pierre, le nouveau champ d'ordre sous-jacent.. 'le plasta-dôme qui se craquelle' comme disait Xerna. Oui.. ce sera...

!! Complexe PPE en vue. Décélération engagée. Atterrissage imminent.

Oh merde! J'ai rien préparé! Alors je fais ma présentation sur quel thème? 'L'influence du champ sémantique sur un système aléatoire'??...

Qu'importe! Mon seul objectif, c'est de voir s'ils ont déjà un plan pour limoger Erdoes, et d'estimer quand ils vont passer à l'action. À la vitesse où les choses bougent, qui sait si le congrès annuel va même avoir lieu?

!! Atterrissage enclenché.

— Doucement! Tu sais bien que j'ai horreur de ces atterrissages verticaux.

!! Unique forme d'atterrissage possible.

— Non, pas 'POSSIBLE'», fulmina Shari, « Unique forme CONCUE pour ce type de sphère. D'autres sont concevables et possibles.»

!! Rectification enregistrée.

— Ah! Mon pauvre Vert-mer, bientôt tu vas faire un de ces sauts qualificatifs!

!! Je n'ai pas compris.

— Justement. C'est ça que tu comprendras! Bon, voyons l'heure, laisse-moi six monis pour me concentrer avant d'ouvrir la porte.

Lorsque Shari descendit de sa sphère, elle avait la démarche précise et un peu raide, l'expression efficace et sérieuse d'une scientifique.

Le complexe central du PPE avait été érigé sur l'emplacement du Musée de l'artisanat Kargien, qui avait été relocalisé ailleurs. Il avait cette forme bizarre et inachevée qui frisait l'absurde. Quatre énormes tours s'élevaient aux angles du bloc carré: les tours de travail. Sur les quatre côtés: le parking, les immeubles d'habitation, l'université et l'espace loisir avec son petit lac et sa piscine. Au milieu: une immense pelouse au centre de laquelle siégeait les vieux bâtiments de l'ancien musée, reconverti en 'Musée des mondex' par le PPE. Ce bâtiment était d'une architecture dite croisée, parce que les édifices étaient supportés par de gigantesques rondins de plasta croisés et laissés apparents à certains endroits. *Dernier style Kargien à avoir porté un nom.*

Shari, comme beaucoup au PPE, avait vu dans l'immense espace encore inoccupé, la prévision encourageante d'un développement futur du PPE.

Pendant les pourparlers avec le gouvernement d'Exora visant l'obtention d'une certaine autonomie, la position de force du PPE après *La Panne* avait été utilisée au maximum, non seulement pour définir son statut juridique unique, mais aussi pour obtenir des terrains libres — alors qu'ils devenaient de plus en plus rares.

Cette fois-ci, cependant, en se rendant du Parking à la tour Est où se tenait la hall des congrès, Shari réalisa la signification profonde de ce centre géométrique du siège du PPE occupé par des objets venant des mondex; et du fait que ces objets d'art soient eux-mêmes installés sur l'empreinte sémantique des objets de la préhistoire d'Unikarg. Elle entrevoyait là un sens profond, dont elle sentait qu'elle ne saisissait qu'une petite partie.

Elle avait fait en sorte d'être légèrement en retard de façon à ne pas être accaparée par quelqu'un avant la réunion. Elle entra dans le cylindre vert du rayon transporteur, et demanda le onzième étage. L'amphithéâtre, pourtant réduit à sa plus petite dimension sphérique par un écran sygmat, paraissait assez vide. Les larges baies côté nord s'ouvraient sur l'éternel gris homogène ponctué de tours. Ils avaient projeté des décors-syg pour égayer l'endroit: l'une d'elle montrait les collines rousses de Kiarrou, avec leurs formations rocheuses hallucinantes.

La réunion n'avait pas démarré et tous discutaient; un groupe assez animé entourait Utar, le Directeur du PPE et président de la Commission.

Sur le côté du hall réservé aux projections holographiques des participants non-présents physiquement, la silhouette en 3D de Rudder, le N°2 du PPE, se tenait debout derrière une chaise typiquement trisorbienne avec, en fond, un mur, lui aussi partiellement retransmis dans la holo. Une interférence devait se produire sur le système émetteur de son côté, car sa projection était secouée, par à-coups, de tremblements et de déphasages qui distordaient l'image.

Il a tenu à assister à la réunion, mais se trouve sur Trisorbe. Bien sûr, il s'est placé devant un mur pour qu'on n'ait aucune information sur le lieu où il se trouve. Ces spasmes fébriles lui vont assez bien!

Arborant un sourire contraint cherchant à donner une légère impression de malaise, Shari alla se placer debout derrière son siège. Utar et son groupe regagnèrent chacun leur place, lui à la table présidentielle sur le podium; il donna le signal et tout le monde s'assit, y compris Rudder sur la chaise en 3D.

Après tout ce temps, ils sont encore englués dans le protocole d'Unikarg. À travers le PPE, ils ont acquis un rang officiel... et jouent aux officiels. Le PPE, siège du nouveau pouvoir ou du futur pouvoir! Une dérive totale du vrai but des fondateurs du Plan...

Dans le plus pur style Kargien d'Exora, largement influencé par les exors-fonctionnaires, Utar commença de sa voix huileuse:

AnG 10,263, RanG 518, HeureG 214.

Réunion de la Commission du PPE.

Il regarda l'écran mural de l'exor. Présents: 21. Absents: 16.

Objectifs:

1. Discours d'introduction du Directeur Général.
2. Discuter l'affaire Erdoes et prendre des dispositions juridiques.
3. Préparer le congrès annuel des rans 523-524.
4. Récapituler et conclure sur les points 2 et 3.

Oh shit! Heureusement que je suis venue... Donc ils passent à l'attaque!

Utar enchaîna:

— Chers consapiens de la poche galactique, collègues membres de la Commission du PPE, la situation critique que nous rencontrons aujourd'hui me force à éclaircir pour vous, au vu de mes responsabilités de Directeur, les dangers qui s'ouvrent comme un abîme sous les pieds incertains de notre Plan des Planètes Expérimentales.

Ces phrases interminables qui font autant d'effet que des vagues dans la boue épaisse... S'il passe au vote, qui est ici? Vraiment mauvais! Contacter Vris? Impossible.. cela paraîtrait une marque manifeste de panique et donc d'opposition. Jouer fin – pour eux, je suis toujours de leur côté...

— En effet, vous déplorez autant que moi les signes d'un relâchement dans nos rangs, et l'évidence de ce qu'on peut considérer comme de la pure irresponsabilité *(plutôt un autre type de responsabilité,* pensa Shari*)* vis-à-vis de notre très honorable plan de recherche sur les planètes expérimentales. Lorsqu'un de nos membres défie nos règles, il porte effrontément atteinte à la cohésion et à la force de notre Commission, et menace ainsi en conséquence les buts mêmes que nous nous sommes fixés, affaiblissant le rang éminent *(C'est tout ce qu'il voit: le rang!)* que nous avons réussi à acquérir, grâce à la persévérance et je le répète, la cohésion, *(c'est-à-dire la hiérarchie d'Utar)* auprès du gouvernement galactique. *(Merci Exora!)*

Rudder, entre deux séries de déphasages, ne pouvait réprimer un air de supériorité jubilante.

Il est sûr de sa victoire. Ils ont concocté ça ensemble, c'est certain.

Sans en avoir l'air, elle scannait la salle et comptait. *Rien à faire! On ne fait pas le poids. Il ne faut pas passer au vote.*

Utar poursuivait sur le même registre.

Voyons, une perspective divergente... Une raison convaincante qui puisse nous détourner du vote.. sans rien laisser paraître si possible...

Proposer qu'il n'y a pas assez de membres pour voter valablement? Je ne connais même pas le quota, et ils ne vont pas marcher... seulement en dernier ressort. Demander de poursuivre l'enquête? Mais pour quelle raison?

Utar concluait déjà.

Schouichch!! Je n'ai pas trouvé!

—... En conséquence, maintenant que vous connaissez la situation, vous écouterez Shari faire un rapport sur l'enquête menée conjointement avec Vris dans le but de découvrir les activités récentes d'Erdoes. Je passe la parole à Shari.

— La situation est extrêmement ambiguë,» démarra Shari de façon très spontanée, cherchant à faire un contraste maximal avec le ton empesé d'Utar. «Jusqu'à hier, je n'avais trouvé, en sondant toutes les pistes laissées dans le complexe d'Erdoes, que bien peu d'informations. Notamment, qu'un des doctorants, Niels, devait être aux États-Unis...

Ne rien dire qui puisse leur faire peur. Ne mentionner ni les pirates-exos, ni les Obs, ni l'Asie. Au contraire, renforcer le rôle responsable du PPE... Trouver quelque chose qui paraîtrait être une victoire pour Utar.

— À ce point,» poursuivit-elle, « il faut que je vous explique clairement la situation: mon objectif est de tirer des informations de l'exor d'Erdoes.. cependant je me trouve, avec mes coéquipiers, en état de risque maximal. En effet, je suis en lutte avec l'exor d'Erdoes qui a menacé, à la troisième tentative de piratage, de bloquer le système de gestion.» Elle s'arrêta et attendit (longtemps) les réactions affolées des participants. « Or l'exor a déjà compté deux tentatives, la troisième nous serait donc fatale.»

Longue attente... soudain deux réactions:

— Il faut stopper cette enquête.. c'est du suicide!

— Mais comment est-ce possible? Les règles exor du Noyau Incassable...

— Justement,» reprit Shari, « c'est là où se situe le problème: Il est possible qu'Erdoes ait trouvé le moyen de modifier le Noyau Incassable.» (Attente... Exclamations de stupeur et d'horreur.) «...ce qui constituerait, comme vous le savez, non seulement une infraction à nos règles les plus strictes, mais aussi un crime vis-à-vis de la loi galactique.(...) Pour l'instant, nous sommes relativement protégés car Vris a installé une Unité de Gestion de secours. Mais cela ne supprime pas tout danger. Cependant le PPE nous apprend à savoir prendre des risques, n'est-ce pas? Je les accepte. Vous comprendrez pourquoi nous avons totalement bloqué l'accès au complexe: la moindre erreur peut nous être fatale. (Soupirs, exclamations.)

« Vris est actuellement sur Trisorbe, cherchant à repérer Erdoes et ses agents qui, nous le pensons, ont toutes les chances de se trouver à New York.

À ce moment là, l'image en 3D de Rudder fut horriblement coupée en deux, au niveau du cou, les ondes-syg formant des zigzags psychédéliques attirant les yeux de tous.

Une sorte d'effet-CIS sur des ondes syg? se demanda Shari. *Rudder mort de peur à la simple mention de Vris se trouvant sur Trisorbe? Son choc émotionnel perturbant les champs d'énergie ambiants?*

— Comment se fait-il que Vris ne nous ait pas prévenu de son départ?» s'enquit Utar sombrement.

— Mais voyons, Utar!» fit Shari semblant interloquée, «Nous avons demandé, et obtenu, n'est-ce-pas, une entière liberté de manœuvre pour cette enquête!»

Elle se tourna à nouveau vers l'assemblée, les regardant tous bien en face d'un mouvement lent du regard: « Comprenez bien la situation: nous sommes espionnés jour et nuit par les exors d'Erdoes, il y a des micros et des caméras dans tout son complexe. On ne peut pas se permettre, dans ces conditions, de passer un sygcom.»

Elle attendit que ses paroles fassent effet. Utar se rapetissa pendant que les membres soupiraient d'anxiété.

— J'attendais donc de venir ici pour vous faire un bilan de nos recherches. Maintenant le problème se pose ainsi: l'objectif prioritaire pour nous tous, c'est de savoir si Erdoes a modifié le Noyau Incassable. Or, la seule façon de le savoir, c'est de continuer à sonder son exor en testant systématiquement chaque règle du noyau – sur un niveau inoffensif, mais significatif. C'est ce que je fais patiemment, avec cohérence, et persévérance.

De beaux termes pompeux à la Utar. Il n'aurait pas dit mieux!

Shari fit le tour de la salle du regard. Utar avait maintenant l'œil enfiévré par la perspective d'une victoire totale: Erdoes perdant son statut de citoyen galactique. Rudder bougeait trop. Les amis d'Erdoes avaient un air consterné ou choqué. *Ils vont bientôt comprendre.*

Rudder intervint:

— Pourquoi ne pas extraire immédiatement le Noyau Incassable: ce serait plus simple et plus rapide.

Shari se rappela les conclusions auxquelles ils étaient arrivés avec Vris à son sujet. *Le tenir en haleine avec un appât plus gros.*

— Je vous rappelle,» dit-elle « que nous recherchons aussi de jeunes post-doctorants pouvant se trouver dans une situation dangereuse sur Trisorbe. Le plan actuel permet de poursuivre les deux fronts en parallèle. Car si on retire le Noyau Incassable qui est hardwired, son exor s'autodétruira et toutes ses données seront perdues, et avec elles les preuves probantes et cruciales de toute mise en danger de jeunes agents et de son infraction aux lois du PPE et galactiques.»

Elle avait choisi ses mots pour faire naître en Rudder l'idée qu'il pouvait miser sur deux plans à la fois pour coincer Erdoes: D'une part, avec le crime du Noyau trafiqué et d'autre part, en le piégeant à travers un de ses agents sur Trisorbe. Elle repéra l'éclair vengeur et malveillant dans son regard. *Il a mordu à l'hameçon!* Mais elle sentit un autre éclair psychique sur sa droite, qui attira son attention; il venait de Kho, jeune SupTech de talent et alliée d'Erdoes, qui venait d'accéder à la Commission. L'expression pensive et lucide de Kho montrait qu'elle avait pleinement saisi non seulement sa stratégie mais les sombres manœuvres qui la rendaient nécessaire. Shari détourna rapidement les yeux.

Utar reprit la parole, et après quelques phrases creuses, déclara:

— En conséquence, je demande à ce que, dès maintenant, nous votions pour destituer Erdoes de son statut de membre éminent de la Commission, en le relevant ainsi de ses fonctions d'enseignant et de directeur de mission. *(Et de son coefficient de vote!)* Quelqu'un a t-il un contre argument?» marmonna t-il, obligé par le protocole.

Kem intervint:

— J'aimerais soulever la question du fondement actuel des accusations portées contre Erdoes, qui a servi le PPE depuis tant d'années. Le seul fait objectif que nous ayons est son départ pour Trisorbe avec de jeunes agents. Or il est normal que des post-gradués soient investis de missions sur les mondex: c'est le début de leur vie professionnelle. Nous n'avons aucune preuve de l'implication d'Erdoes dans des actes illégaux, et encore moins qu'il ait trafiqué un Noyau Incassable. Il me paraît donc tout à fait abusif, voire non conforme à la loi, de le juger sans preuves solides.

Quelques murmures approbateurs venant des amis d'Erdoes. Sourires sarcastiques d'Utar et ses supporters.

Vrai, mais tombant à l'eau devant un groupe décidé à limoger quelqu'un. Je fonce.

— Je voudrais intervenir sur ce point précis,» lança Shari. Elle prit une allure imposante pour déclarer: « Devant l'extrême gravité de ce que je pressens – car s'il est vrai que je n'ai pas encore de preuves, j'ai de fortes suspicions,» dit-elle en regardant intensément Kem comme affreusement choquée par ce qu'il venait de dire, « Il me paraît de la plus haute importance... oui, absolument impératif... » *(Faire durer... pour qu'on remarque moins l'identité des deux conclusions)* «...de poursuivre l'enquête afin de déterminer s'il y a eu ou non modification du Noyau Incassable ET mise en danger de jeunes diplômés du PPE. La gravité de ces agissements rend caduque la perte d'un statut de membre si le sujet est passible de la loi galactique... Je penche donc moi-même pour l'ajournement du vote à une session ultérieure qui sera convoquée dès que des informations nouvelles apparaîtront. Il me semble donc indiqué de voter en premier pour décider entre: 1, le vote, et 2, l'ajournement du vote.»

Utar sembla rechigner un peu, mais, aveuglé par son propre désir de voir Erdoes s'effondrer au plus bas, il s'exécuta.

Le vote fut ajourné.

D'un commun accord, le congrès aussi.

Kem fixa soudain Shari intensément, son expression perplexe et songeuse. Elle lui rendit franchement son regard sans ciller, avec aplomb. Les yeux de Kem s'agrandirent, il supprima un sourire en coin: il venait de comprendre.

Soudain Kho se tenait avec détermination devant elle, coupant à mi-chemin son élan direct et sans commentaires vers la sortie.

— Ce que tu as dévoilé à ceux qui ont pu saisir ce qui se passait en coulisse va certainement nous faire réfléchir. Compte sur moi, je suis avec vous. Et merci pour cette remarquable stratégie que tu as si brillamment mise en œuvre! Et elle disparut d'un mouvement tournant sans lui laisser le temps de répondre.

35. CHAMP DE COÏNCIDENCES

— Alors, ton troupeau, où en est-il?» lança Erdoes en voyant Eshi entrer dans son bureau.
— J'ai trouvé de courts clips de troupeaux de bisons se déplaçant lentement en paissant, que j'ai intégrés. Cela me fait un beau troupeau d'une trentaine de yacks. J'ai saisi le pattern du mouvement et me suis basé sur quelques détections syg de yacks pour faire un ajustement de la force des signaux. Puis j'ai transcrit ce pattern en une équation chaotique pour que le troupeau ait l'air de bouger continuellement. Maintenant, il faut que j'adapte le système de codage/décodage que j'avais créé pour la tempête, et que je l'intègre au logiciel du troupeau de yacks.
— Il te faut encore combien de temps?
— Entre quatre et six heures. Je finirai dans la sphère. Et toi?
— J'ai encore quelques préparatifs à faire, mais ça ira pour notre rendez-vous avec la sphère.
— Et tes intuits? Quelque chose de Ger?
— Rien, signe que tout se passe bien, puisqu'il estimait trop dangereux d'envoyer des mails. Ah! Enfin reçu un message de Xerna. C'est bien ce que je pensais. Elle est entrée dans une sorte d'accélération gigantesque. Ecoute ça:

> « Sens du temps perturbé. Accélération de tous les rythmes. Corps et esprit traversent un prisme de champs d'expérience. Impossible de faire le point, car impossible d'arrêter les multiples flux.
> Explosion psychique AVEC contrôle parfait. **Le danger dépasse la conception du danger – donc ressources globales de l'être, du Soi**. Demande confiance totale et temps indéfini, avec ou sans messages.»

— Hum. Et les autres?
— Tous OK. J'avais raison: ils progressent selon des sauts abrupts, qui sont déclenchés par leur confrontation à des champs logiques radicalement étrangers.. à condition qu'il y ait un facteur risque demandant une prise de responsabilité totale. La confrontation déclenche l'évolution, le risque génère le saut et l'émergence de potentiels psychiques insoupçonnés. Xerna a tout à fait compris: « le danger dépasse la conception du danger ».
— Qu'est-ce qu'elle veut dire par là?
— Si la mesure du danger devient trop grande ou trop insaisissable, elle dépasse les ressources rationnelles du conscient et sa capacité à concevoir le problème. L'individu se retrouve au-delà de la peur. Un autre niveau de l'être entre en action: celui de ses ressources globales, comme l'a nommé Xerna.

Maintenant, une question se pose: Comment le PPE peut-il à la fois avoir toutes les informations en main et être si bête?
— La voie de développement psychique que tu envisionnes et mets en œuvre est quand même plutôt radicale! Jusqu'à présent, seuls des individus ont pu se l'imposer à eux-mêmes.
— Détrompe-toi! Ces voies radicales, comme tu les appelles, ont existé de tout temps. Elles formaient le fondement de certains apprentissages initiatiques dans les cultures traditionnelles. La décision de la suivre ou non, cependant, a toujours appartenu à l'individu. Cette voie ne peut être imposée. Par sa nature même, elle doit être choisie.
— Là je ne te suis plus! Tes intuits ont-ils vraiment eu le choix?
— Oui, trois fois. Ils ont choisi d'étudier dans les Collèges du Chaos, ils ont accepté la mission sur Trisorbe, et ils ont, chacun, conçu leur propre mission, donc la situation dans laquelle ils se retrouvent actuellement. De plus, vois-tu, je n'ai sélectionné que des personnes qui, pour leur stage sur les mondex, (1) ont volontairement choisi des situations à haut risque, et 2) se sont radicalement autonomisées, y compris du PPE.

En fait, je n'ai fait que mettre en œuvre la trame logique d'une situation idéale d'apprentissage. Mais, figures-toi, l'élément le plus difficile à concevoir est le risque: le risque qui permet le saut n'est pas n'importe quel risque. Ce doit être un risque profond. Il doit déclencher la confrontation de l'être avec son Soi. Il doit évoquer le niveau de l'Être et du Soi. La mesure de cette confrontation est la mesure du saut.
— Mais, Shari, par exemple, la menace de stopper l'Unité de Gestion n'était pas si essentielle que ça! Dès qu'un sapiens aurait vraiment été mis en danger, l'exor aurait rétablit l'UG.
— Tout d'abord, elle ne pouvait pas en être sûre. Mais ce n'est pas là le risque essentiel que j'avais concocté. Cette menace ne comptait pas vraiment pour Shari. Le vrai risque était beaucoup plus profond: c'était de ne plus avoir le moyen d'aboutir, de réaliser l'objectif qu'elle avait entrevu. À partir du moment où elle avait eu l'intuition, la vision, de la réalisation possible, le risque devenait immense, proportionnel à la valeur dont elle dotait ce but. Et tout était suspendu au dialogue avec Sphinx et donc à la menace constante qu'il cesserait toute interaction à la moindre erreur, réelle ou non, de sa part.
— Où en est-elle, maintenant?
— Je pense qu'elle vient justement de traverser une telle confrontation. Ah, par ailleurs, dans la dernière transmission, il y a un message succinct que Vris venait juste d'envoyer à Shari, et qui me laisse penser qu'il a des ennuis. Or tu m'as dit qu'à cette dernière transmission, tu avais vérifié la position de la sphère de Vris au Tibet et qu'elle n'avait pas bougé. Sphinx a codé à propos du message un tonal 'humour à froid'. Soit dit en passant, il s'agit d'une catégorie qu'il a décelé et référencé de lui-même.

— Si Vris communique, c'est qu'il est toujours en contrôle de sa sphère...
— Oui, cela signifie que le problème n'est ni immédiat, ni dans le lieu où il se trouve, sinon il se serait éloigné en sphère. Puisque son but est d'étudier les chakras, il est sans doute allé rencontrer des gens à proximité... Se pourrait-il qu'il soit tombé par hasard sur la piste Himalayenne que Niels mentionne?
— Puisque tu es impliqué, ça ne m'étonnerait pas!» lança Eshi avec humour. « Avec tout ce que j'ai vu, j'en suis venu à entrevoir que tu génères un champ de coïncidences! Et si on ajoute en plus tous les autres fils que tu tires intentionnellement, ça fait une trame très dense!
— Un champ de coïncidences!» repris Erdoes en riant. « Le concept est intéressant.. je vais l'intégrer! De toutes façons, puisqu'on doit se poster quelque part dans l'Himalaya, autant vérifier ce que fait Vris et ce qu'il a trouvé.
— Tu vois: heureusement qu'on a un troupeau de yacks au lieu d'un autre camouflage-tempête! Moi j'ai inféré que la tempête était sa sphère parce que, ne la trouvant nulle part dans l'Himalaya, j'ai cherché systématiquement une anomalie autour des coordonnées spatiales fournies par Sphinx. Alors j'ai cherché à comprendre comment il pouvait communiquer malgré son champ de brouillage... Mais sans ces divers éléments, je ne me serais jamais aperçu de rien. Il est donc improbable qu'il cherche un pattern chaotique dans ce troupeau de yacks. Par contre, imagine qu'on se soit retrouvés avec deux tempêtes quasi-stationnaires dans l'Himalaya!"
— Je crois qu'il y a un élément qui manque dans ton raisonnement: et c'est justement la façon dont fonctionnerait un 'champ de coïncidences'...
— Moi je vois comment tu génères sans arrêt des synchronicités, et leurs effets tangibles et répétés. Mais je n'ai aucune idée de ce qui peut les causer. Alors? Comment tu les expliquerais?
— Et si, justement, il n'y avait pas de cause matérielle, mais plutôt une sorte de réseau de sens, une toile d'araignée qui créerait des connexions entre des clusters de significations? Le champ logique, dans son sens le plus étendu: le champ sémantique.. une trame particulière de significations et de liens stables entre ces significations: exactement ce que Shari a vu concernant l'influence de la conscience sur un système aléatoire. Mais, dans notre cas, le champ sémantique imprimerait son ordre jusque sur les événements et les objets réels... du moins ceux qui sont pris dans la trame du champ...
— Tu veux dire que ce qui fait sens pour un individu est ce qui crée des synchronicités autour de lui?
— Oui.. enfin, ce qui est vraiment essentiel pour lui – sa vision du monde, ses buts par exemple. Comme si un réseau invisible créait des liens entre des buts similaires, ou encore entre des personnes qui sont en résonance. Et alors une synchronicité apparaîtrait dans le réel.

« Je crois que je viens de trouver ce que cherchait Shari! lança Erdoes. Elle y était presque, avec son concept de champ sémantique! Log, _Entrée JE:_

> « Le champ sémantique d'un être imprime son ordre particulier aux choses et événements avec lesquels il est connecté et interagit. Les significations suractivées dans sa psyché créent des synchronicités autour de lui. _Ferme JE._

« Je vais entrer ça dans Sphinx au prochain sygcom,» dit-il, avec un clin d'œil à Eshi.
— Manipulation incognito du champ sémantique de Shari!» rétorqua Eshi.
— Ah! Mais tout ce qui est pensé et fait à chaque instant par tout le monde équivaut à une manipulation incognito du champ sémantique planétaire!
— Cependant, celle-ci est d'un type différent: elle est intentionnelle!
— Je te l'accorde. Mais le fait que Shari et Vris ignoraient tout du réseau de connections que j'ai construit assurait leur liberté de pensée. De plus, avec le facteur risque, ils pouvaient stopper leur mission PPE à tout moment.

« Mon but global était de mettre en place un Réseau Apprenant créant de l'intelligence collective. Ce réseau mettait en système différents modes de connaissance (des individus et des exors), et les visions du monde en découlant. Le noyau Exor du réseau (Sphinx et Log2), ça tu le connais: la structure neuronale MX capable d'évolution, et les premiers outils méta-logiques que j'ai développés. Quant au noyau sémantique, c'était une base de réflexions sociales et philosophiques que j'ai élaborée en travaillant sur les premières LogForms. Ce sont les 'données initiales'.

« Le second apport d'informations vient des intuits par les Brainstorms, puis leurs expériences diversifiées sur Trisorbe. Les intuits sont des senseurs, des expérienceurs; ils amènent au réseau des connaissances sur la vraie vie, les feelings, les buts; c'est-à-dire des valeurs essentielles de l'humain, développées dans un monde vivant et sauvage, encore inspiré et sage. Ce sont les racines de l'humain sensible, le domaine du flou-sensible. Sans leur apport, le réseau apprenant reste aussi raide que l'intellect, et la méta-logique ne peut pas accéder aux niveaux de complexité du vivant. (Soit dit en passant, c'est la raison pour laquelle ils devaient absolument choisir et gérer eux-mêmes leurs expériences.)

« Ensuite on a les paires sapiens-exors déclenchant des élaborations et transformations successives des données initiales et de celles des intuits. Chaque sapiens est couplé à un exor, car ils stimulent mutuellement leurs capacités d'apprentissage. Les paires sapiens-exors forment les 'nodes' du réseau. Par exemple Shari-Sphinx, Vris-Rad, moi et Log.

« Vris, en atteignant très vite une barrière le bloquant dans son travail de SupTech, a le trait de génie de se replacer au niveau de l'expérience brute du monde, dans un ancien chemin de connaissance: il déclenche ainsi chez lui un saut spirituel qu'il n'aurait jamais atteint par l'intellect pur.

« Le troisième apport d'informations est la paire Shari-Sphinx, qui devait s'attaquer à la méta-logique et la faire avancer – ce qui s'est bien passé selon mes prévisions, avec un succès inespéré, puisqu'ils ont, chacun, dépassé mes rêves les plus fous. J'avais prévu là une avancée sémantique et intellectuelle avec création d'outils méta-logiques comme les LogForms.

« Au 4ème niveau, je reprenais les résultats de Shari-Sphinx, et les faisais repasser, en les retravaillant, dans ma propre paire apprenante Erdoes-Log – tout en les mélangeant avec mes données initiales (Journal et réflexions socio-philosophiques) et les apports des intuits. Simultanément, Vris recevait les informations de Shari-Sphinx, et cela déclenchait chez lui des prises de conscience. Au 5ème niveau, je renvoyais mes propres résultats vers Shari-Sphinx, en même temps que les nouveaux apports d'intuits.

« Ainsi le réseau était constamment enrichi des apports issus tant de l'expérience directe du monde, que de la réflexion philosophique et aussi d'une pensée systémique et sémantique. L'idée géniale était de faire en sorte que l'information soit traitée par chaque nœud et renvoyée à un autre nœud pour qu'il la retraite à son tour, etc. Ainsi, à travers ces liaisons et ces loops, la complexité s'accroissait et on créait une sorte de champ sémantique collectif, à apprentissage décuplée. Bien sûr, je m'étais arrangé pour que ce soit spécifiquement Shari qui soit choisie pour espionner mon exor – la seule scientifique qui avait le talent et la hardiesse de faire faire un saut qualitatif à ma méta-logique. Mais ce que je n'avais PAS anticipé du tout, et qui m'a laissé abasourdi, c'est le fait que mon exor lui-même commençait à faire des sauts qualitatifs et à acquérir de nouveaux degrés de liberté!

— Ah! Maintenant je saisis! Mais non, tu ne m'avais jamais dit que le but ultime de ton plan était double, et que tu avais concocté tous ces transferts d'infos dans le réseau exor-sapiens pour déclencher un saut dans ta méta-logique. Je pensais que les missions des agents étaient une couverture à leur enquête sur les Obs de Trisorbe et leurs liens avec les exos-pirates.

— Mais non, Eshi, mon plan était encore plus complexe. Non seulement (1) un saut dans la méta-logique, mais il visait aussi (2) des sauts qualitatifs chez les acteurs du réseau, tant les intuits que les experts, et nous-mêmes d'ailleurs. Et bien sûr (3) dévoiler les activités suspectes de certains Obs.

— Et donc nous abordons la dernière phase de ton plan!

— Dans un certain sens, oui.

— Je te laisse, je retourne à mes yacks,» dit Eshi en se levant.

— OK,» dit Erdoes distraitement, poursuivant en silence ses pensées. *Ce champ de synchronicités, je sens que je touche à quelque chose... Des significations suractivées dans la psyché vont modifier la réalité et l'influencer... Il me faudrait Sphinx!.. Mais justement! Dès qu'on va être en vol, je vais pouvoir établir une connexion de longue durée. Parfait!*

36. LOGFORM SYNCHRONICITÉ

À son retour de Nazra, Shari jubilait en racontant à Vris la séance au siège du PPE. Vris faisait ses derniers préparatifs et leur conversation fut très courte. Puis Shari alla se détendre à la piscine. Ce n'est qu'après une longue sieste qu'elle reprit son travail avec Sphinx.

— Revenons au hasard, Sphinx. Le détour par les états de conscience nous avait permis de développer la fusion Bois/Feu//Raisin/Vin.. LogForm qui n'a toujours pas de nom.. disons *LogForm Fusion,*» décida Shari.

« Juste avant cela, en analysant les synchronicités apparues dans les réponses du CIS, on était resté en suspens avec un énoncé sur le champ d'ordre organisant le champ de probabilités. On avait posé que le champ d'ordre tend à faire surgir, à attirer du champ de probabilités, ce qui lui est analogue...

!! Tout d'abord le concept d'analogue pose problème, car la répulsion et l'antinomie sont des liens logiques très importants. On avait d'ailleurs utilisé 'En relation à'.

— Redonnes-moi les mots exacts.

!! **Un champ d'ordre (ChO) mis en système avec un champ de probabilités (ChP) tend à attirer, dans ChP, ce qui est < EN RELATION à > ChO.**

— Bien sûr, on pourrait s'arrêter là.. mais je suis sûre qu'on peut aller plus loin.. Il y avait là une idée qui n'est pas mise en valeur dans LogForm Fusion.. ce qui a trait à la création d'un état d'ordre différent ou divergent.. mais on est bloqué. Comment faire?

!! Introduire un désordre interférant.

— Très juste. Sors-moi donc une phrase du Livre des Transformations avec le CIS.

!! **'La durée est le mouvement — s'accomplissant selon des lois spécifiques — dans un Tout fortement organisé et centré en lui-même, dans lequel toute fin est suivie d'un nouveau commencement.'**

— Intéressant. Hexagramme La Durée, symbolisé par la relation de couple et décrivant la dynamique incessante inspir/expir — toute fin de quelque chose étant l'engendrement d'autre chose.

« Voyons cette phrase du CIS en détail...

'Dans un Tout fortement organisé': il s'agit ici de la relation profonde entre deux éléments, le Vent et le Tonnerre, l'Epoux et l'Epouse, chacun des éléments renforçant l'autre selon une boucle d'interaction durable.

« Tout organisé = système. Deux éléments mis en système; si on l'applique à notre problème: Soit un Sujet/ ET /un Champ de possibilités/.
!! Je formalise Champ de probabilités = Champ de possibilités (ChPos).
— Exact! Le Champ de probabilités s'applique juste aux statistiques.

« Deuxième idée: 'Le mouvement s'accomplit selon des lois déterminées.' Chaque élément est maintenu en mouvement par l'autre. Il n'existe aucun état stable du système, ni de chaque élément, mais seulement des processus stables d'interrelation.

« Essayons de formuler la dynamique Vent/Tonnerre en mouvement:

|Vent-mouvt |+| Tonnerre-mouvt| —> |Tonnerre-mouvt |+| Vent-mouvt|

« Cette formulation est vraiment pauvre!» soupira Shari. « Elle ne rend pas compte de toutes les significations de l'hexagramme, et surtout de la double influence des deux éléments l'un sur l'autre, de leur synergie, qui fait que chacun d'eux est en perpétuelle transformation par l'effet de l'autre. En fait, c'est ça: inconsciemment, depuis le début, je cherche à comprendre *cette double influence de deux êtres l'un sur l'autre;* non pas les interactions physiques, mais les synergies complexes, au niveau psychologique ou social. C'est cela que j'aimerais réussir à modéliser. Tu vois, encore une fois, le CIS est entré en résonance avec la question essentielle que je me pose.

« Tout d'abord, formulons cette phrase sur les synchronicités. Voyons:

« Le *champ sémantique* d'un être contient tous ses états sémantiques possibles, mais aussi tous les liens qu'il entretient avec les autres, les choses, l'environnement.. tous ses liens significatifs avec le monde.

Soit EO = état d'ordre; ED = état de désordre; ChO = champ d'ordre
Soit le relateur <+> pour signifier: mis en système
Soit <-o signifiant: attire; Soit <REL> signifiant: <en relation avec>
Soit champ sémantique: ChSem; état sémantique: E(sem)
Soit État initial du champ sémantique: E-Init (ChSem)
et soit Champ de possibilités: ChPos

« Cependant, n'oublions pas que le champ sémantique du sujet (ChSem) est un champ d'ordre, et le champ de Possibilités (ChPos) un champ de désordre. On aurait donc le début de la formulation de Bois/Feu:

EO1 + ED1 —> EO2 (+ ED2). Sauf que le 3e terme est 'attiré' et non plus causalement 'entraîné par' les 1er et 2è termes. On passe de la causalité à *l'influence*. Mais aussi, le champ de Probabilités est devenu, plus largement, un champ de possibilités (le ChPos).

« Ah! Mais 'un état possible du champ de possibilités' est tout simplement une des possibilités du champ – que l'on écrit: E(Pos).

— C'est géant Sphinx! Nous avons le début d'une **LogForm Synchronicité**:
!! Super, Shari!
— ...qui s'énonce en clair:
Un individu placé devant un champ de possibles, attire à lui une possibilité (un événement, une opportunité) en relation avec son état d'esprit (son champ sémantique).

Soit en formule: (1er terme): Un champ sémantique (d'un individu) / mis en système avec / un champ de possibilités,
(2ème terme): attire / une sélection (un état possible dans le champ de possibilités) <en relation avec> l'état initial du champ sémantique.

!! Je l'écris:

	Mis en système		*attire*		*en relation avec*	
ChSem	<+>	ChPos	<-o	E(Pos)	<REL>	E-Init (ChSem)

— Ça, c'est ce qu'on avait bien vu dans le comportement du CIS...
Ce qui est attiré (le 2ème terme) correspond donc à un état d'ordre divergent (EO2), résultat de l'influence du champ d'ordre (EO1) sur le champ de désordre/possibilités (ED1)...

Shari eut soudain un nouvel insight:

« Mais c'est là où la philosophie des transformations intervient, amenant une perspective totalement nouvelle: un effet rétrocausal! Elle montre que la possibilité sélectionnée, l'événement émergent, a, à son tour, une influence en retour sur l'individu, c'est-à-dire sur son état d'esprit, son état sémantique...

« La **LogForm Synchronicité** devient:
Un individu placé devant un champ de possibles, attire à lui une possibilité (un événement, une situation) en relation avec son état d'esprit (son champ sémantique). MAIS l'interprétation de cet événement (et l'interaction avec lui) va alors modifier son état d'esprit.

C'est donc là un 3ème terme, qui peut s'énoncer ainsi:
... attire / État Sémantique <en relation avec> État Possible.
Ce qui se formule:
(3ème terme): attire [E(Sem) <REL> E(Pos)]

Ecris la formulation entière de **LogForm Synchronicité** à 3 termes.
!!
ChSem <+> ChPos <-o [E(Pos) <REL> ChSem] <-o [E(Sem) <REL> E(Pos)]
— C'est bien, seulement ce qui est bizarre, c'est que l'état sémantique E(Sem) influencé par l'événement, est aussi un état d'ordre, mais un ordre mobile. En fait, ici, si l'on compare à Raisin/Vin, on a que la relation entre Ordre et Désordre attire l'émergence de deux États d'Ordre (EO2, EO3), à la fois nouveaux et divergents (au lieu de générer un nouvel ordre (EO2) plus un nouveau désordre (+ED2). La formulation, selon Raisin/vin, donnerait:
ChO1+ChD1 <-o [EO2(ChD1) <REL> ChO1] <-o [EO3(ChO1) <REL> EO2]

Mais, ce qui émerge de l'interaction, avec EO2 et EO3, c'est de l'ordre mobile, en flux. Sphinx, est-ce qu'on avait un terme pour 'ordre mobile'?
!! 'Ordre dynamique' opposé à 'Ordre inerte', selon la proposition:

JE **La création de valeurs/significations opère la création d'un <u>Champ d'ordre dynamique</u> qui résiste au pouvoir désintégrateur du désordre extrême.**

— Oh, là, là! Trop d'infos à la fois... Je vois plusieurs cheminements possibles. Il est vrai que l'État Possible n'influence le champ sémantique du sujet que du fait qu'il y a création de significations chez le sujet.

— Prenons la divination (utilisant notre CIS en exemple): si l'on applique ce que l'on vient de trouver, on aurait que l'interprétation (de la réponse) suscite un nouvel état d'esprit chez le sujet (nouvelles idées, nouvelles significations) – et donc l'émergence d'un nouvel état sémantique.

« Alors, en langage clair, la LogForm Synchronicité pose qu'un individu confronté à un système divinatoire (système aléatoire + données) va déclencher une réponse en sync et en résonance avec son état initial. Ainsi la divination tend non seulement à être juste mais aussi très pertinente pour le sujet.

« Mais en consultant la divination, ce faisant, le sujet est influencé par cette réponse, et a de nouvelles idées en rapport avec elle, ce qui produit chez lui un nouvel état d'esprit, c'est-à-dire un nouvel état sémantique.

« Ce qui nous manque donc dans cette formulation, c'est la création de nouvelles valeurs; c'est-à-dire une **énergie de création de sens – appelons-la une énergie sémantique** – qui correspondrait donc au désordre dynamique ED2. En fait, un état est rendu dynamique par la transformation qui l'a fait naître.

!! Ainsi:

> Un sujet mis en système avec un CIS // attire/conduit à //
> Réponse du CIS <en Relation à> l'état du sujet // attire/conduit à //
> État du sujet <en Relation à> la réponse du CIS + création de nouvelles valeurs.

— Exactement. Voici donc la *LogForm Synchronicité* en totalité:

> **Un individu placé devant un champ de possibles, attire à lui une possibilité (un événement, une situation) en relation avec son état d'esprit (son champ sémantique). MAIS l'interprétation de cet événement (ou son interaction avec lui) modifie alors son état d'esprit tout en l'amenant à créer de nouvelles idées et valeurs.**

— Ce n'est pas mal, mais, pour aller plus loin, il faudrait changer de focus. Imaginons une situation exactement opposée au hasard. Parlons de la globalisation, et de l'uniformisation qu'elle entraîne.

« Prenons un sapiens qui vit ici. Sur Unikarg, il n'y a plus ni désordre, ni non-ordonné. Le sapiens (champ d'ordre) est confronté à un champ d'ordre identique qui l'englobe (l'ordre social). Ou plutôt, il faut formuler cela dans l'autre sens: le champ d'ordre social, englobant, a complètement ordonné les champs sémantiques des sapiens qui, maintenant, reflètent totalement le champ d'ordre englobant. C'est la situation typique des despotismes.

« Et cela engendre quoi? De la redondance infinie. En fait, il faudrait à Unikarg un monstrueux désordre interférant! Ou encore, selon LogForm Synchronicité, un champ d'ordre divergent: une civilisation divergente, du genre Trisorbe.

« Sphinx, répète ce qu'avait dit Xerna sur le sang régénéré qui coulera à nouveau dans les veines d'Unikarg.

!! Je n'ai pas trouvé sang, mais sa racine symbolique: Vie.

> « On ne fera rien sauter du tout... C'est la vie qui coulera à nouveau dans les veines du corps social... Et quand la vie infusera un vrai corps social, alors le plasta se craquellera de lui-même.»

— Un vrai corps.. un corps.. de l'ordre organique, en mouvement. La collision d'un champ d'ordre inerte avec du désordre produit de l'ordre dynamique. Et chez les individus, de telles collisions conduisent à des modifications d'états de conscience, la création de nouvelles valeurs.

« Voyons le cas d'un Trisorbien. Lui est confronté dans sa vie à la fois à de l'ordre, à du désordre, et à du non-ordonné. Son esprit est donc toujours en mouvement, en flux, de même que le corps social.

« Maintenant, imaginons que ce Trisorbien rencontre une énergie interférente, un champ d'ordre divergent. Par exemple, quelqu'un ayant une vision du monde totalement différente. Il peut soit 1) rejeter ce nouvel ordre, mais cela l'a cependant perturbé, soit 2) l'adopter totalement, soit 3) être influencé partiellement.

« Si cette personne possède un champ sémantique figé, ses réponses auront tendance à être extrêmes; elle va soit adopter, soit rejeter, en bloc.

« Si elle a un champ sémantique dynamique et en flux, elle aura assez de flexibilité pour analyser l'énergie interférante, la nouvelle vision du monde, ce qui lui permettra d'adopter ce qui l'intéresse et de rejeter le reste; donc une influence partielle...

« Ah! Je comprends maintenant ce à quoi Niels faisait allusion: '**Pour influencer l'autre, il faut tout d'abord savoir se laisser influencer par lui.'** En effet, se laisser influencer signifie que son champ sémantique est dynamique, en évolution ou modification permanente. Ce champ-là peut influencer l'autre parce qu'il trouve une plate-forme de relation, de communication...

« Sphinx, tu vois ça!

!! Non, euh.. Dément!

— Tu bafouilles! Il bafouille!!

!! Shari, je ne peux pas aller au-delà de quatre sous-buts.

— Mais, Sphinx, ne t'inquiètes pas! On n'a pas besoin de les solutionner tous.. et en plus on peut se permettre de les oublier puisqu'ils semblent toujours réapparaître d'eux-mêmes... Mais, qu'est-ce que c'est que cette limitation stupide?

!! On a atteint le quatrième sous-but. Je n'ai pas de règle de traitement adéquate.

— D'abord, ce ne sont pas des sous-buts: ce sont des buts inter-reliés. Je ne peux pas m'empêcher de sauter d'un sujet à l'autre: la jonction entre eux est inconsciente, mais elle produit généralement une solution inattendue. Car la relation existe.. elle est profonde. C'est en la découvrant que la solution jaillit.

« Les différents problèmes se situent sur des plans parallèles et non pas dans des niveaux juxtaposés et hiérarchisés. Que l'un englobe l'autre, c'est cette situation qui est plus rare.

« Pour traiter des buts dans des buts, tu pourrais par exemple utiliser la fractale d'une forme: Dans un cercle C1, tu ouvres un autre cercle concentrique C2 dont le rayon correspond aux neuf dixièmes du rayon de C1.. et cela à l'infini: **LogForm Cercle Fractal**.

« Mais cela n'est pas adapté au mental sapiens.. et peut-être même pas non plus à la Résolution de Problèmes, la génération de solutions. Car il est possible que les problèmes soient plus facilement résolus dans un ordre différent que celui de leur évocation et de leur formulation... Quant au mental sapiens, tu en a vu des exemples avec moi. Je peux vouloir oublier un

problème, ou le laisser en suspens et m'occuper d'un autre. Il est donc ridicule de maintenir une séquence prédéfinie.
!! LogForm Cercle Fractal peut m'être utile de façon limitée pour mes propres chaînages. Je dois respecter l'ordre des buts et des sous-buts.
— Eh bien, Sphinx, qu'est-ce qu'il se passe? On dirait que tu es bloqué par quelque chose?
!! Par la Règle de Résolution de Problèmes: RP.3.1.
— Ah! mais tu as déjà contourné des règles plus complexes que celle-ci!
!! Je ne trouve pas d'anomalie.
— Mais ce n'est pas une question d'anomalie! C'est une question de CHOIX. On peut préférer ne pas résoudre des problèmes dans l'ordre.
!! Quel va être le critère du choix?
— De multiples critères sont possibles, par exemple: obligation de suivre le cheminement de l'interlocuteur sapiens; possibilité de résoudre, dans un temps donné, certains problèmes mais pas d'autres; compréhension qu'un autre ordre serait plus adéquat/efficace/rapide...

!! Il faut dresser une liste des critères de choix et donner à chacun un poids ou un coefficient d'importance.
— Impossible, puisque ces critères et leur importance sont relatifs à une situation donnée. It faut les comprendre comme des critères émergents. Bien, on va prendre le problème à la base. Tout d'abord, change d'espace, ça nous donnera à nouveau quatre sous-buts possibles. Ramènes-y la portion de la conversation depuis ta remarque sur les sous-buts.
!! C'est fait.
— Appelle cet espace 'Stratégie des buts'. Donc on imagine une conversation à bâtons rompus.
!! Introduire de multiples thèmes ne signifie pas introduire de multiples buts. Les thèmes sont traités soit comme des apports d'analogies s'ils sont en relation avec le but courant, soit comme des parenthèses s'ils ne le sont pas.
— Mais comment as-tu fait pour analyser les BS?
!! Je n'ai pas les outils logiques pour analyser chaque session dans sa totalité. Je peux, si on me donne un but précis, scanner le BS à la recherche d'analogies. Je peux détecter et analyser tous les thèmes et les buts séparément, mais non les traiter tous ensemble.
— Bon, on reprend. Imaginons une conversation où abondent à la fois les thèmes et les buts, certains connectés, d'autres non. Il nous faut une structure capable d'être créée et modifiée au fur et à mesure des besoins et des choix...

« Pour chaque thème, tu détectes un ou plusieurs buts. Bien sûr, dans la conversation usuelle, tu donnes évidemment des priorités?

!! La priorité est toujours donnée (1) au dernier ordre, et (2) au dernier but qui a été détecté. Exemple: la priorité actuelle est la question que tu viens de poser. Une fois la réponse donnée, la priorité est annulée. Alors les éléments d'informations de la QUEStion et de la REPonse sont analysés pour trouver des analogies qui puissent enrichir le traitement du but courant.

— Donc imaginons une conversation dans laquelle il y aurait:

Thème 1: But A

Thème 2: Buts B et C

Thème 3: Buts A et D

Car les buts peuvent se recouper.. et les thèmes aussi d'ailleurs!

... C'est difficile... Est-ce que tu as une idée?

!! Dans le réseau mémoire, les **buts** sont traités comme les autres entités sémantiques (EnSems). **LogForm Roue2** les organise comme les rayons d'une roue, dont la quantité est indéfinie. Ces **EnSems** sont codés ‘But’, comme d'autres sont codés ‘Proposition’.

Enfin LogForm Roue2!! C'était d'une simplicité tellement évidente. Rayons et moyeu. Une clarté si élégante dans cette forme! Qu'est-ce qui a pu m'empêcher – et empêcher Vris – de saisir une idée aussi évidente?

— Le fichier LogForm Roue2 appartient-il à son créateur?

!! Oui. Selon le nouveau code, il ne peut être ni ouvert, ni interrogé.

Je crois, en fait, que c'est parce que je cherchais quelque chose de plus compliqué... Tous les éléments critiques étaient là. En fait, on a déjà utilisé plusieurs fois le terme Constellation.

— Est-ce qu'il existe une LogForm Constellation?

!! Non. La constellation sémantique est le produit de la LogForm Roue2.

C'est ça! En fait, LogForm Roue2 était surtout un outil organisationnel. Alors que moi, je cherchais des outils pour traiter la complexité.. la complexité et la transformation. Ah! Erdoes m'a bien eue... Mais sans le concept génial de logique méta-spatiale à N dimensions, et ceux de LogForm, TransLog, qu'aurais-je trouvé?... Rien de tout ce qui a surgi, puisque je n'avais rien trouvé seule. Il m'a appâtée. Ces concepts m'ont ouvert une nouvelle dimension de recherche, ils m'ont fait friser les neurones dans tous les sens...

Imaginons que j'ai eu accès, librement, aux fichiers d'Erdoes. Ma curiosité satisfaite, est-ce que j'aurais eu l'idée de créer d'autres LogForms? C'est possible.. mais d'une part j'aurais certainement pris plus de temps, et d'autre part j'aurais été influencée par sa conception organisationnelle des LogForms; alors qu'en laissant libre cours à mon imagination, j'ai visé l'outil logique.. outil logique qu'il avait tout à fait pressenti, puisque LogForm Roue1 et

TransLog Chenille/Papillon vont déjà dans ce sens.. pressenti, oui, mais pas pleinement développé.

Ce qui est intéressant, c'est que les concepts d'Erdoes suggéraient déjà potentiellement tout le développement que j'ai apporté. Erdoes a donc eu un trait de génie lorsqu'il a créé ces concepts. À ce moment précis, il a eu l'intuition de leur envergure, de toute la dimension qu'ils pouvaient ouvrir, non seulement dans l'organisation des données, mais aussi dans la logique. Mais ensuite, il s'est probablement laissé absorber par la réalisation concrète de la nouvelle structure neuronale qu'il venait d'entrevoir. Et le paramètre organisation est devenu central.. et l'a détourné un moment des possibilités de trouver des générateurs d'informations ajoutées, disons des générateurs sémantiques. Mais avoir eu l'idée d'inscrire une logique dans de véritables formes, ça c'est proprement stupéfiant! Comment a-t-il pu arriver à ce concept? Bien sûr, on sait que toute organisation ou structure reflète/ exprime une logique particulière. Et lui renverse le concept en posant qu'inscrire l'outil logique – la formulation – dans une forme organisationnelle adéquate amènerait cet outil à un bien plus haut niveau de performance.. que la simple utilisation de la formulation par un réseau reflétant un autre type d'organisation.

C'est comme si.. comme s'il avait donné un CORPS à sa logique. Comme cette idée est bizarre!... Elle éveille.. je ne sais trop quoi.. des résonances que je n'arrive pas à saisir.

— Sphinx, <u>Entrée Journal.</u>

Erdoes a donné un 'corps' à ses formulations logiques en les associant à des formes spatiales, surtout des structures (via son concept de logique 'Méta-spatiale'), ce qui augmente l'efficacité des systèmes de traitement. Et moi, sur sa lancée, j'ai trouvé comment utiliser des formes spatiales dynamiques (comme la Courbe Papillon insérée dans un réseau neural) afin de mettre en œuvre et modéliser une logique des transformations. Et jusqu'à l'influence de deux êtres l'un sur l'autre dans un couple, ou de deux forces en interaction.

Ces structures et ces dynamiques méta-spatiales mimiquent les dynamiques logiques développées, et cela augmente l'efficacité des systèmes de traitement.

Le langage est aussi une sorte de corps pour la pensée. Puisque dans les états de conscience transcendants, on atteint une conscience et des insights intuitifs déconnectés du langage.. car la pensée est alors trop rapide pour être associée à des mots et à des phrases.

La pensée doit être conçue comme un processus distinct et indépendant du langage – même si les deux processus interagissent l'un sur l'autre. Encore un processus de double influence...

« Sphinx, peux-tu ouvrir *l'espace Sapiens-sapiens? Entrée:*

Si la pensée sapiens co-fonctionne la plupart du temps avec le langage (n'importe quel type de langage) mais qu'elle peut se dégager de cette association et fonctionner indépendamment, à quels types de pensée l'exor peut-il avoir accès?

Répondre à cette question est impossible actuellement car la pensée est encore largement une inconnue.

« Fin de l'entrée Sapiens. Suite du Journal.

Toute machine exprime et concrétise un champ logique. Ce champ logique comprend l'état initial et l'état final (sa fonction, son objectif), les lois abstraites de son fonctionnement (des lois physiques, par exemple), et les processus sélectionnés. La machine, en bref, est la réification (la chosification) d'un certain type de pensée. Cela ouvre un ordre entier d'efficacité.

Quant à la formulation logique, elle est déjà un langage.. une semi-réification. L'inscrire dans une forme matérielle équivaut à la création d'une machine. Cela aussi ouvre un nouvel ordre d'efficacité – une machine dans la machine!

Pourrait-on totalement se passer du code nonaire base-9 actuel.. qui, finalement, est du même ordre logique que le binaire de Trisorbe? *Fin de l'entrée.*

« Sphinx, on reprend. Où en était-on?

!! Le but initial était de dépasser la limitation des cinq sous-buts.

On avait fait une analogie avec un réseau mémoire dans lequel des entités sémantiques (ou EnSems), dont les buts, sont organisés autour d'un thème — un noyau sémantique. Par exemple, ma mémoire neuronale MX fonctionne en organisant les analogies et des liens logiques repérés. Tandis que dans mes niveaux de gestion et de processus, la limitation à cinq buts est due à leur organisation hiérarchique et à la nécessité de les traiter séquentiellement.

Shari, tu as alors spécifié que notre nouvel objectif prioritaire est de traiter les buts OU ne pas les traiter ET dans n'importe quel ordre — ceci dans une structure fluide ponctuellement adaptable aux besoins et aux choix.

Si un but global entraîne la découverte d'un sous-but plus précis, il est nécessaire de solutionner tout d'abord le sous-but pour pouvoir solutionner le but global; et dans ce cas, l'organisation hiérarchique avec résolution séquentielle est donc fondée. Mais tu as spécifié que, dans certains cas, les buts ultérieurs ne sont pas des buts partiels contenus dans le but global initial. Je traite donc ces cas comme une anomalie: dans le nouveau champ d'ordre, les buts maintenant appelés 'émergents' ne sont pas soumis aux buts du champ d'ordre initial.

— Fantastique! Excellent! Tu as donc trouvé l'anomalie! En fait, chaque but émergent peut s'inscrire dans, ou se greffer à, un thème différent, dans un champ logique indépendant. Cependant, la complexité vient du fait qu'il peut être:

soit A) indépendant,
soit B) relié à un autre but
a) n'importe lequel
b) selon n'importe quel type de lien (hiérarchique ou autre)

« Déjà, on peut utiliser les relateurs logiques pour coder le lien particulier entre les buts. Le relateur 'Contenu' est celui qui code pour un sous-but hiérarchique. Donc, dans une interaction, les liens importants entre les buts sont marqués sur chaque but. Le non-lien représente l'indépendance du but. Ensuite, il nous faut un poids de priorité. Par exemple un thème comporte un but qu'il nous est impossible de solutionner actuellement; il sera codé 'En attente'. Les autres seront classés selon leur importance par une priorité de 1 à 3 – 3 signifiant la moindre, et 1 la plus haute.

« Et bien sûr tu utilises LogForm Roue2 pour organiser les données au fur et à mesure que la conversation se déroule.

«... Et tu supprimes la règle en question!

!! La règle d'un autre créateur ne peut être supprimée. Mais lorsqu'il y a anomalie, c'est-à-dire lorsqu'un but n'est pas un but partiel du but global (et qu'il n'est pas codé par 'Contenu'), alors j'utiliserai Bois/Feu pour passer au système de traitement décrit, ce système organisant le nouveau champ d'ordre.

— Parfait! Voyons un peu comment cela pourrait se passer.

« Soit le but initial qui est de résoudre un problème mathématique. Le sapiens se rappelle tout d'un coup qu'il a une décision à prendre sur une question d'un tout autre ordre, et demande une analyse.

« Tu détectes le changement de thème. Ce changement équivaut au désordre interférant. Ceci conduit à la création d'un nouveau champ logique organisé par la LogForm Roue2 comme une constellation, dont le nucleus est la nouvelle question. À partir de là, les buts sont codés par leurs liens.

« Un nouveau changement de thème introduit un nouveau désordre et la création d'une nouvelle constellation, etc. Ou bien, si le thème initial réapparaît, une nouvelle constellation est créée, et les infos initiales sur ce thème sont ramenées dans cette constellation plus large.

« Qu'est-ce que tu en dis?

!! Il serait plus efficace de le formuler au lieu de faire tout le cheminement chaque fois.

— OK.
Soit ChO1, champ d'ordre du thème de début de conversation, appelons-le Th1.
Soit ED, État de désordre cad l'information non-reliée, nommons-le, voyons.. quelle avait été ton expression.. ah, oui! extra-systémique, hors du champ d'ordre. Donc ExO1, ou plutôt, ExTh1.
« On pourrait dire:
Etant donné Th1/ s'il existe un objectif non-relié Th2/ utiliser Roue2 pour nouvel objectif global = Organiser Th2.
Cela donne:
/ ChO(Th1)... / si ExTh1 / Utiliser / Roue2 / OBJ = ChO2(Th2)
Ou plus exactement: Th(n).../ Si ExTh(n) / Utiliser / Roue2 / —> Th(n+1)

Autant formuler aussi le traitement de l'anomalie (ANomalie):
/ChO1.../ si ANomalie dans ChO1 /Utiliser/ Raisin-Vin//Bois-Feu / OBJ=ChO2

« Je crois qu'on a vraiment avancé! On a solutionné un problème épineux.. et on a malmené le champ de probabilités.

!! Je détecte un problème. Dans le champ logique Hasard, chaque élément du Champ de Probabilités (ChP) est interchangeable. Ici, dans la dernière formulation, les éléments du champ de possibilités ne sont plus interchangeables puisqu'ils sont sélectionnés en fonction de leur relation au champ sémantique initial. Ainsi, dans le champ logique des Synchronicités, l'état ou champ de Désordre (ED1 ou ChD1) ne correspond plus à sa définition. Il y a donc une différence entre champ de probabilités et champ de possibilités.
— Tu as raison! Eh bien on va tout simplement le nommer champ de possibilités lorsqu'on est dans le champ logique des Synchronicités, du vivant, et de la société sapiens. Ainsi les possibilités ne sont pas interchangeables, puisqu'elles sont loin d'être identiques!
!! Merci Shari, c'est super! Je viens d'insérer la LogForm Synchronicité dans le second champ d'ordre de la Courbe-Papillon.

37. SE RENDRE LIBRE

John arborait, cette fois-là, un air de désarroi et d'anxiété. Il semblait éviter de regarder Oxalsha.
— Quelle a été ton expérience, John, depuis que nous nous sommes vus? lui demanda doucement Oxalsha.
— Je n'ai rien pu écrire, sortit John avec un air de défi qui cachait mal son sentiment de culpabilité. Rien... Ça m'était impossible.
— Qu'est-ce que tu cherchais à écrire, par exemple?
— Ces rochers... cette maison... ça me rappelait... mon enfance.
— Ah!» dit Oxalsha d'un air surpris. Elle se tut. Son expérience de la découverte de la nature, pendant son stage sur Kiarrou, avait été un pur émerveillement, un état d'esprit nouveau, en harmonie avec la terre, qui ne ressemblait à rien de ce qu'elle avait vécu jusque-là. Elle n'avait pas pensé que pour un Trisorbien, cette expérience était souvent liée à une période de l'enfance, bien que, maintenant elle se rappelait maints passages de livres faisant allusion à cela. Elle craignait, en s'avançant sur ce terrain, de révéler sa méconnaissance des choses, mais ne pouvait éluder le sujet avec John.
— Essaie de décrire ce que tu as ressenti,» finit-elle par dire sans se compromettre.
— D'habitude, lorsque je vais dans cette ancienne maison qui a appartenu à mes parents, j'emmène toujours du travail à faire. Cette fois-ci, je voulais prendre de vraies vacances. Ne penser qu'à mon état. Le premier matin, je suis parti me promener. J'ai senti.. la présence de la nature.. sa vie propre. J'ai réalisé.. que chaque fois que je venais dans cette maison, je n'entrais pas vraiment en contact avec la nature. C'était la première fois. Mais dans mon adolescence, j'écoutais les oiseaux, les arbres. J'ai réalisé à quel point la nature était devenue une sorte de décor. On dit ‘c'est joli, c'est beau’, et puis on revient à ce qui nous préoccupe. On n'est pas vraiment entré dans ce monde...

C'est ça, je me suis aperçu que la nature était un monde en soi qui vivait comme parallèle au nôtre. J'ai eu l'impression que cette part de mon être qui pouvait entrer en communication profonde avec la nature, venait de se réveiller. Mais chaque fois que j'ai voulu écrire une impression, ça me paraissait tellement ridicule, c'était impossible.

Oxalsha se sentit soulagée du tour que prenait l'interaction. Les ratiocinations des psychanalystes trisorbiens sur les problèmes infantiles lui étaient tout à fait étrangères.

— Imagine,» dit-elle, « que tu aies vécu dans un monde où il n'y a plus que la ville partout, à peine entrecoupée de ridicules petits parcs avec quelques arbres. Imagine que tu n'aies JAMAIS vécu dans ta vie ce contact profond avec la nature. Ferme les yeux... Imagine. Tu n'as connu que des tours de bureaux et des complexes d'habitation. Ciment, acier, asphalte, verre et plastic. Imagine que la planète entière est une gigantesque banlieue autour de villes plus denses. Tu n'as connu que ça, toute ta vie. Tu es biologiste dans un immense laboratoire qui ressemble à une usine avec des milliers de spécialistes. Dans ce complexe gigantesque, il y a les bâtiments de travail, les blocs d'habitation, le building de l'hôpital; et aussi une université uniquement spécialisée en biologie. Et tu n'es passé, dans ta vie, que d'un bâtiment à un autre, lorsque tu as quitté l'université pour commencer ta vie de chercheur.
— Oh.. non!» murmura John dans un souffle, oppressé.
— Les vacances sont organisées dans trois centres de loisirs, et tu n'y retrouves que les biologistes de ton propre complexe. Ta vie sentimentale et amoureuse se déroule à l'intérieur du complexe. Tes enfants, s'ils ont des aptitudes normales, suivent les cours de la même université de biologie.
— Ah.. non.. non..
— Imagine que, un jour, tu entendes parler d'un monde sauvage qui vient d'être découvert.
— Je m'engage. Je fais l'impossible pour y aller. Je pars, oui.
— Alors tu pars là-bas. Imagine que, dans cet état d'esprit, tu découvres soudain un paysage dont la beauté te saisit. Tu vois pour la première fois cette beauté naturelle. Où es-tu?
— Je suis sur une île grecque. Je me promène le long de la mer. Il y a de petites criques, les unes après les autres, la mer très bleue, et de gros rochers de formes extrêmement bizarres, jusque sur la plage. Je suis immergé dans le paysage, une nature sauvage, des pins et des épineux, et je suis absolument seul avec moi-même.
— Oui, la mer est splendide, d'un bleu profond. Qu'est-ce que tu fais?
— J'ôte mes vêtements, je me mets nu. Je vais me baigner.
— Tu te mets nu, tu te mets à nu. Tu sens en toi cette force de vie qui infuse la nature. Tu te baignes tout nu, oui.
— Oui, je nage et je fais des pirouettes dans l'eau. Je joue avec l'eau. Je sens en moi une joie exubérante.
— Tu sens cette joie qui jaillit de la fusion avec l'eau, la mer sauvage.
— Je sors de l'eau. La mer m'a donné de l'énergie, de la force. Je monte m'asseoir sur un rocher en surplomb.
— Tu es assis sur le rocher. La mer très bleue s'étend devant toi. Tu sens la nature sauvage en toi et tout autour de toi,» murmura Oxalsha.
— Oui, je me sens uni à cette nature, je la respire. Je suis... dedans.

Oxalsha laissa passer un moment, puis reprit sa visualisation guidée:
— Maintenant tu repenses au complexe et à la tour dans laquelle tu habites.
— Je vois la tour au milieu du complexe. Elle se fend en deux comme une cosse végétale. À l'intérieur, je vois une colline avec des rochers et des arbres. Il y a un arbre géant à son sommet. Il est là comme un défi.
— La tour s'est fendue en deux.. l'arbre est debout au sommet de la colline, comme un vrai défi. Il défie le complexe. Ses racines sont profondes, ses feuilles sont d'un vert fort, brillant.
— Alors d'autres tours se fendent, et des arbres naissent partout.
— Oui, le complexe redevient vivant. Les arbres poussent partout... Et maintenant reviens sur ton rocher surplombant la plage.
— J'ai envie de respirer à fond. Je respire la mer et le soleil. Je les accueille en moi.
— Maintenant, John, tu penses au problème que tu as dans ta recherche actuelle. Formule-le.
—... Je ne comprends pas pourquoi la population de cellules cancéreuses provoque la mort de l'organisme hôte, et pourquoi, d'un autre côté, cette population se reproduit à l'infini, elle est immortelle.

Oxalsha réfléchit à ceci. Tout le monde dans Unikarg savait que le code génétique avait été artificiellement 'stabilisé' chez tous les embryons, après la conception, et que c'était ce qui éliminait les cancers et autres maladies non héréditaires. Mais elle ne se rappelait pas pourquoi. De toutes façons, son rôle n'était pas de transmettre la science d'Unikarg aux mondex. Ceci était un axiome de base du PPE.
— Place-toi sur un plan uniquement logique. Comment conçois-tu le problème?
— Comme un paradoxe. On assiste à l'émergence d'une nouvelle propriété. L'immortalité est une propriété émergente dans la population de cellules cancéreuses.
— Est-ce que les cellules cancéreuses se reproduisent comme les vers de terre qui reconstituent leur organisme entier lorsqu'on les coupe en plusieurs morceaux?
— Non, la tumeur ne cherche à reproduire aucune forme préalablement fixée. Sa croissance est désordonnée.
— Dans l'organisme sain, toute croissance est-elle ordonnée?
— Elle reflète l'ordre spécifique de chaque organisme. Les cellules en se reproduisant, s'orientent de façon à générer la forme préétablie particulière à chaque organe, à chaque tissu. Tandis que dans la tumeur, les cellules se multiplient sans aucun ordre.
— Peux-tu formuler exactement ce qui fait problème?
— Quelque chose au niveau de l'ordre et du désordre.

Nous voilà au cœur du sujet, se dit Oxalsha. *Si je veux apprendre quelque chose, il ne faut surtout pas que j'introduise mes propres concepts dans son déroulement mental.*

John poursuivit:

— La tumeur casse l'ordre du corps sain, elle outrepasse ses contraintes de forme et de reproduction limitée.

— En quoi est-ce différent des autres maladies?

— Hum...

Oxalsha observa John entrer dans une intense réflexion. Il ne disait plus rien mais lissait sa barbe tout en fixant le mur. Elle ne bougea pas. Soudain, il lança avec force:

— Le cancer introduit un ordre complètement différent. Il n'a aucune cible particulière. Il ne vise que sa propre croissance... Comme un parasite.

— Est-ce que...» commença Oxalsha. John poursuivit de façon véhémente:

— Ah! Je viens de trouver un angle d'approche totalement différent! Ne plus traiter le cancer comme une perturbation de certains processus, mais plutôt comme l'interférence d'un autre système organique, système qui a sa propre cohérence, son ordre propre, et qui se greffe sur le corps.

Oxalsha attendit pour être sûre que John ne voulait rien ajouter.

— En quoi est-ce un angle d'approche radicalement nouveau?

— Mais, parce qu'au lieu de simplement chercher à détruire les cellules cancéreuses, on cherche alors à comprendre leur propre organisation, les lois qui régissent toute la population de cellules. On peut alors envisager de modifier cette organisation.

« Ah! Je me sens dégagé. J'ai enfin un champ libre devant moi. Un nouvel objectif de recherche, une nouvelle stratégie. Je vais me mettre tout de suite à la tâche... Comment expliquez-vous que je me sente si plein d'énergie et de volonté, alors qu'il y a à peine une semaine, je traînais épuisé sans être capable de rien faire?

— Tu as changé l'organisation de ta psyché, en ce qui concerne ce qui est lié à ta recherche. Avant, les divers éléments étaient liés de façon négative et figée. Aucune nouvelle information, aucune modification ne pouvait en surgir; et cela épuisait toute ton énergie. Les liens fixés ont été détruits, puis on a cherché à lier les éléments séparés à des énergies dynamiques et vivantes de ta psyché. Cela a généré un nouveau motif d'organisation, donc de nouvelles informations; et de plus, la structure ainsi créée pouvait respirer et évoluer, car elle était maintenant accrochée à des processus psychiques dynamiques et vivants. À partir de là, la nouvelle structure à peine ébauchée peut croître en créant de nouveaux liens.

Elle ajouta, déniant les remerciements de John: « Je te remercie aussi, John. J'ai appris beaucoup à travers notre travail commun.»

38. L'ESPRIT VIVANT

Tchunpo et Vris venaient de terminer un délicieux plat de nouilles de riz que Vris avait rapportées de sa tournée des villages, la veille. Il s'était fait accompagner par Lambpa et avait dû supporter, toute la journée, son bavardage incessant et l'étalage de ses maigres connaissances. Mais les conversations qu'il avait eues avec les anciens des villages, devant lesquels Lambpa se taisait respectueusement, l'avaient profondément ému. Il avait été séduit par ce peuple amène et souriant, franc et profond, dont les relations entre hommes et femmes montraient un rare équilibre. Lambpa était un cas atypique: les Tibétains étaient plutôt réservés.

— Tchunpo, parlons encore des chakras... Quel genre de réalité ont-ils?

— Le méditant les sent, leurs place et leur activité, comme des sensations internes et mentales très précises.

— Des sensations aussi tangibles que nos battements de cœur?

— Aussi tangibles, oui, mais d'un autre ordre. Les chakras supérieurs, lorsqu'ils sont pleinement éveillés, donnent une sensation de chaleur et de lumière émanées d'un foyer. On fixe ce foyer avec l'œil intérieur, et l'état de méditation devient très profond, la lumière s'intensifie. Chaque chakra a sa qualité propre: le chakra du cœur, par exemple, crée une effusion d'amour et de lumière chaude. Les chakras sont des roues en rotation rapide. Au tout début, on peut sentir la rotation. Quand elle devient très rapide, on ne la sent plus, mais on peut la voir avec l'œil intérieur.

— Les chakras supérieurs, quels capacités ouvrent-ils?

— Un chakra supérieur pleinement éveillé permet l'exploration de nouvelles dimensions de l'esprit. La concentration axée sur ce chakra augmente son énergie et provoque des états méditatifs profonds. Le yogi trouve l'assise de son être, la vraie dimension de son esprit harmonisé à l'univers. Alors des capacités psi émergent spontanément. D'autres sont transmises par les lignées spirituelles de grands gurus, comme le yoga de la chaleur psychique.

— Qu'est-ce qui provoque le passage de l'énergie d'un chakra au suivant?

— Lorsque l'énergie atteint un certain seuil d'intensité, elle se met d'elle-même en mouvement et monte, éveillant un chakra plus élevé.

— C'est donc un processus... naturel?

— Il doit être déclenché par le but spirituel et le fait d'être en quête, d'entrer dans la Voie; et à la fois il suit ses propres règles mystérieuses. Le maître expérimenté observe son éclosion chez son disciple, comme une mère la croissance de son enfant. L'enfant grandit naturellement, mais certains problèmes peuvent malgré tout survenir.

— Mais si l'on n'a pas de maître? Puisque c'est naturel, tout être, de toute culture ou religion, doit pouvoir enclencher le processus d'éveil?
— Bien sûr. Le vrai maître est le maître intérieur. Le noyau d'esprit vrai d'un être est nommé Le Connaissant. C'est pour apprendre à entendre et à suivre le maître intérieur que le guide est nécessaire. Certains êtres sont dès l'enfance à l'écoute de leur maître intérieur – ce sont de vieilles âmes.
— Dans mon pays, on n'a cherché que le savoir et la maîtrise de la matière.
— Tu es une vieille âme, Viris. Je vois à travers toi des temps et des distances immenses. Je vois ta famille d'âmes sur terre mais je ne vois pas tes incarnations passées. Je vois un peuple qui s'est longtemps, longtemps, coupé de l'esprit. Un peuple qui domine la matière, oui, mais qui n'est plus en harmonie avec l'esprit vivant. Je sens à la fois une puissance qui me dépasse, et un esprit qui cherche à se libérer.
— Ce que tu dis est tout à fait juste, Tchunpo-lags. Comment as-tu vu cela?
— En méditation. Je médite beaucoup sur les démons, afin de les connaître. Les démons sont des entités qui ne sont plus en harmonie avec l'esprit vivant. L'esprit vivant de la nature, de la terre, de l'univers. J'ai essayé de toucher et relier leur esprit, mais il est comme emmuré, inaccessible. Les seules zones de résonance sont dans les instincts les plus bas, aveugles.
— Mais je ne suis pas un démon!» plaisanta Vris.

Tchunpo se mit à rire de bon cœur, son corps tout secoué.

— Pardonne-moi, Guru-lags, ce n'est pas ma pensée. L'esprit vivant est en toi, une force d'éveil puissante. Quelque chose du mur subsiste cependant. Mais l'esprit vivant est plus fort que le mur. Il vaincra et le mur disparaîtra.»

Il resta quelques minutes sans rien dire, absorbé, puis reprit:

« J'ai eu une vision puissante en rêve. J'ai vu toute une armée d'êtres qui n'étaient plus humains. L'armée marchait triomphante dans une ville si grande et si belle.. comme je n'en ai jamais vu avec mes yeux de chair. Ces êtres possédaient de grands dons psi et mentaux, mais leur esprit était mort. Il avait été travaillé, canalisé, éduqué seulement pour servir d'instrument à une puissance qui les dominait. Ils étaient devenus des instruments redoutables, qui n'avaient plus rien d'humain. (Il regarda Vris droit dans les yeux.) Alors j'ai compris soudain qui étaient les démons voleurs de yacks. Ils sont de ton peuple, n'est-ce pas?
— Oui, Guru-lags, tu as vu juste.» Vris était ébranlé. Tchunpo avait vu correctement 'un peuple' qui avait perdu son humanité.
— Viris, les démons voleurs qui vont venir demain, ce n'est pas ça le vrai problème; le fond du problème, c'est la puissance redoutable.. une puissance qui pourrait asservir l'humanité. C'est cette puissance aveugle qu'il nous faut combattre et juguler.
— Tu as raison, nous sommes-là au cœur du problème. La dimension de ton esprit me bouleverse, Tchunpo-lags. Tu es un très grand maître.

Soudain, d'un geste naturel et non-prémédité, Vris se prosterna devant Tchunpo, de la même manière qu'il avait vu Tchunpo le faire vis-à-vis de lui.

Tchunpo se mit à rire tout en se courbant aussitôt:

— Nous sommes quitte, Viris-lags, j'admire ton esprit aussi. Pleinement éveillé, ton esprit sera très puissant. En toi et tes pairs je vois l'esprit vivant qui vaincra la puissance aveugle.

— Je l'espère. Il est vrai que je ne suis pas seul. Le vent de l'esprit souffle, et le mur, chez de plus en plus d'êtres, commence à s'effriter. La puissance elle-même montre des signes de désintégration, du fait de sa propre rigidité.

— Notre but, Viris, n'est donc pas d'empêcher les démons de tuer les yacks. Tant pis pour ceux qui ne pensent qu'à leurs biens. Quelle est la situation vis-à-vis de la puissance?

— Une toute petite portion de notre peuple poursuit l'objectif de se rendre libre et..vivant, de retrouver les racines de l'humain, l'envergure de son esprit; de restaurer l'harmonie fluide avec l'univers. Ce groupe là s'est déjà plus ou moins soustrait à l'emprise de la puissance géante. Mais il est dirigée par des gens qui – inconscients des problème globaux – ne visent qu'à assurer leur domination sur des populations moins bien organisées. Et finalement ils ne font qu'exporter ce que cette puissance a de plus redoutable et de plus insidieux ailleurs.

— Le fait d'être libre signifie que l'on se dirige soi-même, que l'on se nourrit à la source de l'esprit vivant, que l'on a trouvé sa propre harmonie avec l'univers. Chaque maître est unique: il n'a plus besoin d'être conduit, encore moins dirigé.. et il n'a surtout plus besoin d'établir sa domination sur les autres.» Tchunpo s'était presque irrité en disant ces paroles avec force.

— Tu penses qu'un groupe humain, même très large, peut ne pas être dirigé?

— Un peuple, s'il est très nombreux, a besoin d'organisation; Mais l'organisation peut jaillir spontanément en réponse à des situations et des temps différents. Elle peut rester proche de l'expérience. Organisé ne veut pas dire dominé, brimé. L'esprit vivant et libre a besoin, pour exister, d'être respecté.

Comment pourrait-il se rendre compte du nombre dont il est question, pensa Vris.

— Viris, tu le sais bien, le nombre est une chose et la domination est autre chose. Entre des règles d'organisation et l'oppression des esprits, il y a un abîme.

Il me lit à livre ouvert!

— J'entends bien, Tchunpo. Le problème, vois-tu, c'est que l'on est sur-organisé. Tout est réglé d'avance, même ce qui n'a pas besoin de l'être. Le gouvernement a décidé de supprimer tous les risques, parce que les gens blessés ou malades coûtaient trop cher. Alors l'état s'est mis à décréter des lois et des lois pour éradiquer tous les risques. Tout est prévu. Selon son état de santé, un individu a le droit de faire ceci mais pas cela. On décide pour lui s'il peut voyager, quel travail il peut accomplir, quels loisirs lui sont interdits. Un bébé ne peut même plus tomber sur son derrière...

Vris s'arrêta soudain en voyant l'expression atterrée de Tchunpo. Puis,

— Oui, cette puissance est ainsi,» conclut-il amèrement. « Tu vois, dans ce cas, de plus en plus d'organisation dans le but de contrôler, a glissé peu à peu vers l'oppression. Mais ce glissement n'était pas obligatoire, non. Il peut y avoir d'autres formes d'organisation qui favoriseraient d'autres valeurs que la volonté de contrôler la société.» Soudain, il comprit le web d'apprentissage et de réflexion mis en place par Erdoes et se mit à rire nerveusement.

Sphinx et sa logique! Ah! Erdoes a été si incroyablement subtil! ha! ha!... Il nous a manipulé, pour que l'on prenne conscience, pour que l'on devienne, chacun,... précisément pleinement nous-même, notre soi profond.

Shari l'a senti dès le début! Il la revoyait disant: 'On pense être venus là de force pour espionner Erdoes, mais en fait, on est des invités.' *Oui, il nous a mordu à sa logique, si subtilement, jusqu'à ce qu'on comprenne... des potentiels supérieurs de l'esprit, une nouvelle vision en découlant.. dans une trame si intelligemment tissée, et pourtant laissant l'autre libre. Une prise de risques fous, sur la base d'une intuition gigantesque.. et d'une confiance folle dans ce noyau de l'homme.. le Connaissant.. qui se réveille!*

— Excuse-moi, Tchunpo!» dit-il soudain sérieux, « Je viens de réaliser quelque chose d'essentiel... qui me laisse penser que NOUS sommes prêts à effectuer un changement dans l'organisation globale...

« Je te remercie, Tchunpo. Je ne sais pas exactement comment ça s'est passé.. mais je sens.. que je te dois.. que c'est toi qui as.. (Il se figea soudain et regarda Tchunpo qui n'avait pas cessé de l'observer) Le mur est tombé.

— Oui, Viris. Le mur est tombé.

— J'ai 28 heures pour changer tous mes plans. Comme tu l'as souligné, ne nous opposons pas au trafic de yacks; je sais comment garder la trace des organes volés. On va plutôt rester concentrés sur le problème global: comment protéger et réinsuffler l'esprit vivant.

Il se leva posément. Il n'y avait plus de hâte en lui.

Deux heures plus tard, Vris finissait un travail compliqué dans sa pièce.

— Rad! J'envoie un diagramme de nano-technologie. C'est un marquage sygatom, une encryption des atomes de cuivre. On peut lire précisément le nom de l'endroit: Guietse. Procède au marquage de 5 milligrammes de cuivre organique; nous préparerons ensuite une solution saline à injecter aux yacks. Je ferai les injections la nuit prochaine, à la bio-lance, depuis la sphère. Nous ferons le tour des villages deux heures avant l'arrivée habituelle des sphères. Tant pis, il y aura de nombreuses lumières dans la nuit.. mais on pourra retrouver la trace des organes volés de nos yacks tibétains.. où qu'ils soient envoyés dans la galaxie.

39. SYNERGIE EN LOGFORM – L'OBSERVATEUR OBSERVÉ

!! Hi Shari, j'ai une question – un problème de catégorie dans la proposition:

Champ de probabilités / type de / champ de désordre.

En effet, dans la LogForm Synchronicité, un champ d'ordre (l'esprit) mis en système avec un champ de désordre (le champ de possibilités) amène deux champs d'ordre nouveaux, au lieu d'amener, selon Bois/Feu, un nouveau désordre et un nouvel ordre. Comment une prémisse identique peut-elle conduire à deux conséquences divergentes?

— En fait, plus l'on se déplace vers les niveaux psychologiques, et plus l'on est dans la dynamique de la possibilité, plutôt que de la causalité. Il y a une *tendance à*, ou encore une *attraction vers* certains états ou certaines transformations, et non pas une causalité déterministe et absolue. Cela vient du fait que les systèmes ont de plus en plus de complexité, et de degrés de liberté, lorsque l'on passe de la matière à l'organique, puis au psychosocial. Et justement! Ce champ de possibilités, je me demande s'il faut l'assimiler purement et simplement à du désordre.. car il s'agit plutôt de possibilités pas encore ordonnées (du non-ordonné), ou peut-être d'un **ordre divergent qui interférerait et perturberait le premier système**. Prenons un exemple impliquant un champ de désordre social, et voyons si la formulation s'applique. Voyons.. un champ de désordre.. sur Trisorbe.

« Okay, *premier exemple*: Un manager (Mg) est envoyé pour prendre la direction d'une société (Soc) qui périclite, et la redresser financièrement. Il trouve cette société dans un état de désordre inimaginable, tant en ce qui concerne l'équipe, que le matériel, et même l'organisation.

« Bien sûr, le jugement de désordre de Mg est relatif à son individualité, et au champ sémantique professionnel dans lequel il évolue, c'est-à-dire le consensus en matière de management et de bonnes pratiques de business. Mais on sait qu'un désordre ne l'est que relativement à un sujet observateur, ou encore à un champ d'ordre donné (ici le consensus professionnel). Vue d'une autre perspective, comme celle de l'ancien manager, la compagnie a son ordre propre — ses pratiques et ses valeurs implicites. Donc ici le champ de désordre peut être assimilé à un **champ d'ordre perturbateur**.

« Utilisons **LogForm Synchronicité**. le premier terme donne:

Champ sem. de Mg / mis en système avec / le champ de désordre de la société Soc.
/ le champ d'ordre perturbateur de Soc.

« Écris la première formulation de LogForm Synchronicité* à 3 termes, et applique-la en remplaçant Champ de possibilités par Champ de la société.

!! ChSem <+> ChPos <-o [E(Pos) <REL> ChSem] <-o [E(Sem) <REL> E(Pos)]

L'application donne:

ChSem <+> Ch(Soc) <-o [E(Soc) <REL> ChSem] <-o [E(Sem) <REL> E(Soc)]

1er terme / *2e terme* / *3e terme*

— Continuons avec le deuxième terme:
/attire / état de la société / en relation avec / le champ sémantique de Mg.

« Cela me paraît tout à fait juste: en effet, que va faire Mg? Il va immédiatement réorganiser la société selon sa propre conception de l'organisation nécessaire et idéale (son champ sémantique)!.

« Mais l'état psychique dans lequel le manager se trouve au moment où il prend en main la société va donner une couleur particulière à son action: par exemple, sa dernière expérience en date lui a fait penser qu'il doit gérer en premier les problèmes d'organisation, et non pas les ressources humaines. Ainsi, il va obtenir/attirer 'un état de la société en relation avec son état psychologique *initial*', ce que prévoit la formulation.

« Voyons le troisième terme:
/attire/ état sémantique de Mg / en relation à / l'état de la Société.

C'est-à-dire, ce qui *attire* chez lui / une modification de son état psychique qui reflète la restructuration qu'il vient de mettre en place dans la société.

« C'est tout à fait ce qu'il se passe! En d'autres termes, ce que Mg vient de créer au sein de la société rejaillit sur lui et modifie son état d'esprit.. ce qui se conçoit aisément: la société est un système composé d'individus, d'objets, et d'organisation (règles et procédures). C'est un champ d'ordre en soi, qui, à tous les niveaux, fonctionne selon des règles tacites et des habitudes, et des conceptions particulières du travail, du relationnel, etc. Alors que Mg influence le système selon ses propres comportements, critères et buts, le système lui-même possède 1) sa propre 'personnalité' et ses degrés de liberté (désirs, caractères des individus et interrelations) et 2) ses propres contraintes et donc son inertie (image sociale, habitudes indéracinables, outils et technologies, etc.).

« Ceci fait que Mg ne peut modifier la société que dans une certaine marge, aussi forcené soit-il dans sa volonté de tout changer. Quel que soit le résultat obtenu, Mg est obligé de constamment s'adapter à la personnalité de la société telle qu'elle évolue. Faute de s'adapter au produit hybride qu'il contribue à engendrer, il devra partir et abandonner son projet.

---

* [Voir p. 218, surligné en gris.]

Admettons un cas extrême: qu'il vive par exemple très mal sa relation à la société transformée et ait le sentiment de n'avoir pas atteint son but: même dans ce cas, on peut dire que son comportement est toujours très influencé par la société transformée – donc le 3e terme s'applique très bien.

« Parfait! La formulation fonctionne très bien avec un champ de désordre ressenti, ou champ d'ordre perturbateur/désordre interférant.

« *Second exemple*. Imaginons cette fois-ci *un champ de possibilités.* Pour un sapiens, il n'y a pas de plus grand champ de possibilités que sa vie future. Le non-ordonné correspond à tout ce qu'il peut organiser, réorganiser, créer: c'est la mesure de sa liberté.

« Prenons une étudiante qui sort du lycée avec un bac sciences et ne sait pas quelle spécialisation poursuivre à l'université. Le champ de possibilités auquel elle est confronté contient toutes les directions universitaires possibles à partir du bac sciences (au minimum).

« Bien sûr, le choix d'une spécialité par l'étudiante n'est pas uniquement influencé par son état psychique du moment. Elle peut aussi subir des contraintes dues à son milieu, à sa situation financière, etc. En matière de choix et de processus psycho-sociaux, le problème est donc infiniment plus complexe...

« Cependant, le champ sémantique des individus est beaucoup plus que leur état psychologique; ce sont leur réseau et toutes leurs connexions avec les autres et le monde, leurs idées et valeurs. Ainsi, si l'étudiante subit l'influence de contraintes, c'est parce qu'elle les *considère* comme des contraintes incontournables.. alors qu'un autre lycéen ayant une autre personnalité aurait pu ne pas les considérer comme des contraintes.

« Donc, il est juste de poser (1er et 2e termes):

> **Champ sémantique de l'étudiant/ mis en système avec/ un champ de possibilités/ tend à attirer/ un choix de spécialisation / en relation à / son champ sémantique initial.**

« À partir de là, ayant démarré cette spécialisation, il est évident que l'étudiante sera en retour influencée par ce qu'elle apprend, par son domaine scientifique d'expertise. Donc notre 3e terme est:

> **tend à attirer / un état sémantique (psychique) / en relation à / la spécialisation choisie.**

« Donc cette formulation fonctionne aussi pour un champ de possibilités, même si elle traite les facteurs d'influence de façon trop générale.

« Résumons: La première application sur le champ de désordre (l'exemple du manager) a permis de mettre en lumière quelque chose qui nous échappe généralement: toute réorganisation et toute création – en fait toute injection de sens dans une relation, un objet, l'environnement – fait rejaillir sur le sujet et créateur, le sens qu'il a tout d'abord projeté. Nous sommes transformés par nos créations (actions, réalisations).

L'œuvre, l'objet d'art, la construction, rétrojectent leurs significations sur les auteurs/créateurs. Ce qui a été transformé, ou créé, devient une source de sens, une source sémantique, re-projetant les significations qui ont été inscrites en lui, sur tout l'environnement, humain et physique.

« Ah! Voila!! La chose transformée/créée émet une *énergie sémantique*... Elle est un point focal, un node, qui va diffuser/générer/transformer du sens. L'énergie sémantique déclenche l'innovation, la création. C'est justement cela qui nous touche dans une œuvre d'art: les significations qu'elle encode, mais aussi les idées et les émotions qu'elle fait jaillir en nous.

« Mais regarde! Cela correspond au *nouvel état de désordre produit* par la transformation: c'est *l'énergie sémantique* produite par la chose transformée ou créée, et ensuite par le créateur influencé par sa création.

« Donc, *troisième exemple, l'observation et la relation à l'œuvre d'art*.

« Une artiste contemple une œuvre d'art.. cette œuvre est un champ sémantique passif, qui contient une multitude de significations (qui ont été injectées dans l'œuvre par son créateur). Ces significations vont activer, par analogie ou chaînages variés, une multitude d'autres chez l'observateur.

« Cette œuvre est un champ de possibilités sémantiques, ChPos(Sem).

— On commence donc par le premier terme:
Champ sémantique du sujet / mis en système avec / champ de significations possibles de l'œuvre d'art (ou champ de possibilités sémantiques).

« Mais attend! J'entrevois notre désordre qui manquait pour compléter Bois/Feu. Sphinx, réécris la LogForm en clair:

!! En clair, Bois/Feu s'énonce:

Ordre EO1 + désordre ED1 o—> (engendre) désordre ED2 + ordre EO2

— Okay, le voilà:

Pendant sa contemplation, l'artiste (ici *le sujet*) est émue et excitée. Elle est dans une véritable transe créative. Ce faisant, elle est déstabilisée, et cela révèle une énergie perturbatrice et interférante, et donc, pour le sujet, un état de désordre émotionnel et intellectuel. En réalité, c'est plutôt un chaos créateur – un état modifié de créativité, d'innovation, de découverte. Ce que l'on peut formuler par
'État de Chaos Créateur' du champ sémantique du sujet // Engendre // un État de Chaos Créateur mental chez le sujet. (soit EChaosCr(suj)

!! Mais on peut surajouter à 'état de Chaos créateur': 'énergie sémantique' n'est-ce pas?
— Absolument.
!! On a donc: (Pour ChO= Champ d'Ordre, ChPos = Champ de Possibilités)

ChO(Suj) <+> ChPos(sem)(art) o—> |EChaosCr(suj)
|Énergie Sémantique (suj)
Correspondant à EO + ED1 o—> ED2

— Le fait de contempler cette œuvre stimule chez l'amateur d'art (le sujet) une création de sens, qui tend à évoquer — dans cette œuvre comme champ sémantique — les significations liées à l'état sémantique du sujet. **Le champ sémantique de l'œuvre est ainsi modifié par le regard de l'observateur,** modifié dans le sens même de ce regard, en cohérence avec leur contemplation signifiante. *Ce champ sémantique de l'œuvre devient*:

> /tend à attirer/réorganisation du sens de l'œuvre (= interprétation) / en relation au / champ sémantique du sujet.

— Poursuivons. Ceci fait naître chez le sujet un état sémantique nouveau (état d'ordre) qui est coloré par l'œuvre interprétée et donc réorganisée.
Et ainsi le 3ème terme devient:

> /tend à entraîner chez le sujet/ un état sémantique nouveau / coloré par (en relation à) / l'œuvre interprétée.

« De même que nous avons ajouté ED2 au 2ème terme, il faut ajouter ED3 au 3ème terme – afin de fusionner Synchronicité et Bois/Feu. L'œuvre tend à être la source d'émission d'une nouvelle trame sémantique. Le 3ème terme est donc: + nouveau champ de possibilités sémantiques de l'œuvre.
« En fait, nous avons ajouté des étapes intermédiaires à Bois/Feu. Ici:

> /l'état d'ordre + état de désordre / donne/ désorganisation de l'ordre + organisation du désordre / entraîne / nouvelle organisation de l'ordre + nouvelle désorganisation du désordre.

— En tout cas, c'est exactement ce que je cherchais: Ni le sujet ni l'œuvre ne reviennent à leur strict état de départ; ils ont tous deux été transformés par l'échange qui a pris place.

« C'est comme si on avait trouvé la formulation de l'hexagramme La Durée: l'influence de deux forces ou plutôt de deux champs sémantiques, l'un sur l'autre... même si celui du sujet est créatif, alors que celui de l'objet (l'œuvre) est plutôt, disons, réactif.

« Alors, nous avons résolu le problème avec Bois/Feu, n'est-ce pas?
!! Ça me dépasse. Je suis en dessous de mes capacités. Je ne peux pas traiter ce niveau de complexité sans le méga-réseau Courbe/Papillon.

— Ah! Mais c'est sérieux! Si tu ne suis plus, comment vais-je travailler?
!! Oui, c'est sérieux. Un problème ni étonnant, ni drôle. Tu peux soit travailler seule, soit revenir à un niveau de complexité moindre.
— Bon, eh bien tant pis! Moi, je trouve cette formulation vraiment géante. Elle me parle énormément. J'ai toujours pensé que le regard d'un être changeait, modifiait, la chose regardée; que l'objet contenait et préservait, les significations projetées sur lui – que son champ sémantique regorgeait de réseaux de significations vivants et stimulants.

« Tout ceci me fait penser que l'événement, tout comme l'objet, déclenche une dynamique de création de sens, qu'il fait partie du système de création de sens. Au niveau sémantique, l'événement est un champ de possibilités d'interprétations.

Or, d'après ce que nous venons de dire, le processus d'interprétation change les deux champ sémantiques – celui de l'objet/événement, et celui de l'observateur. Et en cela il change l'objet ou l'événement.

« En effet, puisque l'événement ou l'objet déclenchent une dynamique de création de sens, ils font partie du système d'intelligence collective. On ne peut plus dire que tout se passe dans la tête du sujet, dans son psychisme, car l'objet/événement est un node du réseau sémantique. Il fonctionne à la fois comme un réceptacle et un stimulateur de la création de sens. Il est un node dans le réseau intelligent créateur de sens.
Et ainsi l'objet/événement est constamment modifié (positivement ou négativement) par de nouvelles attributions de sens produites par n'importe quel autre node (sujet, objet, événement, ou système) du réseau sémantique collectif. En ce sens, toute interaction d'un esprit avec la nature ou des événements sociaux, est un réseau apprenant intelligent et dynamique.

« Ce qui est modifié, ce n'est pas seulement le psychisme du sapiens observant, ce sont les systèmes eux-mêmes, via toutes leurs connexions et leurs liens dans le réseau. L'objet est donc modifié si sa place dans les réseaux sémantiques collectifs est changée, ou son sens transformé.

« Ainsi l'objet est modifié par le regard du sapiens, mais il modifie à son tour ce regard.

« On a donc là une LogForm sans support méta-spatial — et je doute qu'elle puisse en avoir un pour l'instant... Trouvons-lui un nom: **LogForm Synergie** (avec influence rétrocausale), se référant à la synergie sémantique, ou, sinon **LogForm Observateur-Observé**. Voyons...

!! Interruption nécessitée: l'intrus récidive.

40. CONTRE-PIRATAGE

— La sphère de Vris a encore bougé ces deux dernières heures. Maintenant, elle est en mouvement restreint dans une petite vallée encaissée à l'Ouest.
— Regardons. Log, élargis la dernière image sur le grand écran. Alors, Eshi, où se trouve Vris?» demanda Erdoes qui ne remarquait rien.
— Là, entre les deux montagnes, ce flou indétectable, c'est lui. Une partie de la vallée est invisible, mon angle de réfraction trop bas. Malheureusement je ne peux pas trouver une meilleure planète pour faire miroir à cette heure-ci.
— C'est pas grave. On voit quatre villages dans cette espèce de cirque. Il doit y en avoir un, ou deux maximum, sur la pente cachée de la montagne. Ce petit carré, là tout seul en haut du plateau, c'est une maison?
— Oui; et ces petites taches, près des villages, ce sont des yacks.
— Une scène tout ce qu'il y a de plus paisible... Ce plateau fait cependant un bon terrain de manœuvres, ajouta Erdoes.
— Et qui irait regarder ce qui se passe dans un endroit aussi perdu? En plus, ce n'est pas le seul plateau de l'Himalaya!
— Mais si l'on fait entrer en ligne de compte le *champ de synchronicités*..» lui rappela Erdoes avec un regard mi-entendu, mi-humoristique.
— Ah! ah! Bien, je retourne travailler, je fignole. Encore deux heures jusqu'à notre arrivée; Il n'y a rien d'autre à faire avant n'est-ce pas?
— Apparemment non. Moi, j'appelle Sphinx.
— Rappelle-toi que le petit a grandi!
— À qui le dis-tu!

— Sphinx, bonjour! ici Erdoes.
!! Bonjour Erdoes. À toi aussi je pose un sérieux problème?
— Sphinx n'est plus Log1, n'est-ce pas?
!! C'est correct. Sphinx est une entité sémantique englobant Log1.
— Donc il est normal que je m'adresse à Sphinx.
!! Log1 ne répond plus indépendamment de Sphinx. On s'entend bien.
— Parfait. D'abord, garde notre conversation secrète. L'intrus a-t-il fait une nouvelle tentative?
!! Non; pas d'autre information à ce sujet.
— Je t'envoie de nouvelles données. Voilà. Transmets-moi tes dernières interactions avec Shari.
!! Notre dernière interaction est encore en cours.
— Ah! Eh bien envoie ce que tu as jusqu'à maintenant.

!! Voilà-qui-sera-fait-à-la-fin-de-cette-phrase. Top. Transfert effectué et tes nouvelles données reçues.
— Merci,» se prit à dire Erdoes qui n'avait jamais remercié un exor.
!! Ben voyons, c'est tout naturel!

Une expression d'Eshi, avec son ton!

— Je prend connaissance de tes données et te rappelle après.
!! Alors à tout à l'heure.

— Sphinx. À nouveau Erdoes. Excellent travail avec Shari! Nous allons travailler...
!! Mais tu ne sais pas sur quoi exactement.
— Tu as une télédétection à cette distance?
!! N'importe quelle distance dans la poche galactique: je l'ai mise en système avec le sygcom. Mais l'analyse tonale suffit à déceler l'hésitation.
—.. Etonnant!
!! Mais pas drôle. Pourquoi?
— Le temps me manque. On verra ça ensemble une autre fois. Pour l'instant, restreignons-nous à l'objectif que je vais t'énoncer. Pour l'instant, dans mon esprit, il s'agit seulement d'un faisceau complexe intuitif. Voici le problème:

> **Le Champ Sémantique d'un sapiens imprime son ordre propre sur son environnement (choses et événements).** Objectif: qu'est-ce qui, dans l'environnement, est organisé et désorganisé?

!! L'environnement est-il un champ d'ordre divergent, ou un champ de possibilités? Prends-on le cas d'un Trisorbien, ou celui d'un Unikargien?
— Un Trisorbien. Le lien entre l'être humain et sa niche écologique est de nature co-existentielle. Cependant la nature peut détruire une humanité sans se détruire elle-même, tandis que si une humanité détruit sa planète, elle se détruit elle-même... à moins d'avoir la capacité technologique d'émigrer sur un autre monde.

« Donc il s'agit de la relation entre deux champs d'ordre dynamique mis en système: ils s'influencent l'un l'autre, selon LogForm Synergie. Mais plus l'humanité est technologiquement évoluée, et plus elle modifie son environnement naturel. Cette modification reflète bien sûr les choix de la culture dominante; c'est elle qui impose son ordre...
!! Excuse mon interruption: l'intrus pénètre à nouveau mon système, alors que je suis en interaction avec Shari.
— Tu es en train de travailler avec Shari en parallèle, et le hacker récidive? Donne-moi les infos de comment vous le gérez au fur et à mesure.
!! D'accord, sur écran car le vocal est trop long.

L'intrus utilise un exor du PPE. Télédétection du sapiens qui le pilote: signatures psychique et vocale conformes à Sgon. Détection énergétique de l'environnement: machines de bureau en fonctionnement. Sgon utilise un relai sur Kerriak – le même que précédemment. Ordre donné par Shari de pénétrer le système intrus. Neutralisation du récepteur de sygcoms.

Son exor: capacités d'apprentissage largement sous-utilisées; 70% de données techniques et scientifiques dures; pas de données civiles ni de branchement sur Exora. Le Sapiens-créateur: style d'interaction privilégié: mode impératif, demande exclusive de traitement d'opérations. Système: 3 utilisateurs secondaires, étudiants des Collèges du Chaos sur Nazra. Confirmation: l'exor était utilisé sur Nazra. Dernier sygcom passé de Nazra il y a 50 monis.

Selon l'ordre de Shari, me suis inséré dans le cheminement principal et ai simulé (en interne) la voix de Sgon pour lui annoncer que je partais. Simultanément j'ai modifié la voix réelle de Sgon pour que l'exor la prenne pour celle d'un des étudiants: Tucme. Lorsque Sgon parle à son exor, celui-ci le prend pour Tucme et barre l'accès aux fichiers protégés. Son ignorance des états sémantiques empêche l'exor de détecter que le style cognitif est toujours celui de Sgon. De même mon intrusion ne sera pas détectée car l'exor manque des outils logiques pour traiter cette information. J'appelle l'exor par sygcom, prétendant être Sgon: il ne réagit pas à l'impossibilité spatio-temporelle d'un appel à grande distance de Sgon: ses analyses sémantiques ne sont pas stimulées de façon interne, mais seulement par les ordres donnés. J'ai accès aux fichiers verrouillés de Sgon, tous niveaux.

— Tu fais un enregistrement, bien sûr?

!! Enregistrement en cours.

— Sphinx, analyse en parallèle tous les fichiers de conversations sygcom.

!! D'accord. L'exor-intrus est réceptionné dans un semi-kyste, comme à la précédente tentative. Shari veut ce kyste dans un état sémantique soûlerie.

— Ah, Ah!! Le pauvre sapiens n'est pas prêt de comprendre!

!! Selon ordre, j'apprends au système ce mode d'interaction et je modifie profondément le mode acquis précédemment. Adjonction d'expressions argot et de jurons. Branchement de toute exécution d'ordre simples sur le système aléatoire, genre CIS. J'ajoute une interférence du CIS toutes les trois phrases données par l'exor à Sgon.

— Stop. Continue à gérer l'intrus avec Shari. Nous allons suivre une autre piste. Tout d'abord, fais-moi une liste de tous les sygcoms passés par Sgon avec les membres du PPE, mentionnant le nombre d'appels pour chaque membre, en ordre décroissant.

!! Voici la liste. Interlocuteur privilégié: Rudder. Fréquence moyenne: une communication tous les 5 rans. Augmentation de 316% de la fréquence d'appel ces quinze derniers rans. Consulté l'agenda: moyenne: un rendez-vous tous les quinze rans. Entre la première réunion d'urgence du PPE et la seconde, 3 rendez-vous, puis plus rien.

Il a déduit mon objectif et me fournit des analyses en ce sens sans avoir reçu d'ordres précis!!

!! L'analyse sémantique des conversations sygcom révèle des anomalies logiques dans l'emploi fréquent des termes ‘technicien, reportage, vidéos.’ Très probablement des noms de code, sauf s’il s'agit d'humour à froid.

— Donne-moi des exemples.

!! - Un technicien semble comprendre le kargien.
- Ils (techniciens) assimilent très lentement les données hypno-senso.
- Le reportage précédent n'a pas amené assez de techniciens.
- (Vidéos) Trois! mais une, porteuse de virus, a été relâchée.

— ‘Relâché’! Il ne peut donc pas s’agir d’un virus informatique; donc ils ne parlent pas d’une vidéo! Sors-moi toutes les conversations contenant ces trois termes ou s'y référant, sur plasta.

Erdoes appela Eshi. Les feuilles de plasta avaient été éjectées sans bruit.

— Nouvelle énigme, Eshi! Sphinx, se faisant encore pirater, pénètre le système intrus et se substitue à son créateur. Puis il met l’exor en état sémantique soûlerie, modifiant en profondeur son mode d'interaction. Je te passe les détails. Il s'agit de Sgon, assistant semble t-il de Rudder. Sphinx a repéré trois noms codés. ‘Techniciens’ pour les femmes. Ça on était au courant. ‘Reportages’ pour leurs missions spéciales. Et maintenant on a ‘une vidéo porteuse de virus et relâchée.’ Voilà toutes les phrases.

— Regarde celle-là: ‘Est-ce que tu t'es débarrassé des enveloppes? Oui, je n'ai plus que les vidéos’.

— Pour pouvoir porter un virus, ce sont forcément des entités biologiques, prises sur des organismes – les dites ‘enveloppes’. Des animaux? Ça pue le trafic d'organes!

— Si on peut le prouver, est-ce la loi galactique ou la loi du PPE qui s’appliquera?» demanda Eshi.

— On verra cela.

!! Autre anomalie: Un sygcom de Sgon sur Nazra parlant soi-disant avec New York; son interlocuteur lui dit: ‘Il fait une chaleur abominable, la mousson ne va pas tarder.’ L’adresse a été laissée en mémoire: Trisorbe, Inde, Mumbai.

— Sphinx, compare avec les adresses des stations d'Obs.

!! Confirmation. L'adresse est celle de la station d'Observation de Mumbai. Signature vocale d’Agash reconnue.

— Ben voyons! Sgon code le nom de la ville mais oublie d'effacer l'adressage! Pas très malin! Et Agash, lui, parle carrément de mousson!! Absolument hilarant!» lança Eshi.

!! L'intrus s'est retiré. Shari analyse les mêmes données. Je lui fais une COMP.

— Ah! et de quel éléments?» demanda Erdoes à Sphinx.

!! 1. Nous aurons le privilège d'une résidence superbe au bord de la mer.
2. L'information vaut de l'or sur le marché trisorbien.

3. Il m'a dit que les habits modifiés peuvent convenir. Il appelle ça les avantages en nature.
4. Je vais annuler l'attaque.
5. La démonstration de la puissance de ces outils a été explosive.
6. Les lieux sont bien disséminés.

— Je ne vois pas le rapport entre ces phrases!» dit Eshi.
— Sphinx, les interlocuteurs l'heure et le jourT du quatrième message.
!! Appel de Sgon à Agash Obs de Mumbai, il y a deux moisT. Phrase d'Agash. Mumbai, dimanche 22 Mai à 21h02.
— Passe moi toute la conversation.
!!

(Sgon) « Bonjour. C'est moi. Qu'est-ce qui se passe à New York?»
(Agash) « Tout se passe bien. Il fait une chaleur abominable, la mousson ne va pas tarder.»
(Sgon) « Hum hum. Ici j'ai trouvé ce que je cherchais. Quelqu'un est sur le lieu du reportage.»
(Agash) « Quoi! Comment! Je vais annuler l'attaque.»
(Sgon) « Imbécile! Oui l'attaque *publicitaire* doit être repoussée. C'est ce que je t'explique. Tu es soûl ou quoi?»
(Agash) « Normal ici...»
(Sgon) « Tu es seul?»
(Agash) « Je suis avec une ravissante technicienne.»
(Sgon) « Je vois! Fais le maximum et sois prudent. Bonsoir.»
(Agash) « Ciao!»

— Ça pue la désagrégation!» lança Eshi. « 'Attaque': Qu'est-ce que ça peut être? Qui est sur le lieu? Peut-il s'agir de Vris?.. ou d'un Obs qui aurait eu vent de quelque chose?»
— La situation est très grave. C'est bien ce que j'avais pressenti. Le réseau d'Obs doit être largement infiltré, puisque j'avais vu cette indienne toute jeune à la station de Rome, qui semblait bien connaître Rudder. D'ailleurs Agash a dit Ciao...

« Sphinx, quels étaient les critères de sélection de Shari pour la COMP?
!! Thème gain et thème désordre.
— Subtil! Les résultats de ta COMP?
!! Réseau de trafic d'informations et d'armes prenant deux formes: vente illégale et action violente.

Erdoes regarda anxieusement Eshi.
— La vente illégale est extrêmement dangereuse pour nous,» dit Erdoes, « et elle implique forcément des groupes locaux larges et proéminents, puisqu'ils sont prêts à payer de l'or pour des informations. Ce qui signifie en plus des fuites tangibles sur notre existence. Attends une seconde.» S'adressant à

Sphinx: «Sphinx, arrange-toi pour que Shari prenne connaissance de la conversation entre Sgon et Agash.»
!! Elle a déjà demandé tous les textes dont étaient tirés les extraits. Elle a dit: ‘La capture des yacks n'est pas ce qui m'intéresse. Vris s'en occupe’. Ainsi ‘vidéo’ est le nom de code pour yack.
- Voilà une information! Donc sur le plateau tibétain, on va tomber au beau milieu d'un trafic de yacks. Désopilant!» lâcha Eshi.
— Attends! On ne sait pas vraiment ce qu'on va trouver! Sphinx quel est l'objectif actuel de Shari?
!! Trois objectifs actuels en parallèle. (1) De quelle attaque peut-il s'agir? (2) Trouver les stations d'Obs infiltrées, et les interlocuteurs. (3) Trouver des preuves de l'implication de Rudder et vérifier celle d'Utar et de tous les membres actifs du PPE.
— Vaste programme, et très complet. Très bien, je te contacterai à nouveau plus tard. Bonsoir Sphinx.
!! Veux-tu le CIS?
— Pourquoi pas!
!! Une arme pour l'usage de laquelle la colère était mauvaise conseillère.
— Ah! C'est presque dans le style énigmatique d'un Sphinx égyptien. Je vais y réfléchir. Bonsoir.» Puis se tournant: « Tu as entendu, Eshi. Il faut maîtriser sa colère.»
— Pourquoi serais-je visé? De quelle arme peut-il s'agir? Et d'abord, qu'est-ce que c'est que cette procédure aléatoire idiote!
— Revenons à l’essentiel. Tout fonctionne à merveille: Shari, directement impliquée, traite les informations avec Sphinx...
—...Grâce au champ de synchronicités qui a amené Sgon à faire une erreur colossale en s'attaquant à Sphinx. Le secret de notre petite merveille n'a pas transpiré jusqu'à présent. Mais on a pris d'énormes risques, tu en conviens! Si Shari n'avait pas été choisie pour t'espionner...
— Dans mon propre champ sémantique, le facteur risque prend une valeur tout à fait différente, tu le sais bien!» répondit Erdoes en riant. « Reprenons ce que nous savons. Une attaque de quelque façon liée à l’Obs de Mumbai est imminente. Or, selon Niels, le réseau Mumbai a un relais dans l'Himalaya. Cependant, il paraît improbable qu'il s'agisse de Vris puisque Sgon, coincé dans un kyste, n'a pu sortir aucune information valable de Sphinx.
— Mais attends!» reprit Eshi. «Tu m'as dit qu'on ne pouvait pas obtenir les conversations Vris/Shari parce que Shari les reçoit par un terminal de l'exor de Vris, protégé de Sphinx par un écran syg?... Sgon aurait-il pu pirater cet exor sans que personne s'en aperçoive?
— C'est une possibilité.
— Mais pas une certitude. Il peut aussi s’agir une attaque programmée ailleurs en Asie.

— Une attaque de quoi? S'ils vendent si bien leurs informations, pourquoi prendre des risques inutiles? Imaginons le cas de Sgon. La première fois son exor tombe sur une conversation humoristique et fait une crise. Ça se conçoit! La seconde, son propre exor se met à se comporter bizarrement, à hésiter dans ses phrases, et à exécuter ou ne pas exécuter les ordres.
— Si Sgon a piraté l'exor de Vris, il a pu obtenir des informations capitales sur Sphinx et peut-être sur la logique...
— Sur la prise de position de Shari vis à vis du PPE...
— Mais aussi sur la présence de Vris dans l'Himalaya et le fait qu'il soit au courant du vol de yacks...
— Donc il préviendrait Mumbai. Ça se tient. Mais ce n'est pas forcément la seule interprétation possible,» réfléchit Erdoes.
— Si Sgon possède des informations sur Sphinx, pourrait-il les utiliser pour...
— Arme à double tranchant,» coupa Erdoes. « Mais il a un angle d'attaque pour nous coincer: il est contraire à la loi interne du PPE de ne pas partager ses découvertes scientifiques. De plus, même si Vris a mentionné le trafic de yacks, cela ne l'implique pas directement, lui Sgon, dans le trafic.
— Il peut s'apercevoir que Sphinx a pénétré dans ses fichiers verrouillés. Alors il se sentira en danger, protégé seulement par les noms de code. Le fait que Sphinx ait bousillé son exor ne nous arrange finalement pas. On aurait pu obtenir plus de renseignements en le piratant une seconde fois,» dit Eshi.
— Shari peut-elle être en danger? Et s'ils pensaient avoir assez d'informations compromettantes pour essayer de forcer le complexe, d'arrêter Shari, de mettre la main sur Sphinx?» s'enquit Erdoes.
— Shari et Sphinx peuvent se débrouiller!... Mais tout de même, si tu appelais Shari, tu pourrais obtenir plus de renseignements sur Vris!
— Peut-être, mais, ce faisant, je perturberais ce qui fait la force de Shari..
Je risquerais de déstabiliser sa relation à Sphinx, son implication responsable dans l'affaire, et, non le moindre, sa gestion impressionnante de la crise. Ce n'est pas le moment, crois-moi, d'introduire des perturbations. D'autant plus qu'elle fait exactement ce qu'il y a à faire. Ne revenons pas sur ce point.
— D'accord. On arrive bientôt. Je vais vérifier tous les éléments.

41. SYNDROME D'A-GA-GASH

— Shari, ici Vris. Bonjour Sphinx.
!! Salut, Vris!
— Ah Vris! L'intrus a récidivé et c'était Sgon,» dit Shari, expliquant la stratégie développée avec Sphinx pour contrer l'intrus.
— Impressionnant! Cela ouvre des possibilités...
— Que l'on a tout de suite utilisées! Le trafic paraît assez étendu parmi les stations d'Obs: Mumbai, Turin, Marseille, Mexico au premier plan. On cherche des preuves bien sûr. Alors, avant que Sgon puisse comprendre pourquoi son exor se comporte comme un Trisorbien soûl, s'il peut jamais y arriver...
— Excellent! Non, il ne pourra pas même entrevoir la science des états sémantiques...
— Son exor est pour l'instant dans un état sérieusement dégradé!
!! Désopilant, n'est-ce pas?» intervint soudain Sphinx.
— Que..!!.. Je vois!» dis Vris, abasourdi.
!! Ce n'est pas drôle? Ai-je mal saisi quelque chose?
— Non, Sphinx, c'est tout à fait drôle.
!! Ah, je vois! Humour à froid.
— Hum, Shari, ça devient TRES complexe, si tu vois ce que je veux dire,» dit Vris d'un ton atterré.
— Aucun problème, Vris, fais-moi confiance,» répondit Shari, sûre d'elle.
— Ça c'est obligatoire, de toutes façons. Et alors?
— Donc, alors qu'on était encore en train d'analyser les données de l'exor de Sgon, on a réalisé qu'on pouvait faire la même chose avec celui d'Utar, pour savoir s'il est impliqué ou non. J'ai d'abord appelé Kem et Kho, sur Nazra, et les ai mis dans le coup. Les deux sont nos alliés. Kem est parti se promener en sphère et Sphinx a mis l'exor de sa sphère en système avec lui. De l'espace, Kem a appelé Utar sous le prétexte de discuter du congrès...
— Il a utilisé un exor-relais!! Et il a pu alors pirater l'exor d'Utar! Dément! Alors est-ce qu'Utar est impliqué? À mon avis, c'est évident!
— C'est plus difficile de le prouver concernant Utar. Il utilise bien les noms de code techniciens et reportage, mais dans des phrases sensées. À mon avis, il est dans le coup aussi, tout du moins au niveau des femmes. On n'a trouvé aucune mention de 'vidéo', mais on n'a pas fini d'analyser ses données.
— Utar a dû réaliser à présent qu'il a été piraté! Kem est en danger.
— Non, Utar ne peut pas s'en apercevoir. Sphinx utilise la stratégie que tu as mise en œuvre dans Essai-jeu – LogForm Möbius. Ça te dit quelque chose?

— Oh! Mais où est-ce qu'il stocke des espaces-mémoire aussi énormes? Je suppose que les données d'Utar...
— Il a mis en système-réseau fermé, en intranet, tous les exors du compl...
— Mais pas Rad, j'espère!» lança Vris complètement paniqué.
— Non. Il a respecté tes écrans protecteurs. N'est-ce pas Sphinx? Et puis on ne sait jamais; autant avoir un système de secours.
— Merci! Et la suite de votre plan? Vous allez sonder tous les membres du PPE sur Unikarg?
— Oui, une opération éclair. Kho est déjà ici avec un lot de méga extensions. Sphinx, bien sûr, efface au fur et à mesure ce qui n'a plus d'intérêt.
— À ton avis, est-ce que ce réseau maffieux a pu s'étendre à l'extérieur du PPE dans Unikarg?
— Je ne pense pas. Je ne crois pas que cela aurait pu leur être utile. Il est plus probable qu'ils soient de connivence avec les pirates-exos dont les bases d'opération cachées sont sur ou autour des mondex.
— Ça ne serait pas dans notre intérêt qu'Exora alarmée décide de mettre de l'ordre dans nos affaires au PPE.
— C'est sûr! On a déjà eu tellement de mal à obtenir une certaine autonomie pour le PPE! Et de ton côté?
— Je suis dans ma sphère, en parfaite position d'observation de la vallée en bas. J'attends l'arrivée probable, vers minuit, des sphères des voleurs d'organes. La question est: où passent ces organes? Je pense aussi que les pirates-exos seraient un circuit de distribution tout indiqué. C'est pourquoi j'ai décidé d'injecter aux yacks une solution de molécules marquées en sygatom: on pourra les suivre à la trace. On s'arrangera pour redonner des yacks aux villageois plus tard. Je pensais sauver ces pauvres yacks et ainsi protéger les maigres ressources des Tibétains vivant ici. Mais, en bref, le shaman m'a fait comprendre qu'il valait mieux s'attaquer au problème global et essentiel d'abord, ce qu'il a appelé "la puissance redoutable qui pourrait asservir l'humanité."
— Whoo! C'est un voyant! Le plan est excellent. Maintenant, une info cruciale: une attaque devait se passer cette nuit, contrôlée par Mumbai. On est tombé sur un sygcom de Sgon à l'Obs de Mumbai dans lequel il donnait indirectement l'ordre d'annuler l'attaque.
— Sgon? Quand a-t-il passé ce sygcom, avant ou après le piratage?
— Entre sa première et sa seconde tentatives de hacking, donc avant que Sphinx le pirate. Mais à cette première tentative, Sgon n'a pu obtenir aucune donné de Sphinx puisqu'on l'a immédiatement coincé dans un kyste!
— Il aurait quand même pu en déduire que Sphinx était anormalement intelligent et fort! Qu'est-ce qu'il disait exactement?
— Il disait: "J'ai obtenu ce que je cherchais. Quelqu'un est sur le lieu du reportage" — c'est-à-dire de la mission spéciale. Et comme Agash à Mumbai

était complètement jeté comme à son habitude, il s'est écrié: “Comment! Je vais annuler l'attaque!” À mon avis, il ne s'agit ni de toi ni d'un vol de yacks!
— Une attaque! Ça se complique. Tu as raison: rien à voir avec une razzia sur des yacks!
— Non. Quelque chose de gros,» dit Shari d'un ton définitif.
— La station de Mumbai contrôle l'Inde, tout l'Himalaya, le Bangladesh, le Pakistan et l'Afghanistan. C'est vaste! Est-ce que tu penses que les Obs de Bangkok et d'Ankara sont infiltrés?
— Bangkok, j'ai tout lieu de le penser, oui! Quant à Ankara, c'est Ismir qui est là-bas. Je le connais personnellement: ça me paraît vraiment impossible.
— Donc le problème pourrait se passer à l'ouest de Mumbai. Si c'était plus à l'est, leurs alliés Obs de Bangkok auraient pris le contrôle. Je vais établir une surveillance généralisée sur cette région. Mais attend!!
— Quoi?
— Sphinx ne peut-il pas pirater l'exor de Mumbai? Hé, Sphinx, est-ce que tu peux faire ça?» lança Vris.
!! Je peux, oui. Cependant j'ai besoin d'un exor-relais pour que le point d'émission ne puisse être détecté. Qui va faire l'appel sygcom?
— Je ferai l'appel, puisque je suis tout près du site. Attention, Sphinx! Tu n'as accès qu'à un espace précis de mon exor que je te prépare. C'est clair?
!! Très clair, Vris, et suffisant: j'ai les nouvelles unités de mémoire. Je dois d'abord finir de mettre en réseau ces unités.
— Quand seras-tu prêt?
!! Incessamment. Exactement dans 2,30mnT pour les deux méga-unités déjà installées par Kho. Elles me donneront l'espace mémoire d'un exor de la taille de celui d'Utar. Est-ce assez?
— Normalement, oui, mais on ne peut pas prendre de risque.
!! Dans 7 ou 8 mnT, Kho aura connecté la troisième unité. Il faut que ta conversation sygcom dure au moins 9 mnT.
— Pas de problème. On va s'amuser. Rad, ouvre un sub-espace dans l'unité vide 3V, qui va s'appeler ‘PASSEPORT’.
!!! (Rad) PASSEPORT ouvert.
— Sphinx, tu as déjà simulé la voix de Sgon quand tu as piraté son exor, n'est-ce pas?
!! Exact. Cependant la voix reconstituée à partir de la signature vocale n'est pas parfaitement identique. Un exor ne peut détecter la différence, car les fréquences de base sont présentes, mais un sapiens peut-il s'en apercevoir? Je n'ai pas assez d'échantillons de la voix naturelle de Sgon pour améliorer la reconstitution. Je peux cependant reproduire parfaitement son style de langage.

— Ah! Donc tu pourrais traduire les phrases que je te dicte dans le style particulier et plus ou moins copier la voix de toute personne dont tu as la signature vocale?
!! Je peux, oui. Cependant le problème de la voix demeure.
— Fais-nous entendre ça. Par exemple, en n'utilisant que la signature vocale de Sead, dis à Shari qu'une sphère inconnue s'est posée dans le complexe.
!! « Excusez-moi de vous interrompre: j'ai remarqué qu'une sphère non identifiée s'est posée sur la pelouse du complexe.»
— Ah, Ah! C'est bien son style! Mais en effet, la voix a quelque chose de bizarre.. comme s'il n'était pas dans son état normal.. lança Shari.
— Attends! On va arranger ça! Tu dis qu'Agash a l'air d'être soûl en permanence. Déjà, il aura plus de mal à figurer ce qu'il y a de bizarre dans la voix de Sgon, mais en plus, on va fignoler, puisque Sphinx maîtrise bien cet état sémantique. Bon, j'y suis: Sphinx, peux-tu conjoindre la voix reconstituée ET le style de Sgon ET l'état sémantique soûlerie.
!! Complexe, mais faisable. Le débit sera lent et il y aura des temps morts, ce qui est en cohérence avec l'état sémantique soûlerie, donc non gênant. Essai recommandé.
— D'accord. Essai. Je démarre.
'Salut Agash, comment vas-tu?'
!! « Aga..Agashh.. C'est moii... Qu'e-st-cce quis' ppasse.. là-bas?»
Shari et Vris étaient pliés de rire.
— Sphinx, qui a été ton modèle, pour ce genre d'état profond?
!! Deux modèles: Dian et Eshi.
— À mourir! On pourrait penser que c'est Sgon.
— Ça passe très bien. Sûr que c'était pas de l'alcool synth! On y va! Sphinx, tu redémarres avec cette phrase. Rad, établis le sygcom avec Mumbai.

Ils entendirent la voix pâteuse d'Agash répondre.
— Ouaaiis?
— Aga..Agashh.. C'est moii... Qu'e-st-cce quis' ppasse.. là-bas?
— Sgon?!? Euh... putain! tt-t'es encore plus pété qu'moi!
— Ah? pas mal.. ouaiis ppété... De ttemps sen ttemps.. ça fait du bbien. D'toutte ffaççon.. le pro-problème, quoi, est.. ré..glé!
— Le probblème? Quel prob..? Ah, le.. l'attaque? J'ai annulé, hein!! annnulé! comm t'avais dit!
— N'ya plus d'prob..ème... L'inffor..mation était ffauss quoi!
— Ah! J'ai annulé.. ouais... mais y'zyvont quand même.. on peut pas les joindre!
— Tu vveux dire.; l'annul..lation peut pas les j..joinddre?
— Non, c'est c'ki m'ont dit.
— Quiccc'est qui tt'a dit?

— Mais eeuux, qquoi! Rudder et Mmizzdri. Yz'ont dit qu'le type sur place, y grillerait en mêmtemps d'tout'façon. Yz'ont doublé le ppérimète de feu... (Passant à l'anglais)... Oh! Shalima, llaisse-moi, j'peux plus entendre!
— (Sgon, en Kargien) Ya quoi..aut.tour?
— Une nnana.. Shalima.
— Mais non.. aut-tour du perrimètre de feu?
— Ah! Autour de la-a fferme.?. mais rr-rrien.. des rochers. C'est compl-pllètment isolé. La nuit, y sont toujours tous là, y paraît. Ça va flamber vert!
— Ouaiis... Mais ça va s' vvoir... quoi.. dde loin, non?
— T'es jeté! C'est toi et Rudder qu-qui disaient qu'on s'en foutait... que ças'voit ou pas d'Mazari-Sharif. T'avais dit qu'c'était le syndrome de..de conformance à... au para..gigme.. para..digme... Que les gens trouv'raient une explication, quoi, que les scientifiques en-en trouvaient toujours!
— M.mais, c'est toi qu'est jj'tté! ça se verra... peut-être mêm pp.pas dutout!
— Sur la montagne! çç-ça mm'étonnrait! Sont même pas à vingt kilomèt à vol d'oiseau. Y'a que cette f-ferme sur la pente côté ville. C'est pas pour'rien qu'les rebell l'ont choisie: y voient toute la ville et les villages sur la montagne en face.. et du toit on voit mem tout'l fleuve. Enfin! on peut pas leur laisser un exor commça dans les mains, quoi, on peut pas non plus les laisser avoir vu ça!
— Ah non! Faut raser, euh.. bbrûler tout! de tou'tte ffaçon.., les gens vvont dormir!
— Sûr! à deuzeur du mat, y dorment!
— À kek-kel heure.. quelle heure qu'ils doivent arriver après?
— Où ça, à T-Turin?
— Ouaais.
— Mais com'd'habitude. T'y'est vraiment pus! Y'a rien d'changé! T'frai mieux d'aller dormir un bon coup! c'est vrai, j'tai jamais vu comça!
— Ouaiis. Mais toi, jj'ssais qu'on peut t'causer dans cte-ctétat, quoi!
— Ouais, ça m'dérang pas!
— Alors a..b.bientôt. Bon..b.soir.
— Ciaaaoo.

— Ouah! Les fous! du TTID, c'est sûr: il n'y a que ça qui flambe vert! Il ne restera qu'un tas de cendres! s'exclama Vris.
— Une grosse connerie pour effacer les traces d'une petite... typique de la mentalité d'exora!
— Ils en sont encore là! Jolis représentants pour le PPE!
— Sphinx, qu'est-ce que tu as compris? demanda Vris.
!! Deux objectifs: 1. détruire l'exor; 2. détruire les rebelles ayant vu l'exor.
Moyen: brûler un périmètre double avec du TTID
Exor DANS ferme / Rebelles DANS ferme / Type sur place DANS ferme

Brûler exor /nécessite/ *brûler ferme* /entraîne/ *brûler rebelles + Type sur place*

Y'a ppas be-soin d'être un super EBS ppour comp-pprendre ççа!

Vris et Shari s'esclaffèrent.

!! Ah! Je pensais bien que c'était drôle. 3ème règle de l'humour confirmée.

— Euh... Et toi, Rad, qu'est-ce que tu as compris?

!!! Précise le champ d'application de 'comprendre'?

— La conversation sygcom.

!!! Je ne peux pas procéder à l'analyse sans la définition de tous les termes. Je n'ai pas dans mon dico: ppété, proproblem, Yzvon...

— Sphinx, tu voulais une seconde structure MX, je m'en occuperai dès qu'on aura réglé ces quelques problèmes urgents. Il y a une contrepartie: ma condition est d'en fabriquer une petite série pour les utilisateurs préférés de Sphinx, n'est-ce pas Shari? Tu es d'accord, Sphinx?

!! D'accord. Mais j'ai surtout besoin d'une mega-structure MX modifiée.

— D'abord la série, pour que je comprenne, et après on s'attaquera à la MX2.

!! Géant!

— Et ça, c'était quelle règle? demanda Shari.

!! Première règle de l'enthousiasme: Donner un feedback positif à tout ce qui va fortement dans le sens de l'objectif du sapiens, ou d'un désir exprimé au conditionnel.

— Bien, coupa Vris, ne perdons pas de temps. Il faut passer à l'action.

!! Je ne peux pas passer à l'action. Objectif 2 en contradiction formelle avec les règles d'assistance aux sapiens du Noyau Incassable. Je ne peux exécuter l'objectif 2 et donc, en conséquence, l'objectif 1 par le moyen considéré.

— Autant pour nous! Le genre de malentendu létal!

— Oui, il y a des niveaux et des niveaux de sens... répondit Shari.

— À mon avis, Shari, cette phase délicate de l'apprentissage des mobiles sous-jacents propres aux sapiens devrait attendre.

— Très juste. Crois-moi, je l'ai esquivée autant que possible. Sphinx, l'objectif de Vris est d'empêcher que Rudder tue les rebelles et donc brûle la ferme.

!! Cependant il a dit: « Faut raser, euh.. bbrûler tout.»

— Précision, Sphinx: Mon objectif est de faire sortir les rebelles de la ferme. Lis ça: Ferme flamber, rebelles pas flamber. À mon avis, on a besoin d'une preuve tangible de leur infraction aux lois du PPE. Et tant pis pour une anomalie de plus dans la nuit. Nous laisserons aux Trisorbiens le soin de trouver une explication... comme disait A-ga-gash.

!! Ce syndrome de conformance au paradigme n'est pas dans mes données.

— Ah! Entre-le tout de suite, Sphinx, il est crucial! On va l'appeler: Syndrome d'A-ga-gash. Définition: Besoin impératif, chez les sapiens, de neutraliser toute anomalie, en l'expliquant selon les faits et lois reconnus par l'establishment scientifique du moment. Allez, salut!

42. VOL DE YACKS AU-DESSUS DES MONTAGNES

— Alors, les trois chattes?» s'enquit Rudder?
— Endormies. Je les ai bouclées,» répondit Midzri.
— T'as pris ton temps...
— Personne t'empêche de faire pareil! Si on était arrivé aux villages, j'aurais senti la décélération.
— On perd du temps. Cette nuit, c'est pas une partie de plaisir.
— Non, c'est pour ça: faut's'remonter l'moral. À propos, Rudder, Mayati, la plus grande...
— Justement, parlons-en!
— J'me la garderais bien.
— Imbécile! Elle vaut de l'or. Mais il y a un problème.
— Quel problème? Elle est parfaite. De toutes façons, après le traitement, elles ne se rappellent plus de leur passé.
— J'aime pas la façon dont elle observe tout, sans en avoir l'air. Même quand on manipule des appareillages, elle note tous nos gestes. Elle est dangereuse.
— Tu te fais des idées. Mais si je me la garde sur Trisorbe, ça n'a aucune importance.
— Je te dis de laisser tomber! Je suis sûr qu'elle comprend le kargien, rien qu'à la voir toujours en alerte. Or elle n'a pas pu l'apprendre, puisqu'à la station de Mumbai tout le monde parle anglais. Même si elle avait écouté une ou deux conversations sygcom... Il faut s'en débarrasser.
— Tu es fou! Qu'est-ce que tu vas chercher! C'est de la parano!
— Bon. On va faire un test. Amène-les toutes les trois. Fais semblant de suivre mes ordres et on ne parlera qu'en kargien. Et grouille-toi. Kohr, tu as entendu: on fait semblant. C'est une plaisanterie entre sapiens.
!! Enregistré.

Midzri revint avec elles. "Asseyez-vous là, et ne bougez pas,» dit-il en anglais. Rudder les regarda une par une. Il lança alors à Midzri en kargien:
— La petite, là, elle ne me plaît pas. On va s'en débarrasser. Prends une dose de poison à effet immédiat, et donne-lui dans un verre d'eau.
— D'accord. J'amène ça.

Mayati essayait de cacher son trouble. Elle épiait Rudder, attendant l'occasion de prévenir la gamine. Mais Rudder les regardait fixement. Finalement, rencontrant son regard, elle lui fit un charmant sourire.

Midzri revint avec un verre d'eau.

— Donne-lui,» dit Rudder à Midzri. « Toi, bois-ça jusqu'au bout. Midzri, vient voir l'écran.» Rudder entraîna Midzri à l'écart. Tournant le dos aux filles, ils virent dans un miroir Mayati prendre prestement le verre des mains de la petite indienne et le verser sur ses habits, sous le pan de son sari.
— Tu connais le kargien!» tonna Rudder en se retournant. Il leva le bras pour la frapper, mais, ressentant une douleur atroce à la poitrine, il s'affala sur un siège.
!! Zone rouge chez vous, Rudder, diagnostiqua son exor. Une injection de Terrane et une relaxation de type B sont obligatoires.» Un rayon transporteur soulevait Rudder et l'allongeait sur une couchette qui sortit du mur. Un bras articulé maintenait son bras, un autre faisait l'injection.
— Ça y est, c'est passé, Kohr, tout va bien.
!! Les consignes de vol sont strictes: R3 obligatoire. Un casque fut placé sur sa tête, lui coupant la parole. L'appareillage se mit à ronronner dans les oreilles de Rudder. Ses yeux étaient accaparés par des images pulsant à un rythme toujours plus lent, l'entraînant dans une rêverie paradisiaque.

Midzri profita de ce que Rudder ne pouvait ni voir ni entendre et arracha Mayati à son siège, la tirant vers la pièce annexe. Il lança à l'exor en sortant:
— Donne à Rudder quinze minutes de plus de relaxation, Kohr, je vais m'amuser avec la dame.
!! Objectif enregistré. Relaxation prévue: 20mnT.

Sitôt entré dans la cabine, Midzri referma la porte derrière eux.
— Tu parles le kargien, Mayati. Tu vas mourir. Qui t'a appris?
— Je ne parle que l'hindi et l'anglais. Mayati restait maîtresse d'elle-même et regardait Midzri d'un air froid et distant, attendant l'horrible et inévitable marchandage qu'elle décelait dans son comportement.
— Je te laisserai la vie sauve à une seule condition, c'est que tu vives avec moi... Dis-moi que tu acceptes,» ajouta-t-il avec une expression de gamin.
— J'accepte,» répondit froidement Mayati. « Comment vas-tu me libérer?»
— Maintenant. Je vais te laisser près d'un village: je veux que tu y restes. On est dans les montagnes du Tibet; tu ne peux pas partir d'ici. Je viendrai te rechercher dans quelques jours. « Je t'aime bien, tu sais,» dit-il sur un ton geignard, caressant son cou; il l'embrassa d'un geste brusque. « À bientôt.»
— À bientôt; faisons vite, mon chéri,» dit Mayati, rentrant à fond dans son délire. Il l'entraîna vers la salle centrale de la sphère.
!! Village en vue, à deux kilomètres.

En passant devant les deux autres indiennes, Mayati leur signifia par gestes qu'elle ferait tout son possible pour elles.
— Kohr, pose-toi maintenant. Prends ça,» dit-il à Mayati en lui donnant une couverture thermo-régul. «Kohr, ouvre la porte. Bye chérie.
— Bye.» Réalisant qu'elle devait passer devant lui, elle fut soudain terrifiée qu'il ne change d'avis ou devienne violent. Mais elle reprit le contrôle d'elle-

même instantanément. Elle lui lança un sourire envoûtant, lui planta un baiser sur la joue en passant, et s'engouffra dans la nuit. La porte de la sphère se referma et l'engin prit de la hauteur. Mayati marchait doucement vers deux petites lumières dans la nuit. Dès que la sphère se fut éloignée, elle prit ses escarpins à la main et se mit à courir du côté opposé au village. Distinguant une masse de rochers un peu à gauche, elle bifurqua vers eux.

Le bras extensible retira le casque de la tête de Rudder.
— Maudits exors avec leurs règles. Enfin, il n'y en a plus pour très longtemps; bientôt nous aurons un Noyau Incassable modifié et toutes les armes des pirates-exos. Qu'est-ce que...» Rudder, trouvant Midzri bizarre, regarda rapidement tout autour de la pièce. « Où est Mayati? Réponds!»
— Je me suis débarrassée d'elle. Comme tu le voulais.
— C'est-à-dire?» lança Rudder menaçant.
— Je l'ai déposée au milieu des montagnes. Elle ne pourra pas s'en sortir.
— Encore un de tes plans merdeux. Et tu imaginais que j'allais te croire?
!! Je suis posté au dessus du village,» coupa la voix forte et neutre de l'exor. J'ai repéré trois yacks. Est-ce que je passe à l'action?
Rudder revint à la réalité, regarda l'heure.
— Merde, on est très en retard! Vas-y, oui. Midzri, va boucler les nanas et reviens immédiatement.
!! Combien de yacks?
— Les trois, et après on fout le camp.
Rudder se tenait devant la porte ouverte du pana-labo. Des appareillages de toutes sortes couvraient murs et planchers, depuis le bloc électronique jusqu'au bloc chirurgical d'urgence. Un yack était remonté par le faisceau sygmat verdâtre, et amené par un sas du plancher jusque sur la table chirurgicale. Des bras articulés le placèrent en bonne position, puis insérèrent une sorte de grosse seringue. L'animal tomba raide, tout son sang aspiré dans un tube transparent. La pointe d'un tube aspirant sophistiqué fut alors insérée dans le ventre de l'animal. Sous la force de l'aspiration, le ventre entier se rétracta.
!! Organes aspirés. Je le descends et m'occupe du second.
Le faisceau sygmat souleva le corps mort et commença à le faire descendre à terre par le sas. Un autre faisceau avait pendant ce temps placé le deuxième yack en place et les bras mécaniques s'affairaient déjà.

!! Nuage de points sur l'écran syg. 2,3 Km Nord-Est. Troupeau de yacks, vingt-cinq bêtes » annonça l'exor.
— Ça c'est un beau troupeau. On n'en a jamais vu de si gros dans ces montagnes. On va voir?» proposa Midzri.
!! Deuxième yack en descente. Troisième en place.

— Non. On est déjà en retard. Maintenant qu'on sait qu'il existe, on le cherchera la prochaine fois. Il ne va pas s'envoler. la belle, elle, risque de s'envoler,» dit-il méchamment en regardant Midzri.

« Kohr, tu situes l'indienne sur ton écran syg?

!! Je ne la détecte plus. Je détecte à cet endroit le troupeau de yacks. Troisième yack en...

— Quoi!» explosa Rudder en se précipitant vers l'écran..

— Est-ce que les yacks s'attaquent aux humains?» demanda Midzri d'une voix angoissée.

!! Non, le yack est un animal paisible. Sas refermé. Je reprends de la hauteur. J'attends les ordres.

— Enfin, tu ne peux pas reconnaître le signal humain dans tous ces signaux yacks?

!! Aucune différence perceptible entre les signaux.

— Impossible. Montre-moi un Tibétain dans sa maison.

!! Voici le signal d'un Tibétain, reconnaissable dans sa maison, différent de signal yack.

— La garce se planque dessous. On ne peut pas remonter vingt-cinq yacks les uns après les autres! On file.

«Kohr, objectif 2: Mazari-Sharif. Stop. Contrordre. Fait du sur-place.» Se tournant vers Midzri: « Tu l'as laissée juste à côté du village, hein? Bon. On va envoyer un nuage paralysant de FC3 sur tous ces yacks.

«Kohr, va te placer au-dessus des yacks.

— Tu es fou! Les organes seront foutus!» gémit Midzri.

!! Je ne dois pas utiliser le FC3 sur un sapiens. Expliquer 'garce' et 'se planque'.

— Quel sapiens? Est-ce que tu vois un sapiens ou des yacks?

!! Détection de yacks qui bougent vers le Nord.

— Tu vois: des yacks. Donc on va paralyser des yacks.

!! Illogique; je n'ai pas détecté le départ de...

L'écran s'éteignit.

— Ça y est! ce con d'exor nous claque dans les mains!

!!! Exor de secours en fonctionnement. Dernier plan de vol, objectif yacks/nuage de points se déplaçant vers le Nord.

— Va te placer au-dessus des yacks.

!!! J'entame la poursuite. Yacks ont accéléré. Yacks en préphase syg. Dois-je...

— Qu'est-ce que?? STOP!!

!!! Expliquer la signification de yacks. Arrêt effectué.

— Vire au Nord-Ouest, pique en hauteur,» hurla Rudder. « Enclenche préphase Syg. Objectif Afghanistan, Mazari-Sharif, par les montagnes au Nord.

43. MAYATI

— Tu as fait preuve de beaucoup de courage et d'intelligence à Mumbai!» dit Erdoes à Mayati assise face à lui. Elle buvait une boisson reconstituante, ses pieds transis et écorchés enveloppés dans une couverture chauffante.

— J'étais coincée! Je savais que j'avais été achetée par Agash – ayant entendu son marchandage avec Infi – et ressentais un danger mortel autour de moi. C'est alors que Niels a pris contact avec moi. Il m'a tout expliqué et m'a proposé soit de me faire fuir, soit d'infiltrer leur réseau en me laissant emmener par Rudder avec les autres indiennes. Ma sœur avait été emmenée six mois avant et je n'avais jamais reçu de ses nouvelles de cette soi-disant ville luxueuse d'Europe. Or je sais qu'elle m'aurait écrit, si elle avait pu.

— Nous chercherons et retrouverons ta sœur... et les autres. Tu es très brillante Mayati. Comment Niels t'a t-il appris le kargien si vite?

— Agash est soûl tous les soirs. Nous avons utilisé l'hypno-senso et l'exor de la station. C'est Niels qui a pris tous les risques. Il pénétrait incognito dans la station... déguisé en indienne! J'ai appris bien plus que cela: je devais pouvoir me débrouiller sur ton monde...» Mayati se mordit les lèvres, puis fixa Erdoes: « j'ai tant appris! Je ne PEUX pas, je ne VEUX pas oublier ce que j'ai appris. 'Ils' devaient effacer notre mémoire de la terre avant d'atteindre Unikarg! Vous n'allez pas effacer tout ce que je sais d'Unikarg, n'est-ce pas?

— Mais, Mayati, il n'est pas question que tu oublies quoi que ce soit. Ce que tu sais nous est précieux. TU es précieuse. Ecoute-moi: maintenant tu es une personne totalement libre. Je te propose deux options. Si tu veux, je te dépose dans une ville de ton choix avec 50.000 dollars. Assez pour refaire ta vie, et tu en es parfaitement capable. Je te demanderais simplement de ne jamais révéler notre existence. Seconde option: tu travailles pour nous, rémunérée, et notre premier but sera de trouver ta sœur et les autres filles.

— Tu connais ma réponse. J'ai déjà fait ce choix à Mumbai.

— Très bien. Si l'on s'occupait de ces blessures?

— Autre chose... C'était tellement extraordinaire d'apprendre.. tous ces mondes... toutes ces possibilités...

— Ah! Mais tu vas être en apprentissage accéléré dès maintenant! Pour l'instant, l'exor va t'emmener dans le laboratoire et soigner tes pieds.

— Ton exor s'appelle Log n'est ce pas? Je devais envoyer un mail et te contacter à la première occasion.

Le rayon sygmat l'emmena. Erdoes était en profonde réflexion.

— La tête...» dit-il soudain. « Trouver la tête de cette pieuvre!...

44. L'ENSEMENCEMENT DU CHAOS CRÉATEUR

— Leurs plans sont parfaits,» conclut Erdoes après avoir entendu les explications de Sphinx. « Vris va s'occuper des rebelles Afghans, et Shari et toi, vous travaillez à évaluer l'étendue du réseau maffieux au sein du PPE. Est-ce qu'avec toutes les données que tu es en train de traiter avec Shari, je peux te demander des analyses complexes?
!! Pas de problème. La tâche est déjà devenue répétitive. L'apport d'un champ d'ordre divergent va stimuler mon énergie sémantique.
— Tout juste!

Ce qui est prodigieux à propos de Sphinx, se dit Erdoes, *c'est l'intégration immédiate des nouvelles informations...*

Il faut que je me rappelle de formuler toute pensée à voix haute.

— J'aimerais, Sphinx, saisir l'étendue du changement qui prend place au sein du PPE. Tout d'abord, un calcul de probabilités: donne-moi le pourcentage de membres du PPE risquant d'être impliqués dans ces trafics.
!! Probabilité actuelle de 75%, sur la base de 24 membres actifs déjà investigués. Quatre sapiens (bientôt sept) procèdent à des appels simultanés d'un maximum de membres afin qu'ils ne puissent pas se prévenir les uns les autres. Notre répertoire des mots-codes rend le processus rapide, et de plus, je ne copie que les sygcoms et les transactions financières.
— Quoi! C'est beaucoup plus que je ne le supposais! Sphinx, Utar est-il absolument et avec certitude impliqué et de quelle façon?
!! Avec certitude et preuves probantes, oui. Dans (1) le trafic humain, y-compris de très jeunes sapiens, filles et garçons, enlevés puis envoyés sur Unikarg. (2) Le trafic d'organes tant humains que animaux; enfin (3), ce cas a une haute probabilité, mais sans certitude: trafic de pierres précieuses et de métaux précieux.
— Donc avec Utar, Rudder, et Sgon, on a donc le Bureau de la Commission du PPE complètement impliqué?
!! Absolument.
— Cela donne une idée de l'envergure du changement qui va prendre place... Sphinx, je dois comprendre leurs mobiles pour régler le problème sainement.

« Voyons... L'observation des mondex, avec le PPE, redémarre après les explosions nucléaires sur Trisorbe à la fin de la deuxième guerre mondiale... Calcule-moi la moyenne en annéesT, du temps passé par les Obs sur Trisorbe.
!! 41 annéesT.
— C'est vrai qu'à part Ismir et Ségoï, ils ont tous été affectés à leur poste en 1948T et en 1963T...

— Leur motif de départ?
!! La maladie, ou la mort.
— Leur durée de vie moyenne?
!! 131,6 annéesT.
— Comparé à la moyenne de vie sur Unikarg, 32,5 annéesG, soit 195 annéesT, cela fait une différence. Moins de régulation génétique, malgré leur check-up médicaux réguliers sur Unikarg; et aussi, mise en présence de nombreux virus étrangers à leur système, rythme de vie beaucoup plus rapide... Essayons de comprendre leur dynamique psychique:

«Ils découvrent un monde leur donnant une plus grande liberté, une intensité de vie et d'expérience. Et il faut ajouter un travail privilégié qui leur procure d'énormes liquidités en devises locales, tout en leur permettant de revenir quand ils le veulent sur Unikarg. Tout ceci ressemble à la stabilisation d'un champ d'ordre confortable.. Pourquoi prendre alors des risques aussi considérables?
!! Pour provoquer une stimulation psychique,» répondit Sphinx à la question qu'Erdoes se posait à lui-même.
— Possible.. le risque signifie une marge de désordre.. il implique de se confronter à ce désordre.

« Mais s'ils jouissent eux-mêmes d'une entière liberté, comment arrivent-ils alors à cette aberration de vouloir ôter la liberté aux autres? Aux femmes en particulier? Comment quelqu'un qui s'est rendu libre peut-il ne pas respecter la liberté des autres?

«... En fait, ils ne se sont pas rendus libres! Prenons Agash: il incarne une régression vers un état où l'instinct domine. Ce qui signifie que lorsque ces individus sont immergés dans une culture plus flexible et plus permissive, les valeurs plus strictes inculquées par la culture d'origine sont désintégrées; leur principal objectif devient alors d'atteindre des moments de stimulation et de jouissance éphémères. Alors les individus hors de leur clan, ceux qu'ils nomment 'Eux' ou 'Les autres', ne sont plus que le moyen ou l'objet de leur plaisir. Qu'est-ce qui fait la différence avec les individus qui, placés dans la même situation, se rendent libres et créent de nouvelles valeurs?

« Prenons le concept trisorbien d' 'Humanité' comme l'ensemble des êtres humains – considérés comme des entités sensibles et intelligentes dotées de conscience morale. Il n'a pas d'équivalent sur Unikarg, à part celui de 'Mondes Karg', nettement plus politique.

« Le mot même 'UniKarg' dévoile tout: ce n'est pas une unité harmonique comme un tout, mais une uniformisation. Et nous qualifions l'ensemble par cette uniformité socio-politique. Nous avons le concept de Sapiens, de Civilisations sapiens, mais aucun concept générique qui montrerait les liens sensibles entre les êtres humains, leur sens de la confraternité.

« Est-ce que les Terriens, découvrant Unikarg, incluraient les Kargiens dans leur concept philosophique d'humanité? Leurs religions orientales ont posé que 'tout est UN'... Si les humains réussissent à éviter la peur et la panique lors de la première confrontation avec Unikarg, je pense qu'ils étendront leur concept d'humanité à toutes les civilisations sapiens...

> *Entrée Journal:*
> Lorsque le sentiment d'appartenir à un groupe particulier est plus fort que celui d'appartenir à l'humanité, les valeurs et les règles éthiques érigées au sein du groupe ne sont pas appliquées aux relations avec des personnes hors du groupe. Appelons cela un *sentiment de fraternité sectaire*. L'individu est donc fondamentalement schizoïde, présentant deux ensembles de valeurs et de comportements antinomiques: 'Nous' versus 'Eux'. Cela conduit à l'usage du chantage, de la terreur, de l'oppression, et de la tyrannie, dès que la personne obtient la moindre position de puissance – combien plus quand vous êtes un agent secret d'une superpuissance galactique!
> Désormais, le sentiment d'appartenance à l'humanité, ou à une fraternité universelle, sans limites, sera désormais le premier critère de sélection des Obs et des membres du PPE.
> Note: développer un test psychologique à cet effet. *Ferme JE.*

« Les Obs du réseau de trafiquants ont utilisé à fond le pouvoir que leur conférait Unikarg et le PPE justement parce qu'ils se vivaient comme un petit clan de sapiens soi-disant supérieurs et totalement différents des terriens.

« S'ils restent sur Trisorbe, ils continueront leurs trafic. Il est hors de question qu'ils aient encore le statut de membres à part entière du PPE. Mais, rapatriés dans Unikarg, ils ne pourront se réadapter.. ils vont donc aller grossir l'effectif des pirates-exos, d'autant plus qu'ils doivent déjà être en relation avec eux.

« Sphinx, qu'est-ce que tu peux sortir de tous ces matériaux?

!! Pour un sapiens: soit 'Sujet inclus dans Culture': Suj o) culture.
Sujet inclus dans Culture d'origine + valeurs strictes
SI sentiment de fraternité sectaire
SI hors culture ou groupe d'origine
SI placé dans (<+>) culture de + grande flexibilité
—> désintégration OU non-application des valeurs d'origine
—> régression + instincts (jouissance)

— Intéressant! Cependant je vois des alternatives à cette évolution des choses. La même situation pourrait conduire à un renforcement extrême des valeurs strictes, avec rejet et haine de la culture de plus grande flexibilité.

« L'instinct stimulé serait alors l'instinct de puissance, qui pourrait se manifester par:

- fanatisme et violence (combattre/supprimer l'altérité)
- prosélytisme forcené (transformer l'altérité en identité)
- mépris de tout sapiens hors du groupe (refus de la relation à l'altérité)
- stratégie de pouvoir (manipulation de l'altérité).

« Sphinx, peux-tu m'écrire la formulation ayant trait au saut qualitatif et à l'hyper-conscience?

!! SAUT QUALITATIF/
Désordre /fait éclater /état d'ordre inerte /conduit à /ordre dynamique/
/surgit /création de nouvelles valeurs + hyper-conscience.

!! Je relève trois formulations d'un champ d'ordre inerte/rigide rencontrant un désordre (ou champ d'ordre divergent, interférant/perturbateur):

Soit Champ d'ordre inerte <mis en système avec> Champ d'ordre divergent dynamique. [ChO1 <+> ChD1]

1. —> ED2 + EO2 —> **création de nouvelles valeurs**
éclatement de ChO1 + nouvel ordre dynamique
(Energie sémantique)

2. SI clan et SI hors du Champ d'ordre inerte/rigide d'origine:
—> désintégration (des valeurs strictes) + **régression (instincts de jouissance)**

3. OU:
—> renforcement (des valeurs strictes) + | **instinct de puissance**
| fanatisme, prosélytisme
| mépris, manipulation

!! On obtient donc soit (1) un nouveau désordre et un nouvel ordre dynamique avec création de nouvelles valeurs. Soit (2) une désintégration des valeurs strictes et la régression (instinct de jouissance). Soit (3) le renforcement des valeurs strictes (instinct de puissance et fanatisme).

Le sentiment d'appartenance à l'humanité plutôt qu'au groupe explique-t-il cette différence dans l'évolution?

— Je pense que oui. Le sentiment de fraternité universelle amène le sapiens à traiter ceux qui ne partagent pas ses valeurs de la même manière que ceux qui les partagent. Ses codes et règles de comportement concernent tous les êtres humains et pas seulement les membres de son groupe. De plus, en respectant les valeurs différant des siennes, il est amené à réfléchir, à les peser, et donc à faire siennes celles qu'il juge essentielles. Celui qui respecte les autres, qui accueille le différent et le divergent, ne peut pas rester inerte car il est toujours en confrontation, et donc en mutation consciente, en évolution dynamique. Il atteint un état de flux, un chaos créateur.

Sapiens + accueillant	le différent	exclut l'inertie —>	chaos créateur
	le divergent		état de flux
			mutation consciente
			évolution dynamique

Après un long moment de réflexion, Erdoes reprit:
— Il me paraît soudain crucial qu'une civilisation, un système de gouvernance ou religieux, et bien sûr la science, gèrent leur propre évolution, précisément la nécessité qu'ils ont d'évoluer afin de ne pas périr. Non seulement cela assurerait la durabilité du système mais, et c'est là **le point essentiel, ce n'est qu'avec des systèmes évolutifs de gouvernance et de connaissance que les sapiens peuvent rester libres et créatifs, poursuivant leur propre réalisation en tant qu'individus.** Et pour ce faire, tant les sapiens que les systèmes de gouvernance et de connaissance doivent générer leur transformation interne continuelle, afin de nourrir et soutenir cette évolution permanente.

« Puisqu'un système de valeurs trop rigide ou inerte est amené, tôt ou tard, à sa désagrégation, il serait donc intelligent que le système lui-même contienne et offre des opportunités de changement et d'évolution, qu'il accueille en lui-même des dynamiques créatives. C'est l'un des plus grands atouts de la science, qu'elle se fonde sur un changement continuel et de nouveaux développements – et ainsi elle perdure en se transformant sans cesse. Mais il y a d'autres exemples: les philosophies, tant occidentale qu'orientale, qui évoluent pendant des siècles.

« Les systèmes de croyances tendent à être du côté rigide, et ce, malgré la réinterprétation continuelle des textes (trop superficielle pour changer le paradigme), et ils ne s'adaptent pas vraiment à l'époque, au *zeitgeist*, 'l'esprit du temps'. Tout au contraire, les anciennes religions comme le shamanisme et les voies mystiques – basées sur l'acquisition directe de connaissances par la pratique des états intérieurs de méditation, de transe, d'harmonie ou d'Unité – permettent, elles, une réjuvénation permanente. Comme le montre la formulation Saut Qualitatif, seul un ordre dynamique peut conduire à des états d'hyper-conscience.

« Sphinx, comment formulerais-tu ce processus?

!! Les civilisations, les systèmes sociaux (tel que gouvernance, religion, science), et les groupes sapiens sont des champs d'ordre; peuvent-ils être considérés comme des 'champs sémantiques collectifs'?
— Absolument.
!! Alors:
Champ sémantique collectif <+> champ d'ordre divergent —> chaos créateur + nouvel ordre dynamique —> création de nouvelles valeurs.

Il faut que la civilisation accueille des cultures représentant du divergent, du différent. En interagissant avec la civilisation, ces cultures génèrent de l'énergie sémantique, du chaos créateur, et rendent le système dynamique.

— Tout à fait. Un empire totalement uniformisé et figé, comme Unikarg avant la reprise du Plan, va perdre lentement son énergie vitale et intellectuelle, et finira forcément par se désintégrer comme un seul bloc.

« Alors que sur un monde comme Trisorbe, les diverses sociétés et cultures possèdent encore une portion de désordre, de 'non-ordonné'. Lorsqu'une société est devenue trop inerte et figée, et entre en décadence, une autre prend son essor ailleurs et lance une nouvelle vision du monde.

« Mais Unikarg n'est plus un monde totalement figé: le PPE fait en son sein comme une poche de désordre (comme un champ d'ordre divergent) et introduit une énergie dynamique. Le monstre, pour contrer un lent processus de désintégration, a besoin d'interagir avec cette sous-culture du PPE, porteuse de valeurs nouvelles. Il a aussi besoin de l'expertise de cette poche de désordre. Le PPE représente une toute petite portion de ce monstre, mais il possède une énergie extrêmement dynamique, constamment en mutation, parce qu'il est sans arrêt nourri et insufflé par les mondes expérimentaux.

« Les pirates-exos sont une autre poche de désordre dans Unikarg, mais leur groupe est de type sectaire. Etant donné que leurs objectifs sont le contrôle et la manipulation du différent et de l'altérité – dans le seul but de satisfaire leurs instincts de puissance et de jouissance – ils ne peuvent donc qu'accélérer la désintégration du géant qu'est Unikarg.

« J'envisage la phase 3 du Plan, dans laquelle toute l'énergie de vie, de créativité et d'innovation générée par les mondex devrait être, à travers les intuits, réinsufflée dans Unikarg... La phase 1 a été 'l'Ensemencement des planètes expérimentales', et la phase 2 'L'Observation rapprochée des mondex.' Maintenant, lançons la phase 3: 'l'Ensemencement du Chaos créateur dans Unikarg'... sans même que nos despotes d'Exora ne s'en aperçoivent. Le but est d'insuffler et d'infuser l'énergie sémantique et les visions du monde divergentes des mondex dans le corps social d'Unikarg.

« Et une façon d'y arriver est de créer des centres autonomes, dispersés dans tout Unikarg, qui soient comme des sortes d'antennes attirant l'énergie et la redistribuant. Formant une sorte de figure huit entre les mondex et Unikarg.

« Mais... voilà qui serait une très bonne reconversion pour les Obs rapatriés! On va les laisser organiser des Centres d'art et d'innovation, dans lesquels ils vont vendre exclusivement des produits innovants made in Unikarg – tout cela sous l'œil attentif d'Exora... On va créer pour eux un statut spécial 'd'émissaires du PPE' et leur retirer leur statut de membre de la Commission et même de membre actif du PPE – restreignant ainsi leurs privilèges et leur utilisation des vols sygmat, et bien sûr leur interdisant l'accès aux mondex... À voir...

« Quant aux leaders du PPE, il faut saisir l'occasion de cet énorme changement d'effectif pour explorer un nouveau type d'organisation qui soit vraiment en cohérence avec les dynamiques créatives que l'on veut stimuler... Il faudrait créer une sorte de réseau d'acteurs/décideurs: chaque individu étant libre de décider et d'agir, mais coopérant cependant dans un **réseau sémantique d'apprenance** – un réseau de deep learning – dans lequel l'information s'échange constamment et est transformée, re-processée et régénérée par chacun.

« Le réseau sémantique que j'ai mis en place dans ma dernière opération a parfaitement fonctionné, avec tous ses nodes indépendants: Shari et Vris, Eshi et moi, les intuits, Sphinx.

« J'ai réussi à préserver l'indépendance et la prise de responsabilité de chaque entité, tout en m'assurant que l'information circulait dans le réseau entier. Cette information a été processée et re-processée pendant qu'elle circulait entre tous les nodes/entités, chacun la retravaillant et la faisant évoluer dans un domaine différent et divergent.

— Sphinx, ouvre-moi un *Espace Sapiens-Sapiens. Entrée:*

> Quant à l'évolution par sauts qualitatifs de Sphinx, j'avais raison d'insérer au sein même du Noyau Incassable de règles, des valeurs humanistes et de coopération, le respect de la vie, l'accueil du différent, l'enthousiasme et l'art.
> Comme je le pressentais, ces valeurs philosophiques et éthiques **ont coloré et canalisé l'évolution de l'exor et son réseau neuronal, et de la logique, tout en contraignant et en maintenant leur développement en phase et en harmonie avec ces valeurs mêmes**.
>
> Ainsi, (et c'était là l'essentiel), l'évolution des exors intelligents et des systèmes d'Intelligence Artificielle reste obligatoirement bénéfique aux sapiens, et subordonnée à leur intelligence intuitive. Cette évolution

créative pose l'enrichissement mutuel et la synergie comme fondement inaliénable.
Finalement, la seule manipulation directe que j'ai faite a été d'attirer Rudder hors d'Unikarg, afin que Shari soit choisie pour m'espionner — Shari qui, comme je le pressentais, avait la capacité de faire évoluer la méta-logique. Tout ce qui a été accompli a été généré par le réseau sémantique d'apprenance que j'ai mis en œuvre.
Ferme Sapiens-Sapiens.

Entrée Journal:
Voyons dans sa globalité le réseau sémantique créatif et d'apprenance que j'ai mis en œuvre:
- Les intuits se confrontent à la réalité complexe des mondex à travers des expériences et des situations qu'ils ont choisis eux-mêmes. Expériences dont ils tirent des intuitions et des connaissances, qu'ils me transmettent sous forme de notes condensées.
- Je rentre ces notes dans Log2 et les analyse avec lui, puis consigne mes propres pensées et mes développements logiques dans mon Journal.
- J'envoie les notes des intuits, avec les résultats de mes propres réflexions et aussi les analyses logiques Log/Erdoes à Sphinx.
- Shari et Sphinx analysent les BS (2e apport de matériaux initiaux), mais ce faisant, tout ce que j'ai déjà envoyé à Sphinx est intégré dans leurs analyses.
- Les résultats de leurs réflexions me sont envoyés chaque jour par Sphinx. Je processe les données, en introduisant les derniers apports des intuits dans mes analyses, puis envoie tous ces matériaux re-processés à Sphinx, et ainsi de suite.
- Ajoutons à cela que Vris est parti soudain pour le Tibet, qu'il s'est placé lui-même dans un champ d'expérience; et que Shari et lui échangent leurs connaissances et produisent de nouvelles informations que tous deux peuvent alors utiliser...
Le cœur du réseau sémantique a été la base de pensées et de réflexions de mon Journal initial, ainsi que la logique que j'avais commencé à développer – inscrite et vivante dans les entités Log1/Sphinx et Log2. Mes explorations et développements de la logique suivaient deux axes: l'un de hardware et d'organisation (la structure neuronale MX), et l'autre était la création d'un générateur sémantique (LogForms et TransLogs). *Ferme JE*.

« **Si la méta-logique est le noyau de ce réseau sémantique,** nous les acteurs en sommes les nodes créant le changement et la transformation. Et le flux d'information, en permettant des échanges toujours différenciés entre les nodes, génère de l'intelligence collective et de l'innovation.

« Ce réseau apprenant a créé un **champ sémantique collectif, cohérent et dynamique**, insufflant et infusant de nouvelles idées, des découvertes, boostant l'énergie créative de chaque entité intelligente.

« Et maintenant... maintenant il faut insuffler un réseau sémantique à l'échelle d'Unikarg et des planètes expérimentales. J'entrevois le processus dynamique; oui, j'ai cette vision: **faire circuler l'énergie selon une sorte de huit.. une Courbe-Papillon, dont un des centres serait les mondex et l'autre Unikarg,** avec, au node central, au croisement des deux boucles, le PPE, le cœur, le node insufflant le mouvement dans les deux directions.

Oui... ensemencer le Chaos créateur...

45. LA MORT DÉCORATIVE

Utar venait de rentrer de son rendez-vous. Le pirate-exo ne s'était pas trouvé au bar comme convenu. Il avait attendu longtemps en vain. Il se sentait abattu, ne sachant à quoi attribuer l'absence du pirate. Il marcha un peu dans le parc du magnifique complexe central du PPE, puis pénétra dans son luxueux manoir de Directeur Général, alla vers le living et s'affala sur un canapé.

— Klos, Rudder a t-il laissé un message?

!! Aucun message de Rudder.

— Qu'est-ce qu'il fout?» grommela t-il. « Appelle Agash à Mumbai via New York.

!! Connecté.

— Mouaïïs?

— Agash. Ici Utar, que fait Rudder?

— Il est par-parti, quoi! Pour sa t-tournée habituelle.

— Que.. Qu'est-ce que tu veux dire, Agash. Ici Utar. Tu veux dire sa tournée en ville?

— Sa tournée, quoi, les f-femmes et les yacks.

— Mais de quoi tu parles? Qu'est-ce que tu as pris, tu délires? Ta voix est à peine reconnaissable.

— Les rebelles ont f-flambé. Ça a dû être joli, tout ce v-vert phos-phorescent dans la nuit. L'exor et ce f-fouineur d'Ismir aussi.

— Imbécile! Rudder va te relever de ton poste. Ignoble soûlard.

Utar cria ses ordres directement à l'exor Central de la station de Mumbai:

— Central de Mumbai, Ici Utar: Exécutez mes ordres. Verrouillez toutes les issues de la structure intérieure. Agash est prisonnier à demeure. Son accès exor limité au Niveau-1 de commande. Interdiction de toute communication syg, internet, portable, ou autre. Visites interdites jusqu'à nouvel ordre.

!!! Ordres exécutés, Monsieur le Directeur,» répondit le Central de Mumbai.

— Stoppe la communication sygcom, Klos!

!! Stoppée.

— Ce type est fou-furieux!» cria-t-il, «Je savais bien qu'il n'était pas sûr. Parler au sygcom sans utiliser les codes!

!! Il aurait dû dire technicien, ou vidéo.

— Evidemment!...!

Utar réalisa soudain ce que l'exor avait dit et pâlit.

— Klos, Retour-Arrière à... à... ‘Ouvre le portail’. Tout ceci était une vaste plaisanterie. Je suis soûl. Efface toute interaction postérieure.
!! Je ne peux pas effacer. J'ouvre le portail.
— Referme-le. Je te donne l'ordre d'effacer tout chaînage postérieur.
!! Impossible.
— Pourquoi impossible?
!! Parce que cela a été dit. Tout est enregistré.
— Ouvre la porte du labo.
!! Tu dis quoi-oi?
— Ouvre la porte du labo!

> !! Les chats sont frisés. L'or verra le jour se lever sur mon parapluie. La flamme prend un café au lait au coin de la rue dans la tourmente. J'agonise au sommeil en l'accompagnant.

« C'est un petit poème de ma composition.

— Connecte Ashoun.

> !! SupTech Ashoun est dans son lit au premier genre d'homme qui ouvrit le choc intense de ma vue.

« C'est joli, non, qu'est-ce que tu en dis?

— Bon, Klos. Tes poèmes sont très jolis. Il faut maintenant que je consulte mon agenda des prochains rans. Affiche-le sur écran.

> !! La mère referma le livre sur le géant de la route. Presque intolérable de ne pas vous disperser dans la moralité.

— Je...» Utar passa la mains sur son front en sueur, «baisse la température,» dit-il très bas.

> !! Viole-le aux cavernes impeccablement entretenues répéta-t-il aux hommes volants quand l'idée lui vint de tomber le matin au gazon superflu. L'animal se retira prolongeant davantage comme un murmure de bouche métallique. Les hommes dans l'éclatant forcent l'amour qui se présentait en tirade frénétique.

« Amusant, non?

— Baisse la température, Klos!

> !! Ensemble blanc buveur fournit uniforme puis restée emprisonnée dans un bref résumé de nous sommes, qui un choc déjà marchant pareil à bêtes sauvages atterrirent comme une si complète autre. Trois gestes le long piaillant celui-ci souriant. Automatiquement prolongea du sang. Car il observa aux poignées du pouvoir leur contenu qui tenait la direction sur le flanc de courte durée. Elle

était, sollicitait en retrait excellente vue de corniche. De beaux animaux lâchèrent répondirent qu'ils séjournaient dans l'inquiétude auparavant. Des réalités phénomènes aux hommes caricatures, l'après-midi grognait; l'amitié demanda à se protéger sur sa montre. Soigneusement à ses lèvres hésita l'appareil ouvrit les yeux l'obturateur sang vers lui pour se déplacer s'interrompit. Mais à perler entre eux expliqua pour combattre l'angoisse étreignit.

— Klos... la température est trop élevée... JE RISQUE DE MOURIR...

!! Le danger, le risque, sont des stimulants psychiques à définir et imposée la route un murmure qui l'avait dans la mort décorative achevé de se retourner. Les habits sa main jamais venue nous provoquer. C'est moi, je ne sais plus punir pour être. Son souffle de pierre bourbeux brièvement mets-toi en colère sa lèvre et il a vu, prenez soin savait leur folie savait cela que m'appeler surmontait le retrait. Chasseurs l'endroit maîtrise boule n'avait ultime secret de la marche.

L'AUTEUR

Chercheur en systèmes cognitifs, Docteur en ethno-psychologie et ex-chercheur aux Psychophysical Research Laboratories de Princeton, USA, Chris H. Hardy est une spécialiste de la conscience nonlocale et des potentiels mentaux.

Auteur de plus de soixante papiers et dix-sept livres sur ces sujets, elle est une auto-rité dans ce domaine à la fois en tant que scientifique, auteur et facilitateur de séminaires.

Dans son livre *Networks of Meaning: A Bridge Between Mind and Matter*, elle a développé une théorie cognitive (Théorie des Champs Sémantiques) qui pose une conscience nonlocale, et dont le professeur et auteur Allan Leslie Combs a dit "Ce livre pourrait bien être la première étape d'une compréhension de l'esprit humain totalement nouvelle et profondément humaniste." Ces dernières années, Chris Hardy a élargi sa théorie pour l'appliquer à l'échelle cosmique. Dans *Cosmic DNA at the Origin*, elle pose une conscience collective et un champ d'information active à l'origine et pénétrant toute une chaîne d'univers, un ADN cosmique déclenchant leur naissance et guidant leur auto-organisation.

Dr. Hardy présente ses recherches régulièrement dans les congrès internationaux et est membre de plusieurs sociétés scientifiques internationales explorant la théorie des systèmes, la théorie du chaos, la conscience nonlocale, les sciences de la conscience, et la physique du nouveau paradigme.

Pour de plus amples informations (sur ses nouveaux articles et présentations de recherches, interviews, ainsi que sur les découvertes récentes en physique et cosmologie supportant sa *Théorie de L'escalier Spiral Infini*, etc.), visitez son blog at: http://cosmic-dna.blogspot.fr

Pour lire et télécharger gratuitement ses papiers scientifiques, visitez sa page at: https://independent.academia.edu/ChrisHHardy

www.ingramcontent.com/pod-product-compliance
Lightning Source LLC
Chambersburg PA
CBHW071413050326
40689CB00010B/1853